Kaempfer's Japan

Tokugawa Culture Observed

by Engelbert Kaempfer

Edited, Translated, and Annotated by

Beatrice M. Bodart-Bailey

HAWAI'I

University of Hawai'i Press

Honolulu

Publication of this book has been assisted by a grant from the Kajiyama Publication Fund for Japanese History, Culture and Literature at the University of Hawai'i at Mānoa.

Printed in the United States of America

03 02 01 00 99 5 4 3 2 1

Library of Congress Cataloging-in-Publication Data
Kaempfer, Engelbert, 1651–1716.
[Heutiges Japan. English]
Kaempfer's Japan : Tokugawa culture observed / Engelbert Kaempfer; edited, translated, and annotated by Beatrice M. Bodart-Bailey.
p. cm.
Includes bibliographical references and index.
ISBN 0-8248-1964-0 (cloth : alk. paper).—ISBN 0-8248-2066-5 (pbk. : alk. paper)
1. Japan—Civilization—1600–1868. I. Title.
DS822.2.K313 1999 98-41190
952'.025—dc21 CIP

University of Hawai'i Press books are printed on acid-free paper and meet the guidelines for permanence and durability of the Council on Library Resources.

Designed by Jennifer Lum

Printed by The Maple-Vail Book Manufacturing Group

To my parents, Erich and Liselotte Bodart

Contents

Book 2

Book 3

Acknowledgments

Some ten years ago in a little coffee shop near Tokyo University's Akamon, George Akita urged me to drop all other projects and retranslate Engelbert Kaempfer's so-called *History of Japan*, this being, in his opinion, the most important work I would ever do in my life. I undoubtedly would have ignored his advice had I known what lay in store for me: ten years of intense work on Kaempfer's large collection of manuscripts and related material, and some of the most challenging, albeit also intellectually most satisfying, years of my life.

I am therefore all the more grateful to all those who supported me when the going was tough and helped to bring the project to its conclusion. It would by far exceed the allotted space if I were to mention by name everybody to whom I am indebted for assistance, especially all those who provided information when following in Kaempfer's footsteps. Nevertheless, I would like to express my special appreciation to George Akita, Junji Banno, Harold Bolitho, Toru Haga, and Tetsuo Kamiki for their encouragement, belief in, and support of my work. I would like to thank all my friends at the Australian National University for their help and friendship over many years, but particularly my very learned room-neighbor during the final years, Igor de Rachewiltz, who helped with so many footnotes and problems of translation that it became impossible to record each instance, as well as Susan and Royall Tyler, who provided both moral and academic support in many different ways.

Research on the route Kaempfer traveled was mainly done during a year at the International Research Center for Japanese Studies, Kyoto, where I would like to thank the staff for their assistance, but particularly Hidehiro Sonoda, who brought me there, and Kazuhiko Kasaya, who always found time to explain the intricacies of Japanese history and help read documents few others could. Sachiko Usui was invaluable with organizational matters. My thanks go also to the members of the Institute of Social Science, Tokyo University, for providing a much appreciated academic home on several occasions, as well as to my present colleagues at the Faculty of Economics, Kobe University. Other scholars to whom I am indebted include Julia Ching, Derek Massarella, Ruurdje Laarhoven, Baas Terwiel, and Hiroshi Watanabe.

Many people have been extremely generous in facilitating my research in various practical ways, and I would like to express my gratitude especially to Ariana Dolgoff, Aki Hatano, Tony Hogg, the Otagaki family, and Fumiko Sone.

Institutional support was received from the Australian National University; the Institute of Social Science, Tokyo University; the International Research Center for Japanese Studies, Kyoto; the Japan Foundation; and the Faculty of Economics, Kobe University. I am grateful to the British Library for making Kaempfer's manuscripts available to me and would like to thank in particular Michael Boggan for his assistance.

John and Mia Bailey I thank for sharing their wife and mother with Kaempfer over so many years.

Finally there is one person who deserves more gratitude than anybody else in bringing about the completion of this translation. This is the well-known former editor of *Monumenta Nipponica*, Michael Cooper. He not only contributed to countless notes but also read every page of the manuscript (except this one) and commented in detail. But perhaps most important of all, he has given me his time, moral support, and friendship when I needed it most.

All shortcomings are, needless to say, my own responsibility.

Translator's Introduction

"What is Dr. Kaempfer up to? Will he not publish anything about his travels?" wrote Leibniz, Newton's famous rival, to a friend in 1711.[1] Merchants and missionaries had traveled to Japan for a century and a half, and scholars in Europe had collated and published their reports. Some of these reports, especially those of the Jesuits, had been learned and detailed.[2] Engelbert Kaempfer (1651–1716), however, was the first scholar to travel to Japan with the purpose of reporting about the country, to study the available material before his arrival, to make copious field notes and sketches, and to turn these into a detailed description of Japan. His methods were in essence those of the modern scholar, and he was thus the first of the growing number of Japanologists. The qualifications Kaempfer brought to this task were not inferior to those of his modern counterpart.

Kaempfer's Qualifications

Kaempfer was born in 1651, the son of the vicar of the Westphalian merchant town of Lemgo.[3] From an early age he attended the local Latin school with his brothers. His father was a well-educated man, and although the family was not rich, Kaempfer was privileged to have a good library at his disposal. Among its books was the then-famous account by Adam Olearius of his embassy to the shah of Persia in 1635–1639,[4] and Kaempfer's desire to travel east may well have stemmed from this time.

As was not uncommon for a young scholar, Kaempfer visited a number of schools. He left Lemgo at the age of sixteen, spent one year at the high school of Hameln, two years at that of Lüneburg, and in between managed a trip to Holland. He traveled through Mecklenburg and Holstein and then enrolled at the Latin school of Lübeck, where he matriculated. His university studies covered a wide variety of subjects ranging from ancient to modern languages, to mathematics, astronomy, and history, and finally botany and medicine. He began these studies at the University of Thorn and continued at Cracow. Afterward he visited Warsaw and Danzig and finally completed five years at Königsberg.

According to his own testimony, he did not receive much financial support from home, was at times so poor that he could afford to eat only hemp gruel, and earned what he could by tutoring the children of the rich. Nevertheless, on his travels he would never fail to call on the most prominent scholars, whose best wishes and compliments are recorded in his autograph book. His professors similarly obliged with their commendations, praising him as a diligent and gifted student.[5]

In 1681 he left Königsberg for Sweden, where the young King Carl XI was gathering some of Europe's most talented scholars. At the University of Uppsala the chancellor, Peter Hoffwenig, a pioneer of Swedish medicine, praised Kaempfer as "a young man remarkable for his scholarship and knowledge of medicine."[6] He also befriended

Olof Rudbeck, the famous professor of natural history and medicine, under whose direction the university had built one of the earliest theaters of anatomy. Rudbeck had, moreover, established Sweden's first botanical garden and had written a large botanical work, something to which Kaempfer himself would later aspire.[7] But it was at the court at Stockholm that Kaempfer found employment. He was offered the position of secretary to the Swedish king's delegation to the shah of Persia under the experienced leadership of the Dutchman Ludwig Fabritius, a native of Brasilia and former officer in the Russian army, who was leading the second delegation to Isfahan.[8] Much of the correspondence Kaempfer conducted with the Swedish court was in German;[9] nationalism had not yet swept over Europe. In Stockholm Kaempfer also met the later famous jurist and historian Samuel Pufendorf, who with his brother Esaias sent him on his journey with words of encouragement.[10]

From the day Kaempfer left Stockholm on March 20, 1683, he kept a detailed diary, permitting us to follow not only the physical tribulations of his journey but also his development as a scholar and researcher.[11] One can sense his feelings of shock and alienation as he traveled through Russia, observing a culture that was Christian yet so different from his own. Certain religious worship he described as barbaric and superstitious and sacred pictures as "horrible" and "atrocious."[12] Later he would rarely make such strong value judgments.

In Moscow the delegation was received with great pomp and had the honor of being presented to the two young czars, the mentally retarded sixteen-year-old Ivan and his eleven-year-old half brother Peter, who would enter history as Peter the Great. They were also invited to dine at the houses of the aristocracy, but Kaempfer's judgment remained negative. "In Russia," he wrote, "are many churches and few who come to listen, many drunkards and few tankards, many prostitutes and few houses of prostitution. The following three are under coercion: the bells, the horses and the women."[13]

Up to Moscow the delegation had endured the hardship of traveling on horseback, but now it boarded boats and used the river system to reach the Caspian Sea. This provided Kaempfer the leisure to sketch his environment, compare his observations with those of Olearius, and note "the errors of the geographers."[14]

From the beginning, Kaempfer traveled with the intention of publishing his notes, but on his stormy voyage to Japan the saltwater flooding his cabin rendered much of this material illegible. Nevertheless, in his first large publication, the *Amoenitates Exoticae* of 1712, Kaempfer still spoke of his intention to publish his Russian diaries, but he died before he could realize the project. His water-stained manuscript has permitted only a fragmentary transcription of this material.[15]

Despite the pomp at the court of the czars, the delegation soon realized that the authority of the government did not reach to its borders. It was warned by the local authorities that traveling merchants had been killed by plundering hordes of Kalmucks, Russian settlements laid to waste, and even the official guards and soldiers robbed of their belongings. The delegation was fortunate to reach the Caspian Sea unscathed, but here new dangers awaited it. Winter had set in, and a fierce storm turned the crossing from Astrachan to Nisabad into a nightmare; the members of the delegation had little faith in the local captain and feared for their lives. In spite of the dangers, Kaempfer was fascinated by the alternating currents of salt and clear water. The bitter taste he discovered in the water he assumed was due to naphtha, or oil, welling from the floor of the sea. Later Kaempfer explained these phenomena in a scholarly treatise that formed part of both his doctoral dissertation and his voluminous *Amoenitates*.[16] Today oil rigs stand where Kaempfer first tasted the bitter water, confirming his conclusions.

The delegation had to wait for three months at Schamachi for permission to travel further. Kaempfer's notes document his activity during this period: he explored famous sites, investigated local customs, and attempted to trace the footsteps of his predecessor Olearius. Moreover, he had quickly acquired fame as a doctor and found himself overwhelmed with patients. In their eagerness to consult him, they did not permit him even to step outside the city gates, and in an attempt to see the "eternal fires" of the Apscheron peninsula before the delegation's departure, he made a daring escape at night, accompanied only by two local guides and an interpreter. This unauthorized trip landed him and his party in jail at Baku, the ancient town that controlled the entrance to the peninsula. Plying the guard with wine, the small party escaped from prison at dawn the next day. In a further bit of daring, Kaempfer donned the clothes of one of his guides and investigated the town on foot before he rejoined the rest of the party outside the city gates. Kaempfer spent two days in the bitter cold of winter on the barren peninsula amid the fumes of open oil wells taking notes and sketching the "eternal fires."[17]

Some ten years of university education had provided Kaempfer with the theoretical foundations to understand the importance of and to conduct scholarly investigations into phenomena that had little meaning for other travelers. Paying scant attention to his personal comfort and even his own safety, he was quickly acquiring the practical experience that later would permit him to write the finest work on Japan of his age. As he sketched and mapped his surroundings, his skills as a draughtsman increased, and his notes were becoming more systematic, detailed, and factual. But most important with regard to his work in Japan later was that Kaempfer was becoming very adept in enlisting others to help him acquire the desired information.

When the delegation finally arrived in Isfahan, Kaempfer succeeded in striking up a friendship with the best-informed foreigner in the Persian capital: the Capuchin friar Raphael du Mans, the interpreter of the shah and himself the author of a work on Persia.[18] Even after Kaempfer had left Isfahan, du Mans would remain his faithful correspondent, fulfilling his various requests for further information. Under the tutelage of du Mans, Kaempfer used the four months the delegation had to wait at Isfahan for their audience with the shah to his greatest advantage. He explored the city and surrounding countryside; a copperplate print shows him sketching on a hill overlooking Isfahan, shaded by an umbrella held by a servant. But he was not content with merely gathering the large amount of information that was publicly available. Posing as the assistant to the architect supervising the repair of the fountains, he even had himself smuggled into the highly guarded women's quarters of the shah's palace. When finally the delegation appeared before the shah in a grand reception, he not only sketched and noted every detail himself but even charged his servant to take notes outside, asking him, for instance, to count the number of dishes that were carried into the hall.

Kaempfer had the practical talent to organize his research efficiently, but he also appears to have possessed some personal charisma that opened doors for the penniless vicar's son from Lemgo. In his autograph book we find a number of references to the magnetism of his eyes that quickly broke down barriers.[19] Moreover, only his charisma could explain the popularity he enjoyed in Persia as a doctor, for his interpreters were often so bad that they failed to pass on his instructions correctly. Thus one of his patients did not imbibe the prescribed diuretic as Kaempfer directed but administered it straight to his sore eyes. He was cured all the same. In Japan Kaempfer prided himself on being on more intimate terms with the Japanese than any foreigner before him.[20]

After the audience with the shah, Kaempfer could have returned to Sweden with the delegation, published his research, and no doubt secured himself a comfortable post at the Swedish court. But he was not satisfied; his dreams of following in the footsteps of Alexander the Great had not been fulfilled. In his letters he speaks of the "thirst for knowledge" that was plaguing him like a fever and driving him to travel further.[21] After much pleading, he was finally given a position as a physician with the Dutch East India Company.

Kaempfer was soon to be disappointed with his new employer. After having to serve in Isfahan for nearly a year without pay and using his own medicines, the company finally ordered him to accompany a caravan on the one-thousand-kilometer trek to Bandar Abbas at the Gulf of Hormuz. He reported the journey in detail in his diary.[22] With even greater thoroughness than before, he measured and described buildings and ruins, water basins, and even their taps, but he also recorded local practices in detail, such as the preparation of coffee, a beverage still largely unknown in Europe. His skills were put to the test when he left the caravan for a detour to Persepolis. He noted that two months would barely suffice to sketch and describe the famous ruins, but then within the three days available to him he produced the finest early description of the site. Shiraz, "the city of poets and wine," where he rejoined the caravan, enthralled him with its beauty; the copious notes and sketches he made during his short stay provided sufficient material for nearly three chapters of his *Amoenitates*.

Kaempfer's arrival in Bandar Abbas on December 28, 1685, was much less pleasant and set the tone for the next unhappy years. The travelers' first task on entering the company's lodging was to bury "the black body of an assistant, the sorrowful result of this infernal air."[23] The doctor was certainly needed in this climate, which was so bad that even the locals left in the hot summer months. But the company made no allowance and continued its operations, despite the frequent illness and death of its personnel. Soon Kaempfer too fell seriously ill and pleaded to be moved. But his desperate appeals were refused, and fearing for his life, he twice escaped into the cool mountains to recuperate without the company's permission. Kaempfer left detailed descriptions of these trips and the research he accomplished in spite of his ill health but said nothing about the admonitions he no doubt received for his unauthorized departure from his place of duty. Reading between the lines—a messenger was sent out to find him and bring him back—one can sense, however, that these unscheduled holidays did much to damage his career prospects with the company and were no doubt ultimately responsible for giving him little choice but to accept employment in Japan.

Kaempfer had had no intention to visit Japan. The fabled courts of Alexander's India were his goal, but when at last he arrived in India, he was deeply disappointed. The Dutch East India Company vessel he was finally permitted to board in Bandar Abbas on June 30, 1688, took him to the coastal towns of South India and Ceylon only, where much of the indigenous culture had been destroyed first by the Portuguese and later the Dutch. He remained in Quilon for six months and succeeded in healing the Dutch governor and his family of a dangerous illness but refused the governor's offer of employment.[24] His aim was now Batavia, a city that was home to some twenty thousand Europeans and fifty thousand Asians serving them.[25]

When Kaempfer arrived in Batavia in 1689 the city was still "the pearl of Asia," with Dutch stone mansions lining clean canals and paved streets. But he was not privileged to enjoy its comforts. Unable to gain either of two available medical appointments, he was sent instead to serve on the Onrust, a little island in the harbor where company ships were being repaired amid much noise. Here he had neither a table to write on nor light to work after dark. In desperation he sent pleas for help to friends and patrons, imploring them to assist him "to come up in the world again."[26] Help finally came in the shape of an offer from the company's governor general at Batavia, Johannes Camphuis, to go to Japan. Perhaps Kaempfer was criticized for lacking commitment as a doctor in Bandar Abbas, but Camphuis recognized him as "a man combining extraordinary learning with superior powers of observation."[27] Camphuis himself had served three times in Japan and was so fond of everything Japanese that he had built himself a Japanese house as a retreat and once a week served Japanese food.[28] It must have concerned him that no accurate, recent description of Japan was available, for this is what he sent Kaempfer to write. He had already collected many documents and books about Japan, and he made these available to Kaempfer to prepare himself for his task. Thus when Kaempfer arrived in Japan he had studied not only what had been published but also the papers of the company and the reports of previous delegations traveling to Edo. Kaempfer was able to produce such detail in his work on Japan during his relatively brief stay in the country because he was already well informed about what he would see upon his arrival. He had, for instance, a list of places the delegation would pass on its journey to Edo and knew not only that there was a *daibutsu* (large Buddha) in Kyoto but also that the figure was sixty feet high and sat cross-legged.[29]

Kaempfer left Batavia on May 7, 1690, spent a month in Siam, and finally set foot on Japanese soil on September 25, 1690, after nearly suffering shipwreck along the South China coast. He had intended to stay only one year but eventually stayed two, leaving Japan the last day of October 1692. A year later he was back in Holland, where his first concern was to submit his doctoral dissertation—ten separate pieces of research—

to the University of Leiden. He was awarded his doctorate early in 1694 and soon afterward returned to his native Lemgo. He purchased the family farm at Lieme, outside Lemgo, from his widowed stepmother with the intention of writing up and publishing his research at an early date in the peace and isolation of the Westphalian countryside. Yet this was not to be. The lack of time for research and writing is a constant theme of the letters he wrote during the remaining twenty-odd years of his life.[30] Innumerable visitors were disturbing his peace to look at his exotic treasures, patients had to be attended and medicines prepared, and the estate made further claims on his time. In 1698 he was appointed as the personal physician to the local duke, which was a great honor but added the duty of traveling to the court at Detmold to his already busy schedule. He lived with his beloved half sister but just before turning fifty decided to marry a sixteen-year-old girl, the daughter of a rich merchant. If he had hoped that her dowry would permit him more leisure, he was disappointed. Instead, the marriage was an unhappy one. Three children were born and died at an early age. Despite the attempts of the court at Detmold to smooth over this embarrassing affair, the marriage finally came to its dramatic end with Kaempfer's refusal to live with his wife and a request for a divorce shortly before his death in 1716. The documents dealing with the divorce and the quarrel between his wife and his nephew Johann Hermann over the inheritance after Kaempfer's death give us a glimpse of some of the turbulent events of that period. Kaempfer was a sick man, but his wife refused to nurse him, even prevented the servants from preparing his diet, and instead heaped verbal and physical abuse upon him. Kaempfer, too, stood accused of physically mishandling his wife.[31]

The final years of Kaempfer's life were marred by tragic events: there was the death of his children and of two of his brothers, the departure of his beloved half sister when, to his great distress, she finally decided to marry, and in the end illness and violent quarrels with his wife.[32]

Yet Kaempfer had also fulfilled a dream that was impossible for most academics of the time, namely, the publication of a work of more than nine hundred pages, richly illustrated with copperplate prints: his *Amoenitates Exoticae* of 1712. Only wealthy men, like the learned mayor of Amsterdam, Nicolaas Witsen, could contemplate such a costly venture. The research of less-affluent scholars, even when their work was recognized in their day, like that of the botanist Rumphius, took more than half a century to appear in print or disappeared unpublished.[33] Decades later, subscriptions were necessary to raise the funds for both the English and German publication of Kaempfer's work on Japan. The fact that for the German edition of 1777–1779 a minimum of two hundred subscribers was considered essential to finance the printing, each paying two Louis d'or—the equivalent price of eighty-four kilos of beef—gives some idea of the cost of publication at that time.[34] Kaempfer's introduction to his *Amoenitates* indicates that he was not indebted to anyone for financial assistance; the Duke of Detmold is merely recognized for temporarily reducing his workload.

Kaempfer's handsome work met with approval and recognition in the European world of letters. Already in its year of publication, Nicolaas Witsen in Holland had acquired a copy and wrote to Leibniz that he had read the work with pleasure. He expressed admiration for both the style and the contents.[35]

Kaempfer devoted one section of five of the *Amoenitates* to a detailed description of the Japanese flora. Only some twenty-four pages of this voluminous work, however, dealt with general conditions in Japan and the Japanese people. In the introduction to the *Amoenitates,* Kaempfer likened himself to a salesman peddling his wares and pointed out that what he presented here were simply pleasantries, or tidbits *(amoenitas),* designed to entice the reader to sample the more solid fare of scholarship he had amassed. He gave a list of three manuscripts ready for publication of which the first was *Japonia nostri tempris (Today's Japan),* a work written in German.[36]

Publication of *The History of Japan*

During the four years that remained of Kaempfer's life he was unable to find a publisher for his manuscript on Japan or for any of the others. On his death the greater part of his possessions, including his manuscripts and collection of rare books and items from overseas, went to his nephew, Johann Hermann Kaempfer, a young man with some medical training, who had assisted and nursed him during the final difficult period. Johann Hermann's medical skills, however, were apparently less solid than those of his famous uncle. He could not live on what he earned as a doctor, and after selling the estate he had inherited, he also began to put Kaempfer's manuscripts and collection up for sale. Derek Massarella has unraveled the complex tale of how Kaempfer's manuscripts and collection eventually ended up in the possession of Hans Sloane and how his work on Japan finally came to be translated by a young Swiss in Sloane's employ, Johann Gaspar Scheuchzer (1702–1729).[37]

When Kaempfer's work appeared in 1727 in London under the title *The History of Japan,*[38] it became an immediate best-seller. Some twelve editions and translations were published in the next decade alone,[39] and as a result the European image of Japan rested on Kaempfer's account. For the next two hundred years writers and scholars cited Kaempfer in their work, and even when he is not acknowledged as a source, most of what was written about Japan can be traced to him.[40] Immanuel Kant used Kaempfer's work for his lectures on world geography and also drew inspiration from it for his political and philosophical writings.[41] Goethe referred to Kaempfer as if everybody ought to be familiar with his work,[42] and even the acid pen of Voltaire praised Kaempfer as an "honest and learned traveler."[43] The encyclopedists used Kaempfer's material extensively, and in a seventeenth-century dictionary on philosophy his name appears together with that of Leibniz as an authority on Confucianism.[44] Kaempfer's work on Japan was so well known that it could be parodied in journals for the learned,[45] and writers all over Europe, including Oliver Goldsmith,[46] referred to it. Kaempfer's evenhanded appraisal of the heathen nation was, however, not always welcome.[47]

It was an age in which the churches were still dominant, and religious and racial

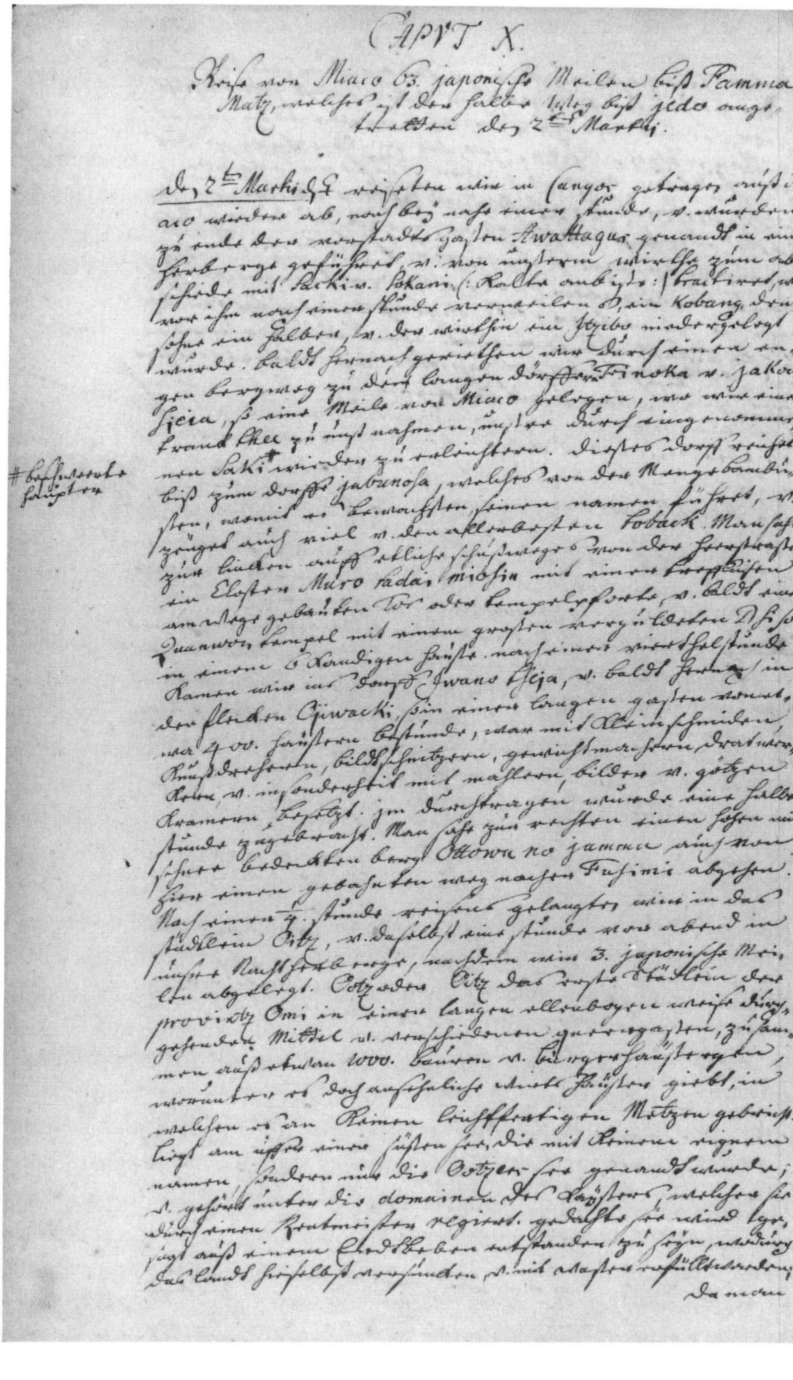

CAPVT X.

Reise von Miaco 63. japonische Meilen biß Famma Matz, welches ist der halbe Weg biß Jedo angetretten den 2ten Martij.

A page from chapter 10, book 5, of Kaempfer's manuscript, *Heutiges Japan,* from which both Scheuchzer and the author translated. (Courtesy of the British Library, Sloane 3060, folio 325 verso) tolerance was the dangerous conviction of a select few. It was the age when, in 1723, Christian Wolff, Leibniz' famous student, was driven from his professorship at the University of Halle for suggesting, as indeed Kaempfer does, that the ethical precepts of Confucianism are comparable to those of Christianity.[48]

The translator of Kaempfer's work, the young Swiss Johann Gaspar Scheuchzer, or his English editors were not free from such commonplace and even valued sentiments of their times. In his translation Scheuchzer, or his editors, did his best to tone down some of Kaempfer's praise of Japan and amplify any criticism. Words and even sentences were inserted, and an attempt was made to turn Kaempfer's dry and mostly matter-of-fact report into a tale of the exotic complete with suitable value judgments about the heathen nation. The puritan sentiments of the presumably Protestant readership were catered to by omitting, for instance, an episode in which Kaempfer's traveling companions paid for the privilege of touching the breasts of "a beautiful whore,"[49] but inserting, on the other hand, a dig at the unreformed by sarcastically comparing the presumed beneficial effects of washing ancestral tablets to that of "any number of Masses, as they are celebrated to the same end in Roman Catholick Countries."[50]

In his introduction, Scheuchzer did not hide the fact that the task of translation was difficult and one he did not cherish. Kaempfer's style he found "very intricate and obscure." Moreover, English was not his native language, and he had to accept others' revisions of his text. Under the circumstances, he decided that the best he could do was "to express the sense of the author, in as clear and intelligible a manner, as was not inconsistent with the nature of the subject, and the genius of the English language."[51]

Scheuchzer apparently completed the enormous task of translating Kaempfer's manuscript, dealing with a subject initially unknown to him, in less than two years.[52] Moreover, to make the work more complete, he added throughout the text passages from Kaempfer's notes, wrote a new opening chapter dealing with Kaempfer's travels to and stay in Siam based on Kaempfer's diary and other writings, and put together a further chapter on Japanese laws Kaempfer had intended to write but never did.[53] Scheuchzer also translated and added relevant passages from Kaempfer's Latin *Amoenitates*. Finally he was personally involved in turning Kaempfer's sketches and various illustrations he had brought back from Japan into copperplate prints, which though not true to the originals, have become the standard illustrations for all translations and editions to this day.[54] Examining the last pages of Scheuchzer's translation, one can sense his utter exhaustion from working under the pressure of time on an extremely difficult text: the final sixty lines of Scheuchzer's translation alone contain some ten serious errors.[55] Two years after the completion of this mammoth task, Scheuchzer died, aged only twenty-seven.[56]

For some time, Germans were able to read only parts of Kaempfer's work in their native language, namely, in a German translation of Du Halde's *Histoire de la Chine*, to which extracts from Kaempfer's work had been appended. These extracts were based on a French translation of Scheuchzer's English version of the original manuscript.[57] On the death of Kaempfer's niece in 1773, however, two more copies of

Kaempfer's manuscript on Japan were discovered at her estate at Lemgo, Westphalia, and it was decided finally to publish a complete German version based on the original.

The task of editing the manuscript was entrusted to the twenty-two-year-old Christian Wilhelm Dohm (1751–1820), who later became famous as a diplomat, statesman, and historian. After some debate and correspondence with more senior scholars in Berlin, Dohm assured the public that the newly discovered documents consisted of a complete manuscript of Kaempfer's work in the hand of Kaempfer's nephew and a second one with only a few sheets missing, written by Kaempfer himself. The two manuscripts have since disappeared, but a comparison of Dohm's modernized version of Kaempfer's text and Dohm's notes with the only remaining manuscript in London indicates that the young editor was not completely telling the truth.[58] Neither was Dohm being truthful when he informed his readers that he was modernizing Kaempfer's original with "micrological exactness." Even the sample passages in his preface indicate that he followed the trend of the English translation in adding negative value judgments to Kaempfer's matter-of-fact description of Japan.[59] Dohm stated that he was aware of inaccuracies in Scheuchzer's translation but nevertheless had no scruples about translating from the English and surreptitiously adding to his own text derogatory sentences Scheuchzer had made up.[60] For Dohm too was of the opinion that Kaempfer had described the heathen nation in much too positive terms and even warned prospective readers that Kaempfer had seen Japan through rose-tinted spectacles.[61]

Kaempfer's account of seventeenth-century Japan has not lost its value with the passage of time. To the contrary, now that historians have turned their attention to the everyday life of the ordinary person, Kaempfer's detailed description of how the average man and woman lived and behaved has become more important than ever. Often Kaempfer supplies more detail on this topic than any Japanese source, for he describes the commonplace, which no Japanese bothered to record at the time. Moreover, most Japanese historical sources were written by members of the samurai class, who had little interest in how the commoners lived. Thus Kaempfer is cited frequently by historians of Japan, both in Japan and in the West.

All existing publications of Kaempfer's work are based on either Scheuchzer's translation or Dohm's modernized version. The discovery, some ten years ago, that no published version of this much-cited account correctly reflects the contents of the original prompted me to set out on an unexpectedly long and arduous path that took me far beyond transcribing and translating Kaempfer's manuscript.

Although we are in a better position today to accept and appreciate Kaempfer's evenhanded appraisal of seventeenth-century Japan, we still must ask why his evaluation was so out of tune with the *Zeitgeist,* the sentiments of his age. What prompted him, the vicar's son, to write so favorably about a heathen nation, a nation, moreover, that kept him and his fellow Europeans imprisoned on the small fortified island of Deshima in the harbor of Nagasaki and treated them, the representatives of the powerful Dutch East India Company, like hostages and criminals? To understand why the heathen nation of Japan won the respect and admiration of the European scholar, it is necessary to examine briefly how certain events in these two societies half a world apart related to each other.

Japan

In 1651, the year Engelbert Kaempfer was born, an eleven-year-old boy succeeded in Japan as the fourth military hegemon, the shogun, of the Tokugawa house. Fundamental sociopolitical changes during the previous half-century made it possible that Ietsuna as a minor could succeed unchallenged to this position and that this mentally and physically weak ruler—known as *sayō-sama*, Lord So-be-it, because of his ready compliance—could remain in office until his natural death some thirty years later. The *pax Tokugawa*, the peace that so impressed Kaempfer, was also unusual for Japan.

Japan had suffered intermittent internal wars since the middle ages. In the eleventh century a new warrior class challenged the power of the emperor at Kyoto and set up a government, the *bakufu*, in the northeast of the country at Kamakura. The leader was given the title of *seii taishōgun,* barbarian-quelling general, yet he was less intent upon subjecting the "barbarians" to the northeast than upon gaining control of the wealth that supported a highly cultured aristocracy in the southwest, at Kyoto, and the large, powerful monasteries throughout the country. An attempt by the imperial line to regain power in the fourteenth century ended in failure. Instead the new military leaders, the Ashikaga shoguns, set up their headquarters in Kyoto, and on their demise, at the end of the fifteenth century, they turned the imperial capital into their battlefield. What followed was a century known as the Warring States Period *(sengoku jidai).* The rule was *gekokujō,* the lower usurping the power of their superiors, and the country was divided into many competing military factions.

Paradoxically it was most probably the introduction of firearms into Japan by the Portuguese in 1543 that eventually ushered in the long peace. The purchasing power and commercial supply lines required to equip an army with firearms and gunpowder eliminated the small players from the battlefield and finally permitted the rise of the first "unifier," Oda Nobunaga.

On Oda Nobunaga's assassination in 1582, one of his generals, Toyotomi Hideyoshi, Kaempfer's Taikō, seized power. War was now no longer sporadic and localized but centered on the Taikō's great campaigns. More often than not, diplomatic and commercial strategies and siege, rather than naked aggression, decided the outcome. After Hideyoshi had secured the submission of the territorial lords, the daimyo, he began to prepare the country for peace. He disarmed the peasants, initiated land surveys, controlled the influence of the foreign missionaries by sporadic persecutions, and moved the battleground overseas by ordering the invasion of Korea. To secure the succession of his house, he appointed regents for his infant son, but the Toyotomi hegemony was not to last beyond the span of Hideyoshi's life. In the spirit of *gekokujō* one of the regents, Tokugawa Ieyasu, seized power after Hideyoshi's death. Even some ninety years after this event, when Kaempfer arrived in Japan, Ieyasu's usurpation of authority had neither been forgotten nor cast in more acceptable terms by his subjects.[62] But the Warring States era had passed, and in only two decisive battles fifteen years apart Ieyasu was able to convince the daimyo that it was more profitable for them to acknowledge his sovereignty than squander their resources in continued warfare. The power of the Catholic missionaries was eliminated by ruthless persecution, among the Westerners later permitting only the Dutch, who declared themselves to be of a different faith, to remain in Japan, secluded on the strongly guarded island of Deshima in Nagasaki.

Ieyasu never held autocratic power over Japan. But his life, which began as a military hostage and witnessed the demise of two hegemons, furnished him with the skills and experience to coerce the daimyo into reluctant support and establish a military regime that lasted until the Americans appeared in the bay of Edo with their "black" (steam) ships in the middle of the nineteenth century. The measures Ieyasu and his successors adopted to secure the hegemony of the Tokugawa house fundamentally shaped the sociopolitical and economic character of the society Kaempfer was to encounter.

Unlike his predecessors, Ieyasu did not establish his government in central Japan, near the great population centers of Kyoto and Osaka, but at Edo, present-day Tokyo, at the edge of a marshy bay in the relatively rugged and uninhabited northeastern part of the country. Here narrow mountain paths controlled overland access, while rough seas and, later, laws forbidding the building of ocean-going vessels made maritime attacks unlikely. In this remote and inhospitable location Ieyasu coerced the daimyo into spending their resources on major building projects: draining the bay, flattening the surrounding mountains, piping in fresh water, and building large mansions for their families and entourages within the outer walls of his castle. Thus grew one of the largest, cleanest, and most "modern" cities of the age, most likely with more than one million inhabitants by the time Kaempfer visited it in 1691.

The system of compulsory residence at Edo for all daimyo and direct retainers of the shogun was institutionalized under the third shogun, Iemitsu, and became known as *sankin kōtai,* the system of alternate attendance. But the presence of wives and children at Edo as a guarantee of loyal behavior by those in the distant domains, as well as frequent attendance upon the shogun, were compulsory from the beginning, especially for the most powerful of the daimyo. A consequence was the rapid development of a system of roads throughout the country with traffic so heavy at certain times of the year that, according to Kaempfer, it could be compared to that of a populous city in Europe.[63] The long peace had brought about a population explosion: some scholars estimate that Japan's population doubled, or even tripled, in one hundred years.[64] New tracts of land were opened in remote areas to cope with the additional numbers, but many sought nonfarming occupations, especially in the rapidly expanding settlements along the highways. Kaempfer's account describes how the Kansai, the area including Osaka and Kyoto, had already grown into one urban sprawl and how, even in mountainous regions, one village followed the next, as if holding hands. Along these highways also agriculturally poor districts found the means to sustain a populace by catering to travelers, providing them with straw sandals, wicker baskets, herbal medicines, and even paper garments, or marketing the meager fare the stony ground provided as unique, local delicacies. The comfort available to the travelers on these roads, especially the main trunk road linking Osaka, Kyoto, and Edo, the famous Tōkaidō, was in all probability far beyond anything Kaempfer had experienced elsewhere in his travels. Official inns were available at regular intervals. With their clean rush matting on the floor, neatly papered sliding doors, verandas, pretty courtyards, and hot baths, they provided in essence the same comforts a traditional country inn furnishes in Japan today. There were restaurants offering elaborate meals with female entertainment and stalls with take-away food for those in a hurry. The roads were drained, swept, sometimes even paved, shaded by trees and signposted, and, within settlements, lit at night. Even private toilets were available at the roadside.

But it was not just the creature comforts, the cleanliness, and hygiene that impressed the doctor from Europe. He was equally astonished by the friendliness and politeness of the populace—even though the foreigners were rarely permitted to profit from it—and their capacity to endure adverse conditions and hard work. Not that the fierce warriors of the previous centuries had been tamed by the *pax Tokugawa.* Kaempfer considered the samurai fiercer than the Russian hussars, and was convinced that the most powerful of them, the daimyo, were merely lurking in the wings waiting to assert their power.[65] Even those who were not permitted to carry the two swords that distinguished a man as a samurai, the commoners, were headstrong, frequently defiant of the law, and reckless in risking their lives for small profit. In Nagasaki alone some fifty persons a year suffered capital punishment for smuggling. Throughout the country the execution grounds bore testimony to the numbers that were publicly crucified or executed, as well as to the cold-bloodedness of the young samurai who cut the bodies into pieces "half the length of a finger" to hone their sword skills.[66] Despite the reckless and defiant character of its populace, Japan was not a disorderly country. To the contrary, every individual, from the highest minister to the lowliest day-laborer, was caught in a complex web of obligations and was, moreover, continuously watched by others and rotated in his task, so that only the most daring found room to stray from the prescribed path.

The apparent paradox between extreme politeness and callousness, scrupulous adherence to innumerable rules and audacious defiance of the law, that emerges from Kaempfer's account was later parodied by W. S. Gilbert in his libretto, *The Mikado or the Town of Titipu*, Titipu most probably being a takeoff on Nagasaki. For Kaempfer, however, such behavior was an expression of the natural stoicism of the Japanese: the stoic acceptance of the conditions of life of a spirited people forced to make a living on a number of mostly infertile, mountainous, and volcanic islands. This inborn stoicism Kaempfer saw reinforced by the philosophy of Confucianism imported from China. The Confucian texts, Kaempfer asserted, were valued in Japan as much as those of the heathen Roman and Greek scholars, the Stoic Seneca and Plato, were in Christian Europe.

Kaempfer's positive appraisal of Japan was to some extent conditioned by the timing of his visit. He was fortunate to arrive in the middle of the Genroku period (1688–1704) when, for a brief interval, the country was free from major natural disasters.

It was an era of unprecedented affluence. Modern Japanese have coined the phrase Shōwa-Genroku, combining Genroku with the era name of the postwar period, in recognition of the fact that Japan did not experience a similar level of prosperity until the modern postwar boom. Kaempfer's positive appraisal was, however, also due to the fact that the reigning shogun was a man much to his taste.

The Dog Shogun

Kaempfer's "great and excellent ruler,"[67] the fifth Tokugawa shogun, Tsunayoshi, has gone down in Japanese history as the infamous Dog Shogun. He earned this disparaging name because he issued laws for the protection of all animate creation, from the child in the mother's womb to the dog in the street.[68]

Tsunayoshi was in more than one way the black sheep of the Tokugawa line. His mother had begun life as a commoner, a grocer's daughter, growing up in the streets of Kyoto. But owing to the quirks of fate and her beauty, she had entered the *ō-oku,* the women's quarters of Edo castle, as a lady-in-waiting and eventually bore the shogun two boys. The elder died in infancy, but the younger apparently distinguished himself by his precociousness and liveliness at an early age, and the father, the third shogun, Iemitsu, became fearful that he might usurp the position of his duller elder brothers. Thus he ordered that the boy not be brought up as a warrior, as was becoming for his station, but be trained as a scholar.[69] His brothers, however, died early or remained childless,[70] and despite strong opposition, Tsunayoshi succeeded to the position of shogun in 1680.

Under this first civilian-educated ruler of the Tokugawa line, the inevitable transformation from warrior to civil society accelerated greatly. Tsunayoshi's laws for the protection of all animate creation, the so-called Laws of Compassion, and the resulting opposition by the military were symptomatic of this fundamental change in sociopolitical direction. To implement the shogun's new policies, a tightening of central control was essential. The first shogun, Ieyasu, had been content to act as *primus inter pares* and to permit the daimyo a great measure of independent control over their domains. But his great-grandson Tsunayoshi saw himself as the all-powerful sun in the sky that lit even the tiniest particle of dust, as a ruler directly responsible for the well-being of even his most humble subjects.[71] Tsunayoshi's ideals were Yao and Shun, the mythical Chinese sage kings of the Confucian classics, who ruled as benevolent dictators, assisted by personally chosen men of talent.

One of Tsunayoshi's chosen men, who had risen from humble samurai origin to a powerful position, was known to the foreigners as "Bingo," the grand chamberlain Makino Narisada, Bingo no Kami. He determined when the foreigners were permitted to see the shogun, just as he controlled all other access to the ruler. Kaempfer's portrayal of him is very positive—he even notes that his physique was rather German—but in Japanese history Tsunayoshi's chamberlains have gone down as the flattering sycophants of a weak ruler. Of Narisada's assistant and later successor Yanagisawa Yoshiyasu, whose reputation was to be far worse, Kaempfer had heard that he entertained the shogun with young women when he visited his house.[72]

Tsunayoshi's attempts to realize his ideals led to conflict with the military aristocracy, who, especially under the thirty-year government of the fourth shogun, Ietsuna, had come to consider it their birthright to govern the country. But it earned him the admiration of those who rose to unexpected honors in the highly stratified society of Tokugawa Japan on account of their ability and learning. These were especially the scholars in all fields of learning that Tsunayoshi patronized and the experts on the Confucian classics he called into his presence for debates and sometimes to advise on political issues. They increasingly found ready employment in the mansions of the great lords, who kept them as an "ornament" of their house and a means of winning the favors of the shogun.[73]

These were people with whom Kaempfer could readily identify, men with a high level of education but of few financial resources. They were also his informers, for generally only scholars seeking tuition in Western science were permitted to befriend him. When alone with them, Kaempfer, in turn, probed them for information on Japan, especially after he had loosened their tongues with sweet European liqueurs.[74] The Deshima interpreters, Kaempfer's daily companions, many of whom were scholars in their own right, also benefited from Tsunayoshi's government. Despite their low official rank, they were now called into the presence of the shogun to show their skills in unheard of, long, informal audiences with the foreigners.[75] For while the Westerners were kept like hostages and prisoners at Nagasaki, they were now more than previously honored by the interest of the shogun.

Like every daimyo and senior vassal of the ruler, the Dutch had been accorded the rather burdensome honor of annually paying homage to the shogun at Edo Castle. Initially there was only a formal and very short audience for the resident head of the trading post, known to the Japanese as *kapitan.* On a number of occasions, however, while the Dutch were waiting for this brief encounter at Edo Castle, they, and no less the Japanese courtiers who attended upon them, were surprised by the sudden and totally unceremonious appearance of the fourth shogun's younger brother, who inspected the foreigners with great curiosity.[76] A few years after Tsunayoshi succeeded as shogun, he began calling the Western visitors into his presence for a second, drawn-out, informal audience, where he not only asked questions but also requested them to act out everyday behavior, dance, and sing. On Kaempfer's second visit to Edo in 1692, the foreigners were even honored with two private audiences.

Kaempfer described these audiences in detail and in memory of the event produced one of his most detailed and valuable drawings.[77] Some European writers castigated the Dutch for permitting themselves to behave in such undignified fashion to amuse a heathen potentate.[78] Kaempfer, however, made it clear, not only in his description but also in his private correspondence, that he considered his performance in front of the shogun an honor. Much to his grief, he was employed by the Dutch East India Company only as a humble physician. But the shogun, this patron of scholars, gave him the recognition he deserved, paid him more attention than even the *kapitan.*

Kaempfer's praise of Tsunayoshi has much to do with this personal encounter with the shogun and his image of him as a patron of learning. This was every European scholar's utopia.[79] But Tsunayoshi matched Kaempfer's ideal also in a much broader sense, namely, as the autocratic, all-powerful ruler. To understand why autocratic government had such appeal to an enlightened and tolerant scholar like Kaempfer, one must take a closer look at his life and the times in which he lived.

Kaempfer's Environment

Kaempfer was born three years after the Peace of Westphalia had ended the carnage of the Thirty Years War and one year after the last Swedish troops had left German soil. In the name of God fertile fields and thriving cities had been laid waste and the population murdered. The plundering armies were followed by pestilence and starvation. It is estimated that the population of the German states was reduced by 40 percent, in some areas up to 70 percent.[80] Kaempfer's birthplace, Lemgo, was spared destruction: the large stone cathedral in which he listened as a child to the sermons of his father, the chief vicar, had dominated the skyline of the town for four hundred years. The houses with their intricate masonry work that lined the marketplace he crossed to reach his "Latin School" had a history of more than a century. Yet if the war had spared the houses, its aftermath destroyed much of the trade on which the small merchant town depended. As in other parts of the Western world, economic pressure found expression in the persecution of women, in witch-hunts. Lemgo had the dubious distinction of burning the greatest number of witches: thirty-eight in three years.[81] The last and bloodiest phase began in 1665 when Kaempfer was in his early teens. For the young Engelbert, the cruel climax was the execution of his own uncle, his father's assistant. Using the pulpit to condemn the senseless burning of innocent women, the assistant vicar angered the city fathers and was declared to be in league with the witches. The power of the local government was such that his imaginary guilt was eventually confirmed by the University of Gießen, and he was executed—the only vicar to die in the persecution. Kaempfer's remark that in Japan punishment was severe but at least could not be swayed by financial considerations could well relate to this incident, for his father and uncle were learned but as clergy not wealthy. This experience apparently still weighed heavily on Kaempfer's mind many decades later, for in his *Amoenitates* of 1712, in an essay supposedly dealing with the establishment of innocence or guilt by the use of crocodiles or fire among the "infidels of the Orient," he wanders off the topic to discuss the history of Western superstition at length. His greatest condemnation is reserved for those who sat in judgment of the alleged witches: "frequently uneducated, biased, if not to say greedy, cruel, and wicked people."[82]

No information exists on how Kaempfer's father, whose duty it was to administer the last sacrament to the unhappy women, dealt with these events. All we know is that he did not resign his post at the time but remained in office until retirement.

Kaempfer's departure from Lemgo at the age of sixteen to visit other schools across the country was not unusual. What was perhaps unusual is that although his so-called *Stammbuch,* his autograph book in which he collected the signatures and good wishes of prominent people he met, gives us a fairly good record of his movements, only one further meeting with his father is documented. That took place in 1680, on the father's seventieth birthday, twelve years after Kaempfer had left home. From Lemgo Kaempfer returned to Königsberg and then went straight to Sweden, to depart from there on his long journey. By the time he returned to Lemgo, his father had long since died.

Although there is no material to indicate whether Kaempfer saw the church, and by extension his father the vicar, as silent accomplices in the crime of witch-hunting, it is safe to say that Kaempfer's religious tolerance owed much to this experience. He could not, like the missionaries before him in Japan, be smugly convinced that his own creed and church were the only way to salvation. He expressed his thoughts clearly when he declared that the Japanese were not atheists but only worshipped the Divine Majesty in a different fashion and provocatively added that they are frequently more pious than their Christian brothers and sisters.[83]

Absolutism

The injustices Kaempfer witnessed in Lemgo in his early teens most likely also shaped his political convictions. These he articulated at an early age, in his high school matriculation thesis submitted at Lübeck in 1672 and printed the following year. In this essay, titled *Exercitatio politica de Majestatis divisione (A Political Discourse on the Division of Sovereignty),*[84] Kaempfer debates the very topical question of whether a ruler was to be omnipotent or ought to be subject to limitations imposed by his ministers and other governing bodies. He carefully cites those scholars who argue for the unlimited authority of the ruler and those who oppose this and then firmly comes down in favor of the former. It was a time when jurists, such as Samuel Pufendorf, were pleading for the natural right of men to govern themselves. Was Kaempfer an archconservative, and how does this apparent conservatism combine with his enlightened tolerance of other religions?

Kaempfer was not alone in advocating what appears incompatible today. The sixteenth-century French lawyer Jean Bodin is similarly castigated for advocating both absolutism and religious tolerance, which are described by one modern commentator "as the improbable twins of the modern state system."[85] Even Pufendorf, the defender of the natural-rights theory, pleaded for the omnipotence of the ruler, and his work is therefore criticized as "honeycombed with juxtaposed and unresolved combinations."[86] Thomas Hobbes too is accused of insincerity when he argues both for the rights of the individual and the authority of the ruler, and similar "inconsistencies" can be found in the political writings of Leibniz.[87]

Such modern criticism ignores the history of absolutism. The term *absolutism* and its negative image in the sense of despotism came into being only in the nineteenth century.[88] It did not encompass the tyranny of a Hitler or Stalin but signified rule by God-given law, the ruler as the defender of the *salus publica:* the general good.[89] Kaempfer states: "A king . . . who is solely intent on his own advantage is degenerate" and insists that the tyranny of the Roman rulers does not deserve to be called sovereignty.[90] The ruler was omnipotent only inasmuch as he did not have to tolerate the interference of lesser men; thus even Louis XIV had to observe the "God-given" laws of Salesian succession and could not elevate the children of his mistress to the status of those born in wedlock.[91] The absolutism advocated by the scholars of Kaempfer's age must be seen within the context of the paradigm change from feudal to modern state; it was an escape from the capricious government of local feudal lords or corrupt practices of powerful city councils. "We Germans," wrote Kaempfer later in life, "are, as is well known, the slaves of our barons."[92] In Kaempfer's time the large state did not possess the means to minutely control the life of the individual, and only the local lord was in a position to do so.[93] What was sought was escape from this personal, erratic "slavery" to the uniform laws and predictable order of the large state, where neither the witch-hunt nor the execution of Kaempfer's uncle could have taken place.

In Kaempfer's age, life was threatened not only by the arbitrariness of local rule but also by the dangers of continuous warfare. His long travels, Kaempfer states in the introduction to his work on Japan, were undertaken because he considered them less onerous than submitting "to the generally prevailing bad conditions and involuntary state of war"[94] in his native country.

Kaempfer calls his native country "Germany," but the political unit with the grandiose name of Holy Roman Empire to which he refers was unable to enforce peace within its boundaries or deter its powerful neighbors from aggression. It was no more than a loose federation of some 355 political units, each of which could enter a virtually limitless combination of alliances within and outside the empire: an extraordinary political "monster," as Samuel Pufendorf called it.[95] Like the daimyo at Edo, the heads of the states gathered at the diet at Regensburg to play a role in the government of the empire, but unlike those in Japan, they did not secure peace for their subjects.[96] For the people of Kaempfer's age who had suffered some two hundred years of mostly religious wars, religious tolerance and the authoritarian state were in theory not contradictions. Whether it was Bodin in France, Hobbes in England, or Pufendorf in Sweden and Prussia, the most fundamental and important right of the individual was to live in peace. The acceptance and celebration of Louis XIV's authoritarianism, Leopold Ranke suggested, mirrored the search of the individual for protection and order.[97]

In defense of the omnipotent ruler, Kaempfer invokes the symbolism of the sun,[98] but he was no admirer of Louis XIV, the self-styled *roi soleil.* It was the threat of this "most Christian" king's army that persuaded him to spend some ten years in distant countries. The sage ruler he was searching for did not exist in Europe: only the Japanese shogun approached his ideal.

In the early nineteenth century, when foreign ships were increasingly seen in Japanese waters and foreign nations were pressuring the Japanese to "open" the country, a chapter of Kaempfer's *Amoenitates* became important in the internal debate in Japan on whether to permit the foreigners access. This essay is known in English by the lengthy title "An Enquiry, whether it be conducive for the good of the Japanese Empire, to keep it shut up, as it now is, and not to suffer its inhabitants to have any Commerce with foreign nations, either at home or abroad," and as *Sakoku ron* (lit., closed country debate) in Japan.[99] First Kaempfer argues that the closure of a country to the rest of mankind was surely against the will of God, who created a world without boundaries. But then he insists that such stringent measures are justified if they secure eternal peace.[100] Japan had emerged from its Warring States Period; Europe had so far failed to do so.

Stoicism

There was another ideal cherished in Kaempfer's age, in the attainment of which Japan apparently had made more progress than Europe. That was in the practice of the tenets of Stoicism, or Neo-Stoicism.

Kaempfer's repeated mention and praise of the stoicism of the Japanese indicates the high regard in which he held such behavior. Moreover, the role Stoicism, or Neo-Stoicism, played in Europe becomes apparent when Kaempfer compares its influence to that of Confucianism in pre-Tokugawa Japan, noting that Confucianism "comprised the greater part of the population and practically held a monopoly on the sciences and the liberal arts." According to Kaempfer the Confucian classics were "valued by all other believers no less than we do the instructive works by Seneca, Plato, and other heathens."[101]

The influence of Stoicism, or Neo-Stoicism, on European thought of the premodern period, the German scholar Gerhard Oestreich argues, has received insufficient attention, considering that Neo-Stoicism became the guiding star for political, social, and military reform. He contends that its general popularity and decisive influence on the important paradigm changes that produced the modern state in Europe has been much underestimated.[102]

The influence of Neo-Stoicism was reflected in the enormous popularity of the writings of Justus Lipsius (1547–1606), an author whom Kaempfer refers to in his work on Japan and whose writings he obviously knew in detail.[103] Lipsius' major work, *De Constantia,* turned the word *constantia,* meaning steadfastness, perseverance, into a fashionable catchword.[104]

In the spirit of the Roman stoics, Lipsius urges the unflinching acceptance of fate, facing it with inner strength, and responding with divine reason lodged in man. Lipsius' sage in search of the truth, taming the passions and settling the mind, yet not retiring to practice spiritual contemplation but leading an active life for the good of society, has much in common with the Confucian sage. Kaempfer often observed in Japan the very steadfastness and unperturbed mind advocated in Lipsius' writings. Even the common, uneducated people faced their lot with exemplary stoic behavior, such as the young

Japanese about to be decapitated who urged his companion to stop praying so that the foreigners would not realize his shameful lack of inner composure.[105]

In a second work, which also won unprecedented popularity, Lipsius addressed those in authority. Here again his counsel, stressing moderation, loyalty, benevolence, and steadfastness, has much in common with that of Confucius. Even more interesting is that his prescription for the modernization of Europe's armies advocates the very principles that had long been cherished and observed in Japan.[106] Military historians have noted that acceptance of Lipsius' principles led to a new chivalry in Europe that was, however, still the exception rather than the rule in Kaempfer's age.[107] It could not have escaped Kaempfer that, here again, Japan had already achieved what was still mostly an ideal in Europe.

The Reliability of Kaempfer's Work

With Japanese government and society fulfilling Kaempfer's ideals in such important respects, should we, as his German editor Dohm suggests, be wary of his rose-tinted spectacles?

I do not think so. Kaempfer's recognition of certain virtues in Japan should rather be seen as a healthy antidote against the many frustrations he suffered as a "prisoner" on Deshima. He makes no attempt to hide these frustrations but, to the contrary, often dwells on them in detail. Moreover, throughout Kaempfer's account there is evidence that despite his tolerance and broad-mindedness, his benchmark remains mostly Europe. Thus Japanese temples, he notes, hardly ever reach the majestic proportions of European cathedrals, houses resemble goat-pens, the native Japanese Shinto religion lacks the essential scriptures, its clergy is unlearned, and the hearts of the Japanese are harder than stone when they ignore a dying priest at the roadside. Only occasionally does he turn the tables and explicitly berate his homeland, as for instance when he states that the Japanese do not suffer under a wide variety of unbearable taxes as do the people of Europe.[108]

Finally, Kaempfer was by temperament much too much the down-to-earth scholar to succumb to unrealistic praise and enthusiastic admiration. In Kyoto at the Sanjūsan gendō (Temple of Thirty-three Bays), the serene beauty of the thousand gilded figures of Kannon had deeply moved the Portuguese Jesuit Lois Frois, and even though they were of a heathen god, they had reminded him of "the ranks and hierarchies of the angels."[109] The prosaic North-German Kaempfer, on the other hand, was much more concerned with enumerating the objects the many arms of the statues were holding and explaining how the figures had been cleverly placed so that each one was in view. Like the encyclopedists, Kaempfer considered it his primary duty to record in detail what he saw, and in this he succeeded to the admiration—or rather horror—of the Japanese. "Somebody who has not been to the eastern part of the country needs only to read what Kaempfer wrote about the subject to be fully informed," warned the scholar Aoki

Okikatsu (1762–1812) in a submission to the Japanese government in 1804. Since the foreigners had succeeded in gathering such amazingly detailed strategic material despite the severe restrictions, he suggested that they be expelled immediately.[110]

I have briefly mentioned above how Kaempfer carefully composed his text, relying not only on what he saw but also on Japanese publications and the record of those who went before him.[111] But is Kaempfer's text totally reliable? For details he could not observe himself, Kaempfer had to rely on informants, and there are times when he was given the wrong information. Thus on his passage through the Inland Sea, he was for a considerable stretch given the wrong information on which daimyo occupied which castle, most probably by someone weary of the constant probing of the foreigner. Also, like every scholar, Kaempfer makes mistakes, which are all the more understandable when one considers that he often could not note down information immediately but had to gather it in secret.[112] Yet we should be wary of labeling a mistake everything that does not accord with what we know about Tokugawa Japan today. Frequently research into lesser-known Japanese sources shows that not Kaempfer but our record is wrong.[113] Moreover, even if Kaempfer's facts are sometimes incorrect in actual terms, they usually reflect the images that presented themselves to him and indicate the level of knowledge of his informants.[114]

The greatest value of Kaempfer's work lies in permitting us to enter the world of late seventeenth-century Japan and see, smell, and hear what he did on the small island in the harbor of Nagasaki and on his travels to Edo. I hope that this new translation does justice to his account.

Notes on the Translation

The simplest and safest way to translate a difficult text is to record all research done on obscure, ambiguous, and difficult words and passages in notes. If this method had been followed here, the notes would have occupied more space than the text, and the main purpose of this new translation, namely, to make available to as large a readership as possible an accurate version of Kaempfer's eye-witness account of Tokugawa Japan, would have been defeated. Notes have therefore been limited to instances where adequate translation was impossible and the available choices significantly alter the meaning of the text.

Having followed in Kaempfer's footsteps for a large part of the journey and having compared Japanese sources with his account, it was also tempting to elaborate in notes on what we know about the subject today and what is still left to see. Further, it might also have been desirable to elaborate more fully on Japanese titles, terms, and customs. But such comments and explanations would again have turned this into a work of unwieldy size, and such material will have to be published elsewhere.

Considerations of size persuaded me also to abbreviate or omit those chapters that do not deal with Japan or do not contain Kaempfer's personal observations and experience. The latter are mainly summaries of Japanese chronologies and similar classical texts that are now freely available. Kaempfer's speculations about the origins of the Japanese also have been omitted. This material is of scholarly but not of general interest and is very different from Kaempfer's vivid descriptions of everyday life. All abbreviations and omissions have been clearly indicated. Again, considerations of size and cost made it impossible to include all of Kaempfer's illustrations. For that same reason, the headings Kaempfer had jotted into the margin—in a not altogether systematic fashion—were turned into subheadings, even though their placement is sometimes awkward. Very occasionally, when its position would have been misleading, a subheading has been omitted.

The text translated is an unedited manuscript. As such, it contains incomplete sentences, ambiguities, incongruities, and repetitions. If these passages had been resolved on the basis of existing knowledge, the translation would have lost its value for research going beyond what is known about the period today. Also statements that a conscientious editor no doubt would have corrected, such as that Kaempfer's party arrived at Hamamatsu "at five o'clock in the late evening," have been translated literally; obvious comments, such as that five o'clock is not "late evening," have been omitted. The same applies to tautological phrases like "sacred deity." However, in those instances where repetitions, omissions, and grammatical errors can obviously be attributed to "a slip of the pen," corrections have been made and recorded in the notes.

To keep the flavor of the original, Japanese terms in the text have not been translated. For the spelling, modern conventions of transcription have been adopted. In instances where Kaempfer provides a number of different pronunciations for the same word, these variations are noted in the notes. Notes are also provided where adjusting the spelling involves more than the usual changes. Japanese terms and personal names are explained in the notes the first time they appear in the text and are listed in the glossary and first appendix if they appear again. Monetary units, weights, and measurements, both Japanese and Western, are discussed in the second appendix.

Sometimes it is difficult to determine whether Kaempfer uses a Japanese word or a Japanese loanword that has acquired its own meaning. Thus Kaempfer's *Benjosen* appears to be based on Japanese *bugyō* but differs from his usual transcription of this term, namely, *bugjo*. Since he uses the term in the sense of "an official," it has been translated as such.

At times Kaempfer uses terms that sound inappropriate or unusual also in the German text. Thus words like *priest* and *church* are used in connection with Buddhism, no doubt reflecting Kaempfer's attitudes toward such topics, and these terms have been translated literally. Again, Kaempfer's *Tempel* is translated as temple, even though the word *shrine* might seem more appropriate when referring to Shinto. Adding the temple/shrine distinction in the translation would have obscured the fact that in seventeenth-century Japan this distinction did not always exist.

Similar problems arise when Kaempfer describes the settlements along his route. Calling a community of only several hundred houses a city might seem inappropriate today, but this is a correct translation of Kaempfer's *Stadt*. This term could, of course, also be translated as town, but that would not have permitted further distinctions between Kaempfer's *Flecken* and *Dorf*. Translating these terms consistently means that, for instance, a town sometimes has more houses than a city, but Kaempfer's choice of terminology was based on the character of the settlement and not simply on the number of houses or inhabitants.

Japanese titles, as other Japanese vocabulary, have only been translated when German translations are part of the text. When a choice had to be made, Kaempfer's German translation, rather than the Japanese term on which his translation was based, has been translated to indicate how Kaempfer saw these positions in terms of his own background. The exception is Kaempfer's *Kaiser*, *Kajser*, or *Kejser*, which has been translated as shogun. If at the time the word *shogun* had been as familiar to his readers as it is today, no doubt he would have used it. He is clear about the distinction between the emperor and shogun; if he uses the term emperor for the former, he distinguishes him as the "ecclesiastical hereditary emperor." More frequently he refers to the emperor as *dairi* or *mikado,* and these words are kept in the translation. The original *caesar,* on which the German *Kaiser* is based, was not altogether inappropriate to delineate the authority of the shogun.

Kaempfer is not always consistent in his use of titles. Thus the Nagasaki *bugyō* (Nagasaki magistrates) are referred to both as magistrates *(Stadthalter)* and governors *(Gouverneure),* and this has not been unified. Again, Kaempfer uses ward headman *(Wiekmeister)* for *otona* but uses street (*Straße* or *Gasse* rather than *Wiek*) for the ward he governs. He does not always indicate whether he uses street in its conventional Western sense or as equivalent for Japanese *machi* or *chō*, and consequently these distinctions have not been made in the translation.

Interpretations differing from the previous English translation of J. G. Scheuchzer, the German "modernized" version of C. W. Dohm, and the Japanese translations are too frequent to mention. Generally only those cases where as yet no final conclusion could be reached are referred to in the notes.

Kaempfer often places parts of sentences in brackets, and these have been retained. Occasionally text is underlined, and this has also been kept. Where Kaempfer's paragraphs are inordinately long, they have been broken up.

Kaempfer's Japan

Prologue

Germany was still troubled by its most Christian and most un-Christian enemies[1] when the Swedish delegation, of which I was a member, received its leave from the Persian court. I decided that the lesser evil would be to embark on even more distant travels and individually and voluntarily endure the resulting inconveniences rather than return to my native country and submit to the generally prevailing bad conditions and involuntary state of war it was in. I therefore said farewell to the delegation (which paid me the honor of accompanying me for one mile beyond the city) with the intention of spending another couple of years looking at other countries, nations, and courts of the Far East. I had never been used to receiving large sums of money from home and always had to rely on my own talents. Therefore, on this occasion also, I examined my qualifications and discovered the means of earning a good living among foreign nations and also of serving, albeit in a lowly capacity, the illustrious community of the Dutch Company in the Indies. This offspring of Japheth[2] enjoys the blessings of Abraham more than any other European nation, dwelling in the huts of Shem and using the labor of Cham.[3] With the providence of God and astute and capable management, the company has extended its arm throughout the whole of Asia to the furthest East, where its interests are promoted by means of excellent men. To come to the point: I was often able to further my aims by taking advantage of their praiseworthy kindness and approval and finally reached the court of this furthest and powerful empire of Japan. As promised recently in my *Amoenitates Exoticae*,[4] I will describe and publish its present condition before dealing with my travel diaries and other works, giving assurance that everything is described and illustrated as I saw it and without exaggeration. The illustrations are perhaps not very attractive, but they are unaltered and by my own hand. The descriptions are at times incomplete, but they contain only facts that deal with the hidden workings of the empire, about which it is as difficult in Japan as in any other nation to obtain exhaustive information today. With the eradication of the Roman Christians, the imprisonment of our own merchants and the Chinese merchants, and the closing of the borders to prevent entry by and communication with foreign nations, the Japanese also closed their mouths, hearts, and souls toward us, the foreign and imprisoned visitors. All those who are in contact with us especially are bound by an oath and sign with their blood not to talk or entrust to us information about the situation of their country, their religion, secrets of government, and various other specified subjects. They are all the more prevented from doing so since the above oath requires all to act as their neighbor's informer. To make an even deeper impression, this blood oath must be repeated and renewed annually.

So much for the foreigners' standing in Japan. The Dutch, who are here as traders, have been aware of this condition for a long time, and they believe that it is impossible for a foreigner to find out anything about this country, inasmuch as there exists neither the opportunity nor the freedom to do so. Even Licentiate Cleyer, the former Dutch resident, claims as much in his letter to Mr. Scheffer.[5]

Yet, my dear reader, it is not quite so difficult as it might appear or as one might expect considering the demands made by the Japanese government upon its subjects and the extensive precautions it has taken. The Japanese are a brave, clever, and imperious people and are inhibited not by an involuntary oath sworn to gods and spirits, which are unknown to them and in which they do not believe, but only by the punishment meted out by the authorities when violation of the oath is discovered. Moreover, in spite of their pride and military ethos, they are a friendly, sociable, and as inquisitive a people as any that exists in the world. They are therefore naturally inclined toward communion and intimacy with foreign nations and are especially hungry for knowledge about their history, arts, and sciences. But since we are only merchants, whom they rank among the lowest class of people, and, moreover, live there confined as distrusted visitors, it is necessary to adjust our behavior to their arrogant and pragmatic spirit and cater to their obsession in a prompt and generous fashion, if we want to draw advantage from this fact. By such means I successfully obtained and enjoyed the total confidence of those in charge of the Dutch and of the interpreters who daily visited our settlement, Deshima, and my house. I was indeed more privileged in this respect than anybody else who has lived here during our many years of confinement. For while I served them willingly and without charge in my profession, with medicines, and with a little instruction in astronomy and mathematics (while cordially serving them European liqueurs), I questioned them about local matters, nature, and secular and spiritual topics with total freedom, and nobody ever refused to inform me to the best of his knowledge (even on prohibited topics, when he was on his own). Even though it was fragmentary, this information that I collected daily from my visitors was very useful, but not enough for a satisfactory description. But fortune presented me with another opportunity and tool in the shape of a learned young man, thanks to whom I could achieve my aims and gather a rich harvest of knowledge on indigenous matters. This young student, twenty-four years of age, was learned in Japanese and Chinese writing and science and at the same time eager to learn; he was sent to me on my arrival as a servant so that he might learn something about medicine.[6] The *otona,* or administrator of our island,[7] on account of our special friendship (and because in his illness he was well served by him as my assistant), permitted this clever fellow to remain with me for the whole two years of my stay and also to travel with me twice to the shogunal court, that is to say, travel with me four times nearly the length of the country. Such experienced and well-informed hands are never permitted to serve the Dutch, at any rate, not for that length of time. In the first year I taught this clever fellow Dutch grammar (without which I would not have made any progress with him), so that he could write the language and speak it far better than any Japanese interpreter before him. I also faithfully taught him anatomy and medicine and, moreover, treated him to an annual salary of considerable size in view of my lowly position. In return he had to look for good information about the situation of the country, the government, the court, their religion and the history of past ages, their families as well as daily events and pass it on to me. There was not a book I endeavored to see which he did not obtain for me and explain and translate the passages I indicated. And since there was a lot of information that he did not know himself and had to obtain by questioning people, offering remuneration, or purchasing it, I never sent him home without some silver to open doors, in addition to special rewards for such dangerous tasks.

That illustrates the expense and difficulties an interested person encounters these days when attempting to obtain information about this closed empire, which I present here to my readers without the danger and cost. Should God grant me life and good health, I will also try to restore and complete my other writings, which have been drenched by sea water and are very much faded. These describe and communicate in the same format the memorable events that occurred during my ten years of travel in Asia through Finland, Russia, Tartary, Persia, Arabia, and the mainland and islands of the Indies.[8]

Book 1

Chapter 1

Journey from Siam to Japan and the Present State of the Siamese Court, Including a Description of the Royal Residence or Capital of Ayutthaya

After I had looked around at the Siamese court for some time, I had the opportunity to travel to the empire of Japan in a vessel called the *Waelstrom,* lying (loaded with local merchandise) in the harbor ready to sail, in which country I was offered the position of physician in a Dutch delegation traveling to the Japanese court. At present there is no other way of entering this empire, which has been closed for nearly a century, and to appear before its exalted majesty than to join this Dutch nation resident in the Indies. The Japanese consider them as the most honest of all the foreigners, and therefore tolerate them, albeit under close supervision, and grant them the favor of having their resident pay their respects annually to the shogun. Before I leave for that country, I will briefly describe the condition in which I left the Siamese court but will reserve a detailed description for another occasion. . . .

Translator's note: With these words Kaempfer began the first chapter of his well-known account of Japan, but they have not appeared in print previously.

Kaempfer's statement that he spent some time at the court of the king of Siam and then joined the Dutch East India Company to travel to Japan was a slight distortion of the truth. As his diary documents,[1] Kaempfer had sailed from Batavia to Siam in the *Waelstrom,* the same vessel in which he departed for Japan a month later, in early July 1690, as described in the next chapter. His visit to Ayutthaya, the capital of the king of Siam, was under the auspices of the Dutch East India Company, which maintained a trading post there in addition to one at Bangkok.

Documentation suggests not only that Kaempfer entered employment as physician for the Dutch trading post at Nagasaki while still in Batavia but also that he had specifically been requested by the company's governor general for the Indies, Johannes Camphuis, to write a work on Japan. Before his departure, he had been given access to a wide variety of material to prepare himself for this task.[2]

It is true, however, that Kaempfer intended to publish a detailed description of Siam in a separate volume, for he also announced this work in the introduction to his *Amoenitates Exoticae* of 1712. He died before he could accomplish this task. Like the remaining material, the relevant notes came into the possession of Sir Hans Sloane and were at hand when J. G. Scheuchzer produced the first English translation of the work on Japan.

The notes consist of a fairly coherent body of writing, especially Kaempfer's diary of his journey from Batavia to Siam. No doubt the good condition of the notes, together with the fact that Kaempfer had included a sizable amount of detail on Siam in his first two chapters of book 1, persuaded Scheuchzer to add them to the manuscript. He created a new first chapter, which begins with Kaempfer's diary of his journey from Batavia. He also added further material to Kaempfer's original chapter 1, which became his chapter 2. In the course of these alterations, Scheuchzer omitted the passage translated above.[3] Preparing the German edition,[4] Christian Wilhelm Dohm incorporated Scheuchzer's alterations, and thus the above passage never appeared in print. Moreover, in this fashion a work named by its author *Today's Japan (Heutiges Japan)* came to include a sizable description of Siam. This has been omitted here.

Chapter 2
Departure from the Siamese Capital Ayutthaya Down the River Meinam to the Harbor, and from There across the Sea to Japan

Translator's note: Kaempfer begins this chapter with his departure from Ayutthaya on July 4, 1690, and a brief description of his journey down the river Meinam to Bangkok, where the Dutch trading post Amsterdam was located. As an indefatigable scholar, Kaempfer not only noted what he saw but added a six-point discussion about the name and flow of the river.

On July 7 Kaempfer boarded the vessel *Waelstrom*, which, owing to the shallowness of the harbor, was riding two miles out at sea. Some time was spent loading the cargo of skins and sappanwood, and on July 11 wind from the land finally permitted the vessel to set sail.

At this point Kaempfer explains the pattern of the monsoon winds. For four months of the year they blow from the southwest, expediting the journey to Japan. A season of violent storms marks the change in the direction of the winds, a period which the Dutch vessels spend in the safety of their Japanese harbor. When the storms have died down and the winds are blowing steadily from the northeast, the vessels depart again for Southeast Asia.

The *Waelstrom*, however, waited in vain for suitable winds to fill her sails. By the time she had left the Gulf of Siam it was July 23. She followed the coastline of Indochina and South China, but the winds were not favorable. When the vessel finally left the safety of the coastal waters of China near Fukien at a latitude of some twenty-five degrees to head northeast toward Japan, it was already August 16. During the next four weeks three violent storms and enormous waves battered the ship. The rudder broke, water flooded the cabins, and provisions ran out. It seemed as if Kaempfer's journey to Japan had come to a premature end. He wrote:

The Sailors Want to Return to Batavia

13 September, early in the morning. When the wooden walls of the ship were sealed with tar, it was discovered that the stanchions,[1] which are like the ribs and props of the body of the ship, had become loose and slack during the onslaught of 6 September. This made both officers and common sailors unwilling to continue tacking against the wind. It was considered advisable to look for a Chinese harbor to take on water (which would not last another month) and then start the return journey to Batavia. Passengers, and those whose opinion counted with the ship's commission, attempted to promote this plan by arguing for it, and it would have been accepted—regardless of the fact that the bookkeeper, buried drunk in his bed, could not signal his approval—if the first mate had not come up with some objections. To help matters, I discovered in a Japanese diary, given

to me for the journey by a good person, that a few years ago a Dutch ship successfully reached Japan in the last days of September. I secretly went with it to the captain. I asked him to consider that the great number of skins would not keep in the hot air of Batavia for a year without rotting and that he would be held responsible for the loss because of his premature return and lack of courage. Then I showed him the above-mentioned passage, which, taken aback, he read three times and then changed his plans without further discussion.

14 September. We were at a polar elevation of 29 degrees 36 minutes; at night the depth of the sea was forty-one to forty-six fathoms.

15 September. Elevation 29 degrees 57 minutes; depth thirty-six.

16 September. Elevation 30 degrees 13 minutes, depth thirty-eight.

17 September. The sun did not permit calculation of the elevation; the depth was forty-seven fathoms.

18 September. Owing to bad weather were again unable to calculate the elevation; the depth was thirty-four fathoms.

On 19 September the elevation was 30 degrees 31 minutes; the depth in the evening was forty-five.

20 September. Elevation: 30 degrees 36 minutes; the depth in the evening was fifty-eight, and at night seventy fathoms. This morning we caught with a spear a yellowish-blue, six-span-long dolphin or dorades, which was delicious and revived our sick stomach.

The Island of Mejima Is the Japanese Hermes

On 21 September we reached an elevation of 31 degrees, 30 minutes. According to the average nautical map this is the latitude of a rocky island in the Japanese sea, called Mejima.[2] It serves the mariners as a Japanese Hermes,[3] and must be passed when traveling to or from Japan. Two hours after calculating the elevation, we saw this island nine or ten miles ahead, but in a northeasterly direction. One therefore must conclude that the island lies further north, around thirty-two degrees. Shortly before sunset, this much-longed-for Hermes presented himself five miles to the north, as pictured in the attached sketch.[4] When, after six hours, we had the island one mile ahead of us on the port side in the bright moonlight (and also when we sailed past it two years later on our return journey), I discovered that it consists of seven or more sharp, rough, and bare cliffs close together, covered everywhere with birds' droppings.[5] It appears to have been the home of seagulls for a very long time, because there were great swarms of them. Fortune blessed us again with another beautiful dolphin. This evening we found sandy sludge at a depth of seventy-eight fathoms.

On 22 September early in the morning we saw Mejima far behind us in a west-southwesterly direction, barely discernible. Soon afterward we noticed a junk from

Nanking, and presently two other Chinese junks coming from Japan; powerful vessels, judging from their shape.

We Arrive in Japan

To our left we saw the Japanese Gotō islands, which are inhabited by farmers, and before noon we sighted the high Japanese mountain chain in front of Nagasaki, our much-longed-for harbor, which was six or seven miles in front of us toward the north-northeast at sunset. We approached it with a northwesterly breeze and few sails and at midnight of 23 September arrived at the mouth of the bay, at a depth of fifty fathoms. Because the entrance to the bay is studded with many cliffs and islands with which we were unfamiliar and which are impossible to avoid at night, we were not able to come closer. We therefore continued tacking until dawn, found sandy soil at a depth of forty-three fathoms, and turned the ship toward the harbor. But the wind suddenly died down, so that we could not enter. We therefore announced our presence with five shots, which were also heard in the Dutch residence seven miles away. In the afternoon four vessels came across to us with Dutch merchants sent by our superior, accompanied by a crowd of Japanese courtiers, scribes, soldiers, and one senior interpreter, to welcome us and claim the mail we brought. After some time we sent them off with seven shots and followed them, but very slowly because of changing winds, up to the so-called Papenberg,[6] situated in the mouth of the harbor and one mile from Nagasaki. We hauled our vessel away from there and forward, up to half a mile from the city of Nagasaki, by warping with kedge-anchors. There we cast our night-anchor in the safety of the harbor at ten o'clock at night. May the supreme God be most humbly praised for His protection.

The Ship's Bookkeeper Dies

Until now we experienced neither death nor illness on our vessel. Only yesterday evening the above-mentioned bookkeeper had a stroke after he was refused further arrack and brandy. This robbed him suddenly of his speech and senses and killed him with terrible seizures after a few hours. Otherwise he was a very clever fellow, the son of a famous ecclesiastical scholar of The Hague. But indulgence led to debauchery and licentiousness early in life.

As soon as we had dropped anchor, two Japanese patrol barges stationed themselves next to us and busied themselves the whole night circling our ship. All Chinese junks departing today were accompanied by a patrol vessel up to the open sea. Not far from us a lord's flotilla, consisting of forty vessels or pleasure boats, furnished with the usual pomp, cast anchor. Their shape is like that of the *Strusen*[7] that travel from Moscow to Casan. This little fleet was a pretty sight at night with its many lights, and the following morning, when they left, with half white and half black sails, which were hoisted at the same time.

24 September. After we had already drifted half the way with a gentle breeze this morning, we were towed further up to two hundred paces in front of the city and our residence by twenty Japanese lighters with oars, which fastened themselves to a rope suspended from the front of the ship. This harbor is enclosed by high mountains, islands, and cliffs and protected by nature against all storms and raging waves. The peaks of the surrounding mountains are furnished with guard houses, and the latter with guards, who have to observe with telescopes what goes on at sea and report it to the authorities of Nagasaki. Thus they had already reported the arrival of our ship in the morning of the day before yesterday. At the foot of the mountains, which make up the shore, are various round fortifications facing the water, on which I saw red stakes as decoration, but no guns. In addition there is a sizable, stately shogunal guard on both sides on elevated ground not far from the shore, covered with drawn curtains for decoration, so that it is impossible to see what there is in the way of guns and battalions.

We Anchor in Front of Nagasaki

In passing we greeted each guard with twelve salutes from our large guns. When we had reached the designated place, we dropped our anchors onto the ocean floor, some three hundred paces from the city and an equal distance from the Dutch residence, the living quarters of Deshima, a closed-off, small island, built in front of the shore of the city.

The Japanese Muster the People on Our Ship

Thereupon two commissioned officials or courtiers of the governors appeared, together with many subordinate soldiers, scribes, and interpreters. All arrivals, with no exception, were mustered, one after the other, according to the ship's roll that we had handed to them. They inspected everybody from head to toe and with a brush wrote his name, age, and servants on a piece of paper. Further, six or more persons were individually questioned about the journey: from where and at what time it had been commenced, how long it had taken, whether we had not landed here or there, and so forth. Each person's reply was carefully written down. Also there were not a few questions about the dead bookkeeper, and the answers were recorded on paper as well. They also inspected his chest and bare skin to see whether he had a crucifix or some sign of the popish religion on him. After a lot of pleading, we managed to have the body collected for burial on the same day, but they did not permit any one of us to accompany the body or see where it was shoved into the soil.

They Take Possession of the Ship

After the mustering, soldiers and scribes were stationed in every corner, and the whole ship with all its cargo was as if taken into possession by the Japanese. A lighter and boat were still left with our people for today for the necessary securing of the anchors, but pistols, swords, and other weapons of the ship were taken away into their custody and safekeeping. And then, the next morning, the gunpowder was stored in barrels. Indeed, if I had not known that this was the common procedure, I would no doubt have thought that we had landed in an enemy country or had been taken for spies. I need to mention also at this point that, as soon as this country came into sight on our journey, on high order and according to an old custom, all persons aboard had to hand the captain their book of psalms and other religious books, as well as the European coins they carried. He packed these into an old barrel, each with the name attached, which was hidden from the Japanese in the ship until departure.

This evening we received from the kitchen of the Dutch refreshments such as chicken, eggs, fish, radishes with leaves, beets, onions, fresh ginger, pumpkin, watermelon, white bread, and a small bottle of *sake,* or Japanese rice beer.

On 25 September, early in the morning, both residents, or directors, of the Dutch trade, Swerus,[8] the departing one, and Butenheim,[9] the new one, who had just arrived from Batavia with three full ships, came from Deshima and boarded our ship. After everybody had been called together, they read us the orders of the Dutch Company and the Nagasaki governors, which consisted mainly of the admonition that everybody was to behave modestly and humbly toward the locals and their laws and in accordance with the customs of the country. After the notice had been read, it was mounted in the ship (apparently according to Japanese custom) and placed in front of everybody's eyes. In the afternoon, I had myself taken to Deshima, on land. For each crossing one has to obtain a new pass here for the guard on land and coming back, return with a different pass from there addressed to the ship's guard. The garden produce that we ate raw as refreshment last night caused us some embarrassing distress, owing to which I had to rush back onto the ship from the still unfamiliar surroundings.

On 26 September I left the ship and went to Deshima with my belongings and moved into the house allocated to me. May God bless us. So much for my journey from Siam, my last port of call, to the empire of Japan.

Chapter 3

The Size and Situation of the Islands and Provinces of Japan

Name

This nation is called Japan by the Europeans, and by its inhabitants by various other names and characters. Among those, Nipon is used most commonly in speech and writing.[1] To give it a more melodious sound, they frequently pronounce it Nifon according to their dialect, while the Chinese from Nanking and other southern Chinese pronounce it Sjippon. According to the characters, it means "the bastion of the sun," because *ni* means "fire," in more elevated language, "the sun," and *pon,* a "fortification."

The most important among the names used mainly in writing, rather than orally, is Tenka, that is, "under heaven," the word "nation" being implied (as if no other existed). Therefore the ruler is called *tenka sama,* that is, "the lord under heaven." Now, however, other countries are also honored with the same expression, that is, Tōjin Tenka, Oranda Tenka,[2] that is, the nation of the Chinese, the country of the Dutch. Hi no moto is the same as Nippon with the addition of the preposition *no*, or "of," and means the root or base of the sun. Awajishima is a very ancient name and means an "earthen froth island," for *awa* means "froth," *ji*, "the earth," and *shima*, "an island." This name is based on the following traditional belief. In the beginning, the first spirit or god stirred this subterranean chaos with a staff. When he pulled out the staff, muddy foam dripped off and formed the Japanese islands. Ignorant of other countries, the ancients believed it was the beginning of the whole earth and, according to its origin, called it by this name. A certain island of this nation, the fourth largest,[3] has maintained this name and still today is specifically called by this name. Other names are Shin koku or Kami no koku, that is, "land of the gods," because *shin* and *kami* stand for the local gods, and *koku* and *kuni* mean a country; in other words, the seat and residence of the gods; Akishima, or, more commonly pronounced Akitsu shima,[4] is a very ancient and much-used name, especially in chronicles and old legends; Honchō, the "true morning";[5] *chō,* meaning "all,"[6] "Japanese provinces" being implied; Yamato, which is also used to denote a particular province of the country; Ashihara, or Ashihara koku; Ka, or Wa. I will omit those used less frequently.

Location

The country is situated between thirty-one and forty-two degrees of north latitude and (according to the maps drawn up by the gentlemen of the Society of Jesus on the basis of a great number of examinations) between 157 and 175.30 degrees longitude.[7]

Size

The country stretches northeast and east-northeast, is of irregular shape, and throughout narrow and of varying width (from the furthest end of the province of Hizen to the furthest end of the province of Ōshū), two hundred German miles long measured in a straight line, not counting the more distant islands and shores under Japanese rule. The country resembles Great Britain, but the land is far more broken up, and just as the former is made up of three kingdoms, Japan consists mainly of three large islands. The largest and most important takes the name of the whole country, Nippon. It stretches from east to west and has the shape of a jawbone, its bend veering toward the north. The second island lies to the southwest of the latter and is separated from it by a strait with many cliffs and islands. It is called Saikoku, meaning "western country," according to its situation, or, according to the number of its provinces, Kyushu, meaning "nine countries." Its circumference is 148 German miles, or, according to Japanese calculation, 140 Japanese miles long, and forty or fifty wide. The third is virtually surrounded by the other two, is roughly square, and consists of four fiefs or provinces and therefore has the name Shikoku, meaning "four countries." These three islands are surrounded by a nearly incalculable number of fertile and infertile islands, some so large, rich, and fertile that they are inhabited and ruled by large and small territorial lords. These will be discussed especially in the next chapter.

In the year 590[8] the hereditary emperor Sushun[9] first divided these lands into *goki shichi dō,* that is seven main highways or areas, to distinguish them.[10] Soon afterward, in 681, the hereditary emperor Temmu[11] further divided the country into sixty-six provinces and delegated their government to as many barons and magistrates. In the last century, an additional two islands, Iki and Tsushima, were wrested from the Koreans, so that there are now sixty-eight in number and name. Areas have kept their names according to this first division of the country until the present, but the unfortunate events of the ensuing period meant that they were split into 604 smaller provinces or fiefdoms. In the first centuries of these monarchs, every baron owned his land peacefully and securely according to the favors bestowed upon him by the hereditary emperor. But afterward a succession quarrel arose among the families of the court which also embroiled the barons of the empire, because they supported this or the other party, and military weapons, such as were unknown until then, were introduced. From then on, they all tried to defend what they owned by their own might, and those who had nothing attempted to gain something by force. The large hereditary fiefs were divided among a number of siblings and by other events, and with their inherited property the various heirs attempted to maintain their noble status and stay in control of land and people. The number of nobles in one fief and the number of fiefs therefore increased to the above number. The last rulers, who took the country by force of arms, have not only maintained and solidified this number in order to govern the country more easily and be better informed of all income, but every year it is split into still smaller pieces on the despotic orders of his majesty. Thus the area of Chikuzen was recently divided between two lords, those of Yanagawa and Kurume, and similarly the lord of Chikugo lost part of his fief to the faraway lord of Iki Tsushima, so that the latter would also have a foothold on the mainland.[12]

The borders of this realm are marked nearly everywhere by high and rugged cliffs, and the country is surrounded by rough seas with rocky shallows, difficult to navigate. Landing is full of danger, especially since the bays and harbors—many of which have not yet been sounded, others of which are shallow—can be entered only by light vessels. It appears, therefore, as if nature has purposely separated this country from others to form its own little world and has fortified and provided it with all the necessities of life, so that it can support itself adequately without relying on other countries.

Japanese Possessions Overseas

Beyond those discussed, there are some far-distant lands that are not part of the Japanese realm but are protected by and take orders from Japan. They are (1) the islands of Ryūkyū or Liqueo, subjects of the lord of Satsuma as their erstwhile conqueror, but not of the Japanese ruler; (2) Chōsen, or the third part of the peninsula of Korea situated at its extremity, which the shogun rules through the lord of Iki Tsushima;[13] and (3) the island of Ezo, which he keeps subservient through the lord of Matsumae, part of the large province of Ōshū.

1. The islands of Liqueo, which they call Ryūkyū and which are marked on our maps by the name of Liqueo, are not Leuconia or the Philippines, but are those which are situated to the southwest of the mainland of Satsuma, or its nearest island, Tane, or Tane ga shima, and according to our map touch nearly the twenty-sixth degree of north latitude. According to Japanese reports, they have such good, fertile soil that rice is harvested twice a year. The inhabitants are mostly farmers, the rest generally fishermen. They are supposed to live happily and merrily, taking their stringed instruments to the fields when plowing, and then as a change enjoying its sound while taking a drink of the local alcohol distilled from millet. Their language proves that they came from China, from where many more fled at the beginning of this century owing to the conquests of the Tartars,[14] and settled in great numbers in these islands as they did also in other parts of the East Indies. They are the very same as those experienced navigators who appear annually in Satsuma as merchants to trade. Some centuries[15] ago these islands submitted to the king of Satsuma as a result of military force, and he keeps them subservient with *bugyō*, or commissioners and magistrates, strong military commanders, and guards. But being far away, they are ruled very civilly and leniently, inasmuch as they only pay him one-fifth of their field produce, while the subjects of this nation must contribute two-thirds. In addition, they annually send tributary presents to the Tartar emperor in China as a sign of their submission. Like the people of Tonking and the Japanese, they are supposed to have a *dairi*, or spiritual hereditary emperor, who they claim descended from a

local lineage of gods. He resides on the northernmost main island of Iayama, not far from the island of Oshima, second in size.[16]

2. Korea[17] is a peninsula jutting out beyond China south of Tartary. According to Japanese reports, since ancient times it has been divided into three regions. The furthest part, jutting out toward Japan, the Japanese call Chōsen, the central part, Korea proper, and the last bordering on Tartary, Hyakusai,[18] even though these names are frequently used one for the other and are also used to denote the whole peninsula. According to Japanese accounts, the inhabitants originate from the Chinese, were often allies of the Tartars, and frequently were under their ruler and subservient to them. They were attacked by the *mikado* Chūai[19] and were made subservient to the Japanese in A.D. 201 by his wife Jingū[20] (who continued her dead husband's war personally and in man's clothing). But after some time they allied themselves with the Tartars and were not attacked by the Japanese until the time of the brave ruler Taikō.[21] One day this ruler read in the national histories how in ancient times this nation paid tribute to his country. He used this as a pretext to execute his plan, which he claimed consisted of opening up a road through Korea to the large empire of China, but in reality was nothing else but removing the barons and lords of his newly acquired empire from the scene, so that he would have a free hand in consolidating his rule. He therefore sent an ambassador to the Koreans to request acknowledgment of the country's rightful submission. But they killed him and thus gave the Taikō the opportunity for a righteous war. He then ordered his barons to invade the country with a large army, which after seven years of great efforts finally overcame the resistance of the inhabitants and their Tartar allies and got the Koreans to the point where they had to accept paying tribute. But because the ruler died, this was not pursued. After the latter's death, the ruler Ieyasu had the Koreans appear at court every three years with a delegation as proof of their submission. After that, they slowly came again under the sway of the Tartars and pushed the Japanese occupation to the furthest corner of their last province, which indeed is still subservient to the present Japanese ruler. The latter is happy to own no more than the Korean frontier as safety for his own country and has it guarded by the lord of Tsushima, who maintains a military guard of sixty people under the command of a *bugyō*. The Koreans are ordered to appear at court only at a time of shogunal succession to take an oath of loyalty to the new ruler. The Korean shore lies at a distance of forty-eight Japanese nautical miles, or sixteen German miles, from the island of Tsushima, and the latter an equal distance from the country of Nippon. The seas in between are dotted with many cliffs and uninhabited islands, which are nevertheless well manned by Japanese guards to inspect passing ships that have to land there and present their goods for inspection. Chōsen supplies the best dried cod and other dried fish, also walnuts, rare herbs and flowers, strong medicinal plants, and among them the excellent and precious root *ninjin,*[22] which, however, is much more frequent in the central provinces of Korea, Hyakusai, and the more distant Tartar province of Sam sui.[23] Beyond these borders the plant is nearly without potency. The country also supplies treasured and expensive earthenware and a few other manufactured goods from

the Tartar provinces of Yupi[24] and Niuche,[25] but they may no longer be used in Japan. Their ships are badly built and can carry their supplies only to Tsushima.

3. Ezo, or Ezo ga shima,[26] is the northernmost island the Japanese own outside their empire. I have been told that the island was subdued by Yoritomo, the first *kubō,* or worldly ruler,[27] and put under the supervision of the lord of Matsumae (an island close by belonging to Ōshū).[28] After a while they grew tired of foreign domination, and they attacked the occupying soldiers and killed them to liberate themselves. Soon afterward the territorial lord sent a large army of foot soldiers, together with three hundred horsemen, to restore order among the rebels. But the lord of Ezo proved that he had no knowledge of this rebellion by sending an embassy to Matsumae and handing over twenty culprits, whose heads were planted on poles along the shore of Ezo, and the crime was herewith atoned for.[29] They are regarded as hardheaded people and are governed strictly and kept in subservience by strong armaments planted along the southern shore. They have to attend upon their lord annually with an embassy and pay an annual tribute of *man koku.*[30] The island is located roughly around forty-two degrees north latitude, right in the north-northeast, above the two areas, or lower mountain chains Tsugaru and Ōmazaki,[31] which in this region surround a wide bay. The crossing is supposed to take a day and, owing to a swift current, which alternately flows to the east and the west, can be done only at certain times, even though the distance between the mainland and the island is nowhere more than forty nautical miles, in some places only five to seven German miles. The island is supposed to have the size of the island of Kyushu but is apparently so much overgrown with shrubs and forests that the only surplus it produces and supplies for the benefit of the ruler is the famous dried fish *kara sake,* which is soaked and boiled like dried cod, as well as a few skins or furs, which the southern Japanese do not use. Because Japanese maps differ from each other I cannot establish the shape of this island: in some the island is depicted as round with many bays; in others it is broken up with many projecting isthmuses and promontories, but it is impossible to say whether these are separate islands. I believe that this country is partly identical with that discovered by de Vries.[32] I also noticed that in some maps the large part in the southwest is marked with the name Matsuzaki, but this has been added in such an obscure and dubious fashion that it could be interpreted as a separate island. I will not discuss the islands that surround it, or those at some distance, because these can be seen on the attached Japanese maps. The inhabitants are described as a rough, strong people, with long hair and beards, skilled in using bow and arrow. They live mostly along the shore and support themselves by fishing. They are described as a very slovenly and dirty nation, but since the superstitiously clean Japanese describe even the fastidious Dutch in this way, I think one may ignore this. Their language is supposed to be somewhat similar to Korean.

Behind this island, toward the north, lies the mainland Oku Ezo, that is, Upper or Great Ezo.[33] This is the country our geographers know exists but do not know whether it is connected to Tartary or America, and consequently where the Straits of Anian[34] or passage from the North Sea to the India Ocean runs. Nor do they know whether it is connected to the two continents and whether consequently no sound or passage exists. However hard I tried to find out something about these northern lands, I was unable to learn anything definite and credible. In Moscow and Astrakhan I met people who either on their journey to China through Siberia and Cathay,[35] others during many years of exile in Siberia, collected various but unreliable information. All of them seem to indicate that to the east an isthmus connects the great land of Tartary to a solid land mass, which they believe is America; they were therefore of the opinion that there is no passage at that point between the ocean and the polar sea. A rough, ungraded map of Siberia, which an exiled bandit had cut into wood, and on which locations were marked in Slavonic writing, showed a number of low mountain ranges extending from the furthest shores to the east. One of them went so far that it protruded beyond the square of the map, and it was impossible to see how it continued. The person who reported this information believed that according to the local Tartars the same isthmus stretched toward a large mainland and was connected with it but that it was very mountainous, full of cliffs, and so ruggedly overgrown that if the earliest people had passed through it to enter America, they certainly would be unable to do so today. This map is the first and the only one that illustrates to the Russian court the extent of their great Tartary and the same that the German councilor or inspector of Muscovite pharmacies, my special friend, Mr. Winius,[36] used as a basis for his Russian and Tartar maps. He incorporated the information of many reports and added longitudinal and latitudinal gradations according to the observations of the learned Mr. Spafarii,[37] court interpreter for Greek and Latin, who around 1680 had been sent by the former ruler as ambassador to Peking. On his way to Peking, he took the northernmost route, and on returning, the southernmost, and on the secret instructions of the curious czar, he did everything possible to discover these lands. At the same court it happened to be my luck that this eloquent man had to serve as my interpreter, which gave me the opportunity to question him. But I discovered that this fishy character was so secretive that he had no inclination to disclose much of what he had learned. However, the very noble Nicolaas Witsen, I.U.D. and mayor of Amsterdam,[38] on his last embassy to his majesty the czar, obliged the grand duke and all inquiring minds to such an extent with his incomparable deportment and amiability that he was given all available information about these countries. On the basis of this, he constructed a map of Great Tartary and the whole of the Russian empire, incorporating all hitherto unknown rivers, mountains, lakes, cities, and provinces with the greatest accuracy, and made it available to the academic world.[39] This map was also used by Mr. Isbrant[40] on his voyage to China. However good and exact this map is, the Siberian shores and the neighboring country of Ezo have not been indicated, and this northern part remains unknown.[41]

Also unknown to the Japanese is the nature of the country beyond Ezo ga shima, which they call Oku Ezo, except that it is supposed to be three hundred Japanese miles long. A ship's captain, who was cast up there a few years ago, reported that among the rough natives he had seen a few people dressed in fine Chinese cloth, which led him to believe that there was a connection with Datsu, or Tartary, or that at least it was not far away. A junk sent out to explore the region in 1684 reported the same when it came back three months later. A well-traveled, experienced captain, who had visited all the areas around Japan, could answer my questions with nothing except that the current between Japan and Ezo ga shima was always flowing alternately to the east and west, and that behind Ezo ga shima it was always flowing to the north. He therefore concluded that there was definitely a passage near Datsu (Tartary) to the northern sea. A few years ago a shogunal junk was sent out from the eastern coast, and after weathering a lot of difficulties between the fortieth and fiftieth degrees, it reached a solid land mass further to the east, which they believed was America. They spent the winter there in a bay, and they could report nothing except that the land stretched toward the northwest. After that it was decided to no longer visit these foreign frontiers. I have seen a variety of their maps showing these seas at the Edo mansion of the Nagasaki governor Tsushima no kami[42] and also at the Sumiyoshi temple by Osaka and other temples. In front of great Tartary and beyond Ezo ga shima they show another piece of land jutting forth, ending roughly at fifteen degrees longitude, further east than the easternmost shore of Japan, and between that and America, a wide passage. On that piece of land one sees the following provinces marked with phonetic letters: Kabersari,[43] Orankai,[44] Sitsji,[45] Ferisan,[46] Amarisi,[47] and between the latter two a very large river, beyond Ezo, running into the sea toward the southeast.[48] But like all maps they are slipshod, without any gradation; moreover, they differ from each other. Consequently one cannot rely on them, especially not on those maps that have the name written only according to its sound in *kana,* that is, phonetic letters, and not according to its meaning, or with proper characters.[49]

Before we finish our description of the country, we have to mention two islands with high-flown names that the Japanese claim belong to their nation although they are some 250 miles east and east-northeast of Ōshū. The smallest, northernmost, and furthest bears the name and character Ginshima, that is, Island of Silver; the other is called Island of Gold.[50] Their state and situation are kept secret from the foreigners, all the more so, since their precious names might induce them to visit the islands. For in 1620, as soon as the Spanish king had been informed about these islands rich in gold and silver situated in the western half of the world, which was recognized by the pope to be his, while the eastern half was to be that of Portugal,[51] he sent an experienced captain to search them out. But since their locality was unknown, he did not find them. Similarly those at Batavia attempted to find them in 1639 by sending one ship[52] and in 1643 by sending two. The latter two were also charged to discover the American and Tartar coasts. They did not merely fail to find them. When the captain of the yacht *Breskens* went on land with a few people at a harbor situated at forty degrees north latitude, he was taken prisoner and brought to Edo[53] bound and was treated as harshly as if he had intended to betray the whole nation.[54]

Finally I must add that in 1675 the Japanese discovered a large island when a barge was cast away from the island of Hachijō by a storm. One suspects that this island is situated three hundred miles east of Hachijō.[55] The island was uninhabited but had fertile soil, freshwater rivers, and fertile trees, including coconut trees, as the fruits that were brought back showed. That, however, should lead to the conclusion that it is situated further south, as these trees grow only in hot countries. The island was given the name of Buninshima,[56] and since it was uninhabited, it was designated with the character for an island without people. The shores were incredibly rich in fish, and there were also crabs, two to three fathoms long.

Hachijō or Hachijō ga shima, that is, "the island eighty fathoms high," which we have already mentioned, is one of the southernmost islands of the Japanese. It lies on the same longitude as Edo, some eighty nautical miles from the mainland, with a chain of many small islands in between. It is the most important among those islands to which, since very ancient times, the great lords who have fallen into disfavor with the ruler have been sent into exile. Here they are imprisoned, surrounded by a shore of steep cliffs the height of which gives the island its name, having to earn their living by weaving. These idle and spirited persons of learning produce the best silk cloth of all Japan, some of which neither will nor can be reproduced by others; nor can it be sold to foreigners or exported. When this fortification receives supplies, or new prisoners, the whole vessel has to be wound up and then let down again by winches, since there is no other access to the island. Thus the island is guarded and fortified by nature.[57]

Chapter 4
The Division of the Japanese Empire into Large and Small Domains, and Especially General Information about Their Revenue and Government

We do not want to leave the description of the country until we have discussed separately the division of the Japanese land into seven large regions or roads, and these into sixty-eight large domains or provinces of the empire, and these provinces into 604 smaller areas or districts, as well as the size, location, produce, and annual income of each province. All this information has been taken from a Japanese description called *Setsuyōshū*.[1]

Translator's note: As Kaempfer states, the text that follows has been taken from a Japanese work. *Setsuyōshū* is a Japanese dictionary of unknown authorship that appeared in numerous editions, some of the later ones with supplements.[2] Kaempfer apparently used an edition of 1680 published by the monk Ekū, which has a supplement corresponding to the information in this chapter. A reproduction of this is now available.[3]

Like Kaempfer's chapter, the supplement lists the seven *dō*, highways or areas, with brief explanations, followed by an enumeration of the domains and districts. In both cases, the list ends with explanations about Iki and Tsushima.

Kaempfer concludes this chapter with additional information about the government of Japan that is unlikely to have appeared in this form in any Japanese publication and therefore may be assumed to reflect his own observations. He writes:

The total income of the above seven areas and their sixty-eight provinces amounts to 2,257 *man goku*.[4]

Kubō or Absolute Ruler of Japan

This is not the place to write in detail about the government of this empire, its principalities and smaller dominions, but only inasmuch as it adds to the understanding of our account. The Japanese empire is governed by their shoguns, and each province by its domain lord, in an autocratic way. The present *kubō,* or monarch, called Tsunayoshi, is the fourth generation and the successor of Ieyasu, who ruled at the beginning of the sixteen hundreds and was the first shogun in his family to seize power. This Tsunayoshi is a clever, just, and strict ruler. In government he follows the ways of his ancestors by ruling with absolute authority. This he does to such an extent that, when the circumstances arise, he disposes of the lands of his subordinate princes and lords as he pleases: divides or exchanges them, or confiscates them completely, as he judges or determines is in the interest of the empire, or in accordance with the achievements or crime of the owner.

Daimyo or Great Territorial Lords

The above-mentioned principalities are ruled by their hereditary princes, called daimyo, that is, of august name,[5] which means large territorial lords. The fortunes of war gave some of them several territories in earlier times. Therefore the lord of Satsuma owns the two neighboring provinces of Ōsumi and Hyūga, the territorial lord of Kaga, also the adjoining province of Noto, which means they are counted among the most powerful princes of the empire.

Shōmyō or Lesser Territorial Lords

The lords of lesser territories are called *shōmyō,* or "well-named,"[6] which means as much as small territorial lords. In the registry of the sixty-six main provinces, their lands, be they islands, such as Gotō, Hirado, Amakusa, Matsuzaki, and so on, or territories on one of the three large islands, are always added to and counted as belonging to the same large province near or in which they are situated.

These lords have come so much under the sway of the last shoguns that they are permitted to live only six months of the year in their hereditary lands, while the rest of the year they spend in the city of the shogun's residence with their families, who reside there as hostages.

Bugyō and *Daikan*

Among the small territories are also shogunal lands or domains that either were set aside for this purpose from the beginning or were confiscated from those who had fallen out of favor at some time or other. For the art of government consists of attempting to break the power of the princes by splitting up larger territories to safeguard the position of the shogun. Of these domains, the large ones are governed by magistrates, who go under the common courtly title of *bugyō,* that is, commissioned men of high rank. The lesser are governed by rent collectors, or intendants, by the name of *daikan.* The income is collected and brought to the treasury.

Chapter 5

The Origin of the Inhabitants

Translator's note: In this chapter Kaempfer discusses the origin of the Japanese. On account of the great difference in language and native religious beliefs, he dismisses the theory that the Japanese islands were settled by the Chinese. He concludes the chapter with the following summary:

Summarizing, we may say that in the first age of plurality after the Babylonian discord of minds and languages, at a time when the Greeks, Goths, Slaves, and Celts left for Europe, when others scattered and spread in Asia, while still others even entered America, the Japanese set out on their journey. Perhaps wandering for many years and suffering great deprivation, they finally reached this furthest corner of the earth. Here they grew into a large nation with the occasional addition of strangers from foreign lands. They spent many centuries under tribal government in the rough fashion of the Tartars, until they finally elected a common leader to rule over them, namely, Jimmu Tennō. Therefore, according to their roots and earliest beginnings, the Japanese must be regarded as an independent nation, owing nothing to the Chinese with respect to their origins. Even though they adopted their code of conduct, liberal arts, and learning—as the Latin people did from the Greeks—they never accepted a conqueror or hegemon from China or any other nation in the world.

Chapter 6
The Origin of the Japanese According to Their Own Fanciful Opinion

The Japanese are very indignant when one wants to trace their origin back to the empire and blood of the Chinese, or other foreign people, for they want to have their origin in their own small world. Yet they do not wish to have come into being like mice and earthworms appearing out of the soil—as Diogenes the Cynic accused the haughty people of Athens who did not want to owe their origin to any other place or nation—but in a far loftier and nobler fashion. Thus they trace their origins back to the race of the gods and eternity (if I may use these words), even though the gods are not considered eternal but were created by the force of the first movement of chaos. They posit two lineages of gods: The first is a race of heavenly spirits or incorporeal gods, who, one after the other, ruled the world, or rather, their country, for an immeasurable number of times and years. The other is a lineage of earthly spirits or human gods, who also ruled the Japanese world one after the other for a long, but definite time and number of years. These begot the third lineage, the people of the Japanese nation. It will be worth the effort to describe this race of gods here in some greater detail according to Japanese books.[1] These books introduce the first rulers of their world not with their own names but with flowery names of praise without indicating the limits of their life span or government, in the following order:

Tenjin shichi dai, that is, the seven generations of heavenly gods.

1. Kuni toko tachi no mikoto[2]
2. Kuni satsuchi no mikoto[3]
3. Toyo kumunu no mikoto[4]

The above three gods had no wives, but the following four created their successors with the help of their consorts, however without cohabitation, in a secret fashion, and thus propagated the lineage of the gods.

4. U hiji ni no mikoto and his wife Su hiji ni no mikoto[5]
5. Ō to no ji no mikoto, Ō to no be no mikoto[6]
6. Ōmo taru no mikoto, Kashiko ne no mikoto[7]
7. Isanagi no mikoto, Isanami no mikoto[8]

The above seven generations are described as spirits, and their story is understood like a dream, but one that has certainly and actually happened, even though the gods are introduced without any delineation of time and appear incomprehensible and impossible to us.

The last couple, Isanagi, the man, and Isanami, the woman, are believed to be the first two progenitors of all inhabitants, not of the large world, which previously was unknown to them, but their little world of Nippon. They carry the additional name of *mikoto,* which is a word of reverence, appropriate for the monarchical bliss of the first gods, even though out of reverence it is sometimes also added to the names of the ancient lesser gods. Those Japanese who know something about Christianity call them the Japanese Adam and Eve. They are supposed to have been resident in the province of Ise, even though there is no information either with respect to their death or where they have disappeared to, just as there is none about the circumstances of their birth. This pre-Adamic Adam was the first who, prompted by the movements of the bird *sekirei*—commonly called *ishi tataki,* that is, stone-beating bird, and known to us as wagtail—had carnal knowledge of his spouse and is supposed to have fathered sons and daughters in human fashion in the province of Ise. However, their children were half-divine and of a different lineage. According to the natural law of the firstborn, as still practiced by the present hereditary imperial line of the third and human lineage, the eldest became the regent and leader of the others. On account of its five generations, this lineage of divine humans is called *chijin go dai,* that is, five generations of terrestrial gods. They are:

1. Tenshō daijin, or, in common parlance, Amateru ō kami.[9] According to the characters with which the name is written, it means as much as "Heaven's shining great spirit." He is the oldest and the only fertile son, whose seeds peopled this small world under heaven. He produced, however, not common creatures but people who were half divine, much nobler, and more perfect beings than those whom they finally left behind after they had lived in this world many millions of years, namely, the short-lived humans of today. Originally all the families of this nation claimed descent from the blood of Tenshō daijin, since his brothers were not blessed and disappeared without heirs. The Japanese hereditary emperors, who are now emperors only in name, are descended from Tenshō daijin in rightful succession as rulers of the country. With his great deeds during his government and with his potent miracles after he disappeared from the view of the world,[10] this Tenshō daijin has, in terms of their tradition, proved himself sufficiently and revealed himself to be the most powerful of all their native gods, the light, the energy, the being and authority within or above all nature under heaven. In the native religion he is honored and prayed to as god, but also believers of related religions, yes, even philosophers and atheists, venerate his name and person with courteous deference as their earliest ancestor. The place where he lived and the temple built in his memory at this location are visited by his compatriots in annual pilgrimage. Moreover, each province and large city has at least one temple in his honor, which is visited and prayed to more and with greater respect than all other temples of the native religion (to obtain blessings in this world). His spouse and the spouses of the chief gods that followed him are not mentioned in the books, but after several hundred thousand years of his government, he was succeeded by his eldest son:

2. Oshiho mimi no mikoto, with his full name Masa a ya katsu katchi haya hi ame no oshiho mimi no mikoto,[11] and after him:

3. Ninigo no mikoto, or, with greater words of praise: Ama tsu hiko hiko ho ninigi no mikoto.[12] His successor was:

4. Demi no mikoto, or, a longer version: Hiko hoho demi no mikoto.[13] The last of this long-living lineage is called:

5. Awasezu no mikoto, or, with many titles: Hiko nagisa take ugaya fuki aezu no mikoto.[14] His life brought to a close the second and silver age of divine humans, about whom more will be said in the first chapter of the second book.[15]

These then are the two divine lineages from which the Japanese claim their descent. They say the first spirit of the first lineage came forth in the beginning of the first movement or first ferment of chaos, as its most subtle force. But after that the next spirit came forth from the previous one in a secret fashion, or, according to one explanation, came forth and was begotten through the movement and force of heaven and the elements under heaven, until the last two conceptions, as if incorporated into a living being, began to procreate by means of the flesh. Thus the second lineage, born half as man and half as god, was begotten and created in a somewhat understandable fashion. Their powers served them to live and govern a superhuman span of time, until the fifth and last of these earthly gods, Awasezu no mikoto, produced a third race, that is, the lineage of the Japanese.

The firstborn of Awasezu no mikoto and his successors, or, if there was none, the rightful heir, receives superhuman veneration and is vested with the government of all the people. They are described as *ō dai,* that is, great lineage, and, although they are no longer called *mikoto*, all of this authority and lineage are referred to as *mikado,* that is, emperor; *tennō,* that is, lord of heaven; *tenjin,* child of heaven; *tei,* prince, and they are also called by the name of the whole imperial court, namely, *dairi.*

So far the cherished and sacred tradition of the Japanese about the origin of their nation. It is beyond the comprehension of a normal brain and not something one can argue with, except if one were to interpret the double lineage of the gods as the golden and silver age, or early men before and after the biblical flood. But that is in vain, for the stories and life spans of these gods are pegged altogether too far beyond the creation of the world and reach altogether too far back into eternity. It appears that in this respect the Japanese are equal to the Egyptians, Chaldeans, Brahmins, and other nations (who in vainglorious imitation all transported their nation and kings back in time) but want to outdo their neighbors, the Chinese. By placing their terrestrial[16] progenitor, Tenshō daijin, many thousand years ahead of the (as the Japanese claim) first terrestrial founder of the Chinese, Tenkōshi (Tien Huang Ti, according to the Chinese), in their chronicles, they want to eliminate all conjecture that they might be descended from the Chinese and also to prevent this forefather of theirs being taken from them and cast as a person from a foreign country. For greater assurance they preceded this by the older clan register of the above-mentioned incorporeal gods, from whom he was begotten, and placed the origin of the incorporeal gods at the beginning and creation of all matter. They consider that this ought to be sufficient to qualify as an independent nation. The Japanese have no answer when asked how Awasezu, the last of their great and so perfect divine humans, could have fathered such a weak race of short-lived humans. They have just as little to reply when questioned why, prior to their first actual emperor, there is no description of the condition of the people, ancestors, and native country. Therefore many of their own writers may call the Japanese microcosm an *atarashii koku,* or *shin koku,*[17] as if it only came about and was first settled at the time of their first monarch. I am of the opinion, however, that this is only the result of looking at China. China's history, emperors, and ancient way of life and government, as well as many memorable events of their empire, were written down more than four thousand years ago, while in Japan this was only done for the first time at the first *ōdai,* or *mikado,* beginning 660 years before Christ. When we consider that at the time this great empire had such a powerful monarchy, which, according to the chronicles, waged great internal wars only a few generations later, often losing many thousands of people through pestilence and famine, it is hardly possible that they came into being at that time—they must have lived here for many centuries and must have constituted a populous nation. The only alternative is to maintain that a little previously they left another large empire and moved into this one, or that they suddenly sprouted like mushrooms out of the ground. Both these suggestions are laughable. One may rather believe that in accordance with Japanese topography, where regions are separated by mountains, rivers, and lakes, they lived divided into many wild tribes and groups for many centuries, until this happy Ninus,[18] Jimmu tennō, brought them under the accord of monarchical government, either by force, by trickery, or by the choice of his subjects and their own preference. Since the time of that monarch, the Japanese describe the deeds of their people with impeccable chronology. Like Tachi no Mikoto[19] among the heavenly gods and Tenshō daijin among the gods on earth, this monarch Jimmu is considered the first and greatest among humans, in whose family the right of imperial might (this is no longer so), as well as worshipful authority, has been vested by succession up to the present *kinjō kōtei,*[20] the 114th *mikado,* that is, for 2,360 years up until the year of our Savior 1700.

Chapter 7

The Climate of Japan and Its Mineral Resources

Japanese Air

This country boasts of a healthy climate. The wind, however, is very strong and always cold and carries a lot of snow in winter, but in the dog days it is unbearably hot. Throughout the year the heavens are generous in their supply of water, especially during the months of June and July, which they therefore call *satsuki,*[1] meaning "water months." But the rain falls neither so continuously nor at such exact times as to permit comparison with a season in the Indies. Moreover, the heavens frequently resound with thunder.

The Japanese Sea and Its Two Whirlpools

The surrounding seas are frequently whipped up by storms, have cliffs above and below the water, and are therefore dangerous to navigate. There are two dangerous, strange whirlpools, one of which is called Hayasaki, situated close to Amakusa, near Shimabara. It is avoided only during the change from high to low tide, for while its surface is usually level with the sea and the water still, at that time the water spins forcefully for a moment and then suddenly plunges to a depth of fifteen fathoms (if one can believe that), pulling unsuspecting vessels to its cliff-covered ground and smashing them in the process. The pieces are supposed to reappear a mile away, or not at all. The other whirlpool, called Naruto, is not far from Kii no kuni, near the province of Awa. Therefore it is called Awa no naruto, meaning "the noise of Awa," because it surrounds a small island of cliffs with great force and unchanging noise, causing the island to vibrate constantly. This whirlpool looks frightening but is not considered dangerous because with its terrifying sound audible from afar it is easy to avoid. Because of its strange movement and property, this Naruto is often cited in their *uta,* or songs, and pensive speech. Sometimes one also sees waterspouts on the seas surrounding Japan, rising from the sea and floating above the land. People paint them like dragons with a tail of water and truly believe that they are water dragons, rising into the air with forceful twisting. They therefore call this kind of whirlwind *tatsu maki,* that is, "dragon whirl."

Japanese Land

Japanese land is mostly uneven, poor, stony, and hilly, yet the untiring labor of its inhabitants has made it fertile. But not to the extent that people are able to survive without the addition of fish, shells, and a variety of seaweed supplied by the sea. To this they add roots and wild herbs from mountains and stony ground impossible to cultivate, which their ancestors in their poverty learned to prepare and turn into food. One may, therefore, well believe that as long as the subjects of this country are not disturbed in their cultivation of the soil and production of food, the Japanese, with their temperate style of living, are supplied with all bodily needs, and that this country crawling with people can exist without the slightest help from foreign countries, like a small, secluded world apart from the rest of the world.

Famous Rivers

The country has many rivers of fresh water with large volumes of water. Many of them are awkward to cross on account of their swift current, caused by the steep drop from high mountains and frequent heavy showers. The most famous are:

1. The dangerous Ōigawa or Ōi river. It has no bridge, is more than quarter of a mile wide, and can only be waded through. In the bottom of the river are large, moving rocks. Its waters gush with the speed and power of an arrow, and it cannot be crossed on horseback without knowledgeable, specially appointed guides (of which five have to guide one horse when the water is low, that is, knee-deep). If they lose their passenger, they lose their lives.
2. The Ōmi river, which is famous because, according to Japanese records, it appeared suddenly one night in the year 285 before the birth of Christ in the province of which it carries the name.
3. Asukagawa is considered strange because it constantly changes the depth of its course, and its name is therefore used for all sorts of innuendoes by poets and lovers.

Earthquakes

The Japanese land is subject to frequent earthquakes, but because they are so common, they are given no more attention than we give to thunderstorms. Common people say: "There, again, is a whale creeping below the earth: it's of no significance." But often the tremors are so strong and last so long that buildings crumble on top of each other, causing great ruin to cities and the loss of many thousands of people, as happened in the presence of P. Ludoo Froes in 1586 (according to his account in the work *De rebus Japonicis a Joh. Hayo*)[2] and also a number of times afterward. A friend who had been in Japan wrote to me from Batavia as late as the year 1704 that in the previous year there had been such a horrendous earthquake that the large city of Edo (which was hit hardest) as well as the shogunal residence fell to ruin, at which time more than two hundred thousand people lost their lives in the destruction and the ensuing fire. It is amazing that some particular locations in this country are never visited by earthquakes, which is attributed to the sacredness of the site and the protection of the local idol or spirit. Others argue that these locations rest on the solid ground of the immovable earth center. Among them are the island of Gotō, the little island of Chikubujima, where the first and most important temple of Benzaiten was built, the famous mountain Kōyasan covered with monasteries, and perhaps some others.

Minerals

The wealth of the Japanese lands, which is greater than that of all other known nations and countries in the world, consists of a variety of minerals, but mainly of the most important metals of gold, silver, and copper.

Sulfur, Burning Ground, and Hot Baths

The mother of these metals, sulfur, is evident at many sites, in smoking mountains and valleys, and hot baths, and shows itself even distinctly in ordinary water. In listing some of these locations I will start with our former residence at Hirado. Not far away was a small rocky island, one which on account of their great number carries the name Kujūkujima, which means "ninety-nine islands." This island, small and insignificant though it may be, has been burning for many centuries, although it is situated in the middle of the sea and surrounded by water. An island opposite Satsuma, which the Japanese call by the Portuguese name Fuogo, and is called Vulcanus by our people, also has an everlasting fire. Higo has a trench that formerly burned but has now stopped, having consumed its nourishment. In the same province is a locality called Aso, where the famous temple of the idol Aso no gongen can be seen, the name meaning "the devoted god of Aso."[3] From the peak of the mountain near the temple half a flame is constantly rising, which can be seen better at night than in the daytime. In the province of Chikuzen near Koyanose, a pit has been burning for a great number of years, but it is a mine of hard coal, which caught fire because of the carelessness of one of the workers. The famous Mount Fuji in the province of Suruga, which in height can be compared only to Mount Tenerife in the Canaries and in shape and beauty compares to no other in the world, sometimes has smoke coming from the cavity in its snow-covered and forever-white-haired head as if rising from a chimney. But frequently floating snow falsely gives the impression of smoke. Chronicles relate that in ancient times the peak was burning until the mountain burst out at the sides, cracked, and in the process lost its flame. Unzen is a large, shapeless, wide, and not very high mountain at Shimabara. It is bare, covered with white sulfur, and like a burned-out lump;[4] there is little smoke, but I have seen the rising cloud from a distance of more than three miles. In many places the ground is hot, and there it is loose and cracked, so that it is dangerous to walk around except in some places where there are odd trees. Because of the smell of sulfur, no birds can survive, and when it rains, the whole mountain seems to boil. On and around this mountain are many cold, as well as boiling hot, waters and springs, and among them a large bath as hot as fire, which has the power to kill the germs of the Spanish poison[5] if one sits in it for a few moments on a number of consecutive days or washes the body in it. But before that, the patient has to start the cure with a less-potent bath a few miles away, called Obama, eat warm food throughout the treatment, keep the body warm, and cover it after the bath to produce sweat.

A few field paths away from this hot bath is a monastery of the Tendai sect, which has given the name of a certain hell to each hot spring, indicating that it is for this or the other government official, artisan, and so forth, according to resemblances in the foam of the water, its noise, the soil at the bottom, and so on. According to their profession, dishonest beer or *sake* brewers would have to reside in the depth of a large, muddy spring, kitchen hands or dumpling makers in a spring that boils up with foam in a similar way, quarrelsome people in one that brings up its waters with deep, subterranean sounds, and so on. Credulous people will listen to this and give a donation. This is the mountain where in an earlier period newly converted Christians were taken and tortured in the hot baths to cause them to apostatize.

One of the most curative and most famous among the hot spas is that of Obama, briefly mentioned above, which is situated three miles to the west of this mountain. It cures many external and internal illnesses by bathing and sweating, among others the French pox,[6] which, however, frequently reoccurs after a little while. I believe this is because neither the cure of this illness nor the use of the baths is properly understood. Higo has a variety of hot baths, near which, I am told, are large camphor trees, which are hollow and full of water. The most important and curative of those is a hot bath at the abovementioned temple, Aso. In Hizen there is a warm bath with plenty of water in the village of Takeo and a smaller one in the town of Ureshino. Both would be curative, if people understood their use properly. I have noticed throughout Asia that no baths were used for more than three, rarely, and at the very most, for eight days by the inhabitants. When the sickness recurs afterward, the water's lack of potency is blamed.

The greatest amount of sulfur comes from the country of Satsuma, from a small island close to its territory. Owing to the abundance of this mineral, it is called Iōgashima, which means "sulfur island," and it was discovered only a hundred years ago. Because of its great amount of steam and weird apparitions, it had previously been believed to be the seat of devils, and it was considered impossible to climb its mountains. But a common man had the courage to seek permission to explore the state of the island. He climbed it with fifty men and found neither spirits nor hell, but on its peak a flat piece of ground covered to such an extent with sulfur that wherever they stepped, smoke or steam arose. This soil now nets its owner more than twenty boxes of silver in exchange for sulfur, and the trees that grow along the island's shore also generate profit. The country of Shimabara, especially the area around the above-mentioned hot bath, produces naturally pure sulfur. But it is not collected out of fear of annoying the spirit residing there and is not even touched, because people have learned that the spirit does not want to part with it. I will omit several other locations because they are not well enough known.

Gold

Gold is supplied by mountains and valleys in various areas. It is gained from the ore, found in certain sands, and often separated and obtained from copper. The shogun controls all gold and other mines in the country. Without his order and consent, they may not be opened and worked. When he has given permission to work a mine, he receives two parts and the territorial lord, as owner of the land, one part, but the latter well knows how to get even.

Sado, an island in the northern provinces, has the richest ore and the finest gold. It even has seams where one catty of ore yields one to two taels of gold.[7] But I have been told that during the last years the seams there and in other mines have become rather poor. This is supposed to be the major cause of the strict surveillance and the miserable terms of the foreign trade with the Dutch and the Chinese. Mountain sand rich in gold is also found here, which the territorial lord knows to use well, without informing or sharing it with the shogun's court. Suruga has always supplied the greatest amount of gold ore; it is separated also from copper found there. Satsuma has, among others, a mine with ore yielding four to six taels of gold from one catty. But mining is prohibited, because a chicken with so many golden eggs is believed to be a rarity. In Ōmura in the bay of Ōkusa was an overhanging mountain, which a few years ago broke off and fell into the sea. Thereupon appeared sand so rich in ore and gold (as I have been reliably told) that 50 percent was pure gold. But it had to be retrieved from the depth of the sea by divers. This rich harvest lasted only a few years. Then mighty waves from the rough open seas entered the bay and covered this ground rich in gold with fathoms of mud, swallowing up these immeasurable riches. Still today poor and unemployed people gather sand on these shores and with many washings obtain some gold, but so little that they cannot support themselves on it. In Chikugo, near the village of Hoshino, is a gold mine that is full of water. But it is situated at such height and in such a position that one could break the rock on the lower side and drain off the water. The work was begun, but then a terrible thunderstorm occurred, which forced the workers to stop the task and made everybody believe that the *kami,* or god, of the soil would not permit it. Because of fear of the god's furor, people were not allowed to continue the work later. The same is said about the mountain rich in gold ore on the island of Amakusa. The water welled forth, filled the mine, and ruined all machinery, and the workers were forced to flee to save their lives.

Silver

Silver comes from the area of Bingo, and in greater quantities from the location of Kitami, situated in one of the large northern provinces, and from others that are not well known to me. If indeed their names and characters are in accord with the truth, then this would include the islands of Ginshima and Kinshima, mentioned in chapter 3 of this book, which are rich in gold and silver and are located toward the east of Japan.

Copper

Copper is the most frequently found metal in this country, and it is at present being mined in the provinces of Suruga, Echigo, and Ki no kuni. The last province produces the finest and most malleable copper in the world. Echigo produces very brittle copper, and therefore seventy catties of it have to be mixed with thirty catties from Ki no kuni to make it malleable. That from Suruga is beyond criticism and also contains a lot of gold. Nowadays they are more skilled at separating the gold than previously: to the great grief of the gold workers and Brahmins of the coast of Coromandel. Satsuma also has copper ore, and recently his majesty has permitted that it be mined again. All copper is refined in the city of Sakai and cast into rods one and a half spans long and a finger thick. They are packed in small, square boxes, weighing one picul,[8] or 125 pounds. It is sold to the Dutch at twelve to thirteen mace[9] the picul and transported to other countries, where it is sold again. A different kind of crude copper is also exported. This is cast into round cakes and is much lower in price. Here brass is more expensive than copper, because calamine[10] is not locally available and is imported at great expense from Tonking in slabs and cakes.

Tin

Tin is produced in the province of Bungo. There is only a small quantity, but it is so fine that it looks like silver. The metal is rarely used in this country.

Iron Ore

Iron ore is mined only where the three provinces of Mimasaka, Bitchū, and Bizen meet, but there it is mined in abundance. It is also purified there and cast into rods two spans long. In this shape it is sold to local merchants and dispatched. I believe that the price is the same as copper, because iron tools are as expensive as those of copper or brass. Therefore household goods, handles, latches on ships, and so forth, which in other countries are made of iron, are here made of copper. A substance of iron is cast into fine, thin kettles and pans, because copper is not used for cooking. Old ones fetch a high price, because they no longer know how to produce them.

Hard Coal

Hard coal is not in short supply. It is often cut in the province of Chikuzen, near Koyanose, and in various northern provinces.

Salt

Salt is produced along the shore from saltwater. It is sprayed over fine, loosely raked sand. After the sand is dry, and the process has been repeated a number of times, seawater is filtered through the sand. The liquid is boiled down, and the salt that remains is bleached by calcination in sealed earthen vessels.

Agate

Agate of beautiful color, some resembling a poor sapphire, others like cornelian, is found in the mountain chain of Tsugaru, in the northernmost and furthest country of Ōshū, opposite the island of Ezo.

Pearls

Pearls, here called *kai no tama,* which means "jewel of shells," are found from time to time around Saikoku in various varieties of oysters and seashells, and everybody is free to collect them. Previously they were neither used nor valued by the locals, until they learned their value from the Chinese, who annually bought them up for their women, for these jewels make up their greatest and most precious adornment. The largest and most precious pearls are found in a small, flat shell or oyster, closed on both sides, called *akoya.*[11] It somewhat resembles the Persian variety, is barely the width of a palm, thin, black, shiny and brittle outside, callow with shiny mother-of-pearl on the inside. Pearls from the shell *akoya* are obtained only around Satsuma and the bay of Ōmura. Sometimes they weigh four to five candareens[12] and fetch a price of one hundred *koban.*[13] Satsuma appears to peddle its harvest to the Ryukyuan Chinese. Ōmura knows how to sell three thousand taels' worth annually to the Chinese. At present it is prohibited by the territorial lord to collect them for eating, as was previously done. I had some collected secretly and with considerable effort from there. It is amazing that among the largest of this variety of pearls there are some with such properties that if they are enclosed in a box with local face powder (a powder from the shell *takara gai*[14]), they put on one or two young pearls, which after three years, when they are ripe, drop off on their own accord. Those who own such a pearl keep it in their family because of its rarity and hand it down as an heirloom to their descendants.

Awabi is a longish, round, deep, plain, oyster shell, open on one side, the length of a span, in width a little less. It is neatly punctured with air holes, rough and chalky on the outside; inside it has the most beautiful cover of mother-of-pearl, on which there are frequently some projections like pearls, but they are not as raised as in the Persian mother-of-pearl. Divers look for them merely on account of their large amount of meat and remove them from the cliffs, to which they cling with the uncovered side, with one blow.

———[15] frequently produces pearls, sometimes of the weight of six candareens but yellow, unshapely, and of little value. In the meat of the shell *tairagi*[16] one occasionally finds a good pearl. It is collected in the bay of Arima between Yanagawa and Isahaya. The shell looks like a shield, of slightly flat, three-cornered, longish shape; curved at the sides, one and a half spans long, and at the end nearly one span[17] wide; is thin, smooth, and transparent like a polished horn, but brittle.

Naphtha

Naphtha of reddish color, called *tsuchi no abura,* which means "oil of the earth," is found in a river in the area of Echigo. Where the river is still, it is scooped up and used as oil for lamps.

Ambergris

A little ambergris is found in Satsuma and in the Ryūkyūs and more frequently at the shores of Kumano (that is, the southern ocean near Kii, Ise, etc.). Most often it is found in the intestines of a whale, which is caught near Japan, and called *hyaku hiro,* which means "one hundred fathoms," from the length of the intestines.[18] In those intestines ambergris is found together with chalky excrements nearly as solid as stone, which are especially situated in the lower intestines and indicate the presence of ambergris when the intestines are cut open. This unsavory location has given this noble product the name of *kujira no fu,* which means "whale dung."[19] When the waves first tear the ambergris from the bottom of the sea and wash it to the shore, or when it is swallowed by whales, it is soft and shapeless, flat, slimy, nearly like a cow-pat, smelling unpleasant. Those who find it frequently form it into a round ball, or compress a number of small pieces into a large lump, turning it into a denser and heavier substance. Others know how to knead white husk flower into the fresh ambergris, increasing the quantity and heightening the color of the black variety. This addition, however, makes it prone to attack by worms and is easily discovered because of sooty remnants when burned. Others mix it with powdered, scented resin, which is revealed by the smell of the smoke. The Chinese detect both additions by using hot tea water, namely, when the substance is finely scraped above the water and does not spread sufficiently. The locals use ambergris only as an addition to other pleasant-smelling spices or substances, to retain the fleeting smell, as they call it. It would have received little attention here, if the foreigners had not taught them its value by paying for it handsomely. Everybody is at liberty to pick it up where it is found and to sell it as his property. When I was there, someone had a piece of grey ambergris weighing 140 catties. When no single person was able to buy it, it was divided and traded to various people for sixty to seventy taels the catty. I have bought the blackish variety there for thirty taels.

The gardens of the oceans nurture a great variety of sea plants, hardly less than those of Amboina:[20] seaweeds that are flat, shaped like a net, or are solid; stony and prickly shrubs; stony bushes of coral; strange growths on cliffs; horns and shells. But no attention is paid to all this. Whatever happens to be found by fishermen and female divers is placed as sacrifice along the shore or at the village chapel of their patron, the local neptune, Ebisu.

A quick note on the minerals that are used to some extent in this country but are not locally produced: for instance, neither antimony nor sal ammoniac is found or used. Quicksilver and borax are supplied by the Chinese. But of the latter I came across two local, natural varieties, which, however, are not used because they are extremely impure. Certain Japanese persistently press newly arrived foreigners for sublimate mercury and pay a high price for it. They turn it into a liquid used against spreading ulcerous disease, and I believe also as a weapon to take their own life, in order to commit suicide when they get into trouble. Natural cinnabar is used for medicine; the man-made variety is imported from China and used as color. It may be traded only by the *shuza,* or privileged cinnabar merchants. The natural variety is very fine, and some of it is so expensive that it surpasses the price of silver.

Chapter 8
The Fertility of Plants in This Country

Because of its gentle climate and the inhabitants' unremitting industry, the country produces many wild and fertile plants. In earlier times bare necessity taught them how to use these without differentiation simply as food to sustain the necessities of life; but later their genius inspired them to use them also for pleasure and decoration. In this chapter I would like to discuss the most useful and most common plants; to those interested in rare and unknown plants, I recommend my *Amoenitates Exoticae,*[1] where we have made a beginning in describing the same.

The mulberry tree deserves to be mentioned as belonging to the most important category. Even though its fruits, the white as well as the brown, taste bad and are not for human consumption in this country, the leaves make up for this drawback. They are used to feed silkworms, which produce a reasonably good silk in many northern and other provinces where this tree grows. This is turned into firm, but mostly rough, material in cities and villages. The most precious and finest is woven by criminals on the island of Hachijō, but this is produced from fine, foreign yarn.

The *kozō,* or paper tree, belongs to the same family. It is a wild tree, but because of its usefulness it is cultivated in the fields, where it spreads its branches with incredible speed and produces a lot of bark. With much pain and labor this is turned into paper, which, in turn, is made into match-cord, ropes, material, clothes, and other things, as I have described to some extent in the above-mentioned *Amoenitates.*

No doubt the most noble tree of this country is the *urushi,* or lacquer tree.[2] Wooden household goods and all tableware are covered and lacquered with its sap in this country, regardless of whether people are poor or rich. Yes, it is even used at the shogunal court, where lacquered bowls are much preferred to silver and golden ones. Another wild variety, called *haji,*[3] has narrow leaves, always grows in thickets and in mountains, but produces little and inferior sap, and it is therefore hardly ever collected. The *urushi* tree belongs to a special family, peculiar to this country, and grows in virtually no other province than Yamato for this purpose. Occasionally it grows in the province of Higo, and from time to time in Shikoku. I discovered that the Indian lacquer tree is of a completely different family, being the true anacardium tree, called *rak* tree by the Siamese. In several places in India it bears fruit, but west of the river Ganges it does not produce sap, be it due to the ignorance of the locals or the composition of the soil. Throughout India and even in Japan it is imported cheaply from Siam and Cambodia, but here it is used only for second-rate bowls or as foundation for the local lacquer, which is much rarer and by far more beautiful.

There are a variety of bay trees. The one with red berries is a *Cannelifera spuria,*[4] or, judging from its mucus, at least a *Cassia lignea.*[5] Its shape and, in addition, the shape and constitution of its leaves are no different from the former, although the bark has little of the sweetness and pleasantness of cinnamon, but more in common with the aromatic taste of costus.[6] This deficiency seems to be only a matter of the soil; for I discovered that also the cinnamon trees of the Malabares, Sumatra, and Java (which have been neglected until now) either do not have the pleasant sharpness of the Ceylonese cinnamon or quickly lose it. Or even that their mucus makes them unworthy to be counted among the family of cinnamon, because cinnamon must produce a pleasant, precious oil, something no *Cassia lignea* will supply. Among the family of bay trees with small black-purple berries belongs also the *kusu,* or camphor tree.[7] On the island of Gotō, and even more so in the province of Satsuma, the village people produce camphor gum from the roots of the tree by ordinary boiling. The price is cheap: one catty of the imported camphor from Borneo (which is natural, and collected from in between the bark, branches, and the broken cut-down old trunk) is exchanged for eighty to one hundred of the Japanese kind.

Cha no ki, or the tea tree, is an unsightly bush, which in this country with its cramped space is permitted in no place except along the edges of fields and similar places that are inconvenient for cultivating other plants. It is, nevertheless, the most useful among the plants inasmuch as the daily beverage consumed in homes and inns is boiled from its baked, rough leaves. Among the high-ranking, the most delicate and youngest leaves are baked, ground, and mixed with hot water to make a soup, offered as a common beverage of tea to visitors and drunk after a meal as a farewell drink.

Sanshō[8] is a prickly tree of average height; its husk and bark yield pepper, and its leaves make a delicious spice for food. The local Riches[9] is used also for this purpose.

There are three different varieties of figs. One of them, called *kaki,*[10] is found throughout the country in large quantities. This is a tree that elsewhere would be called a fig. It has the shape of an old, low apple tree; the leaf is oval, long, and without grooves; the fruit looks like a reddish apple, but its flesh has the consistency and taste of a delicate fig; the seed is like that of a pumpkin, but hard and stony. This is one of the most productive and most useful trees in the whole country. Both rich and poor enjoy its dried fruit as a delicacy. The Chinese improve the fruit greatly by preserving it in sugar.

The second kind of fig resembles the common European type, but it grows on a tree with broad, long, rough leaves without grooves. The third is the European kind, which was imported by the Portuguese. Trees are rare, but bear large, delicious fruit that splits open. The sycamore or wild fig tree[11] is common here, but I will not discuss it because its fruit is not eaten.

Chestnut trees grow in abundance, and generally they produce much larger fruit than in Europe. Most of them grow in the province of Chikuzen. Apple trees like those in Germany or Europe are not known here. There are quite a lot of pears, but they are all of the kind we call winter pear and are of not much use raw. They are of unusual size and generally weigh a pound or even more.

Walnut trees are mostly found in the northern provinces. In the same region grows a tall yew tree, called *kaya,*[12] which has longish nuts the size and shape of the Areca fruit covered by a fleshy skin.[13] The fruit and its nut are not pleasant to eat and are very astringent on the tongue, especially when they are still fresh. When dried, they taste a little better. But their sweet oil is a laxative, and because of their medicinal qualities they are served in desserts. The pressed oil is sweet, nearly like almond oil, and is used as food and medicine. The smoke from these nuts provides the main ingredient of the most expensive and finest Japanese ink.

Another species of nut called *gin nan*[14] has the shape of a large pistachio nut. It grows throughout the country on beautiful, incredibly large trees, with wide leaves shaped like those of the maidenhair fern, which is called *ichō no ki.*[15] The oil is used for many things.

There are two foreign species of oak trees. The fruit of the larger variety is boiled and eaten by the common people.

Natsume, or jujube tree,[16] produces in this country a healthy, delicious fruit larger than I have ever seen before.

Lemon trees are seen from time to time in special gardens, but there are few limes; oranges are found frequently, and there are a number of varieties. The best variety is called *mikan,*[17] resembling a Borsdorf apple[18] in both shape and size. The smell is delectable, but the taste is as sour as wine. *Kinkan*[19] is another rare variety, the size and shape of a nutmeg, extremely sour. In grows on a little bush and is used in dishes and for pickles.

Grapes rarely ripen and therefore are not much cultivated. Blackberries and raspberries are not very delicious to eat, and strawberries are totally without taste and not edible at all. Peaches, apricots, and plums are plentiful. Among the latter are two strange varieties that are white and purple, gritty like mulberries; they are mostly used for pickles. Cherry and wild plum trees[20] are grown only on account of their beautiful blossoms. Cultivation has produced blossoms the size of double-petaled roses, and they burst forth in such quantity that they cover the whole tree like blood-drenched snow. These trees are the greatest ornament of all houses and temple gardens. Apricot trees and other varieties of plum trees are also often cultivated solely for this reason. The most common trees of the forest are pine and cypress of many varieties. The wood is used for making houses, boards, and containers; the branches and other parts provide fuel for the ordinary kitchen fire. The common people, however, use fallen pine cones and needles for this purpose. They gather them daily, and thanks to their efforts the ground is kept clean. These trees are planted as decoration in long rows on the top of mountain ridges and also on both sides of the highways. Great effort is made to have them grow in all sandy and uninhabited places. No pine or cypress tree may be cut without permission of the local authority, and a new sapling must be planted to replace it.

The most common shrub is bamboo, which is used to make a great number of household goods, such as gutters, walls that are to be plastered, the best match-cord, finely plaited baskets, and other goods. In the province of ———[21] a variety of bamboo produces long, knotty roots, which we call rattan,[22] which are exported and used as walking sticks. On account of their long life and intense green color, both pine and bamboo are considered auspicious or lucky by this nation. Therefore they are used to decorate sacred places at festivals and for celebrations. They are also alluded to in congratulatory addresses, verses, and symbols, because people believe that the bamboo shrub reaches an age of several hundred years and that the common pine, called *matsu no ki,* reaches an age of one thousand years, at which time it turns its branches and needles toward the earth. From time to time trees of incredible age have been pointed out to me. *Hi no ki* and *sugi,*[23] two cypress varieties, produce a light, strong, and fine white wood that repels water and can be taken as good cedar wood. For a certain period they may not be cut anywhere in the country, and, if such orders come from the shogun, not even one may be used for the construction of an instrument. However, when no punishment has been set for the crime, prohibitions of this nature are little observed. *Kusa maki,* or evil-smelling *maki* tree;[24] *shii no ki,*[25] a variety of oak; and *isu no ki,*[26] called iron tree on account of its hardness, are trees yielding ordinary wood, which can also be used for building houses. *Tochi no ki,*[27] which is collected from the city of Ejiri, and the root of the camphor tree yield the rarest wavy-grained wood, which is used for counters and lacquered boxes.

There are in this country, as in no other place, a great number of wild plants with incredibly beautiful flowers and leaves, which at certain times of the year bedeck wastelands and mountain forests. They are also grown in gardens and by cultivation brought to even greater perfection. The most important are: *tsubaki,*[28] a large shrub with rose-like flowers, growing in thickets and forests; many rare varieties are obtained by grafting. It is claimed that there are nine hundred varieties with different names in this country fond of names. *Satsuki,*[29] a little shrub with lily-like flowers, is supposed to have more than a hundred named varieties. There are two wild varieties, one with red and one with flesh-colored flowers, that cover many bleak fields and hills with their pleasant color. *Shakunage*[30] a shrub that also has lily-shaped flowers, but much larger than those of the former. There are three varieties, but they are not as common as the previous one.

Momiji, belonging to the genus of maple, has received its name because of the purple color of its leaves.[31] There are two different varieties: the leaves of one turn partly yellow and partly purple in spring, those of the other in autumn. They beckon from afar and afford pleasure to the eye. The same is the case with the *haji* tree,[32] which is also covered with purple leaves in autumn.

Chrysanthemums[33] and lilies exist in great numbers and rare varieties. The former (which have been cultivated to reach the size of a rose) decorate gardens, the latter, the uninhabited mountains. Not to mention local narcissus, irises,[34] clove-pink,[35] and other flowers, with which mother nature embellishes this country at certain times of the year, rare elsewhere. They are, however, like all those mentioned above, without scent; also Japanese fruit does not have the same pleasant taste as that of China and India.

Hemp and cotton are cultivated in their fields as much as space permits. *Shuro,*[36] or hemp palm, frequently grows in uninhabited places and makes up for the lack of flax and wool, because it is used to weave a variety of fine as well as rough cloth. Oil for a number of different purposes is pressed from the following plants: *kiri*[37] is an enormously large but rare tree. Its leaves are like those of a burdock, its flowers grow on a long stem and resemble digitalis, and its seeds are like those of the marshmallow. The leaf with three stems of flowers represents the emblem of the *mikado,* or spiritual, hereditary emperor. *Aburagiri,*[38] a tree of average height, has leaves like those of a plane tree, flowers like plain roses, and seeds like a ricinus. Consequently I have called it Ricinus arboreus folio Alceae. Japanese bead tree,[39] the above-mentioned *tsubaki, urushi, haji,* and *kaya no ki,* then also the cotton shrub and herb, sesame of two varieties, with black and white seeds. Among these, only the oil of sesame and *kaya* is used for the preparation of food, but not very often and sparingly, as people in this country know how to prepare food without any butter or fat.

Grain and leguminous plants and all sorts of garden herbs are grown not only in level fields (which are never used as meadows) but also on steep mountains, up to the highest top. Yes, they are even grown in the holes and niches of rocky cliffs, wherever roots can take hold and rainwater collects. Flat land is plowed with oxen, high ground is cultivated by hand, and both are fertilized some three times a year with human excrement to maintain its fertility. If land is left uncultivated for a year, owners forfeit their right to it according to the laws of the country.

The most important and most useful field produce for human consumption is given the title of *gokoku,* meaning five fruits of the field. According to the quantity of their growth, a field and the year's yield is deemed productive or unproductive and the owner deemed rich or poor. They make up for the lack of meat in this country and serve as basic staple for daily meals and special feasts. The *gokoku* are:

1. *Kome,* or rice, of which there are a number of varieties. The best finds no parallel in the whole of Asia, is as white as snow, and is so filling that a foreigner can only eat little at a time. Boiled in water, it serves as daily bread. The annual surplus is used to brew an oily beer, but only as much as is essential. Consequently the foreigners may export neither rice nor beer in greater quantities than permitted by the authorities.

2. *Ōmugi,* which means "large grain," that is to say, barley, is used only as fodder for horses and other animals; however the flour is used in the kitchen for the preparation of various foods. There is a kind of barley with purplish ears and husks, which looks beautiful in the fields.

3. *Komugi,* which means "little grain," that is to say, wheat, which, as far as I know, is used only as flour for cakes and is very cheap.

4. *Daizu,*[40] which is soy beans; they look like Turkish peas but grow like lupins. These beans stand in high repute with the local inhabitants, second only to rice, because their flour is used to make *miso,* a certain floury paste, which in cooking takes the place of butter. It is also used to make *shōyu,* which is used as marinade or sauce to flavor food, and is served at every meal. It is exported to as far as Holland. The preparation of it is explained in my *Amoenitates Exoticae,* page 839.

5. *Azuki,* or *shōzu,*[41] soy beans also resembling lupins, but they are black and like lentils or Indian cajan. Mixed with sugar, the flour is used as a filling for *manjū,*[42] and is also used for other cakes. Otherwise the following field produce is included in the term *gokoku*: *awa,* or foxtail millet (Panicum Indic. *Tabern.*);[43] *kibi,* or our common millet;[44]

hie, or Deccan grass,[45] *mugi,* that is, all sorts of grain; and *mame,* that is, all sorts of beans, peas, and leguminous plants.

Throughout the country radishes of incredible size grow. Because of the large supply, they are used more than any other field produce to sustain life. But they smell and taste so much of human sulfur, with which they are fertilized, that in Europe people would be put off from eating them by the smell. They are enjoyed raw, boiled when fresh, and preserved dried or salted. Beets, turnips, pumpkins, rock melons, watermelons, cucumbers, aubergines, fennel, carrots, and a local lettuce, plants that we grow in gardens, are all common field crops here. There is no cultivated parsnip here, but some wild parsnip.[46] Parsley, cabbage, chicory, and our kind of lettuce[47] have always been cultivated by the foreigners here and grow very well.

Also the uncultivated forests, mountains, cliffs, marshes, and floors of lakes supply many known and unknown wild herbs. The young leaves of their sprouts, fruits, and little roots are not only used by commoners for their daily, ordinary fare but are also prepared as delicate tidbits for the feasts and entertainments of important people. Most varieties of mushrooms are used; people often die of them. That also happens with other poisonous herbs, when untaught people collect them for food. People know how to soak devil's tongue *(konnyaku)*[48] to remove its sharpness and to turn it into a sweet paste or flour. This is also done with the root of *warabi,* or fernbrake,[49] *ren* or *tarate* (lotus),[50] and *kazune.*[51] After it is ground, the substance is steeped in liquid and strained, leaving a fine flour on the bottom. This is used in many dishes, or simply dissolved in water, it provides a ready meal.

No seaweed grows on the floor of the sea that the inhabitants of this country do not use as food. There are many different kinds. It is brought to the surface from a depth of twenty to forty fathoms by the wives of fishermen, who throughout the country are trained to do this. Then it is washed, cleaned, and separated into different kinds, and each kind is preserved as food in its own way.

Chapter 9

The Country's Abundance of Quadrupeds, Birds, Crawling and Flying Insects

Among the native animals are a number of chimera introduced from China which exist only in the minds and writings of the Japanese, but not in nature. We will discuss and deal with them first.

Kirin, people say, is a fast-moving, winged quadruped, with soft, backward-pointing horns attached to the chest. Its body is that of a horse, its feet and claws those of a deer, and its head is not unlike that of a dragon.[1] It is so saintly that it tries not to injure a single worm or little weed when it walks. It is brought forth by the miraculous powers of the star-studded heavens at a time when a *seijin* is born among men. *Seijin* are persons who more than anyone else are endowed by nature with an enlightened mind, with which they investigate the true state of nature and of divine matters, and discover new facts. People who are considered to have had such attributes are: the Chinese emperors Gyō and Shun,[2] as excellent rulers and discoverers of herbs; Kōshi and Mōshi,[3] as Chinese philosophers; Shaka[4] in India, revealing divine matter, Daruma[5] in China and Shōtoku Taishi[6] in Japan, as luminaries famous for their lives and teachings.

To the above they add two other monsters. One of them is called *sūgu,* which looks like a leopard but on its chest has a set of antlers spreading out and backward on both sides like wings. The other one, called *kaichi,*[7] attempts to look like a fox, but on the chest has antlers standing out, on its head has a horn, and along its back has a row of broad spikes, like a crocodile.

Tatsu or *ja*[8] is a common dragon, about which fables abound in the history of their heroes and gods. People believe that this breed lives on the floor of the sea, where it has its own life and world. The dragon is depicted like a snake but with four legs and scales like a crocodile, with spikes along the whole length of its spine. Its head is monstrous and terrifying; the tail ends (in the case of the Japanese dragon) in a short double-bladed sword. The Japanese rulers sometimes mark their personal utensils, such as forks, knives, and other items, with the shape of this dragon, with its right foot holding a jewel or pearl. But each foot has only three claws, distinguishing it from the Chinese imperial dragon, which has five claws. *Tatsu maki* is a dragon with a tail of water dragging behind, which they believe rises from the sea into the air and causes a gyrating column of water, which we call a waterspout. These can often be observed on these rough seas; at times they rise from the sea and float above land.

Hōō is an extraordinarily beautiful and very large bird of paradise, not much different from a phoenix.[9] It descends from the air and settles on the ground when a very august ruler or other *seijin* is born. Such things are described and believed among these nations as if they were the very truth.

We will proceed from the imaginary animals to the real ones.

Wild and tame four-legged animals are not found in great numbers in this country. The former find few uninhabited locations where, timid as they are, they can hide and breed. The latter are raised only for work; their meat is rarely consumed by the locals on account of their Pythagorean,[10] albeit cold-blooded, beliefs. Consequently these vegetarians know how to use the land of this country with its limited space more profitably than for raising animals. Among the tame animals of this country is the horse, which, although small, frequently compares well with the Persian horse in its dexterity. They are kept for show, for riding, carrying, and plowing. The best come from the provinces of Ōshū and Satsuma, and a stocky, rather small kind, from the area of Kai. Oxen and cows are used only for plowing and pulling carts; using them for producing milk and butter is totally unknown here. There is an extremely long and rough kind of buffalo with big humps on the shoulder and of all colors. It is used only in large cities to pull carts. Donkeys, mules, camels, and elephants are unknown. Sheep and goats were introduced some time ago by the Europeans at Hirado, where they are still bred. They would find good mountain pastures throughout the country, and could be raised to good profit if people were to use the wool, or if one were permitted to eat the meat. There are few pigs, and they were introduced from China. They are raised only in small numbers by the farmers of Hizen, and, on account of their religious devotion, they hardly ever eat them. They are sold only to the Chinese, who arrive every year and slaughter them for their daily fare, even though they are of the same religion.

Kaempfer's drawing of a Japanese dragon. (Courtesy of the British Library, Sloane 3606, folio 454)

Under the present shogun's government there are more dogs in this country than in any other. Masterless dogs lie around the streets, causing great obstruction to passersby. The citizens of each street have to maintain and feed a certain number of them. When they are sick, they have to be cared for in a hut erected in each street, and when they die, they have to be carried up a mountain and buried like humans. On pain of death they may not be mistreated or killed, except by the bailiff himself, when the dogs have committed a crime and deserve to die. This has been commanded on account of the superstition of, and an order from, the shogun, who, just as the Roman Emperor Augustus honored the ibex, holds dogs in special respect because he was born in the Year of the Dog.[11] A citizen carrying a dead mongrel up the mountain to be buried grumbled impatiently about the year of the shogun's birth. His neighbor told him to be quiet and to thank heaven that he was not born in the Year of the Horse, for then their load would have been much heavier. Greyhounds and water-dogs are not known; when hunting, for which there is not much opportunity, ordinary dogs are used. Among cats there is one breed that is kept merely for decoration. It has large yellow and black spots on a white background and has a short, crooked tail, as if it had been purposely broken. It has no desire to hunt for mice but just wants to be carried and stroked by women.

As to wild four-legged animals, the country has deer, rabbits, and wild boar, and many of the sects permit their followers to eat the meat of these three animals at certain times of the year. There are only a few monkeys; they are intelligent, have light-brown fur, short tails, and naked red faces and bottoms. A tramp has a monkey that he claims is 106 years old, which he gets to perform tricks for a lot of money. There are only few bears in the northern provinces, and they are of small size. *Tanuki*[12] is a brownish black animal, has a snout like a fox, and appears to be a small kind of wolf. There are wild dogs, with large, wide-cleft snouts. *Itachi*[13] is a reddish animal like a marmot or polecat. Another larger kind is called *ten.*[14] They live in houses and roofs and are nearly tame. Apparently they catch not only chickens but also fish. There is an abundant supply of rats and mice. People are skilled in taming them to perform all sorts of tricks. This is the amusement and pastime of certain poor individuals, especially in Osaka, a city that serves as common showground for the whole country, where there are all sorts of curiosities and games to be seen for money. There is an abundance of foxes. The Japanese believe that they are often possessed by devils and frequently mention them and their actions in divine stories. Hunters are good at quickly skinning these devils, because their soft fur is essential for paint and writing brushes. People distinguish between the devil *kitsune,* or fox, and *oni,*[15] as they distinguish in Sweden between faun and devil.[16] The country is free of tigers, panthers, lions, and other savage animals.

Highest among the pests I rank white ants, as they are referred to throughout the Indies. They are snow-white, delicate little worms. They live in clumps, like ants, and resemble ants with regard to their size and roughly also their shape. Their chest and head is brownish and hard. The Japanese call them *dō taoshi,*[17] that is, borer, because they eat through anything that stands in their way within hours (except metal and stone) and ruin the most precious goods in the merchants' storehouses. They can be stopped only by scattering common salt. Their worst enemies are the blackish, or true ants. When the latter arrive, the former have to disappear. They cannot survive in the open air, even less so than moles, and protect themselves against it with delicate, thin passageways, which always proceed their trail and are glued to the ground. The substance resembles the nest of the stable fly and digger wasp. I have heard many examples of their quick and ruinous marches and experienced it myself in the living quarters of the commander of the fortifications of Quilon at the Malabar Coast. At midnight I had left my desk and went to sleep, and in the morning when I sat down at it again, I found a fine, enclosed passageway, the size of a small finger, coming up from the floor and running along a bored hole the length of one of the legs, then straight across the untouched top of the desk, and finally down and through half the length of the opposite leg, from where it went down to the ground in a round groove. Many people believe such quick destruction is caused by their excrement. I saw no evidence for that, but instead discovered four protruding tongs on their snout, with which they are able to create such havoc.

Centipedes, commonly called *mukade*[18] in Japanese, and *gokō* according to the Chinese character, are not woodlice or slaters but what people call millipedes in the Indies. They are nearly finger-long, slim, brownish insects, with feet on both sides. In India they are very poisonous, and their bite is more painful than that of a scorpion. There are few of them here, and they are seldom harmful. When people are bitten, they dab on saliva, and it heals. This country's lizards are only of a common variety. There are only a few different kinds of snakes. Among them is a famous kind called *hirakuchi* and *hibakari.*[19] It is green with a flat head and sharp teeth. The snake has its name from the length the sun shines, or the length of a day, because people bitten by this snake will die by sunset. Soldiers are eager to eat its meat because it is supposed to have the power to make those who savor it strong and courageous. When preserved in closed-up pots, calcined, it produces a famous powder, *daōsō,* which is used internally for a variety of illnesses. People say that if this powder is scattered under the dripping end of the gutters of a house, other snakes will appear shortly. I have seen this kind of snake nowhere else except with the Brahmins at the Coromandel Coast.

An unusual large snake, called *yamakagachi,* or, more colloquially, *uwabami,*[20] and also *ja,* which means dragon, hides in the mountains and in water. It is rarely seen, and when one is caught, it is displayed for money.

As for tame fowl, people keep chickens, sometimes also ducks, but for superstitious reasons they are seldom eaten and can be killed only by certain low-class people. On the death and remembrance day of a blood relative, nobody may kill a bird or other living animal for food. Neither chicken nor any other living animal may be killed, yes, not one may even be displayed for sale at the market in the year of the death, or the year of remembrance, of the shogun. This applies also to certain other times when his majesty issues such commands. The cock is more frequently and more easily pardoned than the hen and is greatly venerated by religious people because he can tell the time and forecast the weather. Wild, and by nature timid, fowl have become so tame within the confines of this densely populated country that many kinds ought to be regarded as domestic species. The *tsuru,* or crane, is the most important and one that is privileged by the shogun. It may be shot only on his order and only for his majesty. But it is shot nevertheless in Saikoku[21] and other areas far from the court. On account of their extraordinary age and the strange stories told about them, these birds, as well as the turtle, are considered the most lucky and auspicious animals, and the shogunal chambers and other auspicious rooms are painted with their picture, as well as with pines and bamboo. I have always heard farmers and carriers address them with the name *o tsuru sama,* that is, "Great Lord Crane." There are two kinds, one is snow-white, the other grey, or an ashen color.

There are various kinds of *sagi,* or herons, which differ considerably in color and size. The following three are the most famous: *shiro sagi,* the snow heron; *goi sagi,* the grey night heron: both common varieties; *aoi sagi,* the blue-grey heron, is nearly the size of a crane.

There are two kinds of wild geese, both keeping to their own kind. The first is snow-white, with the main wing feathers pitch black; the other is completely grey or of an ashen color. Especially the grey variety exists in large numbers, and the birds are so tame in this country that they do not easily fly away at the approach of people and appear totally domesticated. They do great harm to the fields but on pain of death may not be hunted, except by those who have bought a license to shoot them at certain locations. The farmers cover their fields with nets or cloth to stop them from being invaded by the geese, but it helps little. I have seen with my own eyes how they have come down and broken in at the sides.

There are various kinds of ducks, and they are no less tame than the geese. There is one kind of which the male is depicted as being of such rare beauty in the book *Kimmōzui,* figure 11,[22] that I could not believe the drawing until I saw live birds myself on frequent occasions. The bird displays multicolored feathers, which are red at the throat and belly, its head is crowned with a thick bush of feathers, the tail stands broad and erect, and the wings are lifted up above the back.

Pheasants are also incredibly beautiful. A large kind has multicolored, gold and pink shiny feathers covering its whole body, and, like a peacock, has a golden-blue, glossy tail the size of half the height of a man.

Partridges are the most common birds, and they may be utilized together with pheasants, ducks, and geese. Pigeons are wild; they are bluish-black and not particularly beautiful. People take care not to have them nesting on houses because it has been discovered that when their dung heats up, it occasionally ignites and causes fires.

Storks remain in the country throughout the year.

The best falcons are caught in the northern provinces and are kept more for show than for hunting.

Goshawks are plentiful here and, as they do throughout the Indies, behave like haughty visitors; as do also the ravens, which are of average size and were first brought to Japan as a present from China.

The magpie, too, was first sent as a rare bird to the shogun from Korea and is therefore called *kōrai garasu,* that is, "Korean raven." But it has not multiplied much in this country.

European blue crows, parrots, and other birds of the Indies are not found in this country.

Token, commonly called *hototogisu,*[23] is a very rare night bird. It is served as great delicacy at grand banquets. When its calcinated ashes are mixed into *sake* that has gone sour, the *sake* becomes drinkable again.

Misago[24] is a bird of prey of the seas, like a goshawk or sparrow hawk. It keeps a hole in a cliff as a cellar to store the leftovers of its catch. Amazingly the catch does not go bad, like fish that has been pickled in marinade or brine, or preserved. It is called *misago zushi,* that is, *misago* pickles.[25] It is expensive and very salty. People who know of such a cellar are well off but must not steal too much at a time.

Seagulls, sea ravens, and also a variety of small birds, such as woodcocks, snipes, swallows, sparrows, and many more common birds breed here as in Europe.

The lark sings much more beautifully here than in Europe. Nightingales sing not as well, although one occasionally finds one with an extraordinary whistle. Rich patrons often buy them for more than twenty *koban.*

As to flying insects, the country has bees, and therefore also honey, but little wax. It has bumblebees, wasps, flies, mosquitoes, fireflies, butterflies, crickets, beetles, grasshoppers, and similar kinds of insects in common with our native country. But in addition it has some special ones that are worth mentioning. Among the butterflies there is an unusually large kind called *yama chō,* that is, mountain butterfly, of which some are totally black, and some have beautiful patterns on their serrated wings in red, white, black, and other colors. *Kōmori*[26] is a fairly large, colorful, rough and hairy, beautiful moth; it is called the same as a bat. There are various rare kinds of beetles. Among them is a black, glossy large one, like the dung beetle, with two crooked, hammer-shaped horns. The larger horn rises like that of a rhino in front above the nose; the smaller one sits on the shoulders, bent slightly more toward the front. The beetle does not move well, stays most of the time in the soil, is rare, and lacks a name.

Nature lovers will be amused by a number of peculiar features of a certain kind of brown beetle called *sebi* or *semi.* They come in three varieties and sizes. The most important of these *semi* are called *kumazemi.*[27] In size and shape they resemble the beetles that at home swarm on a summer's night, but they have no wings with which to fly. Early in summer, at night, they crawl out of the soil, where they hibernate in winter, and into a tree or somewhere else. With their sharp, ragged legs they attach themselves firmly to the wood, a leaf, shrub, or whatever else they can get hold of. Then the shell cracks open the length of the back, and another animal crawls out, shaped like a bee, and larger than the body or armor that contained it previously. After sitting for some hours, it flees quickly. This beetle, which Gesner[28] has introduced under the name of cicada, makes a sharp and incredibly high sound, reverberating distressingly in the ear, that can be heard at a quarter of a mile's distance. This noise is made by a horizontal cleft in the animal's chest, which is normally closed off or covered with a kind of shield, and, at the same time, by the movement of its four wings. The mountains and hedges are full of them and their noise. They disappear slowly during the dog days, and it is said that they crawl back into the soil and turn back into beetles in a further transformation, but this is not certain. Their common name is the result of their sound, *semi* or *sebi,* which they produce again and again, first slowly, and then accelerating, until they conclude their little song with the sound of a button-maker's spindle grinding to a halt. Their music starts after sunrise and lasts only till noon. The empty shells, called *semi no nukegara,* are collected and used for medicinal purposes, and can be bought here and throughout China at the pharmacy. Another variety of this kind, much smaller and therefore called *kozemi,* arrives a few months later and appears when the others disappear. They cry only from noon until evening and continue till late into autumn. They make nearly the same, but a much softer, sound, which has caused ordinary people to call them *tsuku tsuku bōshi.* A third variety resembles the last in size and properties, but it plays its music all day. The female of these three kinds are silent, their chest is closed, but otherwise they are of the same shape and size as the male.

Cantharides[29] are the same color as the Spanish variety but rounder and as big as a young beetle. Their use is unknown here.[30] There is also a foreign kind, called *han myō.*[31] It is supposed to be extremely caustic and is therefore considered poisonous. They live on rice ears, are long and narrow, and smaller than the Spanish variety. They are of blue and golden color with crimson red spots and little lines and therefore extraordinarily beautiful.

The most beautiful of all winged insects, which is rare even in this country and is kept as a treasure by women, is a narrow, round night insect, the length of half a finger, with two smooth wings, and more transparent wings underneath, which are decorated with blue and gold lines running the length, and are as glossy as a mirror. The male is of such extraordinary beauty that people tell the following parable about him: All flying insects fell in love with him, but he kept his lovers at a distance by telling them to fetch some fire first, and then he would return their love. His courtesans flew in blind fervor into a candle and were injured so badly that they forgot about returning. The female is not so beautiful and shiny, but of ashen color and spotted.

Chapter 10
Fish and Shellfish

With the exception of rice, the water provides as much, or much more, for the sustenance of the Japanese as the land: the sea abounds with seaweed, fish, and shellfish. Among them there is nothing, or very little, that in ancient times poverty did not cause them to turn into food, and in later times, cultural development did not induce them to exploit as a delicacy and luxury item. Fish and shellfish are known in Japan as *gyo kai,* or, in more common language, *uokai.* We would like to introduce all those that we have encountered here with their local names, regardless of the fact that the majority are not very special and are also found in our waters. This may serve as preparation for, and better understanding of, a future chapter in which we will deal with Japanese food and cuisine.[1]

Among all the creatures of the sea there is not one fish that better fills the hungry stomachs of the masses than the *kujira,* or whale. It is caught virtually everywhere around Japan, but the greatest quantity is taken in the Sea of Kumano (which washes the southernmost shores of the island of Nippon). Next are the islands of Tsushima and Gotō and the shores of Ōmura and Nomo. The fish are caught with spears, as they are in Greenland, but the vessels are more comfortable. They are small, narrow, pointed at the bow, have ten rowers each, and are extremely fast. In 1680 a rich fisherman of Ōmura, called Gidaiyū, discovered a foreign method of catching whales by covering the animals with nets made out of ropes two fingers thick.[2] Soon afterward, a farmer of Gotō, called Yōemon, successfully followed this method. As soon as the animal feels that its head is restricted, it is apparently unable to swim and remains immobile. Then it is shot with spears in the usual fashion and pulled on land. This method is supposed to require far more preparation and costs much more than the common one, for while the common method costs no more than twenty boxes of silver, the former cannot be executed for less than twenty boxes. But it is very much bigger and more profitable.[3] The whales are of different kinds, sizes, and shapes and have different names, such as:

1. *Semi,*[4] the most important, largest, and a very fat fish. It yields the greatest amount of train oil and the best. It also has very healthy meat to which laborers and fishermen, who have to endure so much hardship by day and during nights without sleep in cold weather, attribute their good health.

2. *Aosagai,* commonly called *kokujira,*[5] which means "little whale." The coat is ash-grey, and it is also smaller than the *semi* and of a different shape.

3. *Nagasu*[6] is a fish twenty to thirty fathoms long. It can remain under water for two to three hours and continue to swim under water for several miles, while others always have to come up for air.

4. *Zatō kujira*[7] is called the "blind whale" after the shape of a *biwa,* or local lute, which in this country is played by blind people, for the shape of the instrument is marked

on the back of the fish. This is a small variety, but occasionally it nevertheless reaches a length of ten fathoms. They are frequent here. But their meat is unhealthy to eat because it produces, so they say, altogether too much heat and causes catarrh, scabies, and smallpox, and brings back all old illnesses. People who know the meat do not buy it, but it is sold at the market under the name of *semi,* like all other whale meat.

5. *Makkō*[8] is only three to four fathoms long and does not get any bigger. With other varieties, *mago* means a young whale, but here it is used as proper name.[9] The fish is caught around the eastern shores of Japan, mostly near Ki no kuni and Satsuma. This kind of whale usually has ambergris in its intestines; it yields no train oil, except from its head.

6. *Iwashikujira,*[10] that is, sardine eater, has a tail and fins like a common fish. We saw it in the month of April between Kaminoseki and Shimonoseki. I believe the fish is the so-called North Atlantic right whale.

Nothing of these whales is thrown away as useless except the large hip bone. The skin is very black, and the meat is so red that it looks like beef. The guts, which are called *hyaku hiro,* a hundred fathoms, on account of their length, and all other intestines are pickled, boiled, and used; the fat is heated to make train oil, or oil for lamps, and the greaves, after they have been fried again, are eaten. The bones are white and cartilaginous. When they are still fresh, they are boiled up as food, but mostly they are scraped and dried and in this fashion preserved for use in the kitchen. Other parts of sinews, white ones as well as yellow, are made into rough cords or strings, used for making cotton and for instruments. The scraps are not wasted but are put to some use in the kitchen. The fins or whale bone are made into delicate gold and silver weights, which are named after them, and are also used for other black ornaments and a variety of handcrafted goods.

Shachihoko[11] is a fish that is generally two to three, sometimes five to six, fathoms long. It has two long teeth protruding from its mouth and above its body. They are sometimes placed above the gables of castles and temples. Fishermen say that this fish is a cunning enemy of the whales, for it crawls into their throats, eats their tongues, and thus kills them. When it crawls into a whale, it manages to bend its head in such a fashion that its horns do not prevent it from entering the fish.

Iruka[12] is a well-known fish that throughout the Indies is called *tennye. Fukube*[13] is a normal-sized fish that the Dutch in the Indies call a blowfish, because it can blow itself up to the size of a large ball. It is considered to be extremely poisonous. There are three different kinds in the Japanese seas, and each exists in large quantities. The first kind, called *susume fugu,*[14] is small and therefore rarely eaten. The second is called *mabugu,*[15] which means the proper and true *fugu.* The Japanese consider this fish to be the greatest delicacy the ocean provides, and it is eaten by everybody after the head, bones, and intestines have been removed and the meat has been freed from all harmful substances by diligent and repeated rinsing. People nevertheless often die of it. This is blamed on insufficient care when cleaning it. People who are weary of life because of an incurable illness often prepare themselves a final meal from the unwashed meat of the fish. The neighbor of my servant in Nagasaki suffered from the Spanish pox[16] and his nose was already beginning to crumble. He decided on this kind of meal and cooked himself his last supper from the unwashed meat, cut into pieces. At his own discretion he added soot from the straw roof to make the poison stronger and more effective. Then he lay down on his deathbed. As he was struggling with death in great terror, he vomited constantly and got rid of a lot of heavy mucus. By this process, however, his stomach was cleansed of the fresh poison he had imbibed, and his whole body fortunately was liberated from the deeply embedded illness, and he recovered unexpectedly. Some years ago it happened in the same city that five people who were given a meal of this fish felt so sick that they suddenly lost their strength and fainted, began to rave and vomit blood; after a few days they died in this condition. But nobody wants to miss this delicacy, in spite of the danger. Throughout the empire soldiers are forbidden to savor the fish. If it were discovered that someone had died of it, his son would lose the right to succeed to his father's position. The fish is sold for a much higher price than ordinary common fish but must be eaten fresh. The third kind is called *kita makura,*[17] which means northern pillow, but I do not know why. That name is also used for people sleeping with their head pointing north.[18] This fish contains an absolutely deadly poison, and no amount of washing can remove it. Nobody wants to eat it, except those who wish to die.

The toad fish is as long as a ten-year-old boy, has neither scales nor fins, but has an enormously large head, snout, and chest. It has a large, thin stomach like a sack, which is filled up through the snout with a large amount of water; it has sharp, fine teeth like a snake, hardly any guts, and small, insignificant intestines. Below its stomach are two flat, cartilaginous feet, shaped nearly like a child's hand, with which it appears to crawl on the floor of the sea. All parts are eaten, without exception. The fish is caught between Kamakura and Edo, and it was at the latter place that I saw it being brought into the kitchen.

Tai,[19] which the Dutch in the Indies call sea bream, is the most important fish in Japan because of the superstitious belief that it is the sacred fish of their idol Ebisu, and therefore considered to be very auspicious, and also because of its beauty and luster under water. It is a rare fish, in shape nearly like a carp. It is red and whitish, and the female has red gills. For grand banquets at court the fish is bought when out of season and sometimes costs up to one thousand *koban.* There is also a blackish variety of this fish, called *kurodai,*[20] or black sea bream, after its color. It is much less valued than the former and is caught around Saikoku.

Suzuki is a so-called baldhead.[21] *Funa*[22] is a fish like a carp. It is used for medicinal purposes, especially against worms. *Namazu*[23] is another kind of fish like a carp, but longer. *Mebaru*[24] is a fish with the whole body blood-red, in size and shape like a carp or bream, with such bulging eyes that the whole eyeball protrudes from its cavity. It is not a good fish, is eaten by the poor, and is caught frequently. *Koi*[25] is a kind of perch or carp, up to one and half *shaku*[26] long; it is caught in fresh water. It swims up waterfalls and jumps upstream and is so strong that even when held by two people, it will tear itself away. It is exported to other provinces, both fresh and pickled. At Dazaifu, or the Tenjin lake, are some that reach a length of four *shaku*. *Masu*[27] is a salmon that is caught mostly in rivers and fresh-water lakes. *Itoyori* is a salmonet.[28] *Maguchi*[29] is a grey mullet. *Sawara* is a Spanish mackerel. *Hio* is whitebait. *Ara*[30] is called Jacob Evers by the Dutch throughout the Indies. *Kuzuna* is a snub-nosed fish.[31] *Kamasu* is a barracuda or pike. *Sasaushinoshita* is a sole,[32] but long and narrow. *Aji*[33] is called "Mas banker" by the Dutch. There are different varieties; the largest, *ōaji,* is considered the best. *Fuka* is a sea-lawyer; *same* or *fuka same* is a ray or shark with pearly skin. The skin is often brought from Siam to Japan because there it is much better and more beautiful. *Ei* is a ray, flat and with a long tail. Among these kinds of fish is one that the Dutch call "Pÿlstaart,"[34] which has a horny or bony little sword at the tail. The Japanese consider it an antidote against snake bites when it is spread on the bite, but it must be cut when the fish is still alive. The Japanese carry it in their breast pocket for this purpose with other house medicines. *Kome* or *ei* is a plaice;[35] *karei* is a flounder.[36] *Bora*[37] is a salmon, has white, very delicate meat, and is called *shōgatsu* fish by the foreigners because it is caught during *shōgatsu,* that is, the Japanese first month. The meat is smoked like the salmon of Bremen and exported. The dried roe, called *karasumi,* is tacked ten pieces in a row on two ropes of straw (like a scarecrow). Because the fish are caught around Nomo and in this area, they are sent from Nagasaki to Edo and to other provinces; they are also shipped overseas by the foreigners. The *karasumi* of other fish receives little attention.

The best *katsuo*[38] is caught around Gotō. The meat is cut into four pieces and steamed, dried, and then served with drinks. The Dutch refer to it by the wrong, and little-known, name of "comblomaas." *Managatsuo*[39] is a flat fish, like a flounder, but on the side has an eye. *Sake*[40] is perhaps a cod. It is dried like cod, is distributed throughout Japan from Edo, and goes under the above name because it smells like the drink *sake.*[41] *Tara* is a kind of dried cod that comes from the northern provinces. The best comes from Chōsen[42] and is therefore called Chōsen *dara. Sayori,*[43] called *suzu no uo* in Nagasaki and "needle fish" by the Dutch, is a span long and has a long, pointed snout. *Tobiuo*, that is, a flying fish, because it jumps across the water, is rarely longer than a foot, very delicious, but is seldom caught. *Iwashi* is a sardine; *kisugo*, smelt or sand-smelt; *eso,*[44] which the Dutch seem to call a "Sandkruper," is a cross between an eel and sand-smelt. *Saba* is a mackerel. *Ayu* or *ai no uo*[45] is called "Mode vis" in Dutch. They are a span long, live in fresh water, and move very fast. *Shira uo*, small smelt or white fish,[46] is caught in the sea in spring in the mouths of rivers. *Konoshiro,*[47] called by the Dutch "Sas Sap," is a kind of herring, somewhat similar to the Swedish herring.[48] *Kingyo,* a goldfish, is a little fish the length of a finger, red, gold at the tail, shiny, and when it is still young is of a blackish color. It is kept in tubs in China and Japan, and now also in the Indies. They have to be fed with young mosquitoes that have not yet grown wings. There is another kind which is silver.

Unagi is an eel; *ōunagi* is another large variety of eel. *Yatsume unagi* means "eight-eyes eel"; in German it is called "nine-eyed."[49] *Dojō,*[50] called "Puÿt Aal" in Dutch, is the length of a finger, has a big head, and lives in wet rice fields and mud puddles, as it does in Germany. There are two kinds: one with, the other without a beard. I have been told that they can be made to hatch in chopped-up straw, mixed with a lot of dirt, when this is mixed in full sunlight with mud to breed them. *Hamo,* a pike conger, is narrower and larger than an eel but can be seen in the sea, just like an eel. *Ika* is a common catfish; the Chinese and Japanese consider it a rarity and a delicacy. It is also easier to catch fish with the meat of this fish as bait. *Tako* is a catfish or jellyfish with long tails or feet, at the end of which are cotyles with which the animal attaches itself. It is cooked right away, also dried, and used as ordinary *sakana*[51] or additional course. *Kurage,* jellyfish, of which there are two. The first is *mizukurage,*[52] or white jellyfish; this is the common variety found everywhere in the sea, which is transparent, watery, and useless. The other variety cannot be found everywhere, is meaty, and is edible after its heat-producing sharpness has been removed and it has been prepared properly. Preparation involves a marinade of alum, in which it is kept for three days to soften, and then it is rubbed and rinsed until the meat becomes transparent. Then it is pickled and stored as food. The skin is removed before soaking the fish in the marinade and, after having been rinsed a great deal, is dried separately and kept for the preparation of food. These jellyfish are sometimes so large that it takes two people to carry them. When prepared and boiled, these holothurians are of the same substance, color, and taste as the so-called birds' nests (Nidi alcyonum), which, as I have been told by Chinese fishermen, are constructed from none other than this very substance.

Namako,[53] which the Dutch on Batavia call "Kaffer Küll," is good to eat. *Imori,*[54] a little poisonous water lizard, is black with a red belly. *Tako no makura,*[55] called the pillow of the jellyfish, is the common starfish and is not eaten. *Kame* is a turtle. On account of its long life, the Japanese superstitiously believe the *ki* or *kame,* namely, the turtle, to be an auspicious and the most noble animal among the amphibians with shell and feet. There is a certain variety, called *mōki* by scholars and *mino game*[56] by the commoners, that has a broad tail like a large, round beard. This tail, if not used in its natural state, nevertheless figures in many auspicious emblems used as decoration at temples, altars, shogunal and aristocratic halls, and throughout Japan. Among the other varieties, the most common is *ishigame,*[57] or *sanki,* that is, stone and mountain turtle, because it is sometimes found in such locations. *Iogame,* or *dōgame,*[58] is a fish turtle, because it always lives in the water with fish. On the easternmost and southernmost shores of Japan, turtles are found of such size that their shell nearly covers a whole person.

Ebi is the name for all sorts of crabs and shrimps found both in fresh and seawater. Only the following varieties have names. *Ebizako,*[59] small, common shrimps, are also always found in abundance around the shores of the Baltic Sea. *Zako* means "various small fry." *Shibaebi* is a common prawn. *Kumaebi*[60] are the same, but blackish when more than a year old, and they are caught in fresh-water rivers. *Kurumaebi,*[61] which means "wheel shrimps," are named after the shape of their tail. *Umiebi,* a large shrimp or crayfish, one foot long. It must be boiled, then it is cut up and is frequently used for *sakana* (a dish of dry snacks). One has to be careful not to eat the black tail, because it occasionally produces stomach pain and cholera. *Shako*[62] is a shrimp with a broad tail. It lives in water with other little fish; it has little meat, and at full moon virtually none at all, inasmuch as, quite different from Europe, all testacea are meatier and heavier during the new moon. This can also be observed in the Indies east of the Ganges. *Kamina,*[63] or *kōna,* is a crustacean living in a colored snail-shell. *Kani,* a crab, is the common European variety found in rivers and is referred to by the general name for its family. *Kabuto gani,* or *unkyū,*[64] is sharp at the front, and has a prickly little sword, but is round and smooth at the back. *Gazami*[65] is of average size, with the upper shell running to a sharp point on both sides. It is also armed with a pair of scissors at the back, but they are smaller than the ones in front. *Shimagani,*[66] that is, a striped crab, is very colorful and studded with spines all over its shell. Only its hind legs are smooth and of cylindrical shape. Incredibly large ones are often caught in the eastern seas and also in the Bay of Suruga. From a street kitchen there I brought back a joint from the foot; in size and shape it resembles a man's shinbone.

Here shells and snails, whatever kind or variety they might be, all serve as food, either raw, dried, pickled, freshly boiled, or fried. They are collected daily on the beaches at low tide, are also caught in nets, and are collected by divers in the sea and brought to the shore. The most famous and most common are the following. *Awabi*[67] have only a simple, one-sided shell, the size of an average Persian pearl shell, but are not quite as shallow. They live deep below the sea, with the open side attached to cliffs, and are brought to the surface by the wives of fishermen (who are always divers). They dive with a spear or long knife, with which they can protect themselves against the rays, and when they come across an *awabi,* they remove it quickly with one thrust before it realizes what is happening. Otherwise it attaches itself so firmly to the cliff that no amount of strength will detach it. The shell is full of a large piece of meat of yellowish-white color; it is of tough substance and without any fibers, and they say that it was the most important food of their poor ancestors. Therefore they always include a course of them when entertaining, in memory and for good fortune. It has also become a social custom that all presents exchanged among the poor as well as the mighty, whether they consist of money, cakes, cloth, or something else, have a shred of the dried meat added or put on top, or at least have a little piece glued on top, to honor the memory and as auspicious symbol, as they call it. The preparation of the meat consists of cutting it in the round to make thin, long strips, spreading them on a board, and drying them. Sometimes a large pearl is found in this shell, but it is of uneven shape, yellowish, and not valued by the Japanese. *Tairagi*[68] is a long, flat, sharply pointed, thin, large shell. Delicious meat is attached to both sides with strong tendons. The best are found in the Bay of Arima, and there they sometimes contain pearls. *Akoya,*[69] a flat shell, in size the width of a hand, blackish, scaly and ugly on the outside, inside like mother-of-pearl. The best are in the Bay of Ōmura, where a precious pearl is found inside. *Mirugai,*[70] a common black shell, like those found in rivers in Germany. *Hamaguri,*[71] a shell of the same shape and size, but thick and very smooth and snow-white inside. The outside is brownish. They are used for entertainment and as pastime by the idle *dairi,* or court of the hereditary emperor, after they have been painted on the inside with interesting figures. The game consists in emptying a bowl of these shells and letting the company present scrabble for them. After they have taken their share, the person able to produce the greatest number of pairs is the winner. Pairs that belong together join smoothly and are therefore easy to recognize. The best and most beautiful are gathered on the shores of Kuwana. *Shijimi*[72] is a small shell like the *hamaguri,* but with thin shells, and it is found in the mud.

Here *kaki* or *uchigaki,* oysters, are of irregular shape, rough, stony, and grow on cliffs attached to each other. There is a large and a small variety; the best, and at the same time large, variety is found in the bay of Kamakura. *Kisa* or *akagai*[73] are white on the outside and have deep parallel running grooves. They are red on the inside. A handle is attached to the shell, and then they are used as a scoop in the kitchen. *Nakatagai*[74] is a large, unshapely, round, striped, black shell. *Asari*[75] is a very small, thin, ash-colored, white shell. *Tei* or *mate*[76] is a hollow, thin pipe of a shell, with a delicious snail living inside. *Umitake*[77] is another famous shell in the shape of a pipe. It is a span long and so thick that one may enclose it with the index finger and thumb. Its meat is pickled in brine or another marinade and kept to be served as food. This shell is found only around Chikugo, and every year the lord prohibits the harvest of the shell until he has sufficiently provided for the table of the shogun. *Takaragai,*[78] called "Kaners" throughout the Indies, are collected from the Maldive and other islands and are taken to Bengal, Pegu, and Siam, where they are used as common local coins and small change. There are different kinds in Japan. The best come from the Ryūkyūs and are used to make white face powder. *Sazae*[79] is a fairly large, tasty sea slug in a spiral, thick, and rough white shell with prickly humps. The entrance to the shell is closed off with a flat, thick, rounded shield, as hard as stone, which is rough on the outside, like a Jewstone, but sharper, and smooth and solidly attached on the inside. *Nishi*[80] is a snail of the same shape, but a little larger. The meat is not as good as that of *sazae;* it clings to the rocks like *awabi.* Common people place the shell on a wreath of straw and use it as a spittoon. *Tanishi*[81] are snails in spiral, black little houses of average size. They are gathered as food from the mud of the rice fields. They close their house with a stony shield. *Bai*[82] is a snail with an ordinary, longish little house. *Rashi* or *mina*[83] is of the same kind, but black and much smaller. Both are collected at low tide from the sand. *Kabutogai*[84] is a small rough shell, oval and not spiral. *Sugai,*[85] a very small spiral shell.

Book 2

Chapter 1
Names of the Gods, Divine Humans, and Emperors Who Are Named in the Japanese Chronicles As the First Rulers of This Empire

Translator's note: As the title explains, this chapter deals with Japan's early rulers listed in Japanese chronicles. Kaempfer relied here in particular on *Shin daiki,* which makes up chapters 1 and 2 of *Nihon shoki.* He himself points out that much of this information had already been discussed in chapter 7 of the first book, concerning the origins of the Japanese. Added to this is a discussion of early Chinese emperors who—as Kaempfer explained—had been added in the Japanese chronologies to fill a gap.

Kaempfer obtained this material from his student, who had to render the difficult text into Dutch. As this information is now available in its original form, it has been omitted from this translation.

Chapter 2
General Information about the Spiritual and True Hereditary Emperors of This Empire and the Periodization of Their Succession

The third and latest period of their *Ō dai shin ō,* or spiritual hereditary emperors of human birth, begins with the year 600 before the birth of Christ, in the seventeenth year of the Chinese emperor Kei ō (in Chinese, Hui Wang) from the above-mentioned family of Chou. There are 114 Japanese emperors,[1] who, until the present year of A.D. 1693, have succeeded in an unbroken line. They consider themselves descendants of the firstborn of the most sacred ancestral father, Tenshō daijin.[2] As they are of sacred birth, their subjects and countrymen look upon them with greater respect than ordinary mortals. Before we introduce each emperor individually, we need to report briefly on the emperor as a person, the periodization of their succession, and their government.

Name

First it must be noted that the spiritual hereditary emperors do not carry the title *mikoto,* as the above-mentioned early rulers do.[3] Instead they are referred to by the honorific *mikado,* and *dai,* also *ō, kō,* and *tei,* which all mean "emperor," "prince," and "great lord." Also the title *tenshi,* meaning "child of heaven," and various others are used. The most usual name in ordinary speech is *dairi,* which actually refers to the whole of the spiritual court. In the same way, he is also called *kinchū sama,* that is, the lord of the spiritual courtiers. In speech, the emperor refers to himself as *chin,* in writing, as *maro.*

The Choice of the First Hereditary Emperor

To come back to our subject, it happened at the above-mentioned time that the inhabitants of this country, living without a fixed form of government, united themselves to choose a head and confer their authority upon him and his descendants. For until that time these free and unattached people, like other tartars and tribes of the steppes, had not been under the authority of any ruler, but each family had been governed and headed by the oldest and most clever member of the clan. Now the Chinese who crossed over to Japan had been brought up under a monarchical system and were used to much more order and peace, and it appears that they persuaded this nation for its own good to hand over supreme authority to the person of the emperor. The choice fell on one of the most respected and sacred families' firstborn, who was believed to be a direct descendant and grandson of Tenshō daijin and therefore had inherited his sanctity and all rights that nature bestows upon the firstborn.

Reverence for and Sacredness of the Emperor

The descendants of this family, who have occupied the throne until the present day, are respected as most sacred personages and born popes. In order to strengthen this belief with his subjects, the reigning aristocrat tends to conduct himself in a very unusual, yet for other nations ridiculous, fashion. It is worthwhile to describe such conduct with a few words to the reader.

He maintains that he may not, on pain of losing his dignity and sanctity, touch the bare soil. If there is no floor cover, he must ride or be carried. He may not expose himself to the open skies, nor let his head be touched by the rays of the sun. With regard to his body, he is not permitted to trim even the tiniest bit of growth, be it the hair on is head, his beard, or his nails. The only permissible exception is when, for cleanliness' sake, it is done while he is asleep and consequently unaware of it. This is then termed a theft, and such theft does not prejudice his sanctity.

Since ancient times the emperor has had to sit every morning for a certain number of hours on the throne, wearing the imperial cap and keeping his hands, head, eyes, and all limbs totally immobile. It was believed that this secured blessings and peace for his empire. For if he turned to one side or the other, or directed his eyes at anything, it was feared that wars, fires, and other disasters would occur in that part of the empire. Nowadays, however, this kind of sitting has been discontinued. Since it has been learned that it is, in fact, the immobility of the papal cap that affords protection and preserves the peace of the empire, the same is suspended motionless over the throne of the hereditary emperor, and the emperor himself, whose enjoyment of life is sacred, has been freed from his former chore of sitting immobile.

His food must always be cooked in new pots and served in fresh dishes. These are all very clean but consist only of earthenware roughly made of common clay in order that they may be discarded or broken without much loss. This is often done so that no other secular person uses these dishes. For common superstition has it that if a person takes his profane nourishment from these dishes, his mouth and throat will swell up. Also his shoes and clothing may not be worn by any *gege,* or person of secular lineage, without incurring some harm on those parts of the body, unless the *mikado* has given permission.[4]

Succession

As soon as the sacred throne has been vacated by the death of an emperor, the ministers of the spiritual court pass on the scepter, without regard to age or sex, to the person whose birth they believe has given him or her the greatest right to succeed. Consequently the throne is often occupied by unschooled young princes, and sometimes an unmarried princess or widow of an emperor. When there are a number of claimants, and the decision of who is to be the next emperor is difficult, the matter is dealt with fairly by permitting each to occupy the throne for a number of years, one after the other. However, the closest in line will occupy the throne for a number of years first. Fathers often abdicate and have their sons occupy the throne for a number of years, one after the other, in order that they and their mothers may enjoy the good fortune of their children, who might not have been installed in this exalted position after their father's death. All such matters are decided at court without much ado and without others outside knowing about it. But it has happened a number of times that when a closely related claimant did not attain what he wanted, he attempted to gain access to the throne by force and strove to get rid of the *dairi* who had been installed in preference to him. This resulted in great wars, lasting over many years and ruining the lands of those aristocrats who became embroiled in it; they did not end until the opposing parties were totally vanquished and whole families were eradicated.

The Greatness and Splendor of the Emperor

The court consists of many sacred descendants from Tenshō daijin, and they are considered nobler than other people. Over many years they have branched off into many families and have grown in number to several thousand people. Every year some are drawn off to become abbots and principals of established, large, and important monasteries, but most of them stay at home near the *mikado* and within the confines of his court and domicile. For every one of them is obliged to serve him and in this service earns his income according to his position and duties.

Upkeep

The court's upkeep is at present taken care of by the secular emperor, the shogun.[5] He devoted the income of the lands around Miyako to the court, but since this is insufficient, he annually contributes something from the bowels of his treasury. But this is given so sparingly that the courtiers cannot live on it, or, at least, cannot live as opulently and splendidly as when the *mikado* himself was in control of the empire and the treasury. Consequently this court exists in splendid poverty: great lords are burdened with great debts because they have to live according to their status, and ordinary servants have to make and sell straw sandals for people and horses, or items of lesser value, so that they can survive at all. But regardless of this fact, the *mikado,* who controls the expenditure of incoming monies, manages to take care of his own person, lacking nothing that might serve his pleasure or well-being, especially since he has another, considerable amount of income over and above that granted to him by the shogun, from responding to the requests of great lords and their sons for court ranks. Like his mighty ancestors, he maintains twelve wives, among whom one is the most important and mother of the crown prince. So many grand and costly ceremonies take place when a wife is chosen and married, when she gives birth, when a nursemaid is chosen, and when the prince is educated that one might think that he was the savior of the country.

Titles and Ranks of the Courtiers

At this sacred court there are many high-ranking positions and various aristocratic or court ranks that are bestowed by the *mikado.* Some have real offices attached to them; others consist only of a title. The latter he bestows for a considerable honorarium also on other important lords of the empire, or at the request of the shogun. These titles are divided into six *i,* or ranks. The first and greatest rank has the title *daijō daijin,* which is considered so high and sacred that it is believed that the soul of the owner of this title will become a *kami,* or god, as soon as it leaves the body. But the *dairi* seldom confers this title. To the same rank belongs also the office of *kampaku,* that is, governor, the second highest personage of the sacred court. The following three titles belong to the second *i: sadaijin, udaijin,* and *naidaijin.* There are no more than three people of each rank at court who can boast of the same title. The third level of honor comprises those who are called *dainagon* and *chūnagon.* Both those names designate also certain offices at court. The fourth rank includes the titles *shōnagon, chūnagon, chūjō, shōshō,* and *jijū.* There are a number of people of each title at court, and they are still further subdivided in rank. They are called *tenjō bito,* which means "heavenly people," and together with the above are called *kuge,* which means roughly "sacred lords." Those of the sixth and last rank are *taifu, go i,*[6] and others of lesser station. As mentioned, these titles can be conferred only by the *dairi,* for when he had to hand over the government to the shogun, he retained not only his position of highest authority but also this prerogative. Therefore, when the shogun wants to endow his minions with court ranks, he has to obtain them from the *mikado* and is unable to confer them by his own authority.

There are two further titles that are common among secular lords of the empire: *mukan taifu*[7] and *kami,* which the shogun bestows upon great lords of his empire and court with the permission of the *dairi.* The first title used to be hereditary and indicates a prince or earl, but the other denotes a knight. I must point out here that a deified soul is also referred to with the word *kami.* But then this word is of a very different nature and is written with a different character. Thus also all native gods and idols are always called and referred to in writing by this word and character.

Dress

To better distinguish themselves from their secular countrymen, whom they consider to be of humble and worldly origin, the court wears special dress. Parts of this dress are varied to such an extent among the courtiers that each person's rank can be recognized, as is indicated by the attached copper plates.[8] They wear very wide, long trousers, and over them what they refer to as ceremonial dress, or dress of honor, which stands out widely and has a long, trailing train suspended at the back. The top of their head is crowned with a black pasted and lacquered hat, of various extraordinary shapes, depending on each person's rank. There is often a stiff veil of black gauze hanging down at the back or attached in a curve at the top. Sometimes they also have round blinkers standing out at the side, like nervous coach horses. At times people also wear a sash or broad band of varying length hanging down from the neck on both sides. This indicates their station and rank, inasmuch as nobody is permitted to bow deeper to other members of the court than is possible with the ends just touching the ground. The women also wear clothing different from that of secular persons of their own sex. Especially the wives of the *dairi* each wear twelve unlined, precious robes with golden flowers, which are gathered in many broad pleats and are so wide and long that it is easier to sit than walk in them.

Pastime

Most of the time at court is spent studying. There are not only learned *kuge,* or courtiers, but also women who write poetry and books. The calendars used to be made at court, but now they are made by a learned citizen of Miyako. But they are approved by the court and then sent to Ise, as a sacred site, to be printed. People also play music, and especially the women are trained to play all sorts of instruments. The courtiers also practice knightly accomplishments, many practice riding and compete in running, others practice jumping, dancing, and playing ball, some practice conjuring tricks and similar things useful for a change of mood and to while away the time. I did not investigate whether theater performances are held, but I believe it is likely because this nation thinks much of such plays and willingly invests time and money in them.

Residence

Earlier emperors did not have their court or residence at a fixed location, but established it soon in this city or that province and frequently changed locations according to each ruler's likes and wishes. In recent centuries, however, they have been firmly settled in Miyako, where the northeastern part of the city is occupied by the court. The court consists of many wooden palaces, living quarters, and streets, like a separate city. Merely to prevent unauthorized persons from entering, it is also separated from and fortified against the city of the commoners with parapets, moats, and gates. The *mikado* resides in the middle, in a large palace that looks impressive from afar with its high multistory tower. He lives with his first wife, and the other wives live in the nearby houses surrounding his palace. Not far away are the quarters of his personal aides and other servants, whose services he requires daily. The retired *mikado* has another palace, together with his family and personal servants. Also the crown prince is provided with a separate court as his residence and for his education. High and low officials, important and humble servants are given certain streets and houses according to their standing, title, and office. The shogun keeps at this court a strong guard of sworn *bugyō*[9] and soldiers. This is allegedly done out of the utmost care expended in guarding this sacred, high family, but in reality much more out of concern for the safety of his own person and his own autocratic authority, which his ancestors usurped from the *mikado*.

The Periodization of the Japanese

The following facts must be noted concerning the calendar of the Japanese. There are two ways of reckoning. The first is the common one, which begins with the government of the first Japanese emperor, Jimmu, 660 before the birth of Christ. They count 2,352 years from that time to the present sixth year of Genroku (which is the 1693rd year after the birth of Christ). This way of reckoning they call *nin nō,* which actually means a high personage or monarch, but more sophisticatedly stands for "the very first."[10]

The other way of reckoning, which they call *nengō,* has been introduced from China, first under the thirty-sixth emperor, to superfluously confirm the counting of years. This is a particular era that begins when the *mikado* names a time with a particular character, for example, to commemorate some event that happened in the empire or at court. He permits the name to continue for only a few years, sometimes only one, but seldom more than twenty, until a new event causes him to cancel it and replace it by a new one. Thus the era name of the present year Genroku (of which we write the sixth year in this present 1693rd year of Christ) means the happiness of nature and the arts, a certain analogy with which the loving *mikado* wishes to honor the greater peace and happiness of his august father, who ceded him the throne.[11] They use this reckoning in their calendars, orders, diaries, and letters. In printed books the year of *nin nō* is also added. It must be noted that a new *nengo* is never used before the beginning of the new year, although they are established a few months earlier, and also that their books sometimes bear the old *nengo,* even though a new one has already existed for one or several years. I assume that this happens when the people do not know the new one, or the character is not as convenient as the old one. Thus the calendars of the first and second years of Genroku are still marked the fifth and sixth year of Jōkyō. The next calendar was marked the third year of the current period of Genroku (it was the year of Christ 1690) and consequently could not be the cause of any errors in the reckoning of time or years. The *nengo* consist of two, rarely more, characters which have to be chosen and combined from a certain table of characters dedicated to this purpose. It is not permitted to use a character not included in this sacred table.

There is still a third system of calculating the time in periods of sixty years, which the Japanese have adopted from the Chinese. These sixty years are produced by linking and repeating the *eto,* or names of their astrological signs, with the names of the ten elements. If the former are repeated five and the latter six times in good order, one after the other, to form combinations, after sixty combinations, each standing for one year, the first one will reappear. With that the old cycle comes to an end, and a new one begins. The Japanese use this cycle inasmuch as each year of their history is given one, but this is combined with the year of their *nin nō* and *nengō.* With this system a reliable correspondence between Chinese and Japanese history is maintained. But in Japanese accounts of historical events the number of the cycle in which they happened is never added, as is done in China. Perhaps this is due to irritation about the fact that the cycle was discovered in China and had been in use many centuries before the Japanese monarchy existed. We do not want to waste our time with year and word chimera in this account but briefly introduce them with their proper meaning.

The following are the *eto,* or twelve astrological signs:

1. *ne,* the mouse,
2. *ushi,* the ox or cow,
3. *tora,* the tiger,
4. *u,* the rabbit,
5. *tatsu,* the dragon,
6. *mi,* the snake,
7. *uma,* the horse,
8. *hitsuji,* the sheep,
9. *saru,* the monkey,
10. *tori,* the cock or chicken,
11. *inu,* the dog,
12. *i,* the boar.

With these signs they also designate the twelve hours of the natural day, as also the twelve parts of the hour into which these are divided. In this way they can clearly indicate in their accounts the time an event happened. But they measure both the day (from sunrise to sunset) and the night in six hours. Therefore in summer the hours of the day are longer than the hours of the night, and in winter the hours of the day are shorter than those of the night.

As for the elements: there are actually only five. But each is given two names and characters to make ten, so that when they are combined six times with the names of the animals, the complete sixty-year cycle is generated. The elements are called:

1. *kinoe,* wood,
2. *kinoto,* wood,
3. *hinoe,* fire,
4. *hinoto,* fire,
5. *tsuchinoe,* earth,

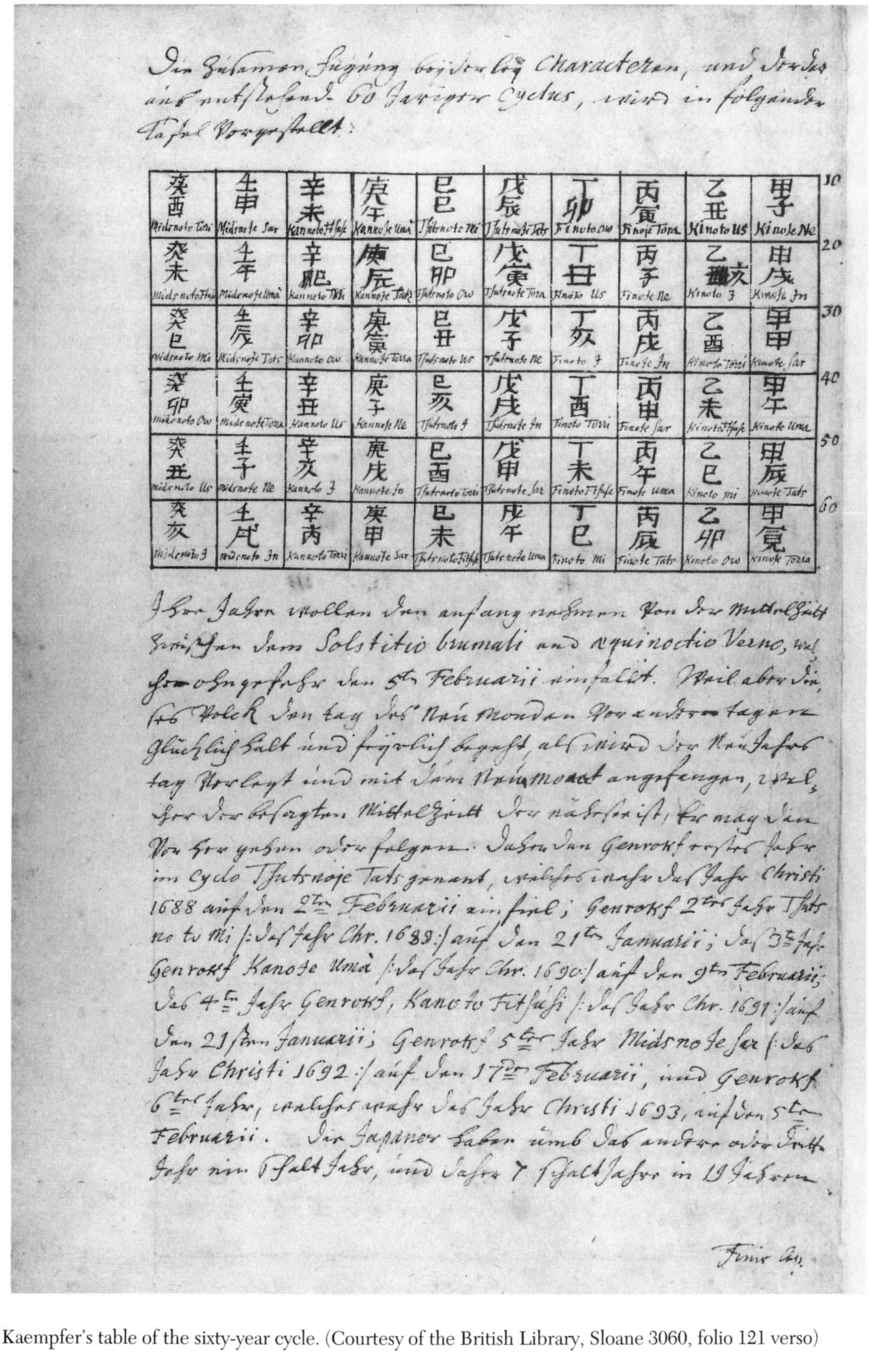

癸酉 Midsnoto Tori	壬申 Midsnoje Sar	辛未 Kanoto Fitsje	庚午 Kanoje Uma	己巳 Tsutsnoto Mi	戊辰 Tsutsnoje Tats	丁卯 Finoto Ow	丙寅 Finoje Tora	乙丑 Kinoto Us	甲子 Kinoje Ne	10
癸未 Midsnoto Fitsje	壬午 Midsnoje Uma	辛巳 Kanoto Mi	庚辰 Kanoje Tats	己卯 Tsutsnoto Ow	戊寅 Tsutsnoje Tora	丁丑 Finoto Us	丙子 Finoje Ne	乙亥 Kinoto J	甲戌 Kinoje Jn	20
癸巳 Midsnoto Mi	壬辰 Midsnoje Tats	辛卯 Kanoto Ow	庚寅 Kanoje Tora	己丑 Tsutsnoto Us	戊子 Tsutsnoje Ne	丁亥 Finoto J	丙戌 Finoje Jn	乙酉 Kinoto Tori	甲申 Kinoje Sar	30
癸卯 Midsnoto Ow	壬寅 Midsnoje Tora	辛丑 Kanoto Us	庚子 Kanoje Ne	己亥 Tsutsnoto J	戊戌 Tsutsnoje Jn	丁酉 Finoto Tori	丙申 Finoje Sar	乙未 Kinoto Fitsje	甲午 Kinoje Uma	40
癸丑 Midsnoto Us	壬子 Midsnoje Ne	辛亥 Kanoto J	庚戌 Kanoje Jn	己酉 Tsutsnoto Tori	戊申 Tsutsnoje Sar	丁未 Finoto Fitsje	丙午 Finoje Uma	乙巳 Kinoto Mi	甲辰 Kinoje Tats	50
癸亥 Midsnoto J	壬戌 Midsnoto Jn	辛酉 Kanoto Tori	庚申 Kanoje Sar	己未 Tsutsnoto Fitsje	戊午 Tsutsnoje Uma	丁巳 Finoto Mi	丙辰 Finoje Tats	乙卯 Kinoto Ow	甲寅 Kinoje Tora	60

Kaempfer's table of the sixty-year cycle. (Courtesy of the British Library, Sloane 3060, folio 121 verso)

6. *tsuchinoto,* earth,
7. *kanoe,* metal,
8. *kanoto,* metal,
9. *mizunoe,* water,
10. *mizunoto,* water.

The combination of both characters and the resulting combination of the sixty-year cycle are represented in figure 3. [See the illustration on page 95.]

Their year begins at a time between the winter solstice and the spring equinox, which is roughly the 5th of February. But since these people believe the day of the new moon to be more auspicious than any other, and celebrate it, New Year's Day is changed to coincide with the new moon, whichever is closest to the above-mentioned time. It may be earlier or later. Consequently the first year of Genroku, called *tsuchinoe tatsu* according to the cycle, began on February 2nd of the year of Christ 1688; the second year of Genroku, *tsuchinoto mi* (the year A.D. 1689), on the 21st of January; the third year of Genroku, *kanoe uma* (the year A.D. 1690), on the 9th February; the fourth year of Genroku, *kanoto hitsuji*, (the year A.D. 1691), on the 21st of January; the fifth year of Genroku, *mizunoe saru*, (the year of Christ 1692), on the 17th February, and the sixth year of Genroku, which was the year of Christ 1693, on the 5th of February. The Japanese add a leap year every second or third year and consequently have seven leap years in nineteen years.

Chapter 3
The Spiritual Hereditary Emperors, and Especially and First of All Those Who Have Ruled the Japanese Empire from the Beginning of the Monarchy until the Birth of Christ

Translator's note: In this chapter Kaempfer discusses the Japanese emperors from the first emperor, Jimmu, believed to have ruled 660–585 B.C., to the eleventh emperor, Suinin, believed to have ruled 29 B.C. to A.D. 70. Here, as in the next chapter, Kaempfer's information is based on two seventeenth-century chronologies. The copies he used were acquired after his death by Sir Hans Sloane and are preserved in the British Library. Both works have notes in his hand, documenting his efforts to transcribe Japanese names and work out equivalent Western dates. The works are: *Dai Nihon ōdaiki,* a chronological account of the first 113 Japanese emperors, beginning with Jimmu Tennō, by Yoshida Mitsuyoshi (1598–1672), first published in 1649,[1] and *Wakan nenpyōroku,* a comparative chronological table of China and Japan from mythical times up to 1689. The work also describes events in China and Japan.[2]

Kaempfer had to rely on his student for translation, and occasionally inaccuracies have crept in. As today this material is available in more reliable form, it has been omitted from this translation.

Chapter 4

The Spiritual Hereditary Emperors Who Lived between the Birth of Christ and the Birth of Yoritomo, the First Secular Ruler, and Ruled with Unlimited Authority

Translator's note: In this chapter, as in the previous one, Kaempfer relies on *Dai Nihon ōdaiki* and *Wakan nenpyōroku*. Entries are generally short and focus mostly on the change of period names *(nengō)* and extraordinary events, such as comets, floods, and famines. However, when he comes to the last entry in this chapter, that of Emperor Konoe (reigned 1141–1155), Kaempfer discusses at some length the birth and establishment of political power by the first Kamakura shogun, Minamoto Yoritomo (1147–1199), and the consequences for the imperial line. This demonstrates that Kaempfer was well aware of the relationship between, and the respective positions of, the shogun and the emperor. Since the information is available in more reliable form, it has been omitted here.

Chapter 5
The Spiritual Hereditary Emperors Who Lived after the Birth of Yoritomo to the Present Day

Translator's note: In addition to *Dai Nihon ōdaiki* and *Wakan nenpyōroku,* consulted for the previous two chapters, Kaempfer here made use of a third chronological table. This work, *Nengōhyō,* contains a list of era names, names of emperors, and horoscope information covering the years 1160–1688.[1] Again, Kaempfer's notes in his copy of this work demonstrate his efforts at transcribing Japanese names and dates.

When Kaempfer came to the split in the imperial line into the "Southern" and "Northern" dynasties in the second half of the fourteenth century, however, his sources agreed neither on the era names nor on the dates of the emperors' reigns. Though he briefly referred to succession quarrels in chapter 2 of this book, Kaempfer here ignored the split of the imperial line. He lists emperors from both the Southern and Northern dynasties, and to overcome the resulting problems in numbering, he assumes that some were not given a number in the official count. Since the information is available in more reliable form, it has been omitted here.

Chapter 6

The Military Commanders and Secular Rulers from Yoritomo to the Present

Ruler Tsunayoshi

Translator's note: This is a brief chapter consisting of a listing of Japan's military rulers since the first Kamakura shogun, Yoritomo. Most of them are given no more than a line, stating their relationship to their predecessor and the length of their government. As with the listings of rulers in the previous chapters, there are a number of errors. Since this information is now available in more reliable form, it has been omitted.

Book 3

Chapter 1
Concerning the Religions of This Empire and Especially That of Shinto

As among all other Asian nations and pagans, in this country also freedom of worship has always been permitted, as long as it does not obstruct secular government. Therefore in addition to the local religion, which originated in this country, a number of other religions have vied to establish themselves. In this century there have been four religions, which at different times have had a roughly equal number of followers. These are:

Shinto, the way of the native gods.
Butsu dō, the way or belief in foreign idols from Siam and China.
Judō, the way of the moralists or philosophers.
Deivus or *Kiristandō,* that is, the way of God and Christ.[1]

On account of the admirable devotion of the Spanish and Portuguese clergy, especially that of the Jesuits, this last-named religion spread so quickly from their first arrival in the province of Bungo in the year of Christ 1549 (after their first ships had appeared at that location in 1543) until about 1625, or nearly 1630, that it had extended to all the provinces and had made its way into many courts. If this had continued, no doubt the greater part of this nation would have become Christian. But the impatience of the padres, who always personally wanted to enjoy the fruits of their labor, and having conquered the nation's souls, also strove to conquer its worldly possessions, provoked the ruler of this empire to utmost brutality, and he unleashed such terror against them and the new Christians as has never been described in the pages of the history of mankind. As a result, the religion was completely eliminated, down to the last believer.

Among the three main religions, sects, or ways of life that prosper and are permitted today, Shinto is the most important in status, but not as regards the number of its adherents.

Shinto, Shinshū

Shinto, *Shinshū,* or *kami michi,* is the belief in the native gods. *Shin* and *kami* mean a native divinity or image of an idol; *dō* or *michi,* the Way, or the method; *shū*, faith, religion; *shinsha*, or, in the plural, *shinshū*, are the people who follow this Way. This religion is more concerned with material well-being than with the state of the soul after death. They believe, nevertheless, in the eternal life of the soul, spent on this earth in a state of well-being. But they have a very sober approach to this topic and do not have much to say about it. Consequently their worship is directed toward those divinities to whom they ascribe power in this material world, each according to his or her function, as in the Aristotelian state.[2] Even though one god is believed to be located in the eternal heaven, and still others have their place in the visible skies, these gods are neither venerated nor prayed to. Being of the opinion *quae supra nos nihil ad nos*, "what is above us, is of no concern," they merely list the names of these gods in the commonly used oath and swear in their name. They worship and venerate only those gods who govern their lands, the elements, animals, water, and other things and who can harm or profit them in this material world. Yet by this devotion the heart is cleansed, and with the help of these Japanese spirits, everlasting well-being is attained.

This religion originated at the birth of the nation. For when the first settlers from Babylon had forgotten the biblical story and the true worship of God by being deprived of the original language and on account of the long journey, they no doubt deified their first leader. Therefore their deceased elders, as well as brave, wise, and revered people, were elevated to *kami,* that is, immortal spirits and souls, to be venerated forever. For the worship of their everlasting names, *miya,* that is to say, houses of living souls, were provided. On days of ordinary worship, or of special celebrations, or when he passes, or otherwise has the opportunity (unless he is unclean and therefore unable to do so), every honest citizen—but now this is almost limited to followers of this sect—must offer his grateful, good heart by bowing humbly and kneeling in front of these *miya,* or temples of idols. From the beginning of his reign, the *mikado,* as descendant in one unbroken line from the first leader, is in this fashion considered to be a living god and one of the greatest divinities among their *kami,* or gods, as soon as he takes the throne of his ancestors. He is a god of such sacredness that no *gege* may visit or set eyes upon him (*gege* is a disdainful, bestial word, which the sacred court uses for other people, to distinguish them from *kuge,* which means people of their own, sacred rank). Yes, he is even visited annually by the bodiless, incorporeal gods, even though they are invisible, and they have to remain with him the whole of the tenth month. Therefore this month has no feast days and is called and recorded by the Japanese as *kami na tsuki,* that is to say, the month without gods, because the gods are not at home in their temples, but are with the *dairi* at the court of the *mikado.*

This living, pontifical pagan deity has the authority to canonize others as gods when, visited by their souls and on the basis of miracles, he has augustly perceived them as such. Then he bestows upon them a distinguished title, or a name, and either he himself or someone else has a *miya* built for them. If the worshippers do well, or some miracles have been noticed, people with gentle hearts and some wealth have similar ones built at other locations, and thus the number of gods grows each century.

These gods and those who have earned the divine title during their government are preceded by seven successive heavenly gods, ruling the other spirits. They are called and described as *tenjin shichi dai,* which means seven generations of heavenly gods.[3] It is claimed that they lived in the most ancient age of the sun, before men and even heaven came into existence, all dwelling together on this earth (since they knew of no other land) for many legions of years. The last in this reign of the gods was Isanagi. Watching the movements of the bird *ishi tataki,* or wagtail,[4] he was induced to have intercourse with his wife Isanami, and through this natural process of propagation they gave birth to another generation of these Japanese rulers of the world, albeit of lesser, human type. According to the number of generations, they are called *chi jin godai,* five generations of terrestrial gods.[5] Among them, the progenitors of the human gods resided in a bizarre fashion, conducting wars and strange adventures, living with other divine, human, bestial, and monstrous heroes and dragons. In this way they earned for themselves the right to have many places in the empire named after them to commemorate their deeds, and many had a special *miya* erected there. After some time, in deference to them, weapons and other antiques, which had always been venerated as relics of this second, silver period, were believed to have a soul. As souls worthy of divine veneration, they, too, had *miya* built for them. In short, their whole theology consists of one enormous, incomprehensible, monstrous fable, which (not to be mocked) they do not easily disclose to commoners or those favoring Buddhism. This religion is so much tied up with the state that it has mainly civil rites and consequently has no teachers or spiritual priests, but instead secular custodians of idols and temples, ignorant of the stories of the gods.

The *shintōshū,* especially the *kannushi,*[6] sometimes teach and preach among young people. Thus when I was there, a *kannushi* from Miyako held daily public explanatory lectures about a passage or commandment titled *nakatomi no barai,* or *nakatomi barai,*[7] first at the Tenjin temple and then at Suwa *miya*. This, however, consisted of nothing else but abstruse stories of spirits and gods. They also teach their theology to others, but in secret. The final topic deals with the origin of all things, which they will teach only after the candidate has given a written and sealed oath to his teachers not to desecrate these mysteries by explaining them to ignorant and nonbelieving laymen. Their work *Ōdaiki*[8] gives the text as follows:

> *Kaibyaku no hajime shūjō fuhyō tatoeba yūgyo no suijō ni uku ga gotoshi. Tenchi no uchi ichi butsu o shō su, katachi ige no gotoshi. Henka shite shin to naru, kuni toko tatsu no mikoto to go su.*[9]

That means: In the beginning when all things began to open, chaos was floating like fish sporting in water. This chaos produced a thing shaped like the shoot of a thorn, mobile and transmutable, turning into a soul or spirit. This is called *kuni toko tatsu no mikoto.*[10]

Chapter 2
The Temples, Beliefs, and Worship of the Shinto Sect

The *shinshū* call the temples of their gods *miya,* which means as much as "houses of remembrance," or the *fana*[1] of the Romans. They also use the words *yashiro* and *sha,* or *jinja,* which, however, properly speaking means the whole surroundings of the *miya* with all its appendages. They call their gods *shin* and *kami,* which, properly speaking means as much as a soul or spirit. To show greater reverence, they add the words *myōshin,* meaning "august and holy," or *gongen,* meaning "just," "stern." But their fellow clerics in other religions call their monasteries prayer houses and temples of their gods *jisha,* or *tera,* meaning temple, and the gods themselves, *hotoke,* while another kind of foreign secondary god tends to be called with the foreign name of *bosatsu* or *butsu.*

Their *miya,* like the temples of other religions, are situated in the most pleasant spots of the country. They are rarely within settled communities, towns, and cities and mostly situated outside. A straight, level, and wide avenue, often planted with native cypress trees, runs from the highway up to the *miya* proper, or its precinct, which frequently has several temples and buildings. But the road always leads up to the front of the most important *miya.* This *miya,* or the precincts of a number of *miya,* is situated either in a shaded park or on the slopes of a mountain with luxurious vegetation, reached by climbing a stately flight of stone steps. An impressive, uniform gate of honor, referred to specifically as *torii,* marks the beginning of such an avenue and distinguishes it from common roads along the highways. It is built of bare rock or wooden posts, with two crossbeams of the same material at the top; the uppermost is curved as embellishment and protrudes on both sides. Between the crossbeams is a stone tablet with the name of the temple, mostly in golden characters. Similar gates of stone are also often in front of the *miya* or wall of the temple precinct. Near the *miya* there is sometimes a washstand of stone for worshippers to clean themselves. And next to the *miya* is a large wooden alms box. The *miya* itself is not at all a splendid structure, but poor and wooden, and frequently consists only of a small, square little house. But it is built of beautiful, strong posts, with the house being slightly higher than the height of two or three men. It is two or more fathoms square and one ell or more off the ground, mostly with a raised, wooden, narrow veranda running around. The house sits on stilts, with one or several flights of steps leading up. The front consists of two lattice doors, through which people can look and pay their respects. The doors are always locked, and frequently there are no custodians or attendants. Other *miya* consist of larger structures, sometimes with an antechamber and two secondary chambers, where the custodians of the temple sit dressed up in their sacred habit in honor of the *kami.* The building has a lot of lattice and is transparent; the floor is covered with mats. The back and the sides are mostly closed off with wooden planks at the outside. The roof is made of tiles or wood chips and protrudes over the veranda running around the house. It differs from that of other houses with regard to the variety of bracketing and duplication of attractive, protruding beams. Generally this is the most decorative part of all temples in this country. At times the roof is finished off at the top with a beam running the full length, and on each side of the house are two protruding thick beams fastened to form a cross, behind which there are others running crossways. This is in memory of the early structures of the temples at Ise, which were only poor buildings, but constructed so ingeniously and uniquely that the weight of those beams kept the whole structure together.

At times there is a flat, wide bell suspended above the door of the temple, which worshippers ring with a wide, knotted string hanging nearby. But this is a new custom, adopted from the *butsu dō*, and was not done in the past. Cut-up paper hangs around inside the temple to express the purity of the site. In the middle there is often a round mirror to show visitors their own blemishes and to assure them that the blemishes and malice of their hearts will be seen likewise by the gods. There is rarely a carved idol to represent the *kami* of the temple, except when its antiquity, some miracles, or the inviolability of its protection make it worthy of such honor. In that case, it is respectfully kept locked up in a chamber at the back called *hongū,* meaning the premier temple.[2] It is kept in the middle of the temple and in the highest place. Worshippers may only salute the door and are not permitted to see it, except on the centenary of the death and remembrance days of the saint. If there are relics of the saint's bones, clothing, a sword, or some miracle produced by his hands, they are also kept in this same, the highest and most holy place.

The most important *miya* of every locality have one or several *mikoshi.* These are small, lacquered shrines with four, six, or eight sides, little sanctuaries built like a temple, decorated with gilded beading, ribbons, mirrors, paper, and all sorts of ornaments. They rest on two carrying poles and are paraded on the *en nichi,* or holiest day of the *miya,* by a procession of *kannushi,* or temple attendants, to the *matsuri,* or annual feast of the god. Some white, cut-up paper hangs inside. At the time of the procession some relics of the *kami,* which are kept in white little shrines, are sometimes placed inside. The highest *kannushi* of the temple removes these from the most holy site of the *miya,* carries them on his back to the *mikoshi* supporting them with both hands, and places them inside, facing backward. During this transfer everybody must step aside, so the relic is not polluted by the uncleanliness of sinners' eyes.

In an outside antechamber or a specially built house these *miya* are hung with many pictures, sometimes also some swords, carved boats, and similar ornaments. Idlers and, on feast days, temple visitors take their pleasure and pass their time inspecting them. These honored ornaments are called *ema.*[3] They are voluntary gifts or gifts made to keep commitments pledged by people distressed by their own illness or misfortune or that of others. After the person's needs have been met, they are donated as embellishments for the temple and the pacification of the powerful idol. This custom they have in common with the Buddhists. These temples and gods are not attended by religious priests but only by married, secular persons. They are called *negi, kannushi,* and *shanin,* receiving their livelihood from the legacy of the donor of the *miya*, or an annual subsidy from the *mikado,* and the gifts of the worshippers. *Mikado* literally means the "august gate," for *mi* means the same as *on, go, ō, gyo,* namely: all-powerful, most serene, august, and so forth, and *kado* means a gate. When these religious priests[4] go out, or are attending their temple, they—like the people at the court of the *mikado*—wear white, sometimes yellow, and other colored choir frocks over their secular clothes. They do not shave their heads, but only their beards, and the front part of their head is covered with a longish, stiffly lacquered hat in the shape of a boat, which protrudes a little in front. It is tied under the chin with a string or attached tassel, with the length of the string indicating their rank, because the rank determines how deeply they must bow. The upper ranks have their hair tied under yet another little ornament of black gauze. To this is attached a small starched piece of cloth, the width of two thumbs and the length of one and a half spans, which stands up more or less straight or hangs down, depending upon the title bestowed by the *mikado.* They are directly answerable and directly under the jurisdiction of the *mikado* only with regard to civil disputes.[5] But in all other matters, they, as well as the rest of the clergy, are governed by two *jisha bugyō,* shogunal temple judges.[6]

It is quite apparent that generally they are very arrogant fellows, considering themselves a better breed than the rest of the clergy, running around like the aristocracy in secular dress and with two swords when they are not in attendance at their *miya.* They refrain from keeping company with secular, common people, and on account of their sacredness and purity, they stay away from the priests of other religions, treating them as unclean undertakers. With this self-restraint they attempt to increase the status of their gods and theology, and this serves them well when they reveal their lack of knowledge and the poor foundation of their wretched and sparse articles of faith and religion in their discourse. For this religion of their forefathers seems incredibly naive, inasmuch as—except for the adventure stories of their gods and the state of the soul after death—they have neither books nor oral traditions like those with which other pagans provide happiness and information for their followers. Consequently not just many fellows of this religious brotherhood but also the rest of their followers split into two sects after the introduction of the foreign, pagan theology. The first is called *yui itsu,* meaning "orthodox," and they keep the ancient belief and customs of their fathers without deviating even the breadth of a hair from the old path of darkness. But there are so few of them that there are more *kannushi* than followers. The second is called *ryōbu,* and they are syncretists. To attain greater enlightenment and for the safety of their souls, they attempt to combine the religion of their fathers with the foreign religion. They believe that the soul of Amida (who is revered as savior by all other sects of the imported religion) entered their highest god, Tenshō daijin,[7] the seed of light, and the sun. Most adherents of Shinto belong to this sect. Even the *dairi* himself, that is, the court of the *mikado*'s family, seems sufficiently convinced that there are vanity and falsehood in this religion, and pretense about his divine status, so that he himself tends to favor this syncretism. For he gave the priests of the Ikkō *shū,* the richest and most splendid sect of the Buddhists, his blood relatives for the posts of archbishop and two other bishops.

His majesty the shogun maintains the religious customs of his forefathers, and annually pays his respects. Yet he no longer does this in person as previously, but for political reasons sends an embassy to the divinity of the *mikado.* He personally visits the temples of his ancestors as well as the gods and temples of his forefathers. Also, while I was there, in accordance with the custom of Shinto, he had two attractive *miya* erected for the Chinese philosopher Confucius,[8] who, like Socrates, is believed to have received his philosophy from heaven. Finally, it becomes apparent that nearly all who believe in this religion (and no less many Confucians)[9] prefer to entrust their souls to the care of the Buddhist priests at their hour of death, to sing the *namu amida butsu* for them, and have their body cremated or buried by them.

The religion of their forefathers does not believe in the transmigration of the soul, as other pagans do. All the same, they abstain from killing and eating those animals that render service to mankind when alive so as not to be unmerciful or ungrateful. But the followers of Shinto believe in the existence of the soul after death at a joyous place, which is situated among the thirty-three heavens and seats of the gods and therefore has received the name *takama no hara,* meaning high, or heavenly fields. The souls of the pious are immediately transported to these fields, but godless and wicked souls, or those who have not atoned sufficiently for their sins, must stay away longer earning their just rewards. With this, the believers of this sect seem to indicate the location as well as the state of bliss. They have neither hell, Cimmerian[10] darkness, nor an unhappy state of disembodied souls in addition to these Elysian fields and places of happiness. As a result, they have no other devil except the fox of superstitious commoners, which in this country is responsible for more tricks than in Aesop's fables. Foxes can possess people like the devil possesses Christians, and they also believe that the souls of wicked people are turned into foxes, called *ma,* or evil spirits, by the clergy.

In their Shinto worship they want to please the gods and attain a place in the above-mentioned fields after death, or those who have little knowledge about the immortality of the soul believe they will obtain secular blessing by naively following the rules. They consist of:

1. purity of heart,
2. abstinence of all that pollutes human beings,
3. celebration of feast and temple days as well as a visit to the holy place of Ise, and, finally, as *opus supererogationis,*[11] in castigating the body.

Purity of heart demands doing, firstly, what the laws of nature and, secondly, what the authorities, as secular gods, demand to be done. However, the gods and spiritual teachers merely created laws and prohibitions concerning outward cleanliness. Since people are not kept back by fear of divine punishment, all opulence and voluptuousness seem permissible. But the laws of nature do not rule them to such an extent that without stronger forces they will keep their cravings within virtuous limits for the sake of the above compensations. Therefore the kindness of the gods had to be limited by the authorities with tough laws against wrongdoing. Consequently what is valued are inner cleanliness with regard to the maintenance of secular laws as well as a clean conscience as dictated by the light of nature.

Outer cleanliness demands avoidance of blood and corpses and abstaining from eating meat. Those who desecrate themselves with one of these may not visit a sacred site or appear before the gods until the effects of this pollution expire. Those who are polluted by their own or someone else's blood are *fujō* for seven days, which means they may not appear in front of the gods until the seven days are over. When anyone building a *miya* is hurt to the point of bleeding, he has been touched by misfortune and, having become unclean, can no longer help to complete the sacred building. When a similar accident happens while one of the temples of Tenshō daijin at Ise is being renovated or built, the whole building has been desecrated and has to be dismantled again. A menstruating woman may not visit a *miya*. People insist that when women are on pilgrimage to the province of Ise, menstruation stops. But I believe that this happens on account of the laborious journey and frequently is not noticed so the journey is not in vain.

The meat of four-legged animals, not including that of foxes, may not be enjoyed without subjecting oneself to great desecration. Those who do remain *fujō* for thirty days. Anyone eating two-legged or feathered game, not including waterfowl, wild chicken, and cranes,[12] is *fujō* for one Japanese hour, which is two European hours.

Killing an animal, watching an execution, being near a dying person, or entering a house in which there is a body means uncleanness for the whole day.

Among all these things that pollute people, nothing is more contagious than the death of parents or blood relatives, for uncleanness spreads through the whole family. Therefore their ceremonial laws determine the time and days of uncleanness according to the degree of blood relationship, wealth, and birth.

The above are the most important cases of outward uncleanness, which are detested by the gods and which generally (except in the case of mourning) make people unworthy to step in front of the gods, unless there are special circumstances. Moreover, such an unclean object may affect a scrupulous saint, trying to keep himself as spotless as a mirror, in three ways: through the eyes looking at this abomination; through the mouth, speaking about it; through the ears, hearing about it. To block those sinful ways, these pagans recommend a symbol of three monkeys, which they have in common with Buddhism and which is often found on public roads, sitting at the feet of Jizō or of another virtuous deity: using their front legs one monkey is covering his two eyes, the other his mouth, and the third his ears.

I knew a person of such outward cleanliness that, if someone visited him whom he suspected of being *fujō*, he had his house cleaned and sprinkled with salt and water from top to bottom. But for this reason others of this clever nation considered him a hypocrite and believed him not to be an honest man because of his inhuman cleanliness.

Chapter 3

Shinto *Reibi*, That Is to Say, Lucky and Sacred Days and Their Celebration

The celebration of sacred days consists of *mairu*, that is to say, visiting the *miya* and temples of the gods and the dead. This can be done on any day but must take place on the so-called lucky, that is, temple, days and holy days, unless this is prevented by the above-mentioned pollution, which the gods detest. Punctilious worshippers add to this pollution further events that carry even a hint of misfortune or those that make people sad. For these gods live in a state of happiness and joy, and they gain little pleasure from visits by people whose hearts are tarnished with blemishes of sadness.

Ordinary devotion is performed in the following way: The worshipper cleanses his body thoroughly, dresses in clean clothing according to what he can afford, and puts a *kamishimo,* a dress of honor, or ceremonial dress, on top. He then goes to that part of the temple compound where there is a stone water basin, draws some water with a ladle placed nearby, and using liberal amounts of water washes his hands to his heart's content. With modest gestures and downcast eyes he moves on to the raised floor or the veranda in front of the lattice grille of the locked-up temple, facing the mirror inside. Kneeling, he bends his head slowly and humbly to the floor and lifts it up again, or, still kneeling, says a little prayer of his own composition about his personal concerns, or a *takama no hara kami todomari.*[1] Then he throws a few coins down through the lattice as a sacrifice or donation, or puts them into the nearby collection box, and with three blows sounds the bell hanging in front of the temple to cheer up the god with the tone, a sound that all gods love. Then the worshipper goes his way, spending the rest of the day walking, feasting, and enjoying all sorts of entertainment.

People perform this short and artless devotion (which may also be performed at other times without dressing up, depending on the occasion) for one or several gods, according to their inclination, or, according to which gods they trust, or to the patrons of their profession and rank, or those which have the power to grant them success in their special request. There is no outward ceremony, and no rosary is used, just as there are no formulas intoned as prayers, unless someone wishes to present his request in his own words. This religion considers all that unnecessary, for the gods look into people's hearts and perceive their thoughts, desires, and requests, just as people see themselves in the mirror. Thus no special preparations are necessary for ordinary celebrations, public festivals, or on remembrance days for blood relations; even on the day their parents pass away, they are allowed to take the same food and drink they usually consume.

Consequently their holy days are secular ceremonial, rather than spiritual, days and are therefore called *reibi,* which means visiting days.[2] On those days people must visit not just the *miya* of Tenshō daijin and other gods and deceased but must call especially on superiors and friends and honor them with greetings of good fortune. On these days they have their banquets, weddings, audiences, and all sorts of public amusements and meetings, which generate happiness and joy and can bring pleasure to the gods. The *reibi* are on fixed days, both the monthly and annual ones.

There are three monthly ones. The first, called *tsuitachi,* is the first day of each month, which more appropriately should be called a secular ceremonial day than a spiritual temple day. From early in the morning people walk around visiting their superiors, acquaintances, and friends to wish them *medetō,* or good fortune, on the appearance of the new moon, spending the rest of the time together with them at temples and other pleasant places, taking *sakana,* a local drink, with snacks and keeping the company of women. Since this celebration is a traditional, secular custom, it is observed in this fashion not only by people believing in Shinto, but by every good citizen, whatever belief he may follow.

The second celebration takes place on the fifteenth day of the month, which is the full moon, and at this time the ancestral gods are visited rather than good friends.

The third takes place on the twenty-eighth. Being the time of the crescent moon, it gets less attention than the former, and temples can hardly complain about an excessive number of visitors. But Buddhist temples have more visitors, for it is a regular monthly day for the worship of Amida.

There are five annual festival days, called *reibi* or *sekku.*[3] On account of their number, they are generally called *gosekku,* which means "five festivals." They are distributed throughout the year to coincide with the most unlucky and uneven days and months and accordingly carry the following names: *shōgatsu,* New Year's Day; *sangatsu sannichi,* the third day of the third month; *gogatsu gonichi,* the fifth day of the fifth month; *shichigatsu nanoka,* the seventh day of the seventh month; *kugatsu kunichi,* the ninth day of the ninth month.

These festivals are in fact nothing other than secular festival days or general holidays, which previous generations established on those days that they believed to be extremely harmful to people on account of their unfortunate lack of symmetry. The happiness of the celebration and the wishes of good luck are intended to distract the *kami,* or gods, and to avoid bad luck.[4] Since, properly speaking, they are not there for the worship of the gods but to generate festive joy, they are acceptable to all religions and sects.

Shōgatsu, or New Year, is celebrated more than others with the greatest solemnity and with ceremonial greetings of good fortune, feasting, and visits to temples in order to start the year in an auspicious manner. Everybody of full age and capacity[5] dresses in his finest clothes and sets out early in the morning to visit his superiors and friends, saying his *medetō,* or "Good Luck," bowing deeply, and presenting a box with two or three fans,[6] onto which a flat, dried piece of mussel-meat[7] is stuck, all to indicate wealth and abundance. The donor's name is on it, so that when his friends are not at home they know who sent it. With important people, a secretary receives the greetings and the presents in the front building, writing them down.

After the morning has been spent in this fashion, and the foundations for the day's enjoyment have been laid by toasts to good fortune drunk here and there, the rest of the day is spent reveling at the house of the senior member of the family. This merry-making and paying compliments goes on for three days, while the entertainment of guests continues the whole month. In the first few days, everything has to be provided in abundance, and everybody must dress up to the best of his ability. Even a poor day laborer hires a *kamishimo* with a sword to join the comedy. Only a few pay equal attention to the temples, mainly to Tenshō daijin.[8]

The second *sekku*, or feast, is called *sangatsu sannichi*. After paying the usual compliments to relatives, friends, and superiors, people amuse themselves as is befitting at this early season: a time when plum, cherry, and apricot trees display their blossoms in an incredible abundance of beautiful flowers, which cover the trees like little light-pink, double-petaled roses, beckoning the visitor from afar. Out of love for their little daughters, and so that the little girls may thrive, people treat their closest friends to meals and entertainments especially on these days. A room is decorated with more than one thousand dolls to represent the court of the *dairi* with *hina*[9] of *kuge*. Each individual has a tray with Japanese food set in front, which includes rice cakes baked with young artemisia,[10] with which the daughters, or if they are under age, the parents, have to entertain visiting friends in this room, offering a cup of *sake* as well.[11]

A rich gentleman living at Ryūzagawa, that is, "Birds River," had a daughter called Bunjo (her husband might have been called Sumiyoshi dai myōjin). She was unable to bear children. She called upon the *kami*, became pregnant, and gave birth to five hundred eggs. She was distraught because she was afraid that nasty animals might hatch from the eggs. She put them in a small box on which she wrote the words *hōjōrō* and threw them in the Ryūzagawa.[12]

An old fisherman discovered the little box far down the river, opened it, and found the eggs. He took them home, but his wife judged that they could not be of great value and would not have been thrown away without good reason. She advised him to throw them away again. The fisherman replied: "We are both old and soon have to die. It doesn't matter what emerges from them. Let's see." Then he incubated the eggs (in the Indian fashion, in an oven with cushions or sand). The eggs opened one after the other: there were children inside. It was difficult to feed them. They took ground artemisia leaves and rice, and with that fare reared the children. But later they needed more to sustain them. The children began to plunder. Their foster parents sent them up the river, where a rich man lived, to obtain some of his wealth. They did not know that it was the house of their own mother. The servant of the woman asked them their name. They answered that they had no name, but that they were hatched from five hundred eggs. They had come because they were poor. If they were given food, they would leave again. The woman asked what had been written on the little box and was told that it was *hōjōrō*. Then she realized that these were her own sons. She took them in as her cherished children and prepared a meal of good fortune, at which she gave each of them a dish of *sakana* to drink and a peach leaf. This is the reason why the peach festival takes place on the third day of the third month. At that festival a branch of a peach tree is placed above a cauldron, and cakes of artemisia and rice are baked. They are called *futsu mochi,*[13] which means artemisia cakes, and they are made in the following way: the artemisia or wormwood[14] leaves are soaked for one night and drained; then they are ground and mixed with rice cooked in water and are stirred over heat again and mixed with boiled and coarsely grated *azuki* (red bean) flower and rice.

This mother of five hundred children later turned into Benzaiten, attended upon by her five hundred children. She is therefore called the goddess of wealth and is worshipped for that reason.

The third *sekku,* or festival, is *gogatsu gonichi,* also called *tango no sekku.* It is similar to the previous one, but, among others, there are usually celebrations for the good fortune of the sons. Boys being what they are, they take good advantage of the occasion and find all sorts of ways to amuse themselves. In Nagasaki this and the following days are spent especially on taking pleasure trips in the bay shouting *peiron, peiron*[15] according to Chinese custom. Roofs (and in the end also the doors) are covered with calamus and mugwort leaves, for artemisia collected during these days is supposed to be the best and strongest for moxa after it has been kept for some three or four years.[16]

In the island kingdom of Mauri ga shima[17] the king, called Peiron, was forewarned in a dream that the island would soon sink. He should watch the image outside the temple, and when its face turned red it was time to save himself. A rogue, who could not believe that this image made of wood by human hands could lose its color, smeared the face with red to frighten the people. The king and his trustful subjects were frightened and, screaming with terror, escaped in boats as quickly as they could. But the offender and his doubting followers remained. Whereupon this kingdom sank all the same.

People from Fuku shū[18] have begun to celebrate this *peiron* festival also in Nagasaki, and it therefore became popular first with the boys and soon afterward with older people.[19]

When the water is low, land appears here and there.[20] This country has the best porcelain clay. At low tide divers still break off porcelain vessels that have grown onto the cliffs and bring them up. They are very thin and slightly green and the rarest existing. They leave a few shells attached to them to show that they are genuine. The vessels are of various shapes, but most of them have narrow necks, and they are used solely to preserve tea. They are such that tea which has gone bad will not only recover its strength if kept in them for one, two, or three years, but will increase in strength by far. That is why the shogun's tea is kept in them, as is further explained in *Amoenitates Exoticae,* 3, paragraph 8.[21]

The fourth festival is called *shichigatsu nanoka* or *shichiseki tanabata.*[22] It is also called *tanomu no sekku,* meaning festival of help. In addition to the usual celebrations, schoolboys especially make merry and enjoy themselves. They erect high bamboo poles with verses attached to them to show some evidence of their progress.[23]

The fifth festival is *Kunichi*, or *Kugatsu kokonoka.*[24] In addition to banquets and amusements, which are the essence of celebrations, this festival requires some special sociable drinking. Everything must be available, and all the food and drink are available for everybody. People visit their neighbors in turn, and no outsider or stranger may walk past without being entertained. It appears that this is very much like the Bacchanalias of the Romans. In Nagasaki this falls on the same day as the celebrations for their divine hunter and deity Suwa, who is honored with all sorts of amusements, such as dancing, plays, and processions. The Japanese call all this only *matsuri,* which means a sacrifice, or *matsuru,* meaning to sacrifice. People are entertained all day watching performances, with the result that a feast day turns into a fast day.[25]

In addition to these main festivals there are still a variety of others, but these are aimed for particular gods and therefore are given less importance. While these festivals in honor of one or the other god are observed throughout the country, they are celebrated with great solemnity only in those localities that stand directly under their protection, of which I will mention the most memorable. Some of these gods are not altogether the oldest and most important but have shown that they are fortunate to be blessed with higher virtues and great accomplishments after some miraculous appearances and assistance have testified to their authority and service in the government of the world, which, among the spirits, is organized like that on earth, conforming in many ways to the principles of aristocratic rule.

Tenshō daijin, the highest Japanese god and patron of the whole country, is honored throughout the country with a general holiday celebrated on the sixteenth of the ninth month. At this time all towns hold a fair and *matsuri,* that is to say, hold public performances in his honor in the presence of his image and his priests. These ordinary *matsuri* and main fairs are celebrated annually with the same solemnity in all cities and towns, two in a row, to honor the highest god of the temple to whose special protection people have committed themselves. In addition to this celebration, the sixteenth, twenty-first, and twenty-sixth of each month are dedicated to visits to his temples, but they are not observed with great solemnity.

Suwa has the ninth day of each month dedicated to him (the commoners add the nineteenth and twenty-ninth), when those whom he favors attend upon him. Celebrations beyond those held monthly are conducted annually on the ninth day of the sixth month. On this day the *kannushi* of the temple have worshippers crawl through a bamboo hoop, braided like the band of a barrel and covered with white linen cloth, to commemorate a certain event that occurred in the life of that saint. His biggest and one of the most solemn festivals of the year is the ninth day of the ninth month, which in Nagasaki, standing under his patronage, is celebrated with three days of joy, a fair, and public dance performances or *matsuri.*

Tenjin[26] has his annual celebration on the twenty-fifth day of the second month and then on the twenty-fifth day of the eighth month. His original and main temple is at Dazaifu, the place of his misery, and in Miyako, where he has worked great miracles. His main celebration is on the twenty-fifth of the eighth month. Pilgrimages are undertaken from all parts of the country to be present there on this day. His monthly festival is on the twenty-fifth of each month.

Hachiman is a brother of Tenshō daijin; his celebration is on the twenty-fifth day of the eighth month.

Morisaki dai gongen is celebrated on the eighteenth day of the third month.

Sumiyoshi dai myōjin.

Shitennō.

Gozutennō or Gion is celebrated on the fifteenth day of the sixth month in Nagasaki. His monthly festival is on the same day as that of Hachiman but is not celebrated.

Inari dai myōjin, the great saint of the foxes, has his annual celebration on the eighth day of the ninth month. He is especially worshipped on the eighth day of each month.

Ōyashiro in the province of Izumo, also known as Izumo no Ōyashiro, is one of the greatest gods and killed a dragon.[27] He is also called Oshioni no mikoto.[28]

Kasuga dai myōjin.

Benzaiten is celebrated on the seventh day of the eighth month.

Kumano gongen.

After these and others of lesser status rank further saints who are considered worthy of an annual festival in one or the other villages, towns, or provinces, but are known only locally and called merely "the saint of this or the other location" without having being canonized and honored by the *mikado* with a special name, or *okurina,* a death or posthumous title.

The above is the common knowledge an alert traveler is able to pick up about the ancient religion of their forefathers. More about the subject is contained in the Japanese history book and chronicle *Nihon ōdaiki,* which deals with the lives and deeds of the Japanese *kinchū,*[29] or great people, and at the beginning of their *Shindai ki,*[30] the history of the important gods.

Chapter 4

The *Sangū*, or Pilgrimage to Ise

A variety of pilgrimages are conducted by this nation. The first, and most important, is to Ise; the second, a visit to the thirty-three most important Kannon temples of this empire; the third is made to some of the most important *shin (kami)* or *hotoke (butsu)* temples throughout the country which have performed miracles and given help to their worshippers. The most famous of these are: Nikkō *dera,* which means "sunlight temple," in the province of Ōshū,[1] Hachiman, and so forth, the temples of the teacher Yakushi, or other ancient and important temples esteemed as places of worship and penance, according to people's own preference. A true Shinto believer goes only to Shinto temples, such as Dazaifu in Chikuzen, where Tenjin[2] died. The last kind of pilgrimage is also performed by the Buddhists; in other words, it is performed by believers from both religions, but each goes to his own gods. The second kind of pilgrimage belongs to neither of the main religions, but the common man believes this to be a good way to obtain prosperity and salvation.[3]

The first is as follows: *sangū* means literally "visiting a temple" and is only used for visiting this, the most sacred temple. This temple commemorates their greatest god Tenshō daijin, or Tenshō kōdaijin, which means literally "high god of the heavenly clan of terrestrial emperors."[4] They refer to the temple as Daijingū, which means "the commemorative temple of the great god," because *dai* means great; *shin* or *kami*, a spirit, god, or immortal soul; and *gū* in this combination and others means *miya* or a devotional and commemorative temple. Commoners call it Ise *miya* in accordance with the name of the province of Ise. They believe that the site was made sacred by the god's birth, life, and death and that he personally gave it the name of Ise.

All those who have visited it say that the temple is situated in flat country, is poorly built of wood and not very high, and is covered with a low roof of hay. It is maintained with great care in the image of the original poor temple of early times, built in their poverty by the first inhabitants and founders of this nation, or, as they call them, the first people. The temple contains nothing but a large, round mirror, made of metal and polished (according to the custom of this country). A few pieces of white paper cut into strips are hung here and there. With the former they wish to symbolize the all-encompassing knowledge and glory of the god, with the latter, the cleanliness of the site. At the same time, it cautions worshippers not to step in front of the god unless their hearts and bodies are clean.

The temple has various chapels in honor of lesser gods, numbering nearly one hundred, which, however, are only shaped like a temple and are often so small that nobody could possibly enter. Each has only one *kannushi* to guard it. Close by live the many *negi,* or lords of temples, or, as they call themselves, *tayū,*[5] meaning "ambassador" or "evangelist," who maintain large houses and lodges to accommodate the travelers. Not far away is the city or town, also carrying the name of the sacred site of Ise. It has many inns, print shops, paper makers, book binders, and builders of shrines, all necessary for this holy industry.

Every honest *shinja,*[6] or rather, every patriot whatever his belief, should visit this sacred site annually, or, at the very least, once in his life, to show due gratitude to the god and founder of his nation by this act of homage. Also, cleansed by this act of all sins, he may enter a happy state after death, or, in the naive eyes of the uneducated masses, he may be blessed with bodily health, food and drink, money, clothing, children, and a family. To strengthen this belief, every visitor personally receives from the *tayū* a box with a letter of indulgence, called *ōharai,* which means "great purification." People who are unable to obtain this personally because of their occupation, illness, or age can buy one annually. In addition to the above *shinshū,* one also sees other Buddhists because they wish to claim the right to be called honest patriots and therefore visit this place of their founder once or several times in their lives. There are also many Buddhists who stay at home but annually purchase the *ōharai* from Ise and, in addition, an annual letter of indulgence from their priest.

This journey is undertaken throughout the year, but especially during the first three months because of the good weather, and is made by young and old, rich and poor, men and women, but people of high rank seldom make it personally.

The shogun pays his respects to this site by means of an ordinary, annual embassy leaving in the first month, while at the same time another is sent to the *dairi.* Other barons and territorial lords do likewise. Rich people make do on their own money; others manage by begging and walking on foot. They carry a rolled-up straw mat on their back as a cover at night, have a walking stick in their hand, and a water ladle tucked into their belt, with which they also collect alms, baring their heads in European fashion. They wear a wide-brimmed traveling hat made of plaited split reed, which, like the water ladle, is marked with their name as well as that of their birthplace or residence, so that they can be identified if they suddenly die on the road. Others of some wealth wear a short white robe without sleeves over their clothes, on which the above names are printed on the chest and back. One meets several hundred of such pilgrims daily. They come in great numbers from the province of Ōshū and the shogunal city of Edo, where often the children run away from their parents to make this pilgrimage. If other parts of the country were visited without a pass, people would run into considerable trouble to the point of risking their lives, but everyday custom provides the liberty that the *ōharai* serves as a pass and is considered enough.

After a pilgrim has left home, his family puts a straw rope over the front door, from which hang twisted strips of cut paper to indicate purity, so that nobody with a heavy *imi*[7] will enter (that is, people who are impure because of the death of their parents). For it has been noticed that at that time pilgrims encounter misfortune or problems; also they may have bad and disturbing dreams. Such symbols of purity are also put up across an avenue that leads to a *miya.*

On this pilgrimage people must practice greater abstinence than ordinarily. Both going and coming back they must refrain from sexual intercourse, which otherwise neither the gods nor the people of this nation seem to consider in any way unholy. Consequently the only punishment it brings is that the parties remain stuck to each other until a potent ceremony by one of their *yamabushi,* one kind of hermit, or another powerful Buddhist priest, permits them to come apart. People strongly believe in this, for they claim that cases happen every year. People who are *fujō,* or unclean, may not show themselves here. If they dare to do so, they and their family would be visited with *shinbatsu,*[8] or revenge of the gods. A *shukke* is a priest of the Buddhist religion, and since he is practicing an impure profession by taking care of the dying and funerals, he may never ever appear here.

After a pilgrim has reached this location—which is visited daily by great numbers, amounting, on some days, to several thousands—he goes to the home of one or the other *kannushi* from whom he annually receives his indulgence as his acquaintance and delivers his greetings, courteously bending down to the floor. On the same or the following day, the *kannushi* in person either leads him and others who have announced their arrival at his house around the sacred site or asks a servant to do so. He briefly mentions the names of the temples and gods, and finally takes him in front of the middle and main temple of Tenshō daijin, where he has him pay his humble respects, kneeling with his forehead touching the ground, and people pray for good health or anything else according to their concerns. After this procession has been completed, the pilgrim is entertained by the *kannushi* either on the same day or, if his devotions have taken longer, on the following days. Also, if pilgrims cannot afford the public inns, he will put them up for the night. But however poor they are, they will make a generous donation from the alms they themselves received, which is never refused.

After the pilgrims' worship has been completed, this *kannushi* hands everybody an indulgence. It is a poor, small, square box, the length of a fan or one and a half spans, two inches wide, and the depth of one and a half thumbs, made of thin boards tacked together. Inside it has a bundle of thin, small sticks of the same material and length, some with clean paper strips tied around: all of it is miserable merchandise purchased for a miserable sum to commend to people that humbleness and cleanliness are virtues esteemed by their gods. A printed piece of paper is pasted on the front of the box. The name of this temple, Daijingū, meaning temple of the great god, is printed in beautiful characters, and at the end in small characters is the name of the *kannushi* who has issued this *ōharai* (for there are many who take people around), with the added title of *tayū,* which means ambassador, or evangelist, an honorific title commonly used by those serving at *miya.*

As soon as a pilgrim on foot has received this *ōharai* with the greatest deference, he attaches the same under his traveling hat over his forehead to protect it from rain. For convenience sake, a bundle of straw of the same weight is attached to the other side. People traveling on horseback have room to keep it in a better place. When pilgrims return home with such an *ōharai,* it is kept as a sacred object throughout the year. After that period is over, it is relegated to another honest place as if its potency had evaporated like smoke. Every year it is put on a board above the height of a man, attached to the wall of a clean room for this purpose. In some cities they are attached to the front of the house, above the door under the front roof. People living in poor accommodations have no cleaner place than a tree in their backyard. This is also where it is placed if one finds a lost *ōharai,* or that of a dead person, on the road.

In order to render service to those who desire this sacred object, and wish to, but cannot, travel as described above, the *kannushi* from Ise annually send large packs and boxes of this merchandise to the cities and villages of all provinces. It is taken by certain emissaries who arrange their journey so that they reach the most important places at *shōgatsu,* the New Year's celebrations, a festival of the most solemn rites of purification. At the same time they bring new calendars, which can be made only by the *mikado* and can be printed only at the above location. The envoy gets one mace or one *bu* for both pieces and sometimes, but rarely, more, according to each person's wealth and preference. People who accept this merchandise once are annually burdened with it, and the next year will again receive three items: one receipt in the shape of a note of appreciation addressed to the purchaser, a new *ōharai,* and thirdly also a new calendar. If he has given a generous donation, which, however, is rarely done by ordinary citizens, he will also be rewarded with a *sakazuki,* a wooden, lacquered drinking bowl.

Ichinohe[9] describes the situation of the Ise *miya* as follows: There are two Ise temples situated about twelve streets distant,[10] one behind the other. Both are poor, the size of about six mats, with *kannushi* sitting inside as guardians and out of respect for Tenshō daijin. Both temples are covered with hay and are poor but have been built without the slightest scratch to the skin. They are of equal importance, but the proper and real chapel of the deity is further at the back on higher ground. This chapel is called *hongū,* which means "real temple" (just as Suwa in Nagasaki is also on higher ground). Both are hung with some mirrors and papers inside.

The first *miya,* called *gekū,*[11] has many *kannushi* and eighty *massha,* which are small temples of lesser importance for the lesser deities placed around, each the size of four mats, with a *kannushi* as guardian and collector of alms, which he keeps for himself.

The second *miya,* which is some twelve streets further away, is called *naigū*[12] and has forty *massha* with their *kannushi* guardians. All guardians of *massha* are called *miya suzume,* which means "temple sparrows."

Meticulous people who want to inspect the temples do this first without the guidance of a *kannushi* and proceed as follows. From the city of Ise they first go to the river Miyagawa, which flows past the city on the side facing Ise *miya,* and bravely wash in it. Having cleansed themselves, they pass through and go beyond the living quarters of the *kannushi* and other merchants situated some three or four streets away from the river and, continuing over sandy terrain, head straight for the *gekū miya.* Having paid their respects, they continue along the right to inspect the *massha* and then return to the previous location. Then they proceed to the other temple of Tenshō daijin called *naigū.* After paying their respects, they do the same tour to pay respect to the surrounding *massha.* Then they head for the hills for some fifteen streets to a mountain situated above and near the raised ocean shore, to pay respect to a little cave called *ama no iwato* (situated some twenty *ken* from the sea), which means "heavenly shore."[13] Here Tenshō daijin hid himself and by secluding himself deprived the world and other planets of light, proving beyond doubt that he was the lord of light and the most important of the gods. The cave is some one-and-a-half mats large. It has a chapel with a *kami* sitting on a cow called Dainichi nyorai, which means great embodiment of the sun, as object of worship. Also here some *kannushi,* who live in two houses above the raised seashore, are waiting. To commemorate his visit, the caller has a little *sugi*[14] sapling planted there (for a few coins). From these tall shores, you can see, at a distance of one and a half miles, a large island that is supposed to have been created in the age of Tenshō daijin.

After this tour of inspection, enthusiasts turn right, proceeding inland for two miles, and inspect a beautiful *butsu dō* temple called Asamadake, where they pay their respects to a Kannon, called Kokuzō bosatsu, and then return to the town of Ise.

Chapter 5

Yamabushi, or Mountain Priests, and Other Religions

In this religion vows are made to pass quickly and without hindrance into the other world, or to attain a place of particular eminence in the heavenly plains, but also simply to resolve a special matter of concern to one's satisfaction. The former is done by entering an order of hermits, whose religious are called *yamabushi;* the latter is achieved by a vow to the gods to perform some act of penance of one's own choosing and visit certain temples for a set period of time. *Yamabushi* means (but the character does not clearly indicate this meaning) a mountain soldier,[1] because, according to the founding rules of the order, they must fight for the gods and lands of their ancestors if required. In reality they are religious and hermits who disdain worldly pleasures to reach the everlasting and are committed to castigating their bodies by climbing sacred mountains and frequent washing in cold water. Those who are rich live in their own houses. The poor wander around the roads begging, especially in the province of Suruga, near the high mountain Fuji, which they climb in the sixth month as an act of penance. Others agree to serve at a *miya,* but these are usually so poorly endowed that they can hardly support a person.

Their first teacher, ancestor, and founder lived more than one thousand years ago and is called En no gyōja, a person about whose birth, parents, and friends nothing was ever known.[2] He also died without children or descendants. He was the first hermit wandering in the wilderness to castigate his body, and with the knowledge he gained, he discovered and marked many routes through this country. His followers are divided into two orders. The first, Tōzanha, adheres to the climbing of Hikozan, a terribly steep mountain in the province of Buzen, right between Buzen and Chikuzen. The mountain is climbed under the greatest danger over several days and is such that anybody climbing it without preparing himself and being *fujō* will be possessed by the fox (the devil) and go raving mad. The other order, Honzanha, makes its pilgrimage to the grave of their founder on a mountain in the province of Yoshino which is called Ōmine, meaning "the great mountain peak," on account of its height. It is supposed to be extremely cold and, owing to its sheer heights, no less dangerous to climb. A visitor who has not cleansed his body and heart will meet the misfortune of crashing down, being smashed to pieces, or, if he manages to avoid this, he will be subjected to punishment throughout his life in the form of illness or another serious affliction. Every member of this order must conduct this pilgrimage once yearly. Those climbing the mountain must prepare themselves well by abstinence from sexual intercourse, forbidden foods, and everything else that pollutes, as well as by washing themselves in ice-cold water several times daily. While climbing the mountain they must make do with eating wild roots and leaves from the mountain.

After the pilgrimage has been concluded successfully, everybody visits the prelate of their order, who lives in Miyako, and presents him with a certain sum of money, which those who are poor have to obtain by begging. In return he receives a higher title or rank, involving also some changes in dress, which determines the amount of respect he receives from his brotherhood. All this is nearly identical to the ranks and manner of the Society of the Blind.[3]

The religious of this order wear secular dress according to the custom of the country, but in accordance with the rules of their order wear various ornaments, each with its own name, meaning, and historical explanation.

Wakizashi, or sword of Fudō, worn in the belt on the left, a little shorter than the *katana,*[4] but also blunt on the underside.

Shakujō, or the little staff of the god Jizō, with a copper plate with four rings on top, with which they make a noise when pronouncing certain words in their prayers.

Hora no kai, a conch shell, twisted like a snail's shell; it is white and smooth with red spots, delicate lines, and beautifully worked by nature, of quite some size: most probably big enough to contain half a liter of water. (They are found near some cliffs washed by the sea and at Arai.) It is carried suspended from the belt, at the side, and has a hole in front into which the owner blows when he desires some alms from a traveler. This produces a sound that is not much sweeter than that of a cow herder.

Suzu kake is a belt worn around the neck, plaited like a carrying rope and covered with a few tassels of different shape and with slight changes to the tassels to indicate the wearer's rank.

Tokin, a hat or decoration worn on the forehead, but only a few are permitted to wear this.

Oi, a pouch or little bag, tied to the back of the shoulder, which contains a book, money, and some clothing.[5]

Yatsume no waranzu is the name for common straw shoes used when traveling, and convenient to climb the mountains of penance. They are intertwined with fibers from the stems of their most sacred flower, *tarate.*[6]

Irataka no juzu, their rosary of rough balls; but this neither is worn in accordance with the founding rules and has been borrowed from the priests.

Kongō zue, a heavy staff which they use when they climb the mountain Ōmine.

The most important of them wear their hair pulled back and cut short at the back. Those of lower rank tie their hair together at the back without cutting it. Many prefer to shave their head according to a custom introduced to this country by the priests of the foreign religion. This is also done with novices and the children of members of this order.

These Shinto hermits, who previously followed the example of their founder and nourished themselves from roots and herbs, constantly roaming forests and mountains and spending their time cleaning and castigating their bodies with cold water, have come to disregard the rigor of the original oath, and in their religious teaching they have added some of the most powerful and miraculous idols of the newly arrived Buddhists to those of their ancestors in their worship and dread of the supernatural. Shortly afterward they willingly got involved with the practice of magic. They pretend that certain ceremonies and words enable them to use the power of foreign and local gods to conjure and chase away evil spirits, search out hidden matter, and bring to pass other supernatural events. Throughout the nation they are also willing to be used for finding thieves and stolen goods, predicting uncertain events, interpreting dreams, healing incurable illnesses, finding wrongdoers, or revealing the guilt or innocence of an accused.

I consider it worthwhile to take a closer look at some of these things. They treat a sick person as follows. The sick person tells the mountain priest the story of his illness, after which the priest notes down the details of the suffering with characters on a piece of paper. He puts the piece of paper in front of the idol and performs his ceremonies, the power of which then enters the letter. He turns the piece of paper into pills, of which the patient has to take one every morning, swallowing it with water; this has to be drawn from this or the other direction, according to the orders of the priest. These distinctive pills are called *goō*. But this hellish treatment is used only for the most dangerous of illnesses, when there is practically no hope. Every illness has a different kind of treatment. Guilt and innocence are determined not only by the power of certain words but also by the presence of the idol Fudō sitting in red flames. This is not done in court (as the trial by water is conducted by the Siamese, or by the Brahmins and other pagans, and yes, indeed, also in various places among us Christians by burning witches) but in secret among the servants, either only by way of incantation, or by trial by fire, or by drinking Kumano *no goō*. If the first method is unsuccessful, trial by fire is used: a fire of coals the length of a fathom is kindled, through which the suspect must walk three times without being harmed in order to be recognized as innocent. People are made to confess by being forced to drink Kumano *no goō*. *Goō* is a letter with characters written on it, and decorated with some black birds, such as ravens, which has been certified by the seal of a *yamabushi*. It is stuck to the pillars of the house to ward off evil spirits and is used for many other superstitions. It is made by *yamabushi* everywhere, but the strongest comes from Kumano. A piece is torn off and given to the accused to drink, which makes him so frightened that he confesses his guilt. With these magical formulas they even know how to handle glowing iron and coals without being hurt, extinguish fire, bring cold water to the boil, and, in turn, make boiling water cold again, to immobilize the sword of a violent person in its sheath, to use it to parry blows, and other abstruse things. Some of these acts are actually performed in accordance with the mysteries of nature; some are illusions. They call this *inusō*, which means "conjuring strokes." Murmuring certain spells, they use the fingers and hands to create the shape of a tiger, crocodile, or other powerful animal for an instant and immediately change it to another shape. At the same, time they raise and change their voice, entering their target with cross cuts, until the power of the obstacle has been cut off and the desired effect obtained.

Their most important and most mysterious *in*,[7] or invocation consists of interweaving their fingers to represent the *shitennō,*[8] or the four most powerful gods of the thirty-third and last heaven. Sets of two fingers are joined together to create a four-sided figure, each side to present one of the above gods. These mountain priests call them Tamonten, Jikokuten, Zōjōten, and Kōmokuten. The two index fingers pointing up straight serve as a telescope, with which they examine the spirits and the illness and perceive and identify in a person's body the *kitsune,* the fox, or the *ma,* the evil spirit or devil, and then are in a position to chase them away as necessary with other powerful ceremonies and words. This symbol in the center represents Fudō Myō ō, that is, the holy great Fudō. He was a penitent *gyōja* of their order who, among other hardships with which he castigated his body, daily burned in fire without being harmed, having the power to control the flames and the knowledge to make use of them. That is also why people light an oil lamp in front of the image of this Fudō, with oil from a black, poisonous lizard with a red stomach, called *imori,* which lives in water.

They are capable of teaching these arts to others for a handsome reward, like a conjurer who empties his bag of tricks. My informant, a man well versed in things

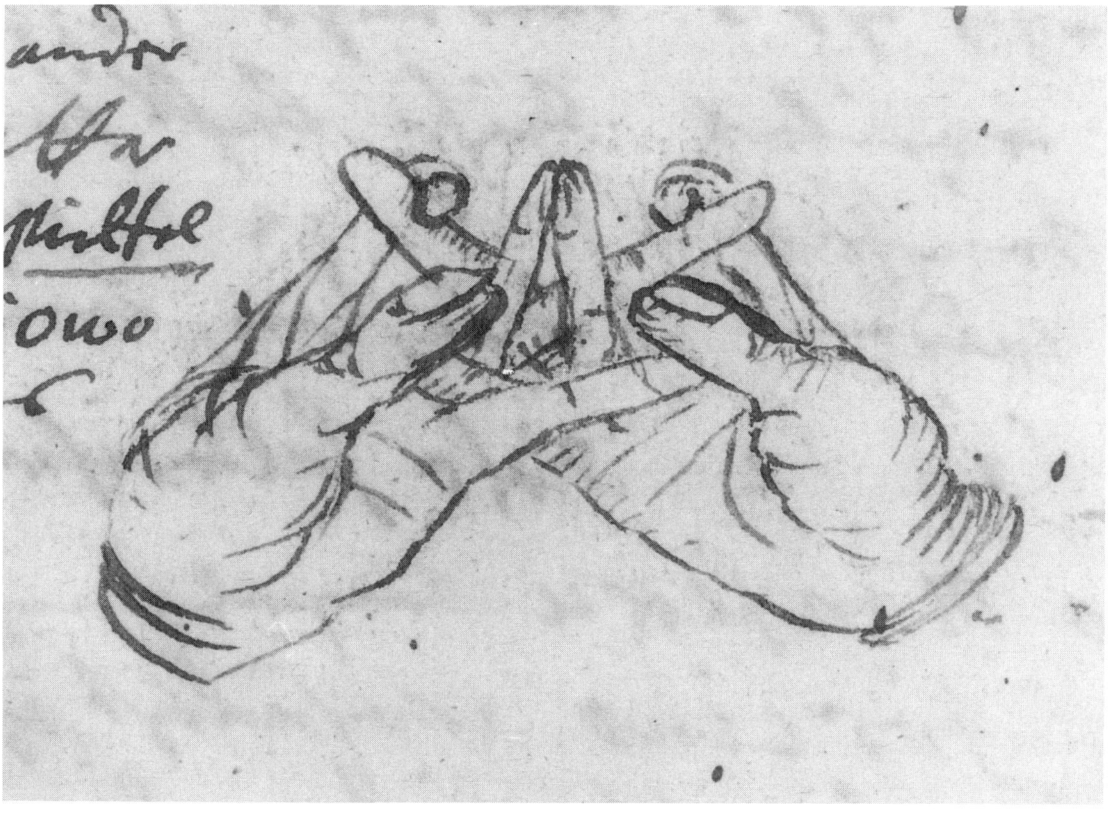

Kaempfer's sketch of a *yamabushi*'s hand position. (Courtesy of the British Library, Sloane 3062, folio 68 verso)

Japanese and my student in medicine, studied under these experts and first had to endure the following trials for six days. He was not allowed to eat any living being and had to make do with herbs and rice only, had to wash himself down in cold water seven times daily, and had to rise up from being seated on his knees and heels 780 times, while at the same time lifting both hands clasped together above his head. He found the last, rising up and sitting down, the hardest. After he had done this two to three hundred times, perspiration was running down his back, and he nearly ran away from his teacher on the last day. But being a strong man and a healthy fellow, he completed the trial, more out of the desire not to disgrace himself than for the sake of the art.[9]

Chapter 6

Butsu dō, or Foreign Paganism, and in General about Its Founder

Butsu or *hotoke* is the pronunciation of the character used to designate a foreign god (which is totally different from *kami* or *shin*), and *butsu dō* means literally "the Way of the Idol," that is to say, the worship of the idol. The origin of this religion can be traced back to the Indian Brahmins. Like the oriental fig tree, it continually dropped new roots from its widespread branches and propagated itself until it had reached and pervaded the furthest corner of the East. The founder of these pagans, after whom they and their religion apparently were initially named, is, in my opinion, the man who is called Buddha by the Brahmins and who is believed to be in large part identical with the god Vishnu, appearing in this world for the ninth time in the flesh as this person with that name. The Chinese and Japanese call him Butsu and Shaka. Through usage, however, this name has become an ordinary word under which they know and serve all gods of this foreign brotherhood and which is also used to salute other holy men and teachers. Ordinary Siamese call this god Phra phuttha chao, which means "holy lord." Scholars call it Sammana Khodum in Pali, or their secret language, or, in Pegu, Sammana Khutama.[1] His native country was Magada *koku,* that is, Magadha province in the country of Tenjiku, which literally means "country of heaven." They use that name in particular for Ceylon, the Malabar Coast, and Coromandel, and generally for all continents and islands of pagan Asia with black inhabitants, such as Malacca, Sumatra, Java, Pegu, Siam, and so forth.

His birth came to pass on the eighth day of the fourth month in the twenty-sixth year of the Japanese emperor Shō ō, the fourth successor of the here famous Shun no Buō,[2] which was in the year 1029 before the birth of our Blessed Lord, or, according to Japanese reckoning, in the year 1027. (When I was in Siam in the year of Our Lord 1690, the Siamese wrote the year 2232 after their Buddha, which could be Shaka, which, however, would add up to only 542 before the birth of Christ.)[3] They say that his father was a king in Magada *koku,* a kingdom of the country of Tenjiku (I believe that is Ceylon), although ordinary Japanese believe Magada *koku* to be Siam.[4] When he was nineteen he left his wife and only son at home and placed himself under the guidance of a hermit, or pilgrim, called Arara *sennin,*[5] who lived on top of Mount Dandoku.[6] The latter exhorted him to lead an austere life and constantly meditate on heavenly, spiritual subjects while sitting in the particular posture of spiritual contemplation where the feet are twisted and placed on top of each other in an unnatural fashion and the hands rest folded in the lap, with the thumbs raised touching each other at the tip. The thoughts are withdrawn with such force from all earthly matter that the body appears devoid of all senses and is unperturbed by outside influence. The Japanese call this devotional act *zazen* and the revelation, or the truth they discover, *satori.* This saint experienced it with such force that he learned the state of heaven and hell, the condition of bodiless souls, their transmigration, the way to bliss, the government of the gods, and other supernatural matter. He transmitted the teaching of this religion to his disciples orally, and many placed themselves under his discipline and adopted his style of life to partake of these mysteries. He died at the age of seventy-nine on the fifteenth day of the second month in the year 950 before the birth of our Blessed Lord.

In general his teaching consisted of the following:

The souls of humans and all animals are immortal. They are of the same kind and differ only temporarily according to the attributes of the subject into which they have been placed.

At death the souls of humans receive their reward in a blissful or miserable region according to the life they have led.

The place of bliss, called *gokuraku,* which means everlasting happiness, is supposed to be divided into many classes according to the merits of the gods and the souls, differing in the extent of splendor and joy, but generally filled with these to such a degree that all consider their own to be the best, do not desire change, and are provided with everlasting joy. The governor general of these heavens is supposed to be the god Amida (whose existence, however, is supposed to have been introduced by the Brahmins shortly after the Ascension of Christ). He instructed this god to act as father of the blessed, and generally as patron of all souls, and to be the good intermediary through whom people can be forgiven their sins by calling his name and reach the state of bliss.

The path that pleases Amida, which everybody must tread to reach the state of bliss, is a righteous life, devoid of all that is prohibited because it is sinful.

The prohibitions are contained in five main articles, called *gokai,* which means five cautions, which every simple person is recommended to look up at as the guiding star[7] of his life. These are:

sesshō: or the law not to take life,
chūtō: not to steal,
jain: not to commit adultery,
mogō: not to lie,
onjū: to abstain from alcohol.

The last was the first and most important law in which Shaka instructed new disciples.

Next are ten precepts, called *jikkai,* which do not differ from the above but consist of a greater number of articles and more details. These *kai* are again divided into a variety of other rules by learned and particularly high-minded people; on the basis of ethical principles, aspects of particular virtues and vices are distinguished, up to the finest degree, thus increasing their number. *Go hyaku kai,* that is, five hundred precepts, are only observed by the religious, who strive for a higher state of bliss. These are very detailed; the diet is prescribed in detail, and all matters are so strictly defined that few priests attain such perfection or are able to observe them regularly.

Those whose sinful life makes them unworthy to enter heaven will receive their just reward, but only temporarily, in the regions of hell, called *jigoku*. This is divided also into many kinds and classes differing in pain and torment, so that people may be punished according to their sins, age, occupation, and crime. In charge of these sinners is Enma, called Enma ō by adding the character for "majesty." This judge of hell has the same name among the Brahmins, the Siamese, and Chinese.[8] To ease the pain and suffering of hell, and shorten the period of damnation into which the souls of the dead enter, the worship and good deeds of those still living, and especially the intercessions of the priests, are extremely helpful. These are directed to Amida. His appeal to the chief judge of hell makes it possible that the severity of justice and his harshness are extenuated, that he treats the damned souls most lightly, and permits them to return to the world as soon as possible.

After penance has been done and sins have been atoned for in this region, the righteous judgment of the above Enma ō will transfer the soul into another body—not that of a human but of an animal whose nature and characteristics bear some resemblance to the person's former sinful life and actions. The soul continually transmigrates from the body of the species to which it has been sent, be it snake, toad, insect, fish, bird, or lesser four-footed animal, to a higher species of animal until finally it is again born as a human being, able to transport the soul to everlasting bliss by leading a virtuous life, or, by sinning, returning it yet again to this miserable cycle.

Among the numerous disciples of Shaka were a number of learned men who left behind their own disciples to spread the faith, and they, in turn, left new men with religious zeal who spread the teaching, until it filled the furthest ends of the world.

The most eminent of those who listened to him are believed to have been Anan and Kashō, or, as they are called with their title placed after their name, Anan sonja and Kashō sonja.[9] They collected into a book what they had heard from his mouth, as well as what they found among his manuscripts on tree leaves. Comparing the teaching's purity with the sacred *tarate* flower, they called it *Hokke kyō,* which means "Book of Beautiful Flowers."[10] On account of its perfection, it is also referred to simply by the general name of *kyō,* or book,[11] and it serves all pagan teachers east of the river Ganges as a general bible. The pains these two men took earned them a place in temples and on altars to the right and left of Shaka, being worshipped together with him as holy devotees and teachers.

Before this teaching spread through China and Korea to Japan, people followed the local *shinshū* or *kami* religion, which taught that the path to well-being was that to their Tenshō daijin at Ise, and except for some apocryphal fables about the events of the early period of gods, few *kami* temple or religious celebrations of other saints took place. These gradually increased over a long period of time with the formation of the state and the first monarch, Jimmu tennō, and the spread of civilization and the arts. In the countries beyond Japan, life was governed by the first simple moral teaching of their Tei Gyō, which means emperor Gyō, who reigned 2,359 years before the birth of Christ, according to their calculation, as well as his successor Tei Shun, that is, Emperor Shun,[12] a wise and righteous farmer, whom the above Gyō pressed to take up the government of the country in preference to his twelve unworthy children (consisting of two daughters and ten sons). These two emperors were considered the first *seijin*. *Seijin* is, properly speaking, a philosopher who through his own genius and without any teaching discovers wisdom and truth, but this title is also wrongly used for the first theologians. Many centuries afterward the first pagan theology of the local teacher Rōshi[13] was introduced. This Rōshi was born in Sokoku, which is the province of So,[14] on the fourteenth day of the ninth month, 346 years after the birth of Shaka, which is the 603rd year before the birth of our Blessed Lord. It is recorded that he was carried in the womb of his mother for eighty-one years and was therefore born white-haired and received the name of Rōshi, meaning "old child." After he was born, he lived for another eighty-four years. It is recorded that he was a reincarnation of Kashō Bosatsu, that is, the god or sacred Kashō, who was the oldest disciple of Shaka. This is most probably why this enlightened man of great intellect had no difficulty in revealing to the simple people something about the state of the gods and spirits[15] and with his unprecedented new teaching about things supernatural to win over the curious and credulous masses.

This teaching soon received marvelous support in its growth through the insightful philosophy of the incomparable *seijin* Kōshi,[16] who was born 399 years after Shaka and fifty-three years after the theologian Rōshi, while the latter was still alive, on the fourth day of the eleventh month in the country of Ro.[17] At his birth, marks and signs of his enlightened intellect and his future as *seijin* were not lacking: for his head showed a number of birth marks that he had in common with the Emperor Gyō, and his forehead was shaped like that of the Emperor Shun. The Chinese recorded that when he was born, music was sounding in heaven, and when he was washed after his birth, two dragons were present. He reached the manly proportions of nine *shaku*, nine *sun*,[18] an unusual size, but in proportion to the size of his intellect. Apart from the tales that have crept into the story of his life, it is certain that he was of enlightened intellect and the most brilliant philosopher ever to inspire the countries of the East to this day, whose books and teaching are still held in such high esteem, as if he had descended from heaven together with Socrates in those barbaric times. In his memory and honor the territorial lords maintain and fund temples. During the time I was there, the present shogun built two in Edo and on his first visit himself delivered a speech in honor of Kōshi's philosophy of the art of government to his councilors and the courtiers present.[19] One finds his portrait in the houses of philosophers, and his name is always pronounced with the greatest respect by all those who study.

With his insight, down-to-earth teaching, and rules of daily conduct, he demolished the supernatural precepts and myths of the teacher Rōshi and the latter's disciples and adherents,[20] and soon support from the superstitious and simple masses increased enormously. He died after completing his seventy-third year, leaving behind many enlightened disciples and new teachers, who put down in writing the knowledge and wisdom they had received from him and at the same time spread it by word of mouth. His precepts are to this very day followed without change as *norma vitae*[21] under the name of *ju,* or *judō,* meaning the philosophical way, or the precepts of living. Others, however, who have taken up *butsu dō* or the religion of other gods, use parts of it, be it with regard to the moral teaching of the nation or natural history, no less than Christians have retained the teachings of the Greeks and Romans and study them for their education.

While this sect of philosophers was flourishing in China, and in the course of neighborly communication was transmitted over many years also to the Japanese, the countries of Laos and Siam and the surrounding countries and islands were converted to the teaching of the Shaka; but this teaching was unable to establish itself properly in this part of the East. In the year 63 after the birth of Christ the first apostles of this great intellect crossed to Japan and were given a temple that, according to Japanese tradition, is still today called Hakubaji, which means "temple of the white horse," because their *kyō,* or bible, was brought on a white horse from West India. However, it appears that with the renown of the philosophical teaching of ethics, the teaching of these apostles was badly understood and had little influence until in the year 518 after the birth of Christ, when a great saint arrived in China from West India, or, in Japanese, from Seitenjiku. His name was Daruma, the thirty-third successor of Shaka, the most important teacher of this pagan religion, comparable to the Khalif among the Imams of the Mohammedans. He settled in China, and reports of his dignity and saintliness, and no less the example of his austere life and devout and persevering worship, secured him a place in the hearts of the people. His devotion was so intense that he did not even hesitate to cut off his eyelids, which had caused him to fall asleep when rapt in worship or fervent meditation and therefore had incurred his anger. With his plausible and comforting teaching of the immortality of the soul and everlasting rewards, he induced the people to call upon and serve the gods, for which they could be rewarded with heavenly bliss. In a very short time this idol worship spread to such an extent that it went from China to Hyakusai[22] (which was the name used for Korea at the time, being that of one of its main provinces), where the first *butsu,* or image in honor of Shaka, was erected in the year 543. At this stage it was impossible for Japan—which at the time followed the sect of the Chinese philosopher as well as worshipped the local gods—to remain ignorant of the new teaching, and, with the closeness and intercourse that existed between these countries, not to have the religion slowly creep in on its own accord and find adherents. The first *bukkyō,* or book of commandments and idols, was brought to Japan and made known in A.D. 550. They recorded that in A.D. 568 a carved idol, an authentic figure of Amida from the central part of Tenjiku, or India, which had turned up only a few years previously in Hyakusai, had revealed itself in the province of Tsu no kuni with miraculous rays. People therefore held it in such veneration that a temple was built in its honor in the country of Shinano, called Zenkōji, which still today is considered to be the most important and largest of that province.[23] At this time Japan was ruled by the hereditary ruler Kimmei, who apparently was not averse to this foreign paganism and permitted its first roots to take hold. He began to have years counted by *nengō,* or era names, and gave the year in which this first temple was built the name of Kongō.[24]

Chapter 7

Judō, the Teaching or the Ways of the Moralists or Philosophers

Judō literally means the way or method of wise men. *Judōsha,* or *judōshū* in the plural, are their philosophers. They do not actually practice a religion but seek perfection and the greatest good in the contentment of the mind resulting from a virtuous and unblemished life and conduct. They believe in only secular punishment and reward, the consequence of virtue and vice. Thus one ought by necessity practice virtue as nature has given birth to us to lead the just life of people, as opposed to dumb animals.

Their founder, the first whose teaching was made public, was the famous Kōshi,[1] born in China 2,238 years ago counting from this fifth year of Genroku, or the 1,692nd year after Christ. He used moral teachings to instruct his disciples in the greatest good and was the first to describe the *Shōgaku,* or book of living ethically,[2] inflicting great damage on the opposing sect of Rōshi, flourishing at the time. After him this sect was continued by the much-praised teacher Mōshi,[3] who established his philosophical Shisho, or Four Books,[4] in this country. Up to this day they have their adherents in all countries where the characters of their writing system are understood.

Their moral philosophy consists of five articles, which they call *jin, gi, rei, chi, shin. Jin* teaches ethical living (consequently *jinsha,* virtuous person); *gi,* law and concern for justice; *rei,* politeness and civil behavior; *chi,* practical philosophy, politics, political judgment;[5] *shin* concerns man's conscience and sincerity of heart.

They do not believe in the transmigration of souls but in a universal soul, or a force common to the entire world, which absorbs the souls of the dead, like the ocean takes back all water, and in the generation of matter permits them to depart again without differentiation. They associate this world soul, or universal nature, with the godhead and endow it with the attributes of the prime being. They use the word *ten,* heaven, or nature, in the actions and fortunes of life, thanking heaven or nature for their food. I have spoken to others who conceded an intellect or perfect incorporeal being as the governing agent, but not as the originator of nature. As the highest creation of nature it is produced by *in* and *yō,* that is, from the action of heaven and receptivity of the earth, the principles of generation and corruption. In this fashion they also accept other forces as spiritual and believe that the world is eternal and that men and animals were produced from the *in yō* of heaven and the five elements.

They have neither temple nor gods, but follow the traditions of their forefathers in observing the memory of and commemorating their dead friends. They venerate their dead friends' *byōsho,* or memorial tablet, according to the customs of their forefathers and in the fashion of other believers by placing meat in front of it, lighting candles, and bowing to the ground (as if they were alive). They celebrate their memory monthly and annually and prepare themselves three days in advance by abstaining from sexual intercourse and all sinful matter, cleaning their body, and putting on new clothes. All this they do as a human gesture, prompted by their grateful and virtuous heart. The body of the dead is kept for three days above ground and placed into a European-style coffin, flat on the back, but the head is raised a little. Presumably to prevent decomposition they sometimes also cover the body with spices and scented herbs. Then they accompany it to the place of burial, where they bury the body in the soil without prior cremation.

Suicide is not only permitted in this sect but is considered an extraordinary act of bravery when committed to preempt the enemy or a shameful death.

These atheistic philosophers will only perform heathen celebrations or special duties for the gods out of common politeness. Instead they strive for virtue, a clean conscience, and honorable behavior in accordance with the teaching of Seneca or our Ten Commandments. Thus they are also capable of looking favorably at the Christian teaching and as a result have come under great suspicion. According to the new laws, which came into effect with the banishment of the Christians, they must, against their will, keep in their houses the image of a god or mount, or paste up, the characters of the name of a god, with a pot of flowers and an incense burner placed in front of it.[6] Generally they chose Kannon or Amida, whom, according to the custom of the country, they assign a place behind the hearth. Of their own free will they may have a picture of Kōshi in public places of learning or, in their own homes, the *byōsho* of their parents with the posthumous name of, or characters for, a learned man. In the past this now-suspicious sect comprised the greater part of the population and practically held a monopoly on the sciences and the liberal arts. But after the martyrdom of the Christians, their numbers decreased yearly and their books were brought into disrepute, even though those books had been valued by all other believers no less than we do the instructive works of Seneca, Plato, and other heathens.

Some thirty years ago it came to pass that the Lord of Bizen, Inaba,[7] an excellent *judōshi* and patron of the liberal arts, attempted to popularize once again in his fief this sect and its stoic manner of living. He founded an academy, appointed learned men and teachers from all parts of the country, and paid them handsomely. Gaining greater understanding and prompted by the example of their superiors, the people no longer wanted to believe in the incomprehensible revelations and fantastic tales or to continue supporting the ignorant rabble of priests, who mostly depended for their living on alms. Consequently these gangs (with which the whole country is packed) nearly died of starvation in this fief. But both the emperor and the shogun were so angered about this matter that they were about to deprive this honest patriot of his inherited fief and would have done so had he not taken the precaution of retiring in favor of his son[8] to prevent his family from falling out of favor. His son, who has governed ever since, demonstrates with his stoic conduct that he is still following his father's path.[9] I want to demonstrate this with only one example, which happened during my time in Japan. Although it will add nothing to the topic, it may serve as an amusing note to end on.

At *shōgatsu*, or New Year's Day, the lord's courtiers and their expensively adorned ladies came to congratulate him and join in the feast according to the custom of the country. Among other presents, he received a pair of peafowls. Everybody was amazed and amused at the sight of these foreign birds. The lord asked them to apply their judgment and guess which of the two was the male and which the female. Out of respect for the ladies, the gentlemen one by one declared the more beautiful to be the female. Their wives, on the contrary, judged the more beautiful to be the male bird. "You are right," replied the lord. "Even nature wants the male to be the better dressed, and I fail to understand how a woman can dress more elegantly than her husband, who has to earn the money for her." An excellent New Year's lecture from a pagan lord!

Book 4

Chapter 1

The Situation of the City of Nagasaki

Gokasho

The *gokasho,* the five most important ports and commercial cities of this empire, are part of the shogunal domains. They consist of Miyako in the province of Yamashiro, Edo in Musashi, Osaka in Settsu, Sakai in Izumi, and Nagasaki in Hizen. Four of them are situated on the large island of Nippon, enjoy fertile soil, domestic maritime commerce, and local manufacture and are blessed with some rich citizens. Moreover, the crowds of aristocratic retinues and common people, constantly passing through their streets, permit them to provide a livelihood also for many other towns.

Nagasaki

However, the last-mentioned of these cities lies among the rugged mountains and the bad soil in the westernmost part of the island of Kyushu. Situated in the most distant corner of populous Nippon, the city is not within easy reach of local food supplies and is now also practically barred from freely importing and obtaining goods from the foreigners. Consequently the city has few merchants, innkeepers, storekeepers, artisans, landlords, or rich people, but consists mainly of common citizens and day laborers, who are able to earn a living by the strength of their arms. But on account of its convenient and sheltered harbor, the city serves as point of arrival for those foreign ships and foreigners who are permitted to land and sell their legally imported goods to Japanese merchants or agents arriving at certain times from various other cities and districts. Moreover, at the time of the last massacre and extermination of the Christians in the year of Christ 1638, the new laws concerning the treatment of foreigners determined with all severity that no stranger, even if a victim of misfortune, may be taken in at any other place, but must be delivered to this city.

Consequently the two nations that are tolerated, namely, the Chinese, or those who go under that name, and the Dutch, cannot land anywhere but in this harbor. If the dangers of an unavoidable storm make it necessary to anchor elsewhere to save vessel and life, they must provide convincing proof of this fact as soon as they are taken to this city.

Harbor

The harbor begins narrow and shallow to the north of the city, with waters running off the muddy soil at low tide and several rivers flowing in from the mountains. At the place where the harbor reaches the city, it has a considerable width of about half a mile and a depth of five or six fathoms. At this point the shoreline turns, and the harbor, just over a quarter-mile wide, runs southwest for a mile between the mountains of the mainland up to the first island or submerged mountain, Takayama or Takaboko. The name means bamboo, pike, or tall mountain.[1] Generally all ships awaiting departure cast anchor here. It is called Papenberg by the Dutch on account of a fantastic tale about some Roman Catholic priests falling headlong off the island. If it were not for some shallow reefs hindering passage, it would be possible to reach the open sea from here within a mile. As it is, vessels have to take a longer route sailing westward between various small islands, keeping close to the mainland on the right until the harbor slowly opens into the sea. The harbor has a number of water gates to allow for the mounting of cannons (which do not exist). Also on each side of the harbor, about half a mile from the city, is an open, unfortified guard station; both have seven hundred men. They also supply personnel for the rowing boats anchored close by and a daily guard ship in the harbor. Not far from the Papenberg, which is considered the beginning of the actual harbor, is an island where in 1640 the last Portuguese ship from Macao was burned with all its fittings.[2] The island has been designated to serve for similar events in the future, and therefore the Japanese call it "location for the burning of molesting ships."

Rarely does one see fewer than fifty Japanese barges and some hundred small fishing boats or other craft in this harbor. Also, except for the few winter months, there are hardly ever fewer than thirty foreign ships at anchor. Few Dutch vessels stay any length of time, at the most three months during the autumn, when the seasonal west winds change to northeast for an easy departure. Their anchorage is within the area of the shogunal guards, at the end of the bay, below the city, close by, or at a distance of a musket shot. There they anchor in soil of clay, in six fathoms of water at high tide, which is reduced by one and a half fathoms at low tide.

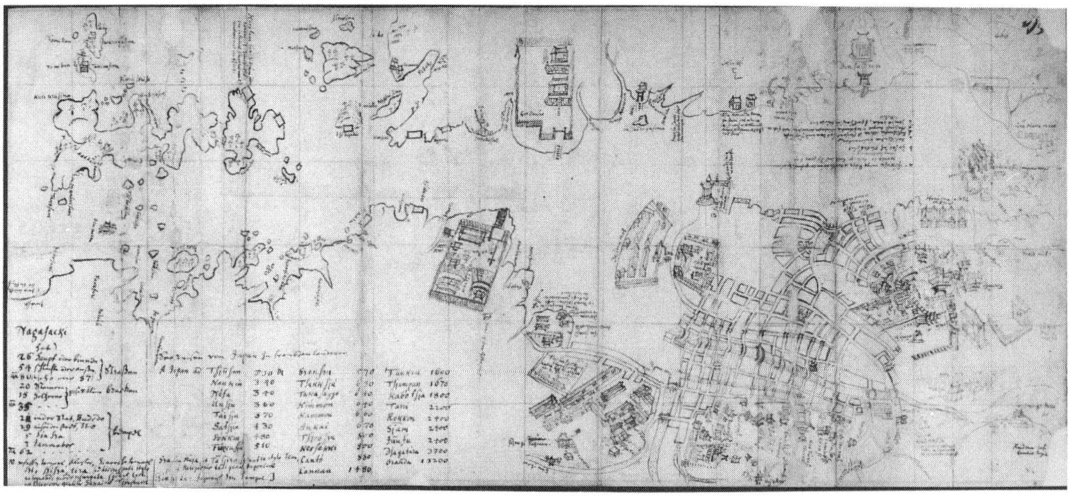

Kaempfer's map of Nagasaki, copied from a Japanese map. (Courtesy of the British Library, Sloane 3060, folio 466)

Position

The city lies at a latitude of 32.36 and longitude of about 151 degrees and is situated virtually at the end and at the widest section of the above-mentioned bay. Because the bay turns to the north, the city has a curved shoreline, and the break in the mountain chain toward the east provides a small valley or base for the city, practically the shape of a triangular half-moon. Thus its length along the shoreline is some three-quarters of a mile, and its width is not much less, since the long main street runs into the valley. The surrounding mountains are not particularly high but quite steep, green, and pleasant everywhere. The slopes are bedecked with greenery and temples rising high above the city and are also covered with innumerable graves, which jut out, one above the other, up to the very top. Other mountains are cultivated up to the peak. All of this provides an amusing and exotic sight. The closest settlements of some size and importance are: toward the southwest, the above-mentioned small town of Fukabori at a distance of five Japanese nautical miles or two short German miles from Nagasaki. It has a small castle and the residence of a *bugyō* who administers the village and its lands in the interest of his hereditary master, the lord of Hizen. The district produces a large amount of firewood and has an income of nearly 30,000 *koku,* even though it is described only as a fief of 10,000 *koku* in the country's register. There is a large pond or lake surrounded by many trees, in which one never detects a single leaf or any dirt. The locals attribute this to the purity of the lake's spirit and therefore out of deference do not like to fish in it. To the north of Nagasaki is the baronial residence and city of Ōmura, situated on the bay and in the district of the same name. A few miles to the east, along the river running into Shimabara Bay, is the small city of Isahaya belonging to the lord of Hizen.

Like most Japanese cities, Nagasaki is open, unfortified, lacking castle, rampart, wall, or moat. Its streets are fairly narrow and winding and, owing to the uneven terrain of the nearby mountains, gently climbing until they come to an end on the slopes close to the temples. Three fresh-water rivers run through the city, the largest and central one running through the eastern valley. All three descend from the mountains, but the little water they carry is sufficient only to irrigate a few rice paddies and operate some tired mills. Yet when there is a downpour, the rivers' waters rise so quickly that they may wash away houses.

Name

The city carries the name of its former hereditary lords, who owned this district with its annual income of 3,000 *koku.* The line began with the man who first brought this area under cultivation, Nagasaki Kotarō, and ended with the twelfth descendant, Nagasaki Jinzaemon. Their hereditary residence is marked by stone ruins at the peak of the mountain behind the city. With the extinction of this family three hundred years ago, the area fell to the baronial house of Ōmura.[3] At that time the site of today's city was occupied by no more than a wretched fishing village and a few fields called only by the name of its harbor, Fuka e, or Iri e, which means long bay, to distinguish it from the town at the head of the harbor still called Fukabori, meaning long pond.[4] Under the care of the new owner and with its own new name, the village grew slowly into a sizable town.

In the meantime, the Portuguese had arrived in Japan. Like the Chinese, they entered Japanese harbors as they pleased and settled in various locations on Saikoku, especially in the provinces of Bungo and Hizen. In the latter they first settled in a village called Fukuda belonging to Ōmura, situated to the left before the entrance of the harbor of Hirado and at a distance of six Japanese nautical miles, or two long German miles, from and on the same shoreline as that city, an area rich in wood. Afterward they also settled in the above-mentioned Fukabori, all the while attempting to promote the Christian faith no less than their trade. This combination (in addition to common elements with the Japanese in their inborn character and disposition) won them the hearts of many commoners as well as those of some of the grandees. The domain lord of Ōmura had already converted to the Roman Catholic faith when he persuaded the Portuguese to settle also here in Nagasaki. This town had already increased to twenty-three streets, and what is now mostly the northern part of the city called *uchi machi,* and now consists of twenty-six streets, he gave to the foreigners as their very own property for the promotion of their nation, trade, and religious worship. This was supposedly done solely for the love of Christ and for the promotion of His church. Or perhaps also because he considered this harbor convenient for the new trade and the trade desirable for his fief. The latter aim was achieved with no less success than the former (even though both ended badly), and this success persuaded also the Chinese merchant vessels to anchor in this harbor and induced many people from a variety of Japanese provinces, cities, and villages to settle here in search of a livelihood. New streets were named after the homes of the settlers, such as Bungo machi, Edo machi, Kabashima machi, Hirado machi, Ōmura machi, Shimabara machi, and so forth. Others carry the proper name of a *bun,*[5] that is to say, one of the first arrivals in this colony, because he financed the street out of his own means. In a short time the village grew into a prosperous and populous trading port which now boasts eighty-seven heavily built-up and densely settled streets.

After the city had gained such prosperity, Taikō,[6] the ruler at that time, severely admonished the lord of Ōmura, expressing his resentment that such an important location had been handed over to the foreigners, and in despair over this unwise conduct felt compelled to annex the same. The arrogant behavior of the Portuguese added fuel to the fire. With their easy success it was painful for them to wear the mantle of humility they had adopted earlier when dealing with the grandees of the empire, and they showed their true colors too early. An old Japanese told me about the following incident, which supposedly tipped the scales in incurring the ruler's displeasure. Formerly, when the above-mentioned ruler used Hakata for his residence, as a convenient location for his military stratagems against Korea, it happened, as so often before, that a Portuguese cleric met one of the nation's, or ruler's, councilors traveling to or from court, and that the priest, without stopping and paying the customary respect, haughtily had himself carried past.

In the heat of anger, the councilor complained bitterly to the ruler about this piece of bravado and the unbearable arrogance and behavior of that nation. The ruler was all the more inclined to condemn the Portuguese as it was against his long-term plans to permit these foreign conquerors of people's minds to have so much wealth at their disposal, allowing them to exert a negative influence on his subjects in the future. Either the ruler was truly displeased by their insolence or he considered the increase and devotion of the Christians harmful to his future plans. In any case, he used the complaint as a cause and opportunity to give these proud strangers a first taste of his displeasure by taking their city and confiscating from their patron, the lord of Ōmura, the attached lands with an income of 3,000 *koku,* for his own domain.

Nagasaki (which for a more pleasant sound many pronounce, but do not write, Nangasaki) is divided into two parts. The first part, *uchi machi,* the inner or old city, consists of twenty-six *chō,* or streets, running in all directions, just as they were originally built. The other part, *soto machi,* or outside city, has sixty-one wards, making a total of eighty-seven.

Some of the most important and public buildings of this city are:

Warships

Some of the ruler's so-called *funagura.* These are five wooden buildings at the northern edge of the city built on low ground at the shore, in which three war junks with their armory are kept, ready to be lowered into the water in case of an incident.

Munition Cellar

The *ensho gura,* or munition store, is on the opposite shore. For greater safety a munition cellar has been dug into the hill.

Governors' Residences

The two residences of the governors-in-residence occupy a plot of considerable width at the end and above other streets. They contain fine houses of ordinary height, with heavy gates at the front courtyard. The newly arrived third governor lives in a temple on Tateyama until the departing governor hands over his quarters when he leaves.

Residences of the Domain Lords

In addition there are about twenty houses and plots belonging to all the daimyo and many of the *shōmyō,* that is, the large and lesser domain lords of the whole of Kyushu (as this

Saikoku or western land, that is, the island on which Nagasaki is situated, is called). Some of the most noble men of their domains, or courts, are always in residence to attend to their lord's duties should an unusual incident occur; for as superintendents the domain lords have to answer for all occurrences in this city. These houses also serve as the lord's residence when he is present.

Deshima

The foreigners live outside the city in two fortified compounds, sealed off and guarded like thieves. The Dutch are situated near the city on an island built in the harbor on a cliff jutting out from the ocean floor, called the island of Deshima, that is, De Island.

Yakuen

The Chinese, and those who go under that name, namely, the people of neighboring nations practicing the same religion, live on an enclosed hill beyond the southern extremity of the city. On account of its former status, the place is known as Yakuen, medicine garden. It is also called Jūzenji, the name of the guard's (or surveyor's) living quarters situated further up on the same hill.

Sixty-Two Temples

There are sixty-two temples in and outside the city, consisting of five *jinja,* shrines to the native spirits and gods; seven temples of the *yamabushi,* or mountain priests; and fifty *tera,* temples to the foreign gods. Of these, twenty-one are located within the city and twenty-nine near or outside the city on the slopes of the hills, reached by flights of stone steps. Though apparently built for religious devotion, they serve no less for public pleasure. With their delightful rooms, verandas, entrances, and other courtyards filled with greenery, their elevated position and magnificent view, they are most suitable for this purpose. They are also the finest buildings of the whole city. Because of their great number, it is impossible to describe them within the limits of this chapter, and we will deal with them separately.

The Prostitutes' Quarter

According to the custom of this country, we will pass from the temples to the *keiseimachi,* or prostitutes' quarter. For politeness' sake it is also called *maruyama,* after the name of the hill on which it is located, and it is frequented no less than the temples. This quarter makes up the southernmost part of the city, and according to Japanese calculation consists of two streets, but to our way of counting, of several streets. It is situated on the slope of a hill and includes the finest houses of the commoners' city, occupied by no one else but the keepers of this profession. Except for a smaller one in Chikuzen, the quarter is the only one on Saikoku where the poor of this island (which, except for Miyako, produces the most beautiful people of Japan) can secure a living for their pretty daughters. On account of the good living that can be earned from the foreigners and locals (the most debauched of all cities), the quarter is well supplied and, next to that of Miyako, is considered the most famous in the country. The girls are traded for a sum of money when still children for a certain number of years (ten, twenty). A well-to-do brothel keeper keeps seven to thirty girls, old and young, under the same roof in separate rooms and daily has them assiduously instructed in dancing, playing instruments, writing letters, and other skills becoming to this sex and appropriate to a life of luxury. The youngest are both students and servants to the oldest and most experienced. As the girls improve in these arts and in good deportment in company, and profit their keeper by being much in demand and frequently asked out, he also awards them higher ranks and gives them better accommodation. Also the fee the keeper charges to their admirers increases. For an elegant affair of one night the price starts from two mace and goes up two *bu,* the highest permissible by law. One of the lowliest, either someone considered past service or condemned to this job for some crime, has to keep the evening and night watch in a specially designated anteroom of the house and for one mace light a candle for passersby. If these prostitutes marry honest people, they pass as honest women among the commoners, since they are not responsible for their profession and furthermore have been well educated. The brothel keepers, on the contrary, however rich they may be, cannot pass as and associate with honest people. They are called by the derogatory and thought-provoking term *kutsuwa,* meaning "horse bit,"[7] and are considered to be subhuman, of the same status as the *eta,* or leather tanners, who are the executioners and knackers in this country. They live next to the gallows, away from honest people. Consequently the brothel keepers must bear the burden of making their male servants or day laborers available to execute the courts' punishment and lend them to the *eta.*

Prison Compound

It seems appropriate to pass from the prostitutes' quarter to *gokuya,* or hell, also called *rōya,* or cage. By that is meant the prison compound, situated in the middle of the city in a sloping side street. It consists of many different huts and separate apartments so that all may be accommodated in accordance with what they deserve. In addition to local criminals, all those caught or accused of smuggling foreign goods or practicing the Christian religion are imprisoned here. Consequently this hell often houses more than a hundred, and even after those sent to their death have been flushed out, there are never fewer than fifty. The compound contains a house of torture, a court building where the less guilty are secretly executed, a kitchen, an inn, a house for strolling, and a *tame*[8] and provides different accommodations for those condemned to death, suspects, and ordinary prisoners with life sentences. The latter are the so-called *bungo sō*,[9] that is, the rabble from Bungo. By that they mean the Christians, of whom they still now keep fifty souls imprisoned here, counting wives and children. Occasionally still more arrive (in 1688 a further three people). They do not know anything about the Christian faith except the name of our true savior, but much prefer to die in their simple belief than to gain their freedom, as they could, by renouncing their redeemer. In September of this ninety-second year it happened for the first time that three people sent some money to the temple of Amida for a requiem on the anniversary of their friends' death. The priests, however, did not want to proceed without asking the governors, and they, in turn, thought it wise to first ask for guidance from the shogunal court. Because of their simplemindedness, and since such severity is no longer required, they are spared execution and have to spend the rest of their lives in this temporal hell on very poor food and water. They will never leave this place except once every two months when they are taken to the governors, where they are examined more out of habit than harshness and following old customs are pressed to name other Christians. Each year they are granted the following recreation: twice they are let out individually to have themselves burned with moxa to guard against pain, as is the custom in this country; six times they are permitted to wash themselves in the *tame* of the prison courtyard, and six times they are free to stretch their legs in a large house in the courtyard constructed for this purpose. To pass their spare, wretched time, they produce a poor hemp yarn that is used for the edging of floor mats. Because they are not permitted any iron, they sew their clothes with bamboo needles. Some also know how to knit socks and other bits and pieces with them. When they do not spend the money earned to have refreshments bought for themselves, they give it to their wives and children, who are kept away in different cells. They also know how to make a drink called *amasake*, that is, sweet rice wine, by fermenting overnight the rice left over from their daily ration. Its sweetness makes it a change and a delicacy. Some occasionally receive clothes from their friends in Bungo, who by now are spared (since there are so few of them and since they are simpleminded and Christians only in name). But the clothes have to pass through many hands and strict censure. Also the governors present them annually with new, poor-quality mats to sleep on. A little while ago some were, moreover, permitted to use a *kogatana*, or small knife.

Thirty-Five Bridges

Among the public buildings we must also mention the bridges of the city. There are twenty stone and fifteen wooden bridges, altogether thirty-five, some big, some small, all solid, but ordinary structures and not particularly memorable.

Streets

The streets of the city are generally winding, untidy, and dirty. Some have smelly gutters, are narrow and on uneven, hilly ground, and therefore run up and down. Others are situated on higher or lower levels, so that they can be reached only by flights of stone steps. All are heavily built up. Each street is divided from the next by two wooden gates, which are closed when trouble is anticipated.

Fire Extinction

Each ward has also a *kaji dōgu,*[10] that is, a place where everything necessary to extinguish fires is located, such as a dug-out well, buckets, fire axes, and straw brushes to extinguish the fire. The ladder is kept by the ward elder. It should be noted that the streets are divided neither at regular intervals nor strictly according to the geometric length of a Japanese *chō* or field path of sixty *ken* or fathom, from which they derive their name. The line is drawn wherever the gates can be conveniently placed so that they roughly have the length of one *chō* and as many neighboring houses as can be governed by one ward elder. Therefore they rarely contain more than sixty or fewer than thirty houses.

Houses of the Commoners

The houses of common citizens and residents are of poor structure, small and low. They either have no attic at all or one that is low and practically useless. The roof is covered with pine chips, generally secured only by other chips placed across. Like all other houses in this country, they are constructed of wood and clay walls. Inside, the walls are nicely hung with colored paper, and the floors are neatly spread with thickly padded woven rush mats. Further, they are divided into separate rooms by papered sliding windows. They lack chairs or benches and have only as many household items as are essential for daily cooking. At the back there is merely a narrow space for one's private business, which, however poor, does contain some little plants, carefully grown to provide a focus of interest for the eyes. The houses of people of distinction, the rich, and those handling foreign trade rise to two stories, are spacious, and are partly built in Chinese style with a large building with bare floor at the entrance and a garden at the back.

Inhabitants

The city has a great number of shopkeepers, craftsmen, artisans, brewers, servants to those conducting the Chinese and Dutch trade, and in addition many poor people and beggars, who are more frequent and brazen here than elsewhere.

A great many of the beggars are *kanjin bōzu* and *kanjin bikuni,* mendicant monks and beggar women. One single street called *yawata machi,* or *hachiman machi,* has more than one hundred. They are poor people with shaven heads who have opted for the devoted, chaste life of the clergy, wearing the black habit of the priesthood to more honestly and easily obtain donations when they wander through the city with their prayer beads or rosaries, pictures, little bell, and other signs of devotion. Some go to a temple to have their head shaved and have themselves consecrated with a few prayers. This is the custom with important and rich old people when embarking on a religious life of seclusion in their own houses. About six times monthly, the priests of the Chinese and other Zen monasteries also send out some of their brothers to beg. This is not necessarily done because of poverty but rather to fulfill their monastic vows to follow the example of the original founder, Shaka.

We should also count the dogs among the inhabitants, as they are maintained like citizens, but here not as carefully as in other cities, especially other shogunal cities. The streets are full of these rascals, which move neither for horses nor for people. If they harm people or deserve to die, only the executioner may kill them on command from high authority. Sick dogs, or those incapacitated by age, are maintained by each street in cages or huts. When the dogs die, they are carried up the mountains and buried no less carefully than people. This is done on the superstitious command of the shogun, who was born under the symbol of the dog, or the year of the dog, and consequently esteems them no less than Emperor Augustus did the ibex. A certain farmer laboriously carrying his dead dog up the hill complained to his neighbor about the year of birth of the shogun, which was responsible for his pains. The other replied: Oh my friend, don't let's complain. If he were born in the year of the horse, our load would be much heavier![11]

Manufactured Goods

Manufactured goods are poorer yet more expensive here than elsewhere (especially for foreigners). However, gold and silver, and items made out of *sōwaas,*[12] which is little used by the locals and mainly by foreigners, are crafted and mined in much better quality here than elsewhere and more precious than anywhere else in the world.

As for food and drink: the soil produces little rice (the daily bread of Asia), and to feed the population it has to be brought from elsewhere, such as Hizen, Higo, Chikugo, Amakusa, or the northern provinces. Garden fruits, some edible herbs and roots, firewood, as well as game and domestic poultry are sufficiently supplied by the surrounding mountains and nearby villages. Shell fish and other fish are overabundantly supplied by this bay and its shores. The rivers of the city produce clear drinking water for every-day use. *Sake,* or the local rice wine (not as good here as elsewhere), is too strong and not used as a daily drink in Japan. A light and much-praised drinking water springs from the crest of the local mountain, Tate. Another well to the east of the harbor close to the city supplies the ships. Even though everything is kept clean and healthy (as everywhere else in Japan), the water tends to produce colic, which the locals also say of *sake,* when drunk cold and in great quantity.

Noise

There is constant noise. During the day this comes from wandering salesmen, advertising their edible and other wares, from day laborers, cheering themselves up with certain sounds when lifting and carrying, and from the oarsmen in the harbor, who measure their progress by the beat of certain noises or songs. At night the sound of the watchmen beating two pieces of wood against each other comes at short intervals from the guard boats in the harbor and the streets of the city as they proclaim their watchfulness and the hours of the night with this loud, annoying clatter. The Chinese contribute to the noise with drums and cymbals accompanying their nightly ceremony of lighting pieces of gold paper and throwing them into the sea as sacrifice to their deity, Maso Bosa, and when they take him to and from the temple.[13] Above all, however, there is the wailing of *namanda* at a high pitch and in complete disorder to the accompaniment of a small bell, punctuated by screams to the point of fainting from the officiating priests and friends, at the house of a deceased after the soul has left the body of the sick and at certain days of remembrance. *Namanda* is a short, abbreviated little prayer consisting of the words *namu amida butsu*. This represents a prayer of mercy to their revered god Amida, the supreme judge of the souls of the deceased, to obtain grace for the soul of the person who has just died. Equal clamor comes from the *nen butsu kō,* brotherhoods or voluntary prayer associations of devout neighbors, friends, and acquaintances meeting alternately in one of the houses for a daily hour of prayer in the morning or, more often, in the evening to intone the *namanda* in a similar fashion as a precaution and the salvation of their own souls.

Chapter 2
The Government of Nagasaki

All shogunal cities have two governors or magistrates each, addressed by their subjects by the more common name of *tono sama*, "highest lord" or "prince," who annually take it in turn to administer the city while the other resides at Edo, the residence of the ruler. This city, however, was given a third magistrate in 1688 as a precautionary measure, considered necessary to permit closer attention to the arrival of foreigners and to ensure the safety of this world-renowned port. Consequently there are always two attending to the administration in monthly rotation, while a third is relieved after two years by a new arrival; he travels up to court again, where he attends upon the high state councilors with gifts, presents the written record of his administration, and replies orally to questions about the cause of and reasons for various incidents. No less important are his personal calls to the private mansions of the councilors and the ruler's favorites to pay the customary compliments upon arrival and to present costly tokens of his respect in return for favors shown and as a sign of submission. The rest of his time is carefully spent obtaining or rekindling the patronage of those who are able to determine whether fortune will smile upon him or not.

He remains at Edo for just over six months, during which time he may enjoy the company of his dear family. After he has received his orders in an open session of the state council and has taken his leave from each member individually, he must leave his family again for a considerable length of time. In the meantime neither he, his nobles, or servants may permit a woman to cross the threshold of his residence here, on pain of incurring the shogun's displeasure. It is considered appropriate that the slightest violation of the shogun's laws results in no lesser punishment than self-immolation, banishment, or lifelong imprisonment, as well as the ruin of the culprit's family.

To the great pleasure of the shogun, these three gentlemen have used their brains to throttle foreign trade to the advantage of the citizens and disadvantage of the foreigners to a point where the latter still just consider it advantageous to remain in the country. As a reward for their excellent service, they were crowned with the honor of receiving the country's knightly title of *kami.* Two have just been honored with this title on their recent journey to the shogunal court, while the third is expecting to receive it on his next visit. The actual meaning of *kami* is all-powerful, worshipful spirit, or an immortal soul, superior and venerable beyond those of ordinary men. The title is supposed to indicate that the shogun wants the man in question to be revered like a god. Generally the name of a certain piece of land is added to the title, which gives it even greater distinction.[1]

These governors are:

Kawaguchi Genzaemon, who has now made the customary change in his personal name but kept that of his family to become Kawaguchi Settsu no Kami.[2] The income of his hereditary fief is 4,700 *koku*. He is a well-built man of fifty, cunning as a fox, and the enemy of all Dutchmen. As administrator he is harsh and unreasonable, as courtier gentle and jovial.

Yamaoka Jūbei, now Yamaoka Tsushima no Kami. This gentleman previously served as marshal or chief constable, ridding Edo of thieves.[3] He and his colleagues personally eliminated more than one thousand thieves, which earned him his post in this administration. The income from his own fief is 2,000 *koku*. He is a gentleman of sixty, of short stature, very humble, righteous, and benevolent, especially as regards his poorer subjects and commoners. Last year when leaving for Edo, he so generously distributed among them all his incidental benefits that some respectable but poor citizens received more than one hundred taels.[4] Either he hopes to make up for the courtly accomplishments of his colleagues with such unsophisticated measures, or such great deeds are the genuine expression of a generous temperament. Whatever the case, he is, nevertheless, still so much accustomed to the practices of his former position that he executes the servants of his mansion without much ado for the slightest act of dishonesty.

Miyagi Tonomo,[5] a good-looking, generous gentleman of noble birth, the same age as the above, with an income of 4,000 *koku* and still without a title.

The magistrate's salary is low. Each receives only 1,500 to 2,000 *koku* of rice, which when sold comes to about 7,000 to 10,000 taels (owing to fluctuations in the price of rice). The so-called incidentals are so high, however, that they would accumulate riches within a few years if these were not used for offerings to the shogun and his court.

Ten *Yoriki*, Thirty *Dōshin*

From the above-mentioned shogunal salary, each governor maintains the staff appropriate to his rank, consisting of ten *yoriki,* people of high aristocratic birth with both military and government functions, and thirty *dōshin,* or military and government officials from the lower aristocracy. They are assigned to him by the shogun, the latter mainly to execute orders, the former also to advise. Previously they were commissioned and directly paid by the shogun, as they are in other shogunal cities. Since 1688, however, they are employed and maintained by the governors themselves. This change was made at the urgent request of the latter, who convincingly showed that they unreasonably resisted the governors' most productive plans simply to demonstrate their authority as *hatamoto* (those standing next to the flag, designating the shogun's independent servants), often impeding the execution of general administrative measures. To distinguish them from hereditary followers (or the military) of the shogun and the territorial lords, they actually should be designated by a lesser title such as *kyūnin shū* for the higher and *shita yaku* for the lower officers; they are called *yoriki* and *dōshin* only by the commoners or to indicate respect. For this reason, the *yoriki* are also honored with the name of *bugyō,* a title that, properly speaking, may be used only temporarily when accompanied by an official lance bearer (to which he has no right on the basis of his own rank) as an indication that he is exercising his lord's power and authority. Court etiquette determines that accompaniment by official lance bearers is permitted only to high-ranking servants of the shogun or commissioned officials.

Here, as throughout the country, the *yoriki*'s duties consist of serving their master with advice and common sense and executing their duties outside the mansion and on errands: acting as military officers in military engagements and as government officials at judicial inquiries and executions, during official missions, and in all other important business where their lord's authority must be represented. They are accompanied by various *dōshin,* guards, government orderlies, and others whose service they may require during their mission. But here they also have to perform lower duties not becoming their aristocratic military rank, such as supervising and guarding the foreigners, storage and sale of the latter's goods, clearing and loading vessels, and so forth. They are not happy about this, and the better nobles will not serve with the Nagasaki governors as, moreover, they are solely dependent upon the governor's favors and badly paid out of the latter's own purse. They differ in rank and conditions determined by the governors. The most important among the local ones are the *kirishitan bugyō,* the inquisitors or public prosecutors of the Christians. Their conditions are extremely poor: in addition to food and an annual formal robe, some receive no more than one hundred taels. With this sum it is impossible to maintain the three servants required by a *yoriki:* a lance bearer, a guardian of the large sword, and a shoe or sandal bearer, let alone their own families. Consequently if they are commissioned, they often use the governor's domestic servants to play these parts and sometimes stay very briefly in the job.

Dōshin

The *dōshin* are the *yoriki*'s helpers and assistants. They are also used as the governor's representatives in less important matters, as commander of the guards on boats, junks, convoys, and guard barges, and as ordinary soldiers, attacking the enemy in person. Finally they are used as constables, for which purpose they always carry a thin, strong rope. Apparently their salary, in addition to board, is no more than fifty taels, out of which they still have to maintain a servant.

Karō

In rank above the *yoriki* are a few *karō,* or elders, consisting of two or three people. As the governor's highest servants and regents, they attempt to sort out by themselves or, as the case may be, with the help of the *yoriki,* all domestic matters as well as some less important external and public incidents, so that their lord may not be troubled by them. They also serve as secretaries on privy councils and as commissioners in important matters. They are always chosen by the lord himself from his oldest, most hardworking and most loyal servants or from among the blood brothers of someone who has died, exhibiting the same qualities as the deceased. Frequently the son succeeds to the father's position.

Lesser Servants

Below the *yoriki* are other personal servants, such as *koshō,* courtiers keeping the lord informed and permitted to enter his personal chamber to supply him with all his needs, *chūgoshō,*[6] pages and valets, as well as some *yūhitsu,* copyists and scribes, in addition to lesser domestic servants and kitchen-hands.

The Pattern of the Local Court

The above make up the entourage of a governor, which at his residence is arranged in the following pattern and order:

At the outer gate in an open room within the courtyard is a guard of *dōshin,* manned in rotation so that there are constantly five or six men seated to attend the door. In addition to the two weapons carried at their side, they are armed with a heavy, strong staff, made out of solid so-called iron-wood, like a carrying pole. They watch all servants entering or leaving, who have to take a marked, square, wooden disk on departure and hand it back on their return, so that the guard constantly knows the number of people in the mansion. They close the gate at seven o'clock Japanese time, which is approximately four o'clock according to ours. After that, no common servants may leave or enter the mansion on their own business or without an express order. Occasionally, when a high-ranking visitor is expected, the number of guards is increased by two to four men, who stand outside the gate presenting their staffs.

Genkan Ban

After that comes the large official and main guard, called *genkan ban,* which is reached by crossing the outer courtyard and is situated in the first open room of the outer mansion, in front of the building's large door, generally reached by three steps. The guards are arranged in a row, their faces turned toward the door, or the outer courtyard. It is manned by *yoriki,* who are obliged to take turns and sit through the hours of their guard duty. For greater prestige, numbers can be increased by unemployed *karō, koshō,* and *chūgoshō.* The latter two are obliged to take their place among the *yoriki*. Any one person from the *genkan ban* may sit at the *genkan chō,* or guard register, and, as is the custom at all noble mansions in this country, note all arrivals and departures throughout the day for the information of their master, should he wish to consult the register in the evening.

Nengyōji Beya

At the side of the *genkan ban* is the *nengyōji beya,* a small room that is the seat of the city's messengers. Four people take turns so that two are always present at the mansion of the presiding governor to attend upon him in the name of the city's mayor, in case he has orders concerning the citizens. The citizens consider it their duty to provide this service so that their own needs may be taken care of and also provide day laborers, artisans, and others. They divide all such duties among themselves proportionally and perform them voluntarily; as soon as a request is made, it is quickly taken care of without the slightest payment.

When the governor leaves the mansion, his official entourage consists of a spare horse led by the reins and the *norimono,* or palanquin, in which he is carried, with four *kachi,* or foot soldiers, in front and four of his most important *chūgoshō,* or valets, at the side. Then following two by two are *yarimochi,* or lance bearers, as well as some of his *karō, yoriki,* and *dōshin,* together with his own and the latters' servants, and lower serfs. On their departure this procession is larger and grander, but in Edo it is much reduced, consisting only of one lance bearer at the rear and a small entourage.

The Extent of the Authority of the Governors

Not only the local civil population of the city is subject to the governors' commands and authority. All foreigners and visitors are also directly under their control, have to submit obediently to the laws and punishments of the country, rely on their discretion and the shogun's mercy for mitigation, and humbly show their gratitude. Under the name of foreigners go the servants of the Dutch company and a second group of foreign merchants, including mainland Chinese and Chinese expatriates from Tunkin, Cambodia, Siam, and other countries.

The responsibilities of the office include the direction of the foreign trade; investigations into smuggling as well as the practice of Christianity, if anything still were to happen on the latter account; arrangements for all new arrivals or vessels and strangers washed ashore by storms, which together with any newly discovered Christians have to be brought to this city from all parts of this western island; strict supervision of all foreigners and precautionary measures to prevent them from turning into a source of trouble; and finally care for the protection and safety of this ocean port.

Supervision of the Governors

The general climate of distrust and the rules of government demand that such important duties are not solely left to the good faith of the governors. Consequently the court keeps an eye on their activity by means of a local representative acting as *daikan,* or shogunal agent. Further the shogun has commissioned the territorial lords of Kyushu to act as superintendents and ordered them to keep themselves informed through their local representatives of any special occurrences, so that in case of hostile action they can move in quickly with large forces. Also, all of them could be used as a source of information, if one party or another were attempting to play a game of deception.

Interpreters

The shogun employs each year a group of interpreters of Dutch, Portuguese, the languages of Tunkin and Siam, three Chinese dialects, and several other tongues for the trade with foreign nations. In most of these languages, however, they are only able to string together broken words without distinction of gender, tense, and number following the idiosyncrasies of their own language: one would require a second set of interpreters to understand the first.

Four Guard Battalions

To guard the foreigners and ensure the safety of the harbor, four guard battalions, all different, are employed to keep watch in general and also to keep an eye on each other.

1. The great shogunal guard. This guard is supplied in annual rotation by the territorial lords of Hizen and Chikuzen by the order and in the name of the shogun. Consequently it carries the name *gobansho* and *goban dokoro,* meaning "great guard" or "shogunal guard house," and is beyond the jurisdiction of the governors. It is situated half a German mile before the city, on both sides of the mountainous coastline, Tomachi being situated on the left and Nishidomari on the right (when leaving the harbor). The guard posts have no fortifications, entrenchments, or cannons and are merely housed in wooden buildings. For decoration, the surrounding courtyard is enclosed with military awnings when ships arrive and enter the harbor, and each must be honored with a special gun salute. Together they have about seven hundred men, and when they are well-manned, each has more than five hundred men serving under a *goban gashira,* or great colonel of the guard. Very few of them are *yoriki*; some are *dōshin,* and the rest are *bushi,* or common soldiers. They keep an eye on the whole bay and also have a large guard barge near the city among the vessels so that they are present whenever an incident occurs.

2. *Funa ban,* or boat guard, consisting of eighteen *bushi,* or common soldiers, and a great number of guard barges manned by oarsmen, with which they keep watch over foreign vessels and make the nightly patrol of the harbor. As soon as a vessel enters the harbor, it is trailed by two of the guard barges, each under the command of an officially commissioned *dōshin.* As long as the ship remains in the harbor, these guard barges rotate every three Japanese hours, and on departure they follow the vessel until the open

sea is reached. The barges are maintained by the streets closest to the sea, which also have to supply the common guards or oarsmen. In turn, the inland or hinterland streets bear the civil duty of providing daily six or, if required, more coolies in the order of the houses and streets, to hold themselves available at the residences of the governors for any necessary tasks.

3. The boat guard is assisted by a third group called *mi okuri bune,* or escorting watch, because they accompany the foreign junks into the high seas after they have been left by the *funa ban.* They follow them to a point where it is unlikely that the vessels will turn back or come across the boats of the natives, which have only eight oars; they patrol the shores to stop the Chinese from landing at other locations and to capture Japanese smugglers: a frequent occurrence. They are actually whalers and are under the command of a man who receives an annual payment of three hundred taels and supervises the catching of whales at the same time. The latter is done only in winter when no foreign ships arrive and takes place along the very same shores where the object of their secondary employment is also likely to fall into their hands.

4. *Tomiban,* called "guard scanning the distance," consists of more than twenty *bushi,* or common soldiers, and still retains the name of their former number, namely, *jūninshū,* "guard of ten people." They live with their families at the southern end of the city on a large hill along the shore, from which they can watch their neighbors, the Chinese, and the houses of the Dutch. Their actual job is to watch the sea from *tomi daka,* watchtowers, on certain headlands surrounding the bay, and to keep the government informed by repeatedly sending fast messenger barges when they sight a vessel, attain certainty of its approach, and chart its progress. The seas are also scanned from a mountain near the city called *hōka san,* "jeweled flower mountain." On this mountain there is always a supply of material ready to light a bright fire if a fleet of ten or more European vessels is sighted, if the arrival of even a few Portuguese ships has been ascertained, or if sudden riots occur in parts of this island of Kyushu. But this has to be done with the advance knowledge and approval of the local government. The fire serves to inform the whole country of any incident threatening the empire, will be observed from certain mountains on Amakusa, and by means of similar fires in Higo and along the mountains of the southern shore, the signal will reach Edo in twenty-four hours.

Administration of the City by Four Mayors

The city and its inhabitants are administered under the supervision of the above-mentioned magistrates by four mayors and their subordinates in such a fashion that by annual rotation one of them carries the duties and the name of *nenban,* literally "annual watch," that is, the mayor governing this year. He has to prepare reports for the presiding magistrate, inform the latter personally of incidents causing concern, and discuss and settle special issues and those matters presenting difficulties to him and his colleagues with the magistrate's advisors, or, with their approval, submit them to the solemn judgment of the magistrate.

The Shogunal Tribunal

This shogunal tribunal hears civil lawsuits, interrogates and investigates the parties, has both sides defend their contentions in the same legal manner, and has cases argued by the above parties with reference to published case law, the government's constitution, proclamations, and judgments by famous men.[7] After judgment has been passed, appeals are impossible, but death sentences may not be executed until approved by the country's supreme council at Edo. The latter is also consulted by return courier in extraordinary, important cases concerning the country, if they permit a small delay.

Toshiyori

The above-mentioned mayors are called *toshiyori shū,* which literally and according to the characters means "elder people" because they used to be selected from among the eldest and wisest civil servants. Later, however, this process deteriorated into hereditary succession, where the son succeeds on account of his father's merits. Now it requires only the approval of the magistrates and that of the shogunal council, to whom the candidate must first personally express his gratitude for such favors. Consequently there now is an eleven-year-old boy, Takashima Gontarō, whose father, Takashima Shirō Hyōe, died last year and who now merely holds his father's title until he comes of age and can take up the position.[8] Another, a real mayor of only twenty-two, is Takagi Genzō, previously called Takagi Seiemon,[9] who five years ago had to change his childhood name and position to that of his father. Thus it is accepted that three blood relatives of the Takagi family serve as mayors and that a fourth is in charge of the surrounding country area. Previously the mayors came under the shogunal court or supreme council, wore two swords as an indication of their aristocratic position, and were preceded by a lance bearer as an indication of their high and direct authority. But after the magistrates were given great power and prestige by the shogun, their aristocratic rank had to be changed to common status in 1683, making it equal to that of mayors in other shogunal cities. At the same time, the supervision and the choice of the *toshiyori* as well as other political prerogatives were put under the disposition and added to the responsibilities of the governors. Nothing has remained of the mayors' former status except that, according to the custom of the country, the outgoing *nenban* has to perform an unnecessary journey to the court to pay his respects to the supreme council as an annual act of submission. After listening to a reading of some articles of a regulation on his second audience, he returns home again. To assist them with their duties, two deputy mayors are employed to administer the *soto machi,*[10] or new city.

Jōgyōji

Jōgyōji are called "constantly remaining heads" because they do not lay down their duties. They administer the streets of the *soto machi,* or outer city, as lesser heads and second lieutenants of the mayors. For in addition to their overall direction, the mayors also have the particular task of administering the *uchi machi* and its wards with the *otona,* or ward headmen. The duty of the *jōgyōji* consists of presiding in monthly rotation over the settlement of ordinary, daily business together with the ward headmen. They are chosen from among the oldest ward headmen by the senior mayors and with the consent of the magistrates. Like the mayors, they receive a poor annual salary from the shogun and get a little more from the income of the foreign trade. But as their subordinates gauge the weight of their authority from their display of pomp, they always live in splendid poverty.

Nengyōji

Below them in rank and service are four lesser officers called *nengyōji,* which literally means "annually resigning heads," as they serve only one year: two people for the *uchi machi* and two for the *soto machi*. They are like representatives of the people and go-between officials of the magistrates and mayors. They attend in twos in daily rotation from early morning until evening at the court of the presiding magistrate. They are housed in a small room next to the *genkan ban* specially designated for this office, so that they are able to transmit the governor's official business as well as various requests from the people after they have been approved by the ward headmen and mayors. They also take orders directly from the governors or as transmitted by his *karō* and pass them to the *toshiyori* or directly to the ward headmen as well as the interpreters of the foreigners. They are also responsible for all services required daily by the court from the community. It is a difficult office, and they rarely succeed in receiving any gratitude from the magistrates. They are chosen from among the best ward headmen of both parts of the city in the manner described for the *jōgyōji.*

The above are the high officials of the general administration of the city. They have no other public council or meeting chambers besides the private house of the presiding mayor.

Chōshi

The so-called *chōshi no mono,* meaning "city messengers," act as general servants in the execution of the administration. They are, properly speaking, lictors and fall under the command of the mayors. Since the decline of the mayors' status, they are also used by the governor's office in the service of the administration and for a great variety of other business. This group consists of approximately thirty families who a long time ago occupied half a street, which is named after them *chōshi machi.* Their number appears to be increasing with the strict supervision of all subjects, since now another *shin chōshi machi,* which means "new messengers' street," is being built. Their name seems to be more respectable than their actual duties, which consist of catching and handling offenders. Occasionally they permit themselves to be used to perform executions. They are versed in the art of wrestling and know how to overpower armed people, half strangling them and keeping them powerless with great agility. To perform their task, they are always equipped with a strong rope. By law, but not in practice, their duties are considered to be of an aristocratic and military nature, and consequently they wear two swords.

Saji

Some of them are of lower standing and are especially called *saji.* They are only permitted to wear one sword. In this guild of *chōshi* the sons tend to learn the skills of their fathers and either take their place or join them.

Bailiff

Much more despised are the so-called *eta.* Properly speaking, they are people who skin dead animals and tan hides, also making shoes and other items. They tend to perform the task of the bailiff: to torture, crucify, and behead. They live apart from other people, outside the city, not far from the execution ground, which is always situated to the west of the city, next to the highway. The brothel keepers are obliged to assist them with their male domestic serfs.

Bell Ringer

The last one in public service is the bell ringer, who measures time with a smoldering tinder and indicates the hours by ringing bells (which for practical reasons have been placed on the mountainside next to the Daikōji temple). The ringing of other large temple bells marks only the rising and setting of the sun and at other times invites followers to listen to the explanations of heathen texts.

Chapter 3
The Government of Individual Streets and Their Inhabitants, as well as the Administration of the Surrounding Districts and Farmers by a Shogunal Official

Here follows a description of the particular administration of each street. This has been organized to curb the liberties of the citizens to an extraordinary degree, greatly facilitating the duties of the government's administrators. The following officials are employed by each street.

Otona

An *otona,* or ward headman, functions as the head or mayor of his street. He takes care of fires and guards and is responsible for the execution of orders from above. He keeps books and registers of all births, deaths, marriages, departures, removals, and arrivals, in addition to recording people's names, date of birth, religion, and livelihood. He investigates and settles everyday incidents and disagreements, punishes petty crime with chains or imprisonment, has delinquents apprehended by his servants in his own district, and has them imprisoned until the authorities deal with them. He hands over to them all criminal cases, informs them of other important incidents, and is responsible for all occurrences in his street. This administrator of the street is elected by the inhabitants from their midst by common vote or written ballot. After the ballot papers have been opened, the names of those receiving the greatest number of votes are submitted by the *nengyōji* to the magistrate with the humble request to entrust one of them with the headship of the street. Their allowance consists of a tenfold allotment from the treasury of the street, or, what amounts to the same, of the money collected from foreign trade.

Under each *otona* are three assistant ward headmen, the *ōgumi oya* or *ōgumi gashira,* the so-called fathers or heads of the great corporation, who, as second lieutenants or advisors, assist him in the government of his street and its inhabitants. For the sake of good order the inhabitants are divided into *gonin gumi,* that is, corporations of five men. Usually there are ten to fifteen in each street; sometimes more, sometimes fewer. These corporations consist of five men, occasionally more, and include only those who own their land. Those living with and under them are not included in this group of five but are placed under them as tenants. Sometimes there are more than fifteen of these subordinate families under one *gonin gumi.* They are not burdened with any official services or payments, except for taking their turn at the *monban* (night watch and rattle guard). But in return they are not allowed to vote, nor do they share in payments from the treasury of the streets. In spite of their poor location, the rents paid for the plots of these city dwellings are high and calculated monthly according to the number of mats covering the floor. In the worst locations each mat costs five condors, in the best ten.

Among this group one man is placed above the other four as *kogumi oya* or *kogumi gashira,* that is, the elder or head of a little corporation. He has to watch the conduct of the others and, together with the other members of his corporation, pay a heavy penalty for crimes committed by any of them.

In addition, each street employs a *hissha,* or scribe. He writes the orders of the *otona*, testimonials, discharges, and passes. He sets out requests, contracts, and oaths and keeps a variety of books for the ward on behalf of the *otona,* such as a register of all dwellings and their inhabitants, with the latter's name, age, and religion, a list of all deaths together with testimonials that the person came to a natural, non-Christian end, a record of all passes issued, together with detailed notes stating reasons and times of departure and return, as well as a diary of daily occurrences in the street.

Takara yaku, that is, "servant of the treasury," is a citizen who keeps the financial accounts of the street and records incoming and outgoing monies. This fund consists solely of the money that the authorities deduct from the price the foreign traders are paid for their goods and is put aside for the support of the citizens and the payment of necessary expenses. The above post is staffed by the citizens themselves in annual rotation.

Nichi gyōshi, meaning literally a delivery person who goes back and forth daily, that is, the street's messenger. He informs the administration of changes of residence, deaths, and other common occurrences. He transmits the requests of the citizens of the street as well as the testimonials issued by the *kogumi oya* to their subordinates, collects the *hassaku,*[1] or contributions to community presents, and carries and issues the orders of the authorities to the *kogumi oya,* or advisors.

Jishinban

Each street has two night watches. The first is the main and citizens' guard, manned at the time of religious celebrations and when necessary also during the daytime. It is called *jishinban,* that is, personal bodyguard, because it is performed personally by the citizens, staffed nightly by three men in rotation. The guard occupies a room or house in the middle of the ward or, depending on the boundaries, a house at the corner of the crossroad. If an incident has occurred in the city, or if there is a suspicion that something happened, the guard is doubled. In such cases, the *otona* himself with one of his deputies or elders joins the guard for a couple of hours during the night until most people have passed to ensure that nothing untoward happens on account of negligence, for which the whole street would suffer. This guard has such authority that anybody who opposes it must suffer with his life.

The second watch, which they call *monban,* is the guard of the gates and the rattle guard, employed to ward off theft and fire. Two laborers or common citizens each sit in a guardhouse at both gates of the street. They constantly visit each other and (like all other guards stationed on ships or land) announce the time of the night by clanging two half-cylindrical-shaped pieces of wood against each other. The citizens take it in turn to pay them and provide for their upkeep and sometimes take on this duty themselves. In other cities, the fire watch has a special watchtower erected beside or on top of a house in the middle of each street.

With these precise arrangements and manifold laws, the citizens are bound with unbelievably hard and stringent discipline to servile obedience and heavy physical duties. However, they do not suffer under a wide variety of unbearable taxes like the people of Europe. And different from other shogunal or ordinary cities, here in Nagasaki this tax, however light it may be, is even refunded to them for their own upkeep from the money pilfered from the foreign trade. We will write about the three above-mentioned topics, namely, the citizens' stringent subjection, light taxes, and refund of the same in as much detail as the limitations of this chapter permit and we have accurate knowledge.

Civil Duties

Crime can never be atoned for by payment of money but only with one's body, or life, or temporary withdrawal of life's comforts. They maintain that if this were not so, rich people would be at liberty to commit crimes: an absurdity. All sorts of possible torments are used as torture but not as capital punishment, which consists of nothing less than crucifixion or decapitation. The exceptions are cases where people are punished for someone else's crime or penalized for wicked acts, where the punishment is permanent or temporary confinement, exile from the province, or just the city, and dismissal from one's position. Such punishment is incurred so easily without one's own fault or knowledge that almost nobody can live assured that he will be spared. The administrators of the street must atone for the crime of their heads of households, the latter for that of the members of their household, lodgers, and guests; a lord must atone for his servants, a son for his father, a corporation for its members, and neighbors for each other. Depending on the person and circumstances, however, punishment may not be as severe.

In addition to the physical duties of providing a variety of guards and attending upon and performing corvée at the courts of the magistrates, the inhabitants are burdened with the following procedures.

All the streets of the city are closed off at times during the day and more often at night. This happens, for instance, when there is suspicion of trouble, to prevent crowds from gathering or protesting, during a search for criminals, and during the frequent investigations of all sorts of other unpleasant minor incidents, of whatever nature they may be. It happens especially on the departure of the foreign junks and ships so that nobody may follow and trade with them. At times like these, the servants of every house are inspected several times during the night to ensure that nobody is absent and possibly out trading. This inspection takes place at varying times and frequency but usually three times a night, in the evening, at midnight, and toward dawn, when all persons have to get up from their resting places and stand when their names are called. The inspection is performed by the administrators of the street, such as the *otona,* who, however, sometimes shuns this bothersome job, an *ōgumi gashira,* two *kogumi oya,* and the *nichi gyōshi,* who reads the names of all the servants, and sometimes only compares the number of assembled persons with that of his register. When the gates are closed, or even when they are open at a critical time, nobody may pass through them except those carrying a *tori fuda,* or small branded wooden docket permitting passage, issued by the officiating mayor. When the docket is shown, the street's rattle guard will accompany the person through their own street to the gates of the next.

Anybody wanting to move into lodgings in another street first asks the *otona* to accept him among his citizens, accompanying his request by a gift of a meal of fish. The *otona* conducts inquiries into his life and then sends his *nichi gyōshi* to find out from the inhabitants of the street whether this new arrival would be acceptable as a fellow citizen. If just one person opposes this, and can charge him with misdemeanor, especially drunkenness and a tendency to brawl, or mentions other suspicions, protesting that he does not want to be blamed for such evil deeds, then the person cannot be accepted. If the supplicant is given permission, he obtains an ordinary testimonial and discharge from the scribe of his own street, which the ward headman authorizes with his own seal. The *nichi gyōshi* takes these documents to the *otona* of the other street, who thereupon accepts the new arrival among the number of his subjects and extends his protection to him. As long as the document is not in his possession, which sometimes happens through neglect, he is not answerable for the man, and the guilt of the latter's crime is still charged to the previous street. This is why the *otona* declares in the document that from this moment on he is no longer responsible for the man he has discharged. After the newcomer has been entered into the street's register, he marks his arrival by treating either only his own *kumi gashira* or all of them to a meal or pays some other form of respect.

Great difficulties are encountered on the sale of one's plot. This may not happen without the consent of all the citizens of the street, who often refuse approval for a whole year because they do not know the buyer or do not consider him suitable, since in the future they will have to atone for his crimes. Once the buyer has taken possession of the house, he has to pay the council of the ward 8 percent, and in the *uchi machi* above 23 percent, of the agreed price, to be shared among themselves and the citizens. Consequently it is called *hachibun,* that is, one-eighth, of which 5 percent is for their pains and 3 percent for a banquet or celebration, for which, however, the money is not used. The new neighbors come to welcome the man in his new house, offering him their help and assuring him of their communal assistance and friendship.

If someone wants to go on a pilgrimage or travel for other purposes, the *kogumi oya* and his colleagues must issue him a testimonial for the authorities, in which they guarantee that the individual is embarking on the journey for an honest purpose and the above-declared reasons and will return within the specified time. For this purpose, the street keeps an extraordinarily large book called *kitte no shitagaki*, that is, signing of the pass, into which the *otona* has the names of the guarantors and their seals entered. The *otona* orders the *nichi gyōshi* to take this written guarantee to the residence of the *nenban toshiyori* to obtain a passport for the applicant. The *genkan ban* accepts the book and presents it to the mayor, who orders his *yūhitsu,* or secretary, to write the pass for the applicant and seal it with the mayor's large seal, which is exclusively used by him. This seal is kept by the *yūhitsu,* is the size of a German gold coin, and consists of the characters of the mayor's *nanori,* the personal name of military men. After that, the pass is carried to the *nengyōji* and confirmed by the latter's name and personal seal or to the *jōgyōji* of the *soto machi,* if the petitioner is resident there. Nothing is paid for all these pains except three condors to the *nichi gyōshi* for a thick, quarto-sized piece of paper, which is generally used for this purpose.

If a crime is committed by the inhabitants or citizens of the street, the administration of the street consults about the matter. That means the *otona,* three *kumi gashira,* and all *kogumi oya* discuss if and how the matter can be dealt with by themselves. If they come to the conclusion that the matter exceeds their powers or the horizon of their common intellect, they defer it to the general city council, which, once it has come to the same conclusion, consults about the matter through their *nengyōji* with the *karō,* or elders of the magistrate, and, if considered necessary, has it submitted to the magistrate himself. Court orders from authority on high are issued in the same way until they finally reach the common citizens through the *nichi gyōshi* or sometimes through the mouth of the *otona* himself. The exceptions are written orders publicized on posters, because they are important and permanent, or come from the shogun.

If a quarrel or a brawl occurs in a street, be it among the locals or caused by passersby, it is the duty of the heads of household of the nearest houses to separate the fighting parties. If one of them is killed, even if it were the aggressor himself, the other, regardless of his blameless conduct in defending himself,[2] will also be publicly sentenced to death (unless he were to forestall this disgrace by disemboweling himself), and the inhabitants of the three closest houses will be locked up in their dwellings for three, four, or more months. Rough boards are nailed across all doors and windows after the inhabitants have purchased the necessary provisions for this imprisonment. The remaining inhabitants of the street, especially those accused of negligence in preventing the incident, will also noticeably atone for the sad occurrence and are ordered to work for, provide corvée, or attend upon the officers of the city for a certain period. The same harsh punishment is meted out to the *kumi gashira* of the street of the culprits, which becomes even harsher if it is known that they were aware of the fact that the offender was inclined to brawl or commit the crime in question. The heads of household or masters of the culprits also have to expect harsh and unavoidable punishment. This severity is practiced for the same reason as *Canon facientis, dist.* 86 states: He who neglected to prevent a crime when he could have is beyond doubt guilty of the same crime.[3]

If someone is excited and rashly draws his sword and this is reported to the authorities, he forfeits his life, even if he did not harm his opponent.

Where a citizen or inhabitant has escaped for fear of punishment, the *kumi gashira* must attempt to find him, searching for him themselves and getting others to assist them, to avoid the established corporal punishment on investigation of the matter.

Hito Aratame

In the last month of the year, the *nichi gyōshi* of each street conducts the *hito aratame,* that is, the registration of all members of the household, including children and old people, specifying their personal name, place of birth, and the *shū,* or religious sect, of the head of the household. But many zealots, especially those belonging to the Jōdo sect, will not permit their head of household to cite a different one from that to which they actually belong. Women are only counted in this inquisition and without further specification added to the total number. After this record of inspection has been completed at the end of the old year, the new year begins with:

Efumi

Efumi means literally to step on the image, as they step on the image of the crucified Christ and on another one of a saint to show that they renounce and curse Christ and his messengers. This desecration of the crucified savior begins on the second day of the first month. Each house and street is visited in turn, and it is conducted at two locations simultaneously, so that each party completes four to five streets daily, and the whole inquisition is completed within the space of six days. Those involved in this process are: the *otona,* three *ōgumi oya,* the *hissha,* the *nichi gyōshi,* and two *monban,* or bearers of the images. The images are about one foot long, cast in brass, and kept in a specially made small box. The stepping on the images proceeds as follows: After the inquisition council has sat down on a mat and everybody, young and old, as well as additional families lodged in the same house and the closest neighbors, if their house is not large enough to conduct the procedure there separately, have assembled and the cast images have been placed on the bare floor, the scribe opens his inspection register and reads the names. As people's names are read, they come forward and walk over the images or step on them. Small children who cannot yet walk are picked up by their mothers and have their feet placed on the images as expression of disdain. After that, the head of the household puts his seal at the bottom of the inspection register so that the inquisitors can prove to the magistrates that the inquisition has taken place in the house. Once this procedure has been conducted in all the streets and houses, the officers serving the inquisition themselves, and finally the *otona,* also step on the same images. The former is witnessed by the *otona* and the latter by the *ōgumi gashira,* and they use their seals to provide testimony and evidence for each other. This inquisition is conducted only here and in the provinces of Ōmura and Bungo, where most Christians lived in the past.

If a member of a household dies, the head of the household must call the *kogumi* to witness that the person died a natural and non-Christian death. After they have assured themselves that there are no marks on the body suggesting either, they provide a written testimonial of this fact stamped with their seal. This is entered into the street register by the *nichi gyōshi*[4] and passed on to the *jōgyōji* in the *soto machi* or the mayor of the district.

Jishi Gin

There are few general levies imposed upon the citizens of the city, and they are paid only by the owners of a family property or house lot and not by other inhabitants. The latter are not considered permanent and proper citizens and are not burdened with any kind of taxes (even though they make up the greatest number of people). Levies consist mainly of two kinds, one being the *jishi gin,* literally, remuneration for land, which is collected for the shogun annually in the eighth month. It is calculated not according to the area but according to the length of the frontage facing the street. For each *ken* (which is approximately one fathom) the payment is four mace in the *soto* and six in the *uchi* city. The depth of the house or family plot is not assessed if it is below fifteen *ken.* If it exceeds that depth, even only by one *bu,* or width of a straw, the frontage has to be recalculated and paid for because this is a payment to the shogun, and the shogun's affairs must be administered with the utmost severity of the law.

Hassaku Gin

The second general levy is more or less a voluntary contribution or gift of honor presented by the (land-owning) citizens to their magistrates and by lesser people to their superiors on the first day of the eighth month. It is called *hassaku gin* after the name of this festival day. In view of their position, the officers administering the city present special voluntary gifts of honor in addition to the communal offering, each according to need and ambition. The gifts are presented individually to each magistrate as well as to the locally resident shogunal revenue officer and the four mayors as the officers' official superiors. As incumbents of their fathers' offices, even the apprentices studying foreign languages each present every governor with twenty-five mace and to the others mentioned a lesser gift.

In the case of ordinary citizens, the money is first collected by each street after the above-mentioned holiday and then presented to the two governors. Donations are calculated according to the plot of the houses, the *kasho* of each house requiring the payment of six mace in the *soto machi* and approximately nine or ten in the *uchi machi.* If each street is counted at fifty *kasho,* this amounts to 4,350 *kasho,* which makes about 2,630 taels. *Kasho* is the area of the original family plot as it was entered and specified according to its size in the register when the street was first established. With the passing of time, various *kasho* were combined into one house, and others were divided into two or split up. This contribution is collected only in Nagasaki, where it was set up at the same time and in grateful acknowledgment of the *hana gin* from which the citizens profit.

Hana gin is the name of the money that has been squeezed from the foreign trade and distributed annually among the owners of house plots from the time that the magistrates started to control the trade. Other shogunal and provincial cities remit only the first-described land tax, payable to their lord. Kyoto was also freed from these taxes and is still untaxed to this date on account of a certain incident and petition to the ruler Taikō.[5]

In addition to these taxes, there are still some smaller expenses that must also come out of the pockets of these same citizens. The most important are the annual expenses in honor of their country's deity Suwa, as the patron of this city. They entail temple expenses of eight hundred *jū momme*[6] for comedies performed at the temple to amuse the deity and the upkeep of the temple when necessary. These things are not paid for from the treasury of the extorted *hana gin* but must be collected through voluntary communal contributions out of the pockets of all landed citizens in proportion to their holding. Finally, there is a considerable sum for the temple celebrations or parish fair for the same deity, celebrated with processions, theatricals, dances, and unusual performances. This is not paid for by all citizens at the same time but financed annually by only ten or twelve streets. Consequently each street needs to shoulder this burden only every seven or eight years. The exceptions are the streets of the prostitutes, which are asked to come to the party annually. This costs each street three to four hundred *jū momme,*[7] since respect for the deity demands that each year new robes, performances, songs, dances, and theatricals be provided for, amply and unstintingly.

Owing to the city's geographical position, this large community of commoners cannot, like other cities, survive from the general produce of the land, nor can it provide taxes from this source. The advantage of the foreign trade, moreover, often results in disadvantages with fatal consequences, constant disturbances, anxiety, and hardship. Thus their common sense, rather than Justinian, has taught them that it is natural that the parties that shoulder the problems should also enjoy the advantages.[8] As soon as control over this trade went to the magistrates, ways were found to harvest its gratuitous fruits under the mantle of much-cited justice, with the unjust claws of an eagle clinging to his prey, to profitably replace the above-mentioned taxes and support the population. They call this money *hana gin,* literally "flower money," perhaps because they expect even greater advantages from the foreigners, unless they are comparing the former to flowers and the profit of the merchants to fruits. These are monies that the magistrates and the remaining flock of heathen officials with their ungodly tricks find ways of pilfering at all times from the prices and profits of the foreigners. Part of this money is distributed among the officials (excepting the magistrates) and lesser men in the employ of the streets and the foreigners in proportion to their services. The other part is distributed to the *kana za,* or public purse of each street, for the disposal of the administrator or ward headman, who again apportions and disburses the "flowers" he collects according to the *kasho* owned. However, he reserves as much for the treasury of the street as he considers necessary to meet upcoming repairs of the street, gates of honor, wells, and fire-fighting equipment as well as pay for corvée and the like. A statement of annual expenditure is taken to each house in turn so that everybody can verify the legitimacy of the expense. Similar distributions of money are ordered by the magistrates two, three, four, or more times annually after the various so-called *kanban,* or foreign sales, have taken place. If someone forgoes his share of the street's treasury, he is also freed from certain obligations to the street, such as corvée, night watch and the like, and will be charged with nothing else but the shogunal land tax and the gift of *hassaku* for the magistrates. However, regardless of the advantages gained and the harsh nature of the duties, I have heard of very few people magnanimous enough to wish to purchase their freedom from the servile obligations of the street by way of these flowers.

This is the way in which the government of the city and streets is structured. It provides a pattern for all civil administration in the shogunal empire and for the provincial cities of the domain lords, as well as small towns and villages, although in the latter the officials have different titles and are treated less severely.

The shogun employs a revenue officer or district magistrate to supervise all matters of government and law enforcement that concern only the administration of the few stretches of land and the small number of villages of the rough and mountainous area extending some miles from Nagasaki. He collects the annual *nengu* from all cultivated land, gardens, and fields as rice or grain tax, or, in the case of fruits, the appropriate sums of money. Here the rice or grain tax amounts to just a little more than half the annual harvest, which the cultivator must deliver gleaned and cleaned to the shogunal grain store (*ōkura* or *komegura*) at Magome (the name of the northern suburb of the city). The amount is determined by estimates of sworn censors who inspect the fields before the harvest or, in plentiful years, have one *tsubo* (the square area of one *ken* or fathom) threshed to calculate the whole harvest on the basis of this sample. The owners of bushland or plots with buildings must raise a small amount of *jishi gin,* or land tax, in accordance with the amount of *tsubo* and in proportion to the fertile or useful area. The total income, when calculated in rice according to the custom of this country, amounts to more or less 3,000 *koku,* depending on the year's harvest. If the rice is converted into cash and each *koku* is calculated as five *jū momme* or taels, it amounts to 15,000 *jū momme* or taels.

Many years ago the administration of these estates was conducted by members of an illustrious family, each generation inheriting the title of *daikan* and the same personal name of Suetsugu Heizō.[9] The dignity of their office permitted them to live in considerable splendor, and they enjoyed such standing and favors at the shogunal court that even the magistrates, although of higher rank, looked up to them, and their misgivings and suggestions were given great weight in matters of government. But in 1676 the splendor and, simultaneously, the eminence of their office came under a dark cloud and was destroyed forever when it was discovered that the *tedai,* or elder of the house, had been in the habit of sending arms wrapped in floor matting and taking out loans on ships going to Korea. The discovery of this crime resulted in the crucifixion of this much-loved member of the household with his accomplice on a little island facing the city called Hadaka jima.[10] His innocent seven-year-old son was executed while his father watched from the cross. This happened after all three had been paraded through the streets of the city with the little son being carried in somebody's arms, quite apart from various other eminent merchants and participants who were involved in this trade and had to suffer the unfortunate consequences. In accordance with the laws of the empire, the old *daikan* was charged with the same crime as his subordinate and was sent with both his sons into exile on an island called Oki no shima in the southern seas beyond the province of Chūgoku. The mother of his sons, the lady of the house, was sent to Hirado. To date (1692) they are still alive, and so is the informer, a personal servant of one of the condemned. In return for his meritorious behavior and his zeal in upholding the laws of his forefathers, he was promoted to the post of ward headman of the foreigners. Owing to the above incident, no mat purchased by the Dutch or Chinese may be delivered unless thoroughly searched.

After this incident, the administration of the above estate was delegated instead to a man named Takagi Sakuemon, who became the shogunal resident agent and was assisted by two mayors.[11] However, he received neither the title of *daikan* nor the independent authority that accompanies that title. Consequently, from the beginning of his appointment, he was not allowed to use the pike, indicating a high official appointed by and acting as representative of the shogun or a territorial lord, nor permitted to wear a second sword, as appropriate for a military aristocrat or his servant. He has the status of a commoner like a magistrate's scribe, without any of the authority appropriate to his office. Therefore he was unable to do anything when he recently caught his servant stealing for a second time and could have him killed only with the magistrate's permission, even though as long as a servant is under contract with a master, his rights are no better than those of a slave. If the master kills the servant in the first heat of emotion, the master is required only to produce evidence of the servant's crime.

Chapter 4
The Temples of the City and the Activities and the Administration of the Clergy

To complete our description of the city, we still have to discuss the temples and their clergy. They belong to different religions and sects and therefore submit to different chief superiors, who are located and hold their religious council in Miyako,[1] the city of sanctity and prayer. The clergy, monasteries, and temple wardens of each sect are governed by their own subordinate heads, superiors, and priors of their order. Although there are various temples and monasteries of the same sect in this city, they do not have a common bishop in Nagasaki and recognize only their above-mentioned chiefs in Miyako.

Among the *shin* or *kami*, that is to say, the native deities, Suwa dai myōshin, that is, the great sacred deity Suwa, is Nagasaki's *ujigami* (the most important deity of a district, city or village, whose duty it is to protect the locality). His shrine is situated near the city on the mountain Tate, and his most sacred personal chapel can now be reached by climbing more than two hundred stone steps from below. This is because recently the shrine had to be located higher up, since the *dairi* (i.e., spiritual court of the hereditary emperor) had conferred this *kami* a higher rank. The temple courtyard proper is located slightly lower on the slopes of the mountain. In its entrance, near the gate, one can see an open, long, overhanging hall for entertainment and comedies, hung with many painted pictures, the usual form of presenting vows and gifts to the *jinja*, or temples of the native deities. Further on one can see some wooden chapels, clean and without surplus ornamentation. In this temple compound, Murasaki dai gongen, that is, the great, stern Murasaki, and Sumiyoshi dai myōjin, that is, the great, sacred Sumiyoshi, are also venerated. For each of them a *mikoshi*, a large monstrance or well-decorated small portable chamber, is stored and maintained. I also discovered a special cubicle among them, built in honor of the deity and the lord of a thousand legs, with many figures of his subjects hung and donated by worshippers.

Various temple feast days are dedicated to this deity Suwa. The most important of these is one of the five main holidays, the ninth day of the ninth month, known as *kunichi* or *kugatsu kokonoka*. As the deity's birthday it is celebrated throughout the country, and here at Nagasaki with an unusually elaborate *matsuri*, since he is the patron of the city. For greater splendor, the *matsuri* begins on the seventh. Also the eighth has been added as a day when rich or pious people try to please the spirit with music played all day at the temple. The music is performed by boys on drums and bells and is the same as that which was played to appease the highest *kami* and general patron of the country, Tenshō daijin, when out of dismay he had hidden himself among rocks.[2] Then there is also the twelfth day of the month of his birth, when, different from other days, only comedies are performed.

The servants of the temple, who should correctly be called *negi* and are wrongly referred to by the term denoting an aristocrat of the *dairi,* namely, *kuge,* are, like generally all wardens of *jinja*, secular people, who, however, pretend to have some special sanctity and stature above other secular people. They live not far from the precinct on the same mountain slope, each with his family in their own quarters, worldly, like ordinary citizen, except that they do not shave their hair and tie it at the back.[3] Also, when they are actually serving at the temple, they put on ecclesiastical robes and various headdresses depending on their rank. They support themselves from the donations the citizens throw them during their procession at the *matsuri* and also during visits to the shrine and at other celebrations, especially those they receive on the eighth, the in-between day of the *matsuri,* when certain people present a gift with the request to have, in return, a serenade performed for the enjoyment of the deity. There are two permanent custodians, one each from among the *otona* of the two parts of the city, who are paid by the city. They are assisted by two men of the same rank, who are replaced annually and not salaried. It is their duty to look after and care for the upkeep and construction of this temple compound, the *matsuri,* the comedies, the welfare of the *negi,* and the appropriate conditions for these *kami.*

The clergy arrange their procession in honor of the *kami* in the following fashion:

1. Two of the deity's ceremonial horses are led ahead, looking as starved as those on which the patriarch of Moscow rides to church on Palm Sunday.
2. Religious insignia, like those used in ancient times and still used by the *dairi,* are paraded one after the other, all for the veneration of the deity. They include some short, broad, gilded lances, a pair of wooden shoes, like clogs from the city of Münster, and a large tuft of white paper attached to a short pole, which is a whisk of ecclesiastical authority.
3. Hollow resting benches for the *mikoshi,* carried upside down to catch alms in them, as well as a proper alms box, each carried by two day-laborers.
4. The *mikoshi,* shaped like an eight-cornered lantern, but so large that one person would have difficulty carrying it, lacquered black with much gilded edging and beading, metal mirrors and ornaments, and a crane projecting on top.
5. Two wooden chambers, which are used instead of a *norimono* to carry the two superiors (as they were used in ancient times and are still in use by the *kuge* or aristocrats of the *dairi*).
6. Two of their own personal riding horses, harnessed, and in the said condition.
7. The whole clergy on foot in good order.
8. A trail of citizens and the common mob in the usual disorder.

As soon as the clergy with their monstrances have entered their ecclesiastical buildings, the deputies of the magistrates arrive with their usual following and in addition are accompanied by twenty long ceremonial pikes, which appear to be crowned at the top with black cocks' feathers, but in reality only have black lacquered pieces of wood. After washing their hands outside the shrine, the four most important step up and in front of the bishops, who are seated in plain view among the *mikoshi,* present their masters' and their own felicitations with extreme, yet in view of the sanctity of the occasion appropriate, humbleness. Thereupon a *negi* pours each one in turn a sweet drink, called *amasake,* from a large golden ladle, but in memory of the poverty of their sacred ancestors of past ages pours it into a wretched small, unglazed earthenware bowl. The drink is a native beer, produced by fermenting boiled rice overnight. It is usually made on the eve of the *kami*'s festival to be drunk the next day in revered memory and as an offering to the ancients, who knew no other than this simple method of brewing. On the first day of the celebrations these two assemblies of high personages arrive only after activities have been concluded. On the third day, however, they arrive before activities begin with the breaking of dawn, since the much-discussed *matsuri* is actually an offering to every *kami,* held for him whoever he might be. But common usage has turned it into an annual celebration, or parish fair, honoring and entertaining the particular saint who has been chosen as patron or *ujigami* of the locality, celebrated on his birthday with public processions, cheering, theatricals, and performances of many strange and marvelous acts.

The *matsuri* is the biggest event that takes place in this and all other cities, and it is therefore worthwhile to introduce it here as a pattern followed in all other localities and as their greatest religious service.

On the said days the event is celebrated not with sermons, prayers, and devotions, but with flamboyant processions through the most important streets of the city and with public performances on a market square set aside for this purpose. During the festival it is called *ōtabi tokoro,* which means "the place of the exalted voyage," from the fact that the deities visit or are conveyed to this locality. At that time a shrine is erected in front of the square; it is open in front, with wings on both sides, made only of bamboo and straw, with the gables of *sugi* branches, all built in the manner of the poverty-stricken ancestors, like a field kitchen or hay barn. A pine tree is erected on each side at the front. The other sides of the square are filled with poor-looking booths for spectators.

All the clergy of this religion arrive here with a considerable following, bringing the *mikoshi* of Suwa and, to keep him company, also that of Sumiyoshi. Murasaki, however, is left at home, because there are neither old stories nor other indications to believe that he receives any pleasure from being paraded around. The clergy that follow are called *ōtomi,* "exalted retinue," or "the following of the great lord." But regardless of its exalted position, the retinue is accompanied by an alms box, and on its arrival, donations are thrown profusely and blindly as if people wanted to stone the clergy. The clergy sit down in front of the temple on three benches placed one behind the other in accordance with their rank, which is also indicated by slight differences in dress: on the first are the two elders as superiors, or people of bishop's rank, in black habits and special headdress, each carrying a short small staff. Behind them are four of the next rank with special black lacquered hats and, like the rest, dressed in long white choir robes. The third rank, wearing black lacquered Jesuit-type hats, fills up the third bench. The rest, who are only servants and porters of the sacred objects, stand bare-headed.

The deputies of the magistrates are seated on raised mats in a hut at another side of the square, where their twenty pikes have been planted for show and respect for the occasion. On their orders the surging mob is kept at bay with staffs, and precautions are taken to prevent riots or accidents. As a further precaution, a constant string of *yoriki* are sent out by the courts of the governors to bring in reports.

The performances one sees here are theatricals, each with eight, twelve, or more actors. They deal with stories of the gods, heroes, lovers, and other fiction, with the text in verse and performed like an opera with music, but sung while dancing. This alternates with one or the other funny act or intermittent speeches in prose. Some performances consist only of dances in which the plot is merely indicated by special or repetitive gestures and hand and head ornaments; sometimes also the whole dance, rhythm and melody, are changed according to changes in the story. This always takes place with the object of the story present, which is practically life-size and carried along and so constructed that it can be erected and dismantled in no time. It might include wells, bridges, gates, pleasure houses, trees, flower gardens, mountains, animals, and so on.

The actors are young women from the streets of prostitution and children and young boys from the other streets. Each group is dressed expensively in its special silk robes of identical color, and they act out their parts with such surprising aplomb and skill that they would not be outdone by a seasoned orator and comedian in Europe. Each street marches along in turn, as follows: First of all a canopy or large silken umbrella is carried ahead as the emblem of the street, with an upright sign in the center on top bearing the name of the street that is about to perform. The musicians follow, dressed in uniforms and with covered faces. The band consists of recorders, hand drums, and voices, sometimes accompanied by a large drum, cymbal, or little bell. The music is unimpressive and poor: it may serve the gods better than the musically trained ear. Also the text is howled slowly by unseasoned throats in a simple tune, which, nevertheless, keeps its measure and frequently varies its beat and thus is adequate to harmonize their slow dances and body and hand movements. These are sufficiently pleasing and skilled, although their feet are obviously more used to a peasant's barn than a French ballroom. After that come the objects and tools required for the performance: the large ones carried by day laborers, the smaller ones, such as chairs, poles, and flowers, by much-adorned children. They are followed by the actors themselves and, after them, the citizens of the street, dressed in ceremonial robes. For greater display they are followed by various bearers of umbrellas and chairs, walking in pairs. They wait next to the square until the performance is finished and then leave again in the same order. Each of these dances or performances lasts about three quarters of an hour, but as some streets only march past with curious objects or in handsome processions, all these festive presentations, which begin at dawn, are over by midday or a little later. The presentations of the ninth day are the same as those of the seventh, except for some variations in the costumes, dances, and the order of all processions, which march in reverse order toward the direction from which they came. Finally, to conclude the event, the two ecclesiastical superiors step in front of the seat of the governor's commissioners and standing express their gratitude for their attendance with nearly as much subservience as previously they paid to them (since they are now off duty and no longer command the respect of their office). The performances differ from year to year, or at least there are new rhythms and dances, for it would be the greatest disgrace if last year's story were dished up without, at least, changing the soup.

I do not hesitate to add a short description of the latest festival performance. It consisted of the following presentations:

1. Dances presented by eight young prostitutes in colorful costumes under flowery white crepe overcoats, with sun hats, fans, staffs, and flowers. They danced in turn and were relieved by two grown-up dancers in different costumes.

2. Representation of a flower garden on each side of the square with a straw hut in the middle, with dances performed by eight prostitutes dressed in red and white, carrying fans, staffs, and flower baskets, moving in and out of the set. They took turns with a skilled dancer who performed alone.

3. A parade of various triumphal carts, with a yoke of buffalo and oxen of various colors, artistically made to look like the real thing, and drawn by well-dressed young men. Its load consisted of the following: a flowering *tsubaki* tree;[4] a mountain with vegetation; a bamboo grove with a tiger lurking in it; a load of straw with a tree with roots and branches; a whale below a cliff, half lying in water; a mountain with well-adorned real boys sitting under a flowering apricot tree, pulled by similar boys.

4. Six flower beds and one green tree was pulled up by boys. Nine boys in identical dress, armed with two swords and muskets, and a farmer danced and moved.

5. A mountain carried by people, a well with a gallery, a large cask, and a house were put down. Then two masked giants with enormous heads representing certain *hotoke,* or Indian gods, began to dance. A third one, an enormous monster with a sword, came out of the mountain, and then, in spite of the mountain's small size, he was followed by seven Chinese, all joining the dance. After a little while the giant shattered the cask, and out came a boy who, after he delivered a long, lively speech, proceeded to dance on his own with the giant. In the meantime three monkeys crawled out of the well. They were life-size and had deer heads and also performed a pleasing dance on the gallery in harmony with the others. After all had returned to their positions, the drama ended.

6. Presentation of a standing round Chinese gate of honor, a pleasure house, and a garden with trees; in between them a dance performed by ten armed boys dressed in green, yellow, and blue striped jackets and formal trousers.[5] A buffoon was holding forth in between. Finally two persons in foreign dress jumped out of the garden's mountain and joined the dance.

7. A parade consisting of a hill covered with bamboo and pine trees and twelve flowering trees, modeled life-like with their flowers, each of a different species and pulled in a different container with a stately retinue dressed appropriately. After that two people dressed in white and eight people in yellow performed a dance playing bells. After a while they were joined in their dance by seven others with flower pots on their heads.

8. A stately parade of a great domain lord and his son, well acted by boys.

9. A hut made of green branches placed in the middle, through and around which ten boys, girded with two swords, wearing black coats and formal trousers, perform a dance, first with branches of flowers and then with bare (imitation) swords, arrows, and spears. They were relieved by various interludes of speeches until finally their servants, with official chests on their shoulders, stepped into the dance and concluded this performance.

10. A stage placed next to a wooded mountain cliff, an armed boy, dressed in yellow and black, stepped onto the stage and talked forcefully and moved around for about half an hour, while eight others in black robes with colorful floral design performed a dance. They were joined by a person and a monkey jumping out of the cliff at the same time, dancing in pleasant harmony with the rest.

11. A well-built young acrobat in front of whom was placed a board and scaffolding without a platform. A split bamboo rod was placed on top of the scaffolding, running the full length, with eight steps to climb up and others to climb down. There was a gate that only had a round hole at the top with a diameter of two and a half spans. He performed some strange acts, the best of which seemed to me the following: lying on the board on his front, or on his back, and instantly jumping straight onto his feet with incredible agility. Walking up the steps with stilts, continuing along the hollow bamboo rod, and changing over his stilts while descending the other steps, finally jumping through the hole of the above-mentioned gate, which, however, was some three fathoms away. He did this, regardless of the fact that the sun hat he was wearing was far larger than the hole, the hat bending and giving during the jump.

12. A parade of certain constructions, life-size replicas of large objects, in their true colors and likeness, but made out of thin material so that each could be carried on the back of a person. All had an exceedingly large drum in front of them, on which some played, others playing bells. They walked as if dancing, but with less movement, swaying their burdens, which even though they were made of light material, were so heavy because of their size that they had to be rested on specially constructed chairs before and after the parade ground and when marching through other streets. The constructions were as follows:

A drawing well with all equipment necessary for extinguishing fires.

A large church bell mounted on its scaffolding, encircled by a dragon.

A mountain covered largely in snow, shaped like a dragon's head, with an eagle on top.

A twenty-four-pound metal cannon, carried upright, with all equipment necessary for loading.

A high load of packs of rice with twelve straw bundles, in accordance with the custom of the country.

A whale in a bowl.

Shellfish, snails, and various fruits larger than life, each carried by one person.

This same religion[6] has a number of other, less splendid temples, such as two dedicated to Tenshō daijin, one to Tenjin, and a few other chapels to deities that are less highly esteemed here. These are not maintained and served by *negi* (the proper servants and secular wardens of the *kami*, or local deities), but are partly kept by a few *yamabushi*, that is, mountain priests (who are supposed to be religious hermits and penitents, but are married and are syncretic secular priests, who could be grouped with the imported *butsu dō* as syncretists of the foreign paganism).[7] Partly they are kept by Tendai (or Shingon) priests, syncretists of the foreign paganism of *butsu dō*, or, apparently, originally of the Lanzu[8] sect. This sect is pronounced *kōshi* in Japanese and was founded by China's first philosopher, Kōshi, whom we call Confucius, and entered into a syncretic relationship with the two other religions. The shogun Gongen[9] was fond of their teaching, and consequently his *ihai*, or memorial or mortuary tablet, is located at Anzenji (a Tendai temple), where prayers for the well-being of his soul are offered daily.

The said *negi*, as servants of the *miya*, or temples of the *kami*, submit to the directions of the *dairi*, that is, the ecclesiastical court of the *mikado*, or hereditary emperor. Especially now one of his high aristocrats, Yoshida dono,[10] has been appointed to their leadership on account of his holiness and at the same time has been vested with the authority to confer not just on the *negi* but also on the deceased souls and deities greater honors, titles, and splendor. However, such matters are often discussed in their council and cabinet of the *mikado*.

The *yamabushi*, or hermit priests, also have their proper spiritual leader in Miyako.

There are some beautiful monasteries and wooden temples here belonging to the four most important sects of the *buppō*[11] or *butsu dō*, that is, the foreign paganism introduced originally from India. Few are situated within the city; many are outside nestled on the slopes and terraces of the mountains and reached by flights of stone steps. They have a host of secondary chapels that are not particularly large or splendid but are pleasing and sober. Inside there are raised altars, life-size gilded images, lacquered columns, gates, and posts, the decorations being sober rather than sumptuous. Each temple is served by monks from its own sect and order. Each sect differentiates between *honji*, the main temple, and *matsuji*, branch, junior, or dependent temple or monastery, so called because they are under the direction of the main temple and its priors. The *honji* of the sects are the following:

Kōdaiji, the main monastery and temple of the *zen shū* or sect of Zen, of the order, or rather faction, called *sōtō ha* or *sōtō shū*. This temple has within its precincts a secondary temple or chapel open on all sides with a draped, gilded image of extraordinary size depicting their first teacher, Shaka, sitting on a gilded *tarate* flower *(faba agip-*

tiaca). Under the temple's direction are various *matsuji,* or lesser monasteries, which maintain a considerable number of clergy, both boys and old monks.

Shuntokuji is also a main temple of the above sect, but of the faction called *rinzai ha*. It has various subordinate *matsuji* and no fewer clergy than the former.

Zenrinji is a temple of the latter order. Its buildings are larger, but it does not have *matsuji.* Its prior is, nevertheless, not subordinate to the former temple but directly responsible to their general in Miyako.

Most people here belong to the above-mentioned temples of the *zen shū.* Their priests travel often and change frequently, and consequently there is an indeterminate, large number of them of some three hundred.

Daionji is the main temple of the sect *jōdo shū.* Several *matsuji* are subordinate to it. This sect keeps the *ihai,* or memorial tablets, of the present line of shoguns, who belong to this sect. A prayer is said for their souls in front of these tablets, or their epitaph, daily, and on certain appropriate days, some food is offered. This duty is rotated annually among the priests. The clergy of these temples are nearly as numerous as those of the previous temples.

Honrenji is the main temple of the sect *hokke shū.* It governs Chōshōji and a few other *matsuji.* It has a small number of clergy and few adherents.

Daikōji is the main temple of the sect and order *omote no ikkō shū,* that is, the Ikkō sect at the front, so called after the location of the residence of their superior in Miyako.

Kōenji is the main temple of the other order of the same Ikkō *shū*, called *ura no ikkō shū*, that is, Ikkō sect at the back, because the residence of their general is located further down.

The monks of both these Ikkō sects may marry and father young priests in their monasteries, although this happens only among the most important monks. In case the number of young priests exceeds the funds of the monastery, they are placed into Ikkō monasteries in the provinces, where the monks are still unmarried. Sometimes they even have to enter the monasteries of other sects, but this is done under the pretext of gaining higher spiritual wisdom.

Neither of the two above temples has any *matsuji,* and they maintain barely twenty full priests and families. However, large numbers of humble folk and generally all the farmers adhere to them since their teaching is very pious and simple both in word and text. The latter are written in plain letters called *kana* to make them accessible to the common people.

There is another chapel (or *matsuji*) of this order called Kanzenji, whose *danna,* or parish, collected to extend the temple, some donating ten, others as much as one hundred *jū momme*. Then last year their *oshō* took the money to Miyako, to place it at the disposition of their general. But he has remained with the money in Osaka, where he is said to have already spent it on high living, while his wife and children are still here. If he does not come back very soon, the *danna* intends to go to another temple.

The above-described clergy of the various Buddhist sects neither have processions nor enact plays. They remain within the precincts of their temples and follow their timetable of chanting and other religious duties, including that of securing their upkeep, some of which they earn by begging or holding services for the souls of the departed. For the rest they have to rely on charity or voluntary contributions from their *danna*. As discussed above, they are subordinate locally to special priors called *jūji* or *oshō*[12] within their sect and its branches, who in turn submit to a general *oshō* of the same sect and faction in Miyako. The monasteries of the Ikkō sect call their priors *shōnin,* and their two generals in Miyako carry the title of *monzeki* or *go monzeki* in memory of their exalted position. This means literally "the deserted seat at the gate," indicating that those seated closest to the high gate have left their seats, and it refers to the fact that the men who adopt this religion and accept the dignity of this office are aristocrats and blood relatives of the *mikado. Mikado* means literally "high gate."

Chinese Temples

In addition to the above monasteries there are three Chinese monasteries of the Zen sect, quite comely, and with a good number of priests, which have in addition several life-size images of a number of Chinese kings and other saints and courtyards decorated with large triumphal banners and other foreign ornaments. The monasteries were donated during the Christian persecution by the various Chinese nations trading in Nagasaki according to the three different languages to which these foreign *danna* belong. They are used for worship and to house the images of their ships, which are given a home in certain chapels but outside the main temple (as long as the ships remain in the harbor). They are brought to the chapel with extraordinary reverence and the noise of large cymbals and drums and carried back in similar fashion at the time of departure. These monasteries and their temples are usually called by the birthplace of their donor rather than their own name (of which they all have a great number) and are as follows:

1. Nankin dera; or temple of Nanking and the country surrounding the city. This is the first temple established by the foreigners and especially by the people from Nanking and neighboring areas that share their language. It has been honored by them with the name of Kōfukuji, which means "temple of restored riches."

2. Chokushū dera,[13] that is, the temple of the area of Amoy, which means that of the people living in the most southern part of China and at the same time of those who live outside China on Formosa and in other more distant countries. It has a *matsuji,* that is, a branch or lesser monastery as subordinate, and is nearly the largest with the greatest number of priests. Its proper name is Fukuji,[14] which means "temple of wealth."

3. Hokushū dera,[15] or temple of the North, the temple of those Chinese who come from the northern part of the country. They call their temple Fukusaiji,[16] which means temple of wealth and sacrifices. Formerly these monasteries were staffed mainly by Chinese priests and were maintained by that country. Since the closure of the country, each monastery is permitted only two native Chinese, and if they cannot collect their

meager upkeep (from sacrifices, requiems, and voluntary donations from their countrymen), they have to rely on the compassion of the shogun, like the other priests within the shogunal cities. The priors of these three monasteries are directly responsible to their own special authority, who lives in Miyako on a mountain called Ōbaku. He claims to occupy the chair of archbishop as the third successor of the archbishop Ingen and consequently to be the head of the clergy of this foreign paganism in Japan.

Ingen

Ingen[17] was born in China, where he occupied the chair of Daruma, the first spiritual magistrate in that country and twenty-eighth successor of the original founder and deity Shaka. His devotion to his work and his countrymen, who lived in three monasteries without a common leader, and his zeal to spread and consolidate the *buppō,* or sect of *butsu,* in the face of the commotion of the *mukuri kokuri*[18] (as they call all Christians and antagonists of their own teaching), who had discredited themselves sufficiently by their harsh code of violence and weapons, induced Ingen to vacate his chair in favor of someone else and go to Japan to establish an office, or archbishop's chair, for the above paganism. He arrived in the year of Christ 1653[19] and was received with great respect. The lords of the provinces came to welcome him, wearing nothing less than *kami shimo,* or ceremonial dress, and took their seat below him. The shogun ordered that he be given a mountain in their holy city of Miyako as a residence, which had to be called Ōbaku, after the archbishop's residence he had left in China. His sanctity came to the test shortly after his arrival, and the result greatly enhanced the esteem in which he was held. He was asked by the farmers of the surrounding countryside to conduct a *kitō,* that is, a holy ceremonial prayer or mass, to draw rain from heaven onto their rice fields, which were being devastated by drought. He answered that he could neither make rain nor assure them that the *kitō* would produce the desired effect but that he would do his best. Thereupon he climbed up a mountain and conducted his *kitō.* The following day the rain poured down so heavily that even the smaller bridges in the city were washed away, and not only the farmers but also the city judged that he had made his *kitō* too strong. The brothers who accompanied him partook of his sanctity and were revered more than others by the people. Even the cook of his very learned entourage from China has been elevated to the dignity of prior of the Chinese monastery of Hokushū dera here in Nagasaki. His enlightened mind has advanced so far in the mysteries of the gods that he uses the name and title of *godō,* which means "godly man of wisdom of all-penetrating mindfulness." He has attained in his mind such *satori,* or truth revealed by devout contemplation, that it cannot be described in simple down-to-earth language. On the Shaka's sacred days, this old kitchen god will place himself on a raised seat in his monastery and accept the respectful salutations appropriate to the gods from thousands of people. He sits in silence and without any movement and very rarely gives a barely noticeable sign to indicate his gracious appreciation. In his hand he holds a small stick with horse hair hanging from the end as his personal token of his mysterious transcendental thought, as the *zazen* priests generally carry such symbols of their own imagination.

Zazen is inner contemplation of spiritual matters and secrets, which, in order to discern the hidden, is done in such depth and with such intensity that the mind is removed from the perception of the senses. After Ingen's arrival, many adherents of *judō*, or the philosophical sect,[20] and no fewer belonging to Shinto, or the local paganism, changed to *buppō*. At that time the eradication of the last vestiges of Christianity was conducted with zeal, and since Christians could easily hide under the cover of the above sects, every house in the whole empire had to own a *zushi*,[21] that is, a place or small altar decorated with one or the other *hotoke*, or deity of that religion. It is the first thing any person moving house will unpack and show to his neighbors, for if he is lacking one, they too are held responsible and have to suffer.

In spite of Ingen's eminence and the unparalleled learnedness attributed to him, neither the clergy, with its divisions into so many quarreling sects, nor the obstinate natives of his own sect decided to place themselves under his umbrella and accept his authority as leader. After his death he was succeeded by someone less learned, powerful, and eminent called Sokuhi.[22] After that the monastery of Ōbaku was headed by someone of their own nation,[23] as authority only over the three above-mentioned Chinese monasteries.

All religious orders and sects in this city, as well as in the whole empire, defer to one or other of these leaders, who enjoy the favor and protection of the shogun. They obediently submit to them and live according to their commands. They humbly accept the favors of the secular magistrates on a great many occasions but for no other reason than that one day they might require their help and protection in civil matters. The superiors of the monasteries are in a position to issue their monks valid travel documents. Beside that they have little say in civil matters and are subject to the secular ruler. The latter has provided all clergy of his domain, regardless of their religion and sect, with two so-called *jisha bugyō*,[24] or, more respectfully, *jisha go bugyō*, who are the shogunal commissioners of the foreign and local idol temples, inspectors, protectors, and secular sextons. After the shogunal councilors, they are the most important bureaucrats of the empire and receive the greatest respect at the shogunal court. They hold their tribunal at Edo which judges civil disputes, concerning mainly such matters as boundary lines, estates, income, alleged injuries suffered by others, and so on, and these are submitted and settled daily in great numbers. Also criminal cases, such as uprisings, treason, and violation of public shogunal laws, which incur capital punishment are heard but are judged as leniently as possible and pronounced only after consultation with and prior knowledge of the appropriate spiritual leader in Miyako. These *jisha bugyō* also generally take care of the clergy's upkeep, religious buildings, and anything else requiring the assistance of secular offices.

Chapter 5
The Arrival, Reception, and Extermination of the Portuguese and Spaniards

Arrival

The Portuguese were the first Europeans courageous enough to venture into the Indian Ocean. In 1497 they sailed with four ships and landed at Calicut to befriend the zamorin, the ruler of these coastal lands. With the annexation of Goa in 1510 they gained their first firm foothold in Asia, and continuing the subjugation of the helpless Indians, they extended their trade through the whole of the East to the furthest and great empire of China. On the journey to the latter country it happened in 1542 that one of their ships drifted to the still unknown country of Japan and landed there in a harbor of the province and principality of Bungo on the island of Kyushu. Japanese chronicles, however, state that the first European vessel landed in Awa on the island of Shikoku, facing Kyushu, and that more or less the next year they arrived in Bungo with only one vessel. They settled there when in 1549 a youth, Georg Alvarest,[1] who had fled to Goa and had been baptized there, returned with a Portuguese ship and showed the fathers of the Society[2] who accompanied him, including the most venerable Francis Xavier,[3] the possibility of converting his heathen countrymen, while to the merchants he demonstrated the profits they could make with their goods in Japan. At that time Japan was not closed. The barons had not yet been subjected to such strict obedience by their rulers; their subjects traveled overseas to trade, and foreign nations were at liberty to visit any part of the country. Therefore these first European visitors were not only free to land where they wanted, but the territorial lords of Kyushu, moreover, vied with each other to induce them to enter their harbors so that their subjects could profit from the trade. Consequently imported goods moved freely through the country. Everybody was craving to acquire something of the foreign rarities and, being ignorant of their value, succumbed to the most unreasonable demands. The newly arrived padres traveled around no less, marketing to these heathens their spiritual wares of the faith of salvation.

Reception

The Portuguese faced no problems importing either their secular or spiritual wares, because they occupied the close-by city of Macao, near China, where they had a store of foreign goods and a supply of Christian fathers. And if they were lacking the latter, they could be supplied by their countrymen and fellow believers, the Spaniards, from the city of Manila, situated in the Philippine Islands, close to Japan. Then there was also the somewhat more distant city of Goa, the Rome of India, packed with monasteries and monks, which delegated its excessive clergy to this most important task. After a short time this nation, therefore, enjoyed the height of good fortune here, inasmuch as the merchants procured the golden ore of the provinces in exchange for Indian and European goods such as raw silk, precious cloth, spices, sweet wine, medicines, and a host of natural and artificially produced goods. The padres, however, won the hearts of the inquisitive populace with the solace afforded by the hitherto unknown religion and made adoption of the Roman Catholic faith attractive through the example of their virtuous lives, performance of good deeds for the poor and sick, and especially the outward splendor of their religious services. In addition, the Japanese had a natural fondness for the Portuguese on account of their lifestyle, their dignified friendliness, and their mental affinity as people of the same latitude, and this resulted in continuing favorable developments for all things Portuguese with regard both to trade and spiritual conversions. To discuss both topics briefly:

Initially the Christian fathers attracted so little faith and attention among the Japanese that even Xavier, the famous converter of heathens, grew weary of the little that could be achieved and left the country. But this was due to their lack of knowledge of Japanese customs, government, and language. They read their sermons and whatever else they wanted to communicate to the people from speeches translated by uneducated interpreters, written in Roman letters. And they did this pronouncing the words (which they themselves did not understand) in such a strange and unintelligible way that mischievous members of their audience could not help but laugh and taunted them. Later, however, when they had learned more about their surroundings and how to use the circumstances to their best advantage, the number of conversions increased rapidly, especially on the island of Kyushu, exceeding any expectations the clergy might have had. For after the padres of the Society had established a residence there, they had the good fortune of converting the three domain lords of Bungo, Arima, and Ōmura. These are the very men who in the year 1582 sent their young relatives with letters to Pope Gregory XIII to demonstrate their deference, an event described by Thuanus[4] and made much ado of in Roman postils. The domain lords' subjects and neighbors followed their example voluntarily and with such zeal that one may indeed say: they took the kingdom of heaven by force.[5] As conversions continued—in some localities faster, in others with some resistance and slower—more and more spiritual reapers were sent from Manila, Macao, and Goa to gather the harvest. Nearly the whole country was converted when the newly initiated Japanese padres began working with the foreigners propagating the Christian faith, for using their own mother tongue they could so much better and effectively show and prove to their countrymen the validity of the Christian faith, as compared to that of their absurd idol worship. However, persecution already occurred during the early stages of propagation. The first edict decreeing capital punishment appeared in

1586, and the first execution took place in the same year.[6] Persecutions increased in severity and force (since the propagation of the Christian faith was damaging to the native priests and temple wardens and consequently led to considerable disorder in the government), but the number of new Christians—with commoners converting publicly, important and great people, secretly—increased at an incredible speed. The letters from the Jesuits in Japan state that in the year 1590 alone, those who had died had been replaced by 20,570 newly converted Christians, and in the years 1591 and 1592 (when the churches were already closed), by 12,000.[7] The Japanese themselves write that the young ruler Hideyori, who was exterminated by his guardian Ieyasu in 1616, and the majority of his courtiers, soldiers, and troops were Christians. For as the new Christians so joyfully met their deaths and could not be dissuaded by any form of torture, curious onlookers were seized by the desire to be instructed in this teaching, which brought such joy to the dying, and finding it full of solace and truth, they became believers themselves.

In the meantime, the secular Portuguese also accomplished their aims. They married the daughters of the richest merchants and procured houses and other riches. Trade, especially, left nothing to be desired. Everyone did his best to fleece the Japanese of their money, primarily with worthless European curios and foreign medicines, hauling more than three hundred tons of gold annually out of the country in this fashion. At that time they could bring in and export again whatever they wished. Most of the time they came with carracks,[8] that is, large vessels; in recent years only gallants, or small vessels, are used. At first the cargo was discharged in the harbors of Bungo and at Hirado, afterward only at Nagasaki. Imports frequently brought twice their value in profits, and exports also brought considerable gains at locations to which they were taken for barter or sale. It is believed that if the Portuguese had continued their trade in this fashion for another twenty years, they would have carted away so many riches from this Ophir[9] that Macao would have displayed as much gold and silver as Jerusalem at the time of Solomon. There is no necessity for me to describe this trade in detail. Let me only state as an example that the amount of goods they imported and sold with large profits here at Nagasaki in the final years of their persecution amounted in the autumn of 1636 to four gallants carrying 2,350 boxes of silver worth 2,350,000 taels, together with 287 Portuguese and their friends from Nagasaki for Macao; in the year 1637, to six gallants carrying 2,142,365.4.1 taels; and in the year 1638, to two gallants with 1,259,023.7.3 taels. I also saw in writing that only a few years previously they carried out of the country one hundred tons of gold in only one single large vessel.

The Fall of the Portuguese

As for the fall of the Portuguese, I have been told by the Japanese that primarily two factors brought about the hatred of the Portuguese. These were the arrogance with which they treated the mighty and the greed they showed toward the commoners. They said that even converted Christians grew impatient with their greed when they discovered that the padres were not just hankering after souls but also after money and land and that, moreover, the secular Portuguese profiteered beyond all acceptable norms. Their arrogance increased with the number of Christian converts, and their spiritual leaders were no longer content to walk on foot (like Christ and the apostles at Jerusalem) but wanted to be carried in stately litters (like the pope and his cardinals at Rome). They also considered themselves of equal and even higher status than the great secular lords. For one day when their bishop happened to meet the most senior councilor of the empire, he declined to pay him the usual respect by stopping, or descending from his litter but instead ordered his bearers to continue walking, and pass him. As a result the councilor not only personally adopted a vindictive attitude toward the Portuguese nation but also complained about their indolence toward the ruler Taikō. The incident was of the greatest detriment for the whole Portuguese nation and also did much to bring about the actual destruction of the Christians. So much so that in the following year of 1597, the destruction took its bloody beginning with the execution of twenty-six people, including the crucifixion of two foreign Jesuits and various Franciscans.

Added to this must be the fact that the Christian faith they propagated was irreconcilable and incompatible with the native religion, which caused great confusion in the community, and it was feared that even greater havoc might be created by the new Christians, who cursed their compatriots, persecuted the *bōzu,* or heathen priests, and in some places had already torn down and broken their gods. Therefore when the clever ruler Taikō and especially his illegal successor Ieyasu had gained control of the country—the former by bravery, the latter by perjury—and they were at pains to eliminate anything that might prejudice the consolidation of their power, they became suspicious of the incredible solidarity of the Christians and their antagonism toward the gods of their forefathers. This was all the more the case with Ieyasu, because his declared enemy, the supporters of Hideyori, consisted to a large extent of newly converted Christians. Therefore these rulers considered it necessary for the preservation of their hegemony to stem the tide of this teaching, which was spreading like wildfire and was irreconcilable with other gods and beliefs. First the propagation of the padres' teaching (the name they gave to the Roman Catholic faith) was strictly forbidden. Next orders went to the governors and barons, or territorial lords, to persuade their subjects to renounce their conversion to Christianity. Soon afterward, those in charge of the Portuguese were ordered to bring no more padres to Japan, and finally the foreign padres were commanded to leave the country. The first order, namely, the compulsory renunciation, was put into effect, but the remaining orders were ignored. To the contrary, Portuguese and Spanish ships secretly landed more and more padres, and the barefoot Franciscans, ignoring the pleas and warnings of the Jesuits, erected a small church at Miyako in contravention of the newly issued prohibition of the ruler and even read their sermons openly to the masses in the streets. Their excuse for their disobedience, which harmed all churches of God and endangered their own lives, was simply that they owed greater obedience to God than to men and that their only desire was to die for the name of Christ. As a consequence, the most cruel persecution and torture of Christians ever witnessed on this globe came about, lasting more than forty years until the last drop of Christian blood was spilled. This also resulted in a permanent ban of the Portuguese and the Spanish nation and their important trade with and navigation to Japan. At no stage previously had the court intended to break with this nation.

When false testimony stirred the Taikō to fly into a sudden rage against the padres, he ordered them to leave the country within twenty days, but shortly afterward he permitted them to build a church near Miyako, though not to preach in it. With that action he wanted to demonstrate that his anger was directed against the religion and not the nation. Nor was it the intention of his successor to break relations with the nation, because their annually imported goods were essential for the good life. Therefore even during the last phase of the persecution of the Christians, when all Portuguese and Spanish teaching was coming to an end, they still wanted to keep the secular merchants and built for them the above-mentioned sealed-off Deshima to continue trading (and separate trade from religion). The final blow, however, came with the fatal discovery of a dangerous venture planned by the foreigners and the native Christians against the person of the ruler as a heathen lord, which happened as follows:

The Dutch, attracted by the profitable trade of the Portuguese, had already arrived in Japan prior to 1600. They established their warehouse and settled at Hirado and received a shogunal patent confirming their right to visit the country and trade freely. The fortunate development of their trade in India made it essential, while the war into which they had entered with the Portuguese made it acceptable, to work against the interest of that nation and its merchants and especially to turn the false accusations with which the Portuguese attempted to blacken the name of the Dutch in the eyes of the Japanese—alleging they were Spanish rebels, pirates, and so on—to their own benefit and to the disadvantage of their slanderers. Therefore, when on capturing a Portuguese ship they found a treacherous letter to the Portuguese king from the Portuguese resident general in Japan, a native Japanese and zealous supporter of the Christian nations called Captain Moro,[10] they were not inclined to ignore this letter but forwarded it to their immediate patron, the lord of Hirado. He sent it to the governor of Nagasaki, as judge and high authority over visitors and foreigners (who was very favorably disposed towards the Portuguese). For this reason Captain Moro and the resident Portuguese denied and fiercely fought the accusation. But neither the goodwill of the governor nor their denials could save the situation, since the script, hand, and seal incriminated them. Instead the letter had to be sent to the ruler, and the author was tied to a post, roasted, and burned alive. The letter revealed the hostile designs of the Japanese Christians against the ruler, the demand for ships and military support pledged by Portugal, the name of the Japanese lords who were to conduct the affair, and the expectation of the pope's blessing for successful completion. The plot was confirmed by another letter of the same Captain Moro to the Portuguese government at Macao, which was discovered and brought back by a Japanese sailor. Consequently it was now easy to completely oust these foreign visitors, who had for some time incurred the suspicion and therefore the hatred of the Japanese court and who were, moreover, still bringing priests into the country in spite of repeated prohibitions. This also led in 1637 to the issue and enforcement of the following order against the Dutch, which was sent by the ruler to the steward of Nagasaki for execution and signed personally by the councilors of the realm. At the same time, the whole country was permanently closed by a prohibition against the departure of Japanese subjects and the arrival of foreign nationals.

> To Sakakibara Hida no Kami[11] and Baba Saburō Saemon[12]
>
> No Japanese vessel nor native Japanese may leave the country.
>
> Those violating this prohibition shall die, and the vessel and all its crew will be kept under arrest until further orders are received. Japanese who return from abroad shall be killed.
>
> Anybody reporting a priest will be rewarded with four to five hundred pieces of silver; for an ordinary Christian a proportional sum will be paid. (One piece of silver weighs approximately five ounces. Consequently 500 pieces are equal to 2,500 taels.)
>
> Anybody perpetuating the Christian religion, and anybody tainted by this evil name, must be imprisoned at Ōmura.
>
> The families of the Portuguese, their mothers, wet nurses, and all other dependents must be banished to Macao. Whosoever carries a letter from abroad and whosoever returns after being banished will be killed with his whole family together with anybody who intercedes for them.
>
> No aristocrat or soldier may buy even the smallest item from a foreigner, and so on. (I am omitting the other sentences which do not have a bearing on the topic.)
>
> In the year Kanei 13, 19th day of the 5th month.[13]
>
> Sakai Sanuki no Kami,[14] Matsudaira Izu no Kami,[15]
> Doi Ōi no Kami,[16] Abe Bungo no Kami,[17]
> Kaga no Kami[18]

Although the enforcement of the shogun's order was very soon under way, the leaders of the Portuguese merchants managed with great efforts to remain a further two years at Nagasaki in the hope of being able to move their residence to Deshima and continue from that location their profitable trade with Japan, which they would no more give up than their lives. For this purpose in 1635 the said island was raised for these visitors from the floor of the bay, close to the city of Nagasaki, to which it is connected by a bridge. The island was fortified with strong gates, fences, and guardhouses, so that the Portuguese could live there as *gōdō*,[19] that is, heretics, removed from any contact with the Japanese, kept and guarded solely for the purpose of trade.

However, the die had been cast, and they were unable to remain beyond 1639. In that year the rest, down to the last survivors with Portuguese blood in their veins, had to leave the country after the court had gained sufficient assurances that the Dutch could service them with all goods that the Portuguese had formerly brought. After that, the Portuguese and Spaniards, together with their sympathizers and relatives, were declared the archenemies of the country, and even the import of goods from these countries such as cloth, leather, wool, and any other produce or product was permanently prohibited. (Only with regard to Spanish wines does the court claim exception.)

Envoys from Macao are Beheaded in Japan

Therefore when in the following year of 1640 two envoys from the government of Macao arrived in the harbor, they were immediately taken into custody on land together with their complete retinue, a total of seventy-three persons (even though they carried no merchandise). Once the court had been informed of their arrival, they were beheaded on shogunal orders in violation of the common law of nations. Twelve of the lowliest were, however, permitted to return to report the treatment of their masters and to communicate that even if the Portuguese king or the god of the Christians were to arrive in Japan, they would be treated no differently. But these messengers never arrived back, presumably because they went down with the vessel, not knowing how to navigate it. In Japanese fashion each condemned man had his own executioner, and therefore the executions took place simultaneously and instantaneously once the sign was given.

In a Japanese manuscript of a Nagasaki citizen living at the time I discovered yet another tragic story that happened before that event, namely, that of a carrack, or Spanish vessel with three decks or floors, which arrived here from the Philippines and was destroyed in this harbor with all its crew in an unprecedented bloodbath. Even though I do not find the story in the journals of the Dutch, which at the time were kept at Hirado but have since been partly lost, I do not doubt its authenticity and therefore have no hesitation in adding it here word by word according to the Japanese record.

The Castilians (as they call the Spanish) had taken a Japanese junk near Manila and drowned the crew. They believed that all traces had been buried in the water, but the news soon reached the Japanese court. After a year a galleon with three decks, or floors, arrived and dropped anchor near Nagasaki. The local government transmitted its news of arrival with express dispatch to the court, which ordered the territorial lord of Arima to burn the vessel with its crew. Three days before this order arrived, sympathetic citizens warned the Castilians secretly of the impending danger and advised them to leave again quickly. But their greed, and in the final instance unfavorable winds, ruled out this course of action. For they spent day and night loading the vessel until it was filled with gold, silver, precious Japanese goods, and the riches they had stored at Nagasaki, while standing by ready to defend themselves and depart. Meanwhile the aristocratic executioner arrived in the harbor with a large force of people and innumerable ships. They immediately encircled the galleon, but it tried in vain to escape because the wind, clamoring for revenge, was against it. Yet the plans of the Japanese could not be accomplished as easily as they had imagined; the extermination was to cost their own blood. Courageously the lord spurred on his people to board the enemy vessel, but no one was willing, until the lord himself stepped on enemy territory and by his example induced his people to follow him. At once they filled the topmost deck or spillway of the ship like a large swarm of bees. On their arrival the Castilians had all descended from the spillway and closed the hatch above them. At this the lord suspected trouble and jumped back into his boat as if to chase up more people. Hardly had he withdrawn than the Castilians blew up the deck crowded with Japanese soldiers with powder from underneath, hurling the enemy into the air. Thereupon a new set of people was ordered to board the vessel and massacre the enemy, who had descended still further, hiding under the second deck. But this deck too was blown up with all the Japanese on it, and repeating this act of violence, they succeed in blowing up their enemy a third time. As a result, the bay was dotted with Japanese as if heaven had showered it with hailstones before they could reach the ship's crew. Consisting of several hundred, the crew still defended themselves for several hours until the last succumbed in battle. This skirmish took half a day and cost no fewer than three thousand Japanese lives. Incredible riches were retrieved from the ocean floor where it took place, amounting, according to hearsay, to some three thousand boxes of silver.

So far the manuscript. I have been told that only a few years ago silver was still found on this spot.

After the country had finally unburdened itself of these visitors in this fashion (even though their padres were still hiding at various places in Japan), the Japanese learned how the Portuguese had gained great access at the Chinese court and to the governors of the provinces. Therefore they considered it necessary to be on their guard and built watchtowers on high mountains and stationed guards in them. To this very hour, the guards are under order to announce by lighting fires if they see more than ten sails or vessels together in the sea. In this fashion the news travels within twenty-four hours over the mountains to the shogunal residence at Edo. Thus, should the vessels attack the country, orders for defense can be issued at an early time. Even at that time a system existed where everybody knew at which location and under which flag he was to report with his weapon when the mountain fires were lit.

Chapter 6
The Situation of the Dutch

At the beginning of the present seventeenth century, very soon after their ships began to travel to Asia and the establishment of their East India Company, the Dutch, enticed by the fertile trade of the Portuguese, began making annual visits to this, the furthest empire of the world. They arrived at the city and island of Hirado and set up their warehouse and living quarters on a spit of land linked to the city by a bridge. Their admission to Japan was all the quicker and easier, the greater their enmity was toward those whom the ruler felt compelled to drive out of the country. Even though the Portuguese still had a lot of influence with the greatest lords of the country, and did much to prevent the entry of the Dutch, they were finally unable to stop the shogun Ieyasu—or Gongen, after his death—from giving the Dutch access to the country in the year of Christ 1611 with a special *goshuin,* which literally means "lofty cinnabar seal" and is a shogunal permit or pass. It is signed by the councilors of the empire and authorized by the red shogunal seal, from the color of which it also takes its name. With this document they were granted in very clear terms, or characters, free trade and access to all provinces and harbors with favorable recommendations to all subjects of the empire. After the death of the shogun they requested to have their privileges renewed and a new pass issued, against the practice of this nation, which considers upholding the laws of its forefathers a sacred duty. This they received, but while outwardly it appeared to be identical in form and shape, it contained much less advantageous conditions. Meanwhile, from the time they settled in Hirado, the Dutch did what they could to profit from the progressive decline of the Portuguese. They did everything possible to please the court, the source of success or failure, as well as the councilors, the lord of Hirado, and any other great men who might proffer help or hindrance. The Dutch spared no cost nor labor to seek out the world's rarest novelties to pay homage to the Japanese annually and to satisfy the ridiculous passion of the Japanese for various strange animals—which nature did not create the way they imagine them—by bringing in as many as possible from the most distant empires of India, Persia, and Europe. The Dutch showed the utmost subservience in everything, even wrongful impositions, to stay in the good books of this nation and conduct profitable trade. Since they valued their lives, they could show no objection when in 1638 the shogun ordered them to tear down as fast as if they were enemy property their own newly built residence and warehouse on the island of Hirado: valuable stone mansions such as Japan had never seen before. The reason was that the buildings were splendid beyond the custom of the country and had the year of the Christian era on the gable. Soon afterward, in the same year of 1638, this heathen court had no qualms in inflicting upon them a cursed test to find out whether the orders of the shogun or the love for their fellow Christians had greater power over them. It was a matter of us serving the empire by helping to destroy the native Christians, of whom those remaining, some forty thousand people, in desperation over their martyrdom had moved into an old fortress in the province of Shimabara and made preparations to defend themselves. The head of the Dutch, Koekebecker,[1] himself went to the location with the one remaining vessel (for in the face of the impudent demand the remainder had slipped out of the harbor the previous day) and in fourteen days treated the beleaguered Christians to 426 rough cannon salvos, both from land and sea. Although this assistance resulted neither in surrender nor complete defeat, it broke the strength of the besieged. And because the Japanese had the pleasure to order it, he stripped the vessel of a further six cannons (regardless of the fact that she still had to navigate dangerous seas) that the Japanese insisted had to be lent in addition to the first to carry out their cruel designs.

It is true that this show of total obedience was instrumental in keeping a foothold in the country when the court was considering completely closing it to all Christians. At the same time, however, they gained a bad reputation among the more high-minded at court and throughout the country, for they judged that people who so easily permitted themselves to be used in the destruction of those with whom they basically shared the same belief and the path of Christ—as they had been amply told by the padres from Portugal and Manila—could not be true of heart, honest, and loyal towards a foreign ruler. I was told this by the locals in these very same words. Thus far from earning the trust and deep friendship of this exceedingly suspicious nation by their compliance, the reputation of the Dutch was ruined unjustly, regardless of their merits. Shortly afterward, in 1641, the Dutch, having assisted in the confinement of the Portuguese by word and deed, were to undergo the same experience. For they were told to leave the island of Hirado with all their belongings and to exchange subordination to a lenient territorial lord for directions from a new and zealous administration directly responsible to the shogun, while retiring under strict guard and manifold supervision within the limits of the prison built for the Portuguese. Submission to these proud heathens into such servitude and imprisonment, forgoing all celebrations of feast days and Sundays, all devotion with religious song and prayer, the use of the name of Christ, the symbol of the cross, and all outward proof or signs of being a Christian, and, added to that, good-natured acceptance of their despicable impudence, an affront to any high-minded soul, all that for the love of profit and to gain control of the veins of ore in their mountains.

> To what does it not drive human hearts, that damned hunger for gold! Virg. 3 Æne.[2]

This jail goes by the name of Deshima, that is, the *island* which lies *in front* of the city. It is also called Deshima *machi,* because it is counted as one street: the street of the in-front-lying island. The island is situated next to the city and has been built up with boulders one and a half to two fathoms from the ocean floor, which at this point is rocky and sandy and at low tide emerges from the water; the island rises half a fathom above the highest water level. It has the shape of a fan without a handle, or a rounded square, following the curve of the city, to which it is linked by a bridge of hewn stones a few steps long,[3] and from which it is separated by a strong gate and sentry. At the northern end are two large strong water gates, which are open only when vessels are discharged or loaded under the supervision of some of the commissioned nobles of the governor. The island is surrounded and enclosed by high planks with their roofs and has a double fence in the fashion of a *Chevaux de frise;*[4] but all of this is weak and unable to withstand any force. A few steps removed from this fortified prison, thirteen high posts emerge from the water, each with a small board with writing. They are orders prohibiting boats to enter in between the posts and approach the island. In front of the bridge to the city, a place for proclamations has been built from hewn stones. Here two orders by the governors are published on raised boards. The first contains instructions for the guarding of the gate, and the second is addressed to the servants of the street of Deshima and all others entering the island. At the time of the sales the headman of our street demonstrates his authority and care by displaying an additional and superfluous poster with nearly identical wording in the street. All these orders, as well as some others, are found in a separate chapter.[5]

The area of the island is estimated to be one stadium,[6] or 600 steps in length and 240 in width. According to my measurements it is 82 ordinary steps in width and 236 in length through the middle, following the curve, being shorter on the side of the city and longer on that facing the sea on account of its shape. Two roads crossing each other run through the whole island, and in addition there is a circular road within the barricades, which can be closed off when necessary. The rain gutters run into the sea in a deep curve, so that they cannot be used for passing anything in or out of the island. Only the street running the length of the island has houses on both sides. Like the whole island, these houses were originally built by a number of citizens from their own funds, and in accordance with the original agreement the owners still receive an unfair rent of 6,500 *jū momme* annually. They are miserable buildings and look like goat-pens: made of clay and pine boards roughly stuck together, two stories high, with the lower having to serve as store and the upper as living quarters. The occupant covers the latter at his own expense with colored wallpaper and padded floor mats in Japanese fashion and installs doors and windows.

Three guard houses are also situated within the limits of the island, one at each end and in the middle. At the entrance there is moreover a place with the necessary equipment to extinguish fires. For this purpose also the fence has a number of water gates, which are nailed down in such a fashion that they can be forced open in an emergency. There is a water course through which the kitchen water is channeled in a bamboo pipe from the river, and this water must be paid for separately on an annual basis. Some of the space behind the streets has been built up by our people at their own expense and contains a building for the sales, two fireproof warehouses (because the other stores do not protect the goods against rain, fire, or theft), a sizable kitchen, a building for the commissioned inspectors of the magistrates, or directors of sales, a house for the interpreters which is used only at the said times, a kitchen and an ornamental garden, a wash place, some private little gardens, a bathroom. Part of the area has been acquired by the ward headman for his living and pleasure quarters, his kitchen as well as an ornamental garden. Of the remaining space some is kept for the stalls, which are erected when the ships are in the harbor, and some for the useless packing material after the goods have been unwrapped. This spot was recently ordained as a bloody execution ground, to be used, as the magistrates assured us, not just for Japanese but also for Dutch smugglers.

This is the state of the enclosure set up for the Dutch, with which they have to be satisfied in this country. During the two to three months of their stay, the annually arriving vessels are permitted to let their men visit the island to refresh themselves in turn after each has been searched and registered. When they have left, the chief must remain here, together with various other persons, about seven, more if desired. (Previously with larger amounts of trade there were never fewer than twenty.) The Japanese could hardly imagine that the nation could come to grief over the presence of the few remaining Dutch. Their small number and the fact that they are unarmed precludes an enemy attack. Neither is it possible for the Dutch to engage in smuggling since all goods and anything else that could be sold is registered and kept under lock and seal by the Japanese. Even the cloth brought for tailoring is kept by the ward headmen until it is cut by tailors, who are under oath. There is even less likelihood that the Dutch could make any forays in matters of religion, because the light of Christian devotion shed by our conduct is too dim to spot even an elephant. But in spite of all this, they are strictly and strongly guarded in this prison from the inside and outside of the secluded island by various guards, companies, and guilds and their sworn members, who in turn contain vigilant outsiders

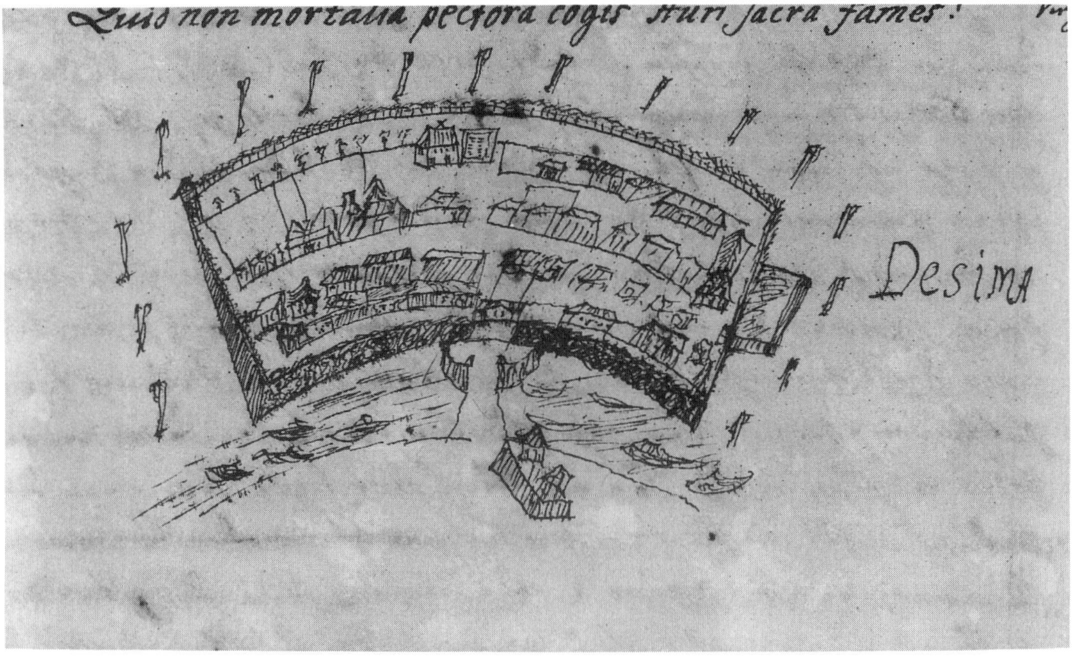

Kaempfer's drawing of Deshima. (Courtesy of the British Library, Sloane 3060, folio 239)

among them, treating us not like honest men but like criminals, traitors, spies, prisoners, or, to say the least, as *hito jichi,* hostages of the shogun, as the locals always (thoughtfully) call us.

The guards employed for this purpose are:

Monban

The first and most important, *monban,* or gate sentry, which occupies the gate house facing the city through which all those entering and leaving must pass, is occupied daily by five and at the time of trading by ten to thirteen men of varying status (not counting their servants). One or two from the city's *funa ban* and an equal number from the *jūninshū* attend daily in rotation, as well as a servant of the *nenban toshiyori,* the officiating city mayor, and a servant from one of the *jōgyōji,* or deputy mayors, acting as heads of the *soto machi.* One of the latter constantly sits next to a book, noting who entered and left, and at what time, and what was carried in and out. The book is kept for the information of the governors, who inspect this diary monthly, or whenever it pleases them. Yet except for the permissible goods carried by the purveyors, they do not permit passage of anything without the special order of the magistrates or guarantee of the ward headman. They are assisted by three sworn inspectors, of whom one or two are constantly seated next to the door, conducting body searches of everybody entering or leaving to find out whether anything is being carried in or out. Exceptions are the representatives of the magistrates and their entourage, as well as the ordinary interpreters and their sons, if they have been registered as apprentices. When the ships are in the harbor, the streets, as well as the purchasers of silk, must each furnish an additional four guards: sharing the profits, they must also share the duties. This results in a great mixture of strangers, and the lack of a common element successfully prevents them from making common cause. And each one is charged with the duty to watch both his fellow guards and those passing by and, as much as possible, also those locked up on the island.

The weapons displayed on the walls of this guard house are iron chains to shackle, ropes to bind, heavy poles to beat, as well as special instruments like morning stars,[7] which are used to catch thieves and escapees and are carried when criminals meet their death.

Mawari Ban

The second guard, *mawari ban,* or watch doing the rounds, is staffed by six lesser citizens or laborers, who are stationed at three places within our confinement and rotate, making the circuit at night with two wooden clappers, with which they announce their watchfulness and the hour of the night according to the custom of the country. They are on the lookout for all unusual occurrences, and especially for fire and theft. They change daily with others and are furnished by every ward of the city on a monthly basis. But at the time of trading, this guard is taken care of by the ward headman, the proprietors of the houses, and the officials of the treasury of our island. Being responsible for all incidents, they take the precaution of employing their own men whom they know and can rely on.

Guards during the Time of Sales and Trade

An additional main fire guard is on duty during the time of trading. It is made up personally of the landlords, scribes, ward headmen, officials of the treasury, and the cooks. During the first round at dusk there is a knock on every door, to ask whether Japanese are present and to recommend caution with fire. The *otona* must join at least one of the night's rounds, at which time he has his iron ward-rod and fire-rod with its rings dragged behind him with great noise according to the custom of the country. In addition, the Dutch themselves have to stand guard against thieves at this time, patrolling the island and the stores, so they are not robbed by the Japanese or the guards themselves.

In addition to the above, there are still other guards responsible for the general supervision of the foreigners. There is especially the *funa ban,* or boat or harbor guard, which patrols outside our island at night with broad, coastal vessels. Yet rather than continue discussing the general guards, I will describe those who are actually employed by the Japanese or hired by the Dutch themselves for their service, assistance, and attendance. Whatever their status, they also have to be regarded as our guards in their capacity as sworn officers and secret enemies, regardless of the fact that they must earn their living and support their dependent family members from our funds, or rather from the riches they unfairly plunder from us.

Otona

Among these a certain ward headman by the name of Yoshikawa Gibuemon wields the greatest authority and has the greatest claim on leadership. In addition to being headman of his street in the city, he is also *otona,* that is, ward headman, and in charge of the island of Deshima. He ranks after the annually rotating head of the ordinary interpreters, over whom he has no authority. His job is to supervise strictly everything concerning the island and its trade and, with the assistance of the interpreters, to take care of the progress of the annual sales and connected matters. Further he must supervise the registration of private goods, keep them in custody, and direct the negotiations for the same. Moreover, he is responsible for the construction of roads and houses, the prevention of fires and all other dangers. He protects and sits in judgment over the servants of the Dutch, the cooks, and the headman of the coolies and day laborers as far as they are under his jurisdiction. He permits them entry, or withdraws them from our service, and hands out passes, or permits, to enter Deshima. His office and oath oblige him not only to observe the above Japanese but also to investigate the pursuits, life, and customs of the Dutch and to keep the same within the limits of shogunal orders. Yet he has never used his authority against the Dutch, nor are they likely to accept it, unless a violation of shogunal orders were discovered, in which case we would be (instantaneously) subjected to his chains and detention.

This *otona* is hated by us on account of his outward severity and the office he occupies but most of all on account of his betrayal of his master.[8] Perhaps he has renounced his evil ways, or was obliged by law to act as he did (as I have been told), for there is no doubt that he is an intelligent man, neither of false nor base sentiment, so well educated in the teaching of Kōshi (Confucius), the traditions of his ancestors, history, and religion that he could be entrusted with writing the chronicle of Hizen. Yet he appears greatly to detest ignorant and brutal men. He has a *nichi gyōshi,* or messenger, to assist him who daily inspects the locks of the water gates and the condition of the barricades and orders construction workers and carpenters and other necessary men. He also has various *hissha,* or scribes, who register the private belongings of the Dutch that can be turned into cash, seal them, and pass them on for safekeeping, quite apart from all the others who are required to follow his orders and assist him. He nets the same benefits from the noble Dutch Company and unlawful share of our trade as the senior interpreters. In addition he benefits from his city streets and the proprietors of our island. He also receives a part of the rent, because he has already bought up nearly one-third of the houses. But his greatest profit stems from Dutch goods, which he acquires through others and in other people's names and then sells.

Deshima *Jishonin*

Among his subordinates are the Deshima *jishonin*, the twenty-four landlords or owners of our houses. At the time of the sales they appear daily, less frequently during the remaining period. They do not just pay attention to the condition of their houses but also observe the inhabitants from a distance, help them with the registration of their arriving and departing goods and household and personal effects, and according to the custom of the country are held responsible for the inhabitants of their houses should something untoward occur.

Oranda Tsūji

The combined fraternity of the *Oranda tsūji,* or Dutch interpreters, constitutes the largest and most important group among the servants of the Dutch, making up a considerable number of approximately 150 (during my presence only 123, as they were incomplete). They are employed to assist us and to discourage foreigners from learning the language, so that they can be kept ignorant of and blind to internal conditions of trade, the city and country, and all events that occur. Their numbers have been inflated so that a greater part of the population can gain their livelihood from this employment and, at the same time, so that they can better observe every move of the foreigners during the time of the sales. I will not neglect to examine this fraternity in detail, for it can serve as example of other well established guilds, but owing to the large amount of detail, it will be discussed in the next chapter. I will also postpone to that chapter the discussion of their subordinates, the Deshima *hissha,* the scribes of Deshima, as well as the Deshima *tsuetsuki,* the inspectors of the porters and day laborers, and the *kanaban nakama,* the guild of the treasury officials, because it belongs to the topic of the annual trade.

Konpura Nakama

Another sworn guild, that of the purveyors, is employed to serve us with the above: the *kai mono tsukai,* or commonly called *konpura nakama* in half-Portuguese. At present they consist only of seventeen citizens or families. Since nobody else is permitted to bring even the smallest item for sale, they alone procure for us what we desire in daily food and drink, household goods, and other requirements from among the permissible wares, at twice or three times the market price. Our immoral and irreligious young men even pay them five German gold coins for a night of pleasure with women who serve the locals for two or three mace. The whore-master only receives one *jū momme* (one-third) of the price.[9] The remainder goes into the treasury of the guild as their profit and also pays for some servants to conduct the bride to the ball.

Cooks

Next are the *daidokoro mono,* or kitchen staff, consisting of three cooks, who serve in monthly rotation and are paid twenty-four *jū momme.* Then there are two common kitchen hands who, in addition, are assisted by one or the other apprentice, or son as future incumbent, as well as by water carriers and servants of the official purveyors. Consequently, except when the sales are on, there are more kitchen hands than Dutch eaters and to maintain them costs more than keeping a table in Europe. On the orders of the governors, their numbers may not be reduced nor may the care of the table be put into the hands of our own people. Formerly the most senior received a monthly salary of six taels, the second of four taels, and the third of three taels. But on orders from the governors, they were given an annual income and from 1674 onward the first had to be paid 150, the second 130, and the third 100 taels. Also other fellow diners, eager to assist the chef, are kept for general requirements, such as a gardener, a servant for housekeeping duties, and a grass carrier or cattlehand. The latter has few cattle because the males are secretly poisoned or have their legs broken at night as soon as they are ready to mate to prevent cattle from being produced to the disadvantage of the purveyors. These servants come from a different street every month, because this service is considered a privilege from which many should benefit, and also because lengthy employment might make them too familiar and frank with the Dutch.

Servants

The Dutch are permitted to use as servants during the day a number of boys or young men who are listed in the books of the *otona* merely as *kozukai,*[10] meaning errand boy. They are the sons of the ordinary interpreters and servants, who are learning Dutch to qualify as their fathers' successors. They are permitted to do so as long as they are still naive and considered ignorant of the Japanese empire, or if favored with a special permit from the *otona.* But they all have to provide a sworn guarantee from a good local man, who stands as guarantor for their conduct. They must, by the way, be commended, for in no other country of the world could one find people caring more faithfully for their masters' property.

Craftsmen

Further, certain craftsmen from a variety of guilds are allowed to enter when they are called to do some work, but they need to have permission from the governors each time. They share the profits with the members of their guild and also present the *otona* and the interpreters with an annual gift.

These are the people who are regarded as ordinary servants and visitors to the island of Deshima, and only they can meet the Dutch and associate with them (but not without an excuse). Yet they are bound by such a weighty oath that persuading them to strike up a candid friendship is not easy. The oath I speak of is one where they must renounce our nation, religion, any communication, friendship, and the promotion of our interests.

The Oath

The oath is taken, here as everywhere else in the empire, according to a general formula laid down in the country's statutes. By this oath the revenge of the highest deities of heaven as well as the most important and stringent authorities of the country is called upon the oath-taker, his family, fellow lodgers, and good friends if he does not abide by the articles he swears to, which are then listed individually according to the above-mentioned general formula. Below that his seal is placed in black oil paint and a drop of blood is smeared on top, which he takes from behind his fingernail. The oath receives less respect from these ungodly people for its frightful supernatural consequences than for fear of inevitable punishment from the secular authorities, for whom violation can be requited only by the blood that sealed the oath.

The clauses vary in importance and strictness according to the position and ability of the person and can be divided into three categories. The first is the most important, containing the most stringent conditions, and is taken by the *otona* and general senior interpreters, as well as junior and apprentice interpreters. It is only taken on the arrival of a new magistrate, who receives the oath in person in his mansion, not by the jurors repeating the formula and raising or placing fingers on the document, but by affixing their seal and blood, as is common in this country. The second set of clauses is used for the oath of all personal interpreters, cooks, officials of the treasury, scribes, headmen of the coolies (inspectors of the day laborers), and purveyors. The oath is received by the *otona* and the senior interpreter in the ordinary monastery of Anzenji of the Tendai sect. The most lenient and simplest clauses are reserved for the ordinary Japanese servants and young personal attendants of the Dutch, as well as the ordinary craftsmen and workers in our streets. It is taken in front of the Deshima *otona.* However, the latter is not satisfied with the oath of a commoner or youth, and consequently each one must produce a trusted citizen as bondsman, who accepts the responsibility for any violation of these clauses by a similar oath. Also the guild of the purveyors demands the same oath from those parties, confirmed only by seal and not with blood, because as heads of the ordinary servants they, too, have to suffer for any misdemeanor.

The distrustful authorities are not content with the detestable oath given by the last two categories, but for added weight have it repeated twice annually. The first time is at New Year, when the picture of the crucified Christ and other religious figures are trampled underfoot. Shortly afterward the renunciation of our Christian nation takes place for added emphasis. The oath is performed a second time when our vessels enter the harbor, to freshly impress the inveterate mind and newly implant feelings of hate. Those people who travel to the shogunal court in our entourage have to take a third oath or pledge before departure swearing that they will even report their companions, will not trust us, report everything they observe about us, not render us any favors, and so on. In addition to the clauses stipulated in the oaths, there are a variety of other orders contained in certain laws and proclamations which the *otona* distributes and publicizes on various points of the island. They direct those permitted to enter for service on our island to avoid us, and contain point by point instructions on how they must conduct themselves in incidents involving the Dutch. Five of those are mounted in the entrance of the *otona*'s living quarters (where he resides during the summer and at the time of the sales). The most important of these concerns the arrival and departure of Dutch goods: each official charged with the investigation of our crates and goods receives a copy of the same as well as a list of prohibited goods to help him in his inspections. A public proclamation from the governors, containing regulations for persons entering and leaving the island, is mounted at the intersection of the crossroads during the months of the sales. In the treasury, the laws governing the treasury officials are displayed and the interpreters, no less, have their own mounted orders.

Finally, in addition to the sworn-in persons, who are employed to visit our living quarters and island ordinarily, the buyers of our annually imported goods and the vendors of the native copper, or their scribes and authorized representatives, mostly from Miyako or other localities, are permitted to enter, but only during the time of the sales and on certain days. At the end of this period merchants of local lacquered wood, copper, and other manufactured articles, who erect their stalls within a designated compound, are also well represented.

None of the above-mentioned persons may enter through the gate unless they carry a permit in the shape of a small wooden docket and are prepared to submit to a body search, which generally is conducted only on departure. Exempt from this inspection is whoever carries two swords within the entourage of a magistrate's deputy senior enough to carry a pike, the ward headmen, eight general interpreters, and some of their natural or adopted sons as privileged students and apprentices to the Dutch language, or, more aptly, freeloaders of the Dutch and their fathers' future successors. They are exempt because the former can be described only as paid and commissioned investigators, and the latter as informers and sworn enemies of the Dutch.

The small docket used as a permit is approximately three inches long and two inches wide. On one side it has the ordinary name of the street headman of the city street in which the bearer is registered with the impression of his seal in black ink, as well as the time of entry and the general ordinary name of the bearer. The other side has a large branded *go mon* (seal)[11] imprint from our ward headman with the wording Deshima *otona*. When the ships arrive, he sends a supply of these brand-marked dockets to all ward headmen of the city, so that they can issue them to Japanese from outside the city arriving for the sales or their own citizens.

Japanese orders addressed to our nation are transmitted to our directors partly by being read to us at the shogunal court by the councilors and partly by the governors of Nagasaki conveying them orally to us through their *bugyō* and our interpreters. When the ships arrive, the directors, in turn, pass the necessary directions on to their subordinates both orally and in writing. These consist mainly in the order to refrain from all forms of smuggling (explained in such a fashion as to impress the newcomer) and to abstain from all outward forms of Christian devotion, as well as to behave properly in accordance with the demands of the locality and the nation. To place further restrictions upon their behavior is unnecessary, for such restrictions are amply indicated by the presence of so many guards and inspectors.

Such are the conditions under which we live all year round, surrounded by sworn officers, confined and imprisoned. We are, however, permitted a few escapes from our prison quarters annually. Yet (without flattering ourselves) we cannot say that these originate from any feelings of gentle leniency, because every time these outings must be justified either by them or by us on grounds of some due payment of respect or some necessity on our part that benefits them. This is well demonstrated by the heavy expenses, and also by the throng of guards and inspectors (an armed enemy or traitor could not be escorted more safely), and finally by the nature of each excursion as described below.

The first takes place after the departure of the vessels when the captain, with a few of his colleagues, makes the annual journey to court and delivers the official presents. This is the same demonstration of commitment all vassals of the empire have to pay annually, and the court considers it nothing less than homage from the Dutch nation. Therefore, on their dismissal, the laws governing their behavior in this country are read to them as they are to other vassals, and in general parlance we are referred to as *hito jichi,* that is, human pawn, in other words, hostages furnished by the Dutch nation. Accordingly we are granted no more liberties on our journey than those accorded to prisoners: we are not permitted to converse with other people, not even with the servants of our inn, unless special permission is granted. There we are allocated the room at the very back, and to prevent us from escaping, its courtyard is carefully locked or nailed up. To guard, serve, and assist us, the magistrate assigns to our entourage a sworn group of soldiers, city bailiffs, servants, and porters, all men unknown to us, in addition to the interpreters and cooks from our island. Further there are horse grooms and overseers for our and other people's luggage, which is carried on horses, all this at the expense of our employer at a cost detailed elsewhere.

Before and after the journey to court, the captain and one of his party proceed to the residence of the governors to express due gratitude for past pains and seek the continuation of their favors in the future. On this occasion he is accompanied by a troop of watchmen, consisting of their soldiers and municipal servants, each having a rope for thieves in his pocket, as well as the *otona,* interpreters, and personal attendants, and he is only admitted after a long wait at the *genkan ban.*

When the Dutch captains present the annual gifts from our employers to the above magistrates on the occasion of *hassaku,* or the first day of the eighth month, they are escorted under similar security.

If some Dutch are called into the presence of the magistrates for a specific purpose, be it to emphasize the importance of a new shogunal order or for some examination or notification, they are accompanied by the same guards and escort, even though often they are not even received by the magistrate himself.

Once or twice annually the resident Dutch are given leave to stretch their legs outside the compound and to look at the temples. This liberty is granted to us under the name of gathering medicinal herbs. Nevertheless, for our guidance and keeping, not only commissioned soldiers but the whole troop of general interpreters, the *otona,* their servants, and those of the whole island are attached to us. All of them must be regaled with a meal at the temple of the Ikkō sect at the expense of our employer, and the courtesy of the priests must be rewarded with gold.

On occasion some of the resident Dutch are sent to inspect the small cargo boats, of which the company constantly maintains five for loading and discharging our vessels. At that time they are given the same escort, which has to be regaled at the next temple at the expense of the same purse.

At the time when the ships are in the harbor the above-described celebration in honor of the city's patron Suwa takes place. The Dutch are permitted the pleasure of watching this from a stand built at their own expense to heighten the splendor and distinction of this heathen festival and to benefit the locals. We are escorted by the said entourage and when passing the guard at the gate of the island are counted four times, or by four separate people, and several times when mounting and descending from the stage, as if one of us could slip through their fingers. An equal number of our slaves is taken and presented as black Dutchmen.

On the arrival of each Dutch vessel a few of the resident Dutch are sent to meet it beyond the harbor to obtain a general idea of its command and condition for the information of the governors and ourselves. For this purpose two specially constructed pleasure and rowing barges are maintained by the noble company to transport the troop of soldiers and watchmen, and every time all of them must be regaled on the island of Iwafu ga shima by the *konpura nakama,* whose kitchen barque accompanies us, again at the expense of the above-mentioned purse.

If a fire breaks out on Deshima, it is ordered that the Dutch be led from the island to another safe place in a fashion that will be described in the last chapter of this book.[12]

These are our days of recreation, if the escort of soldiers and bailiffs qualifies them as such. Nevertheless, it must admitted that even under their yoke one is treated by them, indeed by the whole troop of our wardens (excepting a few), with outward adulation, polite persuasion, expressions of civility, and presents of food, as much as existing conditions permit. Yet this must be attributed to the politeness of this nation and the customs of the country and not to any esteem or affection in which we might be held. The many dishonest actions that the riffraff of Nagasaki inflict upon us confirm that the opposite is the case. I will present only a few general patterns of behavior based partly on my own research and partly on their secret confessions and pieces of evidence furnished. Omitted are the innumerable individual base tricks of the interpreters, as well as the frequent and disadvantageous impositions enforced during the chaotic period of the sales, to which on occasion even the captains are submitted. No Japanese who treats the Dutch with sincerity is considered an honest citizen. This is based on the principle that such behavior would not be in the interest of the common, or the nation's, good, would be in conflict with the shogun's wishes, and, on account of their oath, would violate the wishes of the gods and their own conscience. They argue that when placed under pressure, a true friend of the foreigners must necessarily turn into an enemy of his nation and rebel against the shogun, for if the foreign nation were to attack Japan, it would be their duty to assist the foreigners and betray their own country.

Consequently to cheat the Dutch in the price of goods (if this can be accomplished without injury to their delicate image), swindle or deceive them, curtail the benefits and freedom of the Dutch, to find and suggest new avenues of enslavement and obstruction, are all considered praiseworthy and indications of a true patriot.

If someone is discovered to have stolen property from the Dutch (which the coolies or porters do with great skill during the time of the sales), he will receive a few strokes on his back on passing the sentry at the gate after the property has been taken away or be banned for some time from the island, seldom from the city, in proportion to his crime. But whosoever purchases anything from the Dutch for the purpose of smuggling must, without mercy, shed his blood and die on the cross or by the sword.

The loading and discharge of our vessels, as well as other necessary work, may not be done by our people but must be performed by Japanese coolies and day laborers, while the former stand around idly and watch. They always employ nearly half as many again as necessary, and even if somebody works only half an hour for the Dutch, the whole day must be paid for.

All this riffraff, employed superfluously as burden and vexation for us, must either be maintained and supported directly from our funds, or at least from the wicked deductions from our trade.

The Dutch may not send any letters out of the country without first having the contents noted down by the Japanese and handing a copy to the governors. For this purpose two equal packages are always made up: one they keep, and the other is sent to the departing junk. Private letters leaving or arriving on our own vessels are smuggled (with their consent), but official ones are first presented to the governors.

No Japanese may send either letters or any presents to their relatives (of which there are still some among the Dutch owing to marriages that took place in earlier times), nor may they receive any without first handing them to the governors for them to open and dispose of.

Formerly our dead were considered unworthy of their soil and were thrown into the sea outside the harbor of Nagasaki. Now they are given a shallow grave in a desolate piece of wasteland on the mountain of Inasa. A watchman is employed to guard them and takes such good care of them that there is no sign of a grave, nor is he able to point to one.

Others, be they native or foreigners, can easily press claims upon the Dutch, while the latter can do so only with difficulty. In the former case, they subtract the claim from the payment of goods to the noble company, regardless whether it concerns the company or one of its servants. In the latter case, we are confronted with difficulties and dishonest delays. To end this chapter, I will cite the case of the Koxingian Chinese or robbers,[13] who unlawfully seized our fort Tayoan[14] and the whole island of Formosa. As a consequence, we disarmed one of their large junks at an appropriate occasion in 1660, and even though with its many sealed cross walls or compartments it floated for another thirteen days, only nine people from nearly three hundred survived. Yet on account of this event 27,000 *jū momme* was subtracted from our treasury in the same year as compensation for the plaintiff. However, when in 1672 our new vessel *Kuylenburg* was stranded on Formosa in the neighborhood of Quelang[15] and the same Koxingians fished up our goods after they had killed the people, we were unable to obtain compensation from this court.

Chapter 7

The Dutch Trade in This Country: Firstly, the Guilds Employed for This Purpose

The guild of the *tsūji,* or interpreters, mentioned in the previous chapter, by whose crooked and false mouth our substantial trade must be pursued and annually be conducted, is made up of an excessive number of people: 150 when complete. I will discuss this fraternity in detail, despite its unworthiness, so that it may, at the same time, serve as an example and shed light on the organization of all other guilds and the exact structure of their administration.

Tsūji or *tsūji shū* means literally "by mouth" or "by mouth people" because it is an abbreviation for "people whose mouth is of service." They are not all of the same level and rank and can be divided into two categories. The first, the general interpreters, may visit the Dutch island as they please. The others are admitted only in the final stages of the sales, to use their eyes to watch rather than their tongues to interpret.

Hon Tsūji

The first category of interpreters consists of eight people, who are known as *hon tsūji*, that is, "proper interpreters". They must carry out the duties of this office on all occasions but also observe every move of the Dutch and be responsible for them in all circumstances.

Four of them are *ōtsūji,* that is, upper or chief interpreters, and one of these is the *nenban,* that is, the annual guardian and rapporteur. For one year, that is, during the time of the sales and the remaining period, he, in consultation with the others, informs the magistrate on duty, or only his house steward, of matters concerning the Dutch, their requests, and any incidents. It is he who yields the greatest authority over us, our trade, and everything that concerns us and is the leader of the whole honorable fraternity of the *tsūji.* The remaining four are called *kotsūji,* that is, junior or lower interpreters. They are of lesser status and the assistants and deputies of the former. There is also a *nenban* among them, who is an aide to the upper *nenban* and the head or first man of his class. Both complete their year of presidency by escorting the Dutch to the shogunal court. When this group of eight deals with issues concerning the trade, affairs, or the members of our nation, they have to consult the *otona* of our island, who claims the seat below the senior *nenban* but often finds that the seat below the senior interpreters is left vacant for him.

The *chigyō*, that is, the income or benefits of these regular interpreters, amounts to a considerable sum and consists of the following: a *yaku ryō,* or salary, which was granted to them by the shogun in accordance with their rank after the confinement of the Dutch. It used to consist of a sum of money but now it is a certain quantity of silk, which, as I have learned indirectly, they are permitted to buy and from the sale of which they make the equivalent of their former salary; some (raw) silk, which the noble company offers them merely as compensation for their troubles, or as a present, and of which each senior interpreter is given one bale or 141¾ catty, costing 400 taels to buy, and it is sold again in Japan for approximately 850 taels. Each junior interpreter receives half that amount. In addition the copper companies give them an annual sum in recognition of the trouble taken in the past and so that they may conduct the sales to their advantage. This is neutralized by us with a counter-gift of three to six, or more, hundred taels, depending on the amount and favorable price of the copper. When director Camphuis[1] bought 22,466 piculs of refined slabs of copper and 102 piculs of cakes of copper at twelve and a half taels the picul, he presented them with 1,360 taels and gave each of the senior interpreters a pack rather than a picul, while the junior interpreters received half a pack.

Then there is the *kōsen,* or usual margin, on top of privately purchased goods amounting to 40,000 taels of light or gold coins. This is paid 100 percent by the purchasers but indirectly is at the expense of the vendor, whose goods achieve a much lower price. This amounts to considerably more than 20,000 taels and benefits the two resident governors, the presiding mayor, the *otona,* the above-mentioned as well as the other interpreters. They profit no less from the final, illegitimate sale of some private goods over and above the sum mentioned, which the *otona* and interpreters have people buy solely for their own use and therefore at a lower price. Also included is a sum of 150 *koban,* which the noble company gives them as a food allowance during the time of the sales. Further, there are other special gifts presented to them for certain purposes by the lower servants of the island, the merchants, tradesmen, and even by individual Dutchmen, quite apart from the many obvious and less obvious acts of thieving, with which they manage to pilfer from us on all sides. Among the latter may be counted the wages of the coolies or laborers who are used to discharge and load our vessels. They keep a good part of their wages, for while we pay out six taels for each, they do not hand over more than four, and for this reason always order more than necessary. The two interpreters who accompany us to the court can be counted upon to profit 1,200 taels from us during the journey. For while twenty horses are required for the transport of ourselves and our luggage from Osaka to Edo, and the same number on the return to Miyako, they order twenty more than necessary and charge us fifteen taels for each, even though they pay only eight. The same sort of accounts are made when it comes to the payment of the porters, who are required for this same purpose, so that we have to pay twice 186 *koban* for porters and horses. Our barge is another means for profiteering, inasmuch as they use it to transport merchants' goods from Nagasaki to Osaka and line their own pockets with the freight charges. In addition they receive presents and rewards from the powerful of this empire as well as the noble company. All told, a senior interpreter would make well over 3,000 taels, a junior one, 1,500 annually. Yet this provides only a meager living, because they support their poor relatives—something on which the people of this country stake their honor and in which they put great pride—and in addition a fair amount finds its way to the magistrate and his *karō,* or steward.

The above is the most important band on the island, and the one that does the greatest harm to the privileges, honor, and freedom of our nation. Their basic law is to (1) increase the annual expenses of the noble company in callous fashion in order to obtain benefits for their fellow countrymen as sworn patriots and (2) keep their own villainous acts and thieving from their countrymen as far as possible. For this purpose they attempt to limit our freedom more than necessary in order to prevent us from entering into conversations with the latter and also to keep us ignorant of their language. They greatly obstruct those of us who know the language until a reason can be found to banish them from the country on a spurious order of the governors. The only way the Dutch captain or director of sales can be useful to the noble company (since he is unable to conduct the trade) is by resisting and counteracting increases in the costs, which the Japanese attempt to raise annually in all possible fashion by reducing privileges. For whatever costs or burdens have been accepted once, must, contrary to all reason, be born annually. Consequently a new and inexperienced captain is usually hoodwinked in this respect. On the other hand, they often help him to make profitable sales, but this is made up for by meager returns in the next year.

Apprentices

Next in rank are the *keiko tsūji,* or interpreters in training (not counted in the above-mentioned number of *tsūji*), of whom there are eight or more. They are the natural or adopted sons of the above interpreters, visiting the island daily to learn the Dutch and Portuguese languages, as well as the art of ruling the foreigners. They are used as informers on various occasions and also to inspect the discharging and loading of vessels and departing and arriving sailors and other Dutch, as well as to examine outgoing boxes and household effects. For that they are, nevertheless, presented by the noble company with a small reward of forty taels in total. They also share in the food allowance and various other incidentals.

Nai Tsūji, Private Interpreters

Next in rank are the group of *nai tsūji,* literally, "inside" or "chamber" interpreters,[2] because they have to stay with individual foreigners in their houses. They may visit our island only at the time of the annual sales, after having sworn to abstain from association with us and after each has received a pass in the shape of a wooden docket with burned incisions from the *otona.* Then two to six are allotted to each Dutchman in his room as so-called interpreters, but in reality as spies. For among ten there is hardly one who understands a word of Dutch,[3] unless one of them had been employed in the customary fashion as a servant to the Dutch when young.

There are more than a hundred of these *nai tsūji,* all under the direction of the senior interpreters and especially the *nenban.* Like other servants and guilds in this empire, they are divided into the following classes and ranks:

1. Twelve *kogashira,* literally, "little heads," that is, of the remaining group. Among them are two *nenban,* or rapporteurs, who change place annually. In their year of duty they preside, collect information on all incidents, and present the same to the high fraternity of senior interpreters.

2. *Kumi gashira,* that is, heads of units, referring here to the ordinary, remaining party, for each of them is in charge of those nine or ten who live closest to him in the city. He presides over them as their head, in the name of his superiors informs them of orders issued, commands them as well as answers for them, while the latter in turn must voice any requests directly to him. Among them are also two *nenban* who in their year of duty assist the *kogashira.*

The remaining common band consisting of eighty to one hundred men is divided into two ranks. One set is known as *jō,* meaning "superior," and receives more benefits and more salary than the rest, who are known under the general term of *chū.*[4] Their whole salary consists of a certain sum, taken from the above-mentioned taxes of the merchants, which is determined by the governors and senior interpreters and handed to them in various payments after the sales are over. Depending on the year, this amounts to roughly 6,000 taels, which they divide proportionally among themselves according to rank, so that the twelve most senior each receive a total of 200 taels at the most, and the remaining always have to be content with half that amount or less.

Among them are four *takara yaku,* or attendants of the coffers, who take care of the cash and keep account of these unjustly gathered funds, as well as two *hissha,* or scribes, who all make a meager living from this source.

Only the sons of deceased interpreters are permitted to enter this guild of interpreters. The procedure is as follows. The applicant has a *sojō,* or petition, written for him, and takes it to the *nenban* of the *kumi gashira.* He also pleads his case orally, or sometimes in an indirect fashion. The *nenban* gathers his eleven colleagues and with them ponders whether the applicant is deserving with regard to his father, his age, and his merits and whether the request should be supported and so forth. After it has been approved, he passes the petition to the hands of the *nenban* of the *kogashira,* who reflects on the same points with his colleagues. After their approval, it is handed to the *nenban* of the *hon tsūji,* that is, the rapporteur and presiding officer of the senior interpreters. Here the petition often remains for two to three years until, after frequent requests and intercessions, and also by way of *sode no shita,* meaning, in their manner of speaking, "below the sleeve" (since theirs are so wide that people can insert gifts without being noticed), it finds his favor. Then, as soon as he has received the nod from his colleagues, he passes the request of the person together with all the various approvals to the city magistrate, who confirms it with his *in.*[5] After this the brand-new interpreter goes to everybody in this honorable guild, pays his compliments to secure their goodwill, and in turn receives their felicitations on his admission.

Hissha

Among the attendants on our island may also be counted five *Deshima hissha,* or general scribes. They are employed for the Dutch in case anything has to be calculated or written down with regard to presents, out-goings, expenses of the journey, and so on, tasks that otherwise would burden or embarrass the interpreters. They are the subordinates of the latter and now perform their duties with reduced numbers, because each interpreter maintains his private scribe, and the noble company pays only for the two who travel to the shogunal court. However, they are rewarded with profitable duties during the period of trade.

Commander of the Coolies

Included in this listing must be the *Deshima tsuetsuki,* or inspectors of the coolies or day laborers. There are fifteen of them, and they keep a list of the day laborers, and are in command of them on the island. Below them are still quartermasters of a lesser rank, the actual overseers of the common porters, and all of them must watch over the thieving hands of the coolies. For this reason they have to be well paid and maintained by the noble company. The common coolies, who are used when the ships are in harbor, constantly change. Since this work, which pays twice the normal salary, is shared by the day laborers of the whole city as a special privilege, it passes from ward to ward, and each *otona* maintains a list.

Attendants of the Treasury

Among those attending and commanding are also the *kanaban nakama,* that is, the guild of the attendants of the treasury. They collect the money for goods purchased from the merchants and change it into golden *koban,* which annually are marked by a small stamp and paid to the Dutch through the hands of the interpreters after they have subtracted 1 percent for their troubles and retained some 15 percent or more for the common good of the city according to the annual rate of exchange of the *koban.* Depending on the period, they buy or exchange the coin for fifty-five or fifty-nine *momme,* or units of silver, and sell it again to us for sixty-eight. On top of that, the noble company presents the most senior among them with one hundred and the remaining with fifty taels or *jū momme* annually. This fraternity consists of thirty-six persons, both senior and junior attendants, including five inspectors or chiefs, who work with their eyes only, and four assistants, who collect, keep, and pay out the money and direct procedures with the approval of the former. After that follow the lesser attendants, seated separately, such as: one gold and one silver expert, two men weighing silver, two who call in the money from the merchants, two senior scribes or accountants, *seichō kaki,* who are still joined by various special assistants, servants of senior officials and of our island, to supervise and assist. One person is supplied by each mayor of the city, *daikan, otona,* and general interpreter, in addition to some other favorites, for whom benefits are sought, all going under the name of scribes. Besides the above duties, these men shoulder the burden of being present during the inspection of all arriving and departing private and household goods.

Chapter 8
The Dutch Trade: Details of the Procedure

The annual procedure of the trade is as follows: As soon as the watch has confirmed the arrival of a Dutch ship, which one expects in September at the end of the season of favorable southwesterlies, three people from the post, together with the usual entourage, are sent to meet the vessel roughly two miles outside the harbor. The party carries sealed instructions from the Dutch resident to the captain on how to behave on arrival according to the customs of the country. The interpreter and the Japanese deputy collect the bill of lading and roll of men, as well as the company's letters, and depart quickly to show the letters first to the magistrate and then to deliver them to the Dutch resident. The above-mentioned vessel follows, and on entering the harbor salutes both shogunal guards with two cannon shots and casts anchor in the bay of the city at a distance of a strong musket shot from the water gate. If the wind is unfavorable for entering the harbor, the Japanese send at our expense, but not our request, as many rowboats (which are kept by the commoners for this purpose) as necessary to tow the vessel. In calm seas ten are used, in unfavorable conditions fifty to one hundred. When the vessel enters the harbor two guard barges place themselves behind it. They are manned by soldiers, who, rotating daily, remain with all ships while they are here and until they depart from outside the harbor. As soon as the vessel reaches its anchorage, a group of deputies and day laborers take gunpowder, cannonballs, and individual weapons into their custody and guard them in a certain ammunition store until departure, all at the expense of the noble company. Formerly they also attempted to remove the rudders, but they did not succeed. The next or the same day the commissioners of the magistrates appear with a band of their lesser soldiers, interpreters, and servants and in the presence of the Dutch resident conduct a stringent inspection according to the roll they have received, which specifies the first and family name, age, details of birth, residence, and the occupation of each person, as well as a report on the dead, detailing place and cause of death. A dead monkey and parrot had to be presented and be certified to have died natural deaths. Thereupon the Dutch resident reads to the inspected men a notice in Dutch, instructing them how to behave in accordance with Japanese law, and has it posted on the vessel as well as the island.

The remaining vessels are welcomed in the same fashion. There are two, three, or four annually, depending on how much copper is required and how many are sent from the head office at Batavia. Previously, at the time of free trade, six, seven, and more arrived with the expectation of selling a great amount of goods.

After the inspection, or whenever they consider it suitable, the vessel is unladed. During this time it is occupied for surveillance by *yoriki,* as deputies for the governors, as well as some *dōshin,* one senior, one junior, and one apprentice interpreter, as well as various scribes and servants. At that time the water gates of the island, through which the goods must pass, are opened in the presence of the *karō,* that is, the stewards, and highest officials of the magistrates, and their troupe. While the gate is kept open they, together with some assistants, remain as overseers of the operation in a hall built nearby. Also present to inspect, supervise, and assist is the crowd of ordinary interpreters, apprentices, landlords, scribes, and the necessary coolies. Then the task is set upon by roughly three hundred day laborers, certainly nearly half again as many as necessary. Each vessel is unladed separately in a period of two days which, with interruptions to profit the coolies, turns into three. The goods are taken to the island in flat-bottomed rowboats[1] (which are maintained for this purpose by the noble company) and are placed inside the gate in front of the commissioners' seats. Here they are checked against the bill of lading, counted, recorded, and some carefully chosen lots of each kind are opened. Then all goods are placed into certain warehouses under the seal of the same commissioned officers until such time as they are sold.

The boxes of private individuals are all taken to the above-mentioned location on the island and are unlocked, or, if the key is not readily available, opened with an axe. Anything that could be sold is recorded and kept under their seal. All items considered undesirable, such as arms, cloth with gold or silver thread, and any other goods that are prohibited or improper at the time are kept by the *otona* until the departure of the owner.

Neither foreign coins nor anything bearing the image of the cross, a saint, or rosary may pass. If such items were in our possession, it would be as distressing to them as if bloodshed and fires were raging. Therefore, as soon as a vessel approaches Japan, religious books and foreign coins are packed into a barrel and put away.

Sometimes the new arrivals must consent to a body search on entering and leaving Deshima to establish whether they are smuggling any red coral or amber when coming in and are taking out gold in return. This even happened to a new resident (who afterward served with honor as governor general)[2] but does not occur often.

If someone boards or leaves the vessel, be it for private purposes or to guard the goods of the company, he has to hand over a pass stamped by both commissioners seated at the gate to the deputy on the vessel and on returning must deliver a similar document from the latter to the former. In this fashion they constantly know how many of the crew are on shore and on each vessel.

Around evening, or whenever the deputies and their entourage leave the ships to return home, or come back here, the cabin of the ship is sealed and the Dutch are carefully counted to see whether someone is missing. When this happens, extraordinary commotion breaks out, as, for instance, when during my stay a sailor went missing, drowning at night without anybody's knowledge. This gave rise to such panic among them that work was stopped and attendants ran around aimlessly, fearing, perhaps, that he was a priest and had moved off into the country. The guards at the rear of the vessel were already prepared to cut their bellies had he not soon been dragged up from the bottom of the sea.

The water gates remain closed except on the days when the vessels are unladed and laded, and on all other days the parties, those on the island as well as those on each vessel, remain separated from each other and confined within their limits.

After the cargo from each vessel has been brought in turn to the warehouses in the said manner, it remains there until the Japanese choose to sell it on our island on two or three market days, which they call *kanban.*[3] Unsold goods may remain there until next year's market.

Imported Goods

Our cargo consists of the following goods: raw silk from China, Tunkin, Bengal, and Persia; a variety of woven cloth without gold or silver threads and some other fine woolen material from the above and other countries: especially taffachelas[4] from Bengal and Coromandel, large, white rolled pelangs,[5] white gilams,[6] armozeens,[7] sumongis,[8] sestiens,[9] and florette yarn. There are variety of chintzes,[10] some half-silken, but also some rough, cotton ones (but no delicate, printed, or painted ones), white gunnies,[11] salempores,[12] and percales.[13] From Europe there is woolen cloth and some other woolen and silken pieces, especially ordinary serge and fine serge. From Siam and Cambodia there is sappan or dyewood, which is called brazilwood in Europe. Also wild buffalo and deer hides, ray skins, wax and buffalo horns, cordwains,[14] and treated skins from Persia, Bengal, and other localities (but under no circumstances from Spain or Manila), pepper and sugar, powdered as well as candy, from a variety of East Indian countries. From Ambon and Banda come cloves and nutmeg (cinnamon is no longer desired), white sandal[15] from Timor, camphor de Baros[16] from the islands of Borneo and Sumatra. On occasion quicksilver, cinnabar, and saffron are sent from Bengal. Also from the latter location and from Siam come tin, lead, saltpeter, borax, and alum. Musk from Tunkin, gum benzoin from Atjeh,[17] gum-lac[18] from Siam. From Mocha in Arabia come rose-mallows,[19] or liquid storax, and catechu, commonly called *terra japonica,*[20] from Surat and Siam the root putchuk or costus amara.[21] Again from Europe there is coral, amber, rough molten glass, used for coloring porcelain, mirrors (which are broken here and used for telescopes, magnifying glasses, and spectacles). Less important items are Masang de Vaca[22] (this is a ball of gall from cows from Mozambique), snake-wood, atjar[23] of bamboo, mangoes and other unripe fruits preserved in Turkish pepper, garlic and vinegar, lead and red ochre for writing, sublimate mercury (but not calomel[24]), delicate files, sewing needles, spectacles, cut drinking glasses, fake coral, foreign birds, and a variety of foreign natural and manufactured, new and rare curiosities. They are purchased illegally from the crew of an arriving vessel or from certain individuals. Since the goods do not pass through the *kanban* and are not included in the quota of permitted items, they are often extremely profitable.

Among the imported goods, the Japanese like nothing better than raw silk. It does not, however, bring much profit, and consequently the Portuguese called it *pancada,*[25] meaning "in one lot," a name still used by the Japanese. No less popular are piece goods, or a variety of textiles that return a fixed and reasonable profit. In view of Japan's large population, even a hundred times as much would not satisfy the demand.

Sappanwood and hides also guarantee the importer a safe and good reward. The highest profits are obtained from sugar, catechu, rose-mallows, putchuk, camphor from Borneo, mirrors, and a variety of other items, but only when there is a demand and when the Chinese have imported only small quantities. Coral and amber are treasured in this part of the East, but smuggled goods have satisfied the demand to such an extent in this country that sometimes hardly 50 percent profit can be made. Previously it sold for ten and even a hundred times the purchase price. The price of these and similar curiosities is variable and fluctuates according to the appetite of the purchaser, who, whatever price he pays, is still able to sell them to his compatriots with 100 percent profit. Previously goods were imported in large quantities and generally in seven vessels. Now they arrive in smaller quantities on three or usually four ships, of which one goes via Siam to bring goods from there. Whatever has been brought in excess is deposited and kept in local stores.

The Four Periods of Dutch Trade

The condition of our trade has been subjected to much ill fortune and changes with respect to the prohibition of import and export, curtailment of our liberty, reduction of profits, and with respect to the treatment enjoyed by our people during the early time. I noticed that the period from our arrival until now divides into four distinct phases, and I will discuss these in chronological order so that people interested in this important trade can gain a clear understanding.

What I call the first phase is a period of more than thirty years, from our arrival on the island and city of Hirado, and the granting of immunity by the shogun soon afterward, to 1641, when we had to move our trading post from there to Nagasaki. At the time the trade of the Spanish and Portuguese, then our enemies, was at its height and was based in the city of Nagasaki. We, on the other hand, were still unable to supply the most popular and profitable goods, namely, raw and woven silk. This was due to the fact that we had not yet established a permanent post in the vicinity of the empire of China, which produces the best silk. Moreover, the Chinese, who were at that time still under the government of their native emperor, could only supply us illegally and with small amounts because the country was closed, and they were unable to leave, while we were not permitted to collect the silk from China ourselves. But the others could get as much silk as they liked, since they had established themselves at Macao on Chinese soil. We first visited Tunkin in the year 1637. In Bengal and Persia we were also still strangers and had not yet established our trade and offices in these countries. When fortune and good management opened the door to these countries of plentiful silk for us, and when our trade became well established there, we supplied the required goods together with the Portuguese and Spaniards and sold them freely without restrictions to the highest bidder, managing to market more or less the equivalent of sixty Dutch tons of gold annually. This, then, resulted in large gains for the company, despite the fact that many goods brought less profit than they do now and that our shipping was subject to more danger, running aground, and loss, since at that time the safe route along the Chinese coast was unknown and the dangerous one along Formosa had to be used instead. At that time earnings were exported mainly in silver, generally amounting to twelve to fourteen hundred boxes or 1,400,000 taels, equaling 4,900,000 Dutch florins.

This, then, was the first and golden period in which we enjoyed both reasonable freedom and considerable gains. The basis for such treatment was a *go shuin,* meaning "great red seal" as affixed upon an official document or pass, which was awarded to us in 1611 by the Shogun Ieyasu, who was otherwise called *ōgosho* and was so known after his death.[26] This permitted us to land freely and trade our goods in all harbors and was confirmed in 1617 with a new document, albeit on somewhat less favorable terms, by his son and successor Hidetada, known as Daitokuin after his death. Although we had received and had everything arranged as we desired, we nevertheless frequently experienced dismay, trouble, and vexation in avoiding or forestalling the many hard impositions. To harm us the Spaniards and Portuguese would soon slander us in a variety of ways, with the result that we were wrongfully accused and condemned by the Japanese as pirates, Spanish rebels, oppressors of the Indian kingdoms, and so forth. To our disgrace, we were reproached in the most abominable blasphemous terms that, like the Spaniards, we believed in Christ and that consequently we had fallen foul of the shogunal court. At the destruction of the Christians at Shimabara in 1638 we ourselves had to lend a hand if we did not wish to follow the example of the Portuguese and vacate this golden Colchis.[27] Our hours of prayer and singing had to be abolished, and finally in 1641, after the native Christians had nearly been completely exterminated, and all Spaniards and Portuguese had been banished, we had to vacate the city of Hirado to be imprisoned on another island built in the harbor of Nagasaki, the island De or Deshima, and submit to what amounts to a prison sentence.

The reason for the harsh changes we were made to suffer was mainly the profession of the Christian religion, which was regarded as a plague besetting the country; the painful and costly extermination of so many thousand subjects more and more embittered the court and equally made our nation the object of their hatred and suspicion. But since we were not part of the Portuguese and Spanish camp, since we proclaimed ourselves the enemies and persecutors of the priests, and informed the Japanese of their dangerous ventures against the authority of the shogun, our nation was permitted to stay. But in such a fashion that we had no liberty and opportunity to associate with their fellow countrymen, the Japanese, so that in the future we would not be able to learn what was happening at the shogunal court and in the empire and would not be able to seduce the populace to love us and our religion, which could lead to insurrection and new dangers to shogunal authority. This was feared all the more because they still suspected some thunderous acts of revenge from the Spanish and Portuguese, and it could have been possible for us to ally ourselves with them against the Japanese. Their suspicions were fired, and our change of residence was hastened, by the erection of a warehouse to store our goods, which in violation of the laws of the country was too tall and also had such solid walls that it looked more like a fortress than a warehouse, and under the eaves (which made matters even worse) was the year according to Christian reckoning. A Japanese once whispered in my ear that when the Dutch brought in their packs from the vessel, the bottom dropped out of a crate and instead of commercial goods a heavy brass mortar appeared.[28] Be that as it may, shogunal orders forced them at the pain of death to tear down the building to the very ground with the utmost speed and to exchange their residence at Hirado with the prison at Nagasaki. This concluded the first period of our free trade and movement.

Our ninety-year-old senior interpreter Brasman, otherwise known as Yozaemon,[29] who was already in the service of the company at that time, puts a great deal of blame for these changes on the haughtiness of the Dutch resident Caron.[30] He said that governing Japanese officials could not tolerate arrogance on the part of merchants, who in their nation are considered to be the fourth and lowest class of human beings. The chief judge at Miyako, in charge of foreign affairs,[31] was so insulted by Caron's arrogance that he would neither grant him an audience nor accept the presents of the noble company. As a consequence, he alerted the shogun to the wicked designs of the Dutch in building their dangerous warehouse and brought about a quick change. Caron is the same man who published the short and, in Dutch, first description of Japan,[32] which was afterward translated into many languages. He arrived as a kitchen hand in India. His lively intellect induced him to take up the pen and commerce, which he directed in Japan over a number of years. When he missed out on a high position in Batavia, which he had requested, he went into service with the Portuguese, but went aground at the wall of the fort of Lisbon and drowned before he could carry out his plan to damage the trade of the noble company. At this point I have to mention some vile gossip about the Dutch, which one reads in some writings. Apparently when they were asked by the Japanese authorities whether they were Christians, they had denied this and answered that they were Dutchmen. However, the daily record of the company and other writings kept at our trading post, and also the testimony of the above-mentioned senior interpreter, tell me the opposite and convey to me that they never disavowed their Christian beliefs, but that to their own disadvantage and derision they always and consistently answered and affirmed that they were Christians, but not of the sect of the Portuguese priests. Apparently the gossip arose from the answer given by a Dutchman named Michael Sandvoort, who formerly had run aground along the coast of Japan, and, together with a fellow countryman, had settled as a citizen in Nagasaki. When questioned during the inquisition, he answered to save himself and his friend: "Christians, Christians, dear me, we are Dutch!" After this confession of faith they were left alone.

The Second Period

We will proceed to the second period. As soon as we arrived in the harbor of Nagasaki, we were imprisoned on Deshima and lost all previous freedom. Guards were placed in and outside the barriers that contained us, and we were not allowed to talk to the Japanese, except our servants and attendants. They, however, had to swear by their blood that they would neither disclose to us anything about local conditions nor enter into a friendly relationship with us. As soon as our vessels reached the harbor, they were occupied by the Japanese and surrounded by guard boats. Powder and shot, swords, and all of the ship's accouterments were taken on land and kept in custody by the Japanese until departure. Even the heaviest cannons, as well as the rudder, had to be dismantled and taken away. This was stopped later, however, because of the all too great and unnecessary work it caused. The crew was immediately inspected on the basis of the roll that had been handed over, and each person's age, name, and occupation were noted. Those who went to serve on the island were body-searched, and their sword and salable goods taken into custody by the *otona,* and nobody was permitted to leave or board the ships, which were anchored roughly three hundred paces from the island, without the permission and a pass issued by the Japanese. Our imported goods were unloaded by their own people and stored in our warehouses under their seal. In other words, until now we have been regarded and treated as the nation's enemies and traitors. We were in a situation where our profits were being envied and in danger of being increasingly curtailed. But this populous city and its overlords could not exist without trade, and since the city's livelihood, the Portuguese trade, had recently been stopped, we were permitted to import, as we had done previously, large quantities of goods on six or seven vessels and to sell them with good profit. The largest amount traded was in that same year of 1641 and consisted of eighty tons of gold, while silver was exported in the above-mentioned amount of 1,400 boxes. After that we again requested permission to export copper, which had been prohibited in 1637. This was granted, but in turn the export of silver was prohibited. The noble company has silently been content with this arrangement until the present day, since copper plays a much more important part in the working of the Indian trade: while silver brings a mere 4 percent, copper enjoys a profit of 90 to 95 percent, especially in Surat, to which locality generally some 6,000 boxes are being sent.

In this fashion the great many vexations and unjust impositions, which at that time were much greater than now, were compensated for every year, until after thirty years our trade entered the third phase. This happened in the year of Christ 1672 when we incurred the displeasure of a senior councilor, Inaba Mino,[33] who, together with his colleague Uta,[34] was the most powerful person and in charge of the government of the empire under the peace-loving shogun Genyūin.[35] As a consequence, the golden fleece, which we collected annually from this Colchis, turned into a common pelt, and our trade suffered greatly. I will explain the root of this lamentable evil and at the same time illustrate the vengefulness of this nation.

Mino, or with his title (denoting a great lord) Mino *sama*, a gentleman to whom the shogun felt some obligation, and who in addition to other government duties was especially responsible for the foreigners, noticed that the shogun would be very pleased (pleasing the shogun being the foremost goal and *raison d'être* of these lords) if the temple of his ancestors were furnished with a large European church chandelier.[36] This would be especially so since the Dutch, when at Hirado, had obtained the goodwill and dispensation of the previous shogun with just such a present, and the shogun as well as the whole nation considered the care for this temple as one of the most important aspects of religious devotion and a matter of the greatest piety. He had the Dutch in Japan order the chandelier from Europe, but the Dutch (owing to some thoughtless directives by the governor of Nagasaki), presented the chandelier personally together with the annual presents for the year 1666, hoping to earn the goodwill of the shogun themselves. Mino, disappointed in his expectations, felt insulted to the very marrow of his bones. He was overcome by such deep-rooted hatred toward our nation that even his descendants and all his blood relatives and friends would not be satisfied without fatal or sufficient revenge. The Japanese know how to be patient in these matters until after considerable time there is a chance for reprisal. As soon as Mino perceived such an occasion, he had us chastised in the most painful fashion. When his relative, Ushigome Chūzaemon,[37] became the presiding governor of Nagasaki in 1672 (during the directorship of Mr. Camphuis, later governor general at Batavia), he had this governor change the terms of our hitherto free trade in the most disadvantageous fashion: The governor demanded that a piece or sample of all imported goods going on sale be brought to his residence and had them examined and valued by experts and specialists. At the same time, the merchants arriving from the various cities were inspecting those goods of interest to them. Thereupon not the Dutch directors, but he, the magistrate himself, began to sell the goods to the merchants. After agreements had been reached, he presented the Dutch with a much lower set of prices for which they had to hand over their goods to the merchants, but with the allowance that they could keep and ship back those goods where the set price did not suit them. With this unfair evaluation, the basis of our free trade, which had been granted by the two shoguns Gongen and Daitokuin, was destroyed, and the golden plaster of large profits, which until then had soothed the pain of harsh and unfair treatment, was taken away from us. Indeed, the enforced price was lowered annually on various goods, which nevertheless the Dutch preferred to sell for little profit rather than have to take them back at a loss. Such treatment and the annual decline in prices should really have spelled the end of the Dutch, especially as the Japanese also decided that, in paying us, the *koban* was not to be exchanged according to market value at 59 or 60 mace (within the country the exchange rate is 54 to 56), but at 68 mace. The extra funds from this exchange as well as those deducted from the price of goods as *aidagin*, or broker's fee, were to be kept and used for the common good of the city. Consequently the Dutch were deliberating on how to bring the trade back to its former state. One saw no other avenue than sending a humble petition to the shogun, whom one thought to be ignorant of these measures enforced in violation of the sacred privileges granted by his ancestors. The governor general at Batavia had the petition written in Chinese and had it handed to the magistrates at Nagasaki, since nothing may be presented to his majesty without the prior examination of the stewards. After three years of waiting and lobbying, we received at the end of 1684 the happy news with the sweet message that our sales should again be based on the freedoms we enjoyed previously. But this was linked to a tough restriction, with the result that the free trade conceded to us turned out to be worse than the previous situation, and this seemed to bring us to the fourth and iron period in which we are still today. For this new concession angered the magistrates, because they had not been used and paid as intermediaries in this matter. But they were especially indignant that their right to fix prices had been abolished, eliminating the large profits that they as well as the Japanese inspectors of our trade had enjoyed annually. At one time the *otona* confessed that for him alone this meant a loss of 3,600 taels. Neither did this incident escape the attention of the offended Mino, even though he had lost his office four years earlier at the accession of the present shogun Tsunayoshi and had himself no longer the authority to harm us. But through his son-in-law, the senior councilor Kaga sama,[38] he urged the court to set restrictions and had them enforced here at Nagasaki by his cousin, the presiding magistrate Genzaemon.[39] Together with his colleagues, the latter protested at court that, while such liberties were greatly injurious to the populace they bestowed undeserved large profits upon the foreigners. After their protestations, it was decided that the Dutch would be permitted to sell their goods freely to the highest bidder according to the shogun's concession, but that the goods sold were not to exceed a value of 300,000 taels annually. They would be permitted to import more and store the goods in their warehouses, but not to sell them. Consequently the liberties we regained did us greater harm than the previous price fixing, since it is much more profitable to sell a large quantity of goods with average profit than a small quantity with a larger profit margin. So that it would not look as if these restrictions had been imposed to anger our nation, but appear as if they were the result of a sound political decision in accordance with the wishes of the shogun, the trade of the Chinese nation or community with its many different members was restricted to a sum of 600,000 taels.[40] Finding an avenue for restricting the foreigners in their trade and reducing their profits to an extent that just stopped them from leaving the country (which the court feared and about which it harbored some doubts) without violating previous shogunal concessions earned the magistrates the praise of the shogun and the honorable title of *kami* as a reward for their wise measures.

The Dutch were still unaware of these restrictions when the vessels entered the harbor with their goods in the autumn of 1685. They were all the more joyful about the arrival of the vessels, since they expected that their trade would once again enter a golden phase. But hardly had we set hands to the task of unloading the first vessel than the bad news arrived from the court that our liberty (as well as that of the Chinese) was limited by high order to a certain amount, above which we could not trade. So that this sum was not exceeded by illegal sales, everything had to be unloaded and, like the goods from the remaining vessels, was searched in the usual fashion, registered, and taken to the warehouses. Although the goods are stored there under our key, they are kept under the seal of the Japanese, and we cannot enter the warehouses without their permission and presence.

The sum we are permitted to trade annually, which is half that of the Chinese, amounts to ten and a half tons of gold, according to Dutch calculations, and according to the Japanese, to 300 boxes of silver, that is, 300,000 *jū momme*, or taels (the latter foreign word was introduced by the Dutch and is used by them here), the equivalent of 50,000 golden *koban,* if all is calculated at the highest value at 60 *momme,* or mace of silver. If, however, the noble Company is forced to accept the *koban* at 68 mace of silver and the payment, or permitted quantity of goods, is calculated according to this gold coin, then the sum of 300,000 taels in effect amounts to only 260,000 taels of silver coins. With this measure the government of Nagasaki found a way to provide the much-harassed Dutch trade officials here with some compensation for their harsh treatment, namely, by permitting them to make some private gain and letting them sell their personal goods (which previously they could sell as much as they liked) to the amount of 40,000 taels or $588^{12}/_{34}$ *koban.* This then, together with the previous sum, amounts to the 300,000 taels conceded by the shogun. Since this is an arrangement of the local government, the noble company cannot, as elsewhere, effect any changes, nor does it decrease or harm the company's trade. These 40,000 taels are divided among the Dutch officials in such a way that the outgoing and presiding director or resident is permitted to trade the equivalent of 10,000 taels, the incoming, who has just arrived, 7,000 taels, and the assistant, or number two, 6,000 taels. The remainder is allotted to the incoming sailors, merchants, and scribes according to the good graces of the Dutch director and the Japanese senior interpreter (who jointly determine the distribution).

The above already implies that the Dutch company maintains a resident senior merchant to supervise their trade as director. According to Japanese custom, he is replaced every year by someone else, who arrives from Batavia on the annual cargo vessels together with a deputy and a few merchants, or scribes as assistants, and assists the previous one with good advice until after the sales when the latter departs with the outgoing ships and cedes his position to the former.

The sales are conducted as follows: When the *kanban* (that is the name for the procedure or day of sale), set for a certain day and approved by the court, approaches, the details of our goods are displayed on the gates outside our island, written in large letters so that they can be read from afar. At the same time, the government indicates to the ward headmen, and through them to the visiting Japanese merchants, what percentage of duty (for the benefit of the citizens of Nagasaki) they will have to pay on the different kinds of goods, so that they may arrange their purchases accordingly. This is indeed a shabby trick that permits them to tax our goods indirectly and to mock us with our so-called regained freedom. For they say: "Formerly when your prices were fixed you came with seven vessels and sold many goods; now you arrive with three or four and sell little. Would it not have been better if you had not asked for freedom?"

On the day before the *kanban,* announcements on the gates of all wards invite all interested parties to present themselves on Deshima the next morning. There they are also informed by registers in front of each warehouse of the contents. Since our trade is in the hands of the government of Nagasaki, two house stewards appear as deputies, and the ceremony proceeds under their authority and in their presence. Also the local senior officials of our island are in attendance, and among them the presiding senior interpreter acts as a spokesman and conducts the whole trade, while our three men in attendance (the two senior merchants and their assistant) have little say or impact. Then our triumvir of men ordered to conduct the trade have a sample of all goods displayed, and at the sounding of the gum-gum (a kind of flat bell shaped like a bowl), the merchants enter the store for the deliberations. This is a neat wooden building, erected at the expense of the company. After removal of the sliding shutters it is open, surrounded by a projecting corridor. Inside it is divided into various compartments and comfortably furnished for the procedure. When certain goods are presented for sale, each interested party tenders different pieces of paper, all varying as regards the price of the bid, stating how much they are willing to pay in *kamme, momme, bu, rin, mō, futsu* for each piece or catty of a certain amount of goods. (In this country all major sales are made in this fashion.) Each slip, however, is signed with a false name. The various slips of paper and bids permit them time for reflection and give them the advantage that they can fall back on a lower offer if after the proceedings they regret making the higher one. But since there are so many small monetary units, it is rare that two people happen to make the same offer. When all the slips of paper for the goods on sale have been handed in, our people open them and sort out the higher from the lower offers. Then the presiding interpreter reads them in order, starting with the highest. Three times the bidder is asked to come forward, and if he is silent, the slip is put aside and the next lower offer taken in turn. This continues until a purchaser says: "I am here," steps forward, and imprints his proper name with his seal in black oil-color (the Japanese carry these things on them) on his bid, thus confirming the sale. In this fashion the remaining goods continue to be sold, and the business is completed in two, rarely three or four *kanban,* until the permitted sum of money has been reached. The day after each *kanban* the goods sold are delivered and taken from the island. A shogunal concession restricts the trade in raw silk to certain merchants from the five shogunal cities, and it is generally sold at the very beginning to their greater and our lesser advantage, which is also the reason why they want to coerce us to turn one third of our imports into raw silk. Taxation, or *kan motsu,* is actually little used by the Japanese and has been introduced here to curtail the profit of the foreigners and to divert it to the poor citizens of this place. Previously taxation was tolerable, but once the valuation of the goods by the magistrates had been abolished, the amount was increased to such an extent that the merchants would end up paying much less for the actual goods. This *kan motsu* is termed *kōsen,* or *kasen gin,* that is, honorarium, brokerage, or remuneration for troubles taken, when it is levied, but when it is distributed it is called *hana gin,* or flower money, because it blooms from the foreign trade for the sustenance of the poor. It is distributed in proportion to the civil duties shouldered by each individual (depending on the situation of the ward) and varies between three and fifteen taels. The fact is that without this support the people could not exist in this remote and infertile location and would disperse within a few years. The goods of the Dutch company have to produce 15 percent of their value in a tax, which for the total trade of 300,000 taels amounts to a *kōsen* or tax of 45,000 taels. However, the sale of private goods, which takes place at the very end and on a special *kanban,* is bled even more. For all goods sold by the piece, 65 percent is charged, resulting in tax of 13,000 taels for sales worth 20,000 taels. Goods sold by weight are taxed at 70 percent, so that for 20,000 taels, 14,000 taels is paid. The reason is that people bring their goods on their patrons' vessels free of charge and therefore deserve to make less profit. The Chinese, who do have costs but a shorter journey, are charged 60 percent, amounting to at total tax of 360,000 taels on their goods. Add to this the 5,580 taels paid by our nation for rent of houses and living quarters and the 16,000 taels paid by the Chinese, then the amount that the governing officials and citizens of this city have the pleasure of receiving from the foreign trade annually amounts to 453,580 taels.

As to the profit that the noble company makes on its goods, this differs from goods to goods each year. It usually depends on the fluctuation of prices in Miyako, and this in turn depends on the scarcity of the goods within the country. If years and goods are averaged, one most probably can estimate a gross profit of 60 percent. But if expenses incurred on selling goods here are deducted, a clean profit of no more than 40 to 45 percent remains, so that goods sold for ten and a half tons of gold bring only a profit of some four to four and a half tons of gold. This is not much for a large company that constantly employs more than 18,000 people on land and sea in the Indies with monthly salaries amounting to 260,000 florins and which, in addition, must maintain many valuable ships, warehouses, and fortresses. It would not be worth paying the piper if the goods returning from Japan, especially refined copper, did not bring virtually an equivalent profit.

The above-mentioned expenses vary from year to year and are higher if something has to be built or repaired, more lords and people are to be given presents, or some other unusual expense occurs.

In order to provide those interested with more detail, I will introduce two examples from the last phase of our trade, one illustrating some of our highest expenses, in the year 1686 under the direction of Licentiate Cleyer, and the other showing one of our lowest, in 1688 under the direction of Mr. Bütenheim.

	1686	1688
Food	23,580	13,166
Accommodation	9,791	6,828
Extraordinary expenses	14,097	4,993
Expenses of vessels	10,986	7,589
Presents	107,086	100,789
Emoluments and monthly salaries	8,092	7,318
Rent for Deshima and ammunition store	19,530	19,530
Total in florins	193,162	160,213

I do not consider it appropriate for myself nor pleasant for the German reader if I were to specify the price and profit of each kind of our goods. Merely for reflection I will present the local price of foreign goods at the capital, Miyako, for the past year of 1692 as it was given to me in the following list:

Chinese silk, cabessa,[41] or the best, the picul, or 125 Dutch lb., 665 *jū momme,* or taels. The same, but bariga, or a middle quality, 638 taels. Bengal silk, cabessa, 530 taels; the same, bariga, 406 taels; silk from Tunkin, 440; floretta yarn, 240; cinnabar, 600; cloves, 223; pepper, 23; candied sugar, 21; powder sugar, 14; camphor from Baros, a catty or 1¼ Dutch lb., 33 *jū momme* or taels; putchuk, or Arabian costus, 10; Chinese large white woollen pelangs the piece, 14 taels; armozeens, the piece 7 taels 4 mace; the highest quality of taffachelas from Coromandel, 6.8, second best, 6; taffachelas from Bengal, 4.3; ordinary plain bleached gilams, 4.8.4; sumongis from Tunkin, 3.3; white gunny cloth, 7; common bleached salempores, 3.1; common bleached percales, 1.5.3.

Before we conclude this topic and send our four ships back with the profit of the noble company, let us briefly look at the benefit derived from the privately sold goods, and especially how much the three Dutch gentlemen are able to make here annually. Since these goods are transported free of charge, and therefore sell quickly, they bring a clean profit, which despite the heavy tax is therefore no less than that of the noble company. The two directors, who in accordance with instructions from the shogunal court may remain only three years in annual rotation, take the cream. On arrival they can sell goods to the value of 7,000 taels, and while on duty and departing, 10,000 taels, making a total of 17,000 taels in one year, while the total of their assistant amounts to 12,000 taels. If they are on good terms with the interpreters and know how to oblige them by being generous with the property of others, some of their goods could be lined up with those of the noble company on the first and the following *kanban* days, thus attracting less duty and making a profit of 65 to 70 percent. This does not disadvantage the company, for when the income of the company is calculated up to the permitted sum, these items are skipped. Whatever of their imported or consigned goods exceeds their quota, as well as small, hidden items, such as blood coral and amber, can be turned into cash under the table through the above scoundrels. Usually they buy it themselves, sometimes the *otona* is involved. Formerly a much larger profit could be obtained by selling the goods to outsiders through a middleman who came to the island at the time of the *kanban.* In 1686 a certain resident director[42] did this so crudely that ten Japanese were beheaded and he himself was banished from the country. The incoming resident setting out for the annual audience can use many of his own goods as presents for the shogun and his councilors if the items ordered by the magistrate for this purpose are not available in our warehouses and would otherwise have to be bought from the Chinese. The profit made is his own, earned without any detriment or loss to his employer. If it were not for their scrupulous conscience, they would also occasionally reap some benefit at the expense of their principals. I am not saying that this has anything to do with the expenses of this trading post, which are charged at more than 160,000 florins annually, but comes solely from the purchase of refined copper. The administration at Batavia has given instructions not to buy the picul below twelve to twelve and a half taels, so that the refineries do not get disheartened because of lack of profit. Nevertheless, if our interpreters were to negotiate a price one mace below this sum, then there would be an additional 600 taels on 12,000 piculs, which could not go into the accounts as it is against instructions. Although I do not want to claim that this sort of thing occurs, I can assure the reader that the office of director produces a good annual purse, with which they would not part if offered 30,000 florins. Matters would be different though, if the director were penniless beforehand and had to bring in his goods with half the profit going to his creditors. Furthermore, on his departure and especially on his return he may not greet his benefactors empty-handed, unless he wants to forgo similar overseas appointments in the future. The goods he brings back consist of silk garments received as gifts from the shogunal councilors, which he, in turn, must present to others. There are also foodstuffs, porcelain, lacquered and other manufactured goods that he can sell at 50 percent profit in Batavia and golden *koban,* which previously could be exchanged for 54 taels and traded along the coast of Coromandel at 28 percent profit. But at present they bring very little or no profit. The gentleman would do better to use his remaining funds for the purchase of ambergris and refined copper and send the latter to Malacca at the company's expense, but this is forbidden and not possible for everybody.

Let us finally now dispatch the fleet. For the return freight a good part of the income of ten and a half tons of gold is invested in refined copper. Twelve thousand to twenty thousand piculs are purchased, each of which weighs 125 Dutch pounds. The copper is cast in sticks over a span in length and a finger thick. Each picul is packed in a box of rough pine boards in which it can be carried and transported easily. The copper is distributed among our three or four ships, one of which heads for Batavia while the others separate at Puli Tioman[43] and proceed to Malacca. The governor of that locality will send them to Bengal, Coromandel, Surat, or wherever their freight is required. Also a small quantity of unrefined copper is purchased, which is cast in round cakes and delivered simply in that condition. Sometimes several hundred piculs or boxes of copper casjes, or coins, are bought if they are required in Tunkin or other localities. The copper is supplied by a certain corporation, which is permitted to refine and sell it to the foreigners. In return they have to render four hundred *shu* of silver to the chief judge in his capacity as director of the foreigners. To encourage favorable sales, we annually give our brokers or interpreters a reward of six hundred taels and even more, but these roguish mediators pocket no less a bribe from the other side.

In addition, six to twelve or more thousand pounds of camphor are purchased, which is packed in wooden barrels, as well as several hundred packs of straw containing porcelain; sometimes one or two boxes of gold wire, each containing one hundred bundles, are purchased, as well as a variety of fine chests, boxes, and containers of the best lacquer; quince wood; umbrellas and a variety of artistically manufactured goods of rush, wood, buffalo horn, ray skins, stone, copper, gold, and sowaas, the latter being a metal artificially made from silver, copper, and gold,[44] equal in price or valued higher than fine silver; rolled blinds;[45] paper made transparent with oil and varnish; also paper painted with imitation gold and silver obtained from shells to decorate rooms; rice, the very best in the whole of Asia; a good quantity of *sake,* which is a strong drink made of fermented rice; soy sauce, which is a marinade or sauce to be poured over a roast; preserved fruits, all packed in barrels; cut tobacco; tea; and quince marmalade. Excess funds are carried in gold *koban,* some several thousand pieces.

The vessels may not be laden and taken out of the harbor until the court has given its special permission and the date of departure has been set. On lading, all purchases are again the subject of strict inspection. Moreover, one or several days before departure two landlords, two apprentices, and two scribes attached to the ward headman and the treasury, as well as several coolies or day laborers, appear in each person's room, including those who stay but wish to send out goods and those of men from the vessels who live in the empty houses during the period of the sales. Each piece is individually inspected, recorded, and after the inspection tied up with straw ropes, secured with their seals, and a list of contents is pasted on top for the information of the guards at the gate, who otherwise would open it again when it is taken away. During this inspection all illegal wares are confiscated, if found. These consist of anything that represents the image of a local god, a *kuge,* that is, the courtiers of the *dairi,* or their garments, a printed book or paper, a mirror or some other piece of metal engraved with native characters, silver coins, native woven fabric, and especially anything that goes under the title of native defense, such as the picture of a soldier, a saddle, ship or small vessel, suit of armor, bows, and swords. If the latter were actually found, the owner would at the very least be banished from the country, and the interpreters and servants employed for his supervision, as well as other suspects, would be tortured until the vendor and his accomplices were discovered, for only their blood can atone for this crime. Thus some years ago our resident Dutch witnessed the execution of the magistrate's secretary and his innocent eight-year-old, only son (who wanted to send some hidden sword blades to China). But on my departure the examination of my personal goods was, for certain reasons, carried out only casually by the inspectors while taking a farewell drink. Nevertheless, an old Japanese shaving knife, and also little sticks of wood attached to dolls instead of swords were kept back, because their eyes happened to fall on them.

On departure all must declare any gold they own to the commissioners and openly export the same, so that they can tell from the engraved seal of the treasury whether the gold passed through their hands or was obtained by smuggling. But during the frenzy and clamor of the departure this procedure is not correctly followed. The main purpose of these and many other Japanese measures is to prevent smuggling, which has been strictly and absolutely prohibited by the shogun. Moreover, smuggling brings a greater supply of goods on the market, lowering prices. This disadvantages the city of Nagasaki because it cannot raise as much *kōsen,* or tax. Therefore lawbreakers are given capital punishment, but only the offender is convicted and not, as in the case of other crimes, also the sons. More than three hundred people have lost their lives in the last six or seven years on account of smuggling, mainly with the Chinese (whose departing junks the smugglers follow to buy their unsold goods) and a few with the Dutch. Even during my two years of residence more than fifty died wretched deaths on various occasions, some committing suicide when caught, others being executed by the bailiff, either publicly or in the prison. Recently, in 1691, two Japanese were even put to death on our island in front of our eyes, simply because they had illegally purchased one pound of camphor of Baros from a Dutchman, which was found on one of them (the other one had only lent the money) during the inspection on leaving the island. I will end this painful chapter with the story of their execution after having sent our vessels off first.

As soon as the day determined for our departure approaches, the ships are laded one after the other. At the end their armaments are returned, and the crew is mustered, as on arrival, according to the original roll. As soon as a vessel has been treated in this fashion, it must within the hour proceed to the exit of the harbor two miles from the city and wait there until the last vessel has been dispatched. With its arrival, they are immediately accompanied into the open sea and there are left by the Japanese guards, who until that time were on the ships as well as surrounding them in guard boats. If an enormous storm obstructs our departure, many rowboats, or small vessels, with Japanese rowers are tied to the ships with a long rope to drag them out of the harbor one by one, so that despite all the gods of the sea and the air, the shogun's orders can be executed correctly, even if the vessels may later sink in the storm.

The execution was carried out as follows. The presiding magistrate, then known as Genzaemon and now as Settsu no Kami, indicated to the Dutch resident through our *otona* at daybreak of December 10th that he and his subordinates should get ready to watch the punishment of the offenders. One hour later the herds of interpreters, landlords, cooks, and the whole flock of the island and the judiciary arrived, a total of some two hundred people. Ahead of them was carried the board mounted on a pole on which the reason for capital punishment was written in characters large enough to be seen from afar. Following came the two offenders surrounded by executioners and low-ranking bailiffs. The first was the one who had made the purchase, a lad of twenty-three, in shabby dress, on whom the camphor had been found during the inspection on leaving the island. The other was a well-dressed forty-year-old man, who had only lent the money to the former, his erstwhile servant. Among the executioners one carried an instrument like a rake held upright, with twisted iron hooks instead of the usual teeth, which is used to stop people escaping, because any cloth touched becomes attached. Another man carried a sharp crescent-shaped instrument on a similar handle, which is convenient for cutting, hitting, stabbing, and also for pinning a person firmly against a wall. Next came two courtiers of the magistrates with their servants, acting as commissioners, and a little further behind also two scribes. They went across the island to a vacant plot of land that had been chosen for the execution. We, the seven Dutchmen who remained after the ships had departed, agreed among ourselves not to appear. But since our resident advised us to go, having heard that we would otherwise be urged on with sticks, I did not delay.

I discovered the condemned in the middle of the square in front of the others sitting on their knees, with bared shoulders and their hands tied on their backs. Each had his bailiff at his side; the first had a tanner, since here the tanners are used as bailiffs. The second had his best friend and comrade, whom, according to the custom of the country, he had asked for the last favor of delivering the final blow. Twenty paces away the commissioners sat on one bench, and the scribes were seated on another. The third bench was for our resident, who, however, did not appear. The remaining people stood where they pleased. I had placed myself with my Japanese servant as close as possible behind the second offender, and while they were searching for the remaining Dutchmen overheard a well-spoken exchange between the condemned. For as the elder of the two standing in front was murmuring his *kannon gyō*[46] (this is a prayer addressed to the one-hundred-handed Briarius, whom they call Kannon, taken from *hachi no maki,* that is, the eighth section of the large work *Hokke kyō,* consisting of forty-eight volumes), the younger, standing behind him, scolded him with the words: "You should really be ashamed of yourself to show such fear." The old man answered: "Well, well, I am just saying a little prayer." The young man replied: "You had time to pray earlier. Now it is useless, except that it will make you blush with shame if the Dutch see it." Thereupon he stopped. As soon as the Dutch entered the square, both bailiffs simultaneously struck off the head of their charges with a short sword, so that their bodies fell over onto the bleeding wound. Each corpse was wrapped in a coarse rush mat, the heads were tied into a third mat, and all was hauled from the island to the execution ground at Magome, a village situated outside the city. It is said that young fellows use the bodies to test the sharpness of their swords, until they have been cut into pieces half the length of a finger, after which they are permitted to be buried. But the heads are customarily put on display on poles for seven days.

The remaining procession marched off again without observing any order. When our resident went to meet first the commissioners and shortly afterward also the scribes on the crossroads to thank them for their troubles, cordially inviting them for a pipe of tobacco, he, on the contrary, was served a stern rebuke and given the following warning: He ought to take care that his subordinates did not meet the same fate in the future.

Thus today our place of residence was for the first time stained and initiated with human blood.

Chapter 9

The Treatment and Trade of the Chinese

Since ancient times the Chinese have traded the goods of their provinces, especially raw silk (Greek and Latin speakers therefore gave them the name of Seres[1]) in oriental islands and kingdoms, mainly east of Sumatra and Malacca, and in their last war with the Tartars[2] they settled there in great numbers (to escape the obligatory shaving of the head). They have also always taken their goods to Japan, but only sparingly and in small vessels. For when the policy of the Chinese empire did not permit its subjects to visit foreign countries and foreign nations, only the inhabitants of the coastal regions and the nearby islands took advantage of their location and secretly and illegally sailed to other nations. This continued until the new Tartar government of the present emperor permitted all subjects free passage and trade with foreign nations. This freedom having been granted, they now export their wares in greater quantity than ever before, and, as is the case with other places, they also bring them to neighboring Japan, where they are always received and tolerated by the locals as respected guests because of their common religion, books, learned language, and science. Previously they entered Osaka and other shallow and difficult harbors, until the Portuguese discovered a more convenient one at Nagasaki. Then the merchants taught them to use that city as their marketplace, and the ruler's orders bound them, like other foreigners, to enter this harbor only. For a number of years in the past, both the Chinese scattered through the islands and countries east of the river Ganges as well as the native Chinese, freely conducted their trade there, some on their own account and others for their kings or domain lords, arriving with as many ships, goods, and people, and trading as much as they liked. They happily made use of the freedom granted to them. Some settled as permanent residents. They built three temples according to their different native languages and engaged for them priests from their homeland. In a short time the number of Chinese and junks arriving increased so enormously that the cautious and distrustful Japanese became suspicious. In the last years alone, the Chinese arrived in both 1683 and 1684 in about two hundred junks, each carrying no fewer than fifty men (now only thirty), which brings the number of people who visited this city in one year to ten thousand. Moreover, various junks were at times carrying one hundred people, frequently passengers who came to transport and sell their own goods. But among them were also young people with stipends, or rich Chinese playboys. They came only for pleasure, to spend their money among the people, or, to be precise, among the women, who cannot be bought anywhere in China as they can in Japan and who provided the city with a good source of income. In those very years there was among them a Tartar mandarin with his complete entourage, in command of six junks; but he soon had to depart with them again, since this country—as he was promptly told—tolerates no other lords and mandarins except its own. But this liberty granted to the Chinese was soon curtailed. For the Japanese learned that the Tartar emperor of China gave the Jesuits, their sworn and banished enemy, easy access and also permitted them to convert his subjects from their heathen beliefs. They further learned that the books of the padres (that is how they call the Roman Catholic works) printed in China were hidden among the other Chinese volumes that annually arrived in the country and in this manner reached the people, who were easily taken in again and enticed to become Christians. Moreover, the middlemen themselves were suspected to be under the sway of this teaching and be Roman Catholics. It was therefore decided to curb the past freedom of this nation, and to restrict both their trade and living conditions in the same way as the Dutch had to suffer. The arrival of the above-mentioned mandarin and the annually increasing number of these Chinese and Tartar visitors suspected of being Christians turned their intention into quick resolve firstly to alter the formerly free trade and secondly to limit personal freedom. Firstly, as to changes in the terms of trade: this was restricted already in the following year, 1685, to a certain sum, as was the case with the Dutch. Of the goods they imported, they were permitted to sell only up to the value of six hundred boxes of silver annually, that is, 600,000 *jū momme* or taels, which amounts to twenty-one Dutch tons of gold, twice the amount the Dutch are permitted to sell. They were restricted to carrying goods to this value in no more than seventy junks, and the Japanese specified that the following numbers were to come from the following places annually:[3] seventeen junks from the province of Fu-chou;[4] sixteen from the city and province of Canton;[5] five from Ningpo;[6] four from Chang-chou;[7] four from the island of Amoy and the surrounding shores of the continent; three from Hang-chou;[8] three from the empire of Siam;[9] two from the kingdom of Tunkin; two from Quang-nam;[10] two from the kingdom of Cambodia;[11] two from Takasago, or Taiwan, the island of Formosa; one from P'u-T'o shan, situated near Fu-chou, where there is a famous Kannon temple;[12] one from Kōchi, or Cochin China;[13] and one from Tani, one of the largest islands of Ryūkyū.[14] These are the above-mentioned seventy junks.[15] Further, one junk from Shakatara,[16] or Batavia, and one from Peking,[17] are permitted and are supposed to be fitted in, or be accepted instead of those that stayed behind, were wrecked on the way, or perhaps arrived later. There are often irregularities in this respect, inasmuch as those sailing back in spring after having made their sales cover their ships with new paint and varnish and return once again with different crews and different goods to be accepted without the deception being discovered. Especially when they sail in spring, these clever visitors on occasion tend to be purposely washed up in Satsuma and sell their goods there. Then they rush back for a second load of cargo, which they take to Nagasaki. If on the way to Satsuma they are caught by the guards (patrolling the shores to prevent smuggling), they pretend that they went off the route to the harbor they are supposed to arrive at against their will or without their knowledge.

As to the second point: restriction of their freedom was delayed for three years, and only in 1688 was this nation put behind bars, akin to the Dutch. Their residence was established on the site of the valuable ornamental gardens of the recently disgraced shogunal treasurer Heizō.[18] He had established them as so-called shogunal gardens on a flat hill at the shore, in a corner of the harbor near the city, and until that time local and foreign plants had been cultivated there most interestingly. But prior to their move, various rows of small, wooden two-storied houses, each row sharing the same roof, were built within the compound (which is half again as large as the island De[19]), while on the outside it was well fortified with moats, wooden barriers, a double front gate, and strong guards. All this happened with such speed that what at the beginning of February was still a most pleasant ornamental and flower garden, in May had already acquired the abominable shape of a prison, used to detain the Chinese, for which, moreover, they were made to pay a rent of 1,600 taels annually. There they sit imprisoned during their stay, and, like the Dutch on their island De, put up with this wretched accommodation for the love of profit. There are, however, the following differences:

1. Unlike the Dutch, the Chinese have not been granted the favor of appearing in front of the shogun annually, which means that they save the cost of the three months' journey to court and of many presents to His Majesty and his councilors;
2. Daily various food items are brought for sale and displayed between the entrance gates of their prison, while the Dutch have to maintain a special group of official procurers for their purchase and supply;
3. As partly private and mutually hostile merchants of base character, they are treated much worse by their Japanese superiors and interpreters, yes, are even ordered around and punished for crimes with beatings;
4. They do not leave behind a permanent resident and occupant, but all have to depart on their junks and during the idle winter months must leave their accommodation empty.

Their sales take place during three separate times annually. The first is in spring when the earliest twenty junks arrive; the second in summer, the cargo of thirty junks; and the third, the cargo of twenty junks in late autumn. Those coming after these seventy have arrived have to return without accomplishing anything. Their cargo consists of raw silk from China and Tunkin; further, of silk and cotton weaves in many varieties and names, as also the Dutch import them and as have been described in the previous chapter; sugar from various countries; calamine, to produce brass, from Tunkin; turpentine (from wild pistachio trees), gum lacca, myrrh, agel,[20] and aloes-wood from Champa, Cambodia, and neighboring countries; from the large island of Borneo the costly camphor de Baros; from China the precious Korean root *ninjin* (the wild sugar root);[21] also from China, various drugs and composite medicines, essential for everyday use; and last but not least, various books on philosophy and theology printed in China. As I have mentioned, among these books were a few works about the teaching from Rome. When this was first noticed, the carrier of these books (perhaps being unaware of this fact) had to convincingly vouch not to have had any knowledge of this matter, nor himself to be a Christian, but all the same had to return in his junk with all his goods, unable to sell any. From then on, it was ordered that before being sold, all imported books have to be examined, and a copy of each book must be read and censured. Two local learned men have been appointed by the shogun for this purpose and receive an annual stipend. One of them is the abbot of the monastery Shuntoku, who has to read and censure religious books. The other is a Confucian philosopher and physician of, as he says, the *dairi*, residing on Tateyama.[22] He wears his hair long, tied at the back, as is usual with philosophers, doctors, and physicians. He inspects the books dealing with philosophy and other secular texts.

The usual procedures during the sales are nearly the same as those of the Dutch and can be found in the previous chapter. Only one thing is different. On account of their shorter sea voyage and lower costs, a higher tax is levied on their goods, namely, 60 percent (which has to be paid by the purchaser to the local government for distribution among servants and citizens of the city), which means that they have to sell their goods for that much less than the Dutch. There are restrictions placed on the money they make, inasmuch as they may no longer purchase copper and silver, as some years ago, but must invest it in copper and manufactured goods only. They are not permitted to take even one single *bu* out of the country.

As soon as a junk has sold its permitted quantity of cargo, the *funaban* (that is, the Japanese guard barge that sits behind every ship arriving in the harbor) accompanies it again out of the harbor and into the open sea. On the previous day the image of the sea god P'u-sa,[23] or Bosa,[24] would have been collected from the temple with bells and cymbals (where he had been taken on arrival) and installed again in the ship. This Bosa is a god unknown to the Japanese whom the Chinese merchants and mariners take with them, and to whom they make many vows when in danger. Every night gilded pieces of paper are lit and thrown into the sea in his honor with a great noise of reverberating bells and bowls. Also puppet plays[25] or comedies are performed at night in public streets after a successful journey, if this has been pledged. They apparently also slaughter pigs and other animals for him (no cows, since they do not eat them), but they consume the meat themselves. Since the Chinese merchants leave with many unsold goods, they are sometimes met at sea by Japanese smugglers. These purchase their remaining goods for a good price but are often caught by the cruising boats and handed over to the deadly arm of justice at Nagasaki. Not long after my arrival, on 29 November 1690, eleven such persons were taken from a vessel and brought to the death cells, where they were beheaded a few days later. Not mentioning many others, in the next year, on 28 December, of twenty-three people, ten were executed by sword and the remaining crucified. Five of them were dead, having cut their bellies when caught and thus disemboweled themselves. They were brought to the execution with their bodies preserved in salt.

Neither must I forget to mention the merchants who annually arrive in the large province of Satsuma from the islands of Ryūkyū, or Liqueo,[26] and are permitted to trade there with Japan. This is how they call the islands that run from the above province to the Philippines in a southwesterly direction. These foreigners speak a corrupt form of Chinese, showing that they came from China. Moreover, there are many inhabitants who were born in China and who fled to these islands at the last incursion of the Tartar khan.[27] They have been taken in as fellow citizens by their former compatriots, with whom they were already acquainted through shipping and trade. A few hundred years ago these islands were subdued by the force of arms by the petty king of Satsuma,[28] and, ruled by him with a gentle hand, they have remained loyal to him to this day. They recognize him as their conqueror, but not the shogun as their ruler, and annually bring the residing *bugyō* a small tribute of produce of their fields but send no less an annual present as tribute to the emperor of China. Even though they are not considered foreigners, but to some extent as Japanese subjects, they are, nevertheless, treated as foreigners and outsiders when it comes to trade. Thus they are permitted to enter the harbor of Satsuma with their junks and sell goods to the value of 125,000 taels annually, even though they contrive to sell far more. The goods they bring consist of a variety of silk cloth and other goods as requested from China, where they go to collect them. They also bring some produce of their own fields, such as grain, pulse, *awa mori,* a strong brandy that the farmers make out of their excess millet, *takara gai* and *hime gai,*[29] that is, gem shells and virgin shells, called cowrie throughout India. They are used in Bengal and Siam as the smallest coin and are imported from the Maldives. In Japan they are turned into a white paint used as cosmetics by young boys and women. They also bring transparent shells, filed flat, which are used to make windows, to slide across in winter against the rain; also rare flowers and decorative plants in pots, and little else.

Chapter 10
Some Posters, Passes, and Letters That Have Been Mentioned Above

Translator's note: Kaempfer listed the title of this chapter in the index for book 4, but did not compose the text. His notes, however, contain a body of material that roughly corresponds to this title, and the first translator, J. G. Scheuchzer, transcribed and translated what he could read. The editor of the German version, Christian Wilhelm Dohm, translated Scheuchzer's English text into German.[1]

The material consists of notes and documents in Japanese, Dutch, German, and Latin and appears to have been intended for the personal use of the author only, perhaps as a basis for further writing. His sketch of the notice boards with government orders positioned outside Deshima, which carried some of the orders he transcribed and translated, however, bears a notation in his hand that the drawing should be used to illustrate chapter 9, the previous chapter. This must lead to the conclusion that on second thought Kaempfer decided not to write up this material.

Reworking his notes, Kaempfer might have come to the conclusion that they were simply too sketchy to write up. Indeed, the problem inherent in the material is that the Japanese text occasionally has words missing and does not make sense. Official Dutch and Kaempfer's own translations are imprecise. Consequently Japanese sources have been consulted below.

Orders of the First Shogun, Tokugawa Ieyasu, and the Second Shogun, Hidetada

Translator's note: Kaempfer acquired copies of the original orders by Tokugawa Ieyasu and Hidetada permitting the Dutch access to Japan. The copies are carefully executed down to the reproduction of the shogun's red seal. He also obtained a document that appears to be an official Dutch translation of Ieyasu's order. But this Dutch version is a much embroidered translation, and to demonstrate what potential this provided for diplomatic misunderstandings, both versions are translated. The document, apparently in the hand of a Dutch scribe, states—

Translation of the pass concerning the General United Dutch East India Company, with an office established at Hirado, which his Imperial Majesty of Japan, called Ōgosho sama,[2] gave to the Company at the time of Mr. Jacobus Specx.

With regard to Dutch ships coming to my country of Japan, whatever harbor or location they may land, we herewith give express command to all and everybody in my country, not to molest the same in any fashion or hinder them, but to the contrary, to show them without fail all help, favor, and assistance. Everybody should be watchful that nothing but friendship is maintained, upon which I have given my word, and should take care that what my words have promised will not be violated.

Dated in Japanese style the 25th day of the 7th month, which is 30 August, 1611.[3]

Translator's note: The same order, dated the 25th of the 7th month Keichō 14, which corresponds to 1609 and not 1611, as stated in the Dutch version, translated from the original Japanese reads—

When Dutch ships sail to Japan they can land at any point of the coast, and that shall not be varied. From now on this matter shall be observed without fail. There shall not be the slightest change. The above is ordered.

Keichō 14, 7th month, 25th day.[4]

Translator's note: This order was confirmed by the second shogun, Hidetada, in 1617 (Genna 3). Kaempfer's German translation states—

Explanation of the Shogun's written order by the senior councilors to the territorial lord of Hirado, concerning the behavior of the Dutch.

I send my words in haste.

Dutch ships in Hirado shall trade as before in accordance with the wishes of the captain. Even though we do not issue an order annually, you are ordered (once and for all) to take care that the Dutch do not spread the ways of the padres. You should order thus.

Venerating, venerating, speaking with awe.

Postscript, or rather interscript.

Merchants from Miyako and Sakai should also come to your place to trade as it pleases (both sides). That is how it shall be. It is so.

To Matsura Fisinno Cami donno.

Person, person.

Subscript

Doji Ōjenofske	LS[5]	Nagakatz
Ando Tsussima no Cami	LS	Sigenobu
Itakura Ingano Cami	LS	Katzuge
Fonda Sina no nofske	LS	Massa tsungu

The 23rd day of the 8th month.[6]

Translator's note: The original Japanese order states—

If Dutch trading vessels crossing the seas to reach Japan meet difficult winds and seas, they can land in any obscure or well-known place along Japan's coast. This order is to be observed without change.

Genna 3, 8th month, 16th day.

Hanrei Borowara

Copy of the order.[7]

Because merchants from Kyoto and Sakai are expected to come to your locality, it stands to reason that mutual trade is conducted there.

Immediately and without fail we give notice that while it is understood that the Dutch vessels shall trade according to the directions of their *kapitan*[8] at Hirado as they did previously, it is ordered that they do not spread the teaching of the Catholic priests.

Respectfully,
Doi Ōi no kami Toshikatsu
Andō Tsushima no kami Naotsugu
Itakura Iga no kami Katsushige
Honda Kōsuke no Kami Masazumi[9]
Respectfully addressed to[10] Lord Matsuura Hizen no kami.[11]

Order Read to the Dutch at Edo Castle

Translator's note: The following order of 1677 (Empō 5) was read to the Dutch at Edo Castle when taking their leave. Kaempfer's notes contain a transcription of the Japanese text into the Western alphabet in which, however, some words are missing. There is also a Dutch translation.[12] Here only the Japanese original as cited in *Tokugawa kinrei kō* is translated.

For generations it has been ordered that the Dutch shall trade with Japan, and that every year they shall land at Nagasaki. As before we order that under no circumstances shall you be in contact with the Portuguese and their Christian sect. Should we hear from any country that you are on intimate terms with them, we will stop you coming to Japan. Consequently you shall under no circumstances bring anything of their sect to Japan, and, of course, you shall not carry any objects of the sect on your ships.

If you want to continue to cross the seas and trade with Japan, you must report anything you hear about the Christian sect. You must report to the Nagasaki magistrate if there is a new location where the Portuguese sect has entered and also anything you see or hear on your routes crossing the seas.

You must not capture any Chinese ships crossing over to Japan. If among the countries frequented by the Dutch there is one where you meet the Portuguese, you shall under no circumstances communicate with them. You must write down in detail the name and location of any country where you meet the Portuguese, and the Nagasaki magistrate must be informed annually by the *kapitan* when he arrives.

Addendum

The inhabitants of the Ryūkyūs are people that submit to Japan, and you shall not capture them regardless of where you come across them.

Empō 5, the year of the serpent, 2nd month, 25th day.[13]

Orders Posted Outside Deshima

Translator's note: Kaempfer spent some time studying the two orders mounted on boards at the bridge leading to the island of Deshima. Among his documents are copies in *sōsho* (grass writing) and *kana,* phonetic transcriptions and translations, as well as a sketch. Kaempfer was aware, however, that his Japanese text of one of the orders was not complete, for he added a missing word himself. He did not realize that further words were also missing.

The following translations are based on the orders as published in Japanese sources, but Kaempfer's explanatory headings have been retained; Kaempfer's Japanese has been modernized.

First order in front of Deshima

Jō or *sadamari,* which is the official character and title of the orders.

"If Japanese or foreigners violate the law, conspire to do evil for whatever reason, or, offering a reward ask others to do so, it must be reported immediately and without fail.

"Even if someone has committed the same crime, he will be pardoned and will receive twice the amount of this reward. If someone is accused of hiding the matter, he will be convicted."[14]

Month Day

Tonomo[15]
Jūbei[16]
Settsu no Kami[17]

Deshima machi
Prohibition

"It is prohibited
– that women enter, except prostitutes.
– that monks and mountain priests enter, except the priests from Mount Kōya.
– that people enter who ask for alms or beg for a living.
– to enter inside the posts placed around Deshima or to pass below the bridge.
– that, unless it be unavoidable, the Dutch leave Deshima.
The above order is to be strictly obeyed."[18]
Year of the Monkey[19]
Month Day

Name
Name
Name

Translator's note: Kaempfer wrote the following note on Mount Kōya to explain why priests from there were permitted to enter Deshima.[20]

Kōya is a mountain near Miyako where several thousand inhabitants lead a spiritual life as priests. They are called Kōya *hijiri,* or Kōya priests. No law enforcement officers may enter, and it is therefore a refuge for criminals. All are accepted and given sup-

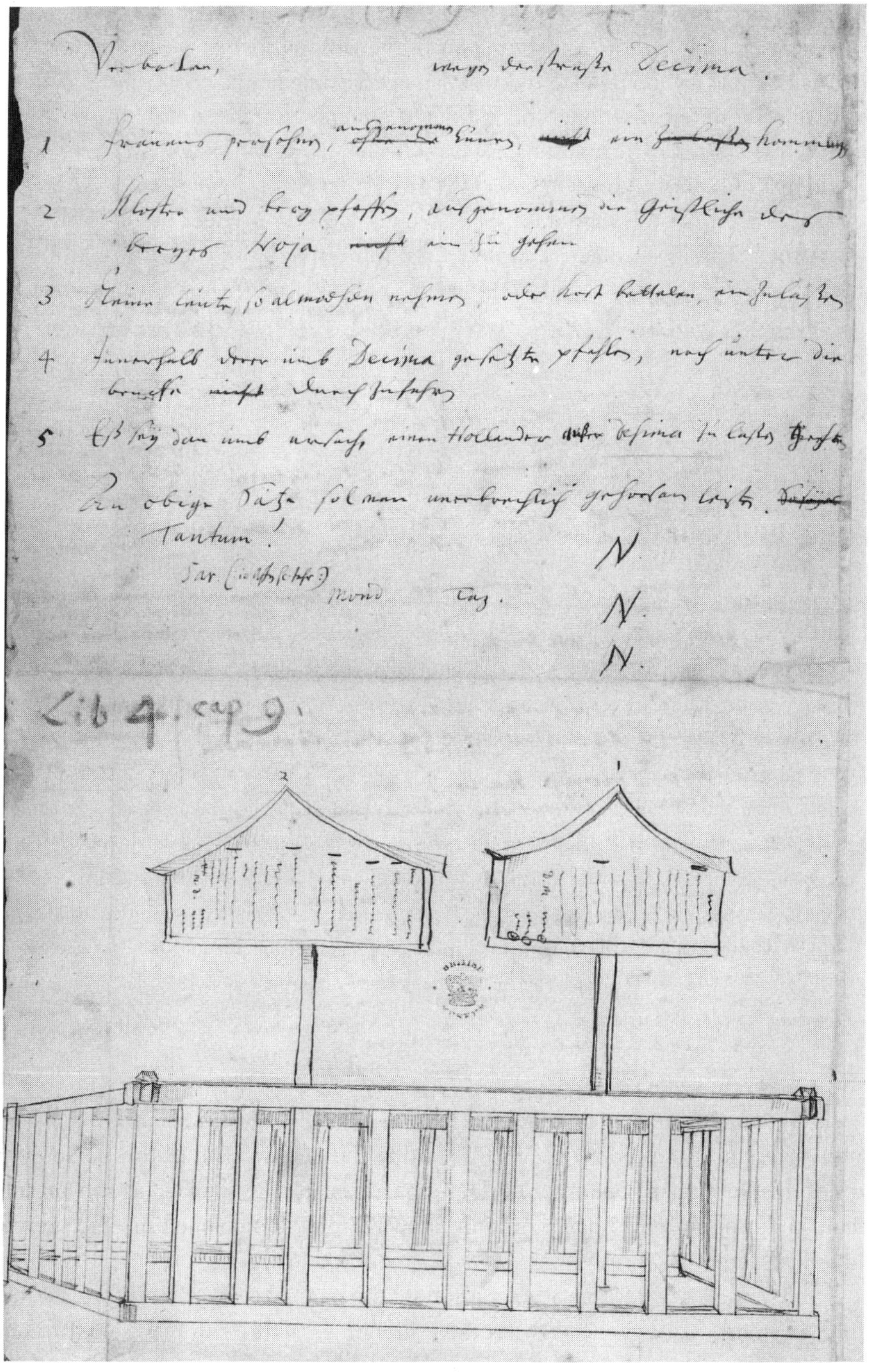

Kaempfer's sketch of boards with orders posted outside Deshima. (Courtesy of the British Library, Sloane 3060, folio 469 verso)

port during their life (but on condition that they serve the common good with their hands and property) as long as they contribute only thirty taels to the finances of the monastery. People can also do a good deed and donate an everlasting lamp by contributing only 120 mace. From the interest, enough oil is bought annually for the lamps (in front of the founder Kōbō Daishi), which receive their oil from a common source, and what leaks is collected in a special container.

The clerics of this mountain are called *hijiri* (the word does not imply the same amount of restriction as *shukke,* i.e., they have more freedom); they travel around the country with textiles or piece goods, in which they always trade. They do not come to Nagasaki, but if they did, they would be admitted to the trade on Deshima like other merchants.

Letter of Employment and Guarantee

Translator's note: In his description of Japan, Kaempfer never hesitated to tackle the transcription of even the most difficult Japanese names. Not once, however, did he mention the name of his faithful servant and student, whom he acknowledged to have helped him greatly to collect the material for this work.[21] The reason is that the young man's activities were highly illegal, as becomes very much apparent from the document translated below. Only recently has he been identified as the later famous interpreter Imamura Genemon Eisei.[22] At about the same time, a Japanese document, which appears to be a copy of his employment contract and guarantee, came to light in the British Library. Strangely enough, this document is dated the 7th month Genroku 5 (1692), only a few months before his employment with Kaempfer terminated on the latter's departure. Presumably the change of date in this copy that Kaempfer took back to Europe as material for his publication on Japan was a measure to obscure the fact that Imamura was employed by him during the relevant years. It is most probably for the same reason that Kaempfer's German translation of this document omits all personal particulars of the employee, such as his name, address, and age. Here the original Japanese document has been translated.[23]

Letter of Acceptance

Genemon, the son of Imamura Ichisaemon of Moto Furukawa machi, aged twenty, adherent of the Jōdo sect. With regard to the employment of this person in the rooms of the Dutchman Kaempfer on Deshima as servant, he shall act as servant to the Dutchman during the day. I have certainly known him well for a long time and therefore stand as his guarantor.

– He shall never listen to any talk about the banned Christian sect. In addition I will not have him violate in the slightest the prohibitions in force on Deshima. I will have him take great care in preventing fires and so forth in the rooms of the Dutch.

– I will not let him have any secret discussions with the Dutch, whatever the circumstances. If someone hands him gold and silver or other items, regardless of who the person is, even if he be a Japanese, I will not let him pass it on. I will never let him sell to, or take from, the Dutch any forbidden items.

– Even if he is asked to sell the smallest thing for the Dutch in the city, I will under no circumstances let him act as an agent, or let him buy the goods himself.

– Under no circumstances will I let him arrange with the Dutch, take measures to hide baggage, or to have it cross the fence, or to have items taken out in someone's pocket. Neither will I let him steal things from the ships at the time when the cargo is being handled and loaded. Furthermore I will not let him assist the Dutch with arrangements to take out goods secretly. If he is requested by the Dutch to do so, I will have him report it at once.

– I will not let him act in violation of the above. If he were to do so, I will in all instances do what is ordered from above. I am guaranteeing this from this day onwards.

The seal of Genemon.
The guarantor from Moto Furukawa machi,
the seal of Irako Yajirō.
To: Lord Yoshikawa Gibuemon.[24]

Translator's note: The remaining material in Kaempfer's notes is too sketchy to produce a translation that would satisfy the demands of the modern historian. Since no Japanese equivalents were available, it has been omitted.

Book 5

Chapter 1
Preparations for Our Journey to Court and a Description of the Local Way of Traveling

The Origin of the Annual Journey to Court

Since the time of the shogun Yoritomo, the founder of the present form of government,[1] it has been the custom that not only the stewards of the shogunal domains and cities but all daimyo and *shomyō,* that is, all greater and lesser territorial lords, appear annually at the shogun's court. They pay homage by offering their respects and presenting gifts; while the greatest of them—one could call them princes or petty kings—call on the shogun personally, the lesser are received by an assembly of councilors. This custom is also enforced upon the servants of our illustrious Dutch company (just as it was upon the Portuguese in their time). Consequently our resident director in charge of trade annually makes his journey to court, accompanied by a physician and one or two scribes as well as a crowd of Japanese of various ranks. These Japanese are sent by their actual superiors, the Nagasaki governors, not just to escort and wait upon the Dutch as guests of the ruler but mainly to serve as supervisors and guards (as if the Dutch were spies or prisoners). For in accordance with Japanese law, the Dutch must be prevented during the journey from entering into suspicious conversations or contact with the Japanese, or from passing the Japanese crosses, images, relics of saints, or anything else connected with Christianity, from selling or giving strange goods and rarities from Christian countries, and, worst of all, from escaping and going into hiding in Japan to continue the teaching of the Christian faith or cause some other trouble. The task is generally entrusted to servants of the Nagasaki governors and also to those who are engaged in or supervise the negotiations of the Dutch, or people who are otherwise known and trusted for their fidelity and honesty. But in spite of their reliability, everyone from the most senior chief down to the lowest servant (with the exception of the grooms, because they change) has to swear on his blood before departure that he will report any of the above violations of these laws that may come to his eyes or ears, either by the Dutch or by his own countrymen and traveling companions. I have twice joined this journey to court and made it with pleasure: once in the year of Christ 1691 with Mr. Henrich von Bütenheim,[2] a gentleman well acquainted with Japanese customs and the Japanese language, an honest, compassionate, and generous person, who knew how to command respect for his person and especially his nation by his fine leadership. The following year I went with Mr. Cornelius Outhorn,[3] the brother of the present governor general at Batavia, an experienced and well-read gentleman familiar with the language, who with his inborn good-natured temperament well knew how to please this unreasonable nation and therefore directed the affairs of his employers to their great gain. In this book I want to introduce the events and memorable occurrences of each day on both these journeys in their proper order. However, before I begin, I will briefly discuss some major points that are essential to understand this account.

Preparations for the Journey to Court and (1) the Selection of the Presents

Preparations for the journey are as follows. First, presents amounting to a certain sum of money are selected for the shogun, his councilors, and some of his high officials at Edo, Miyako, and Osaka. Then they are sorted, assigned, and packed in leather containers, which are, however, again carefully wrapped in straw mats to protect them against all possible accidents on the journey, and finally they are sealed. The presents are chosen by the city governors, who order from our director goods that they believe will please the court one year ahead or select items from the goods that we have available here. Sometimes they also use presents they have received from the Chinese for this purpose, which they thus manage to sell to us most dearly at prices set by themselves or exchange against other goods of ours. Thus rare goods for the shogunal court are often also especially sent from Europe, but sometimes they are not accepted by these judges. For instance, this happened during my time with two brass fire extinguishers of the latest design, which were returned after they had first been tried and then their design copied. This was also the fate of the cassowary bird, sent as a present from Batavia, once they learned that it ate a lot but did not understand anything. After some time has been spent on this process, these goods and everything necessary for the journey by sea are loaded into a barge, which leaves three to four weeks ahead for the small coastal town of Shimonoseki and waits for us there. Formerly our procession also embarked at this time, thus saving the considerable trouble and expense of the present journey on land to the said town. But this was discontinued on shogunal orders since on one occasion we came into danger during a storm and sometimes the journey took much too long. The barge is not used for any other journey and has to be maintained at great expense in the harbor of Nagasaki solely for this purpose. After the most important goods have been sent ahead, the remaining time is spent on preparations carried out with such diligence that one could imagine we were planning an expedition to a different planet.

(2) Appointment of People for the Journey to Court

The first step in these preparations is the appointment of people making up our procession to court. The governors appoint one of their *yoriki,* that is, one of their courtiers or soldiers of the first rank as *bugyō,* or commissioned chief. He has to represent his lord's high status, which is indicated by the pike carried after him. He is assisted by a *dōshin,* or soldier of the court of the second rank, and both these are chosen from among the courtiers of the governor, who is in his second year of office. The two men are joined by two bailiffs, who are granted the honorary title of *tsūshin,* that is to say, official messenger. In accordance with the duty of their office, they, as well as the *dōshin,* are equipped with a solid rope so that they can tie up and overcome a criminal at the order or a glance from the *yoriki.* The above, as well as the official and personal servants of the *bugyō,* are military men and therefore all carry two swords in their belt. These people are called samurai, that is, those who carry two swords, or soldiers, because according to a proclamation that has recently been renewed, no commoners, but only proper soldiers, are permitted to carry two swords. One person from the senior and junior ranks of the interpreters is assigned to us; it is their practice to appoint the person who during the previous year acted as rapporteur between us and the court and the one who presided over the guild during that time. Nowadays these two are joined by one of the apprentices so that at an early age they become well versed in their father's duties by seeing and experiencing them at first hand. All of them take along servants, both as a symbol of status and to attend upon them, with the *bugyō* and senior interpreters taking as many as they like and the others one or two according to their rank. The Dutch captain[4] is permitted to take three, but all other Dutchmen only one. The interpreters assign their favorites who do not know Dutch to this task, quite apart from other guests that make the journey at the expense of our company and with the permission or at the command of the interpreters or governors. These traveling companions are permitted to visit us on Deshima several times before our departure to become acquainted with us from a distance. There are some solid drinking companions among them who would much prefer to deal with us more frankly, but since the oath turns each man into the informer of the next, they fear the presence of others and remain cool and distant to us and our inclinations, without any friendly gesture or genuine service.

The Ordering of Porters and Horses

Porters and horses must also be ordered. This is done by the senior interpreter in his capacity as administrator and purser of the delegation. On his orders all is ready for departure the minute the *bugyō* desires it, and constant progress is assured by a supply of additional porters and horses. Two days before our departure from Nagasaki, porters come to tie up and arrange our packs and do this in such a way that the horses can be loaded and unloaded in an instant. This is not done in German fashion but in a special local way, which deserves to be described.

Preparation of the Equipment (Description of Fixing the Baggage, Saddle, and So Forth)

After a bare wooden saddle (like the pack-saddle of the Swedish hunting or mail horses) has been strapped to the horse with a girth, breast strap, and crupper, a double rope is put across the saddle with which packs balancing each other are fastened on each side as high or low as desired, without the packs being attached either to the horse or the saddle. The packs are stabilized by means of a small, narrow, and long box, called *atotsuke,* which is placed behind the rider and over both packs, and fastened to the saddle either by passing a rope through the hollow rear portion of the saddle or the rings that are located there and pulling the rope tight. The traveler's rugs or bedding are spread on top to form a flat surface and are tied with a softly padded band across the packs after the hollow between the packs has been filled up to make a comfortable seat. The rider sits on this as on a flat table, but quite well padded and comfortably, with his feet crossed under him or stretched out in front as he pleases. But he has to stay very much in the center and be careful that one side does not protrude more than the other so that the packs do not slip and the horse falls. When the horse climbs up and down hills, this is prevented by the servants and grooms, who walk behind and hold on to the packs. Mounting and dismounting is done from the front and is difficult for a stiff-legged person. Unsaddling and unloading is quick when done in the right way: for as soon as one or the other loop has been loosened (after the bedding has first been removed), the packs or bags fall to the ground with the fastening. The ropes used for this purpose are flat, broad, and skillfully made from strong cotton thread. The ends are finished off with small oblong pieces of wood which are very good for tightening and fastening the rope.

The saddle consists of a bare wooden frame with a cushion underneath and a narrow saddle cloth bearing the rider's crest hanging down at the back. On each side of the horse hangs an apron tied loosely under the animal's belly to stop it from being splashed with dirt. The horse's head is covered by a netting of straps or strings to protect the eyes from flies, and the neck, chest, and other parts are hung with cymbals and bells. The packs (which are filled with light goods, or with straw, if they serve only as seats) are square cases made of stiff horsehide, roughly five spans long and three wide and deep. The lid is a little larger and so deep that it covers the container. They are rainproof, but, as mentioned above, are covered with mats and laboriously laced up. People therefore prefer not to open them before they have reached their destination, and daily necessities are kept in the *atotsuke.*

The *atotsuke* is a thin wooden box or case, six spans long and one deep and wide. It contains a convenient drawer of the same length and is closed with a door at the end, through which one can get to the drawer without untying the little box. The *atotsuke* serves as a container for goods needed to be kept handy and no less to hold and secure the two packs, otherwise a rod would be necessary. It is made of gray thick paper and covered with a net of blue rope.

Travel Equipment

Several more pieces, which are attached to the packs and carted along, are necessary to fully equip our traveler and must be mentioned. These are:

A strap and *zeni,* that is to say, small flat brass coins with a hole in the middle, or *pütjes,* with which, when need arises, it is quicker to pay than with silver money, which the vendor must weigh. A person traveling on horseback ties this strap to the ropes of the saddling at the back, while people on foot carry it attached to the back of the belt.

A lamp made of varnished paper folded up in pleats, with the owner's crest painted in the middle. This is carried ahead by one's servants on a pole over the shoulder if one comes to travel in the dark. Otherwise it is carried tied to the very back of the pack covered by a net or small sack, which is dyed or painted with the owners' crest or mark, as are also all other pieces of equipment and clothes of people of high and low rank.

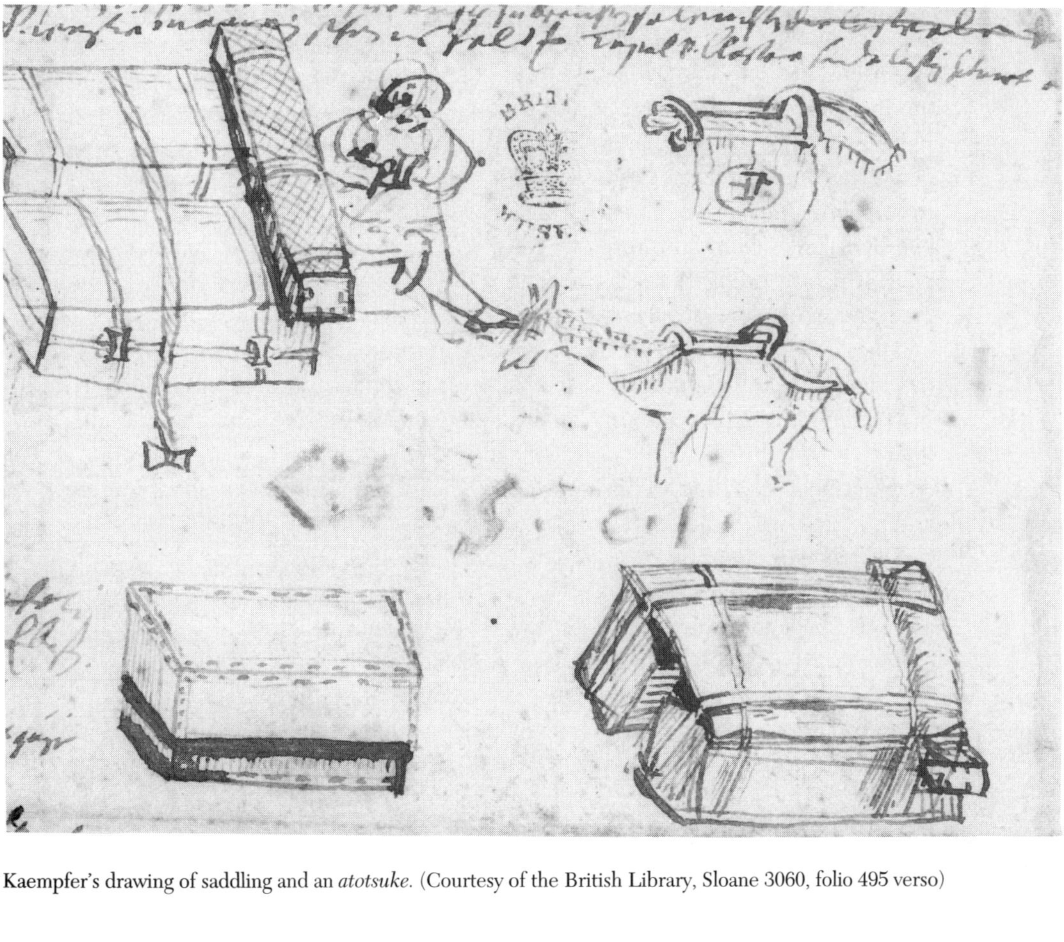

Kaempfer's drawing of saddling and an *atotsuke.* (Courtesy of the British Library, Sloane 3060, folio 495 verso)

A whisk of horsehair or black cock feathers to brush the dust from one's seat and clothes. It is attached at the side to the back of the seat and is more for show than for use.

A water scoop, which is carried in the same fashion on the other side, or wherever else one wishes.

Hoof covers or slippers for horses and servants. These are plaited from straw ropes and have strings of the same material to tie them to the feet. The horses wear these instead of iron horseshoes, which are not used here. On stony and slippery roads they are soon worn out and are often replaced with new ones. The grooms and servants always carry a supply tied to the packs, even though they are available in every village and hut, and street urchins beseech the grooms to buy them. I do not think there is a country in the world where more blacksmiths could make a living than this one, which has none.

Permit me to mention at this point that in addition to the above-mentioned items, I carried something extra, namely, a shabby Javanese box made of bark, in which there was a large compass. I used this in secret to constantly take the bearing of the road, the mountains, and the coastline. But openly I held herbs, flowers, and green branches next to my writing utensils, and thus with the knowledge and under the eyes of everybody, I would be describing and drawing (not just the plants, but under this pretext also everything else I wanted). It would be wrong to accuse me of arousing the suspicions of the Japanese to the detriment of our nation. Until the last day of our journey, all our Japanese companions, and most of all the *bugyō* and his bailiffs, brought me all the rare plants they could find and took much trouble to learn their correct names and properties from people familiar with them. The Japanese, as a reasonable people, are especially knowledgeable about and fond of plants, and they consider botany an innocent discipline, which according to the law of nations should not be obstructed or begrudged. Also, I have never encountered a foreign nation anywhere in the world that hindered me in my botanical studies. On the contrary, most sought to promote them. Moreover, the secretary and most senior councilor of the Nagasaki governor, Tonomo,[5] called me to his office on Deshima in his spare time and had the senior interpreter Shingobei[6] translate the following compliment: His Lordship had great pleasure in hearing from the *bugyō*[7] Asahina Sadanoshin that on the journey I had spent my leisure and found my amusement in this praiseworthy subject of scholarship, a subject which he (Tonomo) himself was extremely fond of, and so forth. But I do not conceal that from the beginning of our journey I did my best to pressure these companions to treat me with extraordinary leniency by providing some with medication and treating them with great deference and by secretly rewarding others for the smallest service.

The traveler must not forget to equip himself with a raincoat. The raincoats are made from two layers of oiled paper and are so wide and long that they cover and protect the horse and luggage as well. The Japanese seem to have borrowed the use of the raincoat and its name, *kappa,* from the Portuguese. Those on foot use capes of the same material when it rains.

To protect his face from the sun, the traveler must also equip himself with a sun hat of split bamboo. These are handsomely and skillfully plaited in the shape of an opened sombrero or parasol and are tied tightly under the chin with smooth cotton ribbons. The hats are transparent and light but become rainproof as soon as they get wet.

They are worn not only by men when traveling but also by the women of the towns and villages on all other occasions, making them look rather attractive.

Also when traveling the Japanese wear baggy trousers ending in narrow pipes covering the calf. These trousers have a slit on both sides to gather in their long skirt, which would otherwise bother them when riding or walking. On top of that, people wear a short coat if they wish. Others wind a wide strip of cloth around their calves instead of socks. Common servants, especially the porters of the *norimono* and the lance bearers, need no trousers, but to move faster they lift up their skirt and tuck it into their belt, so that their bottom and their loin cloth are completely exposed, but this does not embarrass people here.

Just as we do not leave home without gloves, the Japanese of both sexes consider it a point of honor not to be seen without a fan. When traveling they use a fan on which the distance, inns, and prices of food are printed. Or instead they might use a small travel book with the same information, which the boys running around on the road offer to travelers. But the books cannot be purchased by the Dutch (at least not openly).[8]

This is how people equip themselves when they go on a journey. A Japanese who is thus dressed up looks monstrous from afar. For as he is already usually rather short and stocky, the large hat, wide robes, and trousers stick out so much that he appears nearly as wide as tall. People ride in single file on the road. Merchants have their horses, loaded heavily with two or three bales of rice or full cases, led in front of them and follow riding on packhorses. The reins or halter are not held by the rider but by the groom, who walks on the right, next to the horse's head, and with his fellow grooms takes it in turn to sing some wild, heroic songs to liven up the horses and pass the time.

The Way of Riding without a Halter

The European way of riding, where one gets onto the saddled horse and takes the reins oneself, is here, generally speaking, used only in warfare and is the right of soldiers only. It is seldom used when traveling, although often in the city when paying visits. The rider (who in this country sits hunched and awkwardly) holds the reins only out of boredom, and the horse is led to where it is supposed to go by one servant, or two for show, holding onto the muzzle ring on both sides. Saddling differs little from ours. Their saddles are closer to the German saddles than those of some other Asians. The straps of the stirrups are fairly short and on both sides hangs a rough, round piece of pelt to protect the legs, like those of the Tartars. The stirrups are curved, thick, and heavy and are made of iron or *sowaas*,[9] the size of a flat sole, open at the side and without a bar over the foot, so that the feet cannot get caught when the rider falls. They are usually artistically made and inlaid with silver. For the reins they use a beautiful silk cord instead of leather straps; it is fastened not to a bit but to the muzzle rings when the horse is led. I will omit the description of other decorations here.

Before the procession gets on the move, I must mention that people also travel in *kago*, or palanquins: this is the most elegant way to travel and is also used in the cities for outings. Distinguished people use them for show, ordinary people out of necessity.

But there is a big difference between the palanquins of eminent people and those of the lower orders. The former are magnificent and precious structures and are especially referred to as *norimono,* while the latter are far inferior and are called by the common name of *kago.* The usage of these words is according to the speech and habits of the commoners (the masters of the language in all nations) rather than based on distinguishing features: for *norimono* properly speaking means "a thing to sit in"; *kago,* "a basket to carry." Both exist in so many different types and classes that I cannot distinguish a bad *norimono* from a beautiful *kago,* except for the pole on which it is carried. In the case of a *kago,* this pole is poor, solid, and smaller, but with a *norimono* it is large, handsome, and hollow. The latter consists of four thin boards skillfully joined to resemble a narrow, solid pole with a rising curve in the center, and it is therefore much lighter than it appears from the outside. The height and length of these carrying-poles are regulated by law according to one's station, and the eminence and lofty station of rulers and high-ranking lords are mainly indicated by the height of these carrying-poles. Those who consider themselves to be greater than they actually are occasionally use poles with a curve higher than that permitted, but they often fare badly and with much humiliation are forced to remove it. This government regulation does not apply to women, and they are not prohibited from going beyond their station. The compartment itself is an oblong cubicle, and the largest are so big that a person can sit and rest comfortably. The walls are carefully woven from finely split bamboo, sometimes lacquered, delicate, and precious. On each side is a sliding door, and in it or next to it—sometimes also in the front or at the rear—is a small window. On occasion they also have a small flap at foot level so that people can sleep with their legs stretched out. They have a small roof on top, which is quite unnecessarily covered with oiled paper when it rains. They are carried by two, four, eight, or more porters according to the person's rank, resting on the porters' shoulders, but when the passenger is a territorial lord, the porters hold the palanquin up high with their hands. These bearers (who all wear the same uniform with the crest of their lord's family) are often relieved by others walking beside them. More about this elsewhere.[10]

A *kago,* on the other hand, is not so fine, is generally smaller, and is carried by a solid four-edged, or even a makeshift round, pole, which runs under or on top of the small roof. The *kago* that serve ordinary travelers, especially those in which people are carried over the mountains, are often very simple and so small that one has to crouch in it with crossed legs and bowed head. They practically consist of no more than the round bottom of a basket, with two handles running up to the height of the small roof. In these they hump us over all mountain roads that are too steep for horses, with three porters ordered for each *kago,* and they certainly notice the weight.

Chapter 2
A General Description of the Condition and Location of the Route by Water and on Land from Nagasaki to the Residence at Edo

Japan's Highways

Traditionally Japan has been divided into seven districts, and each is crossed by a trunk road or highway, depending on the location. Because all bordering provinces have built special roads to link up with these highways, like small streams running into a big river, one can travel throughout the country on these roads and reach every locality. The highways carry the name of the area, but more about this elsewhere.

These trunk roads are so wide and spacious that two processions can pass each other without hindrance. The one that goes up, as people say here, meaning going to Miyako, takes the left side of the road, while the one that comes down, that is, comes from Miyako, must take the opposite side according to the custom of the country. So that travelers may know their progress, the highways are measured in miles and signposted. The beginning is at the main bridge of Edo, which is honored with the name of Nihonbashi, meaning the Bridge of Japan. This bridge is taken as a common point or center, and throughout one's journey one knows the distance from this main bridge and from the shogun's residence. The distance is indicated on two small mounds facing each other on opposite sides of the road, each planted with one or several trees. Where a district or the domain of a small or large territorial lord ends, wooden or stone posts with characters indicating the border and the names of both territories are placed along the road. Such posts are also used as signposts when roads branch off from the highway, indicating where the road leads and the distance to the next major point.

The Three Parts of the Journey to Court

We take two of the said highways and between these travel a stretch by sea, so that the complete journey to court consists of three parts. The first part is overland from Nagasaki across the island of Kyushu to the coastal town of Kokura. This usually takes five days. From there we cross over a further two Japanese miles in smaller vessels to the little city of Shimonoseki and transfer to our above-mentioned barge, which is anchored there, awaiting our arrival, due to the depth of the water and for convenience sake. The Japanese call this route and district Saikaidō, which means the road of the Western district.

The second part is completed in our barge by sea in more or less eight days, according to the winds, and takes us up to Osaka, or rather, on account of shallows, close to the city of Hyōgo. From there smaller boats are used to transport us and all our luggage a further thirteen Japanese nautical miles to the large commercial and coastal city of Osaka.

The third part is completed in fourteen or more days and takes place over land across the large island of Nippon, or Japan, from Osaka up to the shogunal residence at Edo. The Japanese call this district Tōkaidō, which means "the road along the coast."[1] We spend about twenty days in Edo, during which His Majesty receives us in audience and we also visit the important courtiers. We finally receive leave to depart and then return along the same route to Nagasaki, completing the journey within three months. These three parts by land and sea are at the very least 325 Japanese miles of various lengths, namely, the first part and short journey by land from Nagasaki to Kokura, $53^{1}/_{2}$; the sea route from Kokura to Osaka, at least 136 and at the most 146; the last part and long journey by land from Osaka to Edo, 133 miles and 13 *chō,* which together comes to the above-mentioned 326 Japanese or 200 German miles.[2]

Miles

In Japan miles are not always of the same length. Land miles on the island of Kyushu and in the province of Ise are fifty *chō,* or the length of a street, while other, ordinary land miles are only thirty-six. On good roads I have always found the former to take one hour on horseback or brisk walking, the latter only three-quarters of an hour. One *chō* contains sixty *ken,* or mats or European fathoms, so that the common land mile comes to 2,160 fathoms, the large one to 3,000. Nautical miles outside Japan are two and a half miles for one German mile. Within Japan (traffic between or around the islands) these nautical miles are calculated very roughly and vaguely according to the length of the shore, and I do not know the length, but I am certain that they are much shorter than land miles.

Flat Roads

The roads on the first part on land along the Saikaidō are frequently, and along the Tōkaidō mostly, lined on both sides with a straight and thick row of fir trees to provide shade and enjoyment for the traveler, except where cities and villages along the road prevent this. The ground is always kept clean and level; rainwater is channeled off to the low-lying fields in practical drainage channels, and the road rises up on one side toward a high, carefully constructed earthen bank to stop the rainwater from draining to that side. Thus at all times (except when traveling on loam in the rain) there is a pleasant and fine road to travel on. More so, since the road is diligently maintained due to certain sharing arrangements between neighboring villages and headmen and, like the floor of a farmhouse, is cleaned and swept daily. When an important person travels, the road is swept with brooms shortly before he passes; piles of sand (supplied a few days ahead) are also placed on both sides of the road and kept ready so that, should it rain when he arrives, the sand can be spread to dry the road. If the traveler is a territorial lord of shogunal descent, a hut of leaves with a private side chamber is erected every two or three miles along the road, available for his pleasure or to relieve himself. Headmen have no problems keeping the road clean, since everything that might dirty the road is of use to the farmers living nearby, and one person vies with another to pick it up. The leaves and pine cones that drop every day are raked up and used as fuel instead of wood, which is often in short supply. The children of the farmers gather horse manure for the fields the moment it drops, and the excrement and other droppings of the travelers are also collected and used in similar fashion. To this end travelers can step into a poor little hut along the road next to the farm houses and fields to relieve themselves.

Dung

Worn-out and discarded straw shoes of horses and men are collected in the same little hut and burned; then the ash is mixed well with the above-mentioned matter, and this serves as common dung used as fertilizer throughout the country. Supplies of this evil-smelling mixture are stored in large barrels, kept open and without a cover, which are dug into the soil at ground level in the fields and next to the road in the villages. Their smell of decaying radish (radish is the farmers' staple diet and this smell pervades everything of theirs) often bothers a delicate nose more than the pleasure provided by the sight of the delightful road can compensate the eyes.

Mountains

There are some mountain passes along the route that are stony, steep, and so difficult to climb that horses cannot cross them and people are therefore carried across in *kago,* or baskets to sit in. Yet with their healthy springs, lush green vegetation, and marvellous flowers in spring, the mountains are more beautiful than in most countries, for the flowering bushes and trees that contribute to this beauty, namely, *fuji, tsubaki, satsuki, utsugi,* and *temari kanboku,*[3] are seldom found elsewhere.

Rivers

We have to cross a number of rivers—especially traveling the Tōkaidō—that, on account of the nearby snow-covered, high mountains, run to the sea with such force, particularly after a heavy rainfall, that they overflow their bed of stony shoals and can be crossed neither by bridges nor by boats. So travelers have to wade through these rivers, and horses and riders are entrusted to certain local people to guide them across the water. Specifically engaged for the crossing, these people are familiar with the topography and know how to support the horse carefully with their arms against the force of the river and the rolling stones. *Norimono* are lifted up with the hands and are carried across only by these people.

The most famous of these rivers is the great Ōigawa, which separates the provinces of Tōtōmi and Suruga. This river causes the traveler a lot of anxiety and turns into a barrier when it rains. People then have to wait several days at the river bank until the water has subsided and they can or indeed wish to be taken across. In second place, but of much less concern, are the rivers Fujiedagawa and Abekawa, both in the latter province. Other fast-flowing rivers that are as shallow but not so wide can be crossed by boats. These are built to suit local conditions, with flat, thin hulls so they can bend when gliding over protruding rocks and simply be freed from the rocks without danger. The most famous of these rivers are Tenryū in the province of Tōtōmi, Fujigawa in Suruga, Banyū in Musashi,[4] and Asukagawa in Yamato.[5] The last-mentioned river constantly changes its course, and there is a proverb comparing a fickle person to this river.

Bridges

Other rivers that are deep and do not change their course are always spanned by wide, strong bridges of cedar wood. They are maintained in a remarkable way and always look as if new. The railings on both sides are divided into sections one fathom in length, and two of these sections rest on one pier, except in places where more space is needed for the passage of ships. Since tolls are unknown in this country, there are neither road nor bridge tolls. But in some places it is customary to give a *zeni* or a silver coin to the warden of the bridge in winter.

The most important and, on account of their size, most famous bridges are the following:

1. Seta no hashi. This is the bridge which spans the river Yodogawa at the point where the river leaves a freshwater lake in the province of Ōmi. The middle of the bridge rests on a small island, and it therefore consists of two parts, the first one being thirty-six *ken,* or fathoms, long and the other, ninety-six. The river runs through Osaka and soon afterward flows into the sea; it is spanned by a number of other bridges, of which some are longer than the above-mentioned bridge. One of these is near the small city of Uji, another one near Fushimi, two are near Yodo, and there are seven more in the city of Osaka. In addition, many other bridges span the river's drainage channels or tributaries in this city. On account of its depth, the river is used by small vessels, but only up to Uji.

2. Yahagibashi, near the city of Okazaki in the province of Mikawa, is 208 fathoms long. The river can be navigated only by small vessels coming from the nearby ocean, and they can go no further than the bridge.

3. Yoshida no hashi, with a length of 130 *ken*, is near the city of Yoshida in the above-mentioned province. When the water level is high, local large barges can sail up to the city.

4. Rokugō no hashi in the province of Musashi with 109 *ken*, but this bridge was washed away two years ago (1687)[6] by strong currents. Perhaps it will not be rebuilt because without bridges the large river serves to protect one side of the nearby shogunal residence.

5. Nihonbashi, which means the Japanese Bridge, called thus on account of its importance. The bridge is situated opposite the shogunal castle in the middle of the ruler's city of Edo, and is famous because the distances of all roads must be calculated from this bridge.

Bridges always span the ground on both sides of the river for an additional two fathoms, and two bays continue like wings over the land. So an additional four *ken*, or fathoms, must be added to the lengths I have quoted.

The Sea Route

The sea route we take runs along the coastline of the large island of Nippon, with the coast remaining within view on our left. We never go further than one or two miles from it, so that when a thunderstorm is threatening we can use the harbors. Leaving the straits of Shimonoseki, we have on our left the receding southeastern shores of the island of Kyushu, which we have just left, but soon this changes to the island of Shikoku, and then finally to the island of Awaji and to Izumi on the mainland, where we enter the harbor of Osaka and our journey by sea ends. This sea route has daily a lot of traffic, consisting not just of the processions of the lords on their way to and from the shogunal city but mainly of local vessels of merchants, traveling from one city and province to the next. At times there are so many that on one day one can count one hundred vessels under sail. The coastlines of the said regions are covered with solid mountains, are pretty well settled and cultivated, and have villages, towns, and some castles, as well as a number of good harbors, where ships enter toward evening and find good anchorage at a depth of four to eight fathoms.

Islands

On this route one sees countless islands dotting the ocean, especially in the sea between Shikoku and Nippon. These islands are all mountainous, mostly rock, and barren. A few have good plains and are blessed with clear water and so are inhabited; they are farmed to the very peak of every single mountain regardless of their precipitous heights and the laborious cultivation. For ornamental purposes the mountains of these inhabited islands (and sometimes also the mountains of other districts) are usually planted with a row of pine trees running along the highest ridge the length or extent of the mountain chain. From afar it looks as if the barren heights have been decorated with fringes and it is indeed a pretty and unusual sight. Often these islands have a harbor on one side or on the other, and these are known to all local seamen. They are very useful for domestic navigation, for ships depend on them even when there is just a mild storm. This is because vessels are not built, nor may they be built according to the laws of the country, such that they can withstand high waves and weather a storm without anchoring and taking down the mast to protect the cabin and its freight from rain and seawater. For the deck or upper floor permits the water to run in from above, unless the mast is taken down and the area covered with straw mats and the sails. Also the ship's stern is not closed and is constructed in such an open way that strong waves can smash into the cabin; this can be prevented only by lowering the anchor and using the prow to break the waves and keep them away from the vessel. Moreover, because of their high, shallow, and weak structure, the only way to save the vessels from being ruinously tossed around and smashed is to take down their masts.

Chapter 3
A General Description of Civil and Religious Buildings and Also of Other Structures That We Saw along Public Routes

On our journey by sea we observed the ships, while traveling on land we saw secular and religious structures close to the road, such as castles, cities, towns, villages, post stations and inns, places of public proclamations and execution grounds, temples, monasteries, roadside gods, and other heathen places of worship. We would like to discuss these in this chapter, and what does not fit in here will be dealt with in the subsequent chapters.

The ships or vessels which we see on the waterways and which are used throughout the empire are built of solid pine or local cedar wood and vary in structure according to their use, their original purpose, and the routes they travel.

Pleasure Boats

The ships that are maintained solely for pleasure and travel only on rivers or in small bays are built in various ways according to the imagination of the owner, and many have only oars. The cabin or deck at the bottom is low, and on top of the flat upper deck is a high roofed structure containing rooms with sliding doors and open windows for enjoyment. The top is decorated with many flags and pennants, and all this is better illustrated by providing the eyes with a picture than the ears with a description.

Merchant Vessels

Those vessels that travel the seas between and around the islands of this empire, and serve as means of transport for men and goods, are the largest and best in the country used for the domestic trade between the territories and provinces and therefore deserve to be described in detail. They are usually fourteen fathoms long and four fathoms wide, have sails and oars, and are generally shaped in such a fashion that they taper from halfway the length of the vessel to the front. The lowest timber, or keel, rises out of the water in an arch to a considerable height. The hull of the vessel has hardly any or very little rounding and runs straight to the keel under water. The stern or rear is flat and broad with an opening in the middle running nearly to the bottom, which means that the cabin and all of the ship's interior are open to view from the rear. This makes it easy to handle the rudder, which is located at that point. But after the country was closed, His Majesty ordered that all vessels must have an opening at the stern and that no ships with a closed stern might be used or built. The purpose of this order was to prevent people from venturing onto the open sea and leaving the country. The deck is slightly raised toward the front, but flat and straight toward the side, and consists only of loose planks which are neither fastened down nor attached to each other. When heavily laden, a vessel lies deep in the water. The whole ship is covered with a roof the height of a man, except in front where the anchors are placed. The roof protrudes on both sides the width of an ell and usually can be opened by wooden sliding windows. The part in front contains the cabins for the passengers, divided by sliding doors and neatly spread with solidly padded straw mats. The cabin in the very front is always considered the finest and is given to the most honored passenger. The roof is nearly flat and neatly closed off with boards. As soon as it rains, the sails are spread over the mast (after the mast has been taken down and placed into its bracket, positioning it in line with the length of the ship), and the sailors and common folk also shelter and sleep under the sail. Or the sail is placed in a windward position and used as a temporary gable or roof the length of the vessel and, like a farmer's hut, is covered with shabby straw mats, which are always available for that purpose. Vessels have only one sail, made of hemp, which is fairly large, and consequently also only

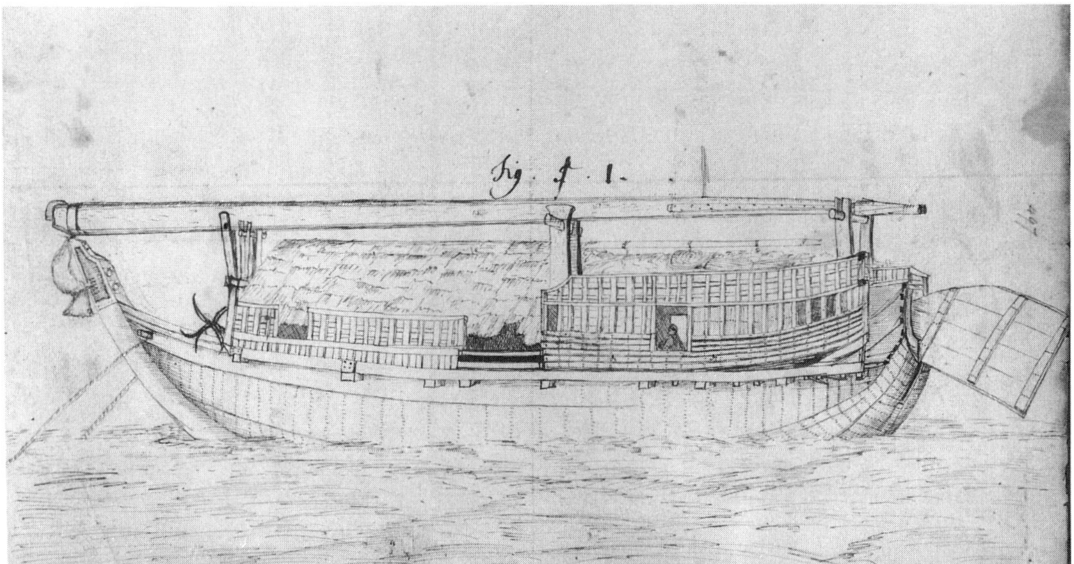

Kaempfer's drawing of a boat with the mast down. (Courtesy of the British Library, Sloane 3060, folio 497)

one mast, which is the same length as the ship and is positioned one fathom toward the rear measured from the center of the ship. The mast is raised by means of a hoisting apparatus and a winch situated in the front of the ship and is brought down in the same fashion. Anchors are iron grapnels with four flukes, and the ropes are spun straw and much stronger than one might think. A vessel of that size generally has thirty to forty oarsmen, who remain in the rear of the ship. When there is no wind to transport the vessel, they usually row standing next to the rowers' benches, moving in rhythm with a song or a few words or sounds to encourage each other and coordinate their movements. In this country people do not row by extending the oars across the surface of the water, but only by moving them down below in the water; this requires less movement and yet moves the ship faster. This way of rowing is also more practical when the ship lies high and there is little room to maneuver. For this same reason the oars consist of two pieces, which are joined below the oar pin in such a fashion that the oar is curved and when used inclines on both sides. The joints, edges, and ends of the timbers of all vessels are tastefully and liberally covered with copper strips and clamps. The prow is decorated with a thick tassel of black ropes, hanging down. When a high-ranking gentleman travels, the sides of the canopy are covered with awnings carrying his insignia and his colors. His official pikes are placed at the stern of the ship next to the rudder; a small flag to indicate the direction of the wind is also planted next to it for the information of the pilot, who mans the helm at this place. When a small vessel lands somewhere, the helm is quickly wound up and pushed on land, so that people can disembark as if they were passing through an open backdoor, walking across the helm as if it were a bridge. We too will disembark here and look at the buildings along the road.

Buildings

The size and splendor of buildings in this country, whether secular or religious, are in no way comparable to those of European structures, since buildings here are always low and made of wood.

Residential Buildings

According to the laws of the country, no secular building may be higher than six *ken*, but even that height is usually reached only by storehouses and rarely by residential buildings. The *dairi,* the shogun, and territorial lords make do with palaces of one story, and even though ordinary city mansions and the houses of common citizens have a second story, the latter is very low and mostly used only for storage. Sometimes the second story has no ceiling and runs straight up to the roof. The reason for this style of building is the frequent earthquakes in this country, which more than low and fragile buildings, destroy tall buildings built of stone. But people are extraordinarily concerned with cleanliness, decoration, and gracious living, things that are more easily accomplished in low, wooden buildings. The whole house is enclosed by a few walls, and rooms are divided from each other by light sliding partitions made of a wooden frame and painted or gilded paper. These partitions can be added or removed quickly and the rooms can be made as big or small as desired. The floor is raised and made of floorboards and then covered tastefully with padded, almost stuffed, fine mats which are expensively edged. (The mats are woven from bleached rushes and throughout the country are made the same size: one fathom long and half a fathom wide.) The wooden entrance with its stairs, the threshold, the windows, posts, and wooden corridors are all varnished. The ceilings are covered with gold or silver paper decorated with flowers, and some rooms are furnished with artistically painted screens. There is no corner that is not clean and well decorated with light material, locally available to the architect. It goes without saying that these houses are much healthier to live in, because they are built of cedar or pine and can be opened up from the front to the back to let the air circulate. I noticed that the rafters of the roof (which is covered with shingles) rest on a large, heavy beam, the heaviest available; also the upper stories are always made of heavier wood. People say this is done so that the lightly constructed building is pressed down and held together when there is an earthquake.

Castles

Castles are generally situated on the shore of large stretches of water or on hills or high ground. They cover a large area and consist of a triple fortress, one separated from the next by guards and, site permitting, one encircling the next. Each fortress has deep, clean moats, stone or earthen ramparts, and strong gates, but no large guns. The innermost fortress is called *honmaru,* which means "the true castle," and is the residence of the territorial lord. Often the residence is resplendent with a white, four-cornered high tower with three or four upper sections, each surrounded with a roof encircling the tower like a wreath. The second fortress is called *ni no maru,* which means "the second castle." This is where the gentlemen-in-waiting, elders, and secretaries live; any spare space is sometimes used for rice paddies. The third or outermost fortress is called *soto kamae,* which means "outer protection," or *san no maru,*[1] or "the third castle." This contains settlements of soldiers and lower court employees, and is open to the public. These castles can be seen glistening from afar, valiant structures with their white walls, guard posts, gate houses with two or more stories, and the beautiful wreathed tower of the residence. Outside the fortress is a wide empty square, called *ōteguchi,* meaning "large frontier mouth," which is used for meetings and mustering the men. The castles can be fairly easily defended and are sufficiently protected against local wars and sieges, which are fought without large guns. Also the castles are quite well maintained. But if any part deteriorates, nothing may be adjusted—let alone one be newly constructed somewhere in the country—without informing and obtaining permission from the shogun. Residential castles are always next to a city, and the city usually surrounds the castle in the shape of a crescent.

Cities

The cities are generally densely settled and have large populations. Streets run straight at right angles as if they were all built at the same time. Most have no walls, ramparts, or moats, and their two gates are no better than those with which the individual streets are closed off at night. In front of these gates one occasionally sees a section of a rampart, but this is built only as decoration. In cities where a territorial lord resides, the two gates are of better quality and are manned by a stately castle guard. But this is done simply out of respect for the resident territorial lord, for the rest of the city opens onto the fields and is only occasionally surrounded by a fence or shallow moat. Cities at the border of shogunal domains are not fortified along the side either; they are located at narrow mountain passes which are impossible to avoid, closed off with strong gates, and manned by a strong shogunal guard to carry out investigations. I counted thirty-three residential cities, which we either traveled through or passed or saw only from afar. In addition I counted seventy-five or eighty ordinary cities or large towns, quite apart from various palaces that are occupied only by local magistrates or have been built as overnight accommodation for territorial lords traveling up or down. What surprises me are the many shops in the cities, often occupying the length of several streets, and I cannot understand where the buyers come from who purchase that many goods.

Villages

The villages along the highways of the large island of Nippon are inhabited by fewer farmers than by the variety of people who live off travelers, either selling goods or providing casual labor and menial services. These villages therefore consist of only one long street with houses lining the highway on both sides. This street often extends so far that one village is linked to the next, and there is rarely more than a quarter of a mile distance between villages. As a result, it happens that two villages slowly grow together and the new village carries two names, because both parts keep their old name. Sometimes, however, the whole village is called by the name of just one part. Readers also need to know that not all names are spelled and written in the same way. To improve the sound, names are often abbreviated or a letter is changed, or the letter *n* is added to a syllable depending on the dialect and the characteristics of the Japanese language which permit such changes. Thus people often say and write Honda instead of Hon Tomida, Mattera instead of Matsudera, Tagawa instead of Takawa, Hirangawa instead of Hiragawa, and Nangasaki for Nagasaki, and so forth. I would just like to mention this here so that readers are not puzzled when the names of settlements are not always the same.[2]

Farmhouses

The farmhouses are so wretched and small that they can be sketched with a few strokes. They consist of four low walls and are covered by a roof of rushes or straw. The floor is slightly raised at the back of the house, where the stove is located, and part of this area is covered with clean floor mats. A row of rough straw ropes hangs in the open door. These do not block the passage but act like a blind, preventing people on the street from looking in. There are few household goods, many children, and much poverty, but people live happily off a little rice and a lot of field and mountain roots.

Fuda no Tsuji or the Place for Announcements

Traveling through any settlement one will always find on all public roads a *fuda no tsuji*, a fenced-in, small area located before the embankment of the street, displaying what they call shogunal edicts, published by the lord of the province under his own name. The edicts are divided into separate articles and written on a square board an ell long or half that length and are mounted on a pole two fathoms high to serve as warning for travelers. There are a variety of these boards, some older than others. The most important, oldest, and largest carry the prohibition against the Roman teaching, the order of inquisition, and specify the amounts paid as rewards for reporting priests and lay Christians. The territorial lords place their own announcements in this same fenced-off area, and consequently so many boards stand next and on top of each other that there is barely enough room. Occasionally rewards of gold and silver coins are attached to the boards for anyone willing to report a certain matter, person, or criminal. These fenced-off areas are usually located at the entrance of large cities and halfway along the street in villages and towns, where they are most easily noticed by passersby. In addition to the above, there are also orders and warnings of the lower administrators, village heads, and road inspectors displayed in uninhabited areas and mounted on rough, low posts. These are of no significance but nevertheless threaten criminals with heavy punishment.

Execution Grounds

In addition there are along the road public execution grounds, recognizable by a number of crosses or posts, reminders of past executions. They are always located outside and on the western side of cities and villages. It is generally said that many laws result in many criminals. The administrators of this country are so careful and so compassionate that they aim to stop any possible crime, and thus they constantly produce new laws. And these are no empty threats, for any transgression invariably results in the death sentence. But, in spite of this, the judges of this heavily populated, heathen country have fewer deaths to account for and less blood on their hands than those in our Christian countries. This shows how fear of an immutable death sentence can keep these obstinate Tartars in order, even though they otherwise do not value their lives highly. But the execution ground at Nagasaki can in no way pride itself on such lack of business. While formerly the place served as a general slaughter house for Japanese Christians, it still continues to reap its bloody harvest, since so many people are punished for transgressing against the shogun's laws by secretly trading with the foreigners. In those so-called smugglers, the desire for a sweet profit seems to be stronger than the fear of capital punishment if they are reported.

Temples: *Tera,* or Buddhist Temples

A pleasant sight is provided by the many *tera,* in other words, Buddhist temples or buildings to foreign gods with their monasteries. These stand out spectacularly among other buildings with their impressive height, stylish roofs, and other ornament. In cities and villages they are located on the highest ground. Outside settlements, they are situated on the slopes of mountains, generally near a clear brook and cultivated forest, because it is claimed that such high and pleasant locations are most favored by the gods. But I think they are also most favored by the priests, because such an environment provides them with more joy and leisure. The temples are made of the best cedar or pine and the interior is decorated with many carved pictures. In the middle is a well-decorated altar with one or several gilded idols and a number of perfumed candles in front. Everything is so well adorned that one could think, were not it for the monstrous idols, that one was in a Roman Catholic church. The temples resemble the Siamese and Chinese pagodas, not only in their structure but also in their interior decoration, but this is not the place to describe them in greater detail. The whole country is full of these *tera,* and there are innumerable priests. The city of Miyako alone has 3,893 of these temples and 37,093 *shukke,* or Buddhist priests, taking care of them.

Miya, or Temples of the *Kami*

The *miya*, the temples of the *kami,* or local idols, are served only by secular persons, but on account of their sacredness, they are also situated on higher ground, or at least at some distance from the uncleanliness of the common road. In the latter case, they have a pleasant, broad path in front, leading the worshipper from the highway to the temple. The path begins at a large gate of honor, which they call *torii.* This gate consists of a fairly broad and high gate structure of wood or stone, finished off at the top with two crossbeams, one half a foot below the other. A board, roughly one and a half feet large, is placed in front and at the center of the crossbeams, and here the name of the deity to whom this temple is dedicated is engraved, usually in gilded letters. Of these grandiose signposts one may indeed say: *parturiunt montes,*[3] because when one reaches the end of the path, which is often several hundred paces long, there is often only a wretched wooden hut or shelter hidden in the bushes, fenced off in front and empty inside. Sometimes it has a round metal mirror in the middle, occasionally with bunches of straw, or, instead, hung with a rope, with strips of papers attached to it like a fringe. Often the *torii* and the path leading away from the gate also have such ropes to indicate the sacred cleanliness of the location. The most magnificent gates are in front of the temples of Tenshō daijin, Hachiman,[4] and the *kami* or saints, whom every location adopts and reveres as patron and guardian angel.

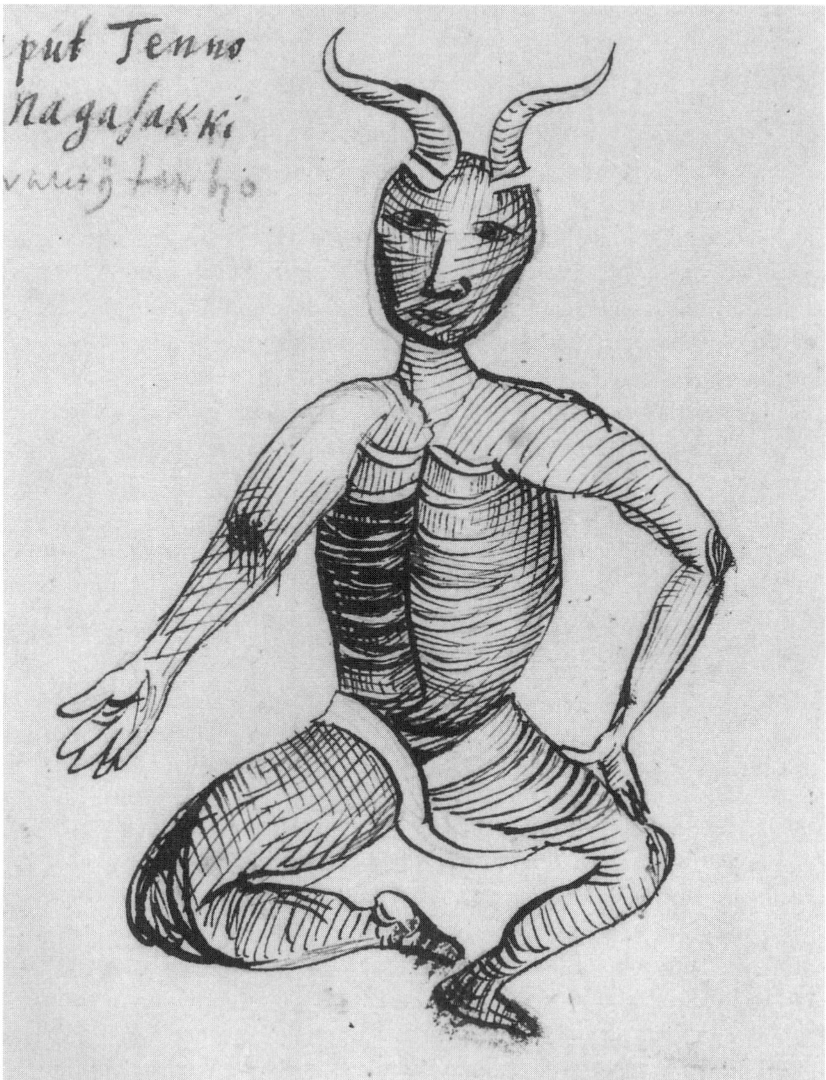

Kaempfer's sketch of the ox-headed Gion or Gozutennō. (Courtesy of the British Library, Sloane 3060, folio 494)

Roadside Idols

Other religious objects on the road include stone statues of *hotoke,* or images of foreign idols, mostly Amida and Jizō, as well as a whole range of monstrous shapes of other gods. On the highways these are placed at road junctures, bridges, monasteries, and sacred spots to honor these places and to stir up religious feelings in the travelers, so that while they follow the road they are reminded of the good and righteous road that men ought to follow in their lives and actions. For this same purpose the images of the above idols and guardians of the road are printed on a sheet or half a sheet of paper and stuck to the gates of cities and villages. They are also mounted on posts near bridges, at the place of public announcements, and at many other locations to attract the attention of travelers. But passersby pay them no visible sign of respect.

Images on Doors

The doors and posts of the houses of common people (because the upper classes do not want to spoil them) always have half a sheet of paper attached to them with a rather indifferent picture of a certain guardian deity of the house. The most common is probably the horned black Gion, also called Gozutennō, which literally means the ox-headed deity, for they believe this deity protects the inhabitants of the house from illness, especially from *sekibyō,* or the pox, which is a great problem for local young people.

Many villages prefer the horrible image of a hairy *ezo*[5] with his hands around a large sword to protect the inhabitants from such afflictions. On the front of new and beautiful houses I have sometimes seen a painted dragon or a devil's head with open mouth, large fangs, and fiery eyes, an image that the Chinese and the Indians, yes, even the Muslims in Arabia and Persia, also place above their doors, so that—as the latter say—jealous glances will be diverted by this spectacle, and harmful envy will not attach itself to the house. Over the doorpost they commonly also have a branch of *hana shikimi,*[6] which is supposed to bring divine blessings, or liverwort herb,[7] to keep away evil spirits, as well as other branches that are less frequently used. Wooden boxes with a letter of indulgence are placed above the door in various villages. These are brought back every year by the pilgrims from Ise, and they believe that these will bless their house with good fortune. Also long pieces of paper are pasted to the door of the house, which people receive in return for a donation to the clergy of the monasteries of the various religions and sects where the household worships. Thanks to certain characters and ritual prayers written on this paper, misfortune is cast out and kept away from the house. These same papers may be placed inside the house and mounted in rooms as well. Many similar charms are also attached in front of doors, and these are directed against a particular plague or misfortune. Among them is also one against poverty. But those houses where I have seen these as a preventive measure could not be recommended to any thief!

Chapter 4

A Description of Post Stations, Inns, Roadside Food and Tea Stalls

Shuku, or Post Stations

The most important towns and villages along our highway all have a station, operating under the territorial lord, where one can always obtain at a fixed price many horses, porters, runners, and whatever else may be necessary for the journey. Incoming and tired horses and men, or those who have been hired only up to this point, can be replaced here. All necessities are available, and the inns are comfortable at these places of exchange or post stations, called *shuku* in Japanese, and so traveling processions will stop only here. The stations are located at a distance of one and a half to four miles from each other. But they are not furnished so properly and comfortably on our shorter overland trip in Kyushu as on the main island of Japan, where we pass fifty-six between Osaka and Edo. The stations are not set up as inns but are merely for stabling horses. There is an open space in front where the transfer takes place so that the public streets are kept clear. The stations have many scribes and accountants, who note down everything accurately and render accounts to the administration of the territorial lord. Prices are fixed throughout the country, and those between each *shuku* are calculated not only according to the distance but also according to whether the road is difficult or easy, whether the animals' fodder is expensive or cheap, and other factors. On an average, one pays the following prices for each mile: for one *norikake,* that is, a horse to ride loaded with two packs and bedding, 33 *zeni;* for one *karajiri,* that is, a saddled horse only, 25 *zeni;* for each porter of a *kago* or other burden, 19 *zeni.* Couriers are available day and night to transport letters of the shogun and the territorial lords. The letters are handed to the next courier as soon as they arrive and are thus carried to the next post station with uninterrupted running. They are handed over in a small, black lacquered box, painted with the crest of the sender, and are attached to a pole carried across the shoulder. These messengers always run in twos, so that if one has an accident, the other can take his place and hurry on to deliver the box. If letters of His Majesty, the shogun, are contained in the box, everybody, even the procession of a territorial lord, must move to the side and let the courier pass without obstruction. The couriers make a certain sound to give notice of this from afar.

Inns

Our highway is well supplied with inns. The best ones are found in those post stations that are so well furnished that even the important lords on their annual journey to and from Edo stop here and occupy rooms. Like other well-built houses, they have only one story, and if there is an upper floor, it is low and perfumed. They are as wide as ordinary residential buildings but are very deep or long, sometimes forty fathoms. At the back they end in a *tsubo,* that is, a house or pleasure garden, closed off neatly with a clean, white wall. The front of such houses consists generally only of wooden sliding doors. During the day, these are always open, and in the absence of important guests, the sliding doors of the inner rooms are also open, so that when passing one looks through the dark rooms into the courtyard as if peering through a field glass. The entrance is raised half a fathom, and wooden verandas covered by secondary roofs project toward the street and the courtyard. Guests with leisure use this to step out of the house and as a seat, and they also might use it to climb straight onto their horse to avoid dirtying their feet with the mud from the street. Some inns have a passage at the side for important guests where they can step straight from their *norimono* into their room without having to pass through a dirty entrance hall. The entrance hall looks dark and shabby, is covered with mats of poor quality, and is closed off with common sliding doors. The kitchen is located here, and this means that sometimes the whole building is full of smoke because there is no chimney and only occasionally a hole for the smoke to escape. This is where lower-class travelers spend their time in the company of the servants of the house and the kitchen hands.

The rear of the house is always kept so pleasant and clean for important guests that not the smallest speck can be found on either the floor, the mats, the posts, walls, or sliding doors and sliding windows. Everything looks brand new. The visitor will find only an empty room without a table, chair, or other household items. But there will be one or more *mezurashii* objects,[1] a piece that is worthy of admiration, something treasured by people of this country and which sometimes is of value and placed there for the guest to admire during a few hours of leisure. The nearby *tsubo,* or delightful and artistically constructed small walled garden, gives equal pleasure to the visitor, permitting him to step outside and refresh his mind. We will look in detail at both of these, but first we will have a brief glance at the room.

Rooms

Rooms in houses rarely have more than one solid wall. This wall is plastered and lightly covered with soil or loam from Osaka[2] and then left in this rough condition without any decoration. Moreover, this wall is so thin that it could be kicked in with one's foot. The other sides are closed off with sliding windows and doors, which move on double runners at the top and the bottom. At the bottom is a groove level with the floor or the mats, at the top a rafter one or two ells below the ceiling so that the panels can be opened up and taken away as one pleases. The sliding paper windows, through which the light enters the room, have hidden, wooden sliding panels on both ends, so they may be covered from the outside when night falls and be separated from the veranda and the courtyard. The area above the sliding panels or their rafters up to the wooden ceiling is plastered as described above. When the ceiling is made of rare wood, it is sometimes left unpainted and covered only with a clear, thin varnish. But frequently the ceiling is covered with colored, flower-patterned paper, matching that of the sliding panels.

Toko, or Alcove

The solid wall always has a *toko.* This is an alcove or a recess raised one foot above the floor and an ell deep; it is generally located in the corner opposite the entrance and is considered the most important and honored place, like that where the Russians put their so-called *bog,*[3] or saint. Usually additional, expensive mats of double thickness are placed in front of this *toko* on top of the already mat-covered floor. They serve as a seat for traveling territorial lords and are taken away when guests of lesser status arrive.

Toko Waki, a Secondary Alcove

Close to the side of this *toko* is a *toko waki,* or a small, secondary alcove with a few small boards in the center, arranged in an unusual manner to please the eye, one board higher than the next. These are known by the special name of *chigai dana.*[4] Usually the host puts a valued book on them, or the visitor may place a book he carries with him on these shelves, because these books, like the Koran with the Muslims, may never touch the bare floor. When the Dutch arrive, the host removes the book. The space above the *chigai dana* is taken up by a wooden cupboard to keep paper, ink, writings, and books. Also in this cupboard the guests sometimes find the sleeping blocks that serve the locals as pillows for their heads. The blocks are shaped like a cube, are hollow, and are made of six thin boards joined together. They are varnished on the outside, smooth and clean, not much longer than one span, while their width and depth is somewhat less, so that turning them in various ways one's head may be higher or lower. The traveler cannot expect any further bedding from his host. Those who do not carry their own bedding use the mat-covered floor as a mattress, their coat as a blanket, and this hollow block of wood as a pillow. A specially raised alcove with an opening to the outside or a window of exquisite shape is often on the wall next to the *toko,* so that the person occupying the seat of honor may look out at the garden, the fields, or some water.

Fire Pit

The floor is covered with precious, solidly stuffed mats and contains a square, lined pit. In winter the mat above is removed and the pit is filled with ashes and topped with coal. Housewives place a small table above this in their rooms and spread a large cover on top; people may sit under this cover and comfortably protect their bodies from the cold air just as they do in Persia under a *kurtsī.*[5] Where there is no fire pit, a metal or earthenware pan, artistically shaped, with two long iron sticks stuck into the ashes, is provided in winter. People are quite accustomed to use these sticks instead of fire tongs or a fork, because no other utensils are used even at meals.

Mezurashii Objects

Among the above-mentioned rarities, which they call *mezurashii,* I have mainly seen the following objects, not in just one but in various inns and at various times:

1. A paper scroll, prettily edged with gold embroidered cloth. It depicted a saint, carelessly painted with a large brush, but the few, rough strokes, often no more than three or four, were so well placed and proportioned that everybody was able to recognize the man and one could not but call it a masterpiece. Or there would be the thoughtful words of a famous philosopher or poet, written by the author himself or sometimes by a man well known for his calligraphy in the country, demonstrating his skill with a few letters or characters written seemingly carelessly and with (feigned) haste; the rough brush moved and spread itself so artistically across the paper that knowledgeable people find much to admire. These works bear the seal of the master and a number of witnesses as proof that they are indeed originals. Serving as safeguard of the room or the house, they are never found anywhere else except in the *toko,* the most honored place of the room.

2. A depiction of old Chinese men, birds, trees, or landscapes painted on a white screen (paravent) or white sliding door by a famous master in an artistic style of feigned carelessness and sketched with rough black lines, which nevertheless look very natural from afar.

3. A vase placed below the *chigai dana* containing various flowering branches. This is always renewed according to the season and the rules of flower arrangement. The latter is considered an art in this country and is studied in the same way as we learn how to carve meat and fish or set the table. Or one may find instead a metal incense burner, artistically cast in the shape of a crane, lion, dragon, or other foreign animal of strange, decorative shape. Once I saw a spa water jug from Cologne with a number of repaired cracks; it had been placed there because it was considered a rare object on account of its distant country of origin, unusual clay, and strange shape.

4. Some strangely patterned wood where the grain curls in a bizarre way, laboriously worked and perfected with all the tricks of the art. Such wood is (generally) used also for the *chigai dana* proper, or the panels framing the window alcove, or the *toko* or the *toko waki;* or it might be used for a sliding door of the room proper or the corridor, or perhaps for some pillars, especially those of the *toko.* The wood is left unfinished and in some parts even the rough bark remains. It is varnished only for cleanliness sake, but the varnish is so thin that the subtle artistry of nature is neither covered nor obscured.

5. Some artistically carved open lattice or foliage work, either only on the small alcove window or on top of the sliding doors of the most elegant rooms.

6. A piece or knot of wood from an old decomposed tree root or trunk, rare on account of its monstrous shape, into which some characters have been carved, hung up somewhere or placed in the *toko waki.*

This is how one or several back rooms of the inns or other well-built houses are furnished and decorated. This dainty cleanliness gradually declines in the remaining rooms, because the stained and old mats and sliding doors are moved from the former to the latter. The most important and largest among the latter rooms is most probably the one where, in addition to earthenware tea bowls and some kitchen utensils, all tableware is kept, sorted, and stored according to special size, shape, and function. This tableware is always made of thin wood and heavily varnished, mostly on a red-colored base. Every time it is used it has to be rinsed with warm water and then dried with a cloth and kept in this condition. If treated in such a way, and if the varnish is fine and the lacquer good and well applied, its clean shine can make this tableware look like new, even after many years of daily use.

Toilet

The veranda facing the garden takes the visitor to the smallest room of the house and the bathroom. The smallest room is at the side of the rear portion of the house and constructed in such a way that one enters by passing through two doors and making two turns. In the entrance one finds a new pair of reed or straw slippers for those who have an aversion against stepping with their bare feet on the floor, which, however, is clean and covered with mats. People relieve themselves by crouching in Asian fashion over a narrow opening in the floor. The pot below is placed there from the outside and filled with light chaff, wherein the dirt disappears immediately. If there is an important visitor, the little board in front of which one crouches over this opening, as well as the door handles, or wherever one touches the door, are always covered with a fresh piece of white paper. Near this room there is a container with water to wash the hands after having done one's business. This generally consists of a long, rough, upright rock, the top of which has been carved carefully into a water bowl, and is furnished with a new bamboo ladle. The water is covered with a small board of pine or cypress wood, and this always has a new handle made of a freshly inserted stick of bamboo, because this kind of wood is always clean and naturally lacquered.

The Bathroom

The bath house is generally in the furthermost corner of the small garden and is built of cedar wood. It contains either a *furo,* which is a steam box or small steam chamber, or only a *sui furo,* which is a hot-water bath.[6] It is heated and made ready every day toward evening, for people in this country are used to bathing daily when traveling; the bath not only removes the sweat but also the tiredness of the limbs. Moreover, owing to the ease with which a Japanese undresses, he is always ready to enter the bath house. As soon as he loosens his belt and with one fling tosses his clothes behind him on the floor, he is totally naked except for a loin cloth. I will briefly describe the shape of the steam box for those interested in this sort of thing. It consists of a cube-shaped box or small chamber, some two ells off the ground, attached to the outer wall of the bath house. The height inside is hardly one fathom; the width and length are roughly one and a half fathoms. The floor is covered with narrow, smoothly planed planks, spaced some inches apart so that the steam can freely rise from below and the water used for washing can drain off. One enters the chamber through a small sliding door at the side; on two sides are wooden sliding windows, so that excessive steam can be let out. The area below the box is sealed off from the ground with a wall, so that the steam can only escape at the side. Underneath this small chamber or box, a kettle has been bricked in from the side of the courtyard, and under it a stove. The stove is closed off toward the bath house to prevent the smoke from getting inside. The kettle protrudes by half its size or so far that it can be filled with the necessary water and herbs, and the protruding section is closed off with a lid; thus when the fire is on, the steam can escape only through the other open side and rise into the box and fill it with steam. The guest is supplied with two tubs, one with cold water and the other with warm, which he may use for his needs or pleasure.

Tsubo, or Small Walled Garden

The small walled garden (the only pleasure we locked-up guests can enjoy) runs along the whole width of the rear portion of the house. It is square, closed off with a back door and white wall like a container, and is therefore called *tsubo;* this generally means a large container or water basin. All good houses and inns have such a *tsubo.* Where there is not enough room, there is at least a grafted old plum, cherry, or apricot tree, the older, more gnarled, and uglier, the rarer and more valued it is. These trees are often trained horizontally the length of the open space, cut bare, and pruned down to one or two branches so that the blossoms are bigger. With their flesh-colored, double-petaled and incredibly rich blossoms, the flowering trees provide exquisite decoration for this corner of the house, but they bear no fruit. Some lesser inns, where there is no open space at the back, have a small open area or atrium with a water basin, at times containing some small gold and silver fish, one or two rare trees, pots with wild flowers, or some miniature trees where the roots have grown into and over pumice-stone cliffs. The plants have no soil and get their nourishment purely from the water into which the rocks are placed. One also finds such things in front of the doors of common people, placed there for their pleasure and as decoration for the house. A complete small walled garden, or *tsubo,* of roughly thirty paces square always consists of the following items:

1. The ground covered partly with beds of rounded pebbles from a river or other water or spread casually with such stones. They are of various sizes and colors, and each kind is placed separately, after the pebbles have been well washed and cleaned. Part of the ground is also thickly covered with rough sand or gravel, always kept smooth with a broom, with oddly shaped boulders in between, which are supposed to serve as a path. All this is arranged in pleasant, artistic confusion.

2. Very few flower-bearing plants casually placed according to the rules of the art. These are often palms or other foreign trees, sometimes also trees on rocks or miniature trees.

3. A mountain or rock in the corner of the garden, expensively arranged according to its proportions and the rules of the art and set up in such a fashion that it resembles the face of a large, rugged mountain. Birds and insects cast in metal are sometimes set among the rocks; frequently there is also a temple, situated, just as they usually are, on a cliff for a pleasant view. Also a little river ought to run through the cliffs.

4. Thick bush or a small forest growing next to the mountain, planted with great care. For a skilled gardener needs to chose those trees that grow well next to each other; he plants them to make the best use of their different sizes and colors of their leaves so that they resemble a large forest.

5. The above-described water container. This too has the most suitable plants placed next to it, namely, those that produce superior foliage, flowers, or fruits when watered frequently. The art of creating this *tsubo* is considered a special profession, as also that of constructing the cliffs or mountains, which is counted as a different one. But more about this elsewhere.

So much about our inns. The treatment a traveler receives there will be discussed soon in a special chapter.[7]

Roadside Food Stalls

There are countless mediocre inns, roadside food stalls, *sake* or beer taverns, cake and sweet stalls along our road. They are even put up in forests and mountains where even a tired traveler on foot and a person of low status can savor a hot, albeit poor, snack and a drink of tea or *sake* for a few coins. These eating houses and roadside food stalls are somewhat meager and wretched, because they belong to poor people who have to scrounge for food, but there is always something to attract the eye of the traveler. It might be a verdant courtyard with its flowering trees, a small decorative hill, running water, and so on, a pleasant sight when viewed through the house, or perhaps even only a herb pot on display, well decorated with branches (the flowers of herbs are not honored with such treatment). Or perhaps the attraction might be one or another dressed-up young wench, calling out to travelers and lovingly offering her warm fare. The snacks, cakes, or small roasts, each on its own special bamboo skewer or stick, are set over the fire in an open stall or open room, so that the passerby can pick them up without losing time and take them along while continuing walking. Besides, when they see people approach, the matrons of the inn, the cooks, and servant girls busily fan the coals so that it looks as if the food is only just freshly cooked or fried. Others beat up tea water or some soup in a small cup to hand the new arrival a pleasantly frothy or chilled drink, should he desire one. And during all that time, their tongues never stop moving as they offer their merchandise, trying to be heard above their neighbors who pursue the same occupation.

Food

The dishes in the roadside food stalls (where they also always serve tea and frequently *sake* as well) generally consist of some of the following. *Manjū:* these are small, round (Portuguese) wheat-flour cakes,[8] the size of a chicken egg, boiled in a closed steamer and sometimes filled with sweet black bean dough. Cakes made of the jelly or gruel of the mountain root *kuzu kazura,*[9] cut into slices and fried. Small fried pieces of eel. Fried, boiled, or smoked snails, mussels, or small fishes. Chinese *karōtsu*[10] consisting of wheat dough thinly rolled, folded up, cut into narrow strips, and boiled. Tansy and other young shoots, mountain roots, and seaweed according to the season, boiled in water and salt after they have been cleaned and prepared for cooking. There are innumerable other, very meager local dishes of different shape and color made of various boiled or fried seeds or root flour which, to satisfy their hunger, people learned to make since ancient times from the produce of the local soil. The common soup or sauce for these and similar dishes is a little soy sauce diluted with sake and covered with sharp *sanshō*[11] leaves, or mixed with thinly chopped fresh ginger or lemon rind, or only sprinkled with dried ginger and *sanshō* or other local spices. Miserable stalls and outside tables also have a variety of biscuits of different colors and shapes on display; they are pretty to look at but have little sugar and are generally so tough that it is difficult to move one's teeth if one attempts to chew them. A poor traveler on foot whets his appetite by consulting a printed guidebook, which they all carry, to find out where these and similar dishes are sold and where they are prepared best and cheapest.

Tea Stalls

Because a traveler rarely drinks anything else, tea is served in all inns, taverns, roadside food stalls, and in many huts set up in the fields and mountains. The leaves used for this are the coarsest, left over after the young leaves (which are usually used for ground tea in this country) have been picked twice, or are those left over from last year. As soon as they are picked, they are fried thoroughly in a pan under constant stirring, yet without permitting the leaves to curl. Then they are packed in large straw packs and put under the roof to be preserved by the smoke. These leaves are used to prepare this beverage for the traveler on foot in a rather careless fashion. One takes a large fist of leaves and boils them, either in a small bag or simply as they are, in water in an iron kettle. The kettle contains a small basket, which keeps down the leaves, so that clear liquid can be ladled out at any time. Half a bowlful is ladled out, tempered by the addition of cold water, and served like this to the visitor. This tea brewed from last year's old leaves has a fairly sharp and awful taste, but the locals consider it healthier and better than that drawn from young, curly leaves in the Chinese fashion, for apparently the strength of the latter goes too much to the head and disappears when it is boiled.

We will ignore a variety of open stalls and workshops in and outside the cities, towns, and villages along our route, which offer the traveler their wares, because they are no different from those in German countries, and I have already elsewhere dwelled on their merchandise and special local manufactured goods.

Chapter 5
The Crowds of People Traveling This Highway Daily and Gaining Their Livelihood Therefrom

An incredible number of people daily use the highways of Japan's provinces, indeed, at certain times of the year they are as crowded as the streets of a populous European city. I have personally witnessed this on the Tōkaidō, described earlier, apparently the most important of the seven highways, having traveled this road four times. The reason for these crowds is partly the large population of the various provinces and partly that the Japanese travel more often than other people. Here I will introduce the most memorable groups of travelers one meets daily on these roads.

Of greatest importance are the processions of the greater and lesser territorial lords, as well as those of the greater and lesser stewards of shogunal cities and provinces, who annually travel up and down this road, that is to say, twice in one year, since they have to appear at the court at a certain time and then have to depart again. They make this journey accompanied by all of their retinue, with a display of as many people and as much expense as their status and wealth permit. To pass the procession of one of the greatest territorial lords takes several days of traveling; since we traveled fast, we would always spend two days passing various groups of the advance party, consisting of lower servants, officials in charge of the baggage, and porters, before finally on the third day we saw the territorial lord himself, traveling in closed formation with his courtiers. It is estimated that the processions of the greatest daimyo consist of about two thousand people,[1] those of the *shōmyō* have half that number, and those of the shogunal stewards of cities and provinces, one or several hundred people, depending on their income and title. If two or more of these large processions traveled at the same time, they would greatly obstruct and inconvenience each other, especially if they were to meet in the same *shuku* or town, where the available houses are insufficient to accommodate even the personal followers of a single daimyo. To prevent this, important lords reserve the inns and *shuku* for certain days—the great lords one month ahead, the lesser, one or two weeks in advance—and announce the time they intend to pass in all the villages, towns, and cities. This announcement is written with a few characters on a narrow board and mounted on a fairly tall bamboo pole at the entrance and exit of each village and town, stating on which day of the month this or the other lord will pass through, eat his midday meal, or stay the night.

The Procession of a Territorial Lord

To provide a picture of these processions, we will watch one of a territorial lord pass by, with its advance baggage train, sedan chairs, led horses, and finally the lord's personal contingent. However, not one of the most important, such as those from Satsuma, Kaga, Owari, Ki no kuni, or Mito, but that of some other, ordinary daimyo, such as we met at various times; their processions are no different and fit the same description, except for their special pikes, personal crests, number of led horses, bearers of *hasamibako,*[2] porters of sedan chairs and their companions, as well as some arbitrary variations in the order of marching.

There are:

1. Several advance parties consisting of quartermasters, scribes, cooks, and their assistants, who prepare the inns for the dignified accommodation of the lord and his courtiers.

2. The lord's personal luggage, some items transported in packs on horses, each marked with a small personal flag and the name of the owner, some carried in large boxes covered with lacquered leather and painted with the lord's personal crest. Each piece is accompanied by various attendants to add to the grandeur.

3. A long trail of lesser retinues of the lord's most senior servants and nobles, accompanied by men carrying pikes, scythes, parasols,[3] and small boxes, and grooms leading horses, all according to each man's birth, rank, and proper station, with the principals in *norimono, kago,* or riding horses.

4. The lord and his personal escort, marching in an unusual formation, as well as various troops of soldiers, each led by a marshal and consisting of:

i. Five horses, some less sprightly than others, each with a groom at the side and two servants following behind;

ii. Five, six, or more burly porters walking in single file with *hasamibako,* or small lacquered boxes, some also with rather delicate, lacquered baskets on their shoulders, containing clothes and other items kept in readiness for the lord, with each porter being accompanied by two attendants walking behind;

iii. Ten or more men bearing arms, walking in single file with scythes, pikes, valuable small swords, and guns in wooden, lacquered cases, as well as quivers with bows and arrows. Occasionally the size of this party is made larger by placing porters of *hasamibako* and led horses in between the men.

iv. Two, three, and more personal, ornamental pikes, with bunches of black cock feathers at the top, dressed and covered with certain rough skins or other ornaments specific to the lord. These are carried in single file and each is followed by a servant.

v. The sun hat[4] covered in black velvet with two officials walking behind.

vi. A sun parasol, covered and accompanied in the same fashion.

vii. Various additional *hasamibako* and personal luggage covered with lacquered leather and with the golden imprint of the lord's coat of arms, each piece accompanied by two attendants.

viii. About sixteen bodyguards in rows of two as advance party of the lord's *norimono.* For this task the tallest men available are searched out and employed.

ix. The *norimono,* or palanquin, in which the lord sits, carried by six to eight uniformed men, who are often relieved by an equally large party of men. The palanquin is accompanied on each side by two or three valets to hand the lord whatever he desires and assist him in getting in and out of the palanquin.

x. Two or three saddled horses with saddles covered in black, the last one carrying a large armchair covered with black velvet on a *norikake* that is also covered in black velvet, with each of these horses led and accompanied by the appropriate number of attendants. These personal horses of the lord are often led by men from his bodyguard.

xi. Two pike bearers.

xii. Ten or more people each carrying two incredibly large baskets, one in front and one behind, suspended from a pole over their shoulders. Their function is to enhance the usual display rather than to be of any practical use. Sometimes these men alternate with porters carrying cases and *hasamibako.* The lord's personal party is followed by:

5. Six to twelve horses with their grooms and attendants.

6. A large rear guard of the lord's servants with their official valets and pike and *hasamibako* bearers. Some are carried in *kago,* or there might only be one *norimono* at the head with the lord's highest minister or steward.

If a son accompanies a territorial lord, he follows with his own retinue immediately after his father's *norimono.*

Watching the procession of a territorial lord, one cannot help but be impressed and praise high enough, firstly, how with the exception of the *norimono* bearers everybody is dressed in black silk, and, secondly, how so many people travel in close and well-ordered formation with only the sound of their clothes, feet, and the horses being heard. But it is ridiculous to see how the bearers of pikes and *norimono* have their clothes tucked in high at the back to publicly display their bare buttocks with only a narrow loincloth down the gap. Also how the bodyguards and bearers of pikes, the sun hat, parasol, and boxes put on a swaggering gait when they pass through inhabited areas and meet other processions. With every step they kick up their heels nearly to their backsides and at the same time thrust the opposite arm forward, so that it looks as if they are swimming in the air. Adopting the same rhythm, the bearers with each step twirl around their pikes, the hat, and the parasol a number of times, and the *hasamibako* are kept in constant motion on men's shoulders. The *norimono* porters bare their arms, tying up their sleeves by threading a string through them, and carry their burden one moment on their shoulders, the next on one hand raised above the head, while the other arm is held stretched out horizontally palm up. The gesturing of this spare arm in combination with their short steps done with stiff knees make a ludicrous display of fear and caution.

Every time a great territorial lord steps into a specially erected hut of leaves or a small farmer's cottage, even just for a short while to have some tea or a smoke or to relieve himself, he leaves the host an *ōban* in return; inns get considerably more for a midday meal or an overnight stop.

Pilgrims to Ise

When on pilgrimage to Ise—which takes place throughout the year but especially in spring—people have to use a stretch of this great road, regardless of from what province they come. So it is crowded with such travelers during the said season as people of both sexes, old and young, rich and poor, embark on this meritorious journey and act of devotion, attempting to the best of their ability to make their way on foot. Many of them have to beg for their board and food along the way; because there are so many of them, travelers are constantly accosted, and this is a great nuisance for people going to the court, even though they approach with bare head and meek voice and say only once: "My dear lord, please give the pilgrim to Ise a coin for his journey." The inhabitants of the city of Edo and the provinces of Ōshū[5] are in the habit of making this journey more often than others, apparently without permission from their superiors. Yes, even unruly children who are to be punished for their misdeeds often run away from their parents to Ise, and when they return with a letter of indulgence, they must be absolved from any punishment. Because there are many of them and they are poor, one often sees them sleeping in the fields; on occasion they are lying at the side of the road, sick or dead. Others pick up the box with the letter of indulgence they drop and attach it to the next tree or bush.

There are also a number of slippery customers who pretend that they are on this pilgrimage, and for as long as they are doing well spend most of the year on the road begging. Others manage to perform this pilgrimage in a rather theatrical and amusing fashion, to more successfully attract people's attention and money. Generally they make up a party of four people and dress in a wide, white linen robe like that of the *kuge* or the courtiers of the *dairi.* Two of them, walking slowly and often stopping, carry a litter decorated with pine branches and strips of white paper, on top of which sits a light-weight replica of a large bell, cauldron, or any other object that features and is significant in the old tales of their ancestors and gods. The third man carries a commandant's staff, which, however, is decorated with a white paper mop to indicate the propriety of this pious performance. He walks ahead, and they sing a song about the object on display in a rough falsetto voice. The fourth man visits houses or approaches charitable travelers, collecting alms. They travel only a short distance each day, for they have all summer to undertake their begging journey.

Junrei

Here and there one finds the so-called *junrei,* that is, those who visit the thirty-three most important Kannon temples throughout the country. They drift around in twos or threes and at each house sing a pitiful Kannon tune; occasionally they also play a fiddle or zither not unlike the vagrants in Germany, but they do not approach travelers for alms. They carry small boards around their necks, each inscribed separately with the name of a temple they have not yet visited and arranged in proper order.[6] They have a linen cloth around their chests and other accouterments peculiar to this pilgrimage. Some like this pious vagabond life so much that they have no desire to earn their living by any other occupation but spend their time traveling the country in a never-ending pilgrimage.

Vows

Occasionally in winter one comes across the strange spectacle of a number of naked people, girded only with a bunch of straw to cover their private parts. They have made a vow to a certain temple and deities to pay a visit in this difficult fashion so that their parents, close friends, or they themselves may regain their health or some other favor. They lead a life of austerity and poverty on their journey, do not beg, and always walk along the road by themselves without much rest.

Shorn Beggars

This large road is, moreover, full of variety of other beggars: often they are young and have their heads shorn. The custom of shaving the head was introduced by Shōtoku Taishi[7] when he zealously spread the worship of *hotoke,* or foreign gods, and has been kept till the present day. When his sworn enemy Moriya[8] violently opposed his spreading the teachings of these gods, Shōtoku Taishi ordered that all men who had adopted this heathen religion shave half their head to distinguish them from those supporting Moriya and that poor children should be shorn completely like the priests. This meant that, being shorn, they had a monopoly on seeking alms.

Among those who shave their heads is an extraordinary order of young wenches called *bikuni,* or nuns, because they are under the authority and protection of convents at Kamakura and Miyako, to which annually they must pay part of their earnings; others pay temples in Ise or Kumano. They usually reside in the vicinity of these temples and hence are called *Kumano no bikuni* to distinguish them from religious nuns. They are nearly the prettiest wenches we have seen on our travels through Japan, because the privilege to collect alms as a nun is generally requested, and easily obtained, by those poor girls who are beautiful and blessed with an attractive figure, since it is well known that these are the most suitable weapons for plundering the pockets of travelers. The begging *yamabushi* make their daughters enter this profession, and they themselves also marry the *bikuni.* Among them are some who have been trained in houses of prostitution and have bought their freedom after having served their term to spend the remaining part of their youth in this fashion. These *bikuni* move in groups of two or three, walk daily one or several miles from their home, and approach genteel travelers who pass in *kago* or on horseback. Each of them attaches herself to one particular traveler, starts up a rustic tune, and as long as it is to her advantage, she accompanies and amuses him for several hours. They look neither religious nor poor, for they cover their shorn heads with black silk hoods and adorn themselves nicely and neatly in secular dress, covering their hands with fingerless gloves and protecting their faces, generally decorated with makeup, with large sun hats. They carry a small walking stick and look like romantic shepherdesses. Moreover, their speech and manner are neither insolent, woeful, vulgar, nor affected but open and modestly restrained. But not to praise these female beggars and their modesty inordinately, I have to mention that, following the custom of the country and their order, they are not too modest to expose their breasts to a generous traveler on the open road. So I can hardly exclude them from the category of loose women and prostitutes, however much they adopt religious tonsure.

Yamabushi, or Mountain Priests

Next in line is the order of beggars that is generally called *yamabōzu,* which means "mountain priest," but which properly speaking ought to be called *yamabushi,* that is, "mountain soldier,"[9] because its members are always armed with a rough sword and are not shorn; and also because they follow the rules of their first pilgrim, the founder of their order, who mortified his body by mountain climbing. Or at least they try to follow his example by adopting his dress and some of his outward behavior. Under the head of their order in Miyako, they, like laymen, are obliged annually to pay a certain sum of money, in return for which they are promoted in rank and receive some decoration with which they indicate their rank to each other. They reside and spend their time in the vicinity of some famous temple of a native god, or *kami,* in the name of which they approach the traveler. They praise the temple's miraculous properties and sacredness in a short speech delivered with a defiant air, punctuated occasionally—to stress a point—by the rattling noise of a staff topped with iron rings; finally, instead of a request for alms, there comes the sounding of a conch or large curved horn. They take their children with them to beg in the same manner and dress, but with their heads shorn, and these children are the most troublesome for travelers. They usually catch travelers at the beginning of or when climbing a mountain path, where one cannot escape because of the slow pace. At various places they team up with crowds of *bikuni* and attack us like a swarm of bees, deafening us with the noise of their singing, trumpeting, preaching, and shouting. People employ the mountain priests for incantations, divination, telling the future, and other superstitious magic, but they are never hired to take care of or administer a temple.[10]

Priests Reading Prayers

There are also other beggars, elderly and, judging from their appearance, respectable men, who are shorn and dressed like *shukke* or Buddhist priests to collect alms more easily. Some of them stand in twos next to each other, each holding a long narrow book, the paper of which has been folded in the manner of official Siamese documents. This is part of their *Hokke kyō*,[11] or bible, and it is printed in characters. They do not understand the text, but they have learned part of it by heart; they recite it as if they were reading the book and in return expect a donation from those who listen. Occasionally one sees some people of the same kind sitting on the bank of a brook performing a *segaki*,[12] that is, a service for departed souls. This consists mainly of washing some small pieces of wood bearing the names of certain deceased persons with a few small branches of the tree *hana shikimi*[13] while murmuring certain words. This is supposed to cool the souls of the deceased in the heat of purgatory, and it also serves as a kind of requiem. If any passersby want to be included in this rite of washing, they throw a *zeni* or florin on the mat spread on the ground, but the man does not give the slightest indication of gratitude, because he has duly earned the money by his skill and devotion. Moreover, showing gratitude is not customary among high-class beggars. Anybody who has learned this ceremony is free to perform it.

Still others, namely, the majority and lowliest of those dressed in this religious habit, sit by themselves on straw mats everywhere along the road. They have a small flat bell shaped liked a shallow mortar in front of them and in a plaintive voice constantly sing or recite the word *namanda,* a contraction of *namu amida butsu,* which is used to call upon the god Amida as an advocate of the souls of the deceased. At the same time, they hit the bell vigorously with a small wooden hammer, because they believe that this will increase their chances of being heard by the god as well as by those passing by.

Kannon Beggars

Along the lanes in the open country there are certain beggars, dressed in either ordinary clothes or religious robes, who have erected a stall and altar on which some of them place a large carved and gilded image of Briareus[14] or Kannon. Others have only some badly painted pictures, such as those of Amida, the supreme judge of the souls of the dead, Emma ō, the supreme executioner or jailer of the damned, or Jizō presiding over the purgatory of the children and other scenes of hellfire and torment, to persuade passersby to do a good deed and give alms when these images stir in them feelings of devotion and compassion.

Silent Beggars

Occasionally one finds some reputable beggars sitting at the side of the road dressed in the same priestly habit and carrying a Jizō staff in their hand. They have made a vow of silence for a certain duration and can therefore only convey their desires to the onlooker with a pitiful expression.

Common Beggars

We will pass over other common beggars, both sick and healthy, who attempt to lighten travelers' strings of coins by begging, singing, playing the fiddle or zither, and performing various amusing antics and artistic feats. Instead I would like to end this account by introducing the reader to some remarkable beggar's music with chiming gongs. Because of the number of gongs, it is called the eight chimes, *hatchō gane;* we saw this on the open road, but only rarely. A boy wears a wooden yoke around his neck and on top a halter to which eight small gongs of different tones are attached by separate straps. He spins around at an amazing speed so that the yoke which serves him as a rest for his arms as well as the gongs fly up and spread out around him. At the same time, he strikes the gongs with a hammer in each hand, beating out a wild melody. Two people sitting nearby accompany him by beating drums, one a large, the other a small drum, the whole ensemble producing a strange sound. People wishing to show their appreciation throw a few *zeni* on the ground in front of them.

Vendors' Stalls

The rest of the crowd on our road consists mainly of petty merchants and farmers' sons, running after travelers till late into the night, beseeching them to buy their wretched

Kaempfer's illustration of a boy playing the *hatchō gane* with a second musician sitting in front. (Courtesy of the British Library, Sloane 3060, folio 516)

wares, such as various biscuits in which you can hardly taste the sugar, cakes made of flour, *sakana,*[15] or a variety of roots boiled in saltwater, as well as printed road guides, straw soles for people and horses, ropes, toothpicks to be used after meals, and other knickknacks made of straw, rushes, bamboo, or wood, depending on the locality.

One also often finds ready groups of porters with *kago,* or palanquins, in and near villages, as well as lower-class servants with untidy and badly saddled horses, offering to transport tired travelers on foot to the next post station or as far as they desire for a small fee. These are people who have delivered something to the nearest post station and are returning without a load.

Prostitutes of the Inns

Discussing the crowds on the road, we cannot omit the prostitutes of large and small inns and roadside tea and food stalls in villages and towns on the large island of Nippon. As soon as they are dressed and made up, from around noon, they sit on verandas constantly eyeing approaching travelers; with amorous cries from here and there, they try to outdo each other calling him to their inn, the prattle ringing in the traveler's ears. This happens especially in those *shuku,* or post towns, where different inns stand next to each other, notably in the neighboring towns of Akasaka and Goyu, because those towns consist mainly of inns, each with three to seven wenches. Therefore these towns are jokingly referred to as the Japanese whore mart or mills with many grinding stones. All the more so as the Japanese rarely pass through these towns without sleeping with this riffraff and generally discover to their dismay that they have returned home with an unwanted souvenir. Caron makes too much of the honor of this sex (perhaps out of respect for his wife, a Japanese) when he maintains that, with the exception of some public, high-class brothels in some of the cities, this profession does not exist.[16] Yet it is impossible to deny that every public inn on the island of Nippon is at the same time a public brothel, where, if there happen to be too many guests, other innkeepers gladly send their prostitutes, because it is they who receive the fixed charges. And this is not a new but an old custom introduced by the famous warrior and first secular ruler Yoritomo some centuries ago, so that his soldiers would not despair of his long campaigns, when the desire for their wives could be eased by locally available means. With good reason the Chinese have therefore dubbed this country "the brothel of China," to which, formerly, those in search of pleasure would travel to spend their money on this riffraff.

Chapter 6

Our Journey, That Is to Say, the Journey of the Dutch, to the Shogunal Court and the Treatment We Receive

Just as the shogun gives every prince and vassal in the empire a day on which he has to set out and begin his annual journey to court, so the Dutch, too, are assigned a day for their departure. That is the fifteenth or sixteenth day of the Japanese first month, which corresponds to February in our calendar. When it comes to that time of the year, we begin preparations for our departure. We first load the vessels with the gifts that we present at Osaka, Miyako, and at court (after they have been allocated and carefully packed), as well as with the food and kitchen utensils required on our forthcoming sea journey, and other large items. This vessel or barge (which has been built solely for this journey and every two years has to be redecorated and refurbished at great expense with new awnings according to the pomp required on such occasions in this country; or, if the barge is old, another one is hired at great expense) is sent ahead to the coastal town of Shimonoseki to wait for us there until we have completed a shorter route overland and are ready to embark for the sea journey to Osaka. Formerly we boarded this barge directly at Nagasaki, but since we were hit once by a violent storm that put our lives in danger, His Majesty gave permission for the land journey to ensure our safety. Some three or four weeks after the departure of the barge and three or four days before our own departure, our resident director visits the mansion of both governors, makes his farewells, and recommends the Dutch who are staying behind to their care. The next day all items of luggage that are to be carried overland by porters and horses are marked with small boards attached to them, giving a general description of the goods and the name of the owner. Then, early on the day set for our departure, the complete gang of those who serve or have anything to say on our island gather around us, and particularly those who have been ordered to accompany us to court. Soon afterward both governors appear with their full retinue, or send their delegates, to extend their congratulations to us, who have been honored with permission to appear before the shogun. As soon as they have received our hospitality and accompanied us on our departure from the island, which takes place in the morning, about nine o'clock our time, we immediately set out on the road. The *bugyō* and Dutch resident director climb into their *norimono*, the senior interpreter, if he is an old man, into his common *kago;* others mount their pack horses and the servants walk. All this takes place in the company of our Japanese servants and the friends of those Japanese traveling with us, who all escort us to the next inn.

The number of people in our procession differs on the three separate sections that make up the journey. On the first stage, the overland journey across the island of

Kyushu, it may amount to a hundred people with the grooms and the escorts ordered by the territorial lords. On the sea journey the number is most probably not much smaller, counting the sailors. And on the third and long land journey across the island of Nippon up to the shogunal residence, the procession comes to some one hundred and fifty men (on account of the goods that have been unladed from the barge and have to be carried overland by men and horses up to Edo). These goods are generally sent a few hours ahead so that they do not inconvenience our procession, and this also serves to announce our imminent arrival to the innkeeper.

One day's journey is rather long and, including an hour's rest for the noon meal, lasts from early morning until almost evening and sometimes until night, so that we travel some ten to thirteen Japanese miles daily. At sea, as a precaution we do not travel at night, and the most we cover in a day is some forty nautical miles.

The treatment we enjoy and must accept is much better on the island of Kyushu than on Nippon, and outsiders treat us with much more honesty than our fellow travelers from Nagasaki and our own servants. When traveling on the island of Kyushu, the stewards issue orders that we receive many of the honors that are generally shown to provincial lords: the roads are swept with brooms, and in towns and villages they are also watered to keep the dust down. The rabble of commoners, laborers, and idle spectators is chased away, and in the houses bordering the road people either sit at a distance in the back rooms or, if they are in the front rooms, kneel behind the blinds, watching our procession in profound silence.

As soon as we pass from one province or region to the next, a nobleman dispatched by the steward meets and welcomes us. Since he himself is not permitted to speak directly to the Dutch, he transmits his lord's compliments to our leader and to our interpreters; at the same time he offers in overabundance the horses and porters requested to cross the province. He places four attendants or bodyguards at the side of each Dutchman and has two impressive-looking marshals, smartly dressed in black silk, precede the procession with their batons and lead it to the border. There he treats our Japanese with *sake* and *sakana*[1] and sends them on their way.

For the crossing of the bays of Ōmura and Shimabara the territorial lords lend us their own pleasure boats and their own sailors; depending on the type of ship, they also have hot meals served, without charging us a penny, for which services, however, we are charged all the same by our thieving interpreters. As mentioned above, on this so-called *saikoku,* or land route over the island of Kyushu, everybody who meets or wants to overtake us pays our procession the respect due to a territorial lord. Individual travelers and riders have to leave the public road and dismount from their horses, waiting until we have passed and bending low their bare heads. Those who have not learned to do this on their own accord are severely reprimanded by the marshals leading the procession. Local farmers and common people traveling on foot leave the side of the road and run into the fields without any instruction, entirely on account of their own good manners, squatting submissively with bare heads. I have seen farmers squatting, with their backsides facing us, since they were too humble to show us their faces! The lowest honor with this gesture also the royal women in Siam and the most noble families among the Indian heathens. This indeed shows great esteem, unless it is paid to us out of respect for His Majesty, to whom we are traveling, or, as our companions wish us to believe, out of respect for the *bugyō,* who represents the authority of the Nagasaki governor. But on the large island of Nippon, we are rarely honored in this way or given similar public displays of respect.

The other treatment we enjoy on this journey with regard to the supply of horses, servants, and porters and with regard to the inns, rooms, meals, and service is, if amply paid for, as good as could be desired. But with regard to our freedom, our treatment is insolent and wretched. We are not permitted any freedom beyond enjoying the sights we can see from our horses or sedan chairs. As soon as a Dutchman gets off his horse (which causes great annoyance unless there is great need for it), the leader or outrider must stop, and with him the whole procession and the *dōshin* and his two assistants must dismount and attend the Dutchman. Yes, these evil specters take possession of and guard us to such an extent that wherever we go, even when stepping aside to follow the call of nature, they will not move from our side. The *bugyō,* or senior leader of our procession, daily studies the articles of the instructions he received for the journey and reads also the reports of the previous journeys to court in order that everything be done in exactly the same way, so as not to forfeit his honor and his life. If he is firmer than his predecessors, then this will reflect favorably on his conduct. Some idiots are so stubborn that no force of nature or incident can persuade them to stop at an inn different from that of the previous year, even if it means traveling late into the night in bad weather and strong winds with much danger and discomfort.

Inns

The inns in which we stay are the same as those in which the territorial lords take up residence on their annual journey and therefore the best available. As with the territorial lords, they are hung with the awnings and emblem of our noble company while we are staying there; following the custom of the country, the colors announce the presence of the noble visitors. We always use the same inns, the only change being that we take the noonday meal in those inns where we want to stay on our return journey, so that the inconvenience caused is evenly distributed, for the overnight stay imposes a heavier burden. The apartment assigned to us is always located at the very back, facing an interesting small garden and therefore the most pleasant. It is also considered the best part of the house, because it is located furthest from the clamor of the rabble on the road and the noise of the kitchen in the front of the house.

The innkeeper treats us with the same ceremony as he does noble Japanese guests inasmuch as he meets our procession at the entrance of the town or even in the open field dressed in his *kamishimo,* or ceremonial robe, with a short sword. He comes up to each person and welcomes him with humble bows; when facing the *norimono* of the *bugyō* and the captain, he bows so low that he touches the ground with his hands and nearly also with his head. He then hurries back home and receives us once again with a similar show of respect in front of his house.

When we arrive at an inn, we are not allowed to pause for a moment (which in any case we would not wish to do, because of the nasty jeering of the children) but are led by our constables through the house and assigned to our apartment. Our only exit is into the small backyard. Any open or unsecured windows and doors facing the fields or back alleys they order closed and have nailed down, so that, as they say, thieves are kept away, but in reality to enable them to guard us like thieves and escapees. On the return journey, however, after we have won their trust, their anxiety is much reduced. The *bugyō* moves into the next best room in whichever part of the house it is situated. The constables, interpreters, and *dōshin* take the anterooms closest to us, to keep an eye on us and to prevent any servant or any stranger from entering our rooms without their knowledge and permission. During their absence they appoint replacements from among their own or our servants to perform this function and watch us closely (even though a general order obliges every single person to do so). Those servants who display more attentiveness and cunning than others in performing this task are likely to be permitted to join the procession also next year as well; the others must wait for two years.

As soon as we enter the room assigned to us, the innkeeper appears with his closest male helper, both carrying a bowl of ground tea, which he passes to each person in order of rank, bowing deeply and uttering submissively: "Ah, ah, ah!," the sound rising from the depth of his chest. They wear formal garments or ceremonial robes and carry a short sword in their sash; this sword is not removed in the house as long as guests are present. Next, smoking utensils are also brought in; these consist of a brass or wooden container or small tray of varying and undefinable shape with a small bowl of glowing coals, a spittoon, a tobacco box with finely cut fibers of tobacco, and some large tobacco pipes with rather small brass bowls. At the same time we also receive a small tray, made of wood either unpainted or lacquered, with *sakana,* that is, little pieces of cake and fruit, such as local figs and nuts, warm *manjū* and rice cakes, a variety of roots boiled in saltwater, sweets, and similar odds and ends. This treatment is extended first to the *bugyō* and then to us.

In the case of Japanese guests, all further service is provided by the maid of the house, who brings them all they need, serves at meals, pours their drink, and serves their food, thus preparing the ground for further friendship. On the journey the Dutch may not indulge in such company. Yes, after they have brought the tea, even the innkeeper and the male helpers may neither enter our apartments nor just approach our rooms up to the sliding doors, and whatever is necessary has to be done by our own servants accompanying us.

Guests are not provided with a spittoon, except for the one on the small tobacco tray. If more are required, pieces of thick bamboo, cut after the node and as long as a hand's width, are used. They bring us candles at night; these are hollow in the middle, for their paper wick is wound around a small round greased stick. The lamps therefore have a spike, on which the candles are placed. They burn down quickly and produce a lot of smoke and evil-smelling vapors, because the oil used is of laurel, camphor, and other nuts. It is quite absurd to watch: when one lifts the burning candle from the lamp's spike, the smoke bursts out at the bottom with a quick puff, causing the flame to run down to the bottom of the candle.

A flat earthenware bowl with whale or cottonseed oil and a reed wick is prepared as a night lamp. This is put on top of a water container or enclosed in a four-sided lamp so that it cannot cause a fire, something that easily happens in these paper houses, and these fires can turn into a large blaze.

Our Japanese eat three meals a day on the journey, not counting the snacks between meals. The first meal is taken as soon as they are up and dressed, before dawn and before our departure. Then there is the noontime meal in the next inn, and the third meal is taken before settling down for the night. Their meals are served in the local manner, just as I have described elsewhere. They eat well, may sing a song while drinking, or amuse themselves with certain games and guessing numbers (because they are not permitted to while away the time with card games) where the loser has to drink. The Dutch, on the other hand, have to take their meals in silence. They get their Japanese cooks to prepare and serve their food in European style. Sometimes they present each Dutchman with a small cup of Japanese delicacies from the innkeeper and in addition to European wines serve plenty of warm rice wine. For all other entertainment the Dutch must rely on the small walled garden during the day and, if it pleases them, the bath at night. They are not permitted to go beyond the prescribed limits or amuse themselves with other servants unless their travel companions from Nagasaki leniently permit this in their own adjoining rooms.

When our procession is ready to leave the inn, the innkeeper is summoned, and in the presence of both interpreters the captain hands him the payment in gold, placed on a small board. The innkeeper comes crawling on his hands and knees with a great show of respect and, receiving the board, expresses his gratitude by bowing until his forehead touches the ground, uttering over and over again: "Ah, ah, ah!" (words that are used in this country to express respect). He attempts to show similar respect to the other Dutchmen but is stopped by the interpreter and soon afterward crawls back, just as he came, on all fours.

Payment for the noon meal amounts to two *koban,* for the night to three, and for this sum the innkeeper has to provide food and drink for the whole procession (except the grooms and the porters). The same sum, not counting other rewards, is paid per day to our innkeepers when we stay longer at Osaka, Miyako, and Edo. For us, who are used to paying double the normal price for everything, this is a small sum, but the amount was agreed upon with the innkeepers many years ago when the procession was much smaller. The innkeepers on the Saikaidō, or short land route, only get some reward for the inconvenience we cause, because there our cooks themselves carry everything that is necessary. When guests leave an inn, they are always polite enough to have their own servants quickly sweep the floor of the room, so not to appear ungrateful by leaving dirt or dust.

The civil treatment we receive from the innkeepers indicates the level of politeness shown to us by other Japanese (but here I must exclude the rabble of our Nagasaki servants). The politeness shown to us on all our stopovers during the journey exceeds that to be expected from any other nation in the world, and the behavior of the people, from the lowliest farmer to the most exalted lord, is such that the whole nation may be called an academy of all forms of politeness and good manners. One may well imagine that the Japanese, who as a clever and curious people very much respect everything foreign, would lavish the best possible treatment on us, were they permitted to do so. Still in some cities and towns the young gentlemen, like rascals everywhere in the world, run after us, shouting certain rhymes or ditties making fun of the Chinese, for which these ignorami take us. The most common of these is: *tōjin bai bai!* which is half-Chinese and means much the same as what at home they would say to the Jews, namely: "Chinaman, haven't you got something to peddle?"[2]

Our disbursements for the expense of the journey consist mainly of the following items, which for simplicity's sake I have calculated roughly and given in round figures:

	Dutch Thalers
Fifty Dutch thalers per day for accommodation and meals, to the innkeepers on the land route for two months, total	3,000
Forty horses and the same number of porters between Osaka and Edo, the number being higher when traveling to Edo and less on our return, each horse at fifteen taels and each porter at six, amounts traditionally agreed upon with the interpreters (who keep nearly half this sum), comes to a total of	3,000
A travel allowance presented to each traveler to cover individual expenses; fifty-four taels for an ordinary Dutchman, others more or less according to their rank, amounts to approximately	1,000
Cost of hiring the barge (or, if it is our own, the proportion of the cost of construction) 420 taels, the sailors: fifty taels, awnings: ninety taels, other expenses for upkeep and improvements: forty taels, amounts to 600 taels, say	1,000
Cost of food, drink, tea, tobacco, and other essentials on the barge	1,000
The usual gifts of money: three hundred taels or five hundred Dutch thalers to the *bugyō* or senior commander of the procession, the same amount to the three innkeepers, their sons, and servants in the above-mentioned three principal cities, amounts to	1,000
Payment to the porters of *norimono,* also payment for *kago,* which have to be used instead of horses in the mountains, on difficult roads,	

and when visiting some temples and places of amusement; the cost of ferries across rivers and bays, the cost of special gifts that must be produced on various occasions, be they emergencies or special amusements, amounting to a total of	2,000
Add to this, the presents for His Majesty, which can hardly be considered precious by such a great ruler and which, if sold, amount to only	2,500
Presents consisting of foreign goods for fourteen of the most important government officials and courtiers at Edo, as well as for the two governors of the same city and the chief judge at Miyako,[3] plus the two governors of that city as well as those of Osaka, a sum that when divided among so many people looks very insignificant but nevertheless amounts to	3,000
Presents for the two governors in residence at Nagasaki (which, however, they receive before our departure) consisting of raw silk and fabrics, which they sell again with profit	2,500
The above amounts to the total annual expense to our noble company for the journey to court	20,000

But before we set out on the road we have to note that in this country a traveler does not consider one day as good as the next for the beginning of his journey but must choose a lucky day. For this purpose he uses a chart of unlucky traveling days that has proved its worth for a great many years and indicates on which day he is likely to have an accident. If he is still at home, he may not commence his journey on such a day, unless he wants to invite misfortune or at the very least end up having made the journey in vain and without achieving his objective. But I must explain at this point that clever Japanese pay little attention to the choice of these and other days and times; mainly common people, mountain priests, and monks in monasteries believe in them. This chart is written up in Japanese domestic, reference, and travel manuals as follows:

Chart of days ill-suited for travel for each month established by the astrologer and visionary Abe no Seimei[4]

Months	Days	Days	Days	Days
1, 7	3	11	19	27
2, 8	2	10	18	26
3, 9	1	9	17	25
4, 10	4	12	20	28
5, 11	5	13	21	29
6, 12	6	14	22	30

To give the chart credence and respect, the visionary Seimei, famous on account of his skill and birth, is said to have established it. His father was a prince called Abe no Yasuna, and his mother was a fox, whom he made his spouse in the following way.[5] One day Yasuna and his servant were at the Inari Temple—Inari being the lord and deity of the foxes—while other courtiers were hunting foxes outside in order to use their lungs for a certain medicine. A young fox that was being chased fled into the open temple and into the lap of Yasuna. As the fox had taken refuge with him and had put his trust in him, Yasuna did not want to hand it over to be butchered and therefore had no choice but to protect the animal from violence, using his fists courageously. He was so successful that, to the humiliation of the courtiers, the fox once again could return to his former freedom. When they happened to get a chance to satisfy their fresh lust for revenge, the disgraced hunters retaliated for this humiliation by killing Yasuna's royal father. But they in turn had to pay for this murder with their own lives and were slain by the hand of the courageous Yasuna.

After the victory, when the knight was sighing with exhaustion and sadness, the grateful little fox appeared in front of him in the guise of a young woman. Her incomparable beauty filled him with such love that he made her his spouse. He fathered this son of heavenly wisdom and the ability to predict the future; he did not know that his wife was the little fox until her tail grew again, and afterward her other parts also slowly changed, until finally the whole body had returned to its former shape.

The above is by no means the least of the very important stories about their gods. The reader will have to bear with us also in the future when on the journey I have no other ancient and remarkable stories to present, except ones similar to this one.

But this man Seimei did not only calculate this chart from the course and influence of the stars; he also used his mystical skills and devised certain words, and made them into an *uta,* or verse. When intoned, this acts somewhat as an antidote, banishing evil powers on those certain days and making them ineffective. The verse is to be used by poor servants who cannot follow the chart, for they have no choice but to set out when their lord orders.

Sadame eshi tabi tatsu hi tori yoshi ashi wa
omoi tatsu hi o kichi nichi to sen.[6]

Chapter 7

Overland Journey from Nagasaki to Kokura, Begun on February 13, 1691, Consisting of 51½ Japanese Miles

On February 10th the resident director, Mr. von Bütenheim, took his leave from both Nagasaki governors and commended the remaining Dutchmen to their protection. The next day the items that were to accompany us were packed and labeled with small boards by the scribes of the procession. On February 13th[1] of this year of 1691 both governors visited our residence with their complete retinue early in the morning, and after they had taken refreshments they accompanied us off our island between eight and nine o'clock. Here we bade farewell to those of our countrymen who were staying behind and set out on our journey. The total route between Nagasaki and Edo by sea and land with all its bends is two hundred German miles long. We pass, or see at a distance, thirty-three impressive cities with castles, seventy-five small cities and towns without fortifications, and innumerable villages. The first part of the journey covers the island of Saikoku[2] and the provinces of Hizen, Chikugo, Chikuzen, and Buzen up to Kokura, and amounts to roughly fifty-five Japanese miles, or some twenty-two German miles. The daily journeys are calculated on the following basis: from Nagasaki to Sonogi: ten miles; from there to Oda: eleven miles; from there to Saga: four miles; from there to Tashiro: seven miles; from there to Iizuka: ten miles; and from there to Kokura: thirteen miles. I noticed that in the province of Ise one mile corresponds to a journey of one hour, or one hour's brisk walk, but in other provinces it amounts to only three-quarters of an hour. Five nautical miles equal three common land miles. Nautical miles outside Japan are calculated at 2½ to one Dutch mile. However, a common mile is made up of thirty-six streets—in Ise, fifty streets—with each street corresponding to sixty mats, or *ken,* but at Nagasaki, to fifty-six. On page 104 of his *Japanese Embassy,* Montanus[3] calculates twenty-five Japanese miles to one degree, namely, from Nagasaki to Edo, 354; from Nagasaki to Osaka, 220 miles; from Osaka to Edo, 134 miles.

Our procession consisted of the following people: a *dōshin,* or, as he is called out of courtesy, a junior *bugyō,* on horseback, followed by his assistant, a city constable. Next, our resident director and the old senior interpreter Yozaemon, otherwise known as Brasman,[4] both being carried, and after them on horseback, one after the other, the merchant Abouts, the physician Kaempfer, and the assistant Dubbels. They were followed by the junior interpreter Tarōemon[5] and by his son as apprentice and then the second city constable, also on horseback. At the end of the procession was the *yoriki,* or, as he is called out of courtesy, the senior *bugyō,* Asahina Sadanoshin, as leader and commander of the procession. He was carried in a *norimono* with his horse led in front of him and a pike-bearer on foot as his steward. His pike was decorated with a ball at the top and a small silver board suspended from it.

As soon as the journey had made some progress and we reached another province, the above order was slightly altered, as the attached illustration shows. Our per-

The Dutch procession to Edo. (Courtesy of the British Library, Sloane 3060, folio 501). Kaempfer numbered the figures and on a separate page (folio 500) gave the following explanations: "1, 2. Japanese and Dutch cooks with their kitchen utensils. 3. Two guides, provided in Kyushu by the government of each domain at its border. 4. The foreman of the procession. 5. The personal horse of the Dutch captain. 6. A *dōshin,* who is a courtly aristocrat and a soldier of the second rank of the governor. 7. The medicine chest. 8. The money chest with its inspector. 9. The captain or representative of the Dutch trade in Japan, with three servants and eight porters, who carry him in rotation, four at a time in his *norimono,* or palanquin. 10. A senior interpreter in his *kago,* or basket, with three servants and three or four porters. 11. An apprentice on horseback with a servant. 12. A government constable on horseback with his servant. 13, 14. One or two assistants or Dutch scribes, each with his Japanese personal servant. 15. A Dutch physician with his personal servant. 16. The junior interpreter with one or two personal servants. 17. The second government constable. 18. The personal horse of the *bugyō* or commander of the procession. 19. The pike bearer of the *bugyō,* representing the power and authority of the governor. 20. The *bugyō* or commander of the procession. In addition to being commissioned to this post, he is also a *yoriki,* or courtly aristocrat and a soldier of the governor of the first rank. He sits in a *norimono* and is accompanied by various servants and carried by six porters taking turns. 21. Some friends of the *bugyō* bidding him farewell. 22. Our friends from Nagasaki who accompany us for three miles when leaving or walk out to welcome us and oblige the Dutch to present them with gifts. 23. Two scribes attached to the procession, who daily travel ahead and make arrangements at the inns. They also keep a record of expenses and a list of goods, people, horses, of the daily journey and inns, and so forth."

sonal cooks and their servants were sent ahead on horseback with their kitchen utensils. Also two scribes belonging to the procession always preceded us; they were charged with arranging the inns, calculating expenses, and keeping a record of all goods, people, horses, daily travel, inns, and whatever occurred. In addition there were our personal servants, grooms, and porters without luggage, who, however, were required to take their turns; all of these were traveling on foot. The horses we were riding were loaded with two packs, with the bedding spread across to form a square table, on top of which one sits comfortably with crossed legs, as mentioned in the first chapter of this book. We were escorted by a group made up of further interpreters, cooks, water-bearers, tailors, and former servants, as well as the sons, grandsons, or friends of important people, all expecting a *bu* as parting gift, as if the Dutch were made of gold!

As soon as we completed the difficult, high mountain pass through the city, we reached the small village of Magome outside the city, which is situated next to the execution ground and is inhabited by tanners, who act as bailiffs in this country. There we had to stop at the house of the man who guards our barge for a drink of *sake* and *sakana* served to us by our interpreters and most senior companions and servants in honor of our departure. On this occasion, however, these beggars not only required rewards for their polite company and entertainment, but the interpreters constantly introduced this and the other young man to the captain to pay him a compliment, explaining who he was and how closely he was related to them. And in this process so many *bu* and silver coins went down the drain that the total amounted to more than one hundred taels. After an hour we set out again and after one and a half hours reached the village of Urakami. About half an hour later we reached a stone pillar at the border, one and a half fathoms high, with characters indicating the border of the district of Nagasaki and the beginning of the district of Ōmura. After another hour we reached the village of Tokitsu, three miles from Nagasaki, situated at the bay of Ōmura, where we ate the cold food we carried for our noon meal but had to pay nineteen taels for *sake* and other various items that we never saw, let alone tasted. Here further friends and companions of our *yoriki* were sent off with presents and left behind.

Up to this point the road is uneven, stony, and mountainous. Except for some fertile valleys, the surrounding area is of the same appearance, but every fertile niche is laboriously cultivated up to the top of the mountains. There is nothing remarkable to describe on this short length of road, but in order not to omit anything I will mention that at the exit of the city nine statues of the patron of travelers, Jizō, have been carved out of rock, one next to the other. A statue of the same Jizō also stands on a stone pillar, which is one fathom high, near the village of Urakami. The statue is half human size, decorated with bunches of flowers and *hana shikimi,* and in front of it are two short, hollowed-out stone columns bearing lamps that are lit in honor of the deity. Nearby is a water container where those who want to kindle the light or make an offering can wash their hands. Before reaching Urakami we saw a stately *torii,* or ceremonial gate, with an inscription attached to the middle, which indicated and sanctified the approach to a local shrine. At Tokitsu we met the steward of the Lord of Ōmura, who on behalf of his lord offered us all possible help for the continuation of our journey out of respect for the shogun and without payment. His offer included two *benzaisen,*[6] or pleasure boats, to row across to the other side of the bay to the village of Sonogi, a voyage of seven and a half Japanese nautical miles. Each of these pleasure boats, which in accordance with local custom were built of solid Japanese wood, had fourteen oarsmen dressed in blue coats with white stripes across. At the back there was a small flag, like a standard, bearing a white rose with five petals on a blue background. In front of this was the commander's usual tuft of paper strips, next to which our *bugyō,* or leader, planted his pike, with the boat's scribe from Ōmura settling down on one side and the helmsman on the other. The *bugyō* and the captain, however, each occupied the main quarters of one ship. We embarked at half past two in the afternoon and arrived before half past six in the evening, having completed today ten Japanese miles. If one takes the land route, traveling along the right side of the bay, the distance amounts to fifteen miles. The bay is very shallow and does not permit the use of large vessels. It stretches toward the sea in a west-southwesterly direction and is connected to it by a narrow strait and is therefore governed by the tides. We saw the residence of the Lord of Ōmura two miles away on the right at the shore, and above it was a mountain emitting smoke, perhaps that situated near Unzen. There are shells containing pearls in this bay, and previously people discovered sand rich in gold where the shore caved in. Ōmura belongs to the large province of Hizen, to which also Nagasaki, Hirado, Gotō, Ureshino, Fukabori, and various other small areas belong. In ancient times they took orders from and were dependent on the king of Hizen, and it is said that in even earlier times Kyushu, which covers one-fourth of the area of Japan, had its own king.

On February 14th we left Sonogi at dawn and after one hour's ride passed a camphor tree famous for its size. The trunk appeared to be six fathoms at the base, but hollow, and was really impossible to measure because the tree stood on top of a hill. One mile further, after we went around the foot of the mountain of Tawara, we reached the border post of Ōmura and entered the small district of Ureshino. The lord of this area is very attentive and generous so that, when one hundred men are requested, he offers two hundred to please even more. The road in front of us was swept by ten people until we reached the village of the same name, where we received fresh horses, each with three grooms, and also were joined by a senior and junior *bugyō* to guide us through the district.

Hot Bath

Near the village, next to a river running on higher ground, was a hot bath, renowned for its efficacy in healing syphilis, scabies, rheumatic pains, and lameness, and we were permitted to inspect it for a short while. The area was neatly fenced off with a bamboo hedge, and there was also a guard house and leisure pavilion. Inside, running along the length of the area, was a roofed corridor with six compartments branching off, each compartment containing a specially stone-lined bath tub the size of one mat. These were arranged in such a fashion that a pipe brought both cold water from the river as well as hot water from the well, and so each person could mix the two according to his desire. At the side, under a separate straw roof, was a rest area. The hot-water spring had been enclosed in a shallow basin, two feet square and under a straw roof, but the subterranean fire caused it to boil with a roaring noise, and it was so hot that nobody dared to dip his finger into it. I noticed that the water had no smell and no taste, and therefore I do not hesitate to ascribe its efficacy purely to the heat. However, our guide took a branch from a camphor tree overhanging the water (the tree was the size of a large oak and the second one of remarkable dimensions we saw), dipped it into the boiling water, and had each person chew a leaf. This soon turned the saliva and the whole mouth a yellow-greenish color, which was supposed to indicate that this was no ordinary water. Further there were two stone-lined tubs near the well, the same size as those mentioned above, where commoners bathed. Steam was rising from the large cold river for quite a distance, perhaps because other hot springs were flowing into it.

There are still other hot baths on this island that are as or more efficacious. I was told of the following: Yumoto, a bath of that name in Arima used to cure lameness; another with similar qualities at Tsukasaki in Hizen. There is one at the seashore at Obama

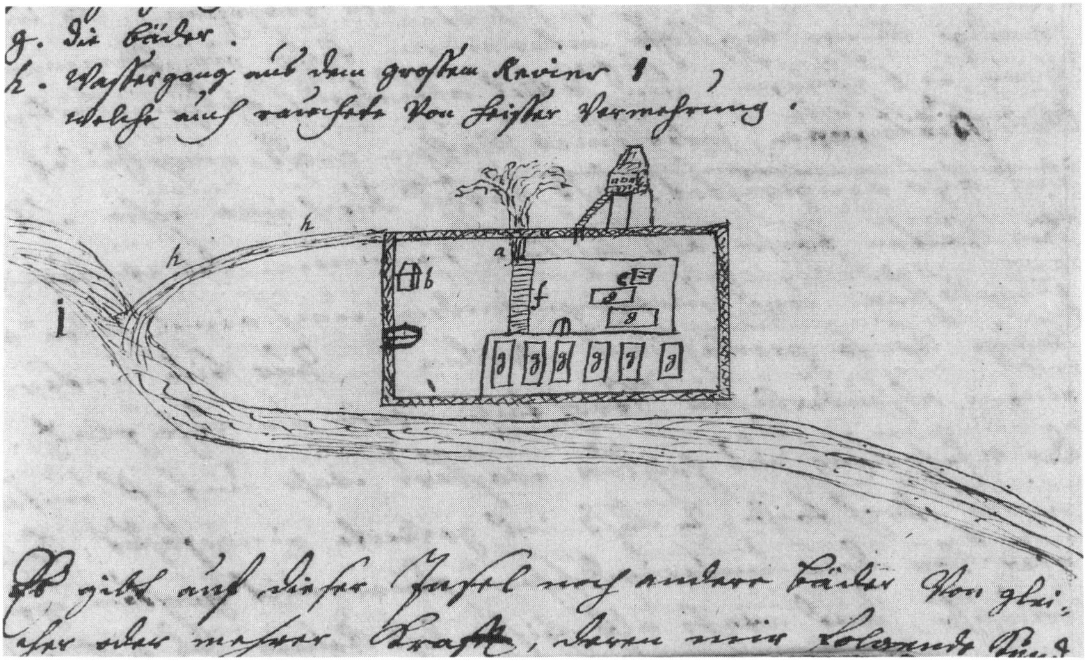

Kaempfer's sketch of the layout of the hot springs at Ureshino. (Courtesy of the British Library, Sloane 3060, folio 305 verso) Key: (a) *kusu no ki*, or camphor tree; (b) guardhouse; (c) hot spring ("Scaturigo Thermarum"); (d) steps leading up to upper pavilion; (e, f) rest area; (g) baths; (h) a channel of water from the large river, which was steaming where the hot water entered.

in Shimabara; at high tide it is under water, and it is small, shallow, and saline, which is considered extraordinary in this country. Three miles from there, at the foot of Mount Unzen, are some springs within a radius of some hundred paces that reek of sulphur and are so hot that they can only be used mixed with cold water. There was a warm lake at Yamaga in Higo, which, however, has dried up, and others that have been listed in detail in the seventh chapter of the first book. Half an hour from here we reached the other half of Ureshino, and two hours later (passing a continuous line of houses on the left) we reached the town of Shiota, where we had our noon meal. At this location people make and fire extraordinarily large water containers, which are used on boats as water tubs. The Europeans call them "martuan," after the empire of Martan,[7] where they are usually fired and from where they are traded throughout India. They can be transported from here on barges because there is a river flowing very conveniently in an easterly direction into a boundless plain.

Porcelain

Here as well as at Ureshino and the surrounding mountains, and sometimes also in Buzen, Japanese porcelain is made out of a greasy white soil, which is found at various locations in the hills and mountains. The earth in itself is firm and clean, but a lot of kneading, cutting, and cleaning is necessary to reach the kind of perfection that makes it possible to produce fine, transparent porcelain. That is how the old tale originated that fine porcelain requires human bones.

After an hour we set out again, passed four muddy rivers spanned by fine wooden bridges; vessels were plying some of the rivers. Before we reached the village of Oda, where we spent the night, we passed the villages of Naruse and Oiwake. Today we traveled eleven Japanese miles between Sonogi and Oda. At the entrance of this village we saw under a very large camphor tree a large sculptured head of an idol, like that of a calf, surrounded by railings mounted on posts. This was the third surprisingly large camphor tree we saw on our journey.

Today we traveled through many fertile valleys and rice paddies, with tea bushes planted along the edges on strips a few paces wide. The bushes were no higher than two ells, had been stripped of all leaves, and looked rather miserable. To the right of this village I saw the finest rice paddies anywhere to be seen. It is therefore not surprising that this province, as well as Hizen, produces the greatest surplus of rice, and there are ten different varieties. Among those the best rice comes from Ōmura, and it is used to supply the shogun's kitchen. Rice from Kaga and Higo cannot compare with that from the paddies of Hizen.

February 15th was a Thursday. We left our lodgings at the break of dawn and traveled the whole day at a good pace, passing through Saga, the capital of Hizen, until we reached our quarters in the village of Todoroki. The day's journey came to a total of ten or eleven Japanese miles, and the road was now taking us through flat and very pretty country. We passed through the following settlements (omitting small villages): half a mile from Oda the long village of Toriimachi, where for the first time we saw the women of Hizen, and we were surprised that such small, young girls, who appeared not even to be of age, were already carrying around infants feeding at the breast. Like all people in this province, they had fine figures and were well behaved but wore such heavy makeup that one could have mistaken them for dolls. As soon as they marry, they completely pluck their eyebrows. A little further on we came through the large, long village of Togawamachi, with a muddy river flowing through the middle and running into the sea at a distance of some four to five miles. There were pleasure boats on the river, and it was spanned by a fine wooden bridge. After a quarter of a mile we reached the village of Ushizu, where we changed porters and escorts. After half a mile we reached the village of Kubota and soon afterward came to the large village or town of Kasenomachi; it consists of the following parts. The first, Tokumanmachi was located on this side of a large river running to the southeast, which was spanned by a bridge of one hundred and fifty paces. The second part, Yakimochimachi, was on the other side of the bridge, and the third part, called Hashinomachi, followed soon after. Especially in the first two parts of this three-part town, silk cloth, paper, and yarn for sails plaited from paper fiber were produced. Outside the town, between the first and second parts, a fellow was hanging on a cross. After a boy had rebuked him for taking some wood, he had strangled the boy in a rage of anger with a piece of cloth until he was dead. The cross, just like others, is of the shape described by Lipsius[8] in his letters: at the top is a long cross beam or piece of wood to stretch out the arms, at the bottom a shorter one to stretch out the feet and in the middle is a protruding stump to rest on. A rope is used to fasten people to the cross. A quarter of a mile later we reached the long suburb of Ōgimachi and then the city of Saga proper.

Saga

This is the capital of the province of Hizen, whose lord, Matsudaira Hizen no Kami,[9] resides here in a large castle. The city is big and extended, and has many inhabitants. It has a strong guard at the entrance and exit, but its low ramparts, walls, and gates are more for display than defense. The streets are wide and run completely straight from east to southwest; the city also has various canals and rivers that provide transport to the sea at Arima, which is called the Sea of Arima at that place. The houses are small and poor and have been turned into workshops and stores in the most important streets, with a black cloth suspended in front as decoration and to embellish the facade. The people are well-built and small; the women especially differ from other Japanese and are so well-proportioned and beautiful that they compare favorably with those in other parts of Asia. However, they wore such heavy makeup that they could have been mistaken for manikins rather then live people, if their bright and vivid facial expressions had not indicated the opposite. For many miles around, the country consists of fertile plains, crisscrossed by rivers and set up with floodgates, which are built in such a fashion that the land can be flooded with water while the rice paddies are ploughed and worked. Together with Kaga, this is the most fertile province when it comes to rice and grains. I would rank it above beautiful Medes[10] if it had an equal amount of cattle and fruit trees, neither of which I saw in great numbers. Today I saw neither a temple nor a priest, except for a *torii* with gilt letters, indicating the presence of a distant building of an idol: it appears that in this province they do not care much for this sort of thing. Hizen is the largest province on Saikoku and includes Nagasaki, Shimabara, Ōmura, Arima, Saga,[11] Karatsu, Hirado, the islands of Gotō, and so forth. These localities are partly attached to the domain of the Lord of Hizen and partly have been appropriated by the shogun and bestowed upon others, who now also have to pay their respects to the shogun with an annual journey to court. But the Lord of Hizen still owns 40,008 villages, enough for the comforts of life.

Satsuma, also one of the provinces of Saikoku, can most probably be called the most important and most powerful, especially since this domain has the bravest soldiers, produces a lot of camphor, and has rich gold and silver mines, even though these are reserved for the shogun. We rode through Saga without stopping and took one and a half hours to pass from the outer suburbs to the other end of the city. Outside the city gates, running toward the southeast, was an avenue densely planted with pine trees, which continued for half a mile. It was here that I saw the first two falcons, which two men carried on their hands in the usual way. I also saw two storks, smaller than the European ones, sitting on a clump of trees in the mountains. Further, I saw for the first time horses used for ploughing. One mile after Saga we passed through the village of Harunomachi, and after two hours, having passed various small villages and rivers, we reached the large town of Kanzaki at about one hour after noon. The town consists of seven to eight hundred houses and was seven miles from our last overnight stop. After we spent one hour on our midday break, we continued our journey as before at a good pace, as everywhere the road was clean, level, strewn with sand, and could not have been better. After some three to four Japanese miles we reached the village of Todoroki, consisting of some five hundred houses, where we spent the night. This was the last settlement in the province of Hizen. Previously the procession spent the night at Tashiro, which is half an hour further along. But on account of an incident four years ago—after some slight verbal disagreement, the senior *bugyō* killed the senior interpreter and then committed suicide; he intended to inflict the same fate on his *dōshin,* who, however, only had his hand cut off—this place is considered ill-fated for our journey and orders were issued that it must be avoided. This afternoon we passed many little rivers and villages, with the largest being Haddi or Faddi[12] (the local pronunciation makes it impossible to distinguish *H* from *F*), Mitagawa, and Nagabaru. We also passed through a pleasant little pine forest, which is unusual for this location. The trees were very tall and large, and the cones were small like cedar nuts. An hour outside Nagabaru we went for half a mile along the foot of the mountains that approach the road on the left but soon left them behind. There we saw a mile away on our right the white castle of Kurume, the residence of the Lord of Chikugo.[13]

On February 16th, a Friday, we set out with fresh horses and traveled through the village of Urino, situated outside the gates of Todoroki, and after half a mile reached the above-mentioned Tashiro, a town consisting of five to six hundred houses, few streets, and high gates. Several years ago this town and the surrounding country was appropriated by the shogun from the Lord of Hizen and bestowed upon the Lord of Tsushima (and Shimabara) to give him some possessions on the mainland, since he only owned the island toward Korea.[14] At this point the *bugyō* who had escorted us through the province took his leave and was replaced by one belonging to the Lord of Tsushima. We changed our horses on the street without stopping and traveled through Imamachi, Haruda, Jūsanzuka, and other smaller villages; we passed various rivers, reaching the town of Yamae after three and half Japanese miles. There we had one hour for our midday break. On the right of Jūsanzuka was a highway to Kurume, and on the left was another one skirting the mountains to Hakata, situated at a distance of four Japanese miles and the residence of the Lord of Chikuzen and Hakata. Yamae is a teeming village of several hundred little houses and has a fine inn, where we lodged. At the entrance to the town stood a camphor tree, which is the fourth camphor tree of an unusual size that we noticed. After we had a meal, we woefully had to sit down in *kago* on account of the mountain path lying ahead, which horses cannot climb. They consisted merely of narrow, four-cornered baskets, open on all sides but with a little roof on top. We were carried in them for half a mile, each of us by two people running at full speed up to the foot of the mountain Hiyamizu; then up this mountain for one mile to a little village without a name, whose inhabitants were all descended from one ancestor, still alive today. The people were very handsome and differed from others in their dress, speech, and behavior. The women especially were so well-behaved, as if they had been brought up in a noble household. After we stretched our legs for half an hour at this place, we traveled up the mountain for a further quarter of an hour and descended again for one and half miles to the village of Uchino, which in German means *im Berg*.[15] Here we stayed for an hour and had something to eat. Then we mounted our horses again and rode through various small rivers and little villages, among which Tendōmachi is the best known. Toward evening we reached the night's lodging at the town of Iizuka, having traveled ten Japanese miles on that day. Iizuka consists of several hundred houses inhabited by townspeople and is situated on the other side of a river carrying small vessels. The others were carried across the river, but I was permitted to walk over the long narrow bridge. Today we traveled through countryside where hills, mountains, and shrubbery alternated with infertile ground, somewhat resembling conditions in Germany. The faces of the people were quite different from those of Hizen. We noticed that the mountain people were rather meek. The only domestic animals we saw were a few cows and horses, used for their labor; we also saw two storks, somewhat resembling ours at home. Fields situated on mountain slopes had tea bushes along a border some eight paces wide, but they were planted in such a way that they could not harm the seedlings.

February 17th. Since today we had to travel thirteen miles—ten to Kokura and three by sea to Shimonoseki—we were escorted out of the inn before dawn by the light of torches (made of pieces of bamboo). During the morning we traveled through Kōbukuro of some one hundred houses and a variety of small villages, and also crossed two shallow, stony rivers in flat-bottomed rowing boats.[16] After five short Japanese miles we reached the town of Koyanose, consisting of two to three hundred houses. The town was located on a river, which was made up of the two said streams and was known after the town as Koyanose gawa. After our noon meal we rode on fresh horses down the river for a short mile and after two further miles reached the town of Kurosaki, situated at the shore of the northern bay and, like most other petty villages, consisting of two to three hundred huts or shabby houses. Along the road were coal mines, which were pointed out to us as something extraordinary. At Kurosaki we mounted fresh horses and after one and a half miles reached two stone border posts, placed at a distance of ten paces from each other and bearing characters. They belonged to the Lords of Chikuzen and Kokura. Another short mile brought us to Kiyomizu, a village outside Kokura, and then, escorted by two officials from the court of Kokura, we arrived at our inn in the city. It was situated very pleasantly in a large plain in the last or third quarter of the city; it was well furnished and overabundantly supplied with all the necessities of daily life.

Kokura

The city of Kokura is situated in the territory of the large province of Buzen, not far from the seashore. Previously the city had many inhabitants and was thriving, but a change in the distribution of the land has brought about poverty and obscurity. The city stretches one mile from east to west, covers a longish, square area, and consists of four quarters: a large castle or residence and three separately closed-off towns. The castle stands in a large square area and is surrounded by moats and low ramparts. The ramparts are built of boulders, rise up from the bottom of the moat, and especially toward the river are fortified and decorated with projecting wooden bastions according to the custom of the country. The castle is situated roughly in the center of these ramparts and is decoratively enclosed by white walls. On the northeastern corner of these walls some cannons were displayed, and there was also a six-storied guard tower, to indicate that this is the residence of a territorial lord. In this castle resides the lord of this small province, Ogasawara Ukon no Kami,[17] a man with an income of fifteen *man koku,*[18] with his servants. The city, and also each of its quarters, has a square shape; all the gates consist of two large portals in between two solid walls. There is always an open wooden guardhouse, and in front of it, on the raised veranda covered by the overhanging roof, are three neat cudgels as well as six pikes, decorated at the top with bunches of black horsehair. Inside we saw three trusty, neatly dressed men seated in one row, facing the gate or the road. The houses of this city are small, the streets are wide and level and run straight to the south and west. There are many good inns and kitchens—the hearths are raised, and they have many grills like ours at home—and the buildings in the rear are decked out with bathrooms and fine, cultivated gardens. The river, which runs through the city and into the sea from the

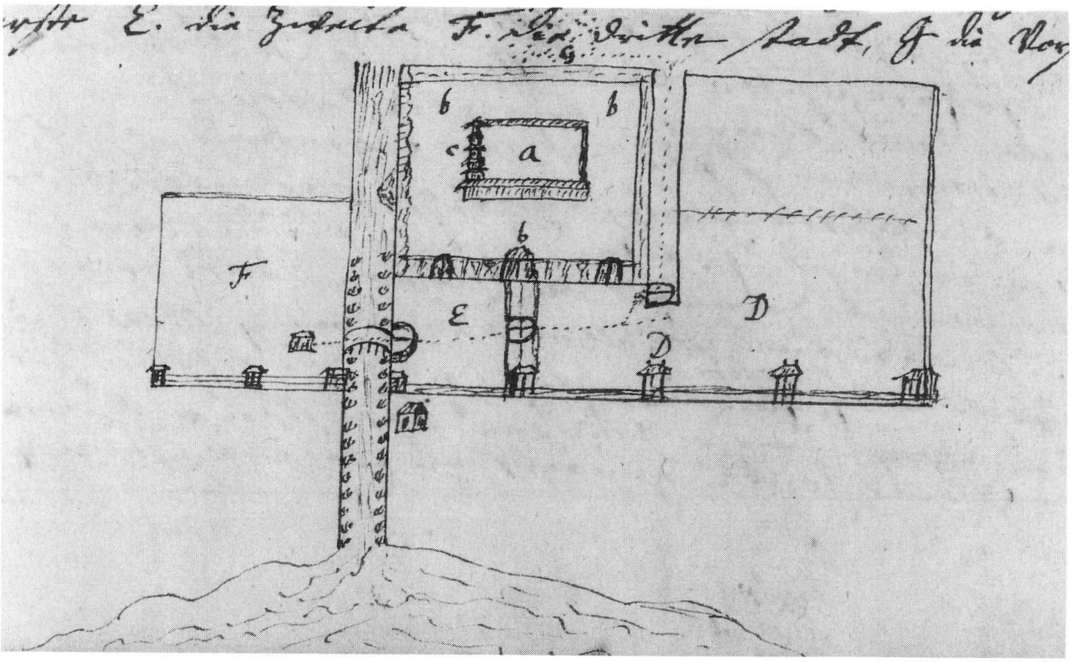

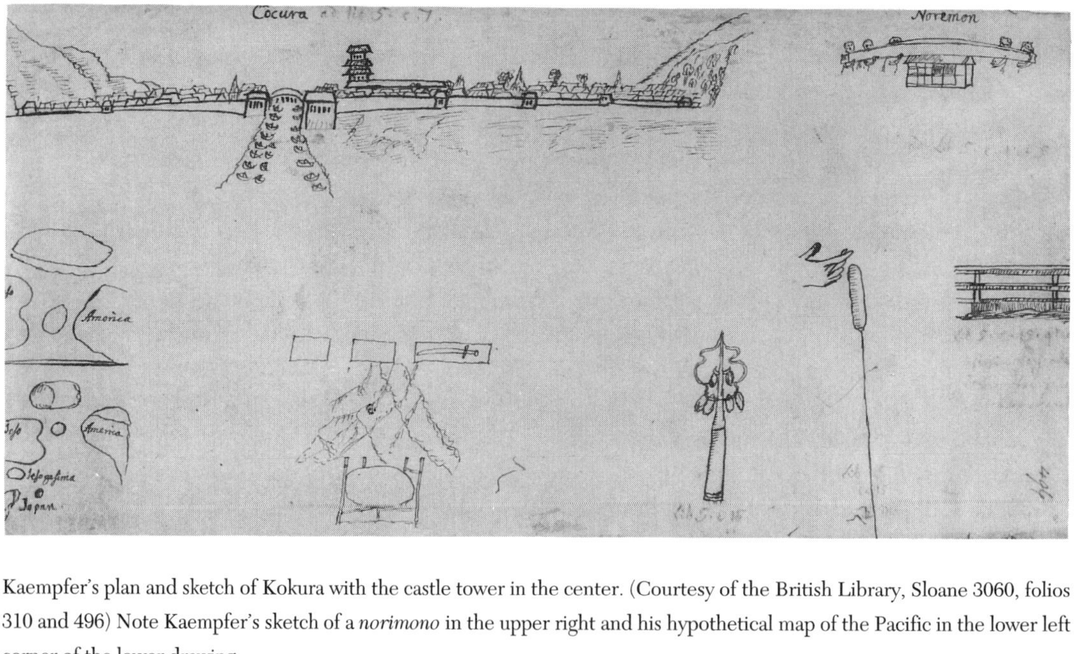

Kaempfer's plan and sketch of Kokura with the castle tower in the center. (Courtesy of the British Library, Sloane 3060, folios 310 and 496) Note Kaempfer's sketch of a *norimono* in the upper right and his hypothetical map of the Pacific in the lower left corner of the lower drawing.

south, separates the last quarter from the other two and the castle and was covered with some hundred small boats. Since the river is shallow, freight-carrying vessels cannot reach the city and have to anchor at Shimonoseki. The river was spanned by a large bridge, some two hundred paces long, beautifully constructed with iron trellises and four rows of wooden pillars. The layout of the city will become apparent from the following notions and especially the plan, where (a) is the inner castle and the residence of the territorial lord, (b) the square of the castle with the houses of the servants and the garden, (c) the tower of the castle, (D) the first quarter, (E) the second, (F) the third, and (G) the suburbs of the city.

Chapter 8

Voyage from Kokura to Osaka, Begun on February 17, 1691, Amounting to 140 or 150 Miles

After we spent one and a half hours at the inn refreshing and repleting ourselves with Japanese food, we again left Kokura under the escort of the two above-mentioned nobles from the local court, who marched at the head of our procession. We arrived at the shore and came to two *chabune,*[1] or small freight vessels, to take us across to Shimonoseki. We discovered that both the large bridge and the wide square in front of our inn were filled with a swarm of spectators, more than a thousand commoners, who knelt down in complete silence on both sides of our procession. Nobody had the courage (perhaps because they were frightened of our leader, or out of respect for him) to get up or make any noise. Thus we left the city of Kokura and at the same time the island of Kyushu, or *nishi no kuni* (as it is called by the common people), which means nine countries or nine provinces or domains.[2] It is also called *saikoku,* which means "western country." Half an hour before sunset we embarked on the two vessels and traveled three miles by sea to our large barge at Shimonoseki; this had arrived five days previously and was to take us on the remaining voyage by sea to Osaka. The small vessel on which I had embarked took five hours and arrived two hours after the other. It went off course and ran aground a number of times, and consequently we arrived late at night. We settled down for the night on our barge, where everybody was assigned his meager space. On the journey from Kokura to Shimonoseki, through a strait between the island of Hikoshima and the province of Buzen, a number of places famous for certain historic events were pointed out to us. On the right, in the territory of Kokura and on the shore of Buzen, there was a green, big, flat plain with trees called Tamashima, which means pearl island. There is a settlement where in ancient times the *dairi,* or spiritual hereditary emperor, had his residence and which therefore still carries the name of Dairi. Between there and the island of Hikoshima a gravestone[3] or memorial stone called Yojibei is poised on a cliff rising from the deep sea in honor and memory of a certain mariner of that name. When the ruler Taikō went to restore order and loyalty, which at present reign among the westerners,[4] the mariner endangered the ruler's life at these cliffs and forestalled his just punishment by cutting his stomach; he was given this memorial in his honor. The location is also famous for the loss of an imperial heir at the time of the wars of the *dairi.* The courageous emperor and war hero Heike[5] had spent many years in bloody wars but finally suffered the misfortune of being chased by his enemy from his residence at Osaka to Hyōgo; he also had to flee these fortifications and then died. The nursemaid of the seven-year-old son he left behind attempted to flee across the sea with him, but when she reached this place and could not shake off the enemy, she grasped the prince who had been entrusted to her, and showing a degree of purpose and determination that is considered courageous and heroic by the Japanese, she threw herself into these tumultuous seas together with the boy. When Heike became aware of his approaching end, he allegedly sent ten ships with silver and gold to China, where a temple has been built in his memory. A similar temple has been built here at Shimonoseki for the prince who drowned. This temple is called Amidaji,[6] and we plan to visit it tomorrow.

Shimonoseki

Shimonoseki is situated at a famous seaport at the foot of a mountain range in the province of Nagato, the westernmost province of the mainland or the large island of Nippon. Because the island of Kyushu is close, the sea is channeled through a strait one Japanese mile wide. This island of Nippon is the largest of the Japanese empire and is shaped like a jawbone. It is divided into fifty-two districts and two large highways, of which the most important is the one from Shimonoseki via Osaka and Miyako along the southern shore up to Edo. That is to say it runs from west to east, but on account of the many mountain ranges, the sea route is generally used up to Osaka. The other highway runs from Edo to the furthest borders of Ōshū for more than forty miles in a north-northeasterly direction. The lord of the province of Shimonoseki, who also travels to court annually, is called Mori Hida no Kami.[7] His residence is six miles from Nagato. The city of Shimonoseki consists of four to five hundred houses, situated along one very long street and a number of short side or minor ones. There are many stalls selling all sorts of essential provisions for the ships. Ships arrive daily because this is a popular harbor where all vessels coming from the west and east anchor, and we saw some two hundred in this harbor. We also saw many stone carvers, who were skillfully making ink jars and all sorts of boxes of various shapes out of grey and black serpentine stone. The stone is quarried in the nearby mountains.

February 18th, Sunday. Today as well as the day of our arrival we remained here according to a long-standing custom and spent the afternoon visiting the stalls of the cutters and the Amidaji temple, which is famous throughout Japan. In any case, contrary winds would not have permitted us to depart. Together with our traveling companions and two city officials to keep the crowds of commoners away, we were taken up twenty-four rough stone steps to this temple; there we saw three small temples consisting of wooden structures and ahead, on our left, the Amidaji temple. A young priest met us and led us into the entrance hall of the temple, which was covered with black gauze[8] like a theater, except for the center, where a piece of silver fabric had been spread. Here, on an altar, stood the imperial prince who drowned, plump and stout with long, black hair. The Japanese worshipped him by bowing down to the ground. On each side, two life-sized persons of imperial descent were depicted. They were dressed in black garments like those worn at the *dairi*'s court. The priest lit a lamp and began to make a speech about this tragic tale; he led us into a secondary hall and showed us images, painted on gilded cupboards, that portrayed some of the other people mentioned in his story. Then we were taken into an open and beautiful audience hall of the monastery, where the abbot, an old, thin, and modest priest, immediately appeared and sat down. Like the young priests in his charge, he was dressed in a robe of black gauze but had a white silver belt hanging from his right shoulder toward his left side. He had a square piece of the same material both in front and at the back suspended from his left shoulder, and all this served to indicate his eminent status in the monastery. When he noticed that we were not approaching and were not paying attention to him, he stood up again and disappeared into the room at the back, which was low and separated with sliding doors. We put down an *ichi bu* (a piece of gold worth two and a half taels[9]) in honor of the monastery and had our marshal take us back to our inn. There we refreshed ourselves with Japanese food and drink and, finally, took advantage of the innkeeper's bathroom and returned to our boat in the evening. There was still another temple, that of Hachiman, who is worshipped here as the first settler and founder of this small city. But the temple was in such bad condition that it was not considered worth a visit.

Early in the morning of February 19th we set out on our sea journey to Osaka. People are reluctant to set out on this journey without reliable winds from the west, because the first day's journey is long, and there are only two harbors on the northern coast, namely, Mukō and Kudamatsu; neither of them is safe during a storm, and they are difficult to enter. The journey is calculated at 136 nautical miles. Others consider it longer, depending on in which harbors a vessel casts anchor at night and the course dictated by the winds. Some mariners have given me the following figures: thirty-five miles from Shimonoseki to the island, harbor, and village of Kaminoseki; from there, twenty miles to the island and village of Kamagari; then eighteen miles to Tomo; then thirty miles to the small city and harbor of Muro; then eighteen miles to the town and harbor of Hyōgo,[10] and from there to Osaka thirteen miles. Others, however, calculate the distance as follows: from Shimonoseki to Kaminoseki, thirty-five nautical miles; seven miles to Kamuro; eighteen miles to Mitarai; five miles to Hanaguri; ten miles to Tomo; three miles to Shiraishi; seven miles to Shimotsui; ten miles to Ushimado; then ten miles to Muro; thirteen to Akashi; five miles to Hyōgo; and thirteen miles to Osaka. That comes to a total of 136 Japanese nautical miles, as mentioned above, or roughly 46½ German miles, and includes all places where it is possible to drop anchor. Usually, however, these places, situated on the mainland on the left, are passed at a distance of half a mile or a whole mile. There are several better-known places, which include harbors, islands, small extended cities, towns, and villages that are marked on my map and do not require mention here. For the first few miles, until it reaches the open sea, our vessel changes its course frequently. Then we take a slightly northerly course for half of the way and a somewhat more northerly direction for the rest. But on account of the innumerable islands we encounter, which we sail around sometimes on the left and sometimes on the right, our course is full of curves. Some of these islands have harbors and villages and are cultivated to the top of the mountains; others are barren and uninhabited. Osaka lies in a line running slightly north of east[11] of Shimonoseki, which is easier to observe on the map. I discovered a declination of the magnetic needle toward the east by five degrees. During our journey the mainland of Nippon lies on our left, one or several miles away, and on the right are the provinces of Buzen and Bungo, situated on the island of Saikoku. Later we have the large island of Shikoku on our right and the smaller island and the province of Awaji.[12]

With steady winds and a fine drizzle we passed at a distance of two miles a palatial residence near the village of Dan no ura, where the territorial lords traveling to court stopped over. It was a further five miles to the village and well-known mountain of Motoyama; there the sea opens up because Saikoku disappears on the right and the shoreline of Nippon recedes into a bay. We counted nearly one hundred vessels under sail; on account of unfavorable east winds, they had to remain moored during the past days. Before evening we had caught up with all of them because our crew and sails were better. After eighteen miles we lost sight of Saikoku and ahead saw the fairly large island of Iwaijima, and then on the mainland the high mountain Kasadoyama still some ten miles before Kaminoseki. Then on the right we caught sight of the high snow-covered mountains of the province of Iyo on the large island of Shikoku; this consists of four large domains and is calculated to be seventy Japanese miles in length. Soon afterward our course took us past dangerous, overhanging, and partially hidden cliffs called Zōsui no kuso, which means "cook's excrement,"[13] where seafarers have to take care. Soon our course took us into a strait, where the island on the right was situated so near to the spit of the mainland that one could only detect a passage when close by. To our left, on the mainland, was the town of Murotsu and to the right, on the island of Kaminoseki, a village of the same name, both with about eighty houses. They were governed by a cousin of the territorial lord of Mori,[14] who transferred the areas bordering his domain of Nagato to him as dependencies. Before the entrance to the harbor is a wooden light tower on a high cliff to guide the ships at night. The island prides itself on a huge image of an idol, called Daishi no daibutsu. The sea we had crossed is called Suō nada, which means the bay of Suō,[15] after the province of Suō along its side.

Ji no Kamuro

From here we sailed another seven miles without interruption to Ji no Kamuro, which means lower Kamuro,[16] and dropped anchor in the dark near the shore together with many other vessels, at half past seven German time. Today we traveled forty-two Japanese nautical miles with constant winds from the west.

Ji no Kamuro is a village of some hundred farmers' huts and a few stately houses, situated at the shore of the province of Aki on a bay surrounded by mountains. It has this name to distinguish it from the smaller village of Oki Kamuro, which means upper Kamuro,[17] situated nearby on the same shore. It is well known among sailors on account of its convenient anchorage.

February 20th. We rowed away early in the morning in calm weather and soon reached Oki Kamuro, a village of some forty houses, facing our anchorage. It is located on the eastern corner of an island, where the mountains are cultivated to the very top. Around noon we reached the island of Tsuwa, situated on our left, with a circular bay opening to the southeast. The shore is lined with some two hundred houses, and the bay provides a safe haven for ships. The mountains in the background are terraced and cultivated to the very top.

From here we traveled with a gentle breeze to the village of Kamagari in the province of Aki, located on the shore between two mountains. It was only a few miles further to the famous harbor of Mitarai, where we dropped anchor in the dark next to many other vessels. Today we traveled eighteen Japanese nautical miles and came across many barren, unknown, and deserted islands and mountain chains. On the right, the province of Iyo stretched for four miles; on the left was the province of Aki. Both had high, snow-covered mountain ranges, but we passed them at full speed.

Thus we left Mitarai on Wednesday, February 21st, one hour before dawn in calm weather. At this point the distance between the island of Shikoku and Nippon is only about one Japanese mile.[18] After we traveled two miles, we saw on the furthest outpost the poor residence or manor of Kurushima belonging to the Lord of Hiroshima of the province of Aki.[19] The domain consists of nine scattered islands and this corner of the

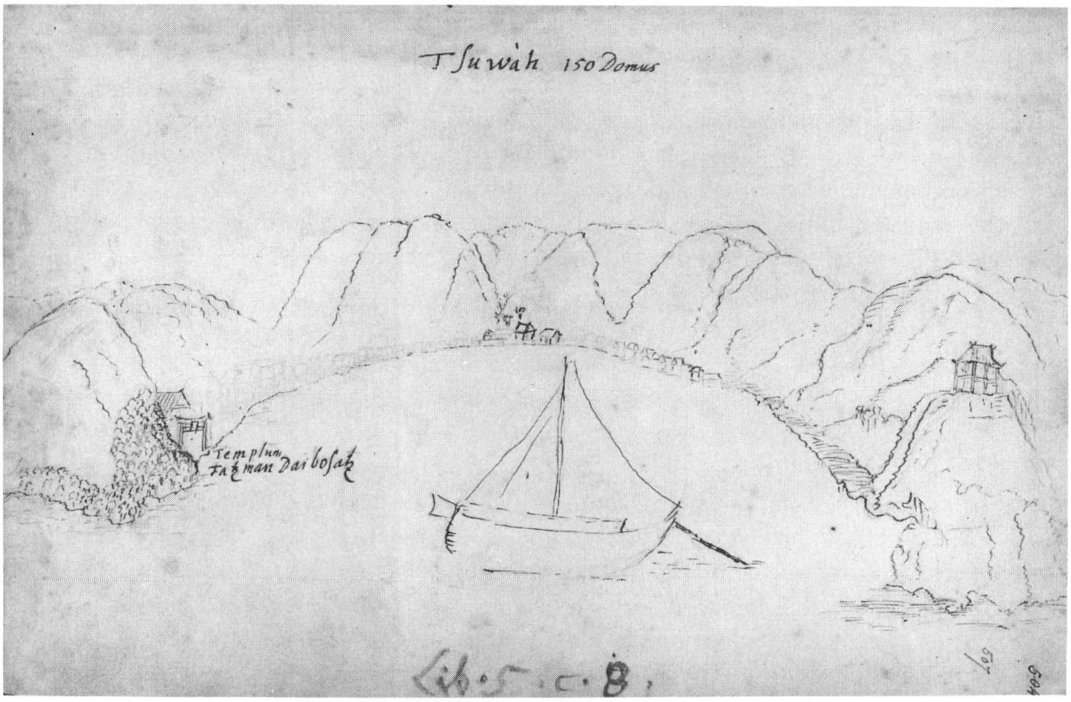

Kaempfer's sketch of the harbor of Tsuwa. (Courtesy of the British Library, Sloane 3060, folio 507)

mainland. Two or three Japanese miles further along the mainland stands a beautiful, large castle, splendid with its tall towers, and the city of Imabari, the residence of the territorial lord Shiro moto dono, son of the territorial lord of Ki no Kuni and son-in-law of the shogun.[20] Five Japanese miles later we reached a narrow strait and the village of Hanaguri situated on these shores; we stayed there an hour to take on fresh water, and during that time many vessels sailed past. Hanaguri is a village of some sixty houses, situated below a mountain range with two peaks; it gets its name from the mountain range, because *hanaguri* means a nostril. Here we saw nine straw huts, like small mounds, built very crudely, in which salt was being produced from seawater. We saw a number of other small fishing villages along the shore close by, and a mile from here is a village called Tarumi with a fine inn. Between the two we saw some ramparts or banks rising from the water, built in such a way that the sea lane, whose width is less than a pistol shot, could be closed if necessary.[21] After a few miles we reached the village of Iwagi on our left with some eighty houses (because there are so many inlets I could not tell whether it is on an island or the mainland).[22] Nearby, on a green, overgrown cliff was a temple, with steps leading up from below and two gates on the shore marking the approach. As we continued, we passed stark mountains, harbors, and villages on both sides of our course. Among them, Shioya, a village of some hundred houses on an island to our right, is worthy of mention, because it produces a lot of salt, and this is why it was given that name.[23] Close by was the small village of Yuge, with some rich farmers and a residence or manor. From there we had favorable winds. Ahead of us on our course was an extraordinary island rising out of the sea like a tall pyramid.[24] To our right we had the open sea, which lies between Iyo and Sanuki, the two northern provinces of the island of Shikoku, and the sea extends so far inland that we could not see the shore. Along the shoreline on our left were some villages.

Soon afterward we passed the famous harbor and town of Tomo, situated on the shore to our left not far from our course. To distinguish it from another place, it is called Bingo no Tomo. It lies on the coast below gently rising mountains and has several hundred fine houses along a road following the curve of the shoreline, as well as a Maruyama, or prostitutes' quarter, and two pretty temples. Large quantities of beautiful mats for covering the floor are manufactured here and exported to other provinces. Behind the city on the slope of the mountains is a stately nunnery or widows' monastery. At a distance of a quarter of a German mile from the city is a famous temple of the god Abuto, who possesses skills to heal certain illnesses, but especially to produce favorable winds for sailors. For this reason, passing sailors and passengers throw a few pennies or coins firmly attached to a piece of wood into the water as a donation for this Abuto kannon sama, which means lord god Kannon (as they call him), in return for favorable winds. The guardian of the temple maintains that such donations always drift ashore and are taken by him; but to make quite sure that he gets them, in calm weather he usually comes out personally to the passing barges in his little boat to request the toll due to his god. In front or next to the little city is an island, nicely covered with bushes and trees, and also the surrounding mountains had some growth of this kind. We continued with favorable winds for another seven nautical miles to the small village of Shiraishi, situated on a small island along the shore to the right of our course; even though it was still one hour before sunset, we stopped and took advantage of the good anchorage, because there would be none for quite some time. This village consists of some fifty houses and is next to the harbor on a narrow bay opening up to the north, in a valley with pretty fields near a mountain, where the god Kōbō Daishi[25] is worshipped in a cave on high. In addition to us, twelve other barges arrived, all following our example of taking the mast down to prevent being tossed about. Today we traveled eighteen miles slightly east of north and north of east.

February 22nd, a Thursday. We set sail at dawn and traveled past many islands across the open sea up to the small city of Shimotsui, situated to the left of our course on the mainland in the province of Bitchū on a shore built up with boulders. The city lies at the foot of a rocky mountain, which—like nearly all mountains on islands that are cultivated—has been planted with fir trees at the top, and they look like a fringe. The city consists of some four to five hundred little houses, most of them rather poor, and is divided into three parts, each part being governed by a *yoriki.* Near Shimotsui to the right is the castle of Shiaku, built of boulders and situated next to a village. Not far from here we again came across an extraordinary pyramid-shaped high island called Tsuchiyama, lying

Kaempfer's sketch of Bingo no Tomo. At the bottom he noted that this drawing was to illustrate chapter 8 of book 5. (Courtesy of the British Library, Sloane 3060, folio 509 verso)

right on our course and visible in the east from as far away as Shimotsui. Here the sea passage narrowed again and then opened up to the left into a large harbor with only a few vessels. The harbor faced south and was part of the mainland province of Bizen. On both sides of the harbor was a village called Hibi. Eight miles further along on the same northern shore we saw the pretty town of Shimachi or Ushimado, where there are also some fortifications, and then after another seven miles the well-built castle of Akō. It was a pretty sight with its white walls, the towers marking the corners of the fortifications and the small city behind it, but apparently the bottom of the sea is covered with a lot of sludge, and therefore it is inconvenient as an anchorage. It is the residence of a small territorial lord named Asano Takumi, whose stipend is only five *man koku.*[26] Three miles further we came to the city and large and famous harbor of Muro.

We arrived there at five o'clock in the afternoon and stayed the night, having traveled today twenty-seven nautical miles with favorable winds. We positioned ourselves twenty feet from the shore, being one of more than hundred barges resting at anchor. While this harbor is not very large, it is protected on all sides from storms and waves, since the entrance is closed off by a narrow mountain jutting out from the mainland toward the west. Consequently when entering the harbor the ship has to take a northeasterly course and then turn south-southeast to reach the anchorage below the city. The city of Muro is situated in the province of Harima along a circular shoreline fortified with boulders at a very pretty and scenic location. The city consists of a long, nar-

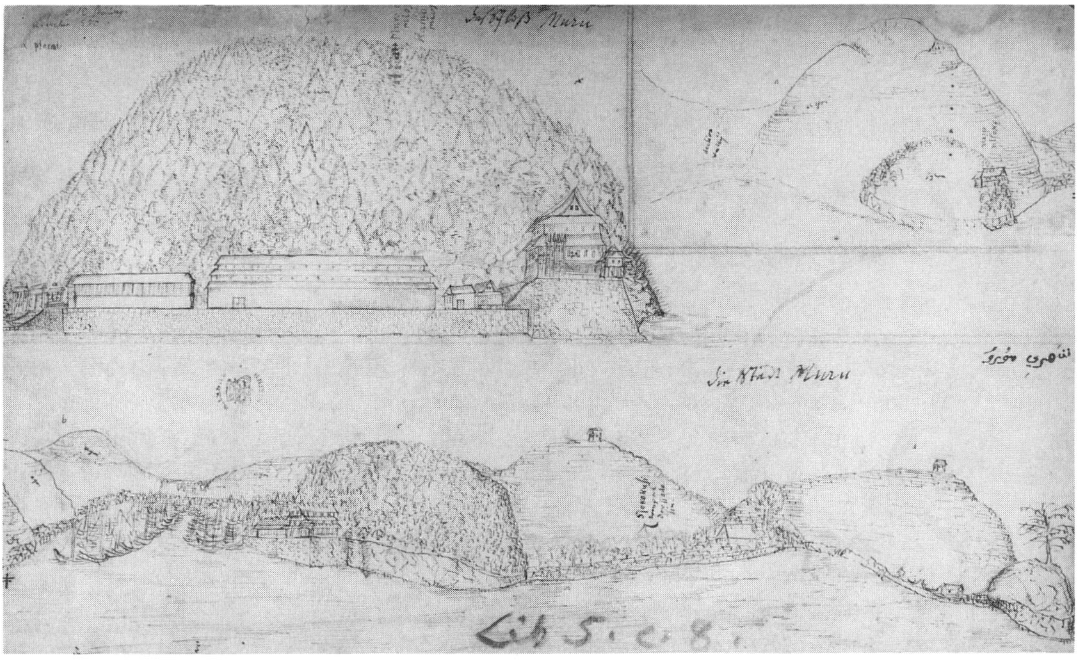

Kaempfer's sketch of the harbor of Muro and the castle. He noted that this was to illustrate chapter 8 of book 5. (Courtesy of the British Library, Sloane 3060, folio 506)

row street following the shoreline and a few short back or side streets running up to the surrounding mountains; it has a total of some six hundred houses. The inhabitants are *sake* distillers, innkeepers, and shopkeepers, who do well with the great number of seamen. The city is governed by a *bugyō*. A lot of different products are made here from horse skins, which are prepared as they are in Russia and then covered with lacquer. They are sold for one tael, four mace apiece. As unkempt as this city is, it still keeps a Maruyama, or brothel, for its pleasure. The surrounding mountains are cultivated up to the top, step by step so to speak, and present a pretty sight from afar. No less pleasant to look at is the said nearby densely cultivated forest, rising up high on the narrow peninsula and shielding the entrance to the harbor. This circular piece of forest, which runs up to a high point in the center, is situated on a rocky outcrop and surrounded by round towers, guard houses, and pleasant buildings that rise fairly high above the ground and provide accommodation for officers and soldiers. On the west of this forest, toward the entrance of the harbor, was an armed guard in a fortress; its presence was indicated by ten pikes and five halberds standing in a row in front, rather than any physical presence of the soldiers. On the other side, the peninsula was linked to the fortifications of the city by a low isthmus but separated from it by walls and gates. Soon after our arrival we set out for the city with our companions and were taken through the back of a large house of a *sake* distiller to the long street and from there to a bath house, where we were forced to clean and refresh ourselves in the sweat house. This house was full with customers, and the owner also provided *sake* and refreshments. Having used the bathing facilities and taken refreshments, we returned to our barge but discovered that the street was filled with spectators. They were squatting and in total silence out of respect, observing their foreign guests.

February 23rd, Friday. We left the bay again at daybreak and rowed some two thousand paces until we reached the open sea and were able to use our sails. We passed the following settlements all situated on the mainland toward the north: Aboshi, a city with some fortifications and a shogunal storehouse. Although this city is in the domain of Harima, it was governed by a shogunal appointee and resident *bugyō*. Himeji[27] is a small city with a magnificent castle with many towers, belonging to the territorial lord Matsudaira Yamato.[28] At both localities the bottom of the sea is full of cliffs, and vessels cannot approach. Takasago[29] is a small city another seven miles from Muro, where the country becomes flat, and this plain stretches ten miles from the coast toward the north and five miles along the shore to Akashi. The latter is an unfortified, small city with many trees, more than four hundred houses, and a deep river flowing through it. It is famous for its *katabira*,[30] or women's frocks, which are skillfully made here out of hemp. Behind the city is a beautiful castle, with tall trees growing inside and around it, so that only two sides of the castle are visible with their gleaming white walls. The middle and end of each wall is adorned with tall, square, three-storied towers. In the middle is the manor of the resident *bugyō* of the lord of Harima, whose fief is believed to be only twenty *man koku* and half the size of Hizen.[31] On both sides of this city, along the built-up shore, we saw various large villages where people earned their living by fishing and producing salt. A long island on the right (with villages and temples along the shore)[32] meant that we passed through a narrow strait for one and a half nautical miles. Formerly this and various other small islands were given to farmers to cultivate and hand down to their descendants (the only obligation being an annual present to the local official), and these farmers are now so rich that some of them own twenty to thirty boxes of gold. Along the above-mentioned shore of the mainland—which here consists of sand—the most important villages are: Yamada, Tarumi, and Shioya, where, again, people earn a living by fishing and producing salt. Then there is the village of Suma with its three parts, where during former wars the imperial faction of the Heike lived for many years (we heard a story about this at the temple at Shimonoseki). Shortly afterward there was the village of Komaga hayashi, consisting of two hundred to three hundred houses, and then at the beginning of the province of Settsu, five miles from Akashi, we came to the city and the harbor of Hyōgo.[33]

Hyōgo

Before we enter this harbor I have to explain that it is sheltered from the open sea toward the south by a breakwater or wide, sandy bank. This piece of land continues on from the mountains on the southeast and runs into the sea for a third of a German mile to shelter the harbor or bay. The bank is not a natural one but was built on the order of the emperor Heike[34] by the hands of men and was settled with houses and fields to create a harbor for his own protection and that of the country. Battling the raging seas and completing the task is said to have been an enormous labor achieved only at the expense of human lives. The work was ruined many times and was twice completely washed away. It did not succeed until a certain man (others say thirty people) had himself buried in the ground, like M. Curtius,[35] pacifying and appeasing the god of the sea. The bay opens toward the east and is somewhat protected by the nearby country of Settsu, but in the south it is sheltered from the high seas by the above-mentioned bank. The harbor is very important for seafarers, the last between Shimonoseki and Osaka, and there were some three hundred barges with freight at anchor.

The city of Hyōgo does not have a castle and is nearly as large as Nagasaki. It is not quite as wide but is longer because it runs right around the circular shore of the bay. The houses on the shore are poor and small; further back they are more stately and larger, and they climb up the forested hills in the background. Behind the hills looms a steep mountain chain that is supposed to produce a lot of ore and gold. We dropped anchor in the harbor of this city around one o'clock in the afternoon, having traveled eighteen miles today with favorable winds.

The 24th, Saturday, we left our large barge early in the morning, because it would have been difficult to take it across the shallows of Osaka harbor, and we were rowed in four small boats up to the area of Osaka after the vessels had been loaded with our luggage. On this journey we saw various cities and castles along the shore, including the beautiful castle and small city of Amagasaki, which was still three miles from the

Osaka roadstead. Ahead of our course in the same southerly direction we saw the shogunal city of Sakai, which, when we entered the river, remained at a distance of four Japanese miles to the southeast. After we traveled today ten miles up to the mouth of the Osaka river, we entered the navigable arm of the river at eleven o'clock in the morning in an east-southeasterly direction. There we were received by our innkeeper from Osaka with two grandiose barges and were taken up the river, passing many new villages and suburbs, built along the shore on both sides of the river in great numbers a few years ago. We passed more than one thousand vessels until we came to the entrance of the city, which is separated from the suburbs by two stately and strong guardhouses on both sides of the river. We then passed under six beautiful, wooden bridges until we were told to disembark and step into the city. We climbed the stone steps of the tall, masoned bank and entered a side street, through which we reached our usual inn at the corner of the first long street. We arrived at one or two o'clock in the afternoon and were assigned some rooms on the upper floor separated by sliding doors; this would have been comfortable to rest in if we had not been bothered by frequent clouds of smoke (which in this country is not channeled into a chimney). As soon as we arrived, we sent our interpreters to the houses of both magistrates to request permission to call on them with some small gifts. One of them, called Odagiri Tosa no Kami,[36] was in Osaka but not at home; the other, Nose Izumi no Kami,[37] had traveled to court as part of the usual duties of his office. The former informed us late in the evening that he would be pleased to see us at eight o'clock in the morning.

Chapter 9
Journey of Thirteen Miles from Osaka to Miyako, Begun on February 28th and Completed on the 29th, as well as a Description of Both Cities

Osaka

Osaka is one of the shogunal capital cities[1] and is situated in the province of Settsu, at a latitude of 34.50 degrees North.[2] It has neither ramparts nor walls and is happily located in a fertile plain and on a navigable river. In the east the city is girdled by a massive fortress, in the west by two imposing guardhouses, which separate the city from the nearby suburbs. The city extends from east to west—that is, from the above-mentioned fortress to the suburbs—some three thousand to four thousand ordinary paces, but its width is less. The large Yodogawa river, with its great volume of water, cuts through the whole length of the northern part of the city. The river contributes much to the flourishing trade and the prosperity of the city, and it is therefore appropriate to briefly describe its course. The river's source, a lake in the province of Ōmi, is one and a half days' journey to the northeast.[3] According to the written record, the lake was created in one night by an earthquake, which caused the land to subside. The river begins at the village of Seta no hashi, where it is spanned by an imposing double bridge, joined in the middle on a small island. The river flows in the direction of the cities of Uji and Yodo and takes its name from the latter. Then it continues on to Osaka. One mile before the city, one arm runs straight toward the sea. But the loss of water is made up by two tributaries—Yamatogawa and Hiranogawa—which enter the river before it reaches the city at the northern side of the castle. Each tributary is spanned by an imposing bridge before the point of confluence. After this large combined stream has passed through roughly a third of the city, a wide man-made canal carries the water into the southern and larger part of the city, the actual town of the citizenry. A few other canals branch off, running the length of the streets, until they converge again into the main stream. This creates a system with a number of deep tributaries that can be used to transport incoming goods leisurely in and out of the city by small boats and thus supply the merchants. As mentioned above, these city canals all run parallel to the streets, forming a regular pattern, and are of fixed width. Here and there they are crossed by beautiful bridges, of which there are more than one hundred; but some canals lack water and consequently are muddy and their banks are not very tidy. A little further down the main stream, on its northern side, a wide but shallow arm branches off. This is a natural arm, which runs quickly toward the west until it flows into the sea. The main river also flows in a westerly direction through the city, but at the end of the city it turns west-southwest. Its winding course runs through the city's suburbs and through villages before it reaches the sea. The river is narrow, but carries a large volume of water and is navigable. Consequently several thousand barges and merchant vessels were traveling back and forth, and territorial lords were also plying the river between the sea and the city. The banks on both sides of the river consist of ten or more steps of roughly hewn boulders rising out of the water, so that one may leisurely embark and disembark from one's vessel. Every three or four hundred paces, or somewhat further, is a wide bridge, beautifully constructed from immaculate cedar wood. All have railings, and some are decorated with brass knobs. I have counted a total of ten, of which three, spanning the wide section of the river, are remarkable. The first and easternmost is a good sixty fathoms long and rests on thirty piers, each consisting of five or more beams. The next bridge is of the same size. The third spans both streams and is 150 fathoms long. The remaining part of the river up to the end of the city is spanned by a further seven bridges. These are considerably shorter on account of the reduced width of the river, however, and some are only sixty or even twenty fathoms long and rest on only thirty or ten piers. The city's streets are fairly narrow, many of only ordinary width. They cross at right angles and run completely straight to the south and west, except in that part of the city which faces the sea, where the streets accommodate the flow of the river and run west-southwest. The streets are not paved, and the ground is clean, but there is a gutter of roughly hewn boulders on both sides. They are closed off from each other at night with solid gates, and the ward headman permits only people holding a pass to leave or enter. Each street has a fenced-off area where one finds various fire-fighting equipment and also a covered well.

In accordance with the laws of the country, the houses are only two stories high, each story not exceeding one and a half or two fathoms. They are built of pine, plaster, and lime. From outside, the front door is visible as well as some open sliding partitions revealing a booth or anteroom, where merchandise is displayed or workshops operate within the gaze of the public. There is always a short, black cloth hanging down from above, as protection against the wind and as decoration, with an attractive emblem indicating the type of business. The roof is not very steep and is covered with flat, black fired tiles set in lime; other houses, those of ordinary citizens, are covered only with wood chips. The houses are nicely decorated inside but do not have tables, chairs, or furniture. The stairs, shelves, and all woodwork are varnished; the floors are covered with valuable, solid mats stuffed with rushes; the rooms are arranged in such a way that they can be made smaller, larger, and closed off with light sliding partitions. The sliding partitions and the walls gleam with gold and silver flower-patterned paper, with which they are lined. The upper sections of the walls are often left bare, because they are covered with orange-colored loam, which is dug up around Osaka and taken to far-off cities because of its beautiful color. Mats, doors, and sliding partitions are all one size: one fathom long and half a fathom wide.[4] All rooms, yes, even the houses, are arranged and even built according to the size, shape, and measurements of the mats. Behind the house is a *tsubo*, that is, a small garden where the owner proudly displays beautifully shaped stones and other decorative features, as I have described elsewhere. Behind this there generally is a sweatshop[5] or bath-house for cleaning the body. There is also likely to be a fireproof place, that is to say, a small house or room covered with thick loam and lime to protect it against the force of a blaze, where people can store their assets and household goods in case of fire.

The city and community are governed by their own ward headmen and mayors, under the supervision and orders of two magistrates, who at the same time act as stewards of the surrounding districts, towns, and villages. They reside here every second year, so that if one is present, the other must be with his family in the shogunal residence of Edo. The same applies to the four other shogunal cities, the only difference being that a third magistrate has been appointed for the government of Nagasaki. Of these, two are present, presiding a year each, while the third has to spend the year at court with his family. In Miyako the two magistrates take it in turn and have to appear only every third year at court. The two magistrates of Edo always remain there and preside every second year. All other laws and civil administration are the same in Osaka as they are in other cities, and I have explained these in detail in my description of Nagasaki. I discovered that there is a difference in the division of the night watch, or the hours of the night, inasmuch as they are indicated by different sounds: the first hour after sunset is announced with a drum; the next with a *gumgum* (a metal instrument resembling an enormous bowl with a large rim, producing a far-reaching sound when beaten); the third, around midnight, with a bell, which is not rung but hit with a piece of wood; the fourth, again with a drum; the fifth with the *gumgum;* the sixth with the bell. The sixth hour is the last and finishes at sunrise. The night is divided into only six hours right throughout the year, and therefore the hours are longer in winter and shorter in summer.

The city has a very large number of inhabitants and is recorded to have eighty thousand fighting men. On account of its good position, its trade, conducted via sea and land routes, it is the greatest in Japan. Its citizens therefore are affluent, and there are also a great variety of artisans and workshops. In spite of the large population, the quality of life is good, as there is an overabundant supply of whatever serves to satisfy and delight the senses. This is why the Japanese refer to the city as the show ground and center of all earthly pleasures, where comedies are performed publicly inside buildings every day and people crying their wares and entertainers flock. People owning something strange, such as some monstrosity, foreign animals, or animals trained to perform tricks or the like, arrive from all over the country to show their tricks and rarities for a fee. When we chose the cassowary (a large Indian bird, which swallowed stones and red-hot pieces of coal) as a present for the shogun, together with many other items, and it failed to win the approval of the censors and had to be transported back to Batavia, a rich patron said that, if he were permitted, he would pay us one thousand taels, for he claimed the bird would make him twice that amount in Osaka before the year was over. Owing to these attractions many people from other parts of the country and rich travelers come here to while away their time and amuse themselves. Even though the territorial lords of the western provinces own houses here and retain people who have to accompany them to Edo, they are not permitted to stay longer than one day and one night when they pass through, and they are not allowed to travel within sight of the castle.

The drinking water is bad and somewhat brackish, but the *sake* is the best in the country. It is brewed at the nearby town of Tennōji and is often sent to other parts of the country and also exported by the Dutch and the Chinese.

The fortress is located in a plain on the eastern, or rather northeastern, end of the city, and one passes it when leaving for Miyako. It was built by the ruler Taikō in the shape of a square, with strong round towers, according to the state of the art of military defense. Its size is such that it takes one hour to walk around it. With the exception of Higo, there is no castle that compares with it in size, splendor, and strength.[6] It is protected on the north by the river Yodogawa, where the river consists of three streams and is larger than its normal size. On the east it is bordered by the river Kashiwaragawa before the river enters Yodogawa, and here the large castle gardens are situated. The southern and western sides border on the city. The outer moats are an extraordinary width and up to seven fathoms deep; ramparts supporting tall walls of rough boulders rise from the water, with neat rows of pines or cedars and some heavy cannons on top. On two sides I noticed a narrow gate in the middle of the wall and a small, wooden bridge leading to the gate. Beyond this I have not inspected the site of the castle, and the following information I have merely learned from the reports of the Japanese.

As soon as one enters the first fortress or fortifications, one discovers a second one with the same architectural features, and after that also a third, or innermost, castle. It is decorated with the usual towers at the corners. There was also a stately, multistoried tower. On the uppermost roof of the tower were two large fish, with scales of polished golden *ōban,* which shone so brightly that one could see them glitter even at Hyōgo. But thirty years ago (calculated from the year 1691) a blaze reduced this tower to ashes. In the gate of the second castle, a polished stone of blackish color has been masoned into the wall; on account of its size, weight, and the way it was brought here, it is considered a wonder, since it is five fathoms long, four fathoms wide, and in the shape of a cube. At the time, the governor of Higo[7] was ordered by the ruler Taikō to obtain large stones for building the castle, and he had this stone laboriously transported on six barges joined together from an island called Inatsumishima, five miles from Tomo. The said ruler had this fortress built for his own safety, purposely utilizing the time when the powerful territorial lords were busy with the war against Korea and were outside the country. A strong military force is stationed in this castle to ensure the safekeeping of shogunal riches, including the annual revenue from the western provinces, as well as to prevent disturbances in these provinces. Two commanders, the most trustworthy favorites of His Majesty, are in command of the castle, and the command is rotated on a three-year basis. It is interesting that as soon as one of them returns from Edo, completing his duties there, the other has to depart immediately without exchanging a word with him, and the necessary information has to be deposited in writing in the office of the castle. They have

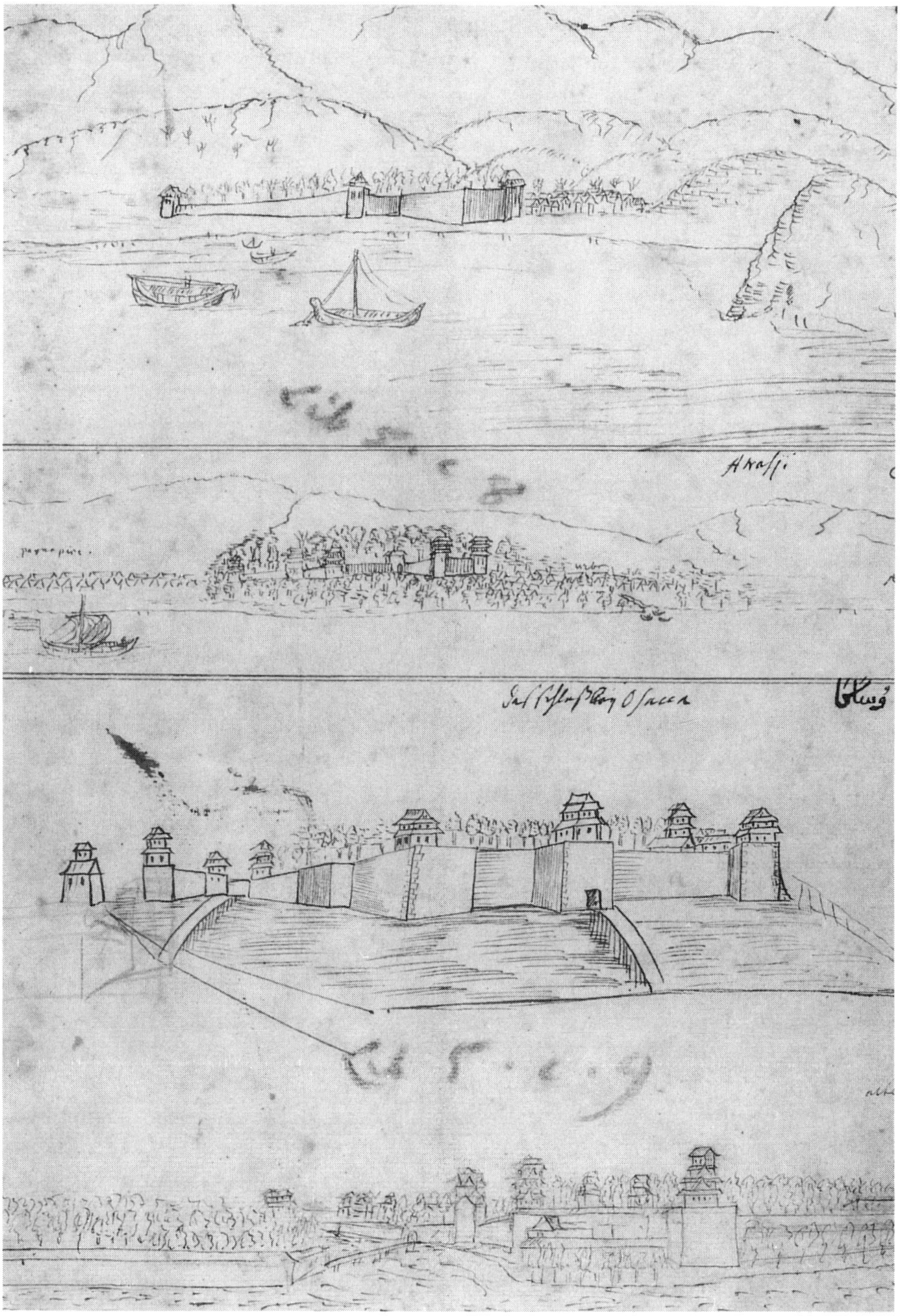

Kaempfer's sketch of Akashi, middle, and two sketches of Osaka castle. Note the name of the locations in Arabic script to avoid detection while sketching. (Courtesy of the British Library, Sloane 3060, folio 557)

nothing to do with civil affairs nor with the magistrates but are ranked above them. This is indicated by the fact that the previous chief judge of Miyako,[8] who was one of the most powerful shogunal courtiers and more or less the shogun's right hand, was transferred from this commandery to that high office.

Audience at Osaka

On February 25th, a Sunday, accompanied by our interpreters and servants, we were carried in palanquins to the house of the magistrate, half an hour on foot from our inn, at the end of the city at the square in front of the castle. We descended in front of the house and all put on black silk robes, because the Japanese consider these the equivalent to festive or ceremonial robes. We walked through a passage thirty paces long into the entrance hall or guard rooms, where we were greeted by two nobles and were invited to sit down until our arrival had been announced. On the left we noticed four sentries or soldiers, and next to them eight courtiers sitting on their heels in a row. This way of sitting is much more respectful than resting cross-legged. The wall on the right was totally covered with weapons, in the following order: fifteen partisans,[9] twenty lances, and some fifteen pikes, which had many curled hooks at the end. We were taken through offices and next through four chambers, which turned into one room after the sliding partitions had been removed, and then into the audience hall. As we were passing, I saw that the walls were decorated with bows one and a half fathoms long, many swords, and also some guns in beautifully lacquered black cases. In the audience hall seven courtiers were sitting in order of rank, and the two secretaries sat down three paces away from us. They treated us with ground tea and entertained us with kind words until soon afterward the magistrate, accompanied by two sons, seventeen and eighteen years old, sat down in another chamber ten paces away from us and talked to us through an opening created by removing three partitions. He was a gentleman some forty years old, of average height, well built, with a large, manly face, quick gestures, affable, and with a soft voice. His robes were black and spartan with a grey overcoat or ceremonial robe, wearing only one common sword. He said to us that the weather was cold now and we had traveled a long way. It was a great honor to visit the shogun, and among all the nations of the world, only the Dutch were blessed with this fortune. Surely we must be enjoying seeing their country after having completed such an arduous and dangerous journey! And finally he said that since the chief judge at Miyako, who issues the permits for travel, had not yet returned from Edo, he would issue us one to the same effect. He said we should have it collected tomorrow and offered to supply us with horses and other things necessary for the journey, should we need them. We, in turn, thanked him for the generous offer, and begged him not to scorn our small presents (consisting of silk cloth, which had also been given to the two secretaries or house stewards). We bade farewell and were accompanied by the said secretaries to the first guard room. We exchanged greetings and then went back to our baskets.[10] Our interpreters permitted us to stretch our feet, and thus we were given the chance to leisurely regard the splendid fortress from the outside. Then we sat down and had ourselves carried to our inn, passing another long street. We would have left presents also for the other governor, but as he was not there, we will have to consult the Nagasaki governor residing in Edo on what we should do. For in this country we have to be extremely careful not to endanger our position by creating harmful jealousies.

On March 26th,[11] a Monday, we rested quietly according to established custom.

On February 27th, a Tuesday, we had to stay another day because some horses needed for the journey to Edo were still lacking. We hired a total of forty horses and forty-one porters (after a long argument with the interpreters, who demanded more). Every year we could do with less if the rascals of interpreters did not arrange to have goods on order transported in our name and at our expense. Toward evening we sent our old senior interpreter to the magistrate to say farewell on our behalf, and he returned with good wishes for our journey and the required permit.

On February 28th, a Wednesday, we left at the crack of dawn in order to reach Miyako today, thirteen Japanese miles, or a full day's journey from here. That is, from Osaka to Sada, three Japanese miles; another two miles to Hirakata; three miles to the city of Yodo; and five miles traveling through Fushimi to Miyako. First we rode over the so-called Kyōbashi, or bridge of Miyako, spanning the first river surrounding the castle; then we went one mile on low dikes along muddy rice paddies, on a road with many bends on account of the irregular course of the large river, which remained always on our left. For half a mile we passed on our left some scattered houses in the suburbs of Osaka. Next we traveled along the dike of the river, which is planted with many *aburagiri* trees.[12] This tree grows here as big as an oak and has flaky grey bark; on account of the season, it had no leaves but much yellow fruit, from which the local people know how to obtain oil. The road and the surrounding countryside is covered with villages, and not many more are needed to turn the whole road to Miyako into one urban street. The largest and best-known of these, none with fewer than two hundred houses, are Imaichi, Moriguchi (where the best cinnamon is produced), Sada, Deguchi, then the town of Hirakata, with nearly five hundred houses, where we arrived in the morning at half past nine, after we had traveled five miles. We stayed only half an hour for our noon meal. There are many inns, tea and *sake* houses, and stalls where one can buy all sorts of warm food for a small sum of money, and each inn has a young prostitute wearing makeup. On the left, on the other side of the river, we could see the white castle of a minor territorial lord, known as Takatsuki, radiant and splendid from afar. Further on we were led through the villages of Kuzuha, with two hundred houses, and Hashimoto, with some three hundred. The last-named village was also full of inns and wenches wearing makeup. Soon afterward we reached the famous small city of Yodo, surrounded and crisscrossed by waterways. The outer city consisted of one road, which led to a stately wooden bridge called Yodo ōhashi of four hundred paces and forty piers, with forty sections of railings above, all decorated with metal knobs. After crossing the bridge and passing through a simple, well-protected gate, we entered the city. The city is pleasantly situated and has well-kept houses; its few streets all run east and south and intersect in an orderly pattern. The city is well supplied with artists and artisans. On the western side the castle, with its walls of rough boulders, rises splendidly from the center of the wide river. White, multistoried towers decorate the corners and center of its outer walls in keeping with local architecture, making it a splendid sight. The outer part of the castle is fortified with rough, masoned walls, reaching far into the city. This is the residence of the territorial lord Honda Shimōsa.[13] Leaving the city, we were taken once more over a long bridge. This bridge was supported by twenty piers and was two hundred paces long, and it brought us to a suburb, the end of which was closed off with a guard house.

Uji Supplies the Tea for the Court of the Shogun

To the right, in the direction of the river but beyond our sight, was the town or unfortified city of Uji, which is famous throughout Japan because it produces the best tea and also each year has to supply the court of the shogun. After a further two hours on horseback we reached the city of Fushimi[14] at two o'clock in the afternoon.

Fushimi

This unfortified small city consists of a few, wide and often long streets, of which some run to the wooded hills to the right. Various arms of the said river flow through and past the city. The central and main street stretches up to the streets of Miyako and is linked to it so closely that one cannot separate the two. One could even consider Fushimi as a suburb of Miyako, inasmuch as the Japanese capital is surrounded by neither strong walls nor ramparts but is unfortified and situated in a flat plain. Today was the Japanese *tsuitachi,* that is, the first day of a new month, on which the Japanese visit temples, go for walks, and amuse themselves in various other ways. For this reason, the long street, along which we traveled for four hours before reaching our inn, was filled with the people of Miyako, visiting the nearby buildings of the idols for pleasure.[15] Noticeable among these pilgrims were in particular the much-adorned women with their splendid robes in the fashion of Miyako, the head covered with a cloth of purple silk gauze hanging down over their forehead and a large straw hat against the heat of the sun. We also saw various strangely clad beggars: some dressed up in mad costumes, some walking on iron stilts, and others with deep buckets on their heads with green trees. Still others were singing, whistling, playing the flute, or striking chimes. Everywhere on this road we saw crowds of vendors, hawkers, and performers. The said temples, located on wooded slopes to our right, were lit up with many lamps, and in them we heard the priests making a lot of noise by beating small bells with hammers. While riding past I saw on my left in a well-decorated chapel or little temple a large, white dog, perhaps made out of plaster, standing in the middle of the large, main altar. The reason was that this temple was dedicated to the patron of dogs. We reached our lodgings in Miyako at six o'clock at night and were assigned our quarters on the second floor (which could have well served as a Westphalian bacon or smoking compartment). Today we traveled through fertile country consisting mainly of rice paddies. There we saw many wild ducks, which were so tame that they did not fly away when people approached. We also saw large, white herons, swans, and a few storks, searching for food in the muddy fields. The fields were ploughed with black oxen, which looked rather poor and thin but are supposed to be very robust.

On our arrival, the interpreters called at the house of the absent chief judge, Matsudaira Inaba no Kami,[16] and also at those of the two magistrates, Koide Awaji no Kami[17] and Maeda Aki no Kami,[18] to announce our arrival and to ask for permission to hand over our usual presents.

Audience at Miyako

February 29th, a Thursday. This morning, having sent our presents ahead and, according to Japanese custom, having had each item presented individually on a special gift tray (this is a little table made of pieces of pine, constructed solely for this purpose), we had ourselves carried across in *kago* at ten o'clock in the morning.

Their residences were at the furthest western side of the city, opposite the shogunal castle or fortress. We were told to descend fifty paces from the palace of the chief judge and walk the rest of the way to show our respect. We were also told to wait at the gate near the general guard of the entrance until we had been announced. Then we were led some twenty paces through the outer courtyard into the entrance hall, which is called the *ban,* meaning guard, because that is where the scribes, sentries, and custodians of the house are; some twenty courtiers and servants were sitting there in a row. Then we were taken through yet another chamber into a third room and asked to sit down. Soon afterward the steward of the house appeared, a man of sixty or more in a grey ceremonial robe. He sat down four paces away from us and in the name of his lord accepted our compliments as well as the presents with a cordial show of gratitude. The presents, which had been displayed in the above-mentioned central chamber, consisted of one bottle of vintent[19] and twenty pieces of all sorts of foreign silk, woolen, and linen material. A set of tobacco utensils with all its different parts was placed in front of us and each was given a little cup of ground tea; each person was served three times by a special servant, while the steward and most important nobles in the room encouraged us to drink. Having stayed just over a quarter of an hour, we bade farewell and were accompanied by the steward to the outside of the first room and by other people we had met up to the gate. Afterward we went on foot to the house of the presiding new governor, who had just recently arrived from the court and was not yet acquainted with the etiquette of receiving the Dutch (as we were told by both scribes, in their capacity as masters of ceremony). There was an ordinary guard at the gate, and nearly fifty people in the *ban,* or entrance hall of the house, as well as some richly dressed boys, all sitting in good order. We were led past them and into a side chamber, where the said secretaries, two elderly men, received us cordially. They treated us with tobacco, ground tea, and sweet biscuits, and talked to us for a long time, consoling us by saying that we would soon see the magistrate. After half an hour, we were taken to another place, where after a short while suddenly the two sliding partitions opposite us were drawn back, opening another room to view. There fourteen paces from us this grand magistrate was sitting in a ceremonial robe over his black dress. He appeared to be some thirty-six years old, was of strong build, haughty and defiant both in his facial expression and gestures. He addressed us brightly: "You arrived in good weather, that is meditai, meditai! That is lucky, lucky!" After we exchanged a few words, we asked that he accept our presents, consisting of twelve pieces of cloth (which had been presented in the said fashion) with warm sentiments. Thereupon he slightly bowed his head to express his gratitude and simultaneously take his leave. As he began to get up, both sliding partitions were drawn closed at the same time in a rather comical fashion. We, however, were asked to stay a little longer, so that the women, who were behind a paper sliding partition riddled with holes, might regard the foreign visitors and their clothing. For this purpose our envoy had to part with his hat, as well as his sword, watch, and other items so they could be inspected, had to take off his coat, get up and have his clothing examined from the back and the front.

After spending an hour in this house, we took our leave with the appropriate humbleness and were accompanied by the secretaries to the large entrance hall of the house and from there led by two lesser officials to the outer courtyard. Since the weather was pleasant, we walked from here to the residence of the second magistrate, a distance of several hundred paces. Here the circumstances and all observances were the same as at the previous house. As soon as we were entertained at the large *ban* at the entrance hall with tea and tobacco, we were taken through various rooms into a well-decorated audience hall, where we saw a small room with shiny bows, arrows, and short guns and pistols in black lacquered cases on the walls. Also the other rooms through which we were led displayed many weapons, just as at the Osaka magistrate's residence. At the end of this hall were two sliding paper panels riddled with holes and behind these were the curious women who had come to look at us. Hardly had we sat down than the magistrate sat down some ten paces away from us, a fairly grey, nearly sixty-year-old, but sprightly, good-looking, and well-built man in black robes and ceremonial dress. He welcomed us, was of amicable disposition, and gratefully received our presents. On this occasion the senior interpreter, who was an old acquaintance of his, presented him with personal gifts, consisting of some European drinking glasses, and at the same time asked for a favor for the son of the junior interpreter. After we were given leave, we had ourselves carried back home, where we arrived around one o'clock in the afternoon.

Description of Miyako

Kyō, or Miyako, is the Japanese word for a city, and on account of its preeminent status (as the seat of the holy *dairi,* which makes it the capital of the whole country), it is never called by any other name than this general term. The city is located in a flat plain in the province of Yamato and stretches three-quarters of a German mile from north to south and approximately half a German mile from east to west. It is surrounded by mountains rich in vegetation and water; they are closer to the city on the southern[20] side and are pleasantly dotted with many temples, monasteries, and chapels, which we will look at on the return journey. A shallow river divided into three arms runs through this part of the city. The large river comes from the lake of Ōtsu; the other two originate in the northern mountains. The three arms flow together near the middle of the city, and at this point the river is spanned by a large bridge, two hundred paces long, called Sanjō no hashi. Then the river takes a course a little more toward the west. At the northern end of the city resides the *dairi* with his sacred family and court in a special small city of twelve or thirteen streets, separated from the ordinary city by moats and walls.

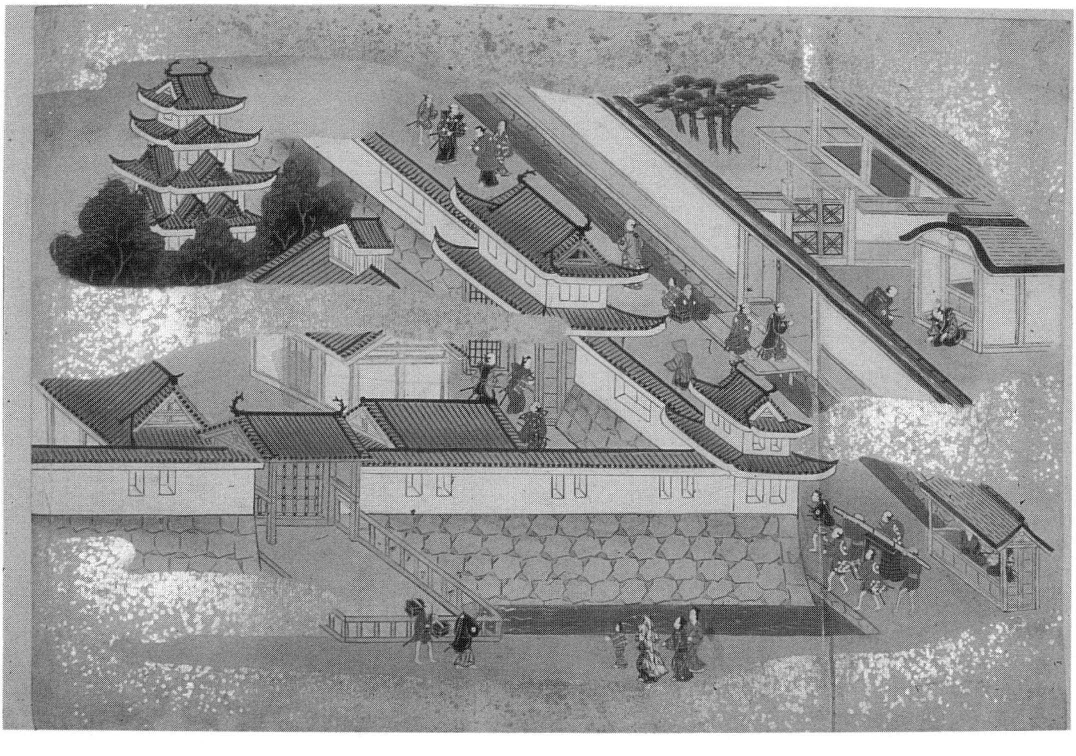

Nijō Castle, one of the fifty illustrations of famous sights Kaempfer brought back from Japan, which he planned to use as illustrations for his text. (Courtesy of the British Library, Add. Ms. 5252, folio 45)

On the western side the city is closed off by a castle built of stone, or a fortress, which was constructed by the shogun for his own safety during the civil wars of the past. Now it is used as a lodging for the shogun when he visits. The castle is laid out in a square in accordance with the drawing which has been copied.[21] Each side is one hundred and fifty *ken,* or fathoms, long, and there is a deep masoned moat, surrounded by wide, empty spaces. A square, high, multistoried tower stands resplendent in the middle, and the moat contains a delicious variety of carp, a number of which our interpreter partook this evening. Residing in the castle and guarding it is an officer with a large contingent.

The streets of the city are fairly narrow and run absolutely straight toward the east and south. Because of the dust and the many people moving around, it is impossible to see the end of the streets. The houses of the citizens are narrow, two stories high, made of wood, plaster, and lime, built as is common in this country, and are roofed with wood chips. One often sees on the roof a wooden watchtower, with water and fire-fighting equipment for an emergency. This city serves as the storehouse of all Japanese workmanship and trade. There are few houses where something is not sold or produced. It is here where they refine copper, mint coins, print books, weave the most wonderful materials with gold and silver flowers, have the rarest dye works, and produce fine carvings, musical instruments, paintings, lacquered cupboards, and other utensils, the most meticulous working of gold and of a variety of metals, especially the best steel, and from it the rarest blades and other weapons. It is here where one finds the prettiest clothing, all sorts of fashionable accessories; artificially moving dolls and toys are also made and sold here. Nobody could think of anything, or find an object skillfully made abroad, that cannot be duplicated here by a master craftsman. For this reason, goods made at Miyako are famous throughout the country and are preferred to others, even if the latter are of better quality, simply because they are labeled as having been made in *kyō.* There are few houses in the main streets where something is not being sold, and one cannot help but wonder where the buyers come from for all these goods and stores. One thing is certain: nobody travels through the city without buying some goods made in Miyako to take home for himself or others.

This is where the chief judge resides, a man of great authority and standing, in charge of the finance *bugyō,* the stewards, and administrators of the smaller shogunal towns and domains of the western part of this country. Also all the territorial lords of the western provinces have to comply with his orders when he acts as judge and intermediary in disputes and disturbances. Without letters of safe conduct in his hand, which must be shown, nobody is allowed to cross the main shogunal passes at Arai and Hakone or permitted to travel to court. The government and civil administration are the same here as at Osaka, as explained above. Without counting the people living in the castle of the small city of the *dairi* and those in the many monasteries, it has been calculated that there is a population of 1,200,000 males and 1,400,000 females, as shown by the *aratame*[22] produced annually in Miyako. *Aratame* is an investigation in which each citizen informs the officials of the number of people in his house and to which sect or temple they belong. For the pleasure of those interested we will end this chapter with the above-mentioned document.[23]

Kyoto Aratame, That is, Investigation of Miyako

tera[24] number/*kazu,* big and small ones, proper and poor ones	3,893
miya[25] kazu	2,127
negi people, servants of the Shinto gods	9,003
yamabushi	6,073
shukke, Buddhist priests	37,093
shokoku daimyō yashiki,[26] that is, residences or estates of all the daimyo, or territorial lords	137
machi, or streets	1,858
houses *ken, jūsan man hassen kyū hyaku shichi jū kyū ken,* or if you prefer 13 *man* 8,979[27] or	138,979
bridges	87
shūshi oboe, that is, memorandum *(oboe)* on the sects	
Tendai *shū*	1,009
Shingon *shū*	18,095
Zen *shū*	16,058
Risshū	9,998
Hossō *shū*	5,513
Hokke *shū*	97,728
Jōdo *shū*	159,113
Dai nenbutsu *shū*	289

Honganji *shū* West and East	
West Nishi Honganji *shū*	54,586
East Higashi Honganji *shū*	99,016
Bukkōji *shū*	8,576
Takada *shū*	7,576
East and West Honganji *shū*, Bukkōji and Takada *shū* altogether[28]	169,754
All sects together	477,557

I understand that these figures contain people favoring the same sect (men, women, children?). *Shū* = sect.[29]

(a) *Nembutsu* is the name of *namanda*.[30] This *namanda* is the prayer they recite. They are Jōdo *shū* people, but poor and uneducated, unable to read or write. A number of people tend to stick together and form a Buddhist fraternity. They take turns meeting in each other's houses to sing the *namanda* to the beating of bells. People in the same fraternity help each other very much. If one of them dies, they bury the person with their own hands, and if they lack the means because they are too poor, they ask for donations. If a rich person wants to join them, he is first asked whether he is prepared to bury his dead brothers with his own hands. If he says no, he will not be admitted. This custom is found throughout Japan. They visit the Jōd*o shū* temple. Hokke *shū* has the same fraternities.

(b) Ikkō *shū* (is very rich), has two branches: East and West. Their temple is called Honganji (*ji* and *tera* are the same). Therefore it is called Honganji *shū*.

(c) Bukkō is the name of a temple. Both are Monto *shū*[31] founded by Shinran Shōnin.

Chapter 10

The Journey from Miyako to Hamamatsu of Sixty-three Japanese Miles, Being Half the Journey to Edo, Begun on March 2nd

On Friday, March 2nd, we left Miyako again, carried in our *kago.* After nearly an hour we were led to an inn at a place called Awataguchi at the end of the streets of the suburbs. Here we were bade farewell by our innkeeper with *sake* and *sakana* (cold snacks), and after an hour's stay we paid him for this one *koban,* half that amount for his son, and a *bu* for his wife. Traveling along a narrow mountain road, we soon reached the long villages of Hino`oka and Yakkochaya, situated about a mile from Miyako, where we drank some tea to clear our heads heavy from the *sake* we had drunk. This village stretched up to the village of Yabunoshita, which takes its name from the large amount of bamboo growing there. The village also produces a lot of tobacco of the very best quality. At a distance of several gunshots from the highway one could see the monastery of Moroha daimyōjin with a fine *torii,* or temple gate, built at the side of the road, and soon afterward a Kannon temple with a large gilded *Jizō* in a six-cornered building. After quarter of an hour we arrived at the village of Iwanochaya and soon afterward at the small town of Oiwake, consisting of a long street with about four hundred houses. Here people were occupied with cutting, turning, carving images, making weights, working wire, and especially with painting and selling pictures and religious images. It took half an hour to be carried through the town. To the right we saw a high mountain covered with snow called Otohayama, and there was also a road branching off to Fushimi. After quarter of an hour we reached the small city of Ōtsu,[1] and one hour before dark our quarters for the night in this town, having traveled three Japanese miles. Ōtsu is the first small city in the province of Ōmi and has a long, central road in the shape of an elbow and various side streets. There are about one thousand farm and town houses, including, nevertheless, some handsome inns, which do not lack easygoing women. The town lies at the edge of a clear-water lake, with no name of its own, but simply called the lake of Ōtsu. The area is under direct control of the shogun and is governed by a tax collector. The lake is said to have been created by an earthquake that caused the land to sink and be flooded with water, and it was noticed at the same time that this caused Mount Fuji (which will be discussed later) to rise. The lake is fairly narrow but extends some forty to fifty Japanese miles to the northwest up to the province of Kaga, and goods from Kaga for Miyako are brought here by boat. The lake produces a great amount of fish, such as delicious salmon as well as carp, sheat-fish, and various other kinds. Swarms of wild ducks settle on the lake like clouds. The lake's excess water flows out in several rivers, one going through Miyako, the other through Yodo and Osaka into the sea.

Along the edge of the lake to our left lies a beautiful and famous mountain, Hieizan, which means pretty mountain.[2] According to the documents, there are three thousand temples and many villages in its surroundings, and therefore it manages to support many priests and farmers. The mountain has always served the inhabitants of Miyako as a refuge and safe haven in times of civil war. Nevertheless, the callous Nobunaga[3] climbed and conquered it, cruelly strangling priests and farmers and burning and devastating the buildings. Behind this mountain is a long mountain range covered with snow, called Hira no take, running along the lake, some two miles from our road. Behind this mountain range are two other difficult and mountainous highways, which are used by some of the lords of the western provinces when traveling to court.

On the 3rd of March, a Saturday, we left our inn shortly before dawn so as to reach today the small town of Tsuchiyama, thirteen miles from here. It took nearly half an hour to reach the end of the city streets. We noticed that each house had a four-cornered paper lantern in front, because a shogunal envoy had just passed before us.

Zeze

The streets of the outer city continued to the pretty small city of Zeze,[4] the residence of the Lord of Hakata, Honda Oki no Kami.[5] On the sides where the gates were located the city was surrounded by low but well-built walls (or at least as far as I could see); the streets were all constructed to run to the east and south, and the houses were painted white. The castle, situated at the northern end of the city, was half-surrounded by the sea and half by the city. It was stately and large, and, according to local custom, embellished with tall, four-cornered towers with many roofs. Not far from the castle we saw a large temple dedicated to the deity Uma no Gongen.[6] Soon afterward we reached the gate where the lord's guardhouse was situated. The black awning that surrounded it bore his crest, a character between two erect clover leaves.[7] From here to Edo the highway is planted on both sides with pine trees except where rocks or dry sandy soil makes this impossible. Moreover, at carefully measured intervals of a mile, the distance is indicated by a round hill the height of a man, with a tree planted in the center, giving travelers an indication of the distance between settlements and the progress of their journey. Half a mile from the said residence we reached a village stretched out along the road, which was called Seta,[8] or variations thereof, depending on each person's fancy. Right through the village ran the river Yodo from the nearby lake, here called Yokotagawa. There was a double wooden bridge where the water was discharged, or the river began, and it was the largest I have seen in this country. It is called Seta no hashi after the name of the village and is famous throughout the country. The two sections meet on a little island, the first section being forty paces long and the second three hundred. Both sections have railings decorated with metal knobs.

Well, I can't resist stopping at this bridge for a little while to tell a story or two that are supposed to have taken place here and the Japanese take as gospel truth. A *ja,* or dragon (which all heathens greatly revere,[9] and which the Japanese draw with feet, hands, and two horns), had his home here at the edge of the lake. A giant centipede the length of two men lived two miles from here on a mountain or high round hill along the highway, which is still called Mukadeyama after the animal, and made the road unsafe. Also at night it would go to the edge of the lake and eat the eggs of the dragon. This led to a fierce fight between the two beasts, in which the dragon won and took the life of the evil foe. In memory of this story a temple was built at this same spot in a part of this village called Tawara Tōta, and the temple was pointed out as proof that the story is true.[10] Another story: In olden times the stone column at the end of the bridge was possessed by an evil spirit, much disturbing travelers and locals. One day the great and much venerated teacher Koos or Ji[11] was passing through, and all the farmers implored him to free them from this terrible burden and ban the evil spirit, which he happily succeeded in doing. They imagined that he would have to go to a lot of trouble, performing prayers and ceremonies. Yet he did nothing else but tie his dirty loin cloth around the column and then said to the people: "My dear friends. The long ceremonies you were expecting will not drive away the devil. Only faith can do it; it is through faith that I perform miracles." Then he went his way. What thought-provoking words from the mouth of a heathen teacher!

From here we traveled one and a half miles through Katagiwara, Shinden, Noji,[12] and other little villages or settlements, and also crossed the river Oikami, which originates one and a half miles from here in the Oikami mountain, and continued until we reached the small city or town of Kusatsu. On this stretch of the way we noticed six boundary markers, which separate the villages and land belonging to the lord of Yodo from the rest of the province of Ōmi. Kusatsu[13] has more than five hundred houses, mostly situated alongside the road, and thus, after we had some tea, it took us nearly half an hour until we reached its end. In this area one finds the type of reed or bamboo known as *hachiku*.[14] The roots are made into walking sticks and are traded in Europe under the name of Rottang. They are cheap, except when for a number of years the lord of the province forbids digging them up, a process destroying the whole plant, because the roots run very deep and have to be traced a long way. *Hachiku* grows also in other areas, but there the roots are short and useless. The roots may be supplied and traded only by certain people of this village, whose occupation it is and who have been appointed by the lord of the province. The roots are prepared as follows: damaged parts are trimmed off at both ends; then they are cut into usable sections; shoots or little roots, which often grow at the joints, are carefully cut off with a pliant knife (this is indicated by the round marks that remain); crooked parts are straightened with the help of fire, and afterward they are carefully cleaned. After a quarter of a mile we reached the village of Mekawa, which carries the name of the small river running through it. The village consists of four hundred houses, which extend along the road up to the village of Tebara.[15] Tebara has some three hundred houses and in turn reaches up to the village of Menoke,[16] of which it is often considered a part; and Menoke is again connected with other little villages or streets, each having its own name.

The houses of Menoke are scattered along the highway, and the village consists of several parts. It is famous for a powdered medicine called *wachūsan,* which was discovered here and cannot be produced anywhere else. This is taken as a remedy for a number of illnesses, but especially the local colic, and consists of putchuk (one of the foreign, bitter costus roots)[17] and various local roots and bitter herbs growing in the surrounding mountains. They are ground to powder together with the costus (after all the ingredients have been dried and cut into rough pieces) and sold in three separate stalls and houses located at some distance from each other. On our return journey we saw that the grindstone is turned by four men the way our mustard seed mills are operated.[18] The remaining work is carried out by two women, who gather up the powder and carry it into the warehouse. There it is wrapped into four-cornered pieces of paper, each side the width of four fingers, on which the name, strength, and dosage have been printed in red and black letters. Each portion of powder weighs a little over two drams and is taken one to three times with warm water depending upon the person and the illness. In these houses the same herbs are also steeped in fresh water and served like common tea to those who care for it. The inventor was a pious, poor man who lived in the settlement of Tebara. He claimed that the deity Yakushi (the local Apollo and patron of medicine) appeared to him one night in a dream, showing him these herbs in the mountains and ordering him to prepare them for the use of his sick fellow citizens. This claim benefited the medicine and its sales greatly, and in a short time he rose from poverty to position and wealth. So much so that he built himself a beautiful residence and opposite his workshop a well-decorated chapel in honor of the deity. In this chapel Yakushi stands erect in a gilded lotus flower (nymphaea palustris maxima or faba Aegyptiaca prosp. alp.) covered by half a shell at his back and over his head. The head was surrounded by a circle or halo, in the right hand he was holding something indistinguishable and in the left he had a scepter; everything was covered in gold. This gilded deity was honored by those passing mainly by bending their body; others approached the chapel bent over and with bare head, rang the attached little bell, and then said their prayers with hands clasped together high in front of their head. Two of the founder's relatives have started the same business in Menoke after they received a copy of the recipe and have similarly enriched themselves. Therefore they too built a similar chapel to this patron. Next to one of them was a small house, where a priest or sacristan was employed to clean the chamber, light candles, and serve the deity with other acts of reverence. Outside Menoke our road took us away from the lake of Ōtsu, which had been close to the road until now. On both sides low mountains began to draw near, among which, on the left at a distance of half a mile, was the fabled mountain Mikami yama.[19] Here the highway had been washed away by a heavy shower, and we therefore followed a newly made stretch around a mountain to our right for half a mile until we joined the old road again. Soon afterward, at eleven o'clock noon, we reached Ishibe, a town of four hundred houses six miles from Ōtsu. We came to a fine inn, where we had our noon meal contrary to our custom, since our usual inn in the next small city of Minakuchi had burned down. After we had our meal, we continued the day's journey to Tsuchiyama, a town at the foot of the mountains with three hundred houses; we reached here at five o'clock in the evening after traveling today twelve Japanese miles. This afternoon we were led continually through large and small villages, one village, so to speak, holding hands with the next. Among them (halfway between Ishibe and Tsuchiyama) was the small town of Minakuchi, which belongs to the junior councilor Katō Sada no Kami.[20] The town consists of three very long curved streets and surrounds a small castle, which has neither ramparts nor moat, but both gates are guarded by soldiers. The last part of the town had been reduced to ashes during a recent fire. Here rushes and split reed are made into fine hats, coats, and baskets.

Today we passed innumerable people of both sexes, mostly on foot, few on horseback. Sometimes two or three people were mounted on one animal, and there were also a variety of beggars. All of them were on pilgrimage to or from Ise, a location in the south of the province to which it has given its name. They busily approached us for coins for their pilgrimage. Often the name of the pilgrimage, their personal name, and that of their native town were written on the upper part of their sunhat so that a message could be sent in case something untoward were to happen on the journey. Those coming back had the box with the letter of indulgence attached to the rim on one side of their hat, and on the other a small bunch of straw wrapped in paper, just to keep the balance.

Sunday, March 4th, we were carried in *kago* from our inn two miles over the rugged mountains of Suzuka to the village of Sakanoshita, a winding and strenuous stretch of road. These mountains are covered with infertile soil (at times peat and sterile soil) but nevertheless have several, albeit small, villages, which support themselves mainly by catering for travelers. We went down the mountains as if we were descending a spiral staircase, through a steep ravine from which a wide flight of stone steps led to a nearby high and rather remarkable mountain. It serves sailors as an indicator, inasmuch as they can tell the impending weather from certain clues provided by the clouds and mist rising from and surrounding the mountain's peak and plan their journeys accordingly. Up in the mountains we saw a temple along the path, and nearby a chapel with a gilded idol to which two monks were holding a prayer session, so that their devotion might induce travelers to part with a donation. It took a quarter of an hour to descend the mountains, and at the foot we saw a chapel with a gilded lion in front. There were some priests in attendance, handing to passersby a sacred object to be kissed and receiving a few coins in return. A quarter of an hour further, close to Sakanoshita, was a chapel carved into the solid rock, which was called Iwaya Kannon, but there were neither priests nor worshippers.

Sakanoshita, a village of about one hundred houses, marks the beginning of the province of Ise. Thanks to its many inns, the village is affluent, and it is situated at a fine and enjoyable spot. In an open chapel here, small, thin pieces of wood, with sacred, powerful words against many illnesses and misfortune written upon them, were offered for sale for a few coins. After we had some tea, we again mounted our horses and after a quarter of an hour reached the small village of Kutsukake, where roasted chestnuts and boiled *tororo* roots,[21] which are common to this area, were being sold. After three quarters of an hour we reached Sekinojizō, a town of some four hundred houses. In many houses people were engaged in turning scraped reeds into copious amounts of match-cords as well as shoes, hats, and other things, with which the children accosted travelers, molesting them with a lot of pleading and proffering. We had our noon meal in this village, after having done only four miles; and we left in a hurry to reach Yokkaichi—still some seven miles away—while it was light. Outside the village, a road branched off toward the south, to the sacred site of Ise, which is a further thirteen miles from here, and in this province every mile is calculated to take one hour (Ise is said to be thirty miles from Miyako). After three quarters of an hour we reached the town of Kameyama, situated on high ground or a flat hill. It is a fine city, with walls as far as I could see, and also gates and guards. The walls surround the southern portion of a castle, which is well fortified with moats, stone ramparts, round towers, and bastions. It took nearly one hour to reach the third guard at the end of the outer city, as the road followed the lay of the land and went nearly in a circle. After a mile we reached a small village called Morinochaya at a short distance before the large village of Shōno; here we were surprised by a heavy downpour and had to travel in the shadow of the houses for a while. From here another road branched off to Ise and is used by the Easterners and Northerners. We continued passing many villages, of which the most important were Shōno, Ishiyakushi, Tsuezuki, Obata, and Hinaga,[22] none of them with fewer than two hundred houses. However, the last-mentioned village (which is half a mile before Yokkaichi) had considerably more houses, since it had an additional settlement of nearly one hundred houses on the opposite side of the river, from which it received its name. The countryside through which we traveled today is mostly mountainous and infertile; other parts are mediocre. From roughly the last two miles before Tsuetsuki to here, we saw low-lying, fertile rice paddies as in the province of Hizen. Before we reached our inn, a shogunal envoy returning from the *dairi* rushed past us. He traveled each day at fast speed since he has to complete the journey from Miyako to Edo within eight days. He was a stately gentleman. His retinue consisted of two *norimono,* various pike bearers, one saddled horse being led, seven mounted servants, and camp followers on foot.

Yokkaichi is one of the larger small cities, with more than one thousand houses situated at a bay facing the southern ocean, which provides a living for the locals. Travelers are their other source of income, inasmuch as the town has a great number of well-appointed inns, in which visitors can regale themselves to their hearts' desire. Among the pilgrims we saw today was a lady in silk robes, well adorned and made up, leading an old, blind man and begging on his behalf. We thought this was rather strange and odd. Even stranger and odder, however, was the begging of some young and delicate *bikuni,* or nuns, who attached themselves to travelers, sang songs with gentle tunes to entertain them, and stayed to divert them as long as desired. They are the daughters of the mountain priests, dedicating themselves to this religious form of begging by shaving their heads. They are clean and prettily dressed, and their shaven heads are covered by a black silk cloth as well as a light traveler's hat to protect them from the sun. Their demeanor was neither cheeky, sorrowful, frivolous, nor smacking of poverty but modest and spontaneous, and one could hardly hope to find women of greater beauty and more attractive appearance under these skies. The whole scene was more like a well-rehearsed comedy rather than real begging. Indeed, the priests could hardly have sent out more skillful beggars than these girls, their daughters, because they quickly win the heart of the traveler and even more quickly the contents of his purse. To distinguish them from other begging nuns, they are called *Kumano bikuni,* and they are always in pairs and only on this stretch of the highway. Every year they have to pay a certain percentage of their earnings to the shrine at Ise.

On Monday, March 5th, we left Yokkaichi at sunrise (the shogunal envoy had left shortly after midnight) and after three miles arrived at eleven o'clock at Kuwana. On the way we passed through fertile, flat country, many rivers, and ten villages. Two of the rivers had bridges, of which the longer was 150 paces long. We had to wade through the others. I have noted the names of the villages in the route map.[23] The most interesting event that might deserve a mention is merely that in a village called Nawao so-called *hamaguri*[24] shellfish were fried over a fire of pine cones and were offered for sale as a snack to travelers on foot.

Kuwana

Kuwana[25] is a large city and first in the province of Owari. It is situated at a harbor or inlet of the sea and consists of three parts, or different cities connected to each other. It took us no less than three-quarters of an hour to reach our inn at the very end. The first and last cities are surrounded by stone-lined moats and low ramparts, which, however, have high masoned walls and also solid gates and guards. The central city has no walls and is surrounded only by water, since the level of the land is low and the whole area is well supplied with water. At the southern end of the last city we saw toward the west a large castle or fortress in which Matsudaira Etchū no Kami[26] resides. The walls of the castle are fairly high, dotted with loopholes, roofed neatly, and intersected with blockhouses at short intervals. The castle occupies a large square, which, however, is rounded off on the eastern side, as can be seen from the attached drawing. It is separated from the town by a deep, stone-lined moat and linked to it by two bridges; the remainder is surrounded by the sea. From the central square rises a tall, white tower, square and with a number of stories and roofs built in Japanese fashion, which give the castle a splendid appearance. The enclosed sketch makes further details unnecessary. This castle was built by the shogun Genyūin, the uncle of the present shogun, for his wife. Since he practiced abstinence from her and all other members of the female sex, he built this as her prison, where she and her nursemaids had to end their lives as innocent exiles.[27]

As soon as the rain stopped and the weather cleared after our meal, namely, at twelve o'clock midday, we boarded four ships with our luggage and horses and crossed the seven and half miles of the bay to the city of Miya. Three miles from Kuwana, the large river Saya surged into the bay at a village of the same name. Large amounts of wood from the province of Owari are floated down this river and transported to other locations.

The bay is shallow and full of marshy banks, which at low tide rise four to six feet above the water. Therefore we changed to smaller boats one hour before we reached the city and also had to transfer our luggage. The boats were pushed with bamboo poles over the bog, two men in each boat, one in the front and one in the back to keep the boat moving. As ridiculous as this boat trip seemed to us, it was, nevertheless, successful, since the bog was as soft as butter at the top and the ground hard; moreover the boats were flat and only big enough to carry eight people or fewer if loaded with goods. As a result, we reached the town in good time with two hours to spare before dark. We saw more than fifty cargo vessels at anchor, but owing to the shallows, they were moored half a mile away. The journey is much easier along the land route, even though there is still a distance of ten miles from the village of Saya to Miya. I am, therefore, not surprised that Ulysses and his Archonauts sometimes took their boats over land, as Rudbeck noted in his work *Atlantica.*[28] All the more so since this is still commonly practiced by the Cossacks, who drag their boats from the river Tanau to the river Volga near the city of Zarich. As it was, the day before we arrived, eight hundred Cossacks had, at this very place, boarded the ships they carried to float down the Volga in order to recapture at Jajik some booty from the Calmuks.[29]

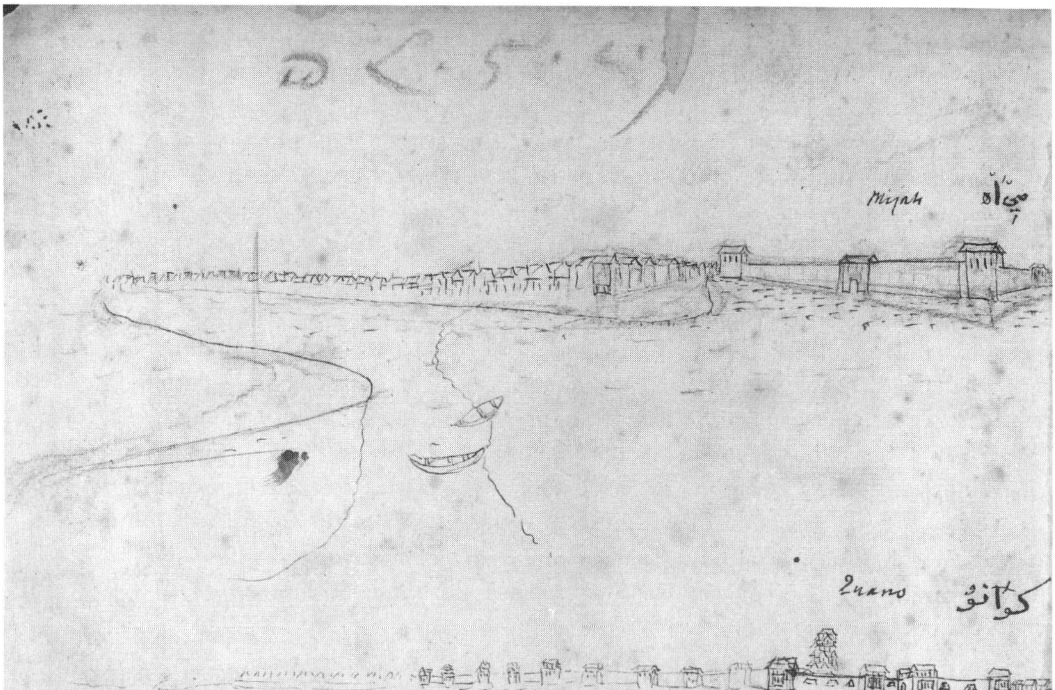

Kaempfer's sketch of Miya and Kuwana. Note the names written in Arabic script to avoid detection. (Courtesy of the British Library, Sloane 3060, folio 557 verso)

Miya

The city of Miya has no walls and only a miserable moat at the entrance and exit. It is populous and also quite large, but not as large as Kuwana. It consists of nearly two thousand houses and has, on the right, a square palace built in the style of a castle, which serves as a residence for the shogun as well as the territorial lords when they pass through. The roads ran at right angles as far as the lie of the land permitted. One row of houses extended two miles out of the city up to the city of Nagoya, which is the residence of the lord of this province. He is a powerful lord of shogunal descent.[30] His castle there is considered to be the third strongest and largest in the empire. When this lord goes to court, he proceeds with the greatest splendor, with an advance party of more than two thousand men, who travel with led horses, halberds, pikes, scythes, guns, arrows, bows, coat-of-arms, baskets, ornamental boxes, and other items of useful and decorative nature. When we Dutchmen meet him on our journey, we have to dismount from our horses, and our envoy must descend from his *norimono,* and all must remain crouched, bodies bent, until he has been carried past. The country around this area is flat, fertile, and well cultivated. In Miya we passed a small Shinto temple built four years ago,[31] which was called Atsuta, meaning three swords.[32] Its location was indicated by two red painted gate structures. In this temple three fabled swords were preserved as relics, which the incarnate gods of ancient times had used in their wars and which previously had been kept in the temple at Ise. The relics were cared for by five Shinto priests, wearing *dairi* hats, pasted and varnished black, and white choir frocks. The first two, being of lower rank, stood on a low-level floor, the next two were sitting behind them on a slightly higher level, while the fifth was at the very back in the highest position in the middle of the temple. There was another temple called Hakken to be seen in this city, which means temple of eight swords, where eight swords of heroes of old were stored. They, too, were cared for reverently as sacred objects by people seated in religious court robes.

On the 6th of March, Tuesday, we left Miya again at dawn, traveling by land, and passed many towns and villages. The most important were the following: Kasadera, consisting of about one hundred homes. This village carries the name of an important idol,[33] in whose honor passersby rang a bell and after the ringing bowed deeply, with some also saying a short prayer. Narumi is a town of four hundred houses and inhabited huts. Arimatsu is a village of one hundred houses where colored cotton dresses are made and sold. Imokawa is a village of roughly two hundred homes. Chiryū is a modest small city and the beginning of the province of Mikawa.

Okazaki

Okasaki is a fine city and the residence of the lord of this province, a place where we had our midday meal, after we had gone seven miles. The city consists of some fifteen hundred houses, of which some are well built, and is surrounded very decoratively with a hedge of bamboo, in some places also by ramparts. The castle is situated at the southern edge of the town, against a hill, surrounded by a moat and white walls set on a low rampart. Moreover, it is fortified with four-cornered guardhouses or firing galleries of stone and, it appeared, with three walls against the hill. The high tower of the residence stood out splendidly on the southwestern side. The outer city had about two hundred homes and was crossed diagonally by a large river, named after the city. Even though the river is wide and carries a lot of water, it is shallow and not used by ships. It descends from the nearby mountains in the northwest and runs swiftly toward the sea in the southwest. The bridge is made of wood, strong and splendidly built, has a length of 158 *ken*, or fathoms, according to what I was told by the Japanese, or of 350 paces according to the measurement of my servant. The distance from the beginning of the outer city to our inn, a magnificent place, was calculated to be half a mile.

In the afternoon we set out again and traveled another five miles to the small city of Akasaka. We passed many small villages as well as the small city or town of Fujikawa, situated some one and half miles from Okazaki, and between the two quite a large river, spanned by a bridge of 130 paces. Half an hour before Fujikawa, near the small village of Ōhira, we were assaulted by three *bikuni*, or young, shaven, begging women, and an equal number of young *yamabushi*, or mountain priests, who came out of the mountain forest. The former were singing, and the latter were preaching, both doing their best to scrounge a donation off us. The former received more, because they accompanied us for a while with their songs. Akasaka consists mainly of a long, built-up street, which has many inns, some of which are very fine. The city has a great supply of dressed-up strumpets, especially in the inns, who have to serve the visitors, and this is why it is also called the storehouse of whores. This morning up to noon we passed some forests or thicket and much arable land, traveling through a plain that stretched from Chiryū to the mountains (which seemed to be five miles away). In the afternoon the country was hilly for two and a half miles before Okazaki; the rest was flat and some of it well cultivated.

On March 7th, Wednesday, we had to remain at our inn till half past eight, because our old interpreter had a painful attack of gout. We then traveled seven miles to Arai, where we had our noon meal, and afterward another three-quarters of a mile to Hamamatsu, where we stayed the night. Settlements that we passed in the morning were: the village of Goyu, with nearly three hundred houses; Kofumura, with one hundred fifty houses; and Shimoji, with one hundred houses or homes. Here we crossed a bridge of three hundred paces into the outer city of Yoshida[34] (three miles from Akasaka). This city of Yoshida is built on raised ground and as embellishment has gates and guardhouses, which are occupied by a number of garrisons. It has about one thousand houses, along one long and a few short, level streets, but the houses are poor and inhabited by rural folk. The suburb at the entrance consists of about one hundred houses and that at the exit, two hundred fifty houses. Both are built along the length of the highway, and therefore it took us one hour to pass through. The castle is in the northeast: three parts are fortified with moats and ramparts, the fourth by the river. The walls are high, white, and handsome, but are fortified neither by towers nor firing galleries, because the castle was merely built to house the grand lords traveling through. The keeper of the castle had placed twenty *bugyō*[35] and high-ranking soldiers along the way to honor our passage. In this town a lot of metal was forged and sold. Perhaps because it was the time of the fair, the farmers, too, brought their goods for sale, such as wood, leaves, hay, peas, and a variety of fruits of the field.

There were no other large villages or towns on the nearly five-mile journey to Arai. The exception was Shirasuka, consisting of two hundred houses, situated on the shore of the sea, where we saw for the first time the marvelously high and most beautiful mountain of the world, Fuji or Fuji no yama. Then, after half a mile we reached the small city of Arai, consisting of about four hundred houses, near the open sea, at the straits of a small lagoon or bay. In this open, small city, where we had our noon meal, the luggage of all travelers—that is, especially that of the territorial lords—is searched by commissioners appointed by the shogun to ensure that neither women nor quantities of weapons are transported and taken back home. Women have to remain in the capital of the shogun to assure loyalty; weapons, however, if transported in large amounts, could encourage revolt and be used against His Highness. Our goods were merely inspected from the outside and not opened. Only my portmanteau, tied behind my saddle, caused problems on account of its weight, which could have indicated that weapons were hidden inside. After sufficient explanations, however, I was saved from having it taken down and opened. After we had been summarily searched, we presented ourselves and lined up in front of the shogunal guard, which treated us kindly and without further ado authorized our departure. So we crossed the half mile of the bay to the village of Maisaka on the other side in a shogunal pleasure boat. This lagoon, which they call Sanaru, has a circumference of seven and a half miles, lies in a curve below the mountains, and runs to a narrow point in the east. There another guard is stationed to prevent people from traveling around the bay to escape the search. At Maisaka we mounted fresh horses and traveled another three miles, passing few villages, to Hamamatsu, where we arrived only at five o'clock in the late evening and stayed the night.

Hamamatsu is a small city of several hundred poor houses and few, but regular streets. Its length is three-quarters of an hour's walk, and it is situated on fertile, flat ground. On the right this continues for one mile to the sea, and on the left stretches four miles to the foot of the mountains. Because of the many open stalls, the streets look pretty in the daytime. In the north, toward the center of the city, one can see a large castle, which, however, is not fortified and is surrounded by a plain wall. Because it was the day of a fair or a holiday, boys were marching in a procession with drums and bells and lit lanterns suspended from bamboo poles.

The countryside through which we passed this morning had few settlements but was flat, quite well cultivated, and especially around Yoshida and the following two miles had corn and rice fields. Afterward an enjoyable combination of bushes and pine forest stretched up to Arai. From there, too, the road was flat, full of bushes, and pleasant, but not well settled. This is the halfway point between Miyako and Edo.

Chapter 11

Continuation of Our Journey from Hamamatsu Sixty Japanese Miles and Thirty-eight Streets to the Shogunal Capital of Edo

On March 8th, Thursday, we set out later than usual owing to the weak condition of the senior interpreter and after two miles reached the rapid Tenryū River. This time the river was divided into two streams, and its banks were quarter of an hour apart. The first stream we crossed on horseback, the second in *prauen*.[1] Then we mounted our horses again and traveled as before through many villages, which are noted on my map, as well as through the cities of Mitsukedai, with two hundred fifty houses (where a handsome *torii,* or gate with crossbeams, indicated the way to a temple), and Mitsuke, of nearly five hundred houses. Then we passed over a bridge of one hundred fifty paces and reached Fukuroi, a town of four hundred homes, where we ate. In the afternoon, two Japanese miles from Fukuroi we were led through the city of Kakekawa.[2] It had suburbs at both ends, as well as a gate and a guardpost. In the north was also a large castle, which, however, was surrounded merely by plain walls, without fortified towers; inside it was embellished with a white, high, three-storied, stately tower. As we were passing through this city the following accident happened: a poor citizen was sitting in the entrance of his house watching our train with his domestics, when behind him a large kettle, where certain fruits were being boiled to obtain oil, caught fire. In an instant the whole house, and because of the strong wind also those in front, went up in flames. We did not notice the fire behind us, but only saw black clouds suddenly covering the sky, and expecting a big thunderstorm, looked for our raincoats. But the storm was blowing the hot smoke into our direction with such force that we had to flee at full speed in order not to suffocate. When we reached high ground and looked back some hundred paces out of the city, everything was covered with smoke and flames, and there was virtually nothing to see of the city except the tower of the castle above the black smoke. But on our return journey we found the castle undamaged and only about half the city—mainly the greater part of the long central road, a total of some two hundred houses—reduced to ashes. From here we rode a further two miles to Nissaka, a town of two hundred houses. There those of us on horseback changed over to baskets and for two miles were carried over the mountains to the town of Kanaya, where we again mounted our horses. After a quarter of an hour we reached the large and famous river Ōigawa. This river runs down from the nearest mountains as swiftly as an arrow with a large amount of water and enters the sea half a mile from here. As it had not rained for a long time, the river did not fill its quarter-of-a-mile-wide bed and this time was flowing in four streams. When the water is high it is impossible to wade through the river; even in dry weather this is not without danger because of the force of the current and the many large boulders the water carries. For this reason local people knowing the area have been appointed to guide men and horses through the river for a certain fee; if they let somebody drown, they inevitably incur the death sentence. The price is fixed according to the depth or height of the water, measured and indicated by a scale on a post in the water near the bank. Even though this time the water was shallow and reached barely above the knees of the horses, each horse was given five guides, two on each side taking hold of the horse below the belly and the fifth guiding it by holding it at the mouth. If the water is higher, each side has six people in two rows, of which two take hold of the horse and the rest hold on to these and each other. The river is very famous in the writings and poetry of the Japanese, and its nature and character give rise to a wide range of allusions. After crossing the river—which took nearly half an hour—we soon reached the town or little city of Shimada, consisting mainly of a street a quarter of a mile long. Here we stayed the night, having done five miles in the morning and six in the afternoon.

Today the land was flat, fertile, and well cultivated until Harakawa, and from there until the night's lodging, mainly infertile and hilly. After Mitsuke (where for half a mile we had the mountains on our left and the sea on our right) we traveled half a mile through bushes, forests, and fields, where the edges were planted with tea bushes. Among today's beggars attempting to obtain alms by various means, we met a boy of about thirteen years, with a wooden construction hanging around his neck, and above it a rope divided into eight strings, each with a flat little bell at the end. Standing on one spot, he spun around at such speed that after a while the construction lifted horizontally, spinning around him, and at the same time he managed to play a pretty tune on the bells with a hammer in one hand. He spun around at such a speed that one could hardly watch without feeling dizzy or having one's eyes affected; my drawing will show the construction in greater detail.[3]

March 9th, Friday. After we left the inn at seven o'clock and had passed through various villages, we came to a large river named Fujiedakawa after the small city Fujieda on the other bank. This river is wide and rapid and dangerous to wade through without the assistance of people who know the river and are appointed for this job. But at the moment the water did not cover the riverbed because of the dry weather. The city had two gates and guards at the entry and exit, but mostly poor, small houses of mud, most of which lined a curved street. It took us more than half an hour to pass through this street and the suburbs at the entry and exit. On the left was the castle of the steward governing this area. Soon after we had left the city a famous castle was pointed out to us on our right, at half an hour's distance from the road. It was called Tanaka jō.[4] One mile further we passed over a bridge of fifty paces spanning a river and entered the village of Okabe, and after traveling another quarter of a mile between the mountains, we came to a town of the same name. Then we strenuously climbed two miles across mountains (in which the above-mentioned river has its source) along a stony road full of turns, down into the plain and to the small city of Mariko, consisting of some three hundred houses. After we had our noon meal there, we mounted our horses and *norimono* and half an hour later reached Abekawa, a village in two parts, on both sides of a large river, which enters the ocean in three streams not far from here.

Suruga

A quarter of an hour after this river we reached the capital of the province of Suruga,[5] which sometimes is also called Sunpu, or, after its castle, Fuchū, but generally after the province, Suruga. The city is open and without gates and otherwise has rather broad, even streets running at right angles and low houses decked with a lot of stalls and goods. People here make and sell colorful paper cloth, worn as clothing. They also turn rushes and split reeds into artistically woven and plaited sun hats, baskets, boxes, and a variety of fine items, which are sometimes varnished. All are sold for a low price. There is also a mint here, as at Edo and at Miyako, where the *koban* (longish, oval flat pieces of gold worth five ducats) and *ichi bu* (longish, square pieces of gold worth two and a half ducats) are minted.[6] The castle is in the northeast, has a square plan, and is surrounded by moats and high ramparts built of square stone blocks. A few years ago, however, it lost its high castle tower, resplendent from afar, in a fire. The cause was pigeon dung that had accumulated for a long time on the top story, and it caught fire through spontaneous combustion, causing the whole building to burn down. Apparently this happens often, and therefore uninhabited upper stories are generally protected from pigeons settling there. The eldest brother of the shogun Daitokuin,[7] the natural son of the shogun Gongen[8] (who held court here), had been the lord of this province, but because he coveted his brother's throne, he was exiled in this castle for many years until he ended his life by cutting his belly.[9] The young people here seemed well mannered and well brought up, because they did not shout after us *tōjin baibai,*[10] as elsewhere. The trip from the entrance of the city to its furthest end took one hour.

Three miles from Suruga we reached the poor but pleasantly situated town of Ejiri[11] not far from the bay of Tōtōmi (because all bays have their own name). The town consists mainly of a long curved road and several hundred inhabited huts, among which, however, were some good inns. The town is cut in two by a deep river, on which some kind of famous wood, hard as iron, is floated down to the sea and transported throughout Japan. It is called Ejiri wood after this town. Not far from here near a village is a harbor, where the shogunal warships are kept to protect this bay, if necessary. A little further along the bay, on a high mountain, lies a fortress called Kunō.[12] It was built in a previous age to store the shogunal treasures, and the Japanese believe it to be invincible. It seems nowadays the rulers prefer to keep these in their castle at Edo under their own supervision. The same mountain also has gold and silver mines, but they are no longer worked. We spent the night here at Ejiri, having traveled all the way through inhabited, cultivated, level country, except for the two miles we were carried through the mountains.

Today I saw many unusual plants along the road and in gardens of houses, such as various grafted flowering trees and also different varieties growing from the same stem. I will set aside their names and description for another place.[13] Before and after Suruga various groups of beggars were waiting for traveling parties, such as the *bikuni,* or young begging nuns, singing songs; the *yamabushi,* or mountain priests, and their lectures, followed by a ghastly loud wailing sound from their conch shells; their sons, or young mountain priests, also in strange robes and also making speeches while rattling from time to time their staffs, hung with rings. There were also some lone pilgrims on the way to Ise, among them a boy whom we asked where was his home. He replied: in the province of Ōshū, in a village eighty miles beyond Edo. What immense devotion from such a simple boy, who deserves God's mercy.

On March 10th, Saturday, we left before sunrise and in the morning traveled seven and half miles to Yoshiwara, in the afternoon five to Mishima. One or one and half hours from Ejiri, we reached Kiyomi, a small city of two hundred houses situated below a mountain covered with pine trees. Good salt is produced here by boiling sand from the beaches after it has been splashed with seawater many times. Also in the villages that followed up to Kanbara, nestled below the mountains along the bay, a few people earned their living by agriculture, but mostly by making salt, an occupation with which the women pass their time. Also a famous plaster is produced here made out of pine resin from the famous mountain; it is sold in small pieces wrapped in bark or reed leaves. We enjoyed the pleasure of climbing up a flight of stone steps from the street of this village to the top of the said mountain, where we found a beautifully situated temple called Kiyomi dera, famous on account of various tales. Here I should not conceal the fact that in this village there were nine to ten stalls or pretty little houses along the highway, each with one, two, or even three well-dressed and painted boys, some ten to twelve years old, sitting exposed in a line in front. They were behaving like women and could be had by rich clients traveling past for a repugnant, damned sum of money. So that those not in the know would not be shocked and a dimwit might find no occasion to flirt with them, they were put in charge of selling the plaster. The senior *bugyō,* our leader, who never left his *norimono* except when arriving at an inn, sat with them for half an hour to pass the time, while we others took the chance to stretch our legs and inspect other things. Before we leave this place I also need to mention that before the village, in the pine forest, there was a small board suspended at the roadside with the following message for passing travelers: that nearby in the fenced-in area was a dead body of a person who had hanged himself returning from a pilgrimage to Ise. Anybody who knew him or had lost him could find him there.

In Okitsu those of us who were riding changed to *kago* and were carried through a fierce river and afterward over the mountain Satta (which had to be climbed laboriously like a spiral staircase, because the usual road along the sea had been washed away) to the village Yui,[14] before which we had to cross a broad, but shallow river. Here we mounted our horses again and after one and half miles we once more reached a large town or small city, namely, Kanbara. Then we left the shore of the bay, which continued still several miles toward the east, and proceeded one and a half miles toward the north (we had traveled toward the northeast for two days) in the direction of the great river Fujigawa to the large village of Iwabuchi, since it is impossible to cross this fierce and dangerous river anywhere else. The river has its source on the high mountain Fuji,[15] situated seven Japanese miles in a straight line from here slightly north of east, and the low mountains surrounding Fuji. From there the river descends with great force and flows into the bay of Tōtōmi. The riverbed is very wide but not always filled with water, and therefore stores had been erected in the middle. The river was flowing down in two streams: we managed to wade through the first, but the second was dangerous, and could be crossed only by boats called *Prauen.* Because of the difficult, shallow, and stony riverbed, these *prauen* have a large flat bottom and are made of flexible planks of wood, which tremble in the waves like leaves and bend when passing over rocks. They were first pulled up high on the bank, then pushed off, allowed to float down the river, and with constant rowing we reached the other side. Here we mounted horses again and after one and a half miles—during which we passed through many village streets, one running into the next—reached the small city or town of Yoshiwara at one o'clock in the afternoon, where we had our midday rest. This town is the closest we come on our journey to the said mountain Fuji:[16] according to the compass (which deviates five degrees to the east here), the distance is six Japanese miles in a straight line, but believed to be seven miles along the winding road to the foot of the mountain or the surrounding fields and a further six miles through the snow to the top. Similar to Mount Tenerife, it is of incredible height, so that in comparison the surrounding mountains look like low hills. Therefore the mountain served us for many miles as point of reference[17] along the way and when plotting the map.

The mountain is conical in shape and so even and beautiful that one may easily call it the most beautiful mountain in the world, even though it is totally devoid of grasses and plants and the greater part of it is covered with a white mantle of snow most of the time. The snow disappears as the heat of the sun increases until it covers only the uppermost peak, but rarely disappears altogether. According to those who have climbed the mountain, there is a hollow, hilly area at the top, with a deep hole filled with water. Formerly flames and ashes surged forth from there and this finally produced this hill-like elevation. The snow always drifts up there from side to side as it is blown about by the wind, so that it looks as if it were smoke. Since the wind never stops at the top, but is constantly blowing, it is worshipped there, and people climb the mountain to pay their respects to Aeolo, the god of wind. The ascent takes three days, but the descent three hours, thanks to a reed or wicker basket, which is tied around the hips to slide down the sand in summer and the snow in winter. The *yamabushi,* or mountain priests, belong to the order of the wind god, and the formula they repeat when begging is the word Fuji sama. The poets and painters of this country never end praising and portraying the beauty of this mountain.

After we had our meal, we went on our way and after half a mile reached the miserable village of Moto Yoshiwara of about three hundred inhabited huts, scattered over half a mile along a stretch of sandy road and fields. Here many village children came up to our horses and *kago,* asking for donations in return for their amusing antics, performing endless cartwheels and romping some twenty or thirty steps ahead of us. We threw plenty of money in their direction and watched with pleasure as they pushed each

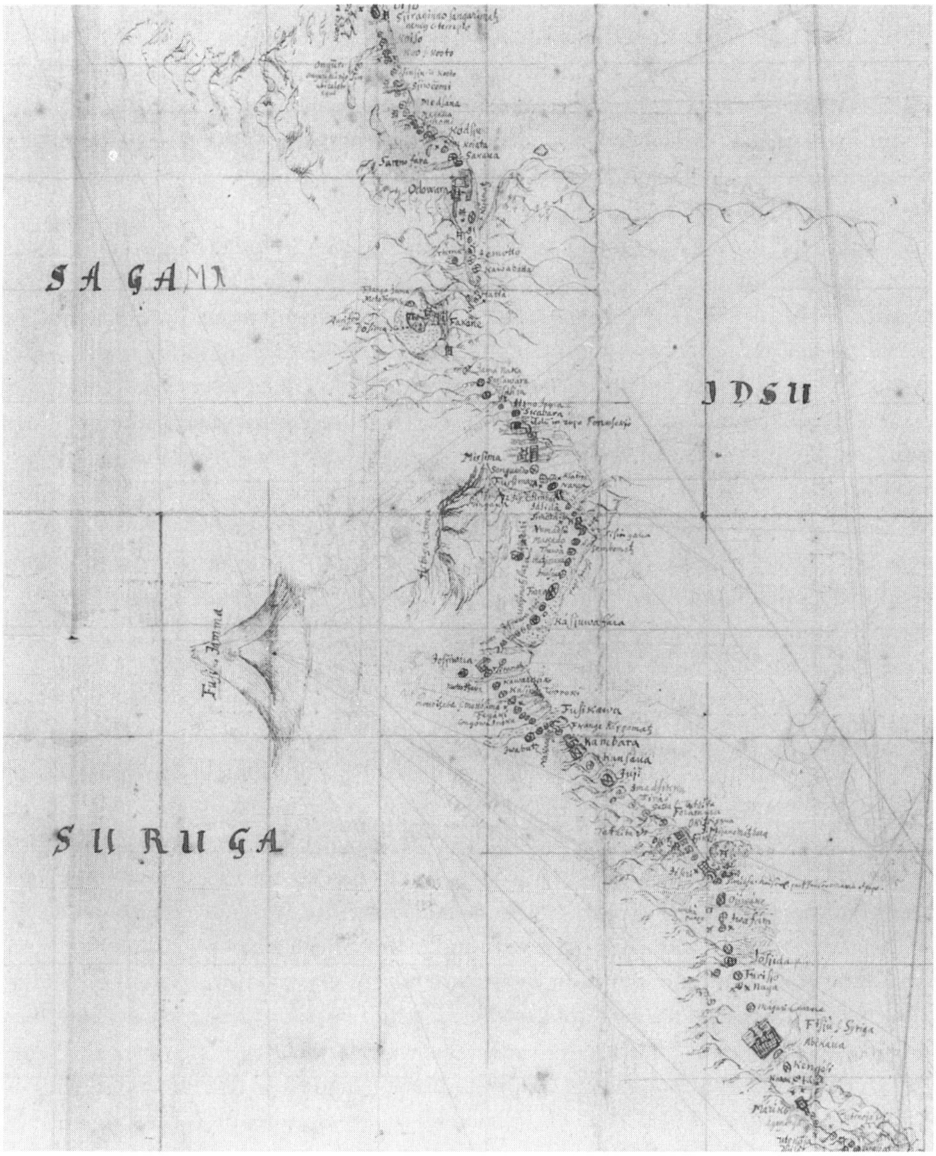

A segment of Kaempfer's map of the Tōkaidō, with Suruga *(lower right),* Mount Fuji *(left),* and Odawara *(top).* Note Mount Fuji on the left. (Courtesy of the British Library, Sloane 3060, folio 510/511)

other over snatching the money from the sand. People generally get a string of *kansen*[18] in Yoshiwara to give some pleasure to those poor village children, who often accompany the travelers for half a mile, or as long as coins are thrown. *Kansen* is a flat metal coin, the size of a three-groschen[19] piece, worth a penny. It has a hole in the middle, through which they thread a string so that they may take it along attached to their horse.

From there to the night's lodging we traveled through many settlements. The most important are: the village of Hara of two hundred fifty houses and the small city or town of Numazu of nearly two thousand. This small city is unfortified and set out like a village; the central road stretches for half a mile. Out of curiosity our servants visited a temple called Kama no miya, or Sannō miya, to see the famous large kitchen and hunting cauldron of the first military commander or secular emperor Yoritomo, or his eldest brother Yoshitsune,[20] which is kept there as an especially rare object. The kettle is supposed to be wider than two mats and was used to cook wild pigs caught on the grand hunts around Fujiyama.

Here we were caught by nightfall and therefore traveled through a number of interconnected small villages in the dark for another one and a half hours until we reached Mishima. We also crossed a bridge, forty-five *ken,* or fathoms, long, spanning a river that had its source between the mountains of Ashitaka and Hakone, flowing through hills and fields until it reaches this place, and then into the bay. Some called this river Sekigawa, but others Kama ga fuchi. The latter name has its origin in the following story: An enormously large *kama,* or hunter's scythe, which was used for the *Fuji no makigari* (that is what the old, great hunts in these mountains are called) was kept in the temple Sannō. One night robbers entered the temple and stole the *kama,* but it became so heavy that they threw it into the river, whereupon a *fuchi,* or deep place, was created in the river, called Kama ga fuchi. The scythe changed into a spirit and now inhabits the river. Mishima is a small city, which according to my estimate consists of six hundred fifty houses, not counting the outer city, and has a central road a quarter of a mile long. It is crossed by two rivers, and a third girdles the end of the town. Because they are fairly deep, all the rivers are spanned by bridges. Formerly this city had various old and important temples and chapels, famous because of the many tales attached to them, but all of them, including the city, burned down in 1686, and in the meantime the city has been rebuilt from the ashes far more beautifully than before. A famous temple that had burned down was rebuilt as before with a large courtyard paved with square stones; we inspected and described it on our second journey.

Today we traveled through a poor and mountainous area up to Kanbara. From there until Yoshiwara, and especially in the area around this town, we passed through a fertile plain with rice paddies which, however, afterward soon turned sandy and infertile, and then again changed to medium-quality soil.

The 11th May, Sunday, we left after sunrise and were carried for eight miles in *kago* across the mountains of Hakone through the villages marked on the map to the city of Odawara. In the morning we went four miles up the mountains: the ground was mainly bare or sometimes covered with reeds and reed grasses. This is an area where my

Japanese *dōchūki*,[21] or travel guide, advises the traveler to be careful. When we reached the highest point we saw at the side a long boundary stone marking the beginning of the domain of Odawara and separating the province of Izu from Sagami. From there our party again tortuously twisted down the mountain paths, and after an hour, or about the length of ten streets, we reached the town of Tōge, generally called by the name of the mountains of Hakone, and situated in the middle of today's journey. Here we had our noon meal.

One should not pass this spot without taking note of its environment and a number of other things: in particular its inland mountain lake. The town consists of some two hundred fifty poor little houses, most of them set close to each other in a long curved street at the southeastern shore of the lake. Located in such high mountains, the lake is, as it were, suspended in the air, but it is surrounded and locked in by further steep mountains so that it cannot spill over. Yet Fujiyama rises still much higher in the air and could be seen from here slightly north of west-northwest. The lake's width is just under half a Japanese mile from east to west and just over a Japanese mile from south to north. I was told that ore containing a large amount of gold is dug not far from the northern shore. On the eastern shore is the high mountain Futagoyama, with a pointed shape. At the foot of the mountain is the village Moto Hakone, and between that and our town lies Tō ga shima, that is to say, the island of tō.[22] Because of its mountainous, rugged shore, it is difficult to walk around the lake, and people use small boats to go where they want. A variety of fish are caught in the lake, of which people could name only salmon (which are very fat here) and herring.[23] We were assured that in ancient times an earthquake had caused this area to sink and turned it into a lake. People prove this theory with the countless *sugi*, or cedar logs, of unusually large size, which are often found deep in the water. On the orders of the domain lord they are cut in the deep and brought to the surface by women divers. As it is, this kind of tree still grows plentifully here, and they are higher and more beautiful here than anywhere else in Japan. The air here is cold and heavy, sultry and unhealthy, so that no outsider can last very long without damaging his health. There are neither flies nor mosquitos, and it is pleasant to sleep in summer but uncomfortable to live here in winter. General Camphuis[24] told me that it was here and nowhere else that he acquired his bodily weakness.

At the end of the town, where the road is very narrow, we stopped at a shogunal guardpost, called *goseki sho*,[25] which, like that at Arai, stops travelers from passing with either arms or women. But it is stronger and more important than the previous one, since this area is, so to speak, the gateway to Edo, which those from the western provinces cannot avoid. Palings and strong gates close off the road before and after the guardpost, and it is fortified naturally by rough mountain cliffs on the right and the lake on the left. Having eaten, we set out again and descended the mountains to our overnight stop through a delightful gorge, full of rivers and cliffs and a variety of beautiful plants. Thus we first passed the shogunal guardpost at the end of the village, where all the Japanese got out of their baskets and off their horses and with bare heads submitted to a body search and inspection of their luggage, which, however, was carried out only superficially. If the guards suspect a woman in disguise, a thorough search conducted by a woman has to take place. A private individual traveling to Edo must present a pass, without which he is imprisoned for three days and then sent on his way. Just outside the gate, on the shore, stood a row of five poor little wooden chapels. The first two had a carved bust of an old woman on their altar and in each sat a priest or a monk, playing the *namanda*[26] on a bell; that is to say, he hit a flat little bell with a hammer, intoning the *namanda* in a most miserable howl in honor of Amida and for the souls of the dead. Those on foot in our train threw the priests some *kansen* or pennies, whereupon each of them received a piece of paper with letters written on it. Baring their head, they took the paper to the shore and fastened it near the water with a stone, because people believe that here under the water is the prison or inferno of children who died before they reached the age of seven and must do penance until they reach salvation. Since these priests teach that the souls obtain relief, if not salvation, when a piece of paper with certain names and sacred characters is cleansed by water, people want to take the occasion to do a good deed, perhaps for their own or related children, believing that as soon as the waves wash away the letters, the souls will also enjoy refreshment. I have seen the priests themselves do a similar washing of small boards with characters. The place of the imprisoned souls of children is called Sai no kawara, and it was marked with natural stones, piled in pyramids on the shore of the lake. Beyond the said chapels is the small temple Hakone Gongen, which is famous for various rare items that are kept and exhibited in the temple.[27] There are four sabers, large and small ones with the handles made of *sowaas*[28] inlaid with gold, one rusted in its sheath from blood. They were used in ancient times by certain war heroes (whose names and stories I will omit) for great deeds. There were also two delightful naturally grown coral stones, two horns of horses, each being two *sun* and six *bu*[29] long and as wide, two unusual shells, two stones, one of which had been found in a cow, the other in a deer, a heavenly *ama*-woven robe,[30] which is worn by angels and with which they can fly, a comb belonging to the first secular ruler, Yoritomo, marked with the insignia of his lord, a little bell carried by Kōbō Daishi, the founder of the N. sect,[31] which he used when he prayed, a letter in the hand of Tokimune.[32] Each of these rare objects (which are called Gongen's treasures) has, owing to the awe with which it is regarded, received its own name, by which it is referred to.

From there we descended for a good mile a winding, stony road, next to and below the mountain Futago. Looking around at one of the trees serving as a milestone, we noticed on our right a beautiful mountain called Komeyama, thickly covered with tall trees, and a strange waterfall up above on our left. Here the water from the above-mentioned lake was bursting forth out of the rock of the mountain Futago in three separate places and, joined by other small streams coming from the side, turned into a river with plentiful water. In this narrow valley the river was soon flowing next to our path, but it soon appeared below us (at a horrible depth), running down toward the sea with great noise. The path was always narrow and often descended from the stony crest of the mountain; it was also twisting much more and far more precipitously than the one we had climbed in the morning. But at the same time it was very scenic inasmuch as in the distance, slightly north of east, one could see the sea between the mountains, framed by the tall rocks of the mountains covered with green trees and all sorts of plants.

Doctors believe that the herbs in this area are especially effective and they are gathered for medicinal use. Among them the *Adiantum* or Venus-hair plant is frequently found with shiny, purplish-black ribs. It is far more efficacious than the common variety found in other places, and so no one travels over these mountains without taking a supply for his personal medicine chest. Because of its superior potency, the plant is called by no other name than simply the general term of Hakone *gusa,* that is, the herb of Hakone.

The most important places we passed this afternoon are: Hata,[33] a village of about one hundred houses, where the small stream Ōsawa was flowing into the above-mentioned river from the right. The river became so large that soon afterward it was spanned—and crossed by us—by three bridges in a row, each nine fathoms long. After the village on our right came the temple Sawa no Tera of the Zen sect. Yumoto, which means warm water, is a dispersed village consisting of two parts. It has its name from the hot-water spring, which has its source beyond the river to the right in a bush. The spring flows into another fairly sizable stream, and then the water runs into the river. Behind the village is Sōunji[34] temple and in the village a double Jizō temple with a number of Jizō columns in front.[35] At this temple they pointed out a miraculous imprint of a right foot on a horizontal stone, made by a son who valiantly revenged the injustice and death suffered by his father. The story or fable is not worth quoting.[36] Iryūda, a small village, to the left of which was a splendid temple situated on a square paved with hewn stones, called Jōtaiji. On one side of the temple was a beautiful fountain and on the other a board with characters written in gold. But in front of the latter was a stone gate called Chōkōzan with writing in gold at the top. Kazamatsu,[37] a poor village, to the right of which, across the river, was a green mountain mentioned in stories, called Ishigakiyama. Here Taikō stood with his armies. The mountain is also know as Shiroyama, which means castle mountain, after the fortifications that Yoritomo built here. From the village a path branched off to the left up a high hill, called Odawara ishi[38] after its famous quarry, where fine stone is quarried; it is transported to Edo, where it is turned into containers for hot coals with which people warm their feet.

A quarter of a mile after the village we arrived at half past four in the afternoon at Odawara no ichi or the outer part of Odawara, a city very pleasantly situated by the sea. The city begins where one hears the sound of the rushing water of the river, between mountains that are covered with green trees and stretch down to the shore on the right side. But on the left the mountains give way to a fertile plain one German mile long. Outside, the city has gates, guards, and a neat, short moat on both sides. Inside, it has clean and regular streets and a broad central thoroughfare. The city stretches lengthwise and more than half an hour is required to pass through the inner and outer quarters. There are roughly one thousand small, but well-built, houses, mostly white, many of them built around squares and in small decorative gardens. In the northern part of the city, the residence and castle of the domain lord was resplendent with its new, white, three-storied tower. The city's temples were in the same direction, on the slopes of the mountains.

Empty stalls indicated a lack of trade and manufacture from which this place suffers, in spite of its closeness to the sea. But the locals do produce the perfumed catechu[39] and turn it into tablets, pictures, flowers, and a variety of shapes and pack it in delicate boxes. It is offered for sale for daily use, mainly by women, because it strengthens the gums and produces good breath. The Dutch and the Chinese import the condensed juice into Japan, and after it has been cleansed and mixed with ambergris, camphor from Borneo, and other substances at Miyako or Odawara, they purchase it again and export it. The elegant dress and refined appearance of the citizens, especially the courtly demeanor of the women, well demonstrated that the people living here are high-ranking and rich, living off stipends and not trade, and have settled here because of the city's pleasant situation and healthy air. The young men were—as at Hakone—rather mischievous and showed their bad upbringing with importune shouts at us. The city and the domain used to belong to the house of Mino Sama, with its last owner being Inaba Mino no Kami, but now it belongs to the shogunal senior councilor Kaga Sama.[40] From here we sent word of our impending arrival to our innkeeper at Edo.

On the 12th March, Monday, we left early and in the morning traveled eight miles to Fujisawa. Soon after we had left Odawara we came to the river Sakawa, which was at the most only three feet deep, but very powerful; when the water rises, this river is so mighty that its banks have been raised and are fortified against destruction with bushes and bags of stones. We crossed the river in flat-bottomed boats and passed in a row the large villages of Sakawa and Kōzu, each with roughly a hundred houses, as well as Maegawa and Mezawa of some two hundred houses. Before reaching the latter, we were led over a bridge fifty paces long. One hour later we passed the small city of Ōiso of several hundred houses, and half a mile further the town of Hiratsuka of over three hundred houses. Before Hiratsuka we crossed a river of the same name and a bridge of a hundred paces. Half a mile further we reached the village of Banyū[41] of about a hundred houses, next to a large river of the same name which is famous among the Japanese. The river roared toward the sea beyond, descending with terrible force. Even though the depth of the water was low enough to wade through, the fast current made this impossible. Therefore we once again used the flat-bottomed boats; with their thin and flexible planks adjusting to the short waves, they are easy to manipulate on a flat bank. The mountains on our left had sometimes been close to the road and sometimes could be seen only at a distance, but here they stopped and an immeasurable plain stretching to Edo opened up in front of us. After we crossed the river, we continued through a desolate area (where, however, the villages of Machiya, Nangō, and Kowada tried to eke out a living along the road) up to the big village of Yotsuya. A mile from Yotsuya, opposite the village of Kowada, close to the shore, a remarkable sharp-pointed rock rose from the sea, looking like a pyramid from afar. And one mile from the shore to the south was the famous robber island of Kamakura, which means "cushion." It looks as if the island is small, round, with a circumference of less than a mile, covered with trees, level but of some height, so that we saw it already from a distance. When high-ranking men have fallen out of favor, they have been seated on this island, and once seated on this cushion, they must rest there for the rest of their lives.[42] The shore of the island is steep and full of rocks, like Hachijō, which makes it impossible to climb up or down. Those arriving and other necessities come by boat and are heaved up with a crane, and once the vessel is emptied, it is lowered again with the help of the same machine.[43] A mile from Yotsuya we arrived at the small city of Fujisawa, where we took our noon rest. But since the inn we normally use was occupied, we had to stay in another. This small city consists of a street half a mile long and is crossed by a river flowing into the ocean a quarter of a mile from here. We had the ocean at our side all day, but here the road turns away from the shore, for the sea runs around a mountainous promontory or cape[44] for roughly six miles south-southeast. Therefore for the next four miles of our journey we had nothing but land on both sides of the road, until at Hodogaya we once again came to the sea. From there our route followed the uneven coastline up to Edo.

Before leaving this place, I must mention that at the outskirts of the same we passed a monastery where there was among other idle rice gluttons an eighty-year-old, grey priest, a native of Nagasaki. He had traveled throughout Japan as a pious beggar to visit all the temples and with this sanctimonious life had risen in the esteem of the common people to such an extent that they canonized him and revered him as a saint while he was still alive. He had his image carved in stone, and after his death it was worshipped as an idol.[45] Those in our train who were fellow countrymen of his went to the monastery during our meal to pay their pious respects to this saint. The priest was more successful than Alexander the Great, whom people refused to worship as a god while he was alive.

After we had lunch, we went on to Kanagawa. Two miles after Fujisawa we reached the small city of Totsuka, consisting of nearly five hundred houses, including the outer city, located on both sides of the river. We took half an hour to pass through the curved central road. Two miles further was the small city or town of Hodogaya. It had several hundred houses on a long street, which first ran to the east and then to the northeast. A recent blaze had reduced many houses to ashes. This small city was again situated on the sea; a river, after crossing the city, ran into a narrow bay, which provided safe anchorage for pleasure boats, and several were moored in the mouth of the river. Here we were overtaken by the dark but traveled another mile along the shore by the light of the moon, reaching the small city of Kanagawa at nine o'clock. We spent the night here, having traveled five miles this afternoon. This town consists of a street half a mile long with some six hundred houses. The town has the name of a river, but there is none.[46] Drinking water was scooped from several holes at the entrance of the city where the water collected. The holes had been made at the foot of a mountain or long hill. The water was of very light color but somewhat brackish. At the nearby bay, muddy silt was exposed after the water had receded.

The road we traveled today was full of people and villages and was fertile. The area was mainly flat or hilly, but rather fertile. In many places the fields were laboriously covered with straw ropes attached to stalks of reeds to scare away the birds. It looked like fine scaffolding.[47]

Tuesday, 13th March, we left before dawn and traveled six miles not far from the shore, through a low-lying, mostly fertile region with many rivers and villages, until we reached our inn at the shogunal capital of Edo. The settlements that have names and are considered most important are: the village of Shinjuku,[48] of about one hundred fifty houses, close to Kanagawa; after one and a half miles, the small city of Kawasaki, with more than three hundred houses, where we crossed a gentle, deep river in *prauen* to the small village of Rokugō on the other bank. Here are kept a lot of boats that are used for fishing in the ocean. One and half miles further we arrived at a small fishing village called Suzu no mori, where we stopped for a while to stretch our legs. This place is famous for its harvest of mussels, which are particularly plentiful on these shores, since the seabed is very slippery and shallow between Kanagawa and Edo. Consequently it is exposed at low tide in many places, and then the mussels, sea slugs, and seaweed (alga) are carefully collected for human consumption. I saw how the alga was prepared in the following way: the collected mussels were covered with two kinds of seaweed. One kind was green and delicate, and the other was somewhat rust-colored or reddish and broad-leafed. Both kinds were pulled off and sorted and then both well rinsed in a bucket of fresh water. The green seaweed was then placed on a board and cut up finely with a large knife, like tobacco. It was rinsed again and put into a two-foot-square wooden sieve. Water was splashed over it several times, which packed it down more solidly, and then it was brushed or pushed onto a comb or grid made of reeds. It was gently patted down by hand and set in the sun to dry. The reddish kind, of which there was little, was left uncut but otherwise treated in the same way and formed into cakes. When they were dry, they were gathered up and wrapped for sale. At the end of that village stood a Hachiman or Mars temple,[49] in the middle of which was a black smooth stone that people call the famous Suzu no ishi, that is, the stone of Suzu.[50] The stone was placed knee high on a bamboo structure and shown to pious travelers to shore up belief in a heathen legend. At the back, chains of cut and plaited white paper were suspended from above and spread out in such a fashion that one was not able to make out anything behind the stone. At the top of the back wall, a bare sword was suspended horizontally, together with two carved small figures of horses, which formed part of the said legend.

Shinagawa

Half a mile from there is the beginning of Edo's suburb of Shinagawa, which is said to be two miles from Edo, or rather from Edo's main bridge (called Nihonbashi, that is, the bridge of Japan). However, Shinagawa is connected to Edo as Fushimi is to Miyako and is therefore considered a suburb. At the entrance to Shinagawa, the execution ground was an ugly sight for the traveler: several human heads and disfigured bodies were lying thrown together with cadavers of dead beasts. A large emaciated dog was rummaging with its hungry snout in a decaying human body. Also many dogs and crows were sitting nearby; they had already satisfied their appetite at this food stall and would again and again find a free meal here.

Shinagawa carries the name of a small river flowing through the settlement and consists mainly of one densely settled, curved street, with the sea on the right and a long hill covered with temples on the left. A few short secondary roads lead to the temples. The temples are fairly big, situated pleasantly, and have gilded idols inside and large, carved images outside. They have tall gates, and flights of stairs built of stone, and one of them was also embellished with a four-storied tower, but they cannot compare with the splendid stone structures of our great Christian churches in Europe. At the entrance to this small city on the left was a large mansion, perhaps that of a nobleman, surrounded by a wall and many other buildings and houses.

After we had traveled three-quarters of a mile through Shinagawa, we entered a small inn, pleasantly located by the sea, for refreshments and to prepare ourselves for the entry into the city. From the inn one could see right across the city with its tall buildings, as well as the large harbor with several hundred vessels and boats. The smallest vessels were closest to the city, and the bigger a ship, the further it was away, up to the large barges and merchant vessels, which were anchored at one and two miles' distance, because shallows prevented them from coming any closer. Because of the beautiful view, the inn is often visited by sons of high-ranking lords, who come incognito, according to the innkeeper. After we spent an hour eating Japanese food and decorating our horses, we set out again. Here the *bugyō* left his *norimono* and mounted a horse, because people of his rank are not permitted to use a *norimono.* We traveled another quarter of a mile through the rest of Shinagawa to the actual and proper suburbs of Edo. The latter were a continuation of the former, and the border was indicated with a poor guardhouse. Here the sea was so close that there was room only for a single row of small houses below the steep hills to the left as the road followed the uneven curve of the shore. But soon the road was doubled up by various other, irregular streets of immeasurable length, which after half an hour's ride became more regular, smoother, wider, and more beautiful. This fact, and the crowds of people, assured us that we had arrived in the city proper.

At the beginning of the city we rode through the fish market, where a variety of seaweed, mussels, slugs, jellyfish, and fish were collected and sold for human consumption. We stayed on the large central road, which runs through the whole city in a northerly direction, though with some curves. We crossed a number of handsome wooden bridges and muddy ditches or rivers, which, similar to a number of other crossroads, were running toward the shogunal castle on our left and toward the sea on our right. Among the bridges is one that is forty-two fathoms long and famous throughout the country, because it is used as the fixed central point from which the distance of all major roads and settlements is calculated. Because of the high esteem in which it is held, the bridge is called Nihonbashi, that is to say, the Japanese bridge. It appears to be some six hundred paces from the outer castle moat, from where the river, which it spanned, was flowing. On the main road, which is roughly fifty paces wide and runs through the whole city in a curve toward the north, we came across an incredible turmoil of people: convoys of high-ranking lords and courtiers, women in beautiful robes in sedan-chairs, and among others a procession of a company of firefighters of nearly one hundred men, on foot and in European military formation, clad in local brown leather coats as protection against the fire. Some carried long pikes, others long hooks over their shoulders as fire equipment, and their captain or leader rode in the middle. We saw many fine stalls: those of merchants and cloth dealers, medicine dealers, traders in idols, book sellers, glass blowers, pharmacists, and people crying out their wares. The stalls were in the entrance of houses under the outer roof, and few were on the street. They were half-covered with a black cloth suspended from above, and the goods were marked carefully with curious signs attached to them. As we passed through, hardly anybody came out into the street to watch as in other cities, perhaps because in this populous city with the shogunal court, people are not interested in such trifling matters.

After we had traveled a good mile along the central road in the orderly part of the city and passed fifty crossroads on both sides, we turned right into the last of these and came to occupy the upper story of a rear building situated on the left at the head of the street, near a wooden clock tower where the time was rung.[51] To reach our quarters we had to walk through a narrow corridor. We arrived at one o'clock in the afternoon, having completed the journey in twenty-nine days.

Chapter 12
Description of the City and the Castle of Edo, Some Events That Took Place There, Our Audience and Departure

The City of Edo

Edo ranks highest among the shogun's free merchant cities, is the residence of the shogun, and because of the grand court and presence of all the noble families of the country, is the largest and most important city of Japan. It is situated in a large, boundless plain in the province of Musashi at a northern latitude of 35°32′ (according to my measurements)[1] and is connected to a long bay, rich in fish and shellfish, which is bordered on the right by Kamakura and the province of Izu and on the left by Kazusa and Awa. The seabed is muddy here, and the water is so shallow that barges carrying freight must anchor up to two miles away from the city to unload. Stretching along the curved shore, the city has the shape of a crescent moon and is, according to the Japanese, seven Japanese miles long, five wide, and has a circumference of twenty Japanese miles. Like other cities, it is not surrounded by any walls but is crossed by several wide moats, as well as high ramparts on which trees are planted in order to stop large fires from spreading. But I noticed that near the castle these were closed off with strong gates, and it may be that they also serve as fortification for the castle. There is a large river running in a westerly direction through the southern part of the city into the harbor. A large arm of this river runs north around the shogunal castle and back south into the harbor in five separate streams.[2] Each of these streams has its own name and is spanned by a fine, high bridge famous throughout Japan. The first is called Nihonbashi on account of its size and excellence. It is the most important bridge and considered to be the center of the whole of Japan, the point from where all distances to other places must be calculated on maps. The second bridge is called Edobashi, that is, the bridge of Edo.

The city is full of people from other parts of the country, monks and citizens. Among their number are the many servants of the shogunal court, and especially the high-ranking noble families from all over the country, who must hold court and reside here. The lords themselves, however, stay only half a year, spending the rest of the time in their fiefs to govern their subjects.

The city is built very untidily, because it was not planned at one time but gradually grew to its present size. But many quarters have straight roads crossing at right angles; they are constructed in this neat fashion when a large fire—which occurs only too often—makes room for them. One sees various burned-out areas that have not been rebuilt, since in this country houses cannot be replaced as quickly as in Moscow, where ready-made houses are sold and put up again on the second or third day after the fire without any clay, lime, or nails. The houses are small and low, and, as in other Japanese cities, built of pine wood and thin clay walls. Inside they have paper sliding partitions and windows, and fine rush mats on the floor. The roofs are decked with pine chips and the whole construction, so to speak, is put together from such light tinder that they easily catch fire. Most of them have a rack or railings on the roof, which hold a bucket with water and two tufts to spread the water, easily reached by an outside ladder hanging from above. With this equipment it is possible to fight a smoldering fire in the house but not an advancing blaze. The latter is fought by no other means than tearing down houses that have not yet been affected by the fire. This is the task of the fire-fighting companies, who must roam the city day and night.

The city is burdened with many monasteries and priests, whose dwellings occupy the most pleasant spots (as is the case with Christians and all other people). Their houses do not differ from those of ordinary citizens but have a few flights of steps lead-

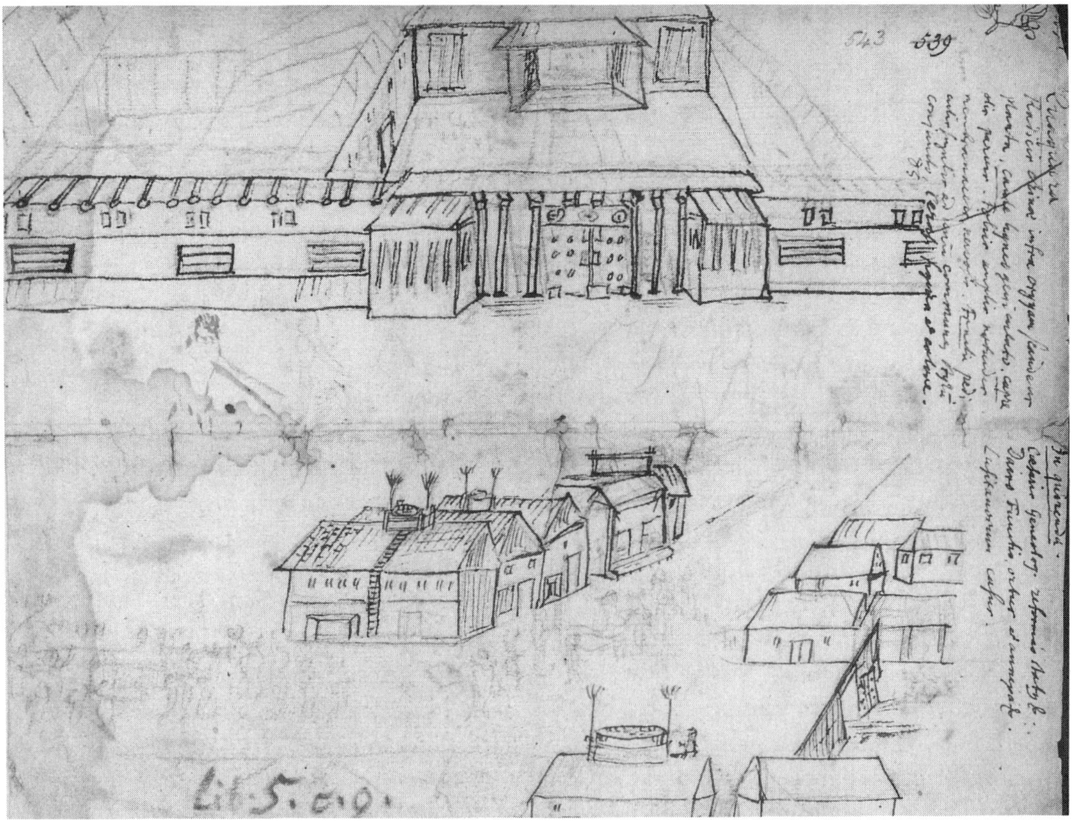

Kaempfer's sketch of a gate house and houses with fire-fighting equipment on the roof. (Courtesy of the British Library, Sloane 3060, folio 543)

ing up to them. But there is always a small temple at the side, or, instead, a fine hall decorated with one or several altars and a number of idols. In addition, all sects and religions maintain magnificent temples especially dedicated to Amida, Shaka, Kannon, and other idols. But they are no different from those that we will inspect at Miyako on our return journey. As can be imagined, this city, where the shogun and the many territorial lords hold court, has many palaces. They are closed off with stately gates and outer courtyards, are entered by lacquered stairs of several steps, and inside are magnificently divided into many rooms. But they are only one story high and are not embellished with towers.

A variety of arts and crafts, trades, merchant guilds, and businesses flourish in the city, but everything is more expensive than elsewhere because of the large number of idle people attached to the court and the monasteries and the difficulties in transporting provisions. The administration of the city consists of ward headmen governing streets, mayors governing quarters, and two magistrates who govern the whole city in annual rotation in the same way as has been described for Nagasaki and Osaka.

Shogunal Castle at Edo

The shogunal castle lies in the northern part of the city; its shape is roughly circular and its circumference five Japanese miles. It consists of two outer castles, a large fortress, which is the residence of the shogun, two fortified secondary castles,[3] and a large park situated behind the residence. The first and outer castle has ramparts, a stone-walled moat, and gates manned by a stately guard. The castle girdles a large square and surrounds half of the shogunal residence, but it has so many intersections, different moats, and ramparts that I was able neither to work out its ground plan nor to properly inform myself by consulting Japanese printed illustrations. Inside the grounds of this castle are the residences of most of the territorial lords. They are arranged along streets and are magnificently built, with heavy gates closing off the outer courtyard. The second, interior castle has ramparts, moats, bridges, and gates superior to those of the first. There is also a larger guard. It girdles a smaller square, adjoins only the front of the shogunal residence, and is surrounded by the first castle. In this second castle reside the most senior councilors, the city magistrates, and some of the most powerful territorial lords in beautiful palaces. The shogunal residence is situated on slightly higher ground or on the top of a hill that has been flattened. It is surrounded by a large moat built of square stone blocks. On the side of the palace, the walls of the moat are built up high with incredibly large square boulders, and the walls are slightly slanted like a steep rampart. At the back the walls are filled in with soil and on top fortified with long buildings and square multistoried guard towers. Also the wall itself has guard posts of stone jutting out in accordance with the art of fortification. The above-mentioned square boulders are only placed on top of each other and not joined with lime or brackets. It is said that this method is used so that the wall absorbs vibrations and is not damaged by earthquakes. Inside there is a square multistoried white tower rising high above all other buildings.

With its many ornamental roofs and decorations the tower gives the castle a grand appearance from afar.[4] So also do the fan-shaped, curved roofs decorated on top and at the end with ornamental dragon heads, with which all buildings are extravagantly covered.

The second castle is small and built like a round citadel without exterior decorations. It has only one gate. Its entrance is via the residence over a high and long bridge. The third castle is situated next to the second and of the same type. Both these castles are well fortified and surrounded by high stone ramparts as well as deep and very wide moats through which the large river has been channeled. In these two castles the sons and daughters of the shogun are reared, if there are any. Behind the residence the ground rises to a hill, and this area is well adorned with a variety of ornamental trees and flower gardens, extravagantly constructed in accordance with Japanese taste. The gardens end with a small hilly forest with two varieties of maple leaves. Their star-shaped leaves vary from green and yellow to red and are a pretty sight. The flowers and colors of one variety are more spectacular in spring, the other in autumn.

The shogunal residence consists of only one story, albeit a very high one. Moreover, it is very spacious with many long corridors and large rooms, which can be increased and reduced in size or closed off by sliding partitions. As a result of this arrangement, there are also many small patios open to the sky,[5] or small central areas, through which the light enters into the rooms when the partitions have been drawn back.

The most important chambers have their own names, such as the waiting room (for those who seek an audience with the councilors or the shogun), the councilors' chamber (where the councilors meet), the hall of one hundred mats (where the shogun accepts the customary homage and presents from ambassadors and the most important territorial lords), the audience chamber, the furniture room, and so forth. These rooms are all constructed according to the finest design of Japanese architectural tradition, with ceilings, beams, and pillars of cedar, camphor, and Ejiri wood,[6] which is patterned by nature and therefore has only a thin coat of varnish in many rooms. But in others it has been covered with lacquer or has been carved and gilded artistically into patterns of birds and foliage. The floor is attractively covered with fine white mats, edged with gold ribbons, and that is all the decoration and all the furnishings found here and in all aristocratic palaces. I have also been told that in the vicinity there is a subterranean hall or cellar, covered on top with a flat, wide tub, filled with water. For reasons of safety the shogun removes himself to this room when it thunders, because any lightning will be stopped by the water. There are also two stores filled with valuables, guarded against fire and thieves by heavy copper roofs and solid iron doors.

The rulers who have held court in this castle are the descendants of the shogun Ieyasu, the founder of the clan. They are: (1) this same Ieyasu, called Gongen[7] after his death, (2) his son Daitokuin,[8] (3) the latter's son Daiyūin,[9] (4) the latter's son Genyūin,[10] and (5) the latter's brother Tsunayoshi, the present shogun. So much for the shogunal castle or palace.

About Daily Events and Our Business in This City

As soon as we arrived, we had the junior interpreter (since the senior was sickly) announce our presence to the commissioners of the realm, as those responsible for foreign affairs, as well as the Nagasaki magistrate in residence here. This governor, Genzaemon (who received the title and name of Settsu no Kami for the measures he took in 1685 to ensure greater benefit for the country from foreign trade),[11] sent an order to our *bugyō*, or leader, that same night, instructing him to lock us up carefully in our rooms and permit no one to enter except our personal servants. Our rooms were isolated from all other human beings, as it were, situated on the upper floor of a rear building. The only access from the road was through a long, closed-off corridor; even the stairs were sealed off with locked doors at both ends. The whole story was closed off by walls on three sides. My room had only a small window high up in the wall, which pathetically gave me merely a view of the midday sun at its height. When we arrived, we heard that four days earlier forty streets consisting of four thousand houses each had been reduced to ashes. Also that evening a fire broke out one and a half to two miles toward the east of our inn, but it was extinguished after the loss of only a few houses.

On March 14th the commissioners and Settsu no Kami sent their kind regards and informed us that they had notified the councilors of our arrival. Today we opened up the presents for the shogun and the others in the presence of our leader and one of the *bugyō* of Settsu no Kami and ordered the appropriate little boxes for the aloes-wood and camphor from Borneo, which were part of the presents.

On March 15th two dressmakers sewed the European cloth for the shogun into the customary folded shape. Bottles to draw off the vintent[12] and the Spanish wines were ordered, as well as wood or pine tables, upon which the cloth is presented. Our leader returned from Settsu no Kami with the order not to permit any outsider to visit us before the audience without his personal permission. That night we again noticed a fire two miles from here, but it did not cause much damage.

March 17th. Our leader, or *bugyō*, came with news from Nagasaki that already fifteen days after our departure twenty Chinese junks with merchandise had arrived. At the same time he enjoined us to ensure that no scraps of paper with European letters were among the dirt thrown out of the window after sweeping the rooms. This morning we saw a fire in the vicinity of our lodging.

On March 18th Spanish vines and vintent were broached into long bottles and flasks, aloes-wood and camphor were put into small boxes, and everything was ordered in the way it was to be presented to His Majesty during the audience. Tonight a fire started one and a half miles, or, in a straight line, one mile, away from here to the west while a strong wind was blowing from the north. It was extinguished in four European hours, after twenty-five streets or six hundred houses (which are very large there) had burned down. It is supposed to have been started by fire-raisers, of whom two were caught.

On March 20th we learned that Matsudaira Inaba no Kami, who was made chief judge at Miyako,[13] has left after his appointment together with another gentleman carrying presents for the *dairi;* this gentleman is to introduce him to the people. Settsu no Kami sent a message today through one of his servants raising our hopes that the audience might take place on March 28th. At the same time, he admonished us to stay healthy and be prepared for that time.

On March 21st our senior interpreter called on the lord commissioners and requested permission to be carried to the audience in a sedan chair. Permission was granted after he confirmed with a written oath, sealed with his own blood, that he was unable to travel in any other way. Today the mayor of Nagasaki, Gotō Shōzaemon, left again after he had an audience with the councilors on the fifteenth day of the second Japanese month and was given his leave on the twenty-first.

On March 23rd we sent our junior interpreter, Tarōemon, to the young lord of Hirado with a bottle of aquavit as a small memento, since in earlier times our nation enjoyed the protection of his father. Today, one hour before noon, in bright and calm weather, there was a terrible earthquake which shook the house with a loud sound. But it did not last longer than the count of fifty. This earthquake taught me that the country's laws limiting the height of buildings are based on necessity. It is also necessary that buildings be constructed of light wood, partitions, boards, and wood chips and then, below the timbers, be topped with a heavy pole, which with its weight pushes together the whole construction so that it does not collapse during an earthquake.

Saturday, March 24th. Even though the night had been sultry and hot, the day was cold with sporadic rain and snow. Today Makino Bingo, councilor and the shogun's favorite,[14] asked our captain for some Dutch cheese. He received a whole Edam and half a Saffron cheese from our own provisions.

On Sunday, March 25th, the presents for his majesty and important nobles at court were sorted in the hope that our audience might take place on the 28th, a religious feast day as well as a holiday. We requested the lord commissioners and Settsu no Kami to have the presents transported. The gentlemen to whom we have to present gifts, or just call upon to pay our humble respects, in addition to his majesty, are the following: five shogunal senior councilors, *go rōjū,* which means "five old people,"[15] who are: (1) Makino Bingo no Kami, (2) Ōkubo Kaga no Kami, (3) Abe Bungo no Kami, (4) Toda Yamashiro no Kami, and (5) Tsuchiya Sagami no Kami. Next are four shogunal lower councilors called *waka go rōjū,*[16] who are (1)[17] Akimoto Tajima no Kami, (2) Katō Sado no Kami, (3) Naitō Tamba no Kami, and (4) Yanagisawa Dewa no Kami. After that come the so-called *jisha bugyō,* or superintendents of temples and shrines,[18] who are: (1) Toda Noto no Kami and (2) Honda Kii no Kami. Finally we pay respects to the young Matsuura Iki no Kami, Lord of Hirado of the family of Hizen.[19] In addition, there are what we call the commissioners of the realm, or rather the Edo treasurers:[20] (1) Tōdō Iyo no Kami and (2) Obata Saburōzaemon. Then there are two Edo governors, Hōjō Awa no Kami and Nose Izumo no Kami. Finally there are the three Nagasaki governors, of whom only the first is present while the others are at their posts. They are (1) Kawaguchi Genzaemon, now called Kawaguchi Settsu no Kami, who is here at present, and (2) Yamaoka Jūbei, and (3) Miyagi Tonomo, both of whom are away.

On March 26th we, unfortunately, learned that the great councilor Makino Bingo, the shogun's favorite,[21] agreed with Settsu no Kami to have our audience postponed by a day, because the death of his brother did not permit him to leave his house before the 29th.

On March 27th, after the noon meal, we had a visit from a shogunal physician, Hirano Sōsatsu, an old, corpulent gentleman, who came to consult me about some illnesses.

On March 28th the commissioners as well as Settsu no Kami informed us through their secretaries that we were to appear in front of his majesty tomorrow. Therefore we were to proceed to court early and wait for them at the great shogunal guard to be escorted further.

Tomorrow, the last day of the second Japanese month, the shogun holds his regular audience. However, Makino Bingo used this day to get rid of us, since he will have the honor of receiving the shogun at his house on the fifth of the third month and needs extra days to prepare sufficiently. This Bingo, or Bengo, used to be the shogun's guardian and foster father before he became shogun. Now he is his most intimate councilor and the only one whom the shogun trusts. Moreover, he enjoys the singular honor of receiving the shogun's words directly from his mouth during the audience and passing them on to us. He is a gentleman of almost seventy,[22] somewhat tall and thin. He has a long, ordinary, nearly German face, has slow gestures, and has a friendly disposition. He is said not to be ambitious, revengeful, unjust, or selfish and consequently deserves to be favored by His Majesty. When this Bingo had the honor to play host to the shogun three years ago, he was graciously rewarded with the shogun's own sword, which is estimated to be worth 15,000 taels. In addition he received 3,000 *koban,* 300 *shu* silver, and some precious materials such as damask and Chinese silk. The shogun also added another 300,000 bales of rice to his stipend of 400,000, so that it now amounts to 700,000 bales. Hosting the shogun is considered an immeasurable honor, but the host sometimes ends up broke because he has to procure the rarest and the best and pay for it all dearly. When the shogun gave a ball[23] for his courtiers a few days ago, Bingo sent him the following items for a *sakana* (this word indicates a small collection of dishes, which people send each other on a tablelike construction made of pine boards): two *tai,* or sea bream, which he bought for 160 *koban,* and a few cod fish for 90 *koban,* reckoning the *koban* at five gold ducats. These two kinds of fish are the most expensive and rarest here; the sea bream (as the interpreters call them) especially are never sold under two *koban,* but are much more expensive during winter and when out of season, especially when a large banquet is being held. On these occasions the purchaser considers it an honor and the vendor his great fortune that such an expensive dish can be procured for such an honored guest. There is a superstitious belief connected with the name of the fish, because it is the same as the last syllable of the word *medetai,* which is used to wish someone good luck.

Thursday, March 29th, the presents for the shogun were taken to court, accompanied by the deputies of the senior commissioners and Settsu no Kami.[24] At court they were, as usual, arranged in orderly fashion, each on a special little wooden table, and lined up in the large audience chamber, where his majesty will inspect them. We followed, a rather poor-looking procession, wearing black silk coats as European robes of honor or ceremonial garments. We were accompanied by three house stewards of the Nagasaki governors, as well as our *dōshin,* or deputy leader, two Nagasaki city messengers, and the interpreter's son, all of them proceeding on foot. We three Dutchmen as well as the junior interpreter were on horseback, riding one behind the other; the horses were being led by servants holding the bridle and walking on the right side of the horses. Horses are also mounted from the right in this country. Previously horses were led by two men, but this has now been discontinued. After that followed the captain in a *norimono* and the old interpreter in a basket. Our personal servants walked at the side and followed as far as they were permitted.

After quarter or half an hour we reached the first castle fortified with ramparts and solid walls. There we crossed a large bridge adorned with brass knobs, spanning a river with many boats, which seemed to be moving in a northerly direction around the castle. The entrance was closed off by two strong gates, with a small guard post in between. As soon as we passed through the second gate and reached the square of the first castle, we had to pass a stately guard post on the right, where, however, the emphasis seemed to be on grandeur rather than strength. The guard post was adorned on the outside with beautiful awnings, tufts, and pikes and with gilded screens, lacquered guns, pikes, shields, bows, and quivers on the inside. The soldiers sat in good order, legs folded beneath them, each girded with two swords over his black silk robe. No sooner had we crossed this area, built up with the mansions of territorial lords (and leaving behind on our left yet another large and busy river), than we reached the second castle, fortified just like the first, but the gates and the great guard inside as well as the palaces seemed to be far more splendid. Here we left behind our sedan-chairs, horses, and servants and walked across the square with our leader toward the *honmaru,* or shogunal residence. Then we passed a long stone bridge, went through bastions sealed off twice, and climbed about twenty paces up a winding road, which was sealed off on both sides with incredibly high walls in keeping with the lay of the land. We reached the great castle guard, called *hyakuninban,* meaning the guard of one hundred men (situated on the left at the end of the above-mentioned road, below the last gate leading to the residence). There we waited for an invitation to proceed, which was to come as soon as the shogunal councilors had arrived at the castle. Two officers of this guard welcomed us cordially and treated us to tea and tobacco. Both commissioners and Settsu no Kami also stopped to greet us on their arrival, quite apart from a number of courtiers unknown to us. In an hour's time the senior and junior councilors had entered the castle, going past us either on foot or carried in *norimono,* and we were called up and led through two splendid gates closing off a square. Walking through the second, we climbed a few steps and reached the forecourt of the residence.

This area, situated between the last gate and the front of the shogunal mansion, was only a few paces wide and in addition to being crowded with courtiers and valets, was well manned with guards. Having climbed about two steps, we entered the shogunal mansion and proceeded into the first chamber to the right of the entrance. This is the usual waiting room for people who are to be received by the shogun or the councilors. The room is fairly high, but once the sliding partitions are closed, it is rather dark, since only very little light enters through a lattice high on the wall to a storage area on the right. But apart from that, the room was beautifully decorated with the ceiling, walls, and sliding partitions all gilded. After we had sat there for more than an hour and the shogun had proceeded to his throne, both commissioners and Settsu no Kami entered and led the captain to the audience hall but left us behind. As soon as the captain appeared, someone shouted in an exaggeratedly loud voice *"oranda kapitan"*[25] to prompt him to step forward and pay his respects. Thereupon he crawled forward on his hands and knees between the place where the presents had been lined up and the high seat of his majesty as far as they motioned him. Crouching on his knees, he bent his head to the floor and then, like a lobster, crawled back in this very same position, without one word being exchanged. This short, miserable procedure is all that there is to this famous audience. Nothing else happens at the annual audience of the important territorial lords. After their names have been called and they have in similar fashion silently paid their respects to express their submission and obedience, they too must crawl out backward.

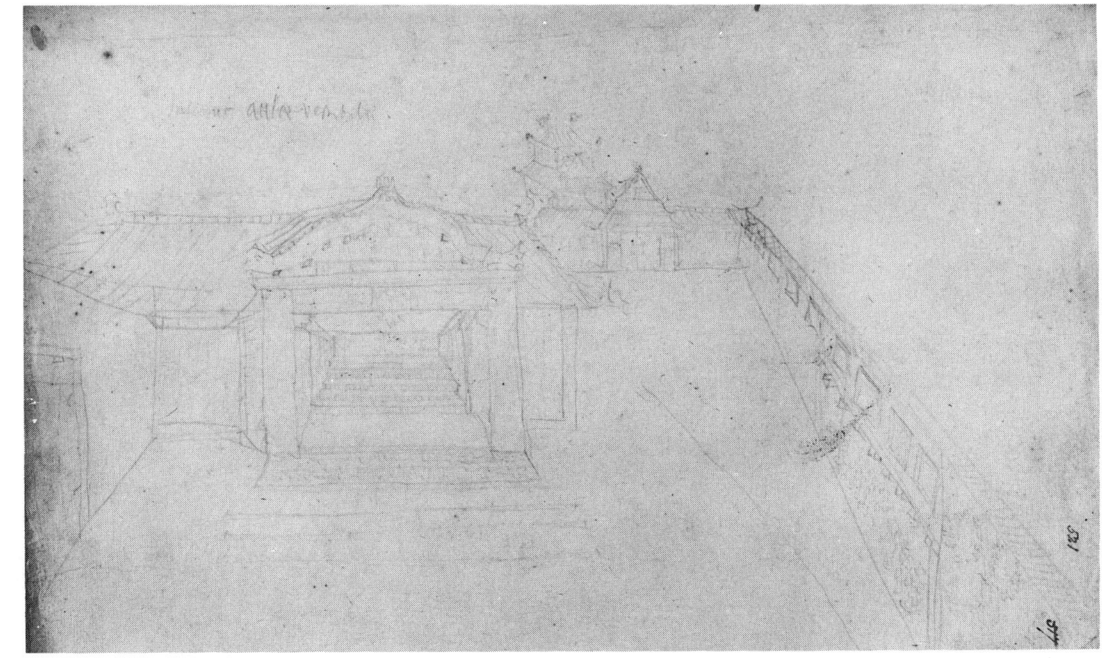

Kaempfer secretly drew the entrance to Edo castle. This is the only known realistic depiction of the entrance to the *honmaru* of the so-called Manji (1658–1660) Edo *jō*, which burned down in 1844. (Courtesy of the British Library, Sloane 3060, folio 521)

Audience Hall

The audience hall is different by far from how Montanus describes it according to his imagination: there is no elevated throne, no stairs leading up to it, no carpets hanging down, no magnificent columns on which the throne, hall, or whole building is supposed to rest. Everything is certainly very beautiful and precious, but no different from what I have sketched. In the second year after the audience, the Nagasaki governor took us to show us the place, and I used the occasion to quickly make this sketch, which was not difficult once the floor mats, sliding doors, and pillars had been counted.

The audience hall with its one hundred mats is open to a small courtyard on one side, from where it receives its light. On the opposite side are two rooms, which open up in the direction of the courtyard. The first of these rooms is fairly wide and is used to seat the councilors when they receive lesser territorial lords, stewards, and emissaries. The other, or last, room is narrower, deeper, and one step higher than the common hall. The shogun sits at the end of this room on a floor raised by a few mats, with his legs folded under him. It is difficult to discern his shape there, because the full light does not reach this part of the room. Also the ceremony takes place too quickly, and the visitor has to appear with lowered head and must leave again without lifting his face to look at his majesty. But the silent presence of the councilors, aristocratic princes, gen-

Kaempfer's sketch of the audience hall with the presents for the shogun laid out on the left. (Courtesy of the British Library, Sloane 3060, folio 512)

tlemen-in-waiting, and other high-ranking court attendants gives the event considerable grandeur.

Formerly the whole venture was concluded with the above-described appearance of the captain. A few days later he was given permission by the councilors to return to Nagasaki after the laws had been read to him and he had promised to keep them in the name of the Dutch nation. It was only twenty years ago[26] that they began to lead the Dutch delegation deeper into the palace to present them for inspection and amusement to the shogunal women, as well as curious princesses of shogunal descent specially invited for the event. On this occasion his majesty and the women are hidden behind the blinds, while the councilors and high courtiers commanded to attend the audience appear in public.

As soon as the obeisances had been made and the shogun had retired to his usual chambers, we remaining three Dutchmen were also called and together with the captain were led through various chambers to an artistically carved and gilded gallery. After sitting there for a quarter of an hour, we were led through further corridors to a hall and invited to sit down. A number of tonsured courtiers (these are religious men, doctors, and kitchen attendants) arrived and asked our name, age, and other trifling matters. Gilded screens were soon pulled up, however, to rescue us from being surrounded and inspected by the swarms of court attendants passing by. During the half hour we were waiting there the court had proceeded to the rooms of the performance, to which we were led through some dark corridors. These corridors were lined by a single row of shogunal bodyguards, followed by other high-ranking courtiers in similar order, right along the length of the gallery and along the foreground of the site of the performance. They were all wearing ceremonial robes and were sitting on their knees and bending low. The details of the site of the performance, the place where we were presented, can be gathered from the sketch.

It consisted of several rooms, some of which opened up to a central area and some were closed off with blinds; each was fifteen mats wide,[27] and each one higher than the next by the thickness of a mat in accordance with the rank of the occupants. In the central area the mats had been removed. It was therefore the lowest area, and we were instructed to be seated on the varnished floor boards that covered it. His Majesty and his wife were seated behind the blinds on the right near to us. I glimpsed the face of the latter twice when the blinds were bent and saw that it was brownish, rounded, and of beautiful shape, with black European eyes, full of fire and vigor. Judging from the proportions of her head, I imagined her to be a tall lady, about thirty-six years old.[28] What I call blinds are hanging mats made of small, split, soft pieces of reed, with interwoven silk threads a span apart. They are painted for decoration and to make them less transparent. When the light behind them is covered up, one cannot make out people at a distance. Only the sound of his voice gave us an indication that His Majesty was present, even though he spoke only in low tones as if he did not want to be heard loudly. Women of the court and the invited princesses of shogunal descent sat behind the blinds in front of us at a distance of four mats. Here and there the joints or gaps in these blinds had been widened with small pieces of paper stuck in between to permit a better view: I counted more than thirty bits of paper and therefore supposed that there were as many people present. Bingo sat on the raised floor of a special room in front of us, being on our side of the blind from behind which His Majesty was speaking. To the left on a special floor sat the senior and junior councilors in two rows according to their rank. Behind us was the gallery, as described, filled with chamberlains and high-ranking courtiers. At the entrance to the shogunal chamber, aristocratic princes, pages, and court priests were peeping out one on top of the other, some from in front and some from behind a screen. That is a description of the stage and the cast; now let us turn to the comedy proper.

As soon as the commissioners had brought us to the gallery, we were greeted by a junior councilor and led to the central area described above. There we all had to show our submission in Japanese fashion with heads on the floor and crawling in the direction where they indicated his majesty to be present. The interpreter moved closer to enable him to hear better, and we others sat beside him in a row. After we had paid our respects, Bingo welcomed us upon instructions from the shogun. The interpreter listened to the words and repeated them to us. Thereupon the captain presented respectful compliments on behalf of his superiors and at the same time expressed his gratitude for the favor of being permitted free trade with Japan. Lying low on the floor, the interpreter repeated the above for the shogun to understand. Whatever the shogun said, Bingo had to receive from his mouth, and then pass it on to the interpreter. The latter passed it on to us Dutchmen. The interpreter could have directly received the words from the shogun and saved Bingo the trouble. But I believe that—still warm from the shogun's mouth—the words are considered altogether too exalted and sacred for this.

Then the farce began, but not before we had been asked a number of meaningless questions. For instance, each of us was asked in turn for our age and name, and since we were carrying a European ink-pot, we each had to write our name and pass it to Bingo, who passed the piece of paper together with the writing utensils to his majesty behind the blind. Our captain was asked: How far is Holland from Batavia? Batavia from Nagasaki? Who was mightier, the governor general of Batavia or the prince of Holland? I was asked: Which internal and external illnesses I considered to be the most serious and most dangerous? How I treated damage caused by cancer and internal abscesses? Whether I had not searched for an elixir of long life like the Chinese doctors have done for many hundred years, and whether our European doctors had discovered anything? I obliged them with the answer: Our doctors are still daily searching for a medicine to preserve people's health to a ripe old age. He asked: Which of them was considered the best? Answer: The latest was always considered the best until experience indicated otherwise. Question: Which is the latest? Answer: A certain alcoholic spirit which when used moderately has the effect of preserving the body's fluids and reviving and strengthening a man's vital spirits. Question: What is it called? Well aware that things esteemed by the

Japanese all have long names, I replied: Sal Volatile Oleosum Sÿlvii. The name was written down behind the blind, and I had to repeat it several times. Question: Where and by whom was the spirit discovered? Answer: In Holland by Professor Sylvius. Question: Whether I knew how to prepare it? The captain ordered me to reply in the negative, but

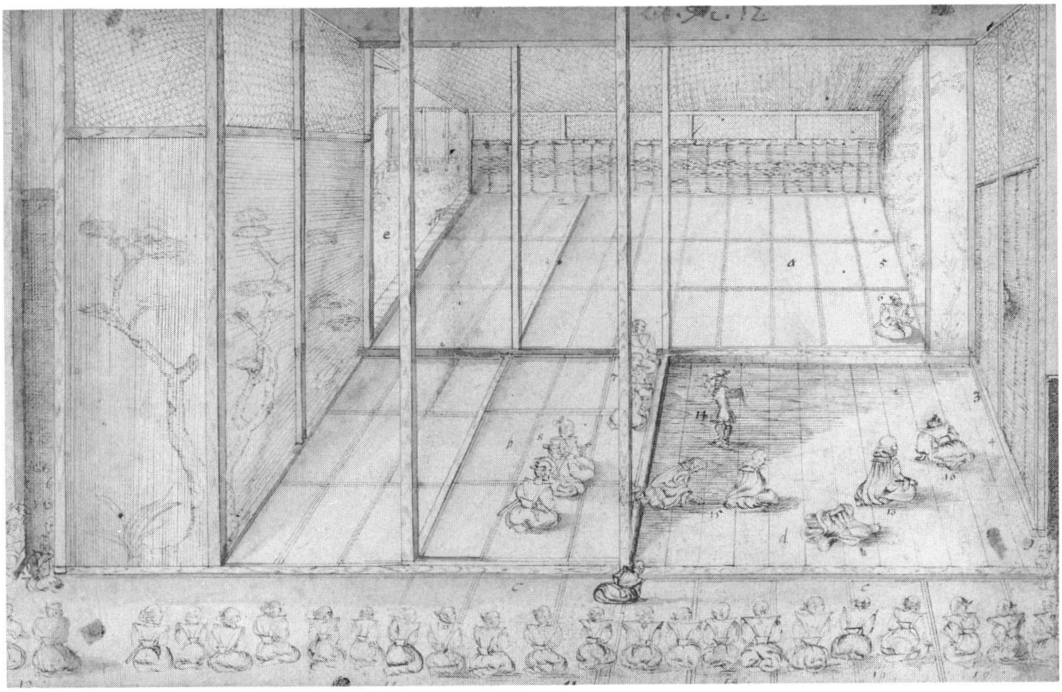

Kaempfer dancing and singing in front of the shogun. (Courtesy of the British Library, Sloane 3060, folio 514) Kaempfer's key to the drawing: (a) The chamber in which the shogunal intermediary is seated. (b) The chamber where the upper and lower councilors are seated, which is one mat lower than (a). (c) The corridor where important courtiers sit according to their rank, which is one mat lower than (b). (d) The place where the Dutch appear for their audience. Since the mats have been removed down to the varnished wooden floor, it is still one mat lower than (c). (e) A side courtyard or small open space, paved with small irregular stones, opened to let cool air come in. (1) The normal seat of the shogun, his spouse, mother, daughter, and so forth during the audience (behind the blind). (2) The highest-ranking ladies of the court, including those of shogunal blood. They had enlarged the slits in the blind with bits of paper in order to see better. (3) The place where His Majesty sat most of the time during the first audience. [Judging from the name of Outhoorn, mentioned below, Kaempfer refers to the first audience of his second visit to Edo. On that occasion the delegation was given two audiences.] (4) The shogunal spouse or daughter, whom I saw a number of times when the mat bent. (5) The normal place of the intermediary when the shogun sits at his usual place. (6) The shogunal intermediary *(gosoba goyōnin)* and junior councilor Bingo. (7) Three senior *gorōjū,* or councilors. (8) Three of the *wakagorōjū,* or lower, junior, or extraordinary councilors. (9) *Gosoba shū,* or senior gentlemen-in-waiting, who walk through the corridor and sometimes stay. (10) *Gosōsha shū,* attendants of the shogunal table and personal servants. (11) *Kōke shū,* titled courtiers of high birth. (12) *Otsume shū,* court guards, seated here and also according to their rank in the corridor. (13) The Dutch captain Cornelius van Outhoorn. (14) Myself, having got up and dancing according to the shogun's orders. (15) Two Dutch scribes. (16) The Dutch interpreter.

I answered: Yes, of course! But not here! Could the spirit be obtained at Batavia? Answer: Yes! Thereupon the shogun asked that a sample be sent on the next ship.

The shogun had first been seated next to the women at some distance in front of us, but now he moved to the side, as close to us as he could behind the blind. He had us take off our *kappa,* or ceremonial robes, and sit upright so that he could inspect us; had us now stand up and walk, now pay compliments to each other, then again dance, jump, pretend to be drunk, speak Japanese, read Dutch, draw, sing, put on our coats, then take them off again. During this process I broke into the following song:

(1)
I am mindful of my obligation
In the furthest corner of the globe,
Oh, most beautiful, who cannot be mine,
Most beloved, who breaks my heart.
Without guile and hesitation,
By the light that shone when I was born,
I gave my pledge to thee,
To remain forever true.

(2)
Why speak of obligation and commitment?
Of promises and pledges?
Your god-given beauty,
Your matchless virtue,
Enchain me,
Capture me.

(3)
Wretched me! Impudently I thought
That the ordeal of wild escape to distant lands
Would permit me to forget you,
My angel.
Yet neither Taurus nor Caucus,
Turks nor heathens,
Indus nor Ganges River,
Can part us,
Can quell the fire.

(4)
Great Ruler, Son of Heaven,
Lord of these distant lands,
Rich in gold and great of power,

By your throne I swear:
All the radiance
Of your wealth and splendor
Of your women with painted faces
I prize less than my angel.

(5)
Away with you, court of empty pleasures!
Away with you, land of immense treasures!
Nothing can give me earthly pleasure,
But the chaste loveliness,
Of my precious Florimene.
Deeply longing for each other,
She for me, and I for her.

At the demand of the shogun we had to put up with providing such amusements and perform innumerable other monkey tricks. The captain, however, was excused so that the light of authority of our superiors, whom he represented, would not be blemished. Moreover, his poised demeanor made him an unlikely candidate for such impositions. After we had been drilled for two hours—albeit always after courteous requests—tonsured servants served each of us with small Japanese dishes on separate little tables; instead of knives we were given two small sticks. We ate just a little. The remains had to be taken away by the old interpreter, carried with both hands in front of him, by him who hardly had the strength to drag his feet. Thereupon we were told to put on our coats and take our leave; we complied immediately, and this brought the second act to a close. Our guides returned us to the waiting room and took their leave. It was already the third hour after noon, and we still had to present our gifts to the senior and junior councilors as listed above under March 25th. We left the *honmaru* on foot, greeted the officers of the great guard in passing, and did the rounds on foot.

The scribes had taken the presents ahead and delivered them to each mansion, and perhaps they had been deposited in a special room, because we did not see them. They consisted of a few pieces of Chinese, Bengal and other silks, also linen cloth and black serge, several yards of black woolen cloth, gingham, pelang, and a pot of vintent. We were well received everywhere by the house stewards and secretaries and, as far as the short visit permitted, well entertained with tea, tobacco, and sweets. An audience of women crowded behind the blinds and sliding doors in the rooms where we were displayed, and they would have liked the Dutchmen to perform a few tricks but were disappointed. We performed only a brief dance in the first mansion, that of Bingo (who had himself carried home along the back way), and each sang a short song in the mansion of the youngest councilor, who lives in the northern castle. After that, we mounted our carrying baskets and horses, left the castle through a gate facing north, and using a route unknown to us, where large ramparts for the prevention of fire and moats were running off on the left, arrived at our inn at sunset.

Friday, March 30th, we rode out to present gifts to the remaining lords. Our Japanese scribes went ahead to line up the presents in the designated audience chambers. The presents consisted of Chinese, Bengal, and other material, linen, black serge, a piece of black woolen cloth, some gingham, pelangs, and a pot of vintent. On arrival one or two servants of the house always guided us to the audience chambers, passing through a number of rooms of which the first or front rooms, as well as the adjoining secondary rooms, were very crowded with spectators. When we sat down, we were served tobacco and ground tea, and soon afterward the first minister, steward, or secretary, either on his own or together with a companion, received our compliments in the name of his superior. The rooms were so arranged that the women could inspect us, and we were therefore detained with a variety of pastries and numerous sweets.

Those who received presents from us today were the two governors of this city, three superintendents of temples and shrines,[29] and two commissioners or superintendents of foreign affairs.[30]

The last two were located at quite a distance; the first one, southwest of the castle, and the other, northeast of the castle at a mile's distance from each other. They greeted us like well-known, high-standing lords: the street was lined with twenty armed bodyguards, who struck an imposing stance with heavy staffs placed at arm's length, keeping the greater part of the street free from the common rabble.

We were received in the same way as at the other mansions but were led further into the building right to the innermost rooms, so that we would not be bothered by outside spectators but be all the more at ease for the women who were to inspect us. The rooms were arranged such that, instead of sliding partitions, blinds stretching the length of two mats were facing us. Behind them these little painted house mites[31] sat and stood not by themselves, but together with friends and strangers who had been invited in such swarms that there was not the smallest space left. As soon as we sat down, seven well-dressed, fine-looking servants entered in one line and brought us smoking utensils. Entering in the same formation, they presented us a little later with some baked food served on varnished trays, and afterward we were given some fried fish in the same manner. There was also always something in a bowl such as a baked or boiled egg, and between these dishes a drink of old, strong *sake*. We spent about one hour, or one hour and a half, in this fashion, whereupon they approached us to sing a song and soon afterward to perform a dance, but we did not comply with the latter request. At the mansion of the first commissioner we were offered sweet plum soup instead of spirits; at the house of the other, the first course consisted of a piece of *manjū* bread dipped into a cold brown sauce, served together with ground mustard and radish. The last course was designed to bring good luck: slices of lemon strewn with sugar and, as conclusion, ground tea. Thereupon we took our leave and arrived back home at five o'clock in the evening.

March 31st. In the morning at ten o'clock we rode out and visited our three Nagasaki governors with only a bottle of vintent (because they had already received their presents at Nagasaki); two of them were residing at Nagasaki. The first, Settsu no Kami, met us in front of his house with quite a following, stood still, and told the senior interpreters to appear in front of him. He commanded them that we were to enjoy ourselves at his home, and we were indeed well received by him, told to wander around the garden and take our pleasure and not to think about Nagasaki but to imagine that we were at the house of a good friend in Edo. We were served warm food and strong tea like yesterday, and his brother and other nobles and friends entertained us with friendly conversation. After we had been entertained for two hours we went to the home of Tonomo sama, where we were led to the innermost and most important chamber. Twice we were asked to move up to the blinds, which were quite wide and hanging on both sides. Behind them were more women than anywhere else. They inspected us, our dress, the captain's weapon, rings, pipes, and so forth with pleasant and respectful curiosity, and all these items were passed in between or under the blinds. The person acting as host and the other noblemen present, seated around us, were also extremely friendly, and the former encouraged us to drink with affable gestures so that it was not difficult to be happy and each sing a song. The overabundance of sensuous pleasures bore testimony to the high status of this family, and while they were similar to those at the first commissioner's, they far surpassed these in intimacy. After about one and a half hours we were given leave to depart. This gentleman lives further to the north or northwest than any of the others, roughly one and a half large miles from our inn, where the city has a lot of shrubbery and hills. The third magistrate, Jūbei sama, lives at the moat in a rather poor house, where only a few women sat behind window-doors[32] near us, making do with holes, which they made by pushing through their fingers as soon as they sat down. And since the mill wheels had been watered more than sufficiently with strong liquid, and therefore were beginning to turn the wrong way, it was just as well that we left in a hurry—or rather were given permission to leave—right after the refreshments. It thus saved our very serious interpreters, unused to such mischief, from becoming upset about having to convey our tomfoolery. Especially as the acting host (not the master of ceremonies, a job performed always by a different person, a household servant), however friendly he was and intended to be, irritated us with his fastidious mien, for we considered ourselves not as merchants but envoys, dispatched not to seek profit but to gain honor. Consequently we left as soon as possible, and in the afternoon of April 1st heard from Iyo sama that our leave-taking at court had been set for the following day.

On April 2nd, before nine o'clock in the morning, we went to court on horseback as was the custom. We waited for one and a half hours in the above-mentioned guard room. After the lord commissioners had paid us a visit and greeted us together with Settsu no Kami, we had to wait as long again in the large front room of the castle, where the floor is covered with thirty-six large mats and which is surrounded by gilded sliding doors. Here we were greeted by the lord commissioners and Settsu no Kami. They called the senior interpreter away to show him the place and inform him of the nature of the scheduled ceremonies. Then our captain was led to a hall on the left, not far from the large front room and the waiting chamber, to be given his leave and listen to the usual orders of His Majesty concerning the trade of the Portuguese and other matters, consisting of five sentences. He returned accompanied by Settsu no Kami, who bade him farewell with a few words and a jovial mien, expressing his hope of meeting him again in Nagasaki. Thereupon we left without paying our compliments to the commissioners, after two hours, arriving at home at about one o'clock in the afternoon. While we were waiting or moving around the castle many sons of noblemen and courtiers came to inspect us. Among them was the grandson of the territorial lord of Hakata, who has only one eye.[33] The other day he was ordered to serve the shogun at court, and the only reason for this is that the shogun wanted a hostage as a pledge of loyalty. Others also arrived and among them one asked for the captain's name, which he had already written on his fan, when immediately an order arrived from Settsu no Kami (which shows how quickly it got out) that nobody else was to learn the names of the Dutchmen. As we left the court we were preceded by thirty shogunal robes on three trays. In the afternoon the robes of the gentlemen to whom we had paid our respects on the previous days arrived, such as: (1) two black robes from the governor Nose Izumo no Kami, (2) ten robes from the councilor Toda Yamashiro no Kami, (3) ten robes from Tsuchiya Sagami Sama, (4) two robes from Hōjō Awa no Kami, the Edo governor, (5) ten robes from Ōkubo Kaga no Kami, and (6) ten robes from Bingo Sama.

On April 3rd the remaining gentlemen sent us their robes, such as three each from the lord commissioners and six each from the junior councilors. All that was finished by one o'clock in the afternoon.

On April 4th His Majesty attended a banquet at the house of Bingo. Therefore the doors of the castle were closed, a practice introduced by this shogun to the surprise of many.

Chapter 13
Return from Edo

Departure from Edo

On April 5th early in the morning at eight o'clock we finally left this very large and populous city after traveling for two hours. The city's last three crossroads and the last river ran toward the sea, roughly four hundred paces away. Noteworthy in this city is the famous bridge Nihonbashi, which means Japanese bridge, forty-two mats long. In the countryside the farmers were hoeing the rice fields up to their knees in mud and water. In many villages tall bamboo signboards had been erected announcing that people were not permitted to use the inns because some territorial lords were expected.

Shinagawa

Today there were no human bones at the place of a skull[1] at Shinagawa, but some one and a half miles from our overnight stop we discovered a human head at the side of the road and many sick pilgrims on the way to or from Ise. We had our noon meal at Kawasaki and later, just before evening, arrived at our inn at Totsuka in dark weather and a fine drizzle. This area is fertile but somewhat hilly with a long, low mountain range toward the sea.

April 6th. We left our inn one hour after sunrise in damp weather and the whole day ran into the advance party and luggage of the territorial lord of Ki no Kuni. All the luggage was marked with the shogunal crest in gold. We met the main party at twelve o'clock noon before Ōiso. It consisted of twenty men marching behind each other with covered guns, the same number carrying large bows and arrows, and perhaps as many again with long wooden poles; among the latter marched a few with lacquered cases of firearms and swords and a variety of pikes. Then followed four horses, the last of which carried a black chair placed on a black seat with two large pike-tufts at the back and three or four black and white feather standards at the side, in front, and behind, as well as other pikes and men on horses. Soon afterward came twelve forerunners and the lord's *norimono.* We stopped at a distance of twenty paces, dismounted from our horses, bared our heads, and when he was slowly carried past us had our interpreter convey a brief message of good wishes. He in turn replied with mild gestures and good wishes for our own journey. He looked some thirty years old, had a brownish, narrow face and similar figure and a serious, yet friendly mien. After him came a number of men on horseback with pikes and some servants and then his magistrate with other people, all in turn accompanied by servants carrying pikes and other followers so that there were nearly one thousand men on foot. They somehow seemed to be crouching together and marched in total silence. This gentleman is of shogunal descent and his son at Edo is promised in marriage to the eleven-year-old daughter of His Majesty.[2] We arrived at our inn at five o'clock in the evening, trailing a large convoy of ill-mannered boys, shouting and running after us rowdily and maliciously.

On April 7th we were carried in *kago* from our inn to Hakone, where we had lunch and were told that close by there was the place where Gongen Kami was defeated. After our noon meal we continued to Mishima, where we arrived one hour before sunset and entered an inn for the night's lodging. There used to be a famous temple here standing on a big, spacious square, well paved with large square stones and next to a pond with very tame fish. Descending the mountains, we noticed that the land ran in a west-southwesterly direction twelve miles toward the sea. Not far from Mishima were a large number of young *yamabushi* boys, as well as young women who accosted us with their songs, the former importunate, the latter a little more bashful.

On April 8th we left our inn three hours before sunrise. The reason for this early departure was to avoid the lord of Owari, who is married to the shogun's sister and who was lodging at the village of Numazu, one and a half hours' distance from us. All the same, the road was full with his men, horses, luggage, and *norimono* as well as his house stewards and chancellors, all moving in complete silence past the lanterns that had been lit in all the houses. These house stewards or chancellors appointed to a fief by the shogun must be regarded as informers rather than stewards, because they are selected from among the shogun's courtiers and companions. From our inn, situated at the bridge of Numazu near the outer city, which consisted of some thousand houses, we proceeded to the city of Numazu proper, where the monks, instead of sleeping, sat at the wayside making ringing sounds and begging from us. Young men on pilgrimage to Ise were here sleeping in the fields. From Numazu the road ran slightly west of north for roughly a mile through various villages, where the local boys, romping and rollicking, begged money from us. Then we arrived at a bridge of roughly one hundred paces, which led us to the right, while the sea remained further to the side and behind us. Next we came to a pretty village and fertile rice fields, which on the right stretched below the mountains and on the left toward the bay, up to Yoshiwara. Traveling through these fields, we proceeded southwest and then west till Fujikawa. Here we used a newly constructed road, built by the territorial lord. Now the road turned much more to the west, and we mounted our *kago* till Kanbara. Next we reached the village of Katayama, and from there we followed a strangely winding road till Okitsu. We continued on horseback to Ejiri, arriving at five o'clock in the evening, and stayed the night but at an inn different from the one we had used previously. Over the mountains from here, at a place called Kuno, are gold and silver mines, but they are no longer worked.

On April 9th we traveled from our inn for half a mile through pretty countryside between mountains and after a great many curves and turns reached Suruga. Here the mountains stop and the land stretches out flat without an end in sight. From there we proceeded to Abekawa and then to the village of Mariko, where we were mobbed by a swarm of beggars. Among them we found a beautiful whore, who came up to our *kago* and enchanted some of our men so much that they gave her a number of coins just to let them touch her breasts. Also close by was a wooden hut, built by a priest, where he displayed a large gilded image with twelve arms. Two arms each held a child in front of the chest, two were lifted up above the head, and the others came out from the back stretching away from the body. The figure had seven little idols on the head; these illustrated the way in which the goddess Kannon has given birth to many divine heroes into this world and thus symbolized the birth of the gods. After many twists and turns in the road, we reached the village of Utsunoya and finally the town or little city of Okabe, where we had our noon meal.

City of Fujieda

After that we continued on horseback and soon reached the domain and castle of the governor of Osaka, called Ōta Settsu no Kami,[3] and then the city of Fujieda, consisting of six hundred houses.

After many twists and turns and also some dangerous stretches of road and mountains, we reached the city of Shimada; from there we proceeded to Ōigawa, where the officially appointed porters of this area had to carry us through the swift currents of water for a quarter of a mile. Every person was given three porters, and each of us received a small piece of oiled paper signed at the bottom, which the scribes or clerks handed out for the fixed price of twenty coins,[4] or sometimes for as much as one hundred, depending on how dangerous the water is. Afterward the scribes have to collect these pieces of paper again from the porters, because a porter forfeits his life if a person comes to grief in the water through lack of care.

City of Kanaya

After we had been happily carried through the river and handed back our piece of paper, we still had to cross a number of different bridges before reaching the city of Kanaya, where we arrived in the evening and stayed the night. Today we saw many upright poles displaying the name of the area as well as the distance of places.

On April 10th we were carried from our inn in *kago* through the city, which consisted of some two hundred houses.

City of Nissaka

Next we reached the city of Nissaka[5] and from there continued to the large village of Haragawa, where we saw many reed fields. Fine reed matting, also made into shoes, is produced and sold here. Next we arrived at a small city where we had to cross a stretch of water in boats and then had ourselves carried in *kago* to the city of Hamamatsu, where we arrived just before the evening and stayed the night.

City of Hamamatsu

Before Nissaka we were accosted by a naked young beggar, who wore only a straw band over his private parts and was otherwise totally bare and naked. He carried a spear in his hand, and his shack or hut was pasted with pictures of divine heroes. We also met many pretty, painted whores. A priest was lying face down in the open field, completely drenched by a downpour. He was dying but made noises to indicate that he was still alive, because he assumed he would be handled roughly as a corpse. The sight would have moved stones but not the heart of a Japanese. In Hamamatsu we were told that a man on his way to Ise (having received permission from his territorial lord to go on this pilgrimage) was lying in a priest's house with a whore, locked to her already for fourteen days (because people believe that this can happen on the way to such holy places). As a result he had already been inspected by friends and some thousand others. On this side of the mountains we saw today many fertile rice paddies and corn fields. Also the low, terraced mountains appeared to be alive with fertile abundance. At the villages of post stations we saw seven poles with boards showing the days on which the future territorial lord is to arrive and enter his domain.

April 11th. Since it had rained hard during the night and continued to drizzle this morning, we left Hamamatsu in *kago.* This city, situated on the slope of a hill, has a stately temple and residence, also gates, guards, and an outer city; it has a total of twelve hundred houses. For about a mile on the left many green, handsome rice paddies stretch down to the sea, but on the right there are hills and mountains some distance from the road.

For the first three-quarters of a mile from the inn the road was level and straight, up to an upright signpost. From there we came to the large and extended village of Wakabayashi,[6] through which the level and straight road continued for half a mile. On the left was the coastline and on the right a pleasant forest. Half a mile later the shore disappeared and in its place we saw the large and spread-out village of Shinohara, with a pillar indicating the distance and direction of places. We noticed stony and infertile fields on our left and on our right the beginning of an extensive bay. On the opposite shore of the bay loomed a large, low mountain range. After half a mile we reached Maisaka, from where we continued for another half mile on a very flat road. At an upright signpost we left our *kago* and continued in shogunal guard boats to Arai. From there we proceeded to the village of Hashimoto; after having passed another small village, we arrived at the large settlement of Shirasuka consisting of five hundred houses, and then ascended to the foot of Mount Fuji. From here the road took us to Banba, or Saruga Banba, and then through a cultivated forest to Futagawa, which is situated below mountainous forests and consists of two hundred houses. At this place we had a rather poor noon meal.

City of Yoshida

We continued to the city of Yoshida,[7] which surrounds the castle with straight, long streets. Here I spied on the left not far from the shore a mountainous island roughly three miles wide. There were also some woods on the right, but otherwise the land was flat and level. We continued further on to Kosakai, and traveling through a forest, we reached Sakuramachi. Here we saw a castle which, together with the above-mentioned island, belongs to the Lord of Owari. After a little while we reached a bridge of eighty paces situated before the city of Goyu—a place crowded with ugly and variously painted prostitutes belonging to the innkeepers—and finally with the evening and the falling of dusk reached the city of Akasaka.

City of Akasaka

This city has houses as large as those of Edo and the largest we saw since our departure from there. It also has a great variety and number of prostitutes, not to be outdone by those of Goyu.

On April 12th we left Akasaka, consisting of roughly two hundred houses, for the large and extended village of Hōzōji[8] of one hundred fifty houses, where string bags were being sold. To the left of this village is a temple school, where the first shogun of the present ruling house is supposed to have studied. But more likely is the story that he was employed in this village as a servant and escaped from his master, an innkeeper, because he was tired of carrying wood. Therefore it is said out of deference that he was brought up here and educated in the arts and sciences.

Fujikawa[9]

Afterward we reached the village of Yamanaka and then passed through the small city of Fujikawa of some two hundred fifty houses. Close by were the village of Shōda, from which we proceeded to a bridge of one hundred forty paces and the large village of Ai no shuku, and soon afterward we reached the city of Okazaki.

City of Okazaki

Even though it was only morning, we had a meal in the beautiful inn that is situated in the outskirts, since we were told that the shogun's highest councilor[10] was returning from a tour of duty at Miyako and was having his noon meal at our usual inn at Chiryū. But instead he sent his cook and advance party to this place for the noon meal. We therefore ate quickly and left, continuing on to the large bridge spanning the river with the most plentiful amount of water we had seen. After this bridge of 428 paces we reached a village situated in a plain roughly three miles wide, and the mountains on our right decreased in height, but another mountain range soon loomed behind them. On our left, however, the mountains continued in the same fashion up to the sea. Here we met Abe no Bungo sama, whose advance party consisted of no more than one hundred men, the main party of no more than six hundred. There were a few men carrying pikes and other men with weapons, followed by eleven stately men dressed in black at the head of the procession. Then came the lord seated in his *norimono.* After we had dismounted and saluted him by sending our compliments, he waved to indicate his gratitude. He did not stop but had our compliments returned by sending one of his servants after us: a solid man of about forty. More men carrying pikes and weapons followed as well as two led horses, which are always accompanied by pikes, and some *norimono* with led horses, pike bearers, and servants. Then followed twelve men on horseback and as many *norimono*. Next we passed a high mountain covered with snow near the city of Kōzoyama, which had roughly two hundred or two hundred fifty houses, and then proceeded to the village of Ōhamachaya, where the horses belatedly received some fodder and rest. From there we went on through a broad wooded plain to Chiryū, consisting of one hundred fifty houses as well as a large residence to accommodate territorial lords on their journey. From there we proceeded to the village of Imokawa, consisting of one hundred houses, where we found a lot of *sake* taverns. Then we reached the small city of Arimatsu of fifty houses, after having passed two villages as well as forests and hills. We traveled through fine country up to the city of Narumi, then past flat fields, and on the left a village situated at the shore. There we had to cross a bridge, leading us to the village of Kasadera and the temple Komatsu, where people were celebrating and someone was invoking the idol Kannon; a similar temple is supposed to exist in Nagasaki. From there we soon reached the village of Tobe or Yamazaki—also called Kasadera by some—consisting of one hundred houses. Next we crossed a bridge of more than forty-five paces and soon afterward reached the outskirts of Miya and then the city proper, where we entered our inn before evening.

City of Miya

We discovered that some gentlemen of the advance party of the territorial lord of Tsushima[11]—who is expected at Kuwana tomorrow—were lodging there already. We passed a *miya*, a Shinto temple, with two gates, located on rising ground on the shore, which had been constructed by the local king four years ago.[12] Five Shinto priests wearing imperial court hats sat in front of the shrine, in one line, each one a step higher than the next. We also saw two priests begging in front of the inn where we spent the night: one had *yamabushi* rings in his hand, the other paper tufts. This temple is called Atsuta, which means temple of three swords.[13] They have been brought here from Ise and are treasured as holy relics. There is also another temple called Hakken, which means temple of eight swords. These belonged to famous heroes of old and are treasured as relics and guarded by the same kind of people as we just saw sitting in front of the temple.

City of Kuwana

On April 13th we set out at sunrise in boats and with a weak breeze from the land sailed past islands and inlets to our inn at Kuwana. We arrived at ten o'clock and after we had a meal left again at eleven. The first part of the city through which our road took us had a well-fortified gate and two guardhouses, a masoned rampart, and a moat, just like the castle itself.[14] The middle section of the city was fortified like the former. The third section of the city had walls, ramparts, and moats but poor gates, yet a good guard. Outside this large and well-built-up settlement was a cultivated plain with a large, high mountain chain four to five miles ahead to our right, with a small, hilly village stretching a quarter of a mile in between the mountains. At nearly half a mile's distance on our left was the sea. Next we came to the village where shellfish are fried and where we had stopped briefly on our outward journey. Afterward we came to two large villages and then to the large village of Tomida. Following that, we reached the village of Hatsu[15] and from there the large town of Yokkaichi, which was packed with the most ugly, thickly painted old prostitutes I have ever seen. After that we came to the village of Hinaga, where our road left the shoreline for about a mile, and then to the village of Oiwake, close to which people were fertilizing the fields by burrowing in dung and dirt. The area was well cultivated up to our inn in the town of Ishiyakushi,[16] where we were received and treated extremely well.

On April 14th we left Ishiyakushi at sunrise in gray, cold, and windy weather. The town consisted of about 150 houses, had no gates, and was totally open on all sides. But at its end was a temple where priests rang bells and made sacrifices in accordance with the ceremonies prescribed by their worship. After that town, we passed through open fields and along a flat stretch of road with a plain of many trees ahead of us. Next we crossed a large river, spanned by a poor bridge, and soon afterward arrived in the small and pleasant village of Kumigawara, from where the road was flat up to the long village of Odamura. Here we met the territorial lord of Nagato[17] with three hundred men and some twenty led horses. He had only eight men in front of his *norimono,* and we did not pay him any respect but passed without stopping. We reached the small village of Kawai, where we met a suite of fifty to one hundred men, after which we reached the village of Wada,[18] from where we proceeded through two small forests and then reached the city of Kameyama.

City of Kameyama

This was a large, pleasant settlement on the flat top of two hills, running right through the middle of a little valley. To the right, next to the main street, was the castle with its moat, rampart, and walls. The city had crooked streets in the shape of an elbow running the length of the settlement, solid gates, ramparts, and walls. It consisted of some two thousand houses, not counting those in the two outer cities. We continued for a mile on a flat road and arrived at the town of Sekinojizō. In this town they produced bamboo torches from scraped bamboo, with which the shops were stacked and the travelers were inundated. This settlement had the greatest number of and the best inns we have ever seen, and it consisted of some six hundred houses. After we had stayed here for a while, we proceeded through much mountainous, winding road to the village of Kutsukake, where large quantities of figs were offered for sale. Passing through a number of scattered houses we reached the open road after half an hour. After another half-hour's journey along the highway, we reached the town of Sakanoshita on the slope of the mountains. Here we ate and after an hour continued in *kago* through the town and along steeply rising, curved, and dark stretches of road. At the start we found in front of us a small temple with a gilded lion that had a horn bent slightly backward. From there steps led up to another temple. After we had climbed this steeply rising, curved road for nearly half a mile we reached the village of Sawa. Then we came through the village of Yamanaka, with a large brook running down the hill, and next through the villages of Inohana and Kanisaka. After that we went through a flat plain situated between the mountains, with only a few scattered hills, to reach the town of Tsuchiyama, where we arrived at our night's lodgings two hours before sunset.

On April 15th the road took us from our inn through mountains, hills, and forests to the village of Maeno,[19] after which we came to the villages of Ōno and Imashuku, situated on nearly flat ground. Soon afterward we were again surrounded by mountains and wooded hills and among them saw many *kobushi,* or lily trees, and, at Shinjōmura, *tsuge* trees resembling boxwood.

City of Minakuchi

From there we traveled through the city of Minakuchi, where the manufacture of hats and other goods made from fine rushes had been established. The residence of the lord of this place, which we spotted only after we had nearly reached the end of the city, was poor and without rampart and moat. After that we soon reached the broad and flat highway, where another mountain range rose high to the left, but on the right we saw a large river not far from the village of Izumi, which was situated along our road. After that the snow mountain and scorpion mountain[20] came into view, the former on our left, the latter on our right. Next we had to pass through the village of Tagawa and soon afterward through the long village of Natsumi.[21] Outside this village, a hut had been set up in the fields, containing a wooden image of a deity with a short beard and no arms. In addition to the image there was a priest in the hut. But outside the hut were two people begging, dressed in ceremonial robes and fine clothes and well equipped with two swords. After that we reached the village of Hari, and soon afterward the village of Kōjibukuro, at the entrance of which stood a similar hut with beggars in ceremonial robes. In the hut itself, however, were two black images. The larger of the two had frizzy hair and held both his hands in front of the body, with the index finger of his right hand pointing at his chest and the left hand holding something. From there our road was very flat and level up to the village of Ishibe, where we had our noon meal. From here we traveled around a mountain to reach the highway proper, after which we passed several villages and reached the large village of Takano, or Takanomura, where many medical powders were being sold. The main shopkeeper and trader of this powder lives in the nearby village of Menoke, through which our road took us. The powders were bitter and tasted bad and were packed in bags made of paper, on which directions for use and efficacy were indicated. Opposite the shop selling the powder was a hut or temple with the most important saint called Kannon in a *tarate* flower, with half a shell extending over his head, which symbolizes a grain of rice. The image held a scepter in the right hand and in the left something I could not discern; above the head was a gilded circle. People approached with great deference and bare heads and rang the little bell or flat mortar; but when they said their prayers, they held their hands in front of their head. Toward the end of this village the tall mountains turned into hills, behind which, however, new mountains loomed again. From here we proceeded to the village of Magari,[22] and the same road led us to the nearby bordering village of Megawa and then to the village of Shin'yashiki.

City of Kusatsu

After that we passed another village and then reached the small city or town of Kusatsu, where people worked the bamboo root called Rottang. After that we came to the small village of Noji, near which, on the right, there was a lake, and beyond that the mountain Hieizan. We passed through a great many turnip fields in this vicinity, as well as through three small villages, and then through a long village called Seta and afterward through the large village of Seta.[23] There we saw a small temple at the shore, which has a fabled history. Here stood the largest bridge we saw in Japan, and beyond the bridge was a village which some called Seta no hashi and others Toriigawa.

City of Zeze

After that we came to the city of Zeze, where the Lord Honda sama is supposed to live (but he has had to remain in Edo for many years).[24] The town and castle are pleasant, and the entrance to the town is well appointed with gates.

City of Ōtsu

From here we arrived at the outskirts of the city of Ōtsu and at our inn. Rottang from Kusatsu had been brought here to be sold. At times this root is very expensive, that is, when the domain lord issues orders forbidding people to dig up the root. This happens because the root is totally destroyed when it is dug up, since it is located very deep in the soil and is very difficult to find. This variety is called *hachiku* and does not grow around Nagasaki, where the root is only the length of a span or an arm. However wretched the place appeared at night, during the day it was so well decked out with stalls that it looked like a little Nürnberg.[25]

April 16th was a Sunday. We left our inn and came to the small town of Ōtani and soon after to the village of Ōsaka and immediately after that to the bordering village of Oiwake. Then, passing through a large green plain situated between mountains, we entered the region of Miyako and soon afterward reached the village of Yamashita and the closely bordering small town of Yakkochaya, in which we had our noon rest. From here we proceeded to the closely bordering village of Yamashina and then to a small village on the other side of some mountains. Next we reached the small town of Keage, which is the beginning of the city of Miyako, and went on to Awataguchi. We passed through some suburbs as well as three rivers; the first was at a distance of fifteen hundred paces from the second, but the other two were only one hundred paces apart. Then we finally reached the city proper, where both to our right and to our left streets extended to an interminable distance. Entering the city, one could see the tower of the castle in the west as shown in the illustration,[26] and we arrived at our inn in Miyako at nine o'clock at night.

City of Miyako

April 18th. After our meal, we left in our *norimono,* having spent the previous day purchasing a few fashionable accessories and having received with the usual ceremonies our gifts of robes from the chief judge, as well as from the governors. Next to those received from the shogun, those of the chief judge are the best. First we went back the length of one street in the direction we came from until after the bridge. From there we turned to the right toward the mountains, being carried through regular, clean, and pleasant streets, lined with small houses, stalls, stores, and workshops, up to the approach or square of the excellent temple Chion-in.[27] When returning from the shogunal court, the Dutch are free to visit the magnificent temples of Miyako on the day of their departure, according to a long-established custom. Situated on the slopes of wooded and rough mountains, these temples are the largest, most precious, and most pleasant in the whole country. But this freedom is granted in such a fashion that we are not permitted to refuse it, or not to take advantage of it, even though our prefect, head, and leader was not in the mood and not at all keen about this visit.

The approach to the temple consisted of a long, wide avenue or square on flat and even ground, continuing below or at the foot of the mountain for some one thousand paces.[28] The gate was magnificent and lofty with two roofs like a tower or temple. We (as do the most eminent people of the country, except for the shogun) paid our respects to the temple by descending from our *norimono* and stepping on the ground with our feet. At the end of this avenue (which was paved with small boulders and sand and on both sides lined with the tall houses of the officials of the temple) we soon turned to the left and then to the right, climbing to the next level, which was covered with fine sand and planted with trees and shrubs. After we had passed two magnificent and very valuable wooden buildings, we climbed some fine stairs to enter a wide and extensive wooden house, with long, spacious, and raised verandas, as is common and customary in Japan. The front of the building was much taller and much more magnificent than any shogunal castle, the gallery was varnished, and the interior rooms were covered with fine matting. In the first and large outer chamber was a chapel with a curly-haired, fairly large image, and the room was well decorated all around with a variety of lacquered ornaments and small images. On both sides were other chapels, which, however, were smaller and less ornate. We were then led to two special chambers where the seat of the shogun was: the floor was a little higher than that of the antechamber, and the seat was raised again by two mats. From here one could look into the said chapel through two doors.[29]

Next to these apartments at the foot of a wooded tall mountain (where there were still other pleasant small temples hidden among the shrubbery of the slopes, and which was leveled with boulders more than one fathom high) was a small Japanese pleasure or miniature garden. That is to say, a narrow space, or piece of flat ground, covered with river sand or stones, where the existing uniformity is carefully broken up with artistically made overgrown, small, and neat cliffs, rare rocks, and well-pruned and twisted trees and turned into a pretty garden. For the special delight of the eye there was a winding, shallow stream of water, running around man-made cliffs in a mazelike pattern to give the impression of a wilderness lake in a narrow gorge, spanned with various ornamental stone bridges. From the many paths and passageways we turned left through a gate to a small temple roughly thirty paces up the mountain, where a tablet with the names of the deceased shoguns is kept.

In this temple of the court low chairs had been placed in front as well as on both sides of the area where the image was located, and on each chair there were three large and one small pieces of paper with written characters, to pray for the soul of Genyūin. In front of this temple were several boxes covered with rough grills for throwing in copper coins, and there was also a small raised seat or floor-level chair. From there healthy, good-looking young priests in charge of us, who appeared to be of no mean education, led us across a separate square to a very fine temple raised on pillars one and a half fathoms in diameter. The magnificent exterior of this temple was dominated by the double-layered tiled roofs, extending far over the outer corridor with their four layers of ornamental red crossbeams, timbers, and rafters, and also the four layers of timbers jutting out one below the other with their yellow-painted edges. Inside, the floor was covered with matting, but otherwise the interior was empty up to the roof. The temple was supported by five times six columns.[30] To the right, in a corner of this temple, was a large area, and to the left another area, making up the central chapel with a lot of images in black, lacquered, and closed-up boxes. The central image appeared to be covered by a cloth and in front of this cloth or curtain stood nothing else but a "know thyself,"[31] that is, a round mirror, and a money box covered with a grill for collecting donations. After we had been guided through this temple, the priests brought us to another building of lesser quality, but nonetheless attractive, because the central room was a chapel adorned for worship; close by was the place designated for our entertainment. We were served by six young priests, of whom the oldest was most probably twenty-six and the youngest sixteen. The beverage was *sake;* the food consisted of mushrooms, fried beans, cake, pickled fruits, roots, and tubers. After an hour and a half we left again, accompanied by two priests up to the border of the approach to the temple, or large entrance square, of this excellent, delightful shogunal monastery, which is supposed to contain twenty-seven other temples within its confines. Some of us went on foot, but others had themselves carried to the Gion temple, called the flower temple, situated at a distance of some thousand paces from the previous location through a wild pleasure wood.

This Gion temple was surrounded by thirty to forty small chapels placed at regular intervals, and also here and there by stalls selling goods or places for shooting arrows; moreover, it was planted with fine and beautiful ornamental trees, as if it had been solely created for the enjoyment of young people. The temple itself was a long, somewhat narrow building. In the middle, a room separated off by a corridor contained a central image and many secondary images, as well as innumerable ornaments. There was also hanging up a Japanese lacquered, fairly large picture of a young woman, about two to three fathoms in length, and the temple was, moreover, well decked with pictures of devils and heroes of all shapes and kinds to the extent that a Dutch vessel, a few weapons or swords, and other strange pieces and oddities had also found a home here.[32] From there we had ourselves carried half a mile through the mountain street called Gion Yasaka,[33] a street of beggars and prostitutes, to the noteworthy temple Kiyomizu.

Kiyomizu Temple

This temple had a remarkably high tower with seven roofs. In the lowest chapel of the tower, which was raised a few steps from the ground, stood one large and several small images.[34] Continuing further toward the mountains, we came to the substantial Kiyomizu Temple itself. On one side the temple is next to the steep face of the mountain, but on the other it is supported by pillars eight and a half *ken* high, reaching down to the steep valley below. There was a large crowd of people milling around here. In the middle of this place,[35] surrounded by railings, was a large round mirror, two alms boxes, and some gongs, which were sounded by those making donations with thick ropes hanging in front of the gongs. Not far from here was a flight of eighty-five steps descending to a spring running down from the mountains in three separate streams. The spring was called Otowa no taki and its water is supposed to have the power to make those who drink from it wise and clever. Otherwise the water was clear and no different from any other spring in Miyako. Here we walked along a small terrace built along the side of the mountain, passing some small temples placed in an irregular line, to reach another large temple belonging to the precinct. Inside it was the same as the others, but it rose perpendicular from the side of the mountain above the valley and had a good view. The most important images had their hands folded in such a way that the index finger was touching the thumb.

Daibutsu Temple

Afterward we had ourselves carried to the large Daibutsu temple, which was situated not far from the highway we take to Fushimi. But before that we entered a whorehouse along the road to receive the farewell meal of our host, for which, however, we had to pay a *koban,* four times the usual price.

The precinct of the Daibutsu temple was on an elevated plot close to the road with large boulders nearly two fathoms square marking the front.[36] The temple was surrounded by a walkway closed off on the outside but open on the inside. Its roof was some three fathoms high and rested on sets of two round wooden columns placed next to each other, with about fifty columns running on each side of the gates.

The main gate consists of a tall, narrow building with columns and a double ornamental roof. Both wings of this building are taken up with the figure of a black, fat hero, placed on a pedestal a fathom above the ground. The statues are naked except for

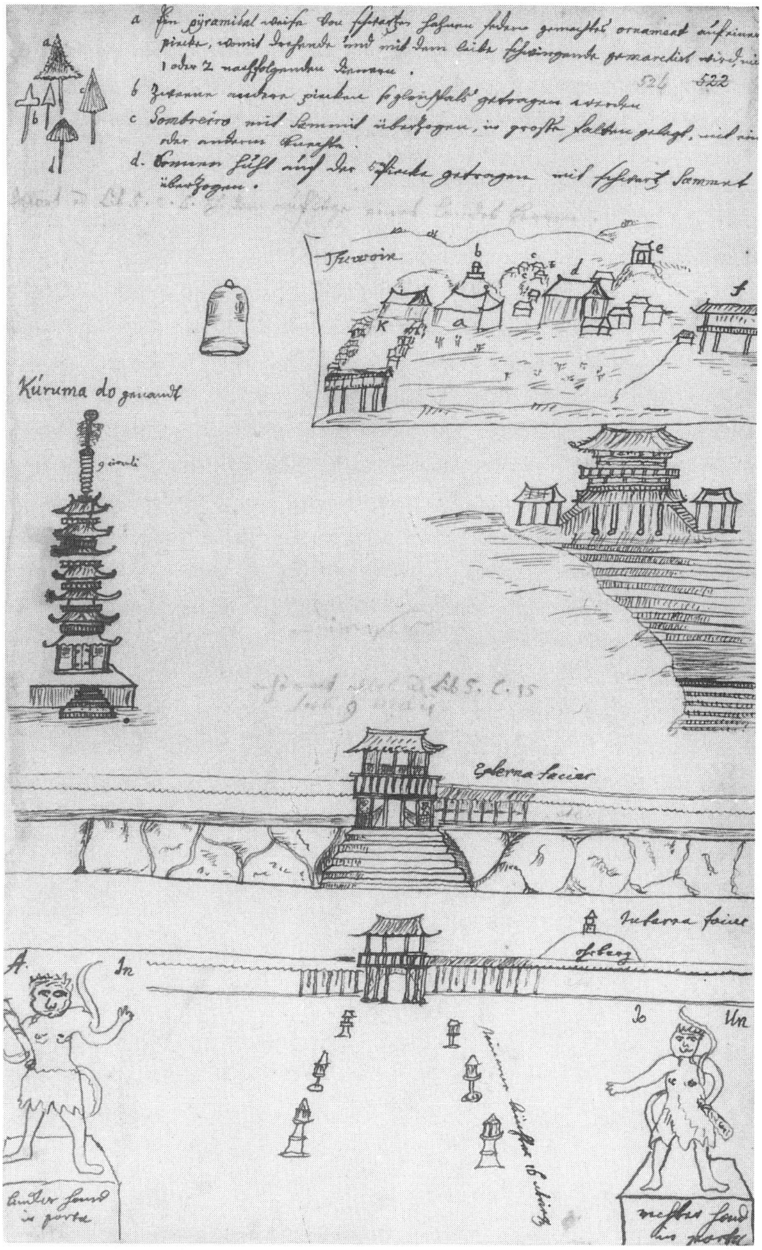

Kaempfer's sketch of implements carried in daimyo processions, above; the layout of the monastery Chion-in, below right; the bell of the monastery on the left; the large gate (Sanmon) of Chion-in, center right; the Yasaka pagoda, erroneously drawn with seven stories instead of five, center left; and the gate and wall of the precinct of the Daibutsu (Hōkōji) below. The bottom view is from the main hall; note the Mount of Ears (Ohrberg) on the right. The statues in the gate have been drawn separately and placed in the foreground. (Courtesy of the British Library, Sloane 3060, folio 526)

a flowing cloth, and their faces are like that of a lion. They are about four fathoms tall and of excellent, craftsmanlike proportions. Each has its special significance.

The Daibutsu temple stands directly opposite this gate and looms high above the houses of the city, being, most probably, the highest in Japan. It has two tall roofs and rests on eight times twelve pillars, which come to a total of ninety-four, subtracting those missing in the middle of the building. Tall doors, running right around the building and stretching to the height of the first roof, permit the building to be opened up. Inside, the building is open to the very roof, where, for solidity's sake, it is filled with red painted beams with many corners, joined in a marvelous fashion. Because of the height, this area is completely dark.

Different from other temples, this one had a paved stone floor and contained no decoration except the large image. The columns were each constructed of several logs of wood, one and a half fathoms wide, and were dyed red like the rest of the wood.

The large image is gilded all over and of quite unbelievable size, so that there is room for three mats in its open hand. It has long cow ears, frizzy hair, a button or crown on the head, and a spot that is not gilded on the forehead. The face could be seen through

The hall and precinct of the large Buddha at Hōkōji, a copy Kaempfer made to illustrate his text of one of the fifty illustrations of famous sights he had brought back from Japan. Compare this with the copperplate print made from the same Japanese original in Scheuchzer, vol. 3, fig. 130. Also compare the entrance gate and the Mount of Ears to the right of the gate with Kaempfer's sketch on page 381. (Courtesy of the British Library, Sloane 3060, folio 515)

Kaempfer's drawing of the large Buddha, most probably the only realistic portrayal of the inside of the temple. Note the figure in the lower right to show the size of the statue. Kaempfer's key to the numbers says: (1) one piece of wood; (2) alms box; (3) flower pot with pine bush; (4) bronze lotus flower; (5) bronze figure of a lion; (6) bronze crane with bronze light placed on a turtle; (7, 8) lights fed by grease and candles; (9, 9, 9) gilded lotus leaves standing upright; (10) lotus leaves with coat of arms standing upright; (11) lotus leaves bending down to the floor; from (a) to (a) twelve paces; from (b) to (b) fifteen paces, that is to say, from shoulder to shoulder. (Courtesy of the British Library, Sloane 3060, folio 544)

the window above the lower roof. Its shoulders are bare. The sculptor had decorated the chest and body with a flowing robe. The right hand was raised, and the left was placed in front and open. The figure sat in Indian fashion, with feet folded below the body, resting on top of a lotus flower. This flower was placed into another flower made of plaster, which, for decoration's sake, had leaves standing erect from the ground. All this was some two fathoms above the ground.

The back of this large idol was framed by an oval-shaped piece of gilded leaves, covered with small idols of human shape sitting on lotus flowers. This flat oval piece was so broad that it covered four columns. The idol was so wide that its shoulders reached from one column to the next. I measured five fathoms from one shoulder to the other. With the lotus flower it was seated on, the idol occupied an eight-cornered area fenced off by a wooden grill in such a fashion that two of the innermost columns supporting the roof had been omitted.

After we had inspected this temple, we passed through another gate, covered only with one roof, into an adjoining courtyard. There we were shown a gum-gum,[37] or bell, as are common in this country, of extraordinary size, hanging in a small building or a wooden tower. It was over a span thick, the depth was nearly the length of an officer's pike, and the circumference was twenty-one feet.

Temple of 33,333 Images

Continuing along this square, we reached a long temple building, in the middle of which sat a large image endowed with forty-six arms, surrounded on both sides by statues, much larger than life-size, of some sixteen black heroes in standing position. Then there were on each side, in straight lines on steps behind each other, rows of gilded idols, standing erect, all of the same shape. The statues had twenty arms on each side, of which the first held a thin shepherd's crook and the others rosaries, axes, and a variety of instruments and ornaments. On top of the head—crowned toward the back by a circle of rays—were seven seated small idols, as if to make up a crown, with the center image smaller than the others. The chest of the figures was hung and decorated with all sorts of symbols and decorations. All these images are life-size, and all are alike and are placed closely next to and behind each other, so that the one behind is always one head higher than the one in front. There are some ten to twelve rows one behind each other, making a total of 33,333 statues, and for this reason the temple is called *san man, san zen, san byaku san jū san tai,* which means the temple of 33,333 images.[38]

Outside the gates of this temple we again stepped into our *norimono* and were carried up to the city of Fushimi in three hours along level ground. Some three-quarters of a mile from the Daibutsu temple, toward the mountains on the left, was a temple where a flower festival was being held. Countless children came from there, dressed in white and colored *katabira,* holding flowering branches. There were all sorts of other mobs, all dressed in white *katabira,* coming from the same location, shouting joyfully and continuously in chorus "yassai, yassa."[39] We continued on our way and were carried through many curved, elbow-shaped streets to arrive finally at our inn in the city of Fushimi. After dinner we boarded our small boats or ships, and during the night made such progress that after midnight we moored at the outskirts of the city[40] to await dawn in order to avoid the most dangerous spots near the bridges.

April 19th. We arrived in the city while it was still dark and disembarked at dawn near our inn.

City of Sakai

After we had been given a positive answer to the request made on our way up to Edo to see copper being refined, to visit the town of Tennōji[41] as the most important *sake* distillery of the country, as well as the shogunal city of Sakai, situated along these shores some four or five miles from Osaka, we returned with great trouble on account of the mad imaginations and stubbornness of our leader.[42] For the same reason he also did not want to take the land route to Hyōgo, and therefore we left on April 21st in two inferior and open vessels and arrived in a few hours—I think some three hours before sunrise—in Hyōgo to cast anchor.[43]

Hyōgo

We were not allowed to stretch our legs on land and went to sleep without a meal after a small and miserable snack, regardless of the fact that our last meal had been the previous day at five o'clock in the afternoon. Our route took us outside the harbor of Osaka up to the port of Hyōgo. Here we met the lord of Tsushima with five or six pleasure boats, of which the central one was lacquered, had a high seat, and was carved and gilded.

April 22nd. We had to remain in this harbor owing to the direction of the wind and on board owing to the lunacy of our master. Therefore the senior interpreter and the other officers amused themselves on shore by themselves, anonymously and without pikes and followers.

April 23rd. In the evening, while we were still anchored at our mooring for the reasons mentioned above, the lord of Chikuzen or Hakata[44]—the latter name being that of his residence—arrived with some fifty large and small vessels under a mounting breeze and the loud swishing of oars in our vicinity. Then they departed again in some confusion as they hoisted their sails to catch the incoming wind. The sails all looked like those of Batavia, with the top and lower section blue and the middle white.

On April 24th we set out with a pleasant breeze at dawn and came to the village of Ejima, situated on an island. After we had taken on some water, we raised anchor and hoisted the sails and in this fashion drifted throughout the night with little wind and the help of the oars.

Early in the morning of April 25th we were near the small town or village of Konnoura, fifteen Japanese miles from Muro. As the sun rose, the wind became favorable and the sea was calm: under these conditions we reached Shiraishi. But owing to an unfavorable gust, we arrived within a stone's throw of the west side of Tomo. Parts of Tomo, with its rough mountain slope down to the sea dotted with temples, are quite an exceptional sight and very spectacular, but the whorehouses[45] and the poor living quarters of the fishermen and others are rather messy and ugly. We passed around this area and moored in the southern bay, which is densely settled with a row of attractive dwellings and storage houses, as good as any I have seen in Japan. Up to one-third of the mountain slopes is cultivated; the rest is steep and overgrown. In the mountains is a beautiful temple and widow's nunnery, a pleasant sight for the eye. Because of favorable winds we raised our anchor late at night and before daybreak were able to drop it again in the harbor of the village of Iwagi.[46] This consisted of some hundred fishermen's huts and other dwellings around the shore near the cultivated area at the foot of the mountain. The distance between the houses was somewhat large, but their situation was very pleasant.

April 26th. Although today the currents were pretty strong and running against us, the wind could not have been better. But we profited little from this, for we wasted the early morning owing to some misunderstandings. Consequently we left around nine o'clock, passing through a narrow strait between mountains. The sea currents were very much against us, but finally we came to an island located in front of Tsuwa, where we dropped anchor at a depth of twenty fathoms. Hoping to catch a breeze that would take us into the harbor, we raised anchor, but in vain, and we soon dropped it again, but closer to the island and at a greater depth of twenty-eight to twenty-nine fathoms.

After raising anchor early in the morning of April 27th, we sailed with favorable winds through the currents and soon arrived at a fishing village, with a harbor the shape of a half circle, situated against a backdrop of high mountains. The mountains were cultivated to the top and had a lighthouse on the cliffs of the foothills. This village consisted of a monastery, a temple, a gallows, and one hundred fifty houses. After taking on water for quarter of an hour, we continued on our journey. Favorable winds brought us to the straits of Kaminoseki but left us there since the straits are only a stone's throw wide, and our oars got us no further than a village called Sagō, situated on an island of the same name.

Because of the rough weather we remained here on April 28th and enjoyed ourselves on shore, outdrinking the officers in charge of us, except for the old under-officer, who during this break demonstrated his authority—which he could well have put aside—with quite inappropriately harsh commands. And he attempted to make us believe that he was sent as a watchdog and spy for the senior officer. This political device is commonly used in the administration of the court, the empire, and the cities; yes, indeed, in all forms of government, so that driven by mistrust and the anxiety of being reported, everybody will live up to the demands of their status and position, ensuring the stability of the government.

City of Senjima

April 29th, with variable and partly favorable winds, we arrived a mile to the side of the city and castle of Senjima, where we dropped anchor after midday and remained till the evening and then sailed away again with a cool breeze. But owing to unfavorable winds, we soon had to drop anchor again close to the shore.

We set sail again early in the morning of the 30th, but owing to strong, unfavorable winds soon headed toward the country of Bungo, situated ahead of us to our left, to reach one of its harbors, six miles from Shimonoseki. But a sudden, violent storm made us and other sailing vessels head straight for land, so that at noon we cast anchor in a heavy storm in a little bay before Mukō[47] with a village of the same name, situated at the foot of massive and high foothills, six miles from Senjima and eighteen miles from Shimonoseki. The entrance to this harbor was narrow, the harbor itself wide and shallow and half-dry when the water receded, so that the local people were able to collect shells. The village was surrounded by mountains, and facing it toward the north was the little town of Mitajiri at a distance of nearly one mile. At various times during the day we saw small whales, which are known as Nord Capers[48] at home. A territorial lord with seven blue sails passed us, but we had to remain here because of the unchanging stormy weather and spend the night in the company of eight other barges.

Early in the morning of May 1st some barges belonging to the lord of Chikugo dropped anchor near us. In the afternoon at five o'clock we noticed some favorable winds coming off the land and immediately set sail and stopped a few hours later a mile beyond Motoyama. Relying partly on our oars and partly on the wind, we dropped anchor at Shimonoseki in the late evening.

City of Kokura

May 2nd we left in two yachts and arrived at Kokura, after we had passed on our left the place where about a century ago the *dairi* had lived. After we had lunch here, we mounted horses and left this formerly flourishing city which, owing to the way the land has been divided, is now poor and obscure. It consisted of three small cities and on one side—which, however, was only narrow and bordering the sea—was fortified with stone ramparts and wooden fences. Nearly two miles from Kokura a large river entered the sea, and not far from there was the large village, or, rather, city of Kurosaki. One and a half miles from here we reached the village of Kōjaku and after an hour came to a small village where coal was being quarried. After another mile we reached our inn at Koyanose, a cramped and inferior accommodation.

On May 3rd we left Koyanose traveling on an embankment and passed the village of Tonno on our left and the village of Nōgata on our right. The mountains rising on both sides were roughly at half a mile's distance from each other. Then we reached the villages of Katsuno and Kotake and after that the village of Namazuda, as well as three villages at some distance from the road and two villages called Kawatsu. There were fine fields up to the village of Kōbukuro, and from there we reached the village of Katashima and then the two villages of Ōya and the village of Tachiiwa, soon afterward arriving at the small town of Iizuka, consisting of some two hundred houses. After our noon meal, we were ferried across the river and arrived at the village of Tentōmachi, bypassing the village of Tarōmaru on our right and soon afterward, not far from the road, the village of Tsubaki. Then we came to the sloping village of Nagao, stretching up to the mountains, and three small villages called Yokoyama, as well as the small town of Uchino, where the inhabitants had beautiful faces but, at the same time, masculine figures. After a brief stop, we were carried in *kago* to the village of Nishiyama, where we came across very demure women—especially when it came to the young girls—who, at the same time, were of extraordinary beauty. From here we proceeded to the night's lodging at Yamae.

On May 4th we left our accommodation and arrived at the village of Futamura and then crossed a river, and after passing through dense, delightful forest we came to the city of Haruda, consisting of some eighty houses. From here the road was very much twisting and turning, over hills and through fields. Half a mile after Haruda were boundary posts marking the end of the province of Chikuzen and once again the beginning of that of Tsushima.

City of Tashiro

Not far from here we saw a small village of twenty houses with a watermill, and then we came to the village of Kiyamaguchi, as well as two small villages close by called Imamachi and Tsunogi, and also to Akasaka and the nearly bordering city of Tashiro, consisting of almost four hundred houses. Then we reached the town of Uriuno, with three hundred houses, and soon afterward we came to our inn at Todoroki, which most probably had some three hundred houses. After our noon meal, we traveled through this settlement, following its elbow-shaped road. On the nearest mountains, not far from the road on the right, a place was pointed out to us where formerly two strong castles had stood. Then we came to the villages of Muratamachi and Nakabaru, up to the large village of Shōzumachi with seven hundred houses. From there we proceeded to the villages of Kiridōshimura and Metabaru and to yet another small village, next to which there were fertile, well-cultivated, and level fields, up to the village of Tate, situated a little to the side of the road. After that we reached our inn in the city of Kanzaki, which consisted of seven hundred houses and winding streets. Here our senior officer let us also have the use of his room, since ours was too small and narrow. The place was full of priests and temples, and so many letters of indulgence were pasted up in our rooms that more recent ones were pasted on top of old ones for lack of space. These letters of indulgence consist of a page-long document folded four times, with a fine printed heading and three red imprints of the seal of the superior of the monastery who has the authority to hand out or sell the letters. Inside there is nothing but a few wretched pieces of pine, split into squares and tied together with cardboard or cord, with a few sacred pieces of paper twisted around. In some inferior letters there were merely a quarter sheet of paper with a few rows of *sōsho*[49] and the red imprint of a seal over the letters or on the side at the end. There were also letters from Ise as well as square, thin, pasted boxes, covered with letters with the same heading and filled with the said sticks. Here our senior officer received a *koban* from the lord of the province to congratulate him on his return, but the senior interpreter got a pickled goose. I don't know what that means. At night the priests here made a lot of music and noise. This place was full with flowers, especially *shaga,*[50] *nazuna,*[51] and *satsuki*[52] of all sorts of colors, growing both in gardens as well as in the forest.

On May 5th we left our inn and came to the village of Kataherajuku and then to the village of Ane and further to the village of Harunomachi, which had two hundred houses. Then we arrived at the town of Takao, where we had to be ferried across water, and soon after reached the city of Saga.

City of Saga

Along various bends and stretches of winding road we reached the village of Ōgimachi and in similar fashion proceeded to the village of Kase. This village consists of two parts with an empty square along a river in the middle, which is the execution ground of the city of Saga.

Execution Ground of the City of Saga

Five wretched sinners had recently been put to death, of whom four had been crucified and the head of the fifth set on the pole of a cross. Small guard stations had been erected on both sides and were well supplied with guards. The men had set fire to a house that had burned down in Saga and had been caught again after they had escaped the first time. The first man had hanged himself, and therefore his body had been pickled and brought here, so that he could be crucified with the others. The head, however, was that of an innkeeper, who had concealed the crime and therefore was considered subject to the same punishment. After we had left this place of Kase, we rode over a bridge of one hundred twenty paces covered with peat and arrived at the village of Kubota, situated, according to my estimate, at a distance of roughly one and a half miles from a tall mountain range. Within one mile I counted ten large villages. From here we reached the town of Ushizu, consisting roughly of one hundred houses, and soon afterward the village of Shinmachi, bending and curving around a mountain. Here we had to have ourselves ferried across some water, which moved with the tide. Then we arrived at the village of Togawa and, after an hour, the village of Teramachi and soon afterward the village of Torimachi. Next we passed through a small village and soon arrived at our inn in the town of Oda. From here we proceeded to the villages of Ōmachi and Iōji and were ferried in wooden barges to the village of Yakigome. But then we went over a large bridge, spanning a river running into the sea. Next we came through a number of scattered villages to the town of Naruse, where firewood was stored from the many densely forested mountains and where we were ferried across in barges. We reached a small village and had high mountains and thick forests on both sides of the road. A signpost led us to another small village, situated in a plain running level down to the sea, with various other villages roughly half a mile apart. After we had traveled just less than an hour from the signpost—of which we saw a good many on our journey—we arrived at the village of Shioda, where a river flowed eastward, with many boats carrying wood.

Baking of Porcelain at Shioda

Here there lived a man baking porcelain, producing all sorts of large earthen pots and porcelain. We were lodged in an attic of a very smoky house and had to put up with it for the night.

We left our night's lodging early on May 6th and soon arrived at the village of Ichirimatsu, from where we traveled along yesterday's river for an hour and ferried across at that point. Soon afterward we reached the village of Mino, situated at the foot of, and curving around, a mountain, which meant that we followed the curve as we traveled through. On the other side of the river we came to the large village of Ōkusano, situated on one side of the foot of the mountain. Passing the river and uneven, hilly country, we reached the village of Imadera and, passing through a large, wide valley, the village of Shimojuku. Then we came to the village of Ureshino and to the large, scattered, and extensive village of Eboshiiwa. Afterward we traveled through a narrow valley, passed a pointer, or signpost, and came to three small villages in a row within a quarter of a mile of each other. Then we came to the mountain of Tawara, where the large village of Fudōyama is situated on the right, and then came to Hizenban, that is to say, the border guard of Hizen, together with a small village called Tawarazaka. Near this village were two border posts standing close to each other. Even though the first was planted lower owing to the slope of the road, it was much taller on account of the particular provincial lord's greater authority and larger domain. Then we came to a small village of eight houses, where our leader, a senior officer of Tango sama, Lord of Hizen,[53] said farewell to our officer.

Camphor Tree

We continued our journey over the mountain range of Tawara and saw a very large flowering camphor tree. After that we came to a wayside column or signpost and a few scattered houses or a village. But then we reached a number of small villages and, passing through a wide fertile valley, arrived at Sonogi, as it is properly called, or Sinogi, as others pronounce it. We waited here for quite some time before boarding our vessels in order not to arrive too early at Tokitsu and thus be urged to complete the remaining part of our journey today. Moreover, it would mean that we would prevent the usual honorable reception and the welcoming party of Japanese friends—that were both to be expected tomorrow—from fulfilling their function. The weather changed to heavy rain, continuing throughout the night and also the next morning. As we could no longer wait for the rain to stop, we left Tokitsu on May 7th and completed the remaining and practically worst part of the journey to arrive on our Deshima at noon. But before reaching the city we had to exchange our *kago* for horses and then dismount some thirty paces before the island. However, after some deliberations, our superior and our leader had themselves carried through the gate. Let us, therefore, give praise, glory, and honor to our gracious God for happily accomplishing our first journey to court, which is herewith completed.

The following events happened here at Deshima and Nagasaki before we embarked on the second journey to court.

On May 8th our barge arrived early and cast anchor near Deshima.

On May 9th two officers arrived together with their retinue, the water gates and the storehouse were opened up, and everybody had their belongings from the boat delivered. The extraordinary mistrust among people here is amazing: our leader entered through the land gate and left through the water gate, but the officer, who was an outsider, entered through the water gate and left through the land gate, so that there was a senior officer as supervisor standing at each gate when they were being closed.

On May 11th our director and Abouts[54] went to the governor to pay the appropriate compliments on their return.

On May 12th vessels and officers arrived from Chikuzen to replace those from Hizen, as is done annually.

On May 28th the first junks of the spring season left, roughly some twenty in four days.

June 1st was a Japanese holiday, on which they played "Pelag," as our people call it.[55] During this event the Japanese practice their boating skills in rowing-boats and barges, trying to beat each other by rowing as hard as they can, which causes great amusement. They often shout "Pelo" and play chimes and small bells at the same time. On that occasion all houses put out flags made of thick paper or cardboard, as well as other ornaments. But it was strictly ordered that only the young were permitted to amuse themselves in this fashion.

On June 3rd smugglers who had traded goods with the Chinese were caught during the night. One attempted to commit suicide but was quickly caught by the bailiff or guard and only injured himself slightly. But because he was stopped and put into prison, he angrily bit off nearly the whole of his own tongue, because he wanted to eliminate his shame by a heroic act of suicide.

Around this time the Japanese *satsuki,*[56] or rainy season, begins, which indeed starts off with constantly wet weather, heavy rain showers, and winds. In this rainy month the rice is planted, the work of girls and women.

On June 20th we inspected our barges, one of which was judged to be old and useless. We took lunch in the temples in the foothills. During these days many special barges left for various locations, and other barges of the autumn season[57] arrived daily. To stop all secret trade, Nagasaki was always kept closed at night, and all passersby were searched.

June 30th. The previous night a Chinese junk of Batavia arrived flying the flag of the prince, but coming from a place in China.

On July 10th the night market, which had been permitted to operate for seven days, was ended, and the great festival of Gion, celebrated in honor of a holy Japanese idol, began.

On June 16th the cooks and servants on our island had to seal an oath with their blood that they would not associate with us.

July 20th. At about this time two libertines[58] were found dead on the road. One had killed the other with his sword and then killed himself by cutting his own throat. A few days previously a servant cut his own stomach; another cut his own throat because he had been insulted by another servant in the house of the governor and could not get the mayor's permission to revenge himself since the incident had taken place in the governor's house. A few days afterward someone was found under the bridge with his head not completely severed.

July 30th. During these days five fellows were brought as prisoners from Amakusa; they had attacked the village of Isahaya and had been caught in the act. They had been motivated by the news that the Chinese had secretly brought goods to the village, which they attempted to seize and rob but could not find.

Also around this time many junks arrived, including two large ones from Siam that had traveled for sixty days. The one that had left later was the first to arrive, bearing the message that they had sighted Dutch ships in the Siamese harbor.

On August 1st the festival of Tanabata, as it is commonly called, was celebrated. Another name is Shokujo. In memory of a certain legend, every husband joins his wife on this night and discharges his obligation. The following morning good wishes are exchanged and celebrations begin.

August 3rd was a special temple festival, a day celebrating Kannon called *sen nichi mairi,* which means "going a thousand days," because going to church on that day is so beneficial and counts as much as going to church one thousand times on other occasions. There is only one of these temples in Nagasaki.

On August 8th was the festival of *bon,* when the night is spent at the graves with burning torches and lanterns. This festival began on the previous day and continued also the following day, August 9th. People believe that the souls of the dead, both the good and the evil, move about and visit the places of their past.

On August 10th we received the news that our vessel, called the *Wahlenburg,* would arrive soon.

On August 11th the above ship arrived in the afternoon and cast anchor in front of the island.

On August 12th we again had news of the arrival of another ship, called the yacht *Wieck op See,*[59] which appeared the next day.

On August 15th the command ship *Wahlenburg* was unladed (after the inspection had been completed), which took four days.

On August 16th the Lord of Hirado arrived, and on the 18th he inspected our island and residence of Deshima.

On August 22 the yacht *Wieck op See,* which had sailed via China, was discharged; it took a total of three days.

August 23rd. We had sighted a ship yesterday, and some of us, including myself, went to meet it. We had our noon meal on the island of Iō, two German miles beyond Nagasaki at the end of the harbor. From there we went ahead for another mile in smaller vessels, which we had taken along, to welcome them.

On August 24th the above-mentioned vessel, *Boßwieck* from Batavia, cast anchor here. The ship was inspected on the following day, after which it was unladed for three days.

During these days we received news from Edo that Kenmotsu sama,[60] a governor who had been suspended, had died. He was suspended from office and died under house arrest because in 1680, when Dr. Cleyer was in charge of our trade, he ordered eighteen Japanese, who had secretly conducted trade with our men, to be crucified and beheaded without contacting the court.

September 7th was the moon festival, as the Japanese call it. In Chinese it is called "the light of the moon." It is celebrated by joy rides at night, both on land and at sea. But people in Nagasaki are distressed because owing to the illegal secret trade, neither business nor profit is possible, and the festival does not get much attention.

On September 9th, Dutch goods arrived.

September 10th was the first trading day for the above goods.

On October 1st, four apprehended smugglers were brought here in the boats of the whalers. Also previously, on September 25th, four persons who had been caught out at sea committing the same crime had arrived here as prisoners.

On October 2nd the boat of the smugglers was brought here with four other men, of whom two had cut their stomachs and had therefore been pickled. Last night one man cut his stomach, because he was involved in smuggling with the Chinese. However thoroughly the investigation was conducted at night with the gates shut, others escaped and fled into the mountains.

On October 4th another man escaped, and one more cut his stomach for the same reason. The latter was a Chinese assistant interpreter who also had advanced money. The leader of the illegal traders, who was caught, bit off his own tongue in order not to give away his accomplices. He also tore his robe, however strongly it had been tied, and made it into a rope with which he strangled himself.

A book was discovered in the possession of one of the prisoners which contained the names of his accomplices, lists of the goods purchased and sold, as well as the names of interested parties and those who had advanced gold. This exposed the trade and many citizens were caught. Consequently a thorough investigation was conducted day and night. Also large contingents of night guards were stationed in each ward, and in all streets the inhabitants were inspected three times a night. This began with the departure of the Chinese junks. Further, three people were caught in Nagasaki and taken to be tortured. The nightly inspection takes place after the gates have been closed to find out whether one or the other went out to the Chinese, who spend a long time cruising the sea below the ramparts, waiting for residents. But enough arrive from other locations, such as Chikuzen and Karatsu, where these inspections do not take place.

On October 6th another person escaped. Therefore all streets were sealed off, and all the Japanese on our island had to return home. A ward headman was dismissed and put under house arrest because he let a prisoner of his street escape from his house. From each street where someone had escaped, more than a hundred people had to go into the mountains to search for the fugitives.

On October 7th further citizens, some two or three, were taken in because they had been given away by the prisoners.

October 10th. Ten days ago the sales, but only the public ones, were held as customary. Beginning our sales on the 11th was extraordinarily late.[61] The reason was that the governor was occupied with a very intricate case relating to smuggled goods in which a hundred residents and many people from outside, as well as friends, were implicated. Therefore nobody was permitted to disturb or distract him for some fourteen days, and nobody was allowed to see him unless it was an absolute emergency.

On October 14th, Saturday morning we twice had a very strong earthquake. Neither of them was longer than the count of twenty or thirty. On the roadstead the pilot fell out of his bed. On land, the ravens and dogs made a lot of noise, having been disturbed in their rest.

On October 21st a coolie or bailiff was caught at the gate with camphor, and the vendor, Mr. *Reinß*, whose name the culprit confessed, was taken to the mayor. But on the orders of the governor, the coolie and the merchant, for whom the camphor was purchased, as well as the merchant's innkeeper, were all chained and taken into custody by the ward headman.

On October 22nd and the following day all ships were searched in the presence of two interpreters to locate all sorts of things, such as the so-called serum of long and eternal life by Silvius.[62]

On October 24th three captives who were caught trading illegal goods that they had purchased from the Chinese arrived from Hizen. Two escaped, but the third was unable to break out and therefore cut his stomach. As a result all coolies and servants had to leave their work and return to their wards to search for the escapees.

On October 25th the death sentence pronounced by the governor was transmitted and read to our director by the scribe and officer. The two people in question were to be decapitated, and it was requested that *Reinß* leave the country. He was to be taken on board and handed over to the highest organ of justice at Batavia. There he was to be sentenced in view of the fact that so many of their own people had lost their lives in this affair. Otherwise in future they would do this here themselves with the necessary severity, although on this occasion they were prepared to forgo it.

On November 1st nobody worked because it was a Japanese holiday throughout the country. It is called *kunchi*[63] and today is the last day. It begins on October 27th.

On November 5th representatives of the governors arrived and we were called in front of them. It included the two captains,[64] the ship's crews, and all other Dutchmen who were on the island at the time, down to the last boy. Thereupon the captains were rebuked in a long and decorous speech, saying that Japanese laws ought to be observed and that their strict prohibitions, on account of which their own people were punished so severely, ought not to be treated so lightly and carelessly. This punishment was to take place at the same square and in our presence. We were again reminded of the two Japanese who had secretly traded two catties of camphor; they were to be executed, and we, on our part, should also deal with this matter with severity and prevent a reoccurrence. Otherwise in future the vendor would also lose his head.

November 6th the yacht *Boßwieck* left and proceeded up to Papenberg.[65]

November 7th, the yacht *Wieck op See* did similarly.

November 9th, at noon, the command ship *Wahlenburg* left with the captain and the remaining persons.

Early November 10th we received, as usual, the news from those at the guard stations on the mountains that the ships were already out of sight. There was also an inspection today, but they only looked into our rooms. Tonight between nine and ten o'clock we had a terrible tremor pushing vertically from below. Yet it passed so quickly that I counted only to twenty, but one of my glasses broke. The earthquake returned after midnight, but with less violence, and all this happened while the air was calm. After that there were three more quakes a little slower, and finally another two, but not so strong.

November 23rd Mr. Dieck[66] passed away gently with God's blessing.

On November 24th, at midday, he was buried on the western slope of Inasa, a small mountain, or Inasa no yama, accompanied by three large and two small *prauen*.

On November 30th I sent a letter to Dr. Cleyer with the Chinese junk sailing to Batavia.

On December 1st all sorts of cloth had to be taken to the governors so presents for the shogun could be chosen.

On December 2nd and the following three days an inventory was made of the belongings of the dead man.

December 7th. Today, Tuesday, the governor Settsu no Kami, previously called Genzaemon, arrived back in Nagasaki. There were a number of officers waiting who had been sent to congratulate him on his arrival as a gesture of respect toward the shogun. They came from Hirado, Ōmura, Amakusa, Shimabara, Karatsu, and other small neighboring daimyo or territorial lords of Kyushu. If an important territorial lord personally welcomes him, he assumes an inferior position to show his respect to the shogun, after whose state of health he inquires. After the ceremonies have been completed, he again assumes his superior rank. Today and on the previous days the last twenty Chinese junks left.

On December 9th, Sunday, the three city governors paid their customary annual visit to our island after they had done the same with regard to the Chinese peninsula.

On December 10th we had the first indication of Settsu no Kami's antagonism toward the Dutch, inasmuch as he had us informed early in the morning that we fellows should get ready to watch the workings of justice, which very soon was to be shown in action on our island, as it was applied to two delinquents who had to die on our behalf (that is to say, the two I mentioned on November 5th for having traded camphor). This indeed took place after about one hour. Consequently we had to appear on the order of our director—who himself had been requested to appear but without success—after we were urged rather rudely a number of times. Two senior officers and secretaries sat on small benches and the third bench was empty. The swarm of interpreters, both the ordinary and extraordinary ones, as well as the apprentices, landlords, and all those who belong to the enclave or island amounted to some two hundred people. These included a few coolies or bailiffs and hangmen serving the court, standing close by. The two candidates sat on their knees, one behind the other, hands tied to their bare back. Each had his own hangman standing next to him who, within an instant and simultaneously, with neither a word nor ceremony, cut off the heads of their charges as soon as we arrived and turned our eyes upon the scene. The bodies were each wrapped separately in a straw mat, while the heads were tied separately in another, and then were carried off our island and residence on carrying poles. When we were leaving—and also when we arrived—a board listing the crime and cause of the death sentence, as well as a toothed hoe of iron and a sharp, half-moon-shaped implement, were carried in front of us. These are two weapons found outside all guardhouses. The iron hoe has sharp hooks to stop fugitives: if it touches someone just lightly, it attaches itself so strongly that the person cannot get away. The other instrument is used to push, hit, and pin a person to a wall. Shortly afterward both the officers and secretaries left in two groups and the others followed slowly.

December 11th. Today I heard from the two interpreters Yozaemon[67] and Zenbei,[68] that the third interpreter, Shōdayū,[69] alone was responsible for the execution of the two men. It was unnecessary, and he should not have reported a crime involving only ten taels, the sum the man was caught for, while the others were prepared to remain silent. They told me that the previous day they had also prepared a document to the governors to save the men from being executed, declaring that the camphor in question had been stolen and not purchased on the island. But that bloodthirsty dog opposed them and refused to sign.

Here the judges do not act according to their conscience and do not pay respect to any inborn sense of justice but arbitrate and judge according to what has been done and has been proven,[70] applying strict laws with the utmost severity.

Around this time Jūbei sama[71] had one of the officers attached to his household executed because the man was drunk and started some indecent mockery and quarrel. Another man, however, who scolded and tried to stop him, but only annoyed him with his scolding, was put into prison. In the residences of their aristocracy such executions apparently take place within their own walls[72] five or six times a year.

On December 20th the governor, Jūbei sama, left at two o'clock at night. But in spite of continuous heavy rain, good manners did not permit that either the inhabitants of our island or the officials of the city abstain from accompanying him. During that night coolies or bailiffs had to attend to him at a river on the route to Isahaya, with the result that one died of the cold while another is still fighting for his life.

On December 28th, twenty-eight persons were sentenced for smuggling, of whom thirteen were crucified and the rest executed. Among them were five who had cut their bellies when they were caught: they were pickled and subjected to the same punishment. There are still many in prison who committed the same crime and can hardly expect better treatment.

On January 18th, 1692, we received the news that of the four escaped smugglers, three had been imprisoned in Osaka, since the governor Settsu no Kami had sent out spies. They were happily sitting together; thanks to their confessions, a lot of others will join the merry chase.

January 19th. During the night a ruffian stepped out of a brothel and cut down three men coming toward him but did not kill them. Chopping people down like this is common in Nagasaki at night.

On January 20th we got the news that the territorial lord of Agata[73] had five thousand *man koku* of his land confiscated by the shogun because some thousand farmers fled on account of excessive burdens imposed by his young secretary. The administration has been turned over to his predecessor until another territorial lord is appointed.

February 1st and the following days we spent loading our barges for Kokura for the approaching journey. We had also spent the previous days with sorting, locating, and examining the goods that we are supposed to take as presents for the shogun and which are examined and chosen by the governors.

Chapter 14
The Second Journey to the Shogun's Court

On March 2nd, 1692, we left the island of Deshima early in the morning at eight o'clock. We were accompanied by the *yoriki* Sasamori Hanzō, the *dōshin* Shimada Sukeemon, as well as two city messengers of Nagasaki, the most senior interpreter Shōdayū, and the junior interpreter. We rode up to the eastern edge of the city to Sakurababa, where we drank to our departure with our interpreters and friends in the Tenjin temple,[1] which is administered by *yamabushi.* Thereupon at ten o'clock we left in our *kago,* traveling on winding mountain roads up to Tōge, or the peak and top of the mountain. From there we came to the village of Himi, with the large fishing village of Aba not far away on our right. We again mounted horses, that is to say, at Himi, and rode to the village of Yagami, where we ate and were bade farewell by our friends and companions with *sakana* and *sake.* But this time they were, so to speak, knocking on the door of a deaf man's house inasmuch as they received no presents from us. We traveled without delay to the village of Koga and then to the village of Isahaya, where on the left of the road large, protruding, and overhanging rocks are a remarkable sight. Also we had to cross three large bridges and after that arrived at Isahaya at seven o'clock in the evening. At eight o'clock, having eaten a sparse dinner, we left in three ships of the Lord of Hizen, accompanied by a small vessel and a boat for running back and forth. We used our oars and arrived before midnight at the village of Takesaki, where we dropped anchor for several hours to find out whether the weather was going to be adverse, in which case we would mount our horses again and continue overland. This is the bay that our skippers call the Bay of Arima, famous for the war with the Christian rebels. The water is very shallow here, and therefore it is important to pay attention to the tide when leaving. We left by ship and arrived this morning, March 3rd, in the mouth of the river of Yanagawa. We reached the bridge and the gates of the outer court of the castle after traveling up the curve of the river for roughly three-quarters of a mile. Seen from a distance of quarter of a mile, the castle tower made a fine sight. We thanked the skipper and inspector who had brought us here, and even though they had entertained all our men with Japanese food and *sake* on the boats this morning, they would take money neither for the transport nor their troubles, saying that they had been ordered by the regent of Hizen not to accept any, since the Lord of Hizen had not yet returned from the court. Before we entered the mouth of the river, we were met by a craft from Yanagawa to guide us. Yanagawa consists only of a handsome mountain town and a tower. There is a pleasant river with many vessels and streets with fishermen, as well as a few fine city streets. After we had lunch here, we left and first arrived at a village, the border of Kurume and Yanagawa, and then traveled through some scattered villages past flat cultivated fields crisscrossed by many water channels up to the village of Yokomizo. From there we went through the village of Tokoromachi and up to the village of Jikkenbashi. Before that, there was a river dotted with small ships and carrying much water, running toward Saga. We were taken across this river without unloading the horses. We rode through a scattered village and past others and came to the town of Daizenji, and to the town of Koga, or Kurume Kogamachi. Then we arrived at the city and castle of Kurume, which is surrounded by well-kept moats and is well supplied with fine gates and short bridges over the moats. We arrived at our inn in Kurume at five o'clock in the evening. From the border of Kurume up to here we were accompanied by five men walking ahead; they took leave of us the next day on their knees and with humble gestures. Only one accompanied us to the border of that province. Here they almost bolted and locked the doors of the house as well as those of the courtyards, claiming that this was done to safeguard us from thieves. I was so bold as to point out with some solemnity that this was a gross insult to us, because it made people believe that we were prisoners and criminals or Portuguese who were being taken to court, while we were traveling as free men and friends of the shogun to be received in audience. However, everything had been ordered by the senior interpreter, the devil incarnate and sworn enemy of the Europeans.

This city consists of a number of long streets and a few transverse ones, all uniform and on level ground but lined by about one thousand wretched little houses. It is unfortified and open with miserable gates and portals. It was remarkable that there was not a single person, neither along the road on which we traveled nor in front of the houses, but they all hid behind blinds. Yet the crossroads running off the main street were full of people who had adopted a crouching position. In this small part of Japan all who came across our way our leader sent off the road and into the fields and told them to dismount from their horses, which they did, kneeling with bared heads and waiting until the procession had passed.

On March 4th, we left shortly before daybreak. After a mile we passed the turnoff on the right to Fuchū, an old castle, and then with the horses loaded were taken across the strong currents of Miyanojigawa, a river flowing to Saga. On the banks of the river is a village called Miyanoji. After that, we came through a village where the houses were scattered far apart and which was mainly inhabited by people tilling the soil. This was the end of the territory of Kurume and the beginning of the shogun's lands. Therefore the forerunner from Kurume, who had accompanied us until now, took his leave by kneeling down. From Yanagawa till here our journey took us along embankments and fine, flat rice fields. But this next special area belonging to the shogun consists of bad, black peat.

We continued on our way and passed through the village or town of Matsugasaki of about one hundred fifty houses, and then through the village of Matsuzaki, and soon afterward through a small village and river up to the border posts of the shogun's lands and the beginning of the territory of Chikuzen, or Hakata. Here we turned into the highway of Akizuki coming from Chikugo. Not far from here we arrived at the village of Ishibitsu and soon afterward at the town of Yamae, where a territorial lord returning from the shogunal court had lodged the previous night and everything was still clean and strewn with sand.[2] After we had our noon meal, we continued our journey in *kago* with two forerunners from Chikuzen, whom we followed up to the village of Uchino, where we mounted our horses at the inn. Here we received two large bream and also were entertained by women with *sake.* Every horse was given two fellows for safety's sake and two men in front, who had to get us through the river. Afterward we reached the village of Aemachi and a temple that had been built there. From there we reached the village of Nagaya and a river running off to the right. Further along we came to the village of Mameda and soon afterward to the village or town of Tendōmachi, then to the village of Akimatsu, and finally to the small city on the opposite side of the river. It had poor bridges and a small village as an outer town. Its name was Meshizuka, but it was generally referred to as Iizuka. Here we entered an inn and were accommodated for the night.

On March 5th, we left early in the morning at four o'clock with bamboo torches. After one hour we reached the village of Kōbukuro and after two hours the village called Kotake, or bamboo.[3] After that, we came to a river crossing and the village of Akaji, and after roughly another hour we reached the other river crossing near the village of Sakai. Then we reached Nōgata on the other side of the river, which is the residence (but without a tower) of Ise no Kami,[4] a son of the lord of Chikuzen. After that we came to the large town or city called Koyanose, where this year the people were very dirty, perhaps because of the hard coal.

After the Hiyamizu mountain range, the country was exceptionally beautiful, and we traveled along embankments today. But the road ahead was hilly and of rather poor soil. Having had a little lunch here, we traveled on to the village of Chayanoharu, and to a village and high mountain road called Ishizaka, and then to the village of Kōjaku, and to the village of Uenoharu. From there we reached the village or town of Kurosaki, where because of the slippery, muddy, and wet condition of the road we exchanged our horses for *kago,* which here are always available in specially appointed houses. We were carried to the village of Nadanoki, and then to the village of Kimachi, and afterward to the outer city of Kiyomizu with a temple of the same name. From there we were carried to the city of Kokura.

City of Kokura

We were entertained in Japanese fashion as usual by the innkeeper here and waited until eleven o'clock at night, since the *bugyō* was writing his letters and the tide was coming in. We left in two barges and on March 6th at two o'clock in the morning entered the inn at Shimonoseki as usual. Food was first brought for the Japanese and then for us, but we did not feel like eating. The other barge arrived only at six o'clock, because it did not have as many oars. We boarded our barge but had to remain here until the next day, because the wind was against us, and, at any rate, this was how it was always done.

On March 7th, the wind came from the west and was favorable but too strong, and we had to remain here because we were told that the waves were too high for the boat we had in tow. It snowed and was very cold today.

On March 8th, we left at four o'clock in the morning in moonlight with calm skies and sea and a constant west wind blowing. We traveled east-southeast toward the island of Himeshima, east-southeast of Shimonoseki. On our left was the district and village of Iwaya. On our right, between Himeshima and Buzen (where the terrible mountain range was all covered with snow, as was also that of Nagato on our left), we could see the high seas at a point between southeast and east of southeast. Himeshima is some three to four miles from here. However, Iwaya was roughly one and a half miles north of us, with one or two islands of Kanju offshore. Mukō is roughly eighteen miles from Shimonoseki.

At twelve o'clock we passed through Kaminoseki, with the island of Yokoshima close to our right, and to the left the mountain and island of Senba, and straight ahead to the right we continued toward Heguri. Soon after two o'clock we passed the island of Oki Kamuro on our left and after half a mile had Itsushima[5] on our right. At half past three we had a village and small bay on our left, but on the right was the island of Yūshima,[6] and half a mile from there the island of Tsuwa no Marushima. From there we traveled two miles to Tsuwa, a harbor and an island, and half a mile later we reached the village of Nuwa, where we arrived at sunset and cast anchor. Today we traveled forty-seven nautical miles.

On March 9th, we left again early in the morning, but the wind died down and was so gentle that we did not make much progress. Nevertheless, tacking against the wind, we still managed to reach Mitarai at four o'clock in the afternoon, and we cast anchor together with some thirty or more other vessels. Among them were two barges with prostitutes, who made the rounds peddling their merchandise to interested travelers.

On March 10th, we sailed away at daybreak with favorable winds and thanks to constant winds sailed past the straits of Hanaguri on our left. On the right we traveled around Kurushima. It has a poor residence and consists of nine scattered islands and some area on the mainland. There are some fine houses in the close vicinity, and it is under the authority of Hiroshima in the province of Aki. Two nautical miles further to the southeast, on our right, was a large, fine castle with a magnificent tower, called Imabari. The city and the residence of the son of the Lord of Ki no Kuni[7] was on the side of the castle closest to us. From here we sailed toward the east and before sunset reached Shimotsui, a small city of about four hundred or perhaps more houses, situated along the edge of the sea, which was held back by boulders. The houses are clustered in three settlements and are governed by three *yoriki*. The city lies at the foot of a rocky mountain, and—like all other inhabited islands—the top of the mountain is covered with *matsu* trees,[8] looking like a fringe.

March 11th. The winds died down somewhat, and suspecting the approach of a severe storm, we took down our mast but then continued our journey into the night. A terrible storm came from west-southwest, however, and as we were not in the harbor proper, but at quite some distance from it, we had to cast six anchors to moor. This happened on account of the orders of the devious senior interpreter, who begrudged us the pleasure of the city and the company of the other vessels. But when I reproached him the next day, saying that his stubbornness had brought us in great danger and that it would have been his fault if something untoward had happened, he pretended that the purpose had been to be all the better prepared to set sail the next day.

March 12th. After the storm had died down and the winds had somewhat abated, we set sail in broad daylight and cast anchor in the harbor of Muro at three o'clock in the afternoon. We had traveled twenty nautical miles today. This time there were 150 vessels in the small harbor and it was totally crowded.

On March 13th, we left at daybreak with a gentle breeze. Five nautical miles after Himeji the winds became so weak that we returned to Muro, since it was already past noon. We reached Muro at three o'clock. Himeji has a large, beautiful tower, castle, and city but no harbor, port, or anchorage: the ground is supposed to consist of flat rocks.

On the 14th, we lay still owing to storms.

On the 15th, we left early and arrived at about two o'clock in the afternoon at Hyōgo, where we changed over to other vessels and barges. We reached the harbor of Osaka at nightfall, and between six and seven in the evening our innkeeper fetched us in pleasure boats.

City of Osaka

On the 16th, we rested.

On March 17th, we had our audience with the governor. In addition to the guard mansion, we were led through another two chambers with weapons in the alcoves, such as twenty muskets with brass locks, as well as bluish-black bamboo torches, containers with gunpowder and whatever else is necessary to load them, and the same number of large lacquered bows, longer than the length of a mat, each with a leather shooting glove attached, and the same number of lacquered quivers. The other corridor contained as many weapons again.

Having sat briefly in a small chamber, we were led to a large room. After a little while the governor appeared and sat near the alcove. But soon he moved closer and sat at a distance of two mats. After the usual compliments, he asked after our rank and age with very friendly, unpretentious gestures. Then he spoke to us about the illness of a member of his family, of which that particular person had already suffered for ten years, in the hope that we might cure it. When I asked to see the person, he answered that the illness afflicted the private parts and that he would therefore ask me to send medication for the illness without an examination. This was done in the afternoon. They looked at our hats, had us write, draw, and sing, and they mentioned dancing and other performances, but we refused. After a while they bade us farewell. This gentleman was fine-looking, his face was pale and long, he was some fifty years or older, he showed curiosity seeing and listening to us, spoke about our dress, and asked the captain to take off his coat.

The other governor had gone to the shogunal court, and we therefore paid our compliments to the steward in the guard mansion. The house was situated some fifty paces from the ordinary road, but we had to get out of our *kago* and in spite of the rain walk the distance on foot. We returned home before noon, packed our belongings, and left on March 18th before sunrise. But we did not travel on the ordinary road, since it was unusable, and instead traveled on embankments for nearly two miles. The first place we reached was the fine temple Montodera, and then we came to the village of Noda and next to the village of Chichi wa Nagara, where the village of Kasugae was situated a mile from our inn. After that we reached the villages of Tomobuchi on our right and Shinnagara on our left on the other side of the river. Further we came to the village of Kema and, facing it, on our left, to the large village of Sarashi. The bleaching-ground for Osaka, operated by the local inhabitants, is located there on the shore.

After that we reached the village of Akagawa, and then the large village of Nagi, and the village of Imaichi, where the ordinary route from Osaka came close to the embankment on the right. But we continued on the embankment and came to two villages situated on either side and then to the village of Ōgire. Next there was the village of Sada, where on the right we saw the temple Tenjin with its large stone gate and square, known as Sada Tenjin. From there we reached the village of Shimenochaya, or Shimeno, next the village of Deguchi, and soon afterward the city of Deguchi proper, where we saw a temple called Ikkōshū.[9] From here we arrived at the village of Hirakata at the foothills of a large mountain range, where we had our noon meal. We continued, passing the villages of Nagisa, Shuke,[10] Hinoue, and Kusuha and the famous village of Yamazaki, situated at the foot of a mountain near a river, where there are two famous monasteries and a temple on the summit of the mountain.[11] From there we reached the city of Yodo. Along the road not far away on the right was the city of Yawata. Above this city is a forest covering a tall mountain slope with many fine houses and buildings—perhaps monasteries—as well as the Hachiman temple.[12] Many people and priests travel back and forth along this road, and the mountains stretch with no end in sight past Miyako. After we passed the outer city of Yodo and the bridge known as Yodo ōhashi, with its forty posts above and twenty pillars below, we reached the city proper. It is a fine city, beautifully built, with a castle and a watermill on the river. On the other side is another part of the outer city and a Benzaiten temple. From there we reached Fushimi and passed an Inari temple, where the road was crowded because it was the temple's feast day. Toward evening we reached our inn at Miyako, near Shōgan temple of the Jōdo sect.

City of Miyako

March 19th. Having already announced our arrival to the stewards last night, we were taken to our audience this morning at ten o'clock. That is to say, we first went to the residence of the chief judge, where we had to dismount at a distance of twenty paces on account of the large entrance courtyard; this was surrounded by twenty fellows, each with his guard stave positioned in front of him and armed with two swords. At the entrance to the left sat a special guard of about six men. Crossing the square, we entered the large guard room of the scribes, where forty or more soldiers and officers were sitting in good order together with two scribes. After exchanging deep bows, we were led to the waiting chamber. We had our compliments sent to the steward, informing him that we were calling as usual on our journey to Kubōsava to extend greetings to the gentlemen in the name of our lords on Jacatra,[13] and to offer this small gift (consisting of vintent and pieces of cloth, which were arranged on ceremonial stands according to the custom of the country and kept in the large guard room) as a token of our good will. After the presents were once more checked by the interpreter and compliments had been exchanged back and forth, we received the answer that the chief judge was delighted by our arrival and our presents, that the presents would be accepted, and that we were invited to an audience. The valets of the mansion carried the presents into the audience chamber and arranged them along the side, but we were seated in the middle of the chamber, facing another chamber with two open sliding doors. In the meantime the honorable womenfolk arrived at a place still further ahead of us. But they disappeared after we had caught a glimpse of them for a short while through the slits that had been made in the paper (the windows at the back had been obscured so that we would not see them clearly), and suddenly that part of the chamber became light. Then the chief judge entered with brisk steps and sat down at two and half mats' distance from us. His expression was animated and he was laughing, but he neither bowed nor inclined his head. He immediately welcomed us and said that he was delighted by our arrival, as well as by our good health and the pleasant weather. After these words had been passed on to us with thanks, we mentioned the reason for our presence and entreated him to accept our presents with a kind heart and to bestow on us the usual passes. He answered that he was delighted with the presents, and that we would receive our passes. Then he inquired after our age, and he would have enjoyed communicating with us further if the submissive words of the interpreter had not irritated him and been unintelligible: the steward at his side could barely understand them, and the chief judge himself could scarcely guess their meaning. The audience took place with the greatest propriety, and everybody was silent when another person spoke. The chief judge sat stiff and upright, but the interpreters and we were lying completely bent over. After having invited us to stay for some food, the steward left again, and we were led back to the previous location in the waiting chamber. Soon two tobacco boxes of a rare kind were placed in front of us, and in addition—as was also before the audience—ground tea and two large baked figs, sweet biscuits, and other such things were placed in front of us on ceremonial stands. After that, one of the stewards appeared with two passes, which he handed to us. The captain received them, bowing and lifting them up to his forehead, and then handed them to the interpreter for safekeeping. We paid our compliments to the steward and bade farewell, but he accompanied us up to the front of the main guard, where once again we bade farewell, bowing deeply and bending our knees, and then marched off. This gentleman was tall, strong, and corpulent, had a large head, pleasant features, a round face, average nose, and pleasant disposition, and was about thirty-three years of age. He walked clumsily as if there were something wrong with him but otherwise was cheerful and uninhibited.

Afterward we were taken to the other governor, who seemed to be a grumpy old man. Out of necessity, however, he put on a friendly, smiling face and did not make us wait long. After we had some tea and tobacco, he had us come to his rooms, where he was already sitting at a distance of four mats, and welcomed us. He was alert when he received our compliments, which on account of the soft voice of our interpreter were passed on to him by his steward. Soon afterward we returned to our previous place, where we said our farewells to the steward, and after we had greeted the guards and made our final bows to the steward in the antechamber, we stepped into the courtyard and there into our *kago*. This gentleman was also corpulent, of not unpleasant figure, fresh and good-looking, about fifty-six years old, and had an alert expression.

From here we were carried to the third governor, who, as was his custom, made us wait for quite some time. But after the audience had taken place (which he conducted, as in the previous year, with a friendly, smiling face, with conversation and welcoming words, but without wishing to inspect anything belonging to us), he had us entertained with tea, tobacco, and biscuits. Also his two stewards, who were already fifty years old, were very humble. They showed us a thermometer, which they had received from us as a gift some thirty years ago. Those present drew closer, and we had to explain to them the indicators of the day and the moon and the grading of the thermometer.

March 20th. We left Miyako and after we had reached the large bridge, we had farewell drinks in the outer city. Then we reached the village of Hino'oka Tōge, located between the mountains, two miles from Ōtsu. Afterward we came to the long and rich village of Yabunoshita, where an excellent, fine tobacco is produced and lots of bamboo is growing. Then we came to the bordering village of Yakkochaya, where a quarter of a mile from the road to the left is the monastery of Moroha daimyōjin. It has a large gate on the road, and there is also a Kannon temple with a large, gilded, famous image of Jizō in a six-cornered building. Close by was the village of Iwanochaya, and soon afterward the village of Oiwake, where to the right we saw a large, high mountain covered with snow. After passing various villages here and there, we arrived one hour before evening at our inn in the city of Ōtsu, since it was mostly raining and snowing today.

On March 21st, we left our inn at five o'clock in the morning, first came to the Hachiman temple, and soon afterward to the city gate, castle, and residence of Zeze. Thereafter we came again to some famous temples and also to another Hachiman temple. Then we reached the following places: the villages of Katagiwara, Shinden, Kusatsu no nojiri, the large town of Kusatsu, the village of Tebara, which borders on the village of Menoke, where they make the bitter powder, and after that the village or town of Ishibe, where we ate. After our noon meal, we passed through the following places: the villages of Kōjibukuro, Hiramatsu, Hari, Natsumi, Yoshinaga, Tagawa, the large village of Izumimura, the village of Kitawaki, and after that the city of Minakuchi. Subsequently we came to the villages of Shinjō, Kosato, Imashuku, Ōno, Tokuhara, and Maeno, where they sell a glue-like substance in every house. It is solid and tastes like thin, hard-baked gingerbread and is called *amakashi.* From here we reached the village of Matsu no Omura and thereafter the small city of Tsuchiyama, where we entered our lodgings at six o'clock in the evening.

On March 22nd, we were carried over the mountains of Sakanoshita at the break of day. After a quick meal, we mounted horses and rode through mountains and valleys to Sekinojizō, consisting of one elongated place, where they made bamboo torches. The place has many fine inns and temples, but the young people are nasty and badly brought up. The settlement consists of a street half a mile long. After we had eaten our noon meal, we rode away and came to the following places: first, the road to Ise, then Sekigawa, Ochibari, Nojiri, Nomura, the city of Kameyama, the outer city of Nabeyamachi, the bordering Shinmachi, the unenclosed town of Shōno, the unenclosed town of Ishiyakushi. Then we passed more villages, such as Ōtani, Kotani, Shimizudani, Tsuetsukimura with its temple, Unememachi, Ogosomura, Oiwake, Tomari, Hinagamura, Akahori, Hamada, and finally in the evening reached our lodgings in the small city of Yokkaichi. Here we experienced the deceitfulness of our interpreter, who called together those traveling to Ise and warned them not to defile themselves by coming too close to us.

On March 23rd, we set out at daybreak on horseback and arrived at Kuwana at nine o'clock. But because of the prevailing wind and rain we could continue our journey neither by sea nor land. Therefore we stayed and spent the night here where Matsudaira Etchū no Kami resides.

On March 24th we left in three vessels and continued by sea since the weather was suitable. To make up for the time we lost yesterday, we had our noon meal quickly and immediately left again, arriving in Okazaki shortly before evening.

City of Okazaki

There we had our evening meal and left again for Akasaka, where we arrived at eleven o'clock at night. We gave free rein to hunger and thirst because the hard journey from Okazaki to here had made us hungry.

On March 25th, we left at six o'clock in the morning, and when we arrived at Arai, the shogunal captain of the guard honored us with a present as usual. He sent burdock roots with the excuse that it was the commemorative day of the shogun's death and that therefore he did not want to send fish.[14] After stretching our legs for fifteen minutes, we continued with favorable winds and arrived at Hamamatsu in the evening.

On March 26th, we left Hamamatsu early in the morning, at about six o'clock, and had our midday meal at Fukuroi. First we continued riding for a while and then were carried up to Shimada, where we arrived at seven o'clock at night, in moonlight, after we had safely crossed four rivers an hour earlier.

On March 27th, we left Shimada for Okabe and from there were carried in *kago* up to Mariko, where we had lunch. Through Fuchū and onto Ejiri.

On March 28th, we left a little before daybreak, ate in Yoshiwara, and spent the night in Mishima.

On March 29th, we left early at daybreak in *kago.* We had terrible weather on the way and up to Hakone. Here the air is always too sultry and unhealthy, so that no visitor can stay very long. We felt as if we were in the clouds and after our meal left in similar weather, arriving at Odawara around evening.

On March 30th, we left in pleasant weather at half past six in the morning and after lunch continued until eight o'clock in the evening, when we arrived at Kanagawa. In our usual inn lodged the regular shogunal envoy Ōsawa Ukyō sama,[15] who customarily once a year pays respect to the emperor in the name of the shogun. On this journey he was constantly in front of us, causing us obstruction and delay, as also today at noon when we had our midday meal in a town. Three of them are used for this annual dispatch.[16]

On March 31st, at five o'clock early in the morning we once again set out, and after we had refreshed ourselves at Shinagawa, we rode on and at twelve o'clock arrived safely—thanks be to God—in our usual quarters in Edo. Our *yoriki* had himself carried into the city in his *norimono,* no doubt having received permission from the Nagasaki governor, in order to show us that he was not of lower rank than our captain. The two governors, Tonomo and Jūbei, soon had us welcomed by their *yoriki*. The senior interpreter had himself carried to the lord commissioners and to Jūbei, as the Nagasaki governor in charge, whose duty it is to expedite our audience. He announced our arrival and was promised that the senators would be notified and that, if possible, our audience would take place on April 28th.

On April 1st, we received the compliments of Settsu no Kami and other commissioners. The following days were spent unpacking the shogunal cloth, mirrors, and other items and polishing them up, as well as with bottling the vintent and sorting out the gifts to honor the courtiers. While this was being done, Jūbei sama, our *bugyō,* and our interpreters were constantly present; everything had to be done in Japanese fashion by Japanese sent to us, and had to be paid for dearly.

April 8th. Yesterday and today we had terrible storms from the west, which meant that temperatures dropped considerably; all the people were so afraid of fires breaking out that they were constantly on the alert and wore trousers over their long skirts. Our cases were packed again, and the fire guards went into every nook and cranny of the streets, making a lot of noise with their rings and clappers, or rattle sticks, trailing behind.

Today Tonomo's son sent his compliments in return for our congratulatory message on the delivery by his beloved, who gave birth to her second child and first son. Around this time we heard that last year the shogun had built a *miya* in honor of the wonderful Chinese politician Confucius, who taught the art of government, and that this year he had built the lecture hall[17] of this same *miya,* which he visited the day before our arrival. The day before yesterday the shogun came to speak on the subject of the art of government in the presence of his councilors, and on the spot gave such an excellent discourse or lecture that those prostrated in his presence were overwhelmed with emotion.[18] Today the shogun was the guest of the young junior councilor Yanagisawa, who lives outside the castle. When the shogun visits, he is served by young women.[19] Some eight days ago our attendants and servants brought along a man from Nagasaki, whom they claimed was a hired hand and porter of our goods, to have his wound dressed, since he had suddenly been attacked by a large street dog, and his calf had been bitten badly. When we asked him whether he had taken revenge on the dog, he replied: "Do you think that I am also going to risk my life?" Nobody is permitted to kill a tame hen or a rooster. If one dies on him, he has to inform the officials in charge of the street, and that applies also if a dog or another fellow lodger dies.[20]

April 17th. Last night a street burned down a mile from here toward the northeast.

Early in the morning of April 18th an earthquake occurred in calm weather and lasted the duration of one Lord's Prayer or perhaps a little longer.

April 20th. Before evening we received the order to appear before His Majesty tomorrow.

April 21st. Although the present heavy rain had already started two days ago, we nevertheless had to mount our horses at eight o'clock and ride up to the second castle enclosure in the company of the various *bugyō* of the three governors. Passing it, we entered the third enclosure and reached the main guard, where Jūbei sama was already waiting for us. After we had waited there until half past ten, by which time the councilors had arrived and we had changed our wet shoes and socks, we moved into the castle and waited until twelve o'clock. Then the captain offered his presents and immediately joined us again in the waiting chamber. Thereupon we were called to the audience and were led by Jūbei sama around the left of the hall in which the presents had been arranged and around the chamber where the shogun's throne was raised by a number of mats. Next we were led through other magnificent corridors, gilded and paneled at the top, up to a long antechamber, from which we were straightaway to proceed to the audience. There were about ten or twelve high-ranking young nobles seated here in addition to the commissioners and other high-ranking courtiers walking around. We were led back again into a corridor so that we would not get tired of sitting but were able to freely stretch our legs. For this purpose also the sliding doors to a small garden were opened up. Immediately the sons of important nobles arrived to congenially greet and inspect us. Also the lord commissioners had a golden ring shown to us, into which a magnet was set with twelve Japanese zodiac signs[21] and a European coat of arms and other things. As we were inspecting and explaining it, we were called to the shogun. Therefore we were led along a corridor to our left, where eighteen chamber guards were sitting, wearing their own special robes over ceremonial dress. Then we passed another row of twenty courtiers, until we reached the place of the shogunal audience, where six councilors were sitting on the left; on the right, in a corridor, a number of personal attendants were seated. Further to the right two women and the shogun were behind the blinds, and in front of the blinds was the orator Bingo sama. The shogun asked him to welcome us, have us sit upright, take off our coats, state our name and age, get up and walk, first act and dance, and then sing a song and pay compliments to each other, punish each other, get angry, prevail upon a guest, and hold a conversation. Then he had us act like two people close to each other, such as a father and his son, like two friends parting and arriving, or friends meeting again, a husband parting from his wife, people hugging children and carrying them, and so forth. He had him ask after my occupation and among other things whether I had ever cured any serious illness. The answer: not here in Nagasaki, where we were kept imprisoned, but certainly outside Japan. He went on to ask about our houses and whether our customs were different. Answer: Yes. He asked after our funerals. Answer: That we only observe the day of the funeral. After our prince: What was his rank? Was the general[22] of lesser rank and below him? Whether the latter governed by himself. Whether we did not have prayers. Answer: No. Whether we also had idols like the Portuguese? Whether there were thunder and earthquakes in Holland and elsewhere. Whether thunder also ignited houses and killed people. We also had to read, but I had to give the names of many ointments and perform a dance; then we had to dance altogether. In the meantime the captain was asked about his children and their names and also how far Holland was from Nagasaki. At this point the shogun had the sliding doors on the left opened up for cool air. Then we had to put on our hats and walk around and talk for quarter of an hour and soon take our wigs off. A number of times I spotted the beautiful woman next to His Majesty, whereupon the shogun said in Japanese that we were looking so intently in his direction and that we knew they were there. He soon changed his seat and joined the group of women seated in front of us and had me approach the blinds and once again take off my wig. After that, we had to leap and dance with each other, go for a walk, and the captain and I had to guess the age of Bingo. He answered fifty, but I said forty-five, and they laughed a lot about that. We had to play husband and wife, and the women laughed heartily about the kiss. Then we had to show how we saluted people of lesser rank, women, nobles, a king. After that, they said I was to sing another piece by myself, and I did this to their satisfaction by singing two, which they all liked so much that they asked whether one had to learn this as an art.[23] Then we had to take off our coats, and one after the other step in front of the blinds and bid farewell in a most exuberant fashion, as we would to a king in Europe, and after that we left. Judging from people's expressions and laughter, they were all very pleased, and it was four o'clock when we left His Majesty after two and a half hours. Having saluted the lord commissioners and Jūbei (after two of them led us away, just as they had brought us), we went to Bingo's residence, where we were well entertained. After that we went home as the sun was setting.

On April 22nd, we rode to the residence of the new commissioner of temples, the son of the lord of Hirado, where the house was crowded. The person who hosted us was a fool, had not the slightest predilection for politeness or manners, so much so that it appeared as if he were one of the high-ranking in disguise. We were served biscuits by the women. After people had inspected our hats and swords, the host said: Let them sing something, which they said we should do in honor of the old lord as his former protégés.[24] From there we rode to the residence of both the lord governors within the castle precincts. There, in the courtyard, we also saw an office, a lot of weapons, and counters crammed full with papers. At the house of the first we received only a cup of tea, and neither were there any women as in all the other houses. From here we still rode to two others, and finally to the two lord commissioners, where we were entertained splendidly, and in return we sang them each a song. At the first commissioner's we were served the following: (1) tea, (2) tobacco and what comes with it, (3) philosopher's or wise men's syrup, (4) a piece of boiled bream in brown soup, (5) two pieces made of ground fish, beanflower, and spices, (6) rolled-up omelets, (7) a piece of fried fish served on a skewer of green bamboo, (8) and finally two pieces of lemon with sugar. Between each course we drank a bowl of *sake,* which was as good as ever I had tasted. Twice they also served us a goblet of plum wine, which was deliciously sweet; also the food was rare and delicate, but no rice was served. We finished off with a cup of tea and after an hour and a half bade farewell.

At the other commissioner's we received after tea and tobacco: (1) two long pieces of *manjū* bread, which one dipped into a brown soup, with a little bit of ground ginger, (2) a hard-boiled egg, (3) four pieces of ground fish fastened together on skewers and fried, (4) three pickled little carps' stomachs with brown sauce, and (5) two pieces or mouthfuls of fried goose meat in an unglazed bowl. We drank a lot of rounds here, and the physician of the commissioner, who wanted to entertain us, also received his share. Behind the blind, two and a half mats in front of us, sat a fellow, and at times he was joined by women. Near the courtyard on the left, the women remained in the corridor. From there we rode home and arrived one and a half hours before evening.

April 23rd. After we were thanked and received the compliments of the gentlemen we visited yesterday, we were told this afternoon that we were to take our leave from the court tomorrow afternoon at three o'clock. The reason why we did not pay our respects to the governors today is that it is the death anniversary of the shogunal father Ieyasu.[25] Therefore they would not have been able to serve us fish today, nor is one permitted to entertain guests, out of respect for the shogun. He lies buried at Gosho, a temple behind Atago,[26] two miles from our inn. Previous shoguns are buried at Nikkō, three days' journey from here. That temple is supposed to be covered with pieces of gold, that is to say, with a lot of *ōban.* The fence surrounding the temple is supposed to consist of knobbed lacquered posts, as I heard from my attendant, who visited me today, having been brought along by a high-ranking person, as otherwise he is not permitted to come.

At seven o'clock in the morning of April 24th, we rode to court accompanied by the three *yoriki* of the three governors. We waited in the *hyakuninban*, that is, the hundred-man guard, until we were led up to the castle. For this we must first receive notice from the governors and the commissioners. After we had waited in the waiting chamber for half an hour, the captain was called in front of the councilors and the annual order was read to him by one of the commissioners (this happens annually as decreed). This says that any Chinese or Ryukyuans traveling to Japan are not to be treated badly by us, that we do not import any Portuguese or their servants, and that we are permitted to trade freely and enter the country. The answer is: *kashikomarimashita.*[27] After that the captain receives three trays with presents, each more than two mats in length and each bearing ten robes, and also a congratulatory letter as an indication of the shogun's favor. The captain creeps up to the presents and puts a corner of the cloth over his head, and that is it. After that, the captain joined us again, and the robes were carried out of the castle on the above-mentioned trays up to the *hyakuninban,* where they were packed in cases together with some of the trays. As soon as the captain had joined us, the governor told us to wait, saying that we were to be given a meal by the shogun. After we had waited about half an hour, we were led into a chamber, where we were received by two men with shaven heads wearing ceremonial robes, perhaps the shogun's table and kitchen masters (the most important of these *osoba bōzu* sits next to the shogun when he eats and first tries everything). The interpreters were led to a different chamber, where they were supposed to eat. Soon the sons of various gentlemen and high-ranking young courtiers came to see us for a talk. In the meantime, a four-cornered rough little table of pine wood, held together with wooden pegs, was set separately in front of each of us. On each were five fresh and warm white cakes, called *amakashi,* as tough as glue, then two hollow pieces of bread, with a circumference of about two spans, baked out of flower and sugar, covered with white sesame. Next to that stood a porcelain bowl with a few slices of raw salmon, marinated or pickled, with a little brown soup like soy, but not as strong, rather sweeter, and two sticks of wood. After we had eaten a little out of courtesy (for we had already had some food at home and also eaten fresh *manjū,* made with a sweet substance of sugar and beans, at the guardhouse), we were urged to eat more and asked whether we would like a bowl of tea. The answer: Yes. The kitchen master ordered some for us, but it was only hot water in miserable, irregular, brown varnished bowls, called *mezurashii.*[28] Here too, just as in the waiting chamber, our hats and clothes and whatever we had on and with us were inspected. Having eaten this breakfast, which was pretty bad and by far below the standard of a good citizen, let alone that of a shogun, we returned to the waiting chamber.

Second Audience

After we were made to stay there for an hour, we were led again to the shogunal audience chamber by the governor, this time following a different route. We were told to sit down close to the audience chamber, where we had waited just prior to the last audience, or had been told to go for a walk in the corridor. The sliding doors and chambers that had previously been closed were now opened up, and the appearance of the court had changed so much that it looked completely different from the last time. In nearly every large room we saw courtiers seated and waiting to serve, as is their duty. In a large room and two corridors new, large posters had been put up, with five lines of writing, with only seven characters each. (Either I had missed these the previous time or we had come a different way.) While we sat here for about half an hour, others also arrived, including a priest, aged about thirty, dressed in white and blue silk, with a beggar's bag of the same colors. Timidly and somewhat embarrassed, he asked our name and age, something most of the others who came to inspect us wanted to know too. We also saw a priest dressed in orange-yellow robes, but he remained in the corridor and did not come over to us. Three water jugs for washing, perhaps made of silver, were carried into the inner shogunal chamber. But soon the water jugs were carried out again on a small two-storied or roofed-over black-varnish table.[29] The lower board of the table was cluttered with a confusion of bowls and trays, which led us to conclude that a meal had been consumed in the shogunal chamber. After that, we were immediately taken to a side corridor, close to the shogunal entourage, and after we had waited there about to the count of two hundred, a junior councilor and the lord commissioners led us in front of the shogunal blinds to the same spot where we had sat previously. (However, the latter remained behind when we entered the shogunal hall.) His Majesty was seated and remained seated on a slightly raised seat in front of us behind the center blind. Bingo sat in the middle toward the paper wall or sliding doors. The three senior and four junior councilors sat in their places. Only a priest seemed to crouch behind the blind on the right, and the place where the *gosobashū*[30] had previously prostrated themselves was separated by a screen and was empty. However, some were seated in the corridor. There were some twenty-five behind us, and along the same row but out of the sight of the shogun were eighteen gentlemen to carry out his orders. Also on the opposite side of the corridor surrounding the hall people had been placed in the same order. When the audience began, more came so that the corridor was pretty crowded.

We prostrated ourselves in Japanese fashion but were told to come up in front of the blind and each salute the shogun in European fashion. After that was done, the shogun asked me to sing a little song, in which I wished him prosperity.[31] Thereupon I began, just as I had done the previous year, to sing a song in memory and in honor of my old Florimene, who had remained faithful to me with all sincerity. "I am mindful of my obligation, In the furthest corner of the globe, Oh, most beautiful, who cannot be mine, Most beloved, who breaks my heart, and so forth." The final part of my song went: "A hundred thousand ducats, a hundred thousand million, are less valuable than the loveliness of my noble Florimene, and so forth." The shogun asked after the meaning. The answer: "May the gods in heaven shower a hundred-thousand-fold good fortune, grace, and happiness upon the shogun, his family, and his whole court." After that, we had to take off our coats and walk in a circle, which the captain did too. Then we demonstrated how one pays compliments when meeting good friends, how one bids farewell to one's friends, father and beloved, how people punish each other and reconcile again. After that, a priest with a wound on his foot was ordered to come. (It was a fresh sore on the shin of no great significance, or an old boil with a ring of inflammation.) He had put a small round daub of ointment on the wound, spread very thickly over a European piece of cloth. I was told to take his pulse and inspect the wound. I did the former and judged the patient to be a healthy, strong fellow. The latter I did by simply lifting up part of the plaster and closing it again, saying that there was no danger and the wound should get better with the plaster. I advised him only to somewhat curb his consumption of *sake*, which judging from the wound (but in reality from his nose) he seemed to take too liberally. This very much pleased the shogun and his whole court, so much so that they all laughed heartily. Thereupon the shogun ordered two others of his physicians to appear. They were personally called by Bingo, because they were in the inner chambers of the shogun and he had to step around the blinds on the left to call them. They arrived immediately, and they too were dressed and shaven like priests. One was blind in the right eye, and the other was not much better off, but besides that they were fairly healthy chaps. Since I had heard that they were the shogun's physicians, I gave them the opportunity to take my pulse first. After that I, in turn, felt theirs and judged both to be healthy. The first was by nature cold and could do with an occasional nip of brandy to improve his circulation. The constitution of the other was a little too hot, his head was weak, and he suffered from ailments of the head, which was also obvious from his appearance. Thereupon the senior of the two asked me at what time an abscess became dangerous and when, how, and in the treatment of which illness people were bled. He also indicated that he knew about our ointments and mentioned their names with awkward pronunciation, and I helped him with my awkward Japanese. And since the names I was saying were partly Latin and partly awkward Japanese, the shogun wanted to know in which language we were conversing and what language the Dutchman was speaking. The answer: Japanese, but badly.

After this performance had been concluded, a tray with wooden sticks was placed in front of each of us, positioned so that it stood in front of the third blind facing the shogun. On them were: (1) two little hollow loafs of bread covered with sesame, (2) one piece of white striped refined sugar rolled together, (3) five pieces of coated *kaya no mi,* or stones of the tree Kaya,[32] which are very much like our almonds, (4) one square, flat little cake, and (5) two pieces of gingerbread rolled like a funnel, brown and thick, but somewhat tough. On one side was a round imprint in the shape of the sun or a rose, on the other the emblem of the *dairi:* this emblem is a leaf and the flower of a large tree called *kiri.*[33] The leaf is similar to that of the bardana, the flower resembles a digitalis, a number of them on a stem the length of a span. (6) Two reddish-brown, square slices made of boiled bean flower and sugar, which was crumbly or brittle, (7) two similar pieces of yellow color but made of rice flower and very tough, (8) two square pieces of a similar nature, made of baked cake cut in square pieces, the center of which was of a different substance, like sticky crumbs. (9) A large *manjū* cooked in a bowl, stuffed with brown bean sugar, a substance like theriac.[34] (10) Two of the same sort but smaller and of normal size.

We took a little of this food, and the interpreter was instructed to save everything for each of us; for this purpose he was supplied with thick white paper and painted cord for good fortune. When the interpreter was loaded with the above, we were ordered to put on our coats and to step in front of the blind, one after the other, to pay our respects on our departure. After that had been done, we were led beyond the corridor by two gentlemen, one of whom was the most junior councilor, to where the gentlemen of the fourth and fifth rank—eighteen of each—sat according to seniority. Thereupon the commissioners and the governor came up to us and led us further until finally only the interpreters—who, loaded with the food we had been presented with, scarcely managed to follow us—led us to the waiting chamber. The governor bade his farewells in front of the waiting chamber and, like the others, congratulated us on the extraordinary favors that the shogun had never before in living memory bestowed upon the Dutch to such an extent. After that we soon left, and after we had saluted the guards in passing, we mounted our horses in the outermost castle. At that moment, the governor Jūbei, now called Tsushima no Kami, was carried past us and opened his *norimono* to greet us and to say something to the *yoriki.* His procession consisted of eight forerunners and four men walking beside his *norimono,* one man carrying a pike, one rather poor white horse, and three men carrying luggage. We proceeded to his residence, where he opened the sliding doors and seated himself in front of us together with a young gentleman and the secretary of the young commissioner. He welcomed and congratulated us personally and urged us to enjoy the food, which was soon served after we had been given a cup of tea. There was boiled fish in a fine soup and after that boiled oysters served with vinegar in the shell, and we were told that he had ordered that dish because he knew that the Dutch liked it. Then small pieces of fried goose meat were served, also fried fish and boiled eggs, and in between all that we happily emptied bowls of drink. When we had finished eating, our hats, swords, tobacco pipes, and pocket watches were inspected and carried away (because there were no women here and consequently no *uta*[35] or dancing). They also fetched two maps, of which the first was well printed but without any names. Otherwise the map was accurate; perhaps it had been copied from a European map. The next one was a general one, set out in an oval shape with names in Japanese written in *katakana.*[36] The area north of Japan was portrayed as follows: a country twice the size of China lay behind Ezogashima, divided into various provinces. A third of it was beyond the arctic circle, and that portion or more also extended further to the east than Japan. At that same place there was in the middle a large bay facing east, or America, with a curve like that of a rounded-off square, so that there was no other opening between Ezo and America. However, between them lay an average-sized island, and in front of that, to the north, a long island, the eastern extremity of which was on the same meridian as the corner of America. Since this island lay west of Ezo, it closed up all of the opening. Also, all other countries to the east, which are unknown to us, had been turned into islands and could be circumnavigated.

After that we rode to the residence of Genzaemon Settsu no Kami sama, where we were also entertained well. There were many strangers present, but even though they were unknown to us, they treated us in a very familiar fashion. Among them were the brothers of Jūbei and Genzaemon. The latter had a son with bad feet, and the brother of the former had pimples on his face, for which they asked for advice. The ladies were in front of us, crowded together behind a light blind, and we not only sang them a song but also performed a dance. At Tonomo's residence everything was, as in the previous year, in abundance and splendid, and that is why we sang three songs and merrily rode home. We arrived home after sunset and on the way passed the temple Kōrinji,[37] where the shogunal water had been closed off. It is thirty to forty fathoms deep.

This evening various junior councilors, as well as one of the governors, had sent their robes during our absence. They had been received by the *yoriki* in our name, but some people were waiting with the gifts. Most of them also gave a present to the interpreter as well as to the son of the innkeeper, who introduces us to them. The reception of the presents takes place in the following fashion: coolies carrying the robes in boxes march ahead, one of them carrying the board or tray for the presents. The tray is taken up to the front, and the robes are placed on it. On top of them a paper for good fortune (consisting of some flat strips, plaited at the end, wrapped into a piece of paper around which a number of gilded, or silver, or other colored paper strings are wound, always an uneven number such as three, five, seven, eleven, and so on) is placed. Then one of the delegates, a house steward, is led forward by our *yoriki* (in the presence of other leaders, the robes, the innkeeper, and the interpreters). He sits down on a mat facing the captain and pays the following compliment: XX sends word that you had your audience and took your leave and also enjoyed pleasant weather. That is *medetai.*[38] Your presents pleased him, and as acknowledgment he sends you a few robes. While saying this, he hands over a large piece of paper with the number of robes and sometimes also their color written in large letters. This is handed to the interpreter and then to the captain, who holds it up above his forehead and, inclining his head (everybody kneeling or seated), has the following conveyed: XX helped them in obtaining an early and successful audience. For this, he expresses his deepest gratitude and asks that he remain the patron of the Dutch. He also would like to express his gratitude for the presents and will inform his superior at Jacatra accordingly. Thereupon a cup of tea is served, in addition to smoking utensils, and after that some distilled spirits and a tray with five silver plates bearing confectionery is put in front of the visitor. At the same time, he is invited to try a little of the Dutch drink (distilled at Batavia) and to take into consideration the sincere hearts of the Dutch rather than this small offering. Thereupon he is poured a brandy glass of vintent, or as they call it, *sinti,* which is lifted up to the mouth with both hands, Japanese fashion, sipped three or four times, and then emptied with feigned eagerness. Even the last drop is sort of slurped up, and the rest is shaken out onto the tobacco, or in between the mats, or onto the wrapping paper. Then the lower edge of the rim is wiped with the thumb or paper and the glass handed to the captain, who has it filled up for himself and then passes it back in the same fashion. The first person takes it back, has it filled up by someone else, and passes it to the *yoriki,* who again passes it on in the same fashion. Then more is served of a different kind until all varieties have been tried and praised as *mezurashii.* Finally the glass is returned to the captain, who has another drop poured and ends the round; he also orders that the drink be taken away. In the meantime, the innkeeper has wrapped the biscuits in paper and wound a few cords of good fortune around it. On his departure, the delegate passes this on to his servants. Then he takes his leave, expressing his gratitude for the courtesy and the *mezurashii* drink. The captain has his greetings and respects conveyed to the delegate's lord, thanking him for his pains. The *yoriki* pays a compliment of a similar nature, and then the visitor is accompanied to the outside, where both parties again bow down to the ground.

On April 25th, Bingo sent ten beautiful robes, and the young lord of Hirado, who has recently been made commissioner of temples and shrines (succeeding to the post of the man who has become chief judge in Miyako),[39] sent five decorated with flowers, more beautiful than any others, excepting those from the shogun. The other magistrate of Edo (who sits in judgment over crimes of hitting, beating, theft, and the like) sent two poor robes, as his colleague did yesterday. The following number of robes are presented: The shogun, thirty. Bingo and the four senior councilors, ten each. Each of the junior councilors, six. Each of the three commissioners of temples and shrines, five. Each of the two Edo magistrates, two. That makes a total of 123 robes. Of those, the company is sent the thirty robes from the shogun, and the remaining 93 are for the captain. Everything was finished at two o'clock in the afternoon.

On April 26th, we were busy packing and we hired fifteen horses for the journey and the necessary coolies. This morning we had a fairly strong earthquake with slow movement, pushing from side to side, lasting most probably a slow count of forty. After midnight, around two o'clock, there was a terrible earthquake, which lasted so long that one could easily have counted to a hundred.

Chapter 15

Second Return Journey from Edo to Nagasaki

Departure from Edo

April 27th. This morning we departed in the name of God soon after daybreak at a quarter past seven and at nine o'clock reached the end of the city where the boards with edicts are located.

Shinagawa

From there we reached Shinagawa, which was divided by a large stream, and another smaller river could be seen at the end. There is a very tall, large temple and tower called Myōtsūji here.

The Fishing Village of Suzu no Mori

At an hour's distance from there, immediately after the execution ground, lies a fishing village known as Suzu no mori, where shells are harvested and the shore is full of them. At the very beginning of this village on the right is a Hachiman temple, and in the middle of the temple the stone Suzu no ishi, a smooth black boulder, is kept on a little bamboo stand, just over knee high. Under the ceiling an ax or sword and various horses[1] were suspended. Behind these hung white plaited paper strips obscuring the rest of the temple. After that we reached Kawasaki at lunchtime at one o'clock. After we had eaten there, we traveled up to Kanagawa, where we arrived at four o'clock and had to stay for the night as the interpreters maintained that owing to the arrival of the Lord of Ki no Kuni[2] all inns and accommodations had already been booked, and that therefore we were unable to travel any further.

On April 28th we left Kanagawa early in the morning at five o'clock and came to the long village of Hodogaya or Shinmachi consisting of four hundred to five hundred houses. At the beginning of this village was a large river and bridge with many boats carrying wood, which was loaded here. From there we reached the village of Kashio, where both on the right and the left stood square stones with images. Next was the village of Totsuka, consisting of three hundred houses, a large river, and a bridge.

Roadside Stone Images

After that came the village of Harajuku and the town of Fujisawa with a river and bridges and some roadside stone images. At this point we passed the Lord of Ki no Kuni. We counted eighty led horses, more than fifty *norimono,* one hundred or more ordinary pikes, thirty-six pikes with feathers and drooping bushes or horsehair, thirty to forty men carrying bows, excluding those men who were still inside the houses, thirty boxes with the gilded emblem of the shogun and other gilded coats of arms, and many more. After the town, the road made a number of curves before it took us to the village of Yotsuya. And at the end of this village, near a fork in the road was a seated image called Fudō. The image had copper-colored hair, a long coat, something on his shoulder, red flames behind him, the right foot placed on a stone, and the left foot hanging down; there was a short ax, knife, or sword in his right hand on his knee, and slightly higher up in his left hand was a double rosary. From here we reached Yawata, where there is a Hachiman temple on the right, and soon afterward came to the village of Hiratsuka, at the end of which was a river with a bridge the length of forty-five mats. Right afterward we came to the village of Kōrai and then to the village of Ōiso, where we ate. We went on and passed a forest on the left, but on the right was a fine field. Subsequently we came to the two villages of Koiso and then to the villages of Shio'umi and Umesawa, at the beginning of which was a bridge eight to ten mats long, but the bridge at the other end of the village was fifty to sixty mats long. Further we came to the two villages of Maegawa, situated at the shore, and then to the village of Kōzu with a bridge eighteen mats long. After that we came to the fine village of Sakawa, and finally to the village of Sannōhara, and at last to the city of Odawara.

The City of Odawara

Odawara has gates and moats and also the castle of the councilor Kaga sama, as well as various streets. I counted seven hundred to eight hundred houses up to the inn, where we arrived at six o'clock at night.

On April 29th we were carried from our departure at dawn and reached the following places: the village of Kazamatsuri, the village of Iriuda with the famous temple Jōtaiji with large gold letters on the gate called Chōkōsan.[3] Further we reached the village of Yamazaki and soon on the left on the other side of a bridge the two villages of Yumoto, with the temple of Sōunji.[4] To the right in a bend of the river were hot baths and a few villages close by.

City of Hakone

Afterward we came to the villages of Kawabata, Hata, Kashinoki, Moto Hakone, Hakone Gongen and soon afterward to two small *miya* or smoke baths,[5] which are supposed to be the purgatory of children, as well as to four temples that had been erected, with their *namanda* and the like.

Creation of the Lake by an Earthquake

Finally we arrived at the city of Hakone proper at eleven o'clock, lunch time, where we ate and were told how formerly the lake had been created by an earthquake. We left again at twelve o'clock and reached the villages of Yamanaka, Sasahara, Mitsuya, Tsukahara, Hatsunegahara, and Kawaragaya, at the end of which was a bridge of twenty mats, and then we arrived in the city of Mishima.

City of Mishima

In Mishima I counted six hundred fifty houses, not including those of the suburbs, and inspected the place where the temple had burned down, which was one hundred paces wide and three hundred paces long. This place was surrounded by trees and a stone wall. The highest point of the temple, where the idol had stood, was fenced in with bamboo to which a large number of pieces of paper were attached.

Tame Eels and Fish

Behind, in the bushes, a little temple had been built, and nearby stood a black wooden horse; there was also a shallow stone-lined lake with many tame eels and other fish. After Mishima we came through a number of interconnecting villages to the village of Nagasawa, which had a Hachiman temple at its end and soon afterward on the right another temple with a bridge forty-five to forty-nine mats long.

City of Numazu

After a few villages we came to the little city of Numazu, arriving at our inn at six o'clock in the evening. Previously our people had seen the large cooking and hunting pot of Yoritomo here.

Hachiman Temple

On April 30th we left our inn early in the morning and first passed a Hachiman temple, where there had been a large fire on April 8th, the day on which we had had a fierce storm in Edo. But they had already erected many new huts. After we passed a number of villages, such as Hara, Yoshiwara, and others, we had our noon meal in Kanbara. Then we walked for a while over the mountains up to Okitsu, passing the villages of Kanzawa, Yui, Imajuku, and others. We arrived at five-thirty at Ejiri for the night.

Ejiri

A mile from here we looked at a beautiful temple situated on a mountain slope.[6] The temple was reached by climbing some sixty steps. It was extremely pleasant. Water was gushing down into an irregular pond surrounded by overhanging trees. The remaining slope was equally steep and thickly wooded with all sorts of trees, especially pines. We saw a completely white sea urchin with bent spines today. In Ejiri finely plaited basketware was offered to us for sale, which came perhaps from Abekawa or Suruga.

On May 1st we left Ejiri at dawn to escape the rain predicted by a sailor from Edo. We were carried in *kago* from Abikawa, which is also called Fuchū or Sunpu,[7] into the midst of a swarm of young *bikuni* and *yamabushi.* Up to the right was a little wooden temple with a stone figure called Jizō bosatsu or Utsuno jizō, and not far from that stood a similar temple, Hana tori jizō. Soon afterward we came across begging Kannon *yamabushi* with rattles. I saw the picture of Kannon along the road here, near a priest, who had a *yamabushi* rattle as well as a small bell, which he used when praying and begging.

Image of Kannon

This carved and gilded image of Kannon had many arms, of which two were above the head and longer and larger than the others. Both these arms held only one child each. On its head were a total of eight figures, of which six formed a kind of crown; two were placed a little higher on the parting, and one standing figure was in front of the forehead. Perhaps this image was supposed to indicate the many incarnations and apparitions of the idol Amida. We had lunch in Okabe, where we heard that on April 8th, when we had terrible weather in Edo, the people here returned from the fields, and when the parents could not find their children, they were told that their children doubtless were still in the houses that had caught fire, and they jumped into the burning houses to be with them.

City of Kanaya

We arrived in the inn at Kanaya at four o'clock.

May 2nd. We left in *kago* early in the morning at four o'clock and arrived at the village of Shinden. Nearby this village we found a round boulder at the road with a circumference as large as a traveler's hat. This stone was called Yo naku no matsu no ishi,[8] because a tree had been turned into a stone. The stone is very hard and cannot be carried away. Soon afterward we came to the city of Nissaka at the slope of a mountain, and close by was a Hachiman *miya*. Then we came to Yome ga ta, which means "ricefield of the beautiful daughter," where there was a memorial stone in remembrance of this young woman.[9] The fields between the mountain and the road were narrow, and her mother ordered her to hoe a field the size of one street.[10] But she fell down dead while working on the spot where the stone was erected. Soon afterward on the left were mountains containing alabaster. We ate at Mitsuke, and from there we were carried to the city of Hamamatsu, where we arrived at five o'clock in the evening. Here one of our *norimono* carriers was treated with *uchibari*[11] by two servants, but more about this can be found in my *Amoenitates Exoticae,* book III, chapter XI.

On May 3rd we left early in the morning at five o'clock and traveled the same road to Maisaka. Shortly afterward we left by boat and after three-quarters of an hour arrived at Arai, where for the price of one *bu* (that makes two and a half ducats) we were permitted to stay at the inn until the horses had been loaded. This price included refreshments for our *bugyō* and interpreters but none for us. From here we reached Saruga Banba, where *kashiwa mochi*[12] are sold (but that name was wrong, since they were plain rice cakes and these trees are not found in this area). In this area we passed many hills where frequently *tsubaki* with purple and flesh-colored flowers were growing, and we stopped for lunch in Futagawa. After lunch we passed the village of Iimura no chaya and then the outer city of Yoshida, with one hundred sixty houses, and then arrived in the city of Yoshida proper, which had about six hundred houses.

City of Yoshida

The city had a castle with many, but not very high, towers. The outer city on the other end consisted of two hundred forty houses, and there was a very large bridge supported by about 326 pillars. After that we passed the villages of Yotsuya, Kofu, Goyu, and other villages until we reached our inn in the city of Akasaka at five o'clock in the evening.

City of Akasaka

May 4th was a Sunday. We were woken by the restless Shōdayū at half past one in the night to get ready for our departure, and at half past two we passed through the city in bright moonlight. We reached the village of Nagasawa, the long village of Hōzōji, where there is a famous temple and an important school,[13] the villages of Yamanaka, Fujikawa, Kanbasaki, Shōda, the long village of Ōhira, and after that we reached the city of Okazaki, consisting of some seven hundred houses.

City of Okazaki

The city and the castle are situated on a hill at the foot of the mountains, but the castle is separated from the city by walls and moats. The moats are spanned by a bridge of 156 arches, or the length of 208 mats. Both the city and its first suburb have fairly large houses. As the mountain chain stretches to the left toward the sea, the road continued through fields. Next came the villages of Utō, Ōhama, Ushida, and the town of Chiryū, where we ate. After we had our meal, we again mounted our horses at twelve o'clock and reached, among others, the villages of Imagawa, Ano, and Arimatsu, the town of Narumi, and the village of Kasadera, where the sea Musashi Shiro[14] was pointed out to us.

City of Miya

From here we reached the suburbs and the city of Miya. At the entrance of the city a temple had been erected in which an immense wooden image was seated, which was called Shōzu ga uba.[15] This image filled up the whole temple; the left hand was placed on the left knee and the right was placed upright on the right knee. There is in this city still another temple for the same idol, which is very old, built without columns, and put together very skillfully by the skillful carpenter Hidano Takumi. And there was yet another temple here, called Atsuta,[16] which I discussed in chapter 13 of this book in the entry for April 12th. The inn here is pleasant and has a fine ornamental courtyard.

May 5th we boarded our barges early at five thirty and left our inn with a gentle breeze and pleasant weather, and after we had passed some islands, we arrived at nine thirty at our inn in Nagashima. The castle here was situated on the shore and had no tower. After we had been well entertained, we left at eleven o'clock and came to the following villages: Yasunaga, Honda, Yawata, Hazumura, Hazutongū, Oiwake, Ogoso, and to another village where they sold *manjū,* after which we arrived at five o'clock in the evening at our inn in the town of Ishiyakushi.

May 6th we departed early at four o'clock and in the main passed through the following localities: the villages of Shōno, Kumigawara, Tomida, Odamura, Kaizenji, Wadamura, the city of Shinmachi, or rather the suburb of the city of Nabeyamachi.

City of Nabeyamachi

Nabeyamachi, which was called Kameyama in chapter 13, under the entry for April 14th. Then we came to the village of Nojiri, the town of Seki, where nearly every house sold torches made by scraping *niwa take.*[17] At this place there is on the left the temple of Amida, and soon on the right the temple of Jizō, in front of which was a stone vessel where worshippers could first wash their hands. After that we arrived at the town of

Sawa, also called Sawabenoki no shita, and also at Sakanoshita, where we had lunch. Thereupon we came to the village of Yamanaka, where a *miya* had been built, and to the village of Tsuchiyama, where we met many travelers for Ise, and to a few more villages until we reached our inn in the city of Minakuchi.

City of Minakuchi

On May 7th we left our inn and at the same time the city of Minakuchi at dawn and came to the villages of Kitawaki, Izumimura, Natsumi, Hari, and Kōjibukuro and to the town of Ishibe.

City of Kusatsu

From here we reached the village of Takanomura, the village of Menoke, where they make bitter powder and drink this instead of tea, and the village of Tebara and after that came to an inn in the small city of Kusatsu at about at ten o'clock.

City of Zeze

After we had eaten at Kusatsu, we passed the villages of Kusatsu no nojiri, Oikami chaya, Shinden, Seta, and then came to the city of Zeze.

City of Ōtsu

After that we arrived at the city of Ōtsu, where we had to stay the night since the interpreter did not wish to travel any further, even though it could hardly have been much after two o'clock.

May 8th we left Ōtsu early in the morning and passed the village or town of Ōtani, the village of Yakkochaya, and the nearby Yabunoshita. Then we reached the village that is situated at the mountain of Hino, near which a tall stone had been erected with the inscription *namu amida butsu.* Opposite this stone two fellows had been sentenced and nailed to a cross. Before as well as after the stone and the cross, but at a little distance and out of sight of the cross, sat a priest[18] on a shabby blanket. Along the road seven tablets had been put up, each bearing the name of a dead person, and above them was a white flag with the words *namu amida butsu.* The priest was wearing a lacquered sun hat and had a little tablet in front of him on which there was a bell turned upside down, which he struck while singing *namu amida butsu.* This priest also had a bucket of water next to him, beside which stood a board from which a few pieces of paper with writing on them were dangling into the water. On both sides a bunch of *shikimi*[19] had been attached. Then the priest took a little stick with a few short branches of *shikimi* tied to the end and continuously washed or rinsed the small boards with the writing, while praising the souls of those whose names he had written. Passersby threw him small coins, perhaps so that he might pray for their souls. But he would have been wise to say a prayer for his own soul, for his eyes revealed the scoundrel he was. From there we soon reached the city of Kyō[20] and the place where previously we had drunk on our departure. First we came to Yamashina Kyō and soon reached the road where one branches off to Kurodani temple on the right and to Gion temple a little further on the left. Then we came to the large bridge Sanjō no hashi, and finally, one hour after sunset, we reached our inn at Miyako.

City of Miyako

On May 9th the chief judge made the captain a present of five fine robes; the two governors each sent five *shu*. These five *shu* are wrapped in paper and are placed in the middle of a gift board, on which there are five folded letters, each bearing a special heading, and one *shu* of silver as well as a cord of good fortune. Today we inspected a lot of merchandise with the servants of the mansion acting as go-betweens because the merchants themselves are not allowed to visit us upstairs. Twice we had to hand back goods (such as small idol boxes) for which we had struck a bargain, for they carelessly had been put together with the goods that were inspected and brought up to us. All pictures and similar things that we had managed to purchase had to be taken downstairs again. And all that happened on the order of our two scoundrels of interpreters. Besides, the prices we had to agree to were not much less than those on Deshima, because experts in the prices were always present.

May 10th we bade farewell, after we had taken a little Japanese food, for which the wife of the innkeeper received a *koban* as usual. Thereupon we mounted our *kago* to look at the temples. First we went to the most magnificent monastery I have ever seen, which also serves as accommodation for the shogun when he travels and is called Chion-in.

Monastery Chion-in

The monastery belongs to the Jōdo sect worshipping Amida and is supposed to have been established or founded eight hundred years ago.[21] First we inspected the large palace, where the shogun usually stays and where the picture and memory of the shogun Genyūin[22] is worshipped in a small shrine or chapel. Up on the left, behind the miniature garden, was a path to a chapel situated on one of the terraces of the mountain slope, where the ashes and bones of the said shogun are kept.[23] As soon as we arrived in the inner chambers, the *oshō,* or abbot, of the monastery was notified. He had his lodgings on a steep and thickly wooded but pleasant mountain shelf or hill, and he came down from there with many well-groomed boys as well as another beautiful boy who had his head shaven and was wearing monk's robes and ten other young priests with shaven heads. The abbot was an old, friendly, and healthy man with a wholesome colored complexion wearing a wide violet or purple robe as underclothes and an Edo-style pair of trousers[24] of the same color. His alms bag was embroidered in gold relief. He stood watching us from a distance and had us served a cup of tea by some other priests, for which we pressed a *bu* wrapped in paper into the hand of the person that served us. On our departure, he had rows of priests seated on both sides of the chamber, and he himself sat at the end behind a *paravent* or screen, perhaps to display his lofty position. From here we walked along a corridor raised a little above the ground to the large secondary temple, which rested on five sets of six very thick wooden columns. With the outside columns there were seven times eight rows.[25] In the middle of this temple was a small lacquered chapel with Amida and many other very beautiful ornaments. Also on both sides were chapels that were no less magnificent. This building was as big as a large European church. The mats had been taken up and moved into a corner, and everywhere there were lamps in front of the images.

We did not inspect the other apartments and temples and only climbed some four hundred paces up a hill to a large *gum,* or bell. This bell appeared to be no smaller than the second largest bell at Moscow and even surpassed it in height or length. But it was out of proportion because of its awkward height and because the rim was turned in, contrary to our bells, where the rim curves out. This surely must muffle the sound in the bell. The bell was hit with a log while we were there, but we could see that the log was seldom used because it was still new and tied down. In other aspects the casting of the bell was fairly rough and crude. The bell was nearly a foot thick, but its height is said to be sixteen feet. The bell's circumference was twenty-eight feet and eight inches. One foot is ten *sun.* Half a foot is called *go sun,* which equals the distance between a stretched out thumb and index finger. However, this span is a little smaller than ours, and the Japanese count four feet to one *hiro,* that is, the size of a man or a fathom, so that here one *ken* or the length of one mat (which we call a fathom) has an additional two *shaku* (feet) and three *sun* (inches).

After that we were led by the two priests who were accompanying us to the other gate of their mountain or monastery and sent off. We arrived at a magnificent building resting on four sets of four pillars,[26] which had an additional wing on both sides with steps to climb up. Then we descended twenty stone steps, then two and finally three stone steps to reach the wooded foothills, which are part of the city and mainly occupied by temples. We sent our *norimono* ahead and walked for a quarter of an hour through clumps of bushes and trees to reach a level area where there was a Gion temple with some twenty to thirty small *miya,* or chapels, with lamps and bowls of food on trays in front of them.

Gion Temple

At the entrance opposite the temple sat the *kannushi* in white frocks with lacquered stiff hats tied on their heads. Our interpreter asked us for a few coins to give to them. Leaving the temple, we passed a stately *torii* and continued walking along the mountain streets, which were full of prostitutes. Each innkeeper can keep only two prostitutes, so that no one enriches himself more than the other. For the most beautiful the price is three mace for one session, the lesser ones cost two *mace,* and the bad ones one *mace,* but that is for the whole night.

Kuruma Dō Temple

Climbing up one of the small streets, we passed a small temple on the left called Kuruma dō, which stood in the same line as the houses. To the right was a small altar for offering incense to Amida and other idols, and opposite that, a few paces away, was a similar, but bigger altar with burning lights. To the left, surrounded by a large wooden fence, was a large six-cornered lantern covered with thin black cloth, which could be turned like a wheel and supposedly could be used for telling the future and discovering hidden events. I also heard that there was a large sacred book, describing their religion, inside the lantern. But the only thing people were prepared to say was that it had wondrous and rare properties and was indeed a miraculous object.[27] The senior *bugyō* was taken inside by the innkeeper, and I entered at the same time, but the rest had to wait outside in the narrow street. After Kuruma dō, we climbed up the mountain and passed a stately tower with seven roofs and five stories.[28]

Kiyomizu Temple

Finally we arrived at Kiyomizu, consisting of a large temple and two small temples on stilts on a mountain slope. We did not notice any great changes from the previous year. The temple was full of pictures; remarkable were those of a large battle and the city of Osaka and a host of other interesting scenes. In the upper part of the compound, above the spring, was a temple with an old woman[29] and similar objects, including a large number of pictures, a water basin, and other objects designed to heighten the enjoyment of the surroundings. From here the visitor descends more than one hundred stone steps to a spring from which the temple has its name. Afterward we walked into a brothel—all part of the local custom—and were entertained by the innkeeper, who was rewarded with a *koban,* while the innkeeper's wife received one *bu* and the two prostitutes the same amount.

Daibutsu Temple

After an hour or an hour and a half we climbed into our baskets and had ourselves carried to the large Daibutsu temple. In front of the outer courtyard was a round hill with a gravestone, which is called the burial of ears, for this is the place where Taikō buried the ears that he had cut off his enemies when he came back from the war with the people of Ezo.[30]

The precinct of the Daibutsu temple was raised by enormously large stones, which were roughly chiseled on the side facing the road. The courtyard of the temple was surrounded by a red latticed, roofed walkway with fifty latticed sections on each side of the gate. It was open on the inside facing the temple, and on each side of the gates were two rows of round pillars, each row containing fifty, which brings the number of pillars on each side to a hundred, making a total of four hundred if the square was perfect. All pillars were made of wood and painted red.[31]

The visitor climbs approximately eight stone steps to enter the gatehouse, which on each side has two formidable black, or dark red with black, giants, called Aun or Inyō or *niō,* standing half a fathom above the ground behind a grid. The one on the left has his mouth and hand open; the right one has his mouth closed and hand turned in, holding a staff half hidden behind his back. This symbolizes the two complementary elements of nature, such as the active and the passive, giving and receiving, the process of opening and closing, heaven and earth, creation and decay. From here the visitor passes through a portal and into a fine courtyard, with sixteen stone pillars on each side where lamps can be lit, as well as a water basin and other items.

The Daibutsu temple proper rests on large columns, each several fathoms thick. Some columns are made of a single tree, others are put together from several trees like the masts of our ships, so that the width remains the same throughout the column, and all the columns as well as the many crossbeams high up were red. To the right of the Daibutsu temple was a small chapel lacquered black, containing a mirror the size of that dedicated to St. Stanislaus in the city of Cracow. Inside the temple sat one or more female vendors. In front of this and the next temple we noticed guards with strong poles in our honor. The ground is covered by rough square stones.

Kannon Temple

Then we came to the temple of Kannon, with the image of Kannon in the middle, and at the side was that of the repentant Shaka, very emaciated, as well as several *niō,* not much taller than an average man; the others were unknown to me.[32] In addition there are on both sides statues standing on long, wooden stairs or steps running the length of the temple. There are ten statues behind or above each other, but each statue has its own square support or bench; they are gilded all over and life-size. On both sides there were fifty statues placed next to each other running to the far end of the temple, but they were placed in such a fashion that there were two sets of five in one line behind each other with every second one filling the gap between those in front. Thus there stood five hundred statues on each side or altogether one thousand life-sized Kannons, making 1,033 with the central group. But when counted with the statues that these figures are carrying on their heads and in their hands, the total number comes to 33,333. These Senjū Kannons[33] were totally gilded with a gilded circle around their head, with some twenty or more hands. Two hands or one pair were placed palms against each other high in front of the chest like a man praying, of two further hands the right held a *Jizō* staff, the left a three-pronged weapon or pike. The other hands were not idle: each held something or they held each other. In front of this choir of the gods were railings running the whole length, and there were also some railings between the first inner row of statues, where there are a number of passages. Arrows were shot outside the temple at the far end of the raised corridor and parallel to the building. And I discovered in their chronicles that some people shot more than several thousand arrows in one day.[34] The target is at a distance of one hundred and seventy paces.

After we had inspected the above temples, we were carried to our barges and vessels without stopping at Fushimi, for with five territorial lords being entertained there, the inn could not offer us the space to dine in the usual fashion. Therefore we soon arrived at Yodo, where on the left the road was signposted to Nara or Nara no Miyako, the location of the old Kyō, where there are also Daibutsu.[35] The present Miyako is called Hieizan no Miyako. After that we arrived at Yamazaki, situated on the right at the foot of a mountain, together with the famous temple Yamazaki Sengen. On the left was the famous temple Yawata no Hachiman. We reached the outskirts of Osaka as night was falling and entered our inn after midnight.

May 11th we had a rest, and our captain received several *shu* of silver from each governor in return for the presents previously presented.

On May 12th we were carried to Sumiyoshi and from there back to Tennōji, for the entertainment provided by our innkeeper, who met us there. After we had once again left this place, we soon reached open fields, where on the left close to the city was a compound surrounded by a wall. In the middle was a tall, large building with a central chimney like a furnace for casting bells. Here the dead were burned, which is also done in the open area if there is no room in the building. On the road between Sumiyoshi and Tennōji were several small villages on both ends of the way and in the middle, as well as a long, terraced hill with pines. Manure was being spread for the sowing of the cotton seed, and people did that with extraordinary diligence.

Sumiyoshi Temple

Sumiyoshi consists of a large precinct in an ornamental forest to the left of the road to Sakai. A tall stone *torii* and a wide path lead the visitor to a tall bridge the shape of half a wheel, spanning running water. This round bridge is very old and for history's sake is being restored with bits of cloth and other pieces and is difficult to cross. However, close by on each side was another bridge that could be crossed easily and without effort. After that we reached the courtyard of the temples, where we ignored some on the right and straightaway walked up to the front of the main temple, where the white *kannushi* who take care of the temple were sitting. Through the middle of the temple one could see as far as two doors, behind which is concealed the *daimyōjin,* to whom people paid their respect. To the right of this main temple (which at its side as well as in secondary buildings had many pictures hanging up, including a map of the world in which Ezo was linked with Tartary) was a rest and tea corner and also a pond lined with hewn stones with a stone bridge where tame fish can be eaten by those who wish to do so.

(a) is the entrance in between pillars of stone lanterns

(b) the round wheel-shaped bridge

(c) the main temple where the white *kannushi* are sitting

(dd) the stone bridge of the fish pond

(e) a resting place, built like a gate, where tea is boiled

(ffff) some temples where *kuge* were waiting

(α) Aioi no matsu,[36] a pine, which was separated into two from the base up. One part of the tree had soft and small needles and was called the little woman; the other part had longer and stronger needles and was called the little man.

(β) a long small church or chapel, from where the idols were carried in procession

(χ) a large, extremely magnificent temple

(δ) two temples facing each other equally delightful, built like a tower with two roofs and a central corridor.

After we had briefly inspected the above, and eaten our fish at (dd) and had also drunken some bowls of tea in return for one *bu* at (ee), we again climbed into our baskets and had ourselves carried to Tennōji along the so-called old route. Here we went along a wide avenue lined with lanterns and, at the side, with hedges, and went through a magnificent roofed gate. In the temple square we faced a very delightful square tower with eight stories[37] and the same number of roofs ornately decorated. Behind the tower we went somewhat to the right and came to the main temple of Shōtoku Taishi where the main figure was kept in the middle. On the right, however, was another image one and a half ells high surrounded by the idols of the four elements and a double cloth. Everything was black with smoke, for the place was full of burning lamps both inside and outside. After that we were taken to a long temple where five large idols stood erect with many others above them in various rows. Then we were taken to a small room where water rich in iron or vitriol was welling up in a basin and where the long continuous flow of this water had produced the shape and form of a turtle. Therefore the water is called turtle water. A small bamboo utensil was close by to scoop a drink from behind the railing.

From here we were taken to an inn, several streets away. With old annexes and a nearby Kannon temple, it stood on the steep slope of a tall mountain with a view over the whole area of Osaka and the sea behind it. After we had been entertained liberally by the innkeeper for several hours, we again climbed into our baskets to return home. But

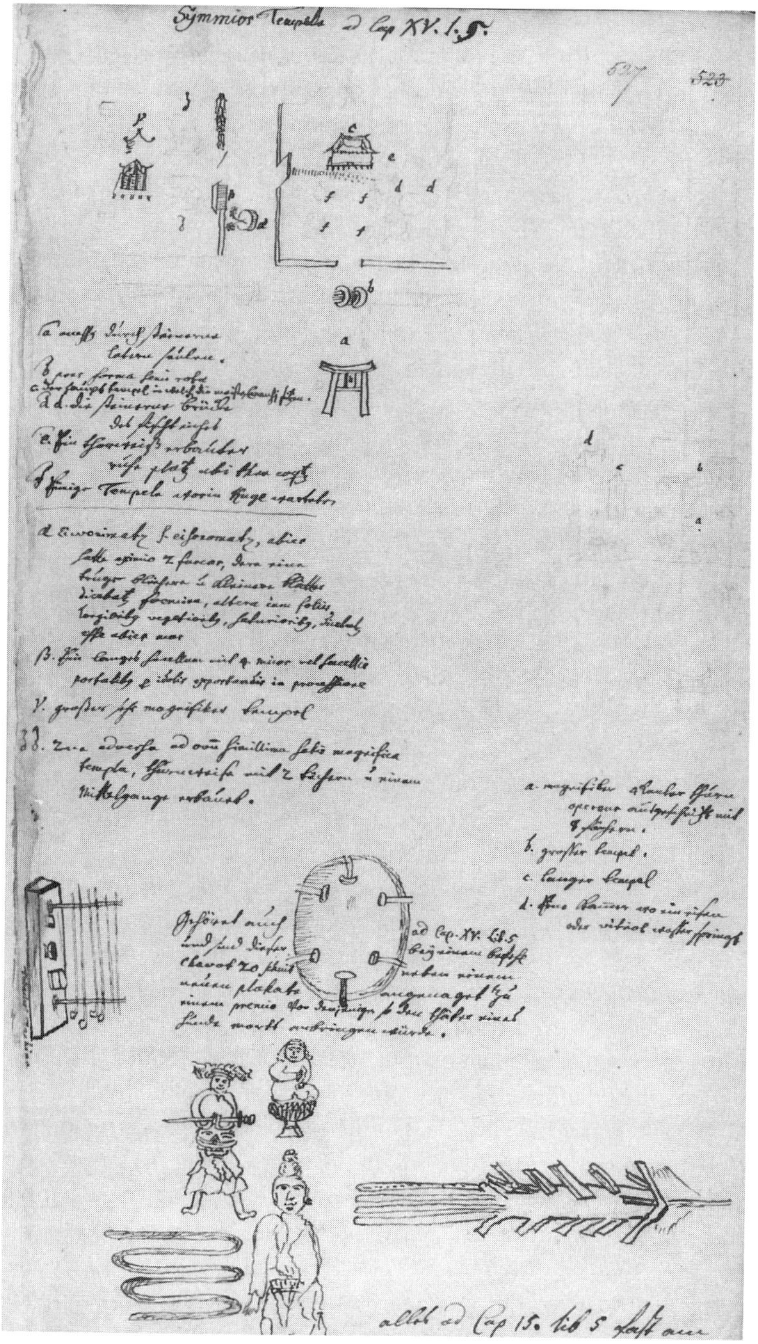

Kaempfer's sketch of the Sumiyoshi temple showing a pipe stand *(above)*, a piece of silver nailed to a poster as reward *(center)*, and statues from Fukusaiji in Nagasaki *(below)*. It is likely that further details were drawn in pencil and that these have faded. (Courtesy of the British Library, Sloane 3060, folio 527)

we soon dismounted again to inspect the temple Ikutama, situated on the left at a lake in the forest at the foot of the mountain. Then we were carried through the streets of the outer city, which were full of temples. We reached Osaka hira no machi and shortly afterward on the left came to a garden that looked spectacular with its flowering *fuji*[38] trees, and a little later, between five and six in the evening, we arrived at our inn.

On May 13th we left Osaka in our *kago* at eight o'clock in the morning, having sent our bedding ahead and dispatched our luggage along the sea route. We first arrived at the village of Kitano, situated on the left as a continuation of the city, and soon on our right passed the village of Hama. Then we came to the village of Sanba, next to the village of Shinke, and after that to the village of Jūsō, as well as to the village of Mitsuya, where there was a small, long temple with the idol of Sōfukuji.[39] This place was situated two miles from our inn, and our innkeeper entertained us here to bid us farewell. Then we came to the village of Kajima and crossed the river Kanzakigawa. The river comes from Jūsō or Ichibangawa, was full with vessels traveling up to Fushimi, and is wide and craggy and also very winding.

City of Amagasaki

Then we came to the village of Nagasu and after that to the city of Amagasaki. The castle, with its tower and well-built stone fortifications, was situated in water and totally surrounded by the river, crowded with ships. The river also ran around and through the city, which consisted of some two thousand houses. The streets through which we were taken by our two leaders were watered ahead of us, and also the people were kneeling humbly in front of their doors. Here and the road we had traveled were full of young calves, which are raised to plough the land. For this land is the best there is in Japan, and wheat and barley are produced in abundance. Apart from that, however, I did not think the soil was very good, as I had the impression it contained too much sand, but the high level of fertility is reached by using human excrement. Further we reached the village of Imazu. In the fields on the right of the entrance of the village six stone images with some writing had been put up, just as at Amagasaki. Then we arrived at the village of Ashiya and afterward at the village of Hama Mikage,[40] where stones are quarried and then transported to the shore in carts with three solid wheels pulled by oxen. From there they are taken by ships to mills and other places where the stone is worked. The carts were low, and when the stone is rolled off, the first or front wheel is taken off. Here and at other places that are usually dry, such stones began to drift away after twenty-four days of continuous rain. This is hard to believe, but it happened recently and is widely known. The river is called Sumiyoshigawa, and the village where the people working the quarry live is called Sumiyoshi. Close by was another quarry called Toganokawara and the village of Midoro, where there is on the left a large fish pond and on the right the very high mountain Mayasan, with a temple in the forest at the highest point of the mountain slope. Not far from here was another fish pond with a building, from where a road to a large mountain temple was turning off. From there we were carried up to the town of Kobe, situated on a bay, from where we crossed over to Hyōgo in vessels and barges.

City of Hyōgo

On May 14th we left Hyōgo by ship early in the morning with favorable winds and passed the straits of Akashi in a fine drizzle. Here the winds died down, and we therefore continued with our oars during the night until we reached the island of Kurakake, where we cast anchor. Today we saw the Lord of Hizen march past along the shore. He traveled on land. It takes thirteen days for the stretch from Osaka to Shimonoseki. It is noteworthy that the territorial lords take no longer than thirteen days from Miyako to Edo, except those related to the shogunal family and the Lord of Satsuma (who takes some forty or more days).[41]

On May 15th we left at daybreak with a cool breeze from behind, bright skies, calm seas, and good weather and had our noon meal near Ōzuchi and Kozuchi and then continued to an uninhabited island opposite Shimotsui, where we went on land to fetch water. We discovered that the place was full of horses belonging to the Lord of Bitchū. In the morning the Lord of Nagata rowed past us with sixty barges, and in the afternoon the Lord of Yanagawa passed with ten barges.

On May 16th we set sail before dawn with constant winds and calm seas and arrived at half past nine at the island town of Yuge, consisting of white houses and a residence. Soon afterward we had Iwagi on our right and then sailed through the straits of Hanaguri, whereupon we passed Mitarai and then Nuwa and Tsuwa, which were hidden from sight behind the islands. From there we went in a straight line past the island of Kamuro, turned slightly, and in the evening sailed through the straits of Kaminoseki, where more than one hundred large and small vessels had cast anchor. We continued rowing for a further mile to permit us a quick departure the next morning. Today's journey amounted to fifty nautical miles, which here are calculated at the same length as land miles, which is normally not the case with distances traveled on the high seas.

May 17th. Since today we had the same pleasant weather as yesterday, we set sail early in the morning and arrived with twenty other vessels in the mouth of the straits of Shimonoseki sometime in the afternoon. There we changed to small vessels. We arrived in Kokura at seven o'clock in the evening.

City of Kokura

On May 18th we left Kokura at six o'clock on horseback for the town of Kurosaki. From there we reached the villages of Uenoharu and Kōjaku and then arrived at the village of Koyanose, where we had our noon meal. After lunch we rode to the village of Nōkata, with many villages on the right of the road, and after that we passed a number of different villages until we came to the large village of Katashima and to Iizuku, where we were given fresh horses for the third time. Then we reached the villages of Tentōmachi and Nagao and finally the town of Uchino, where we arrived in the dark with torches.

On May 19th at five o'clock in the morning we were carried from our inn by torchlight and traveled over the mountain to the town of Yamae. After half an hour's break there, we exchanged our baskets for horses and continued riding up to Matsuzaki, where we were given fresh horses. From Matsuzaki the road branches off to the large temple of Hikosan, situated ten miles away. Two large fellows with shaven heads, their swords at their sides and bedding on their backs, were traveling that road. Supposedly they were *yamabushi* priests, and soon afterward they were followed by another fellow on horseback who apparently was of the same persuasion.

City of Kurume

Thereupon we arrived at the outskirts of the city of Kurume, which consists of nearly two thousand houses. After we had been led up to the gate by a guide, we came to the guard, which had lined up at the head of the street. Four men with weapons placed themselves in front of our procession and two behind. Far ahead of us the road was being sprinkled with water, and once that had been done, not one person could be seen on the road. Instead people kneeled in the rear buildings and looked at us from afar and were so silent that not a single voice could be heard. We passed the place of public edicts at the edge of the castle moat, where next to a new notice twenty *shu* had been nailed down as a reward for anyone who would hand over the murderer of a dog. It must be noted that frequently here and there some people get their pelt beaten because of dogs.[42]

Sulfur Mountain Unzen, Hot Spa at Obama

From Kurume we proceeded to the village of Ojimamachi, from where a level road leads to the mountain of Unzen. At the foot of the mountain is Obama, a hot spring located at the shore toward Nagasaki. No sulfur may be removed from this high sulfur mountain because it is said that the spirit of the mountain, the idol Gongen, wants to keep it for himself and cherishes it, and therefore it is prohibited to remove any sulfur from the mountain. The sulfur is partly yellow and partly green, and one side of the mountain has been scorched white, but there is no burning fire and only thirty old, parched hot spas, to which the priests have given the names of various hells.

Hells

The place where the water wells up in the round shape of a *manjū* is called the hell of the pastry chefs; where it is like bubbling *sake*, the hell of the *sake* distillers; and where it surges like people hitting each other, the hell of the ruffians. Another place is called that of disobedient children and so forth. Any silver carried by the priests or other travelers turns black here. At high tide Obama is covered by the sea and flooded. After Ojimamachi, we reached Yokomizomachi and then the village of Yakabe, with two border posts, where the officials accompanying us said farewell. We, however, proceeded to the village at the outskirts of Yanagawa and arrived at our inn, located on this side of the bridge outside the city. This was a different inn from the one we used previously when traveling up to Edo, and we were told that it was the custom to change over. Today I observed radish seeds being dried on the fields and then being threshed with flails. Also at many locations *cha,* or tea leaves, were being picked, and the *cha* bush was picked totally bare, so that nothing was left but the bare branches, and the many different baskets seemed to indicate that the leaves were sorted right away. People had already started to plant the rice, which—as noted previously—was done by women. First the soil is hoed while submerged in water, then ploughed with oxen (which are smaller than those used for pulling carts) or horses while submerged in water, and finally beaten with a short hoe into mud. A few hours after the evening meal, we left in three barges, but when we reached the sea, the skipper did not want to leave before the morning because he was entrusted with our safety and well-being on pain of death by self-disembowelment.

On May 20th we rowed with the same bearing up to Takezaki and from there to Isahaya.

On the 21st we left Isahaya at dawn, traveled to the village of Kuyamakaitsu, to the village of Koga, to the river Kusunogawa, and to the town of Yagami, where we arrived at nine o'clock, had our noon meal, and dressed up for our entry into Nagasaki. We were met here by our servants and some others who had come to welcome us. The place has been calculated to be four miles from Isahaya and three miles from Nagasaki, and both roads are steep. However, those four miles are reckoned at fifty streets, but normally this distance would only amount to about two miles. Yet here they are counted as three miles because owing to the arduous road the wages paid are equivalent to those usually paid for three miles. After we had a meal, we arrived at the border posts between Hizen and Nagasaki, where one can see the village of Aba on the left, the place from where people cross over to the hot spa of Obama. Shortly after those border posts we arrived at the town of Himi, and from there we proceeded to Tōge and then finally arrived in Nagasaki at about twelve o'clock.

Arrival at Nagasaki

Thanks be to God for his gracious protection, health, and innumerable other favors which in his mercy he has bestowed upon me during this and many other journeys. Glory, honor, praise and thanks be to God. Amen.

The following incidents happened here in Nagasaki until our departure for Batavia.

When we entered our island we heard that ten days ago orders had arrived from Edo that no animals, with the exception of fish, may be killed, unless they were for the

Dutch or the Chinese. Moreover, livestock and birds were forbidden to be traded, and we noticed on our arrival that the stalls selling birds had been covered up. Yet the birds were still being sold, though not on public streets but in front of houses.

A few days after our return the Chinese traded with the Japanese roots of ginseng, aloes-wood, and musk through the prostitutes and other people, and three were tortured and confessed that they had purchased them for one thousand taels only. Nowadays delinquents confess immediately because Settsu no Kami has invented a new instrument of torture where the naked body is pulled over short spikes or sharp needles, resembling the so-called witches' chair of Lemgo, where even the innocent confess immediately.

On May 31st the captain, myself, and Mr. Dubbels went to the residence of the lord governor to convey our gratitude. The audience was conducted similar to those held in the houses of the powerful at Edo.

June 1st. Tonight three suicides were discovered. Two had hanged themselves; one of these seems to have been a citizen who hanged himself because of smuggling, and the other was a priest where no reason was known. The third had cut his stomach because of poverty.

On June 14th the first Chinese junks left, and there are now altogether twenty-four. Seventeen have held their first *kanban,* or day of sale.

June 16th. The day before yesterday and today vessels crowded with people shouting the *nenbutsu,* that is to say, *namu amida butsu,*[43] went around the bay or harbor. These vessels are provided by the streets or wards where a plaguelike epidemic is beginning to spread like wildfire to chase away the evil spirit that is raging here. (This spirit is generally called *ekirei,* which stands for the dangerous illnesses of the country or the spirits, just as it says in the Book of David: the angel of the Lord smote his camp with pestilence.)[44] For the same reason, they also circulate the *hyakuman ben,* or one hundred thousand.[45] This is a large monster of a rosary with 108 large balls, which old people sitting down as well as young ones hold on to. This rosary is pulled around in a circle, passing from hand to hand, and every time people shout joyfully: *namu amida butsu, namu amida butsu,* and so on. This *hyakuman ben,* or one hundred thousand, in a circle is also performed in the temples when the epidemic is beyond control.

June 22nd was the death anniversary of the shogun,[46] on which, according to the usual ritual, six (thieves) are released from prison and their lives are spared, but they are banished to a distance of ten miles from here.

On June 23rd it became known that since last year the Chinese had secretly sold five boxes of silver and had traded it mainly in Osaka. Among three junks there is hardly one which takes its goods home again without selling half of them to the Japanese who secretly follow the Chinese vessels.

On June 24th the *hyakuman ben* was performed all day in the streets near Deshima at the houses where high fever is epidemic and where also written characters have been put up. The place where the one hundred thousand in a circle was celebrated was covered at the top against the sun. It was a terrible noise void of any reason: everybody shouted as they pleased.

On June 26th we visited the temples of the city together with the ordinary interpreters, apprentices, mayors, and others.

1. Shōshūdera, or better, Fukusai, a Chinese temple reached by climbing fifty steps and passing through a round gate in the forecourt. In front of the temple and facing it was the chapel of an idol with a sword, called Idaten.[47] The temple proper stood on pillars, was lacquered and square, and was divided into three sections or areas. In the middle section was a Kannon or Shaka, on the right the picture of a Chinese emperor with three bodyguards, on the left a red young man, dressed normally and wearing a crown. Behind him were other Chinese. In front of each image a torch of bark was burning, measuring the time. But to improve the odor, little scented candles had been added to the torches. There was hardly any smoke, and only one of the three was lit. The floor was covered with bricks, and there were round straw cushions on which the priests sit. Close by was another temple of no less beauty. At the edge of the mountain was a large, long space and path along which stood the houses of the priests and other small temples or chapels, which were furnished and decorated with life-sized images well proportioned, carved to look very natural. We were well entertained here with Chinese food, and the father prior, a sprightly, large, and friendly man, appeared at a short distance from us in the splendor of his purple habit.

2. Suwa, reached by crossing a number of mountain streets and by climbing two hundred steps. From there we were taken still higher to the chapel of the divinity, which is reached by way of a lacquered staircase (which we are not permitted to use and therefore climbed another one made of stone). This upper part was added only one or two years ago, when the divinity of Suwa was given a higher rank by the emperor. There were various small chapels, among them one for the performance of plays, as well as an open building for the storage of a variety of images for worship and also a chapel of the deity of a thousand legs, with a number of figures suspended in front of it. The *kannushi* were in secular clothes and had short hair brushed back. They lived close by at the edge or on the slope of the mountain.

3. On the other side of the mountain was Shuntokuji temple, which caught fire some two years ago when some boys were playing with matches. Consequently there was only one image of Shaka to be seen in the chapel. In this temple lives the inspector of religious or Buddhist books, which are imported to be sold. He belongs to the Zen sect.

4. Kōfukuji, or Nankin dera, where we only went as far as the large forecourt and saw nothing else. The temple is supposed to rise up higher and apparently can be seen above Nagasaki.

5. After a further walk up the mountain, we reached an open chapel where the *daibutsu* totally covered in gold sat on a lotus flower. Near this chapel is a Kōdaiji, or Zen *shū* temple.[48]

6. Daikōji of the Ikkō sect, where we arrived around noon and had our meal with the whole crowd. Part of the front of the building was used as a temple and divided into a number of sections or areas. The one furthest back contained the idol Amida.

Many people gathered in front of it, and soon afterward, when the crowd had grown even larger, a priest arrived who was a preacher. He went to sit in between the chapel and the common people and read a text for three quarters of an hour, or perhaps an hour. Then he read a common prayer and all joined in. Then the other priests stepped in front of the image and sang some more passages, and that concluded the gathering.

7. Sōfukuji, or Fukushū dera, a Chinese temple. In this temple stood the disciples of Shaka in various postures: one was throwing a ring, another had the image of Shaka in his breast, and yet another had eyebrows that had grown several ells, and so forth. All were experiencing *satori* or meditating. In an open area stood an enormously large kettle, which previously had been used during a famine. At that time the father prior of the monastery himself went out to beg alms for the poor and then boiled the rice in this kettle (the rice is boiled up as thin as soup).[49] He even pulled down a temple and used it as firewood. We passed a few other temples, including a Gion temple, and further looked at:

8. Kiyomizu or Seisuiji[50] temple, situated high on a steep slope; we had to climb a long passage and many steps. On the left were six images of Jizō, each with a waterbasin of stone, as is commonly found in Japanese cemeteries. There was also a small *shikimi* bush, with which every passerby moistened the images. The square temple containing the images of their ancestors was closed. To the side was a stone statue of Kannon, which must be worshipped from both sides.

July 1st. Around this time we inspected the barges of the company, and those that were in bad repair were discarded. Then we went to the temple Shōtokuji on the nearby promontory of Magome, and after we had eaten, we returned home on foot. But on the way we were taken to a temple of the Hokke sect, where the priests showed us every nook and cranny in a friendly and intimate fashion. They marveled at us and our belongings and were pleased with our visit. The flags with which they decorate their temples and chapels and with which they announce joy and triumph are very much like those used by the Roman Catholics in their processions. They are made of beautiful and precious material and shaped nearly like the Cajemans[51] flags in front of the temples in Siam. After that the officer in charge of us took us to the Chinese temple Fukusai, which was close by and which we had also previously looked at. We arrived back home at three o'clock in the afternoon.

On July 25th the smugglers who had traded goods with the Chinese junks were sentenced. They consisted of the Japanese on guard duty, who had cut his own stomach and whose body, together with that of another man who had committed suicide, was pickled and put on the wheel,[52] and two who were decapitated. All this was done at Magome, the usual execution ground. Eight people who refused to confess were tied up and put into ships and banished to Gotō to live a life of misery.

July 30th. Yesterday seven barges of the Lord of Satsuma arrived. They brought with them two men from Batan,[53] who are at the same time vassals of Ryūkyū and had been brought from there to Satsuma. They had been called before the governor so the nature of their country and their language could be investigated. They were well-behaved, one thirty, the other twenty-five years old according to their own explanations. They used stones to indicate nearby islands such as Tambaku, Babasan,[54] and so forth. One of them seemed to be a learned man. They sat on the bare floor in front of the residence with a guard on each side, who sat on raised mats to indicate the difference. The men were shaven like Poles, and both had two or three holes in their ears as decoration. They used the left hand instead of the right and paid their compliments like the people of the East Indies, performing their greetings with hands placed together lifted up to the forehead or bending and touching the ground with their forehead with their hands in that same position. The Japanese look after them and keep them confined in the prison. This journey with his barges is costing the Lord of Satsuma more than ten boxes of gold, for the largest barge had eighty oars and the others had to have at least forty. And in addition he has to compensate the gentlemen who joined the delegation out of respect for their lord and the shogun.

August. In this month all our vessels arrived on the same day one after another; the last two came from Siam.

October 1st. After our company had held its second *kanban,* or sales day, the governors received tokens of our esteem. Around this time fifty Chinese of a barge, who had been imprisoned in a room for some time, were taken to a junk to be banished from the country. Apparently three people have been decapitated, one crucified, one junior interpreter cut his stomach, and the rest were exiled. The cause was one picul of ginseng root, which they had hidden in a junk to smuggle.

On October 25th and on each of the two following days one of our vessels left for the Papenberg.

Departure for Batavia

October 29th. After having said our farewells, taken food and drink, and distributed our presents, we were taken to board our flagship *Pampus,* which was laden with some ten or a thousand boxes[55] or piculs of bars of copper, and with the north wind sailed to the Papenberg.

On October 30th we approached the other three vessels from which I collected my Japanese printed and handwritten material, which had been secretly laded and distributed.

On October 31st we left the Japanese harbor at dawn with a northeasterly breeze on a southwesterly course. And with that I will conclude the narrative of Japan for now.

Appendix 1

List of Persons

As explanations are contained in the notes the first time a person is mentioned in the text, generally only those names that appear repeatedly are included here. Only information relevant to Kaempfer's text is supplied. Sources consulted are mainly *Kansei chōshū shokafu* and *Nihonshi sōran* (1993).

Abe Masatake (1649–1704). Bungo no Kami, Mimasaka no Kami, became *rōjū* in 1681 (Tenna 1.3).

Abe Tadaaki (1602–1675). Bungo no Kami, *rōjū* 1633–1666 (Kanei 10.5–Kanbun 6.3), but remained *rōjū* nominally until 1671 (Kanbun 11.5).

Akimoto Takatomo (1649–1714). Tajima no Kami, Settsu no Kami, *wakatoshiyori* 1681–1693 (Tenna 2.10–Genroku 6.9).

Andō Naotsugu (also: Naomasa) (1544–1635). Tsushima no kami.

Arima Kiyozumi (1652–1702), Suō no Kami, lord of Agata (Nobeoka) castle. His land was confiscated on 22.10, Genroku 4 (1691).

Arima Toyouji (1569–1642). Lord of Kurume castle, Chikugo, 1602–1642.

Arima Yorimoto (1654–1705). Nakatsukasa no Taifu, Lord of Kurume castle, Chikugo 1668–1705.

Asahina Sadanoshin. *Yoriki* attached to the Nagasaki *bugyō* and leader of the Dutch procession to Edo in 1691.

Asano Naganori (1667–1701). Takumi no Kami, inherited his fief of 53,500 *koku* in 1675, was ordered to commit suicide after injuring Kira Yoshinaka within Edo castle, and was revenged by the so-called Forty-seven Ronin.

Asano Tsunanaga (1659–1708). Aki no Kami, governed 1673–1708.

Baba Toshishige, Saburō, Saemon (?–1657). Nagasaki *buygō* 1636–1652 (Kanei 13.5–Jōō 1.1).

Bingo. See Makino Narisada.

Brasman. See Yokoyama Yozaemon.

Buijtenhem, Hendrick van (also: Bütenheim, Hendrik). Dutch resident director at Nagasaki 1684–1685, 1687–1688, 1690–1691, 1692–1693.

Camphuis, Johannes (1635–1695). Dutch resident director at Nagasaki 1671–1672, 1673–1674, 1675–1676; from 1684, governor general of the Dutch East India Company at Batavia.

Caron, François (1600–1673). First arrived in Japan in 1619; headed the Dutch trading settlement at Hirado 1639–1641.

Chūai. Japanese emperor, believed to have ruled 192–200.

Cleyer, Andreas (also: Andries Cleijer) (1638–1698). Dutch resident director at Nagasaki 1682–1683, 1685–1686.

Daitokuin. Posthumous name of Tokugawa Hidetada.

Daiyūin. Posthumous name of Tokugawa Iemitsu.

de Vries, Marten Gerritz (1602–?). Sent by the Dutch East India Company to discover the so-called Gold and Silver Islands believed to be situated in the vicinity of Japan.

Dohm, Christian Wilhelm (1751–1820). Diplomat, statesman, historian, and editor of Kaempfer's manuscript *Heutiges Japan (Geschichte und Beschreibung von Japan).*

Doi Toshikatsu (1573–1644). Ōi no Kami, *rōjū* (1638–1644) (Kanei 15.11–Shōhō 1.7). (Some sources state that he was *rōjū* from 1610 to 1638 and *tairō* after this date. This discrepancy is due to the fact that the positions of *rōjū* and *tairō* were not as yet clearly defined.)

du Mans, Raphael (1613–1696). Capuchin friar; translator and advisor to the shah of Persia.

Genyūin. Posthumous name of Tokugawa Ietsuna.

Genzaemon. See Kawaguchi Munetsune.

Gesner, Conrad (1516–1565). Swiss physician and naturalist, published *Historiae animalium,* a compendium of recorded knowledge concerning animal life, 1551–1587.

Gongen. Posthumous name of Tokugawa Ieyasu.

Gotō Shigenao, Shazuemon. Nagasaki *machi toshiyori.*

Hirano Sōtatsu. Shogunal physician.

Hōjō Ujihira (1650–1704). Awa no Kami, Edo *machi bugyō* 1681–1693 (Tenna 1.4–Genroku 6.12).

Honda Masanaga (1645–1711). Kii no Kami, *jisha bugyō* (1688–1695) (Genroku 1.11–Genroku 9.10).

Honda Masazumi (1565–1637). Kōsuke no Kami, *rōjū* until 1622.

Honda Yasuyoshi (1647–1718). Oki no Kami, Lord of Zeze castle 1679–1714 (Empō 7.6–Shōtoku 4.3).

Hotta Masamori (1606–1651). Dewa no Kami, Kaga no Kami, *rōjū* from 1633 to 1651 (Kanei 10.5–Keian 4.4).

Ijsbrants (also: Isbrant), Evert, Ides (van Glückstadt). Traveled to China 1692–1695 as ambassador of the czars Ivan and Peter I.

Ikeda Mitsumasa (1609–1682). Lord of Bizen.

Ikeda Tsunamasa (1638–1714). Lord of Bizen.

Imamura Genemon Eisei (1671–1736). Engelbert Kaempfer's student, assistant, and interpreter at Deshima. He later became famous as an interpreter.

Inaba Masanori (1623–1696). Mino no Kami, *rōjū* 1657–1681 (Meireki 3.9–Tenna 1.12.8).

Inaba Masayuki (1640–1716). Mino no Kami, was transferred from Odawara castle to Takada castle in Etchigo 1686 (Jōkyō 2.12.11).

Ingen Ryūki (1592–1673). Chinese monk of the Buddhist Ōbaku sect; came to Japan in 1654; founder of the Japanese Ōbaku sect and of Manpukuji, Uji, Kyoto.

Ishikawa Noriyuki (Norifumi) (1634–1707). Tonomo no Kami, from 1669 Lord of Yodo castle.

Itakura Katsushige (1545–1624). Iga no Kami, Kyoto *shoshidai* 1603–1620 (Keichō 8.3–Genna 6).

Iyo sama. See Tōdō Yoshinao.
Jimmu. Japanese emperor believed to have ruled 660–585 B.C.
Jingū. Japanese empress believed to have ruled 201–269.
Jūbei sama. See Yamaoka Kagesuke.
Kafuku Kizō (?–1718). Nagasaki interpreter, also known as Zenbei, Kiso, Kizo by the Dutch, promoted to junior interpreter *(ko tsūji)* in 1689 (Genroku 2), to inspector *(tsūji metsuke)* in 1697, retired 1711 (Shōtoku 1).
Kaga sama. See ŌkuboTadatomo.
Katō Akihide (1652–1712). Sado no Kami, Etchū no Kami, *jisha bugyō* 1689–1690 (Genroku 2.8–Genroku 3.10), *wakatoshiyori* 1690–1712 (Genroku 3.11–Shōtoku 1.12).
Katō Kiyomasa (1562–1611). Higo no Kami, Lord of Kumamoto castle.
Kawaguchi Munetsune, Genzaemon (1630–1704). Settsu no Kami, became *metsuke* in 1671, Nagasaki *bugyō* 1680–1694 (Empō 8.3–Genroku 6.12.15).
Kōbō Daishi (774–835). Kukai, Buddhist priest and scholar, founder of the Shingon sect of Buddhism.
Koekebecker (also: Koeckebakker, Couckebacker), Nicolaes (Nicolaas). Resident director of the Dutch trading settlement 1633–1638.
Koide Morihide (also: Morisato, Aritoshi) (1649–1699). Awaji no Kami, Kyoto *bugyō* 1690–1696 (Genroku 3.1–Genroku 9.5).
Kuroda Nagakiyo (1667–1720). Ise no Kami, resident at Nogata, younger brother of Kuroda Tsunamasa.
Kuroda Tsunamasa (1659–1711). Hizen no Kami, Lord of Hakata (Fukuoka) 1688–1711.
Kuroda Yoshiyuki (1682–1710). Son of Kuroda Tsunamasa.
Lipsius, Justus (Joest Lips) (1547–1606). Belgian humanist, classical scholar, historian, author, proponent of Neo-Stoicism.
Maeda Naokatsu (1630–1706). Aki no Kami, Kyoto *bugyō* 1673–1692 (Empō 1.2–Genroku 5.3).
Makino Narisada (1634–1712). Bingo no Kami, *sobayōnin* (grand chamberlain) 1682–1695 (Tenna 1.12–Genroku 8.12).
Matsudaira Naoakira (1656–1721). (Echizen) Wakasa no Kami, Lord of Akashi castle.
Matsudaira Nobuoki (1630–1691). Inaba no Kami, took up his post as Kyoto *shoshidai* 1691 (Genroku 4.2) and died that same year in Kyoto.
Matsudaira Nobutsuna (1596–1662). Izu no Kami, *rōjū* from 1633 to 1662.
Matsudaira Sadanobu (Hisamatsu) (1667–1702). Governed 1676–1702.
Matsudaira Sadashige (1644–1717). Etchū no Kami, Lord of Kuwana castle.
Matsuura Takanobu (1591–1637). Hizen no Kami, Iki no Kami, domain lord of Hizen 1603–1637 (Keicho 8–Kanei 14).
Matsuura Takashi (1646–1713). Iki no Kami, domain lord of Hirado 1689–1713 (Genroku 2–Shōtoku 3), became *jisha bugyō* 25.11, Genroku 4 (1691).
Minamoto Yoritomo (1147–1199). Became the first shogun of the Kamakura bakufu in 1190.
Miyagi Masamitsu, Kenmotsu (1634–1691). Nagasaki *bugyō* 1681–1686, died in house-arrest August 1691.

Miyagi Masazumi, Tonomo (1637–1696). Echizen no Kami, Nagasaki *bugyō* 1687–1696 (Jōkyō 4.8.–Genroku 9.2). He had previously served as *metsuke*.

Mokuan Shōtō (1611–1684). Second abbot of the Ōbaku sect.

Mononobe Moriya (?–587). A descendent of an ancient clan who opposed the introduction of Buddhism. With his defeat, the clan became extinct.

Mori Mototsugu (1671–1718). Hida no Kami, succeeded as domain lord in 1690.

Mori Yoshinari (1668–1694). Governed 1682–1694, Lord of Hagi castle; his domain included Nagato and Suo.

Motoki Shōdayū, Ryōi, Eikyū (1628–1697). Senior interpreter on Kaempfer's second journey to court; physician, translator, and commentator of Japan's first Western anatomical work, *Oranda zenkunaigai bungōzu,* presented to the bakufu in 1682, published in 1772.

Motoki Tarōemon. Junior interpreter on Kaempfer's first journey to court.

Nabeshima Mitsushige (1632–1700). Tango no Kami, Lord of Hizen, governed 1657–1695.

Nagasaki Sadatsuna, Kotarō. First domain lord of Nagasaki.

Nagasaki Sumikage, Jinzaemon (1547?–1622). Thirteenth-generation domain lord of Nagasaki.

Naitō Masachika (1645–1596). Tamba no Kami, *wakatoshiyori* 1690–1694.

Narabayashi Chinzan, Shingobei (1648–1711). Interpreter and physician, founder of the Narabayashi house. He became a senior interpreter in 1686.

Nose Yorisuke (also: Yorihiro) (1658–1698). Izumi no Kami, Osaka *bugyō* from 1688 to 1690 (Genroku 1.5–Genroku 3.12), when he was appointed Edo *machi bugyō*. When Kaempfer arrived in Osaka the first time in the twelfth month of Genroku 3, Nose had finished his duties, but his successor had not yet arrived.

Obata Shigeatsu Saburōzaemon (1642–1717). Bitchū no Kami, Kazusa no Suke, *sakuji bugyō* 1689–1707.

Oda Nobunaga (1534–1582). The first of Japan's three great unifiers.

Odagiri Naotoshi (1650–1706). Tosa no Kami, Osaka *bugyō* from 1686 to 1692.

Ogasawara Nagashige (1650–1732). Sado no Kami (Etchū no Kami), *jisha bugyō* in 1691 (from Genroku 3.12.3–Genroku 4.int.8.26), Kyoto *shoshidai* 1691–1702.

Ogasawara Tadao (1647–1725). Ukon no Kami, Lord of Kokura castle, governed 1667–1725.

Ōkubo Tadatomo (1632–1712). Kaga no Kami, *rōjū* 1677–1698 (Empō 5.7–Genroku 11.2), became lord of Odawara castle in 1686.

Ōsawa Mototane (1656–1697). Ukyō no daibu.

Ōta Sukenao (1658–1705). Bitchū no Kami, Settsu no Kami, Lord of Tanaka castle.

Rumph, Georg, Everhard (1628–1702). Employee of the Dutch East India Company and botanist.

Sakai Tadakatsu (1587–1662). Sanuki no Kami, *rōjū* from 1631 to 1638.

Sakai Tadakiyo (1624–1681). Uta no Kami, senior councilor *(rōjū)*1653–1666, then great councilor *(tairō)* to 1680.

Sakai Tadataka (1648–1720). Uta no Kami, Lord of Himeji castle.
Sakakibara Motonao (1586–1648). Hida no Kami, Nagasaki *bugyō* 1634–1640.
Sasamori Hanzō. *Yoriki* attached to the Nagasaki *bugyō*.
Scheffer, Sebastian. Publisher of Andreas Cleyer's *Specimen medicinae Sinicae* in Frankfurt.
Scheuchzer, Johann Gaspar (1702–1729). Translator of Kaempfer's manuscript *Heutiges Japan* into English *(The History of Japan)*.
Settsu no Kami. See Kawaguchi Munetsune.
Shimada Sukeemon. *Dōshin* of the Nagasaki *bugyō*.
Shingobei. See Narabayashi Chinzan.
Shōtoku taishi (574–622). The son of Emperor Yomei who acted as regent for his aunt, Empress Suiko, and is credited with having introduced Buddhism into Japan.
Sō Yoshitoshi (1568–1615). Tsushima no Kami.
Sō Yoshizane (1639–1702). Tsushima no Kami.
Sokuhi Nyoichi (1616–1671). Third abbot of the Ōbaku sect.
Spafarii, Nikolai, Gavrilovich (Milescu, Nicolae, Spâtarul) (1636–1708). Romanian scholar and diplomat. He came to Moscow in 1671 and served as translator in the Russian Foreign Office. From 1657 to 1678 he headed the Russian embassy to Peking.
Specx, Jacobus (Jacques). Dutch resident director at the trading settlement at Hirado 1609–1613, 1614–1621.
Suetsugu Heizō Masanao (?–1630). Became Nagasaki *daikan* in 1619.
Suetsugu Heizō Shigetomo. Nagasaki *daikan* 1669–1676.
Sugawara Michizane (845–903). Heian statesman banished from Kyoto to Dazaifu, deified and popularly referred to as Tenjin.
Sushun. Japanese emperor believed to have ruled 587–592.
Sweers, Balthasar. Dutch resident director at Nagasaki 1689–1690.
Tachibana Muneshige (1569–1642). Hida no Kami, Lord of Yanagawa castle, Chikugo, governed 1585–1637.
Taikō. See Toyotomi Hidoyoshi.
Takagi Sakuemon Muneo (1657–1697). Took over the duties of the Nagasaki *daikan* in 1676 at the demise of Suetsugu Heizō, but the position was downgraded to *machi toshiyori*. In 1671 he succeeded to his father's position of *machi toshiyori* and to the headship of the house in 1675.
Takagi Seiemon Shigekata, Genzō (1681–1705). After the death of his father in 1685, he succeeded to the headship of the house in 1686 and was made *machi toshiyori* in 1688.
Takashima Shigemura, Shirō Hyōe (?–1691). Nagasaki *machi toshiyori*, father of Shigenori.
Takashima Shigenori, Shirō Hyōe, Gontarō (1681–1715). Succeeded to the headship of the house in 1691 and became *machi toshiyori* in 1695.
Tarōemon. See Motoki Tarōemon.

Temmu. Japanese emperor believed to have ruled 673–686.
Thou, Jacques-Auguste de (1553–1617). French statesman, bibliophile, historian.
Toda Tadamasa (1632–1699). Yamashiro no Kami, *rōjū* 1681–1699.
Toda Tadazane (1651–1729). Noto no Kami, *jisha bugyō* 1687–1699.
Tōdō Yoshinao (1632–1706). Iyo no Kami, *ōmetsuke* 1688–1692.
Tokugawa (Kii) Mitsusada (1626–1705). Retired 1698, a member of the *gosanke*.
Tokugawa Hidetada (1579–1632). Daitokuin, the second Tokugawa shogun.
Tokugawa Iemitsu (1604–1651). Daiyūin, the third Tokugawa shogun.
Tokugawa Ietsuna (1641–1680). Genyūin, the fourth Tokugawa shogun.
Tokugawa Ieyasu (1542–1616). Gongen, the first Tokugawa shogun.
Tokugawa (Kii) Tsunanori (1665–1705). Betrothed to Tsunayoshi's daughter Tsuruhime in 1685.
Tokugawa Tsunayoshi (1646–1709). The fifth Tokugawa shogun.
Tonomo. See Miyagi Masazumi.
Toyotomi Hideyori (1593–1615). Son and successor of Toyotomi Hideyoshi, defeated by Tokugawa Ieyasu at the battle of Osaka.
Toyotomi Hideyoshi (1536–1598). Referred to as Taikō; after Oda Nobunaga, Japan's second great unifier.
Tsuchiya Masanao (1641–1722). Sagami no Kami, *rōjū* 1687–1718.
Tsuruhime (1677–1704). Tokugawa Tsunayoshi's only daughter; betrothed to Tokugawa (Kii) Tsunanori in 1685.
Tsushima no Kami. see Yamaoka Kagesuke.
Ushigome Chūzaemon Shigenori (1622–1687). Nagasaki *buygō* 1671–1681.
van Outhoorn, Cornelis (?–1708). Dutch resident director at Nagasaki 1688–1689, 1691–1692, 1695–1696.
Vinius, Andrei Andreevich (1641–1717). Inspector of pharmacies in Moscow.
Witsen, Nicolaas, Cornelisz (1641–1717). Mayor of Amsterdam, director of the Dutch East India Company, patron of E. Kaempfer.
Xavier, Francis (1506–1552). Founder of the Jesuit mission in Japan.
Yamaoka Kagesuke, Jūbei (1624–1705). Tsushima no Kami, Nagasaki *bugyō* 1687–1694.
Yanagisawa Yoshiyasu (1658–1714). Dewa no Kami, at first *sobashū* (chamberlain), later *sobayōnin* (grand chamberlain), but on Kaempfer's visit was ranked with the *wakatoshiyori*.
Yokoyama Yozaemon Brasman (dates uncertain). *Ko tsūji* in 1656, *ō tsūji* in 1665, retired in 1692 due to illness after thirty-seven years in service.
Yoshikawa Gibuemon. *Otona* of Deshima at the time of Kaempfer's visit.

Appendix 2
Money and Measurements

For a large part of its recorded history, Japan used foreign currency, mostly Chinese. Although coins were struck in Japan for a period in the late eighth and early ninth centuries, they were not minted again on a national scale until the close of the sixteenth century.[1] The coinage used at the time of Kaempfer's visit was mainly the so-called Keichō (1596–1615) coinage, minted by the first Tokugawa shogun, Ieyasu, after 1600.

There were three different gold coins, the *ōban,* the *koban* or *ryō,* and the *bu.* The *ōban* and *koban* were oval-shaped, measuring 147 × 92 mm and 71 × 38 mm and weighing 44.10 *momme* (approx. 165 grams) and 4.76 *momme* (approx. 18 grams) respectively. The exchange rate between the *ōban* and *koban* varied, but at Kaempfer's time it was generally seven *koban* to the *ōban.* The third gold coin was the *bu,* worth one-quarter of a *koban.* The *bu* was square in shape, measuring roughly 17 × 11 mm and weighing 1.2 *momme* (4.5 grams).

Two types of silver coins existed: the oval *chōgin,* weighing about forty-three *momme* (162 grams), and the round *mame'itagin,* varying between one and five *momme* (3.75 and 18.75 grams). The exact value was determined by the coins' weight, that is, scales had to be used at each transaction. As Kaempfer noted, the common units of weight used for monetary transactions were *kan (kamme), momme, bun, rin,* and *futsu.*[2] These units stood in a metrical relationship and were often used like figures to the right of the decimal point in the West. Moreover, ten *kan* (37.5 kg) of silver counted as "one box." On average, there were sixty *momme* of silver to one *ryō,* or *koban,* fifteen *momme* to one *bu.* There was also the measurement of *shu,* with sixteen *shu* of silver to one gold *ryō,* or *koban,* and four *shu* to one *bu.*

There was one common copper coin referred to as *sen, zeni, kansen,* or *mon,* Kaempfer's "pütjes" or "casjes." This was a flat, round coin with a square hole in the middle, four characters denoting Keichō *tsūhō* (Keichō currency) being placed around the square sides of the hole. The coins were modeled on the equivalent Chinese coin, which had four characters reading (in Japanese) Eiraku *tsūhō.* Some coins in circulation in Japan were of Chinese origin, with the two characters for Eiraku changed to Keichō.[3] As Kaempfer notes, *zeni* were carried on a string to cover small expenses when traveling. One thousand *zeni* made up one *kan,* and four thousand *zeni,* one *koban* or *ryō.*

As might be obvious from this brief summary, the fact that specific fixed-weight coins coexisted with coins of varying weights and values, that some coins were referred to by terms denoting also units of weight, and that units of weight existed in great numbers lent a certain complexity to the monetary system. In addition, there were regional preferences for gold or silver as well as units of weight, and exchange rates fluctuated both regionally and daily. To add to the confusion, parts of the community created their own terminology: thus in the pleasure quarters the term *momme* was used for *ryō,*[4] presumably to bypass the government's ceiling on prostitutes' fees. As Kaempfer points out, when bids were received for goods, generally no two offers were directly comparable on account of the many different possibilities of expressing monetary values.[5] It is also telling that a Japanese work written as late as the Ansei period (1854–1860) still bemoaned the complexity and confusion of the Tokugawa monetary system.[6]

Apart from the monetary system was the calculation of samurai income. Here the unit was rice counted in *koku* (47.654 U.S. gallons, 5.119 U.S. bushels) for high-ranking samurai, or *fuchi* for low-ranking ones. The latter unit was based on the consumption of rice per person per day, with the daily consumption set at five *gō* (0.9 liters). Thus a low-ranking samurai might receive a five-person or a thirty-person *fuchi.* The monetary value of the income depended in both cases on the fluctuations of the price of rice.

Trading in Japan, the Dutch had to come to terms with the complexity of the system and, moreover, relate it to their own coinage. They either adopted Japanese terminology, changing the pronunciation to familiar sounds, or translated Japanese terms. Thus Kaempfer refers to both *momme (momi),* the Japanese term, and *maas* (or *mas*), the

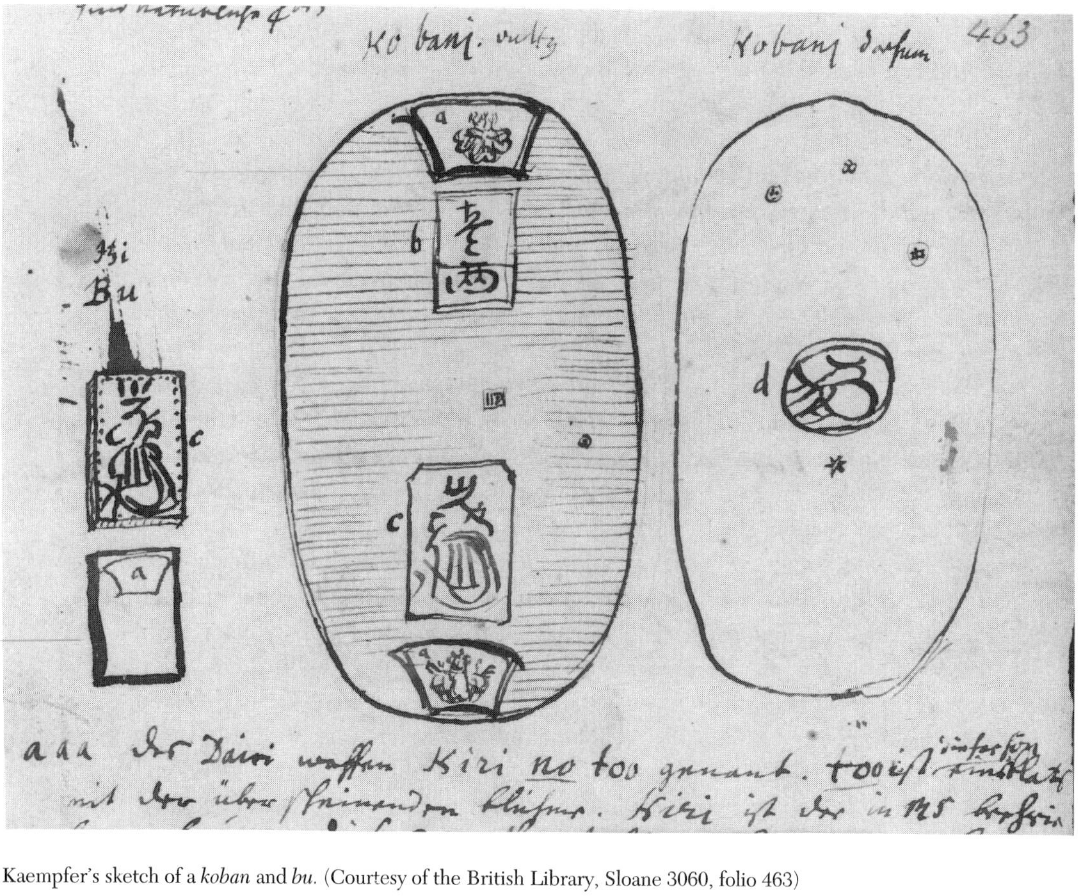

Kaempfer's sketch of a *koban* and *bu.* (Courtesy of the British Library, Sloane 3060, folio 463)

Dutch for "mace," which the Japanese in turn render as *masu*. But since the Japanese usually referred to *momme* in tens, and this corresponded roughly to the tael as used also in other Asian countries, the Dutch picked up the term *jū momme* (Kaempfer: *sjumomi*). But for the purpose of trade, the tael of different Asian countries all had their own exchange rates, so the equivalent of ten *momme* should be, but not always is, referred to as "Japanese tael."[7] But the accustomed correspondence was altered in 1671, when the Japanese government decided to change the country's normal exchange rate fluctuating between fifty-six and sixty *momme* for the *ryō* to sixty-eight, applicable to the foreign trade only.[8]

Finally, the Dutch coinage was not based on a simple decimal system either, but consisted of various issues of rijksdaalder, ducats, ducatons or rijders, florijns, guldens, and so forth, often fluctuating in their exchange rate to each other.[9] Under the circumstances, it is understandable that Kaempfer at times makes mistakes when explaining monetary equivalents. Thus he repeatedly states that one *koban* or *ryō* equals five ducats, and one *bu* equals 2.5 ducats, even though there were four *bu* to the *koban*.[10]

Equivalents for Japanese monetary terms can be found in the glossary. The table of coin/bullion/weight equivalents below may be of some help when reading the text; it at least graphically illustrates the complexity of the system.

1 gold *ōban* = 7 gold *ryō*
1 gold *koban* = 1 gold *ryō* = 4 gold *bu* = 16 silver *shu*
1 gold *koban* = 6 silver *ryō* = 6 taels = usually 60 *momme* or mace of silver, sometimes 68 *momme* or mace of silver
1 silver *ryō* = *jū momme* = 11/3 gold *bu*
1 gold *bu* = 2/3 silver *ryō* or tael = 15 *momme* or mace.

1 gold *ryō* = 60 *momme* = 6 tael
1 gold *ryō* = 4 gold *bu*
4 *bu* = 6 tael

1,000 *mon/zeni* = 1 *kan (kanmon)*
4 *kan* = 1 *ryō*

Other Measurements

Measurements of distance were only marginally less complex. Kaempfer notes that the measurement of *chō* (now 119 yards, 109 meters) had regional variations. Sometimes, but not always, these variations were related to the difficulty of the road, distance being calculated according to the amount of effort required to travel a particular stretch of road rather than the distance covered. At other times, the expense of food and fodder was taken into consideration. In this way it was possible to keep charges for porters and pack horses uniform per *chō* without disadvantaging those who worked on difficult terrain or in expensive areas.[11]

There were miles and nautical miles, which again were not uniform. This does not seem to bother Kaempfer as much as it might trouble us today, and he is delightfully vague in describing them. Within the space of a few pages he explains six Japanese nautical miles as "two long German miles" and four Japanese nautical miles as "two short German miles."[12]

Kaempfer notes that building dimensions were always calculated in *ken*, a measurement he describes as constant throughout the country. There were, in fact, regional variations. Here, as in the example given above, it must be kept in mind that the accuracy of measurements counted upon today was not expected in the seventeenth century. Even the meticulous scholar Kaempfer does not consider it unscientific to explain to his readers that five Japanese *sun* (now six inches, 15.15 cm) is "the distance between a stretched-out thumb and index finger," adding that this Japanese span "is a little smaller than ours. . . ."[13] Moreover, rather than keeping to one well-defined linear unit, he seems to enjoy using a large variety of measurements.

Although Japanese measurements are also contained in the glossary, for convenience' sake they are listed here with Western terms of weights and measurements used in the text that might be unfamiliar to the reader. Values given are standard modern equivalents.

bu	.12 inch, 3.03 millimeters
candareen	Chinese weight and monetary unit, estimated at about 6 grains Troy, the pound Troy containing 5,760 grains
catty	625 grams
chō	see *machi*
ell	25 inches, 63.5 cm
hiro	.994 fathom, 1.82 meters
ken	linear: 1.99 yards, 1.82 meters; square: 3.95 sq. yards, 3.32 sq. meters
koku	47.654 U.S. gallons
machi	linear: 119 yards, 109 meters; square: 2.45 acres, .992 hectares
picul	one man's load = 100 catties, 133.33 pounds
shaku	.994 foot, 30.3 cm
span	distance between tips of thumb and little finger: 9 inches, 22.9 cm
street	when used as measurement: see *machi*
sun	1.2 inches 3.03 cm

Notes

Translator's Introduction

1. Leibniz to Bierling, 7 July 1711 (in Latin), in C. I. Gerhardt, *Die philosophischen Schriften von Gottfried Wilhelm Leibniz* (Hildesheim, 1961; facsimile Berlin 1890 edition), 7:499. (All translations are my own unless otherwise stated.)

2. The most famous of those works collated in Europe is Arnoldus Montanus, *Atlas Japannensis, Being Remarkable Addresses by way of Embassy from the East-India Company of the United Provinces to the Emperor of Japan,* translated by J. Ogilby (London, 1670). Among the reports of the Jesuits, the works of Luis P. Frois (*Die Geschichte Japans,* translated and edited by G. Schurhammer and E. A. Voretzsch [Leipzig, 1926]) and Joâo Rodrigues (*This Island of Japon: Joâo Rodrigues' Account of 16th-Century Japan,* translated and edited by Michael Cooper [Tokyo, 1973]) are the best known. However, only extracts of these appeared in the premodern period, making Kaempfer's report all the more valuable to his contemporaries.

3. For a more detailed description of Kaempfer's life, see B. M. Bodart-Bailey, *Kenperu to Tokugawa Tsunayoshi* (Tokyo, 1994). Major sources for Kaempfer's life are two works by Karl Meier-Lemgo: *Engelbert Kaempfer, der erste deutsche Forschungsreisende, 1651–1716* (Stuttgart, 1937) and *Engelbert Kaempfer erforscht das seltsame Asien* (Hamburg, 1960).

4. A. Olearius, *Vermehrte Newe Beschreibung der Muskowitischen und Persischen Reyse . . .* (Schleswig, 1565; reprint, Tübingen, 1971).

5. See Karl Meier-Lemgo, ed., "Das Stammbuch Engelbert Kaempfers," *Mitteilungen aus der lippischen Geschichte und Landeskunde* 21 (1952):142–200.

6. Meier-Lemgo, "Stammbuch," 163.

7. See Wolfgang Muntschick, "The Plants that Carry his Name: Kaempfer's Study of the Japanese Flora," in *The Furthest Goal: Engelbert Kaempfer's Encounter with Tokugawa Japan,* edited by B. M. Bodart-Bailey and Derek Massarella (Folkstone, 1995).

8. E. Kaempfer, *Die Reisetagebücher Engelbert Kaempfers,* edited by Karl Meier-Lemgo (Wiesbaden, 1968), 5.

9. This can be found in British Library manuscript, Sloane 3063.

10. Meier-Lemgo, "Stammbuch," 162.

11. The following account is based on Kaempfer's manuscript, British Library manuscript, Sloane 2923. A partial, and not always reliable, transcription is contained in *Reisetagebücher.*

12. Sloane 2923, f. 120.

13. Sloane 2923, f. 147.

14. Sloane 2923, f. 122 v.

15. Letter to Joachim Kaempfer, in Engelbert Kaempfer, *Geschichte und Beschreibung von Japan,* edited by Christian Wilhelm Dohm (Lemgo, 1777–1779; facsimile, Stuttgart, 1964), 1:XXVIII (henceforth "Dohm"). The date given, 1688, appears

to be a misprint for 1690. Engelbert Kaempfer, *Amoenitatum exoticarum politico-physico-medicarum fasciculi V* . . . (Lemgo, 1712), "Praefatio," (b) 3 (hereafter cited as *Amoenitates*). For a transcription, see *Reisetagebücher.*

16. *Amoenitates*, 253–262; Engelbert Kaempfer, *Disputatio Medica Inauguralis Exhibens Decadem Observationum Exoticarum* . . . (Leiden, 1694), translated by H. Hüls and Rohtraut Müller-König in *Engelbert Kaempfer zum 330. Geburtstag*, edited by Hans Hüls and Hans Hoppe (Lemgo, 1982), 36–41.

17. This is reproduced in *Amoenitates,* 268.

18. *Estat de la Perse,* 1660.

19. Meier-Lemgo, "Stammbuch," 176–177.

20. See Kaempfer's Prologue below.

21. Meier-Lemgo, *Engelbert Kaempfer erforscht das seltsame Asien,* 56.

22. The following account is based on Sloane 2912.

23. Sloane 2912, f. 69 v.

24. Letter to Pater Du Mans, Sloane 3063, f. 65–65v.

25. J. L. Blussé, "The Story of an Ecological Disaster: The Dutch East India Company and Batavia (1619–1799)," in *Strange Company: Chinese Settlers, Mestizo Women and the Dutch in VOC Batavia* (Dordrecht, 1986), 18–19.

26. Sloane 3063, f. 65v–66.

27. Onno Zwier van Haren, *Proeve, op de leevens-beschryvingen der nederlandsche doorlugtige mannen: behelzende het leeven van Joannes Camphuis* (Tezwolle, 1772), 63.

28. François Valentijn, *Oud en Nieuw Oost-Indien* (Dordrecht, 1724–1726), 4:322.

29. For details about Kaempfer and Camphuis' relationship and Kaempfer's preparations for Japan, see B. M. Bodart-Bailey, "Writing *The History of Japan,*" in *The Furthest Goal: Engelbert Kaempfer's Encounter with Tokugawa Japan*, edited by B. M. Bodart-Bailey and Derek Massarella (Folkstone, 1995), 17–30.

30. See especially his letters to Daniel Parvé in Sloane 3060.

31. For details, see Kaempfer's will, Staatsarchiv Detmold, L 16 O K, and Heinrich Schwanold, "Engelbert Kämpfers Testament," *Lippische Mitteilungen* 5 (1907):41–61.

32. A detailed discussion can be found in Bodart-Bailey, *Kenperu to Tokugawa Tsunayoshi,* 204–218.

33. Witsen published his *Noord en Oost Tartarye* in Amsterdam, 1692, 1705. Rumphius' work was published finally in 1741 as Georgius Everhardus Rumphius, *D'amboinsche Rariteitkamer, of eene Beschryvinge van aller Hande. . . .* (Amsterdam, 1741–1750). See also J. P. Lotsy, "Over de in Nederland aanwezige botanische handschriften van Rumphius," *Rumphius Gedenkboek* (Haarlem, 1902). The writings of Herbert de Jaeger in Batavia, whom Kaempfer much admired as a scholar, completely disappeared. See Derek Massarella, "Epilogue," in *The Furthest Goal: Engelbert Kaempfer's Encounter with Tokugawa Japan,* edited by B. M. Bodart-Bailey and Derek Massarella (Folkstone, 1995), 158–159.

34. Hans Hüls. "Zur Geschichte des Drucks von Kaempfers 'Geschichte und Beschreibung von Japan' und zur sozialökonomischen Struktur von Kaempfers Lesepublikum im 18. Jarhhundert," in *Engelbert Kaempfer zum 330. Geburtstag*, edited by Hans Hüls and Hans Hoppe (Lemgo, 1982), 195–204.

35. Manuscript, Niedersächsische Landesbibliothek, Hannover, LBr 1007, f. 54, 54v. See also Massarella, "Epilogue," 158.

36. *Amoentitates,* Introduction. This has been translated in John Z. Bowers and Robert W. Carrubba, "Drug Abuse and Sexual Binding Spells in Seventeenth Century Asia: Essays from the *Amoenitatum Exoticarum* of Engelbert Kaempfer," *Journal of the History of Medicine and Allied Sciences* 33.3 (1978):320–322.

37. Derek Massarella, "The History of *The History,*" in *The Furthest Goal: Engelbert Kaempfer's Encounter with Tokugawa Japan*, edited by B. M. Bodart-Bailey and Derek Massarella (Folkstone, 1995).

38. Kaempfer's manuscript: *Heutiges Japan,* British Library, Sloane 3060; Johann Gaspar Scheuchzer, trans., *The History of Japan* (London, 1727); cited here is the three-volume edition, Glasgow, 1906 (henceforth "Scheuchzer"). For the complete title, see the bibliography. The manuscript is not in "High-Dutch," as the extended title states, but in "Hoch-Deutsch," that is, standard German.

39. See the bibliography in Hans Hüls and Hans Hoppe, ed., *Engelbert Kaempfer zum 330. Geburtstag* (Lemgo, 1982), especially 227–233.

40. For instance, Sir W. S. Gilbert's libretto of *The Mikado or the Town of Titipu*, first produced in London, 1885. Compare especially the personnage of Pooh-Bah with Kaempfer's description of Nagasaki officials.

41. Geography: see B. M. Bodart-Bailey, "The Persecution of Confucianism in Early Tokugawa Japan," *Monumenta Nipponica* 48.3 (1993):293–294. Political: In his *Vom ewigen Frieden,* Kant relies on Kaempfer's discussion on the closure of Japan, *Amoenitates*, book 2, chapter 14, pp. 478–502, translated into German in Dohm, 2:394–414. Philosophy: The *"Urwesen"* of Kant's *Kritik der reinen Vernunft* has many similarities with the "world soul" of Confucianism as described by Kaempfer (*Kants Werke*, reprint, Berlin, 1968, 3:414 onward).

42. J. W. von Goethe, "Vorschlag zur Einführung der deutschen Sprache in Polen," cited by P. Kapitza, "Japan in der deutschen Literatur des 17. und 18. Jahrhunderts," *Bonner Zeitschrift für Japanologie* (Bonn, 1981), 3:53, 57.

43. ". . . Kemper, ce véridique et savant voyageur." F. M. A. de Voltaire, *Essai sur les mœurs et l'esprit des nations* (Paris, 1963), 2:315.

44. Johann Christoph Gottsched, *Erste Gründe der gesamten Weltweisheit* (Hildesheim, 1983; facsimile of the 7th edition of Leipzig, 1762), 11.

45. Matthias Claudius, *Ein Tropfen aus dem Ozean,* edited by Gunter Albrecht (Berlin, 1975), 50–51, 249–278.

46. *The Citizen of the World,* in *Collected Works of Oliver Goldsmith,* edited by Arthur Friedman (Oxford, 1966), 2:454–457.

47. See, for instance, Goldsmith, above.

48. Julia Ching, "China und die Autonomie der Moral: der Fall des Christian

Wolff," in *Gegenentwürfe: 24 Lebensläufe für eine andere Theologie,* edited by Hermann Häring and Karl-Josef Kuschel (Munich, 1988), 192–193.

49. Scheuchzer, 3:105. Compare with page 370 below.

50. Scheuchzer, 2:343. Compare. with page 270 below. See also B. M. Bodart-Bailey, "Kaempfer Restor'd,' *Monumenta Nipponica* 43.1 (1988):15–16.

51. Scheuchzer, 1:lxxxix and next, unnumbered page.

52. See Massarella, "The History of *The History,*" 112–114, 117.

53. For details, see B. M. Bodart-Bailey, "Preliminary Report on the Manuscripts of Engelbert Kaempfer in the British Library," in *British Library Occasional Papers,* edited by Yu-Ying Brown (London, 1990), 26–37; book 1, chapter 1, and book 4, chapter 10, below.

54. On the difference between the originals and the copperplate prints, see Jörg Schmeiβer, "Changing the Image: The Drawings and Prints of Kaempfer's *History of Japan,*" in *The Furthest Goal: Engelbert Kaempfer's Encounter with Tokugawa Japan*, edited by B. M. Bodart-Bailey and Derek Massarella (Folkstone, 1995), 132–151.

55. Bodart-Bailey, "Kaempfer Restor'd," 23–24.

56. Scheuchzer, 1:xviii.

57. See Dohm, 1:xxix–xl.

58. Dohm, 1:xli; Massarella, "The History of *The History,*" 124–129; Bodart-Bailey, "Preliminary Report," 32–37.

59. Dohm, 1:xlii–xlvii.

60. Dohm, 1:1, xli; for details of changes by Scheuchzer and Dohm, see Bodart-Bailey, "Kaempfer Restor'd."

61. Christian Wilhelm Dohm, *Nachricht die Urschrift der Kämpferischen Beschreibung von Japan betreffend* (Lemgo, 1774).

62. Kaempfer mentions Ieyasu's usurpation of authority a number of times, as, for instance, pp. 181 and 182 below.

63. See p. 271 below.

64. Personal communication with Professor Hayami Akira, International Research Center for Japanese Studies, Kyoto.

65. *Amoenitates,* 495, translated into German in Dohm, 2:409.

66. See p. 223 below.

67. *Amoenitates*, 502, translated into German in Dohm, 2:414.

68. For details, see B. M. Bodart-Bailey, "The Laws of Compassion," *Monumenta Nipponica* 40.2 (1985).

69. *Buya shokudan*, in *Kokushi sōsho,* edited by Kokushi Kenkyū Kai (Tokyo, 1917), ser. 2, 86–87.

70. Tsunayoshi's elder brother, Ieshige, fathered a son who later became the sixth shogun, Ienobu (1662–1712), but the existence of this child brought up by a retainer was kept secret for a long time, since the mother was of low birth and not an official concubine.

71. Hotta Masatoshi, *Yōgen roku*, in *Zoku zoku gunsho ruiju* (Tokyo, 1906–1909), 13:31.

72. On Tsunayoshi's chamberlain government, see B. M. Bodart-Bailey, "The Significance of the Chamberlain Government of the Fifth Tokugawa Shogun," in *A Northern Prospect: Australian Papers on Japan* (Japanese Studies Association of Australia, 1981), and "Tokugawa Tsunayoshi (1646–1709), A Weberian Analysis," *Asiatische Studien/Études Asiatiques* 43:1 (1989). On Yanagisawa Yoshiyasu: B. M. Bodart-Bailey, "Councillor Defended, *Matsukage Nikki* and Yanagisawa Yoshiyasu," *Monumenta Nipponica* 34.4 (1979).

73. On the sentiments of a scholar permitted to appear before the shogun, see Olof G. Lidin, *The Life of Ogyū Sorai, a Tokugawa Confucian Philosopher* (Lund, 1973), 67–68.

74. "Prologue," below, p. 28.

75. On how Kaempfer's student and assistant rose to an important position as an interpreter, see Paul van der Velde, "The Interpreter Interpreted: Kaempfer's Japanese Collaborator Imamura Genemon Eisei," in *The Furthest Goal: Engelbert Kaempfer's Encounter with Tokugawa Japan*, edited by B. M. Bodart-Bailey and Derek Massarella (Folkstone, 1995).

76. Sloane 3061, f. 96v–97.

77. See illustration on p. 363.

78. Goldsmith, 2:454–457.

79. After the publication of Kaempfer's work, Matthias Claudius (*Ein Tropfen aus dem Ozean*, 258–259) transported the scene and imagined the German playwright Gotthold Ephraim Lessing (1729–1781) at the feet of the shogun.

80. W. Treue, *Wirtschaft, Gesellschaft und Technik in Deutschland vom 16. bis zum 18. Jahrhundert, Handbuch der deutschen Geschichte,* 12 (Munich, reprint 1974), 117.

81. Karl Meier-Lemgo, *Engelbert Kaempfer, der erste deutsche Forschungsreisende,* 4. Some towns burned greater numbers of women relative to their populations. See W. Niess, *Hexenprozesse in der Grafschaft Buedingen* (Buedingen, 1982), 177–179, 302–303.

82. "*saepe homines indocti & praejudiciis effascinati, ne dicam avari, crudeles & impii!,*" "Investigatio Inncentiae per Crocodilos & Ignem, apud Gentiles Orientis hodie usitata," *Amoenitates Exoticae*, 458. For a more detailed treatment, see Bodart-Bailey, *Kenperu to Tokugawa Tsunayoshi,* 29–42.

83. *Amoenitates,* 490, translated in Dohm, 2:404.

84. *Exercitatio politica de Majestatis divisione* (Danzig, 1673), translated into German by R. Müller-König, in *Engelbert Kaempfer zum 330. Geburtstag*, 15–29.

85. Peter Gay, *The Enlightenment: An Interpretation* (London, 1967), 298–299.

86. Leonard Krieger, *The Politics of Discretion: Pufendorf and the Acceptance of Natural Law* (Chicago, 1965), 2.

87. See, for instance, G. W. Leibniz, *Politische Schriften,* edited by H. H. Holz (Frankfurt, 1966), 15, 18–21, 26, 27, 29.

88. Gerhard Oestreich, *Geist und Gestalt des frühmodernen Staates* (Berlin, 1969), 180–181. (I thank Professor Watanabe Hiroshi for drawing my attention to Oestreich's work.)

89. Ernst Walter Zeeden, *Europa im Zeitalter des Absolutismus und der Aufklärung* (Stuttgart, 1981), 50.

90. Kaempfer, *Exercitatio politica,* 26–27.

91. Zeeden, *Europa im Zeitalter des Absolutismus,* 51.

92. Sloane 3063, f. 54v; Engelbert Kaempfer, *Die Briefe Engelbert Kaempfers,* edited by Karl Meier-Lemgo (Wiesbaden, 1965), 45.

93. Oestreich, *Geist und Gestalt,* 180–181.

94. "Prologue," 27.

95. *De statu imperii Germanici*, 1667, cited in Treue, *Wirtschaft, Gesellschaft und Technik,* 102. The states of the empire obtained the right to enter alliances with outside powers only at the Peace of Westphalia, but such alliances had already been concluded during the war.

96. Comparing the two political institutions is not easy, but judging from the German terms Kaempfer used for political offices in Japan, he saw some similarities. See also Mark Ravina, "State-building and Political Economy in Early-modern Japan," *Journal of Asian Studies* 54.4 (1995):997–1022.

97. Zeeden, *Europa im Zeitalter des Absolutismus,* 51.

98. Kaempfer cites words attributed to Alexander the Great: "Just as the world cannot be ruled by two suns, the state cannot be governed by two authorities concurrently." Curtius Rufius, *Historiae Alexandri Magni Macedonis*, book 4, ch. 11, cited in Kaempfer, *Exercitatio politica,* 24.

99. Scheuchzer, 3:301–336. The translation of the title of Kaempfer's essay by Shizuki Tadao in 1801 coined the Japanese term *sakoku,* which is now generally applied to the Tokugawa period. Ronald P. Toby, *State and Diplomacy in Early Modern Japan* (Princeton, 1984), 12–14.

100. Kant was later to echo these sentiments in his essay "Vom ewigen Frieden."

101. See p. 133 below. In the pre-Tokugawa period, Confucianism formed the basis of government and statecraft and was studied in Buddhist monasteries. See Bodart-Bailey, "The Persecution of Confucianism," 301–303.

102. This is the leitmotif of Oestreich, *Geist und Gestalt,* but see especially pp. 11–15, 33–44.

103. In book 5, Kaempfer cites Lipsius' correspondence on the shape of the cross. See p. 294 below.

104. The work was published in more than fifty editions in its original Latin text alone and was translated into most European languages.

105. See p. 223 below.

106. Lipsius pleads for a strict military code of conduct, based on discipline and ethical behavior, which is achieved through exercise, order, self-restraint, and reward and punishment. Oestreich, *Geist und Gestalt,* 20.

107. To the amazement of a visitor, the armies of Maurice of Orange-Nassau, trained in the spirit of Lipsius, could be permitted to enter a market and mix with civilians without the fear of plunder or rape. Oestreich, *Geist und Gestalt,* 23, 30.

108. Page 160 below.

109. Michael Cooper, *They Came to Japan* (Berkeley, 1965), 340.

110. Aoki Okikatsu, *Tōmon jissaku,* in *Nihon keizai taiten,* 20 (Tokyo, 1966–1971). (I thank Professor Hiraishi Naoaki for pointing this out to me.)

111. For a more detailed analysis, see Bodart-Bailey, "Writing *The History of Japan.*"

112. I have pointed some of these out in B. M. Bodart-Bailey, "The Most Magnificent Monastery and Other Famous Sights: The Japanese Paintings of Engelbert Kaempfer," *Japan Review* 3 (1992):28–29, and B. M. Bodart-Bailey, "Kyoto Three Hundred Years Ago," *Nichibunken Newsletter* 9 (May 1991):8–9.

113. See Bodart-Bailey, "The Persecution of Confucianism."

114. On how this can constitute a valuable source of oral tradition, see Carmen Blacker, "Forgotten Practices of the Past: Kaempfer's Strange Description of the Japanese Emperor," in *The Furthest Goal: Engelbert Kaempfer's Encounter with Tokugawa Japan,* edited by B. M. Bodart-Bailey and Derek Massarella (Folkstone, 1995).

Prologue

1. The Holy Roman Empire, of which Kaempfer's native Westphalia was part, was threatened by Louis XIV of France in the West and the Ottoman Turks in the East.

2. This expression is used to denote the Indo-European family.

3. Kaempfer refers to the Old Testament, Genesis 9:25–26: "Noah said, Cursed be Canaan; a slave of slaves he will be to his brothers. Blessed by the Lord be Shem, and let Canaan be his slave. God enlarge Japheth, and let him dwell in the tents of Shem; and let Canaan be his slave." Shem, Cham, and Japheth were the three sons of Noah; Canaan was the son of Cham, who had incurred the displeasure of Noah. Kaempfer's "Abraham" should most probably read "Noah."

4. *Amoenitates,* "Praefatio," 3.

5. Andreas Cleyer (also Andries Cleijer), Dutch resident at Nagasaki 1682–1683, 1685–1686. Sebastian Scheffer, publisher of Cleyer's *Specimen medicinae Sinicae* in Frankfurt. On Scheffer, see Eva S. Kraft, *Andreas Cleyer: Tagebuch des Kontors zu Nagasaki auf der Insel Deshima* (Bonn, 1985), 45, 47, 52.

6. Kaempfer refers to Imamura Genemon Eisei (1676–1736), who later distinguished himself as an interpreter and interviewed the priest Sidotti. Kaempfer kept his name secret because the work he did for Kaempfer was highly illegal. See Paul van der Velde, "The Interpeter Interpreted," 44–48.

7. Kaempfer refers to Yoshikawa Gibuemon, whose niece married Imamura Genemon in 1697 (Paul van der Velde, "The Interpreter Interpreted," 48).

8. Kaempfer refers to his travel diaries and notes, some of which were partially transcribed and edited by Karl Meier-Lemgo as *Die Reisetagebücher Engelbert Kaempfers.* His plan to publish these did not materialize.

Book 1

Chapter 1

1. British Library, manuscript Sloane 2921.

2. For details, see Bodart-Bailey, "Writing *The History of Japan*," 17–43.

3. For illustrations of Scheuchzer's omissions, additions, and discussion, see Bodart-Bailey, "Preliminary Report," 27–33. For a discussion of the Thai material, see B. J. Terwiel, "Kaempfer and Thai History: The Documents Behind the Printed Text," *Journal of the Royal Asiatic Society* No. 1 (1989).

4. Christian Wilhelm Dohm, ed., *Geschichte und Beschreibung von Japan*, 2 vols. (Lemgo, 1777–1779).

Chapter 2

1. Kaempfer: "Steven": strong erect poles on each end of the keel supporting the weight of the ship. (Johann Christoph Adelung, *Grammatisch-kritisches Wörterbuch der Hochdeutschen Mundart* [Vienna, 1808], 4:365.)

2. Kaempfer: "Matsuma" and "Matsima." The largest Southern island of the Danjo island group located at 32° north latitude and 128°15′ east longitude; also known as Onnashima or Meshima. However, Kaempfer was most probably passing Tori no shima, which is situated slightly further to the north but fits his description better with regard to size. (I thank Keith Mitchell, Cartography, RSPAS, ANU, for making the appropriate naval chart available to me.)

3. Hermes is the Greek messenger god.

4. Kaempfer's sketch can be found at British Library, SL 2921, folio 36 verso.

5. Maps show the Danjo group consisting of six separate islands.

6. Literally, Papists' mountain: Takabokojima.

7. Kaempfer: "Struven": flat river boats used in Russia and Prussia with huts or small houses on the deck, oars, and sails (Adelung, *Grammatisch-kritisches Wörterbuch*, 4:460). Russian: *strug*.

8. Balthasar Sweers, resident, 1 November 1689–21 October 1690.

9. Hendrick (Hendrik) van Buijtenhem (Bütenheim), resident, 21 October 1690–9 November 1691.

Chapter 3

1. Here the modern form, Nippon, will be used.

2. Kaempfer: "Hollanda."

3. Hokkaido was not counted as part of Japan proper (see below) and hence Awajishima was the fourth largest island after Honshu, Kyushu, and Shikoku.

4. *Akitsu* = dragon-fly. The legend goes that Emperor Jimmu, looking at the land from the top of a hill, said it resembled "a dragon-fly licking its hinder parts." Jean Herbert, *Shinto, The Fountainhead of Japan* (London, 1967), 110, 405.

5. "The true imperial court"; also used to denote the whole country.

6. Further meanings of the word *chō* are "the country ruled by the emperor," "the place where people assemble." Nihon Daijiten Kankō Kai, ed., *Nihon kokugo daijiten* (Tokyo, 1980), 7:478.

7. Excluding Hokkaido, the latitude is about correct, but its longitudinal position, excluding Hokkaido, is roughly between 130 and 142 degrees east.

8. Kaempfer: "im Jahre vor Christi Gebuhrt 590," literally, in the year 590 before the birth of Christ. This is a slip of the pen, for in the next sentence Kaempfer says "soon afterward" and then gives a higher number, indicating that he was aware that these were A.D. and not B.C. dates.

9. Sushun is believed to have ruled A.D. 587–592.

10. *Goki shichi dō* = the five imperial provinces (Yamashiro, Yamato, Kawaguchi, Izumi, Settsu) and the seven main highways. This division is generally traced to the *ritsuryō* system of the eighth century A.D.

11. Believed to have ruled A.D. 673–686.

12. In 1620 Chikugo (and not Chikuzen) was split between Tachibana Muneshige, who became lord of Yanagawa castle, and Arima Toyouji, lord of Kurume castle. Kuroita Katsumi, ed., *Tokugawa Jikki,* in *Shintei zōho kokushi taikei* (Tokyo, reprint 1976), 2:201, Genna 6.11.27; 2:203, Genna 6. uru 12.8; Oda Akinobu, ed., *On'eiroku haizetsuroku, Nihon shiryō sensho* (Tokyo, 1970), 6:57. The daimyo of Tsushima, Sō Tsushima no Kami Yoshitomo (1568–1615), had received land in Hizen (not Chikugo) in 1600 and received further lands in Hizen in 1605 (*On'eiroku haizetsuroku,* 3, 28). Kaempfer's suggestion that domains only decreased in size is not correct.

13. Japan's presence on the Korean peninsula is grossly exaggerated but somewhat modified in the detailed text below. The Japanese had a small trading settlement at Pusan, administered by the Sō family of Tsushima, but were not permitted into the rest of the country. Also the Chosŏn dynasty had already unified the peninsula in 1392. There is, however, a possibility that the terminology as explained by Kaempfer was still in use at Nagasaki.

14. Kaempfer refers to the Manchu conquest of China completed in 1644.

15. The Ryūkyūs sent tribute to Japan through Satsuma during the Muromachi period but were subjected by the lord of Satsuma only in 1609.

16. Kaempfer's text is garbled. The Chūzan dynasty was resident at Shuri on the main island of Okinawa. However, since it was the largest island of the group, it might have been referred to as *ōshima* (large island). Alternatively, "Oshima" might refer to Amami Ōshima, which is second in size to Okinawa jima. "Iayama" might refer to Yaeyama, although this island chain lies to the southwest. Yaeyama was, however, an independent kingdom before the conquest by Shō Hashi in 1422. Mitsugu Sakihara, *A Brief History of Early Okinawa Based on The Omoro Sōshi* (Tokyo, 1987), 207.

17. Kaempfer: "Coréÿ oder Coræa."

18. Kaempfer: "Fakkusai": Kudara, Paekche, which was not bordering "Tartary" but occupied the southwestern part of the Korean peninsula. With regard to Chōsen, see note 13 above.

19. Believed to have ruled 192–200.

20. Jingū Kōgō (regent), 201–269.

21. Toyotomi Hideyoshi (1536–1598).

22. Ginseng.

23. Kaempfer: "Sjam Soi": most probably San-sing, the common name for d'I-lan-hien, at the confluence of the rivers Mou-tan-kiang and Soungari. Lucien Gibert, *Dictionnaire historique et geographique de la Mandchourie* (Hong Kong, 1934), 779.

24. Kaempfer: "Jupy": The Ch'ing-dynasty work *Ning-ku-ta-chi-lia* of Wu Chen-chen says that the people of Fei-ya-k'a are called Wu-chi and also Yü-pi (lit., fish skin), as they wear fish-skins. Sei Wada, "The Native of the Lower Reaches . . . ," *Memoirs of the Research Department of the Toyo Bunko,* no. 10 (1938), 102. Pierre Larousse, *Grand Dictionnaire Universel Du XIXe* (Paris, 1866–1869), defines the term as a people of Manchuria, in the southeast at the border of Ousouri and at the foot of Mount Schota-Aline. European maps used the term for the unexplored area north of Japan, roughly corresponding to Eastern Manchuria. See Vincenzo Maria Coronelli, *Isola del Giapone e Peninsola di Corea,* Venice 1692, and Guillaume Delisle, *L'Asie,* early eighteenth century, in Hugh Cortazzi, *Isles of Gold: Antique Maps of Japan* (New York, 1983), 146, 160.

25. Jurchen, also Jürched, Jou-tchen, Niu-tchen; a Tungusic people, ancestors of the Manchu. In Coronelli's map of Asia, the term "Royaume de Niuche" denotes the area north of Korea, to the west of Yupi (Cortazzi, *Isles of Gold,* 160).

26. That is, the island of Ezo.

27. Minamoto Yoritomo (1147–1199) became the first shogun of the Kamakura bakufu in 1190.

28. One of the Japanese maps Kaempfer brought back showed Matsumae as a small island separate from Hokkaidō. British Library, Or.75. f. 12 (2), reproduced in exhibition catalogue *Doitsu jin no mita Genroku jidai, Kenperu ten* (Tokyo, 1991), no. 26, p. 44.

29. The episode is known as Shakusha'in no ran and happened in 1669.

30. Ten thousand *koku* of rice (1 *koku* = 5.119 U.S. bushels).

31. Kaempfer: "Sugaar und Taijasacki."

32. Kaempfer: "Vriesen"; Marten Gerritz de Vries, born 1602, death unknown. In 1634 de Vries was sent by the Dutch governor general of Batavia, Antonio van Diemen, with two vessels, *Breskens* and *Castricum* (also: *Castrecom*), to discover the so-called Gold and Silver Islands and the shoreline of America and Tartary. See Numata Jirō et al., ed., *Yōgaku shi jiten* (Tokyo, 1984), 634; Montanus, *Atlas Japannensis,* 319–380, etc. The *Castricum,* with de Vries aboard, claimed an area corresponding to Etorofu as property of the Dutch East India Company. Kunashiri Suidō, the strait between the islands Kunashiri and Etorofu, was for some time named after de Vries. See La Pérouse:

Carte General, undated, Jan Jansson, *Nova et Accurata Iapoinae Terrae Esonis*, Atlas leaf, 1659, in Cortazzi, *Isles of Gold,* 135, 139; Larousse, *Grand Dictionnaire,* 15:1434.

33. Kaempfer refers to the "mainland," as contemporary maps placed Hokkaidō between Japan and Eastern Manchuria. See the maps Jan Jansson: *Nova et Accurata Iaponiae Terrae Esonis* . . . Atlas leaf, 1659, Amsterdam, and Guillaume Delisle: *L'Asie*, early eighteenth century, in Cortazzi, *Isles of Gold,* 139, 160–161.

34. Kaempfer: *"fretum anianum"*; believed to exist between China and America, that is, the Bering Strait. See Montanus, *Atlas Japannensis,* 339.

35. Kaempfer: "Kataÿa," a variation of Chinese K'i-tan (Khitan). The Khitan dominated Northern China, and the name was retained for this area.

36. Andrei Andreevich Vinius (1641–1717), *The Great Soviet Encyclopedia* (New York, 1974), 5:475, states that his father, Andrei Denisovich Vinius, had come from Holland. As also in other respects the entry does not accord with the information provided by Kaempfer (e.g., it notes: "From 1692 to 1674 [*sic*] he was on diplomatic assignments in France, Spain, and Great Britain," while Kaempfer met him in Moscow in 1683 as inspector of pharmacies), this might well be a mistake. Vinius wrote in Kaempfer's autograph book in 1683. Meier-Lemgo, "Das Stammbuch Engelbert Kämpfers," 169–170.

37. Kaempfer: "Spitharÿ." Nikolai Gavrilovich Spafarii (Nicolae Spâtarul Milescu, 1636–1708), Romanian scholar and diplomat. He came to Moscow in 1671 and served as translator in the Russian Foreign Office. From 1675 to 1678 he headed the Russian embassy to Peking. *Great Soviet Encyclopedia,* 24:381–382.

38. Nicolaas Cornelisz Witsen (1641–1717), mayor of Amsterdam from 1682 to 1705. I.U.D. = iuris utriusque doctor = doctor of law.

39. Witsen, *Noord en Oost Tartarye.* British Museum, *General Catalogue of Printed Books* (London, 1964). The first edition appeared in 1692 but is extremely rare. J. F. Gebhard, *Het Leven van Mr. Nicolaas Cornelisz Witsen* (Utrecht, 1881), 1:425.

40. Evert Ijsbrants (also: Isbrant, Ysbrants) Ides (van Glückstadt) traveled to China 1692–1695 as ambassador of the czars Ivan and Peter I. His book, *Driejaarige Reize naar China* (Amsterdam, 1704, 1710), acknowleges that he was guided by Witsen's map. Gebhard, *Het Leven van Mr. Nicolaas Cornelisz Witsen,* 427.

41. The Cosaque Semen Dejnev (Dezhnev) reached the Bering Strait in 1648 and lived there for six years, but his description was only discovered in 1736. V. V. Barthold, *La décourverte de l'Asie* (Paris, 1947), 217.

42. Yamaoka Jūbei Tsushima no Kami, Kagesuke, Nagasaki *bugyō* 1687–1694.

43. Presumably Kabarovsk. Here and for the following four names Kaempfer's original transcription has been kept.

44. Orang-k'ai; also Ou-liang-hai, Ouriangha.

45. Tsitsikar, also Ts'i-tsi-ha-eul, also known as Pou-k'ouei, Long-kiang, capital of the province of Hei-long-kiang. Gibert, *Dictionnaire historique,* 229.

46. Hei-long-kiang.

47. The Amur River basin.

48. The Amur River.

49. The maps Kaempfer saw most probably were popular world maps based on Matteo Ricci's map of China with difficult Chinese characters replaced by *kana.* See *Bankoku Sōezu, 1645,* Kobe City Museum; Cortazzi, *Isles of Gold,* 42.

50. The islands are marked on Abe Yasuyuki, *Bankoku chikyū yochi zenzu,* woodblock print, 1853 (Cortazzi, *Isles of Gold,* 118), with Ginshima being the larger, nearly the size of Kyushu. They were first mentioned in a letter written by Fray Andrés de Aguirre to the viceroy of Mexico, 1584–1585; he had heard that a Portuguese ship had been blown there, nine days' sailing from Japan. Dahlgren suggests that the islands never existed, while Chassigneux argues that they were identical with Okinawa. E. W. Dahlgren, "A Contribution to the History of the Discovery of Japan," *Transactions of the Japan Society of London* 11 (1913):250–252; Edmond Chassigneux, "Rica de Oro et Rica de Plata," *T'oung Pao* 30 (1933):70.

51. Kaempfer refers to the papal bulls of 1493. In 1494 a circular line of division extending from pole to pole, passing 370 leagues west of the Cape Verde Islands was agreed upon by Spain and Portugal. Donald F. Lach, *Asia in the Making of Europe* (Chicago, 1965), 1:56–57; O.H.K. Spate, *The Spanish Lake* (Canberra, 1979), 27–29.

52. The expedition of Mathys Quast on the ship *Engel.* See Cortazzi, *Isles of Gold,* 41.

53. Kaempfer: "Jeso." This must be a slip of the pen, especially since these pages of the manuscript are not in Kaempfer's hand. See below.

54. Kaempfer refers to De Vries' expedition mentioned above. In a storm de Vries' vessel *Castricum* was separated from the *Breskens,* under the command of Henry Cornelius (Hendrich Corneliszen) Schaep. As the *Castricum* carried the supplies, the *Bresken* saw itself forced to enter a Japanese harbor. In June and July 1643 the *Bresken* landed at Yamada Ura, Iwate ken, and on the second landing the captain and ten people were taken prisoners. They were taken to Morioka and then to Edo and after much questioning finally handed over to the Dutch resident at Nagasaki, Jan van Elserack. Numata et al., *Yōgaku shi jiten,* 634; Montanus, *Atlas Japannensis,* 319–380. Kaempfer had studied Schaep's diary. See Bodart-Bailey, "Writing *The History of Japan,*" 28.

55. The island lies a few degrees east and south of Hachijō.

56. Also: Mujintō; Kaempfer: "Bunesima"; in the Ogasawara island chain: the Bonin Islands. Most probably first sighted by the Spanish vessel *San Juan* in 1543 and then discovered by Ogasawara Sadayori (dates unknown) in 1593. They were conferred to him as fief by Ieyasu but not settled. In 1675 the Izu *daikan* sent out a ship to survey the area. In 1823 American whalers took posession of the islands, and in the ensuing territorial dispute with the United States at the beginning of the Meiji period, the 1675 "discovery" was cited as a major fact. See Yasuoka Akio, "Ogasawara Shotō kizoku mondai," in *Rekishi daijiten;* Lionel Berners Cholmondeley, *The History of the Bonin Islands* (London, 1915).

57. Hachijōjima is situated 290 kilometers south of Tokyo. Kaempfer's description has been censured by Ernest Satow as "almost like a passage from the Arabian Nights," criticism that has been repeated by Murdoch and Boxer. James Murdoch, *A His-*

tory of Japan (Kobe, 1903), 432n2; Boxer, *A True Description,* 40–41. Kaempfer's statement that whole boats with supplies and people were wound up appears to be based on a misreading of the German text of Caron's description, which is ambiguous and could be interpreted this way. See Fr. Caron and Jod. Schouten, *Wahrhaftige Beschreibungen zweyer mächtigen Königreiche Jappan und Siam* (Nürnberg, 1663), 93. Kaempfer's statement that grandees were banished there is correct and has been criticized erroneously. See *Kokushi daijiten,* 11:602.

Chapter 4

1. Kaempfer: "Sitzi Jossu."

2. The first printed edition of the work is believed to be the *Manjuya-bon setsuyōshū* of the late Muromachi period, published most probably between 1532 and 1570. See Kenneth B. Gardner, *Descriptive Catalogue of Japanese Books in the British Library Printed before 1700* (London: British Library, 1993), 279–280.

3. Nakada Norio, *Ekū hen setsuyōshū taizen kenkyū narabini sakuin* (Tokyo, 1975), 510–516. J. G. Scheuchzer's record shows that a *Setsuyōshū* was among Kaempfer's books purchased by Hans Sloane (Scheuchzer, 1:lxxxvi). Sloane's collection was taken over by the British Library, but this work is no longer in the library's collection. Gardner's *Descriptive Catalogue* lists four different *Setsuyōshū,* but all were acquired from Ernest Satow in 1884.

4. *Man goku* = 10,000 *koku,* therefore 22,570,000 *koku* (1 *koku* = 5.119 U.S. bushels).

5. Literally, large family.

6. Literally, small family.

Chapter 6

1. Kaempfer obtained his information from the first two volumes of *Nihon shoki,* titled *Kami no yo.*

2. Kaempfer: "Kuni toko Dàt Sji no Mikotto." Usually, Kuni no toko tachi no mikoto. Sakamoto Tarō and Inoue Mitsusada, ed., *Nihon shoki,* in *Nihon bungaku koten taikei* (Tokyo, 1967), 76. In the following, Kaempfer's spelling will not be given unless it differs markedly. Translations are from Herbert, *Shinto,* but since Herbert cites these deities with the title of *kami* instead of *mikoto,* his "Deity" has been replaced with "Augustness." Here: "His Augustness Standing Eternally on Earth" (Herbert, *Shinto,* 235).

3. "His Augustness the true Soil of the Land" (Herbert, *Shinto,* 247).

4. "His Augustness the Luxuriant Integrating Master" (Herbert, *Shinto,* 235). Herbert uses the spelling "Toyo-kumo-nu. . . ." Here that of *Nihon shoki* in *Nihon bungaku taikei,* 76, has been adopted.

5. "His Augustness Mud Earth Lord" and his younger sister (not wife), "Her Augustness Mud Earth Lady" (Herbert, *Shinto,* 235).

6. "His Augustness Elder of the Great Place" and his younger sister, "Her Augustness Elder Lady of the Great Place" (Herbert, *Shinto,* 235).

7. Kaempfer has the latter name as: Oosi wote no Mikotto. "His Augustness Perfect Exterior" and his younger sister, "Her Augustness Awful (or Venerable) Lady" (Herbert, *Shinto,* 235).

8. "His Augustness the Male who Invites" and his younger sister, "Her Augustness the Female who invites" (Herbert, *Shinto,* 235).

9. Amaterasu, described in *Nihon shoki* as female, but as was common at the time, Kaempfer refers to the god as male throughout.

10. A reference to Amaterasu secluding herself in a rock cave, thereby casting the world into darkness. *Kojiki,* chapter 17; see Donald L. Philippi's translation (Tokyo: University of Tokyo Press, 1968), 81–85, also Herbert, *Shinto,* 300–301.

11. Also: Masa ka a katsu kachi hayabi ame no oshi ho mimi no mikoto, translated by Herbert as "His Augustness Truly-conqueror-I-conquer-conquering-swift-heavenly-great-great-ears." He was born from the jewels in the left bunch of Tenshō daijin's (Amaterasu's) hair (Herbert, *Shinto*, 293).

12. Also: Ame nigishi kuni nigishi ama tsu hi daka hiko hiko ho no ninigi no mikoto, translated as "His Augustness Heaven-plenty Earth-plenty Heaven's sun-height Prince Rice-ear ruddy plenty" (Herbert, *Shinto*, 354).

13. Also: Ama tsu hi daka hiko ho ho demi no mikoto, "His Augustness Heaven's sun-height prince great rice ears lord ears" (Herbert, *Shinto*, 366).

14. Also: Ama tsu hi daka hiko nagisa take ugaya fuki aezu no mikoto, "His Augustness heaven's sun-height prince wave-limit brave cormorant-thatch-meeting-incompletely" (Herbert, *Shinto,* 386).

15. This has not been included in this translation.

16. Kaempfer: "erdichteten"; Scheuchzer omitted the first mention of this word and translated the second as "fictious." Here it has been taken as derived from *erdicht,* "terrestial," in line with Kaempfer's description of Tenshō daijin at the end of the chapter and in view of the fact that this chapter is not in his hand, and the extra syllable could well have been added.

17. "New country"; correctly, *atarashii kuni*, but Kaempfer has "Kokf" for *koku.*

18. The legendary founder of Nineveh and the ancient kingdom of Assyria.

19. Kuni toko tachi no mikoto; see above.

20. "The present emperor." Kaempfer: "KinSan Kiwo tei." He refers to the emperor Higashiyama, who reigned from 1687 to 1709 but was the 113th emperor.

Chapter 7

1. *Satsuki* was the fifth month of the old Japanese calendar and thus corresponded to June/July.

2. *De Rebus Japonicis, Indicis & Peruanis Epistolae Recentiores* (Antwerp, 1605). This contains a collection of letters edited by John Hay. The letter referred to was written by Luis Frois (or Froes), S.J. (1532–1597). See Cooper, *They Came to Japan,* 15.

3. *Gongen* designates avatar, an incarnation of Buddha.
4. Kaempfer: Latin "massa."
5. Venereal disease.
6. Venereal disease.
7. One catty = 16 taels = 625 grams.
8. Malay-Javanese *pikul,* a man's load, equal to 100 catties, 133.3 pounds.
9. One mace = one momme, one-tenth of one tael.
10. A zinc ore.
11. Pearl oyster: *Pinctada* subalpine.
12. Chinese weight and monetary unit; one candareen is estimated at about six grains Troy (the Troy pound contains 5,760 grains).
13. Japanese monetary unit: one *koban* = one *ryō* = six taels.
14. Cowrie or porcelain shell.
15. There is a blank in the manuscript.
16. Also *tairagai:* a pen razor or fan shell, *Pinna pectinata.*
17. Normally the distance between the tips of the thumb and little finger: nine inches.
18. *Hyaku hiro* (100 fathoms) was used in common parlance as a generic name for whales and for anything found in the intestines of animals; it also means "intestines."
19. *Kujira no fu* means "whale bowels/viscera." "Whale dung" would be *kujira no fun.*
20. Kaempfer refers to the famous research of his contemporary, Georgius Everhardus Rumphius (Rumph), published in 1705 and 1741 as *D'Amboinsche Rariteitkamer, of eene Beschryvinge van aller Hande. . . .*

Chapter 8

1. Lemgo, 1712. Wolfgang Muntschick, *Engelbert Kaempfer; Flora Japonica (1712)* (Wiesbaden, 1983) contains a facsimile reproduction of the chapter on Japanese plants and partial translation.
2. *Rhus verniciflua* Stokes. Scientific names are from Makino Tomitaro, *Makino's New Illustrated Flora of Japan* (Tokyo, 1962). Scientific names are given only where there is no, or a loose, Western equivalent.
3. Old name for *yama urushi; Rhus tripocarpa* Miq.
4. Kaempfer refers to the genus *Canellaceae* = cinnamon, calling the tree a "false cinnamon."
5. *Cassia* is an inferior kind of cinnamon; *lignea* = wood.
6. *Saussurea Lappa* Clarke, fam. *Compositae;* P. A. van der Lith, et al., *Encyclopaedie van Nederlandsch-Indie* (Gravenhagen, n.d.), 3:285–286.
7. *Cinnamomum camphora* Sieb. Kaempfer describes the production of camphor in detail in *Amoenitates,* 770–773. Also Muntschick, *Engelbert Kaempfer,* 40–44.
8. Japanese pepper tree; prickly ash; *Xanthoxyum piperitum* DC.
9. Kaempfer's Riches could not be traced; perhaps ricinus.

10. Persimmon.

11. In *Amoenitates,* 803, Kaempfer identifies the tree as *itabu* (also *inubiwa*) = *Ficus erecta* Thunb.

12. *Torreya nucifera* Sieb. et Zucc.

13. Kaempfer: "Areck." Presumably Kaempfer refers to *Areca Catechu,* the betel-nut palm.

14. Ginkgo nut.

15. Ginkgo tree.

16. Kaempfer: "Lothus baum"; also Chinese date tree; *Zizyphus Jujuba* Mill. var. *inermis* Rehd.

17. Tangerine.

18. Kaempfer: "porstäpffel"; an apple of the reinette type, red, with firm flesh, maturing late in the year.

19. Kumquat; *Fortunella japonica* Swingle.

20. Kaempfer: "Kriecken" = bullace; *Prunis insititia.*

21. Blank in the manuscript. Kaempfer mentions in book 5, chapter 10, that this kind of bamboo is found in Kusatsu, in the province of Ōmi.

22. Kaempfer: "Rottang"; in narrow terms rattan denotes species of the climbing palm genus *Calamus,* but the word comes from Malay *rōtan* (*raut* = to pare, trim, strip) and was apparently used in this wider sense.

23. *Chamaecyparis obtsa* Endl. and *Cryptomeria japonica* D. Don.

24. Usually *inumaki; Podocarpus macrophylla* D. Don.

25. Chinquapin; *Castanopsis cuspidata.*

26. *Distylium racemosum* Sieb. et Zucc.

27. Japanese horse chestnut; *Aesculus turbinata* Blume.

28. Camellia; *Camellia japonica* L.

29. Azalea; *Rhododendron indicum* Sweet.

30. Rhododenron; *Rhododendron Metternichii* Sieb. et Zucc.

31. *Acer palmatum* Thumb. momi = red silk cloth.

32. Old name for *yamaurushi;* wax tree; *Rhus trichocarpa* Miq.

33. Kaempfer: "Matricaria."

34. Kaempfer: "Irides."

35. Kaempfer: "Carÿophÿll" = *caryophyllaceae.*

36. *Trachycarpus excelsa* Wendl.

37. Paulownia tree; *Paulownia tomentosa* Steudel.

38. Tung oil tree; *Aleurites cordata* Muell. Arg.

39. Kaempfer: "Asa diracht Avicennæ"; Jap. = *sendan; Melia Azedarch* L. var. *japonica* Makino.

40. *Glycine Max* Merrill.

41. *Phaseolus angularis* W. F. Wight; the beans are generally of a very dark red color.

42. A bun or dumpling with bean-jam filling.

43. The modern scientific name is *Setaria italica* Beauw.

44. Kaempfer: "Milium vulgare nostras"; *kibi* is Chinese millet; *Panicum Miliaceum.*

45. Kaempfer: "panicum vulgare, juba minore, semine nigri cante"; the modern scientific name is *Panicum Crus-galli* L. var. *frumentaceum* Trin.

46. Kaempfer: "Pastinaca hortensis"; "sÿlvestris."

47. Kaempfer: "lactuca nostras."

48. Kaempfer: "Dracunculo"; *Amorphophalus Konjac* K. Koch.

49. Kaempfer: "Filix"; *Pteridium aquilinum* Kuhn.

50. Kaempfer: "Faba gÿpt"; *Nelumbo nucifera* Gaertn.

51. Also *kazura no ne* = arrowroot.

Chapter 9

1. Kaempfer could describe this and other fabulous animals in such detail because they were portrayed in the illustrated encyclopedia *Kimmōzui* by the Confucian scholar Nakamura Tekisai (1629–1702), the preface dated 1666. The eight-volume edition Kaempfer brought back from Japan is still in the British Library (see Garder, *A Descriptive Catalogue,* 265–266). A reproduction has been edited by Sugimoto Tsutomu (Tokyo, 1975). *Kirin* as well as *sūgu* and *kaichi* below are on pages 1 *(ura)* and 2 *(omote)* of vol. 12 (p. 164 in Sugimoto's reproduction).

2. Yao and Shun, mythical sage rulers of ancient China.

3. Confucius and Mencius.

4. The historical Buddha.

5. Bodhidharma, the twenty-eighth patriarch in line from the Buddha and first patriarch of Zen in China; he lived in the sixth century.

6. 574–622, second son of the emperor Yōmei, regent to his aunt Empress Suiko; he was responsible for political reforms and establishing Buddhism in Japan.

7. Kaempfer: "Kaitsu oder Kaisai."

8. Kaempfer: "Tats, dria, oder Dsjà."

9. *Kimmōzui,* p. 1 *(ura),* vol. 13 (p. 172 of Sugimoto's reproduction).

10. Pythagoras, Greek philsopher and mathematician, sixth century B.C., who believed in the transmigration of souls.

11. See pp. 94–96 below for an explanation of the twelve-year cycle and astrological signs. See Bodart-Bailey, "The Laws of Compassion," 164–167, for the reason for protection of dogs and other living creatures.

12. A raccoon dog.

13. A weasel.

14. A marten, or Japanese sable.

15. An ogre, monster. *Kitsune* is the normal term for fox. The fox-devil is more of a trickster than an ogre.

16. Kaempfer: "Dieblen."
17. Literally,: to break down a hall or temple.
18. *Mukade namako: Orphnurgus insignis* Fisher.
19. *Natrix vibakari* (Boie).
20. Anaconda, boa constrictor, or python.
21. Kyushu.
22. The ducks described by Kaempfer are contained on p. 4 *(omote)* of vol. 13 of *Kimmōzui* (p. 174 in Sugimoto's reproduction; the little cuckoo and fish hawk mentioned below are on pp. 173, 178).
23. A cuckoo; *Cuculus poliocephalus.*
24. Kaempfer: "*Misàgo* oder *Bisago*"; fish hawk.
25. *Zushi* refers not only to pickled but all raw fish.
26. Generally known as *kōmoriga.*
27. *Cryptotympana japonensis* Kato.
28. Conrad Gesner (1516–1565), Swiss physician and naturalist, published *Historiae animalium,* a compendium of recorded knowledge concerning animal life. The earliest Latin editions are dated Tiguri, 1551–1587, the first German edition, Zurich, 1563.
29. A genus of coleopterous insects of the family of *Trachelidae. Cantharides vesicatoria* = Spanish Fly.
30. The dried Cantharides vesicatoria was used externally as a vesicant and internally as a diuretic and aphrodisiac.
31. Tiger beetle: Epicauta gorhami.

Chapter 10

1. This chapter was never written.
2. This method had already been discovered in 1677 by Wada Kakueimon from Kii. Kokushi Daijiten Henshū Iinkai, ed., *Kokushi daijiten* (Tokyo, 1984), 4:775.
3. I presume Kaempfer means that much larger fish can be caught.
4. *Eubalaena glacialis* (Borowski): right-whale. The explanations below rely mainly on Abe Tokiharu, *Illustrated Fishes of the World in Colour* [Genshoku gyorui daizukan] (Tokyo, 1987); Ichthyological Society of Japan, ed., *Dictionary of Japanese Fish Names and Their Foreign Equivalents* [Gyorui zukan] (Tokyo, 1981); Nose Yukio, *Encyclopaedia of Fishes* [Sakana no jiten] (Tokyo, 1989); and Urada Tōru, *Dōbutsu bunrui meijiten* (Tokyo, 1972). Although I have attempted to give exact translations, it should be noted that the present scientific classification did not exist at the time Kaempfer wrote and that names were applied in a much looser fashion.
5. *Kokujira* can refer both to *Eschrichtius gibbosus* (Erxleben) and Rhachianectes glaucus: California gray whale.
6. *Balaenoptera physalus* (Linné): finback whale.

7. *Megaptera novaeangliae* (Borowski) or *Megaptera nodosa:* humpback whale.

8. *Physeter catodon* Linné or *Physeter macrocephalus:* sperm whale.

9. Kaempfer spells the name of the fish *mako* and seems to take this as a homophone of *mago* = descendant, grandchild.

10. Black right whale, rorqual, fin whale: *Balaenoptera borealis* Lesson.

11. A fabulous dolphinlike fish.

12. A dolphin, a porpoise.

13. Usually *fugu:* swellfish, globefish, blowfish, balloonfish, puffer.

14. Dialect for *shōsai fugu,* vermiculated puffer: *Takifugu vermicularis* (Temminck et Schlegel).

15. Purple puffer: *Fugu vermicularis prophyreus* (Temminck et Schlegel).

16. Venereal disease.

17. Scribbled toby: Canthigaster rivulata (Temminck et Schlegel).

18. Because the Buddha died with his head pointing north, a dead person is laid out in the same way.

19. Kaempfer refers to *madai, Pagrus major* (Temminck et Schlegel). Nose, *Encyclopaedia of Fishes,* 392–393.

20. Black porgy: *Acanthopagrus schlegeli* (Bleeker).

21. Kaempfer: "Kahlkopf." The closest in German is "Kahlhecht," bowfin: *Amiatus calvus,* which, however, is a fish native to North America. The nineteenth-century dictionary *Waran jii,* ed. Sugimoto Tsutomu (reprint Tokyo, 1974), explains Dutch "kaalkop" as a certain fish which Kaempfer defines as *suzuki,* indicating that the word was not part of the general vocabulary. *Suzuki* denotes the order *Perciformes,* the perchlike fishes, in general, and a Japanese sea bass, *Lateolabrax japonicus* (Cuvier), in particular. Fishes of the order *Perciformes* are often given names describing them as bald or naked (i.e., the nakedhead large-eye bream, naked-headed snapper, barenoses, Dutch: Kaalneuse, etc.), and I suggest that Kaempfer's "Kahlkopf" was in line with that perception and custom.

22. Crucian carp, a Prussian carp, etc: *Carassius auratus* (Linnaeus).

23. Catfish.

24. Black rockfish, Japanese stingfish: *Sebastes inermis* Cuvier.

25. Carp: *Cyprinus carpio* Linnaeus.

26. One *shaku* = 30.3 cm = .994 ft.

27. Trout, sea trout, salmon trout.

28. Kaempfer's "Salmonat" could also be a mistake for "Salmoniden," meaning "a salmon-related fish." However, *Itoyori* or *ityoridai* is a besugo, golden thread, red coat: *Nemipterus virgatus* (Houttuyn).

29. Usually known as *bora: Mugil cephalus* Linné.

30. Sawedged perch: *Niphon spinosus* Cuvier et Valenciennes.

31. Usually known as *amatai,* horsehead *(Branchiostegus),* which Kaempfer calls "Stumpfnase" = snub nose.

32. Kaempfer: "Suzuki Scharfisch" (meaning: Suzuki is a Scharfisch). As

"Scharfish" is old Dutch for a sole and Kaempfer had described the fish *suzuki* earlier, I have taken *suzuki* to be a mistake for the Japanese for sole: *sasaushinoshita,* a word that could easily be misunderstood by a foreigner. See Noel Chomel, *Algemeen huishoudelijk-, natuur-, zedekundig- en konst- woordenboek* . . . (1778), 6:3248.

33. A horse mackerel, a saurel.

34. Sting ray.

35. Kaempfer: "Come oder Jèi Schollen." Kaempfer had mentioned previously that "Jèi," modern *ei,* is a ray. *Kome* is dialect for *yanagimushigarei: Tanakius kitaharai* (Jordan et Starks), willowy flounder. At the time, "Scholle" was used for *Pleuronectes platessa,* a plaice (Urada, *Dōbutsu bunrui meijiten,* 792).

36. Kaempfer's "Butte" is now used for *Bothidae* (Jap.: *hirame*) but at the time was used for *Pleuronectes flessus* (Jap.: *karei*), a flounder. Jacob and Wilhelm Grimm, *Deutsches Wörterbuch* (Leipzig, 1860), 2:37; Urada, *Dōbutsu bunrui meijiten,* 791–792.

37. Black mullet, bully mullet, common grey mullet, etc.: *Mugil cephalus* Linné.

38. Oceanic bonito.

39. Butterfish, harvest fish, pomfret, etc.: *Pampus argenteus* (Euphrasen).

40. A dog-salmon.

41. The word *sake* is also used for the fresh fish. The word is believed to have its origins in the Ainu language.

42. Korea.

43. Japanese halfbeak fish, hemiramph: *Hemiramphus sajori* (Temminck et Schlegel).

44. A lizard fish.

45. Sweetfish, Japanese samlet, etc.: *Plecoglossus altivelis* Temminck et Schlegel.

46. Also glassfish, Japanese icefish: *Salangichthys microdon* Bleeker.

47. Dotted gizzard shad, spotted sardine, etc.: *Clupanodon punctatus* (Temminck et Schlegel).

48. *Clupea harengas membras.*

49. Lamprey; in German: "Neunauge."

50. Loach; *Misgurnus anguillicaudatus* (Cantor).

51. Snacks served with drinks, not to be confused with *sakana* = fish.

52. Aurelia.

53. Trepang, sea slug.

54. Newt, water lizard.

55. A large burrowing cake urchin: *Clypeaster japonicus.*

56. *Chaetomorpha chelonum* var. *japonica.*

57. *Clemmys japonica* (Temminck et Schlegel).

58. Also known as *suppon:* a snapping, mud, or soft-shelled turtle.

59. Also: *ebijako, Crangon affinis* De Haan 1849.

60. *Penaeus semisulcatus* De Haan.

61. *Penaeus japonicus* Bate.

62. Squilla, mantis-shrimp.
63. Abbreviation for *kani mina,* old name for *yadokari,* a hermit crab.
64. Horseshoe or king crab.
65. Blue crab.
66. Today *takaashigani:* a giant Japanese spider crab.
67. Abalone.
68. Pen, razor, or fan shell.
69. Pearl oyster.
70. Also *miru-kui,* a trough shell.
71. Clam.
72. Corbicula.
73. Ark shell.
74. Known today as *tobugai, karasugai*: a fresh-water mussel.
75. A short-necked clam.
76. A razor clam.
77. An edible bivalve of the family *Pholadidae: Barnea dilatata.*
78. Cowrie shell.
79. Turban or wreath shell.
80. Spiral shellfish.
81. Mud or pond snail.
82. Ivory shell.
83. Known today as *kawanina*: a marsh or black snail.
84. Known as *uni:* a sea urchin.
85. A small sea snail of the family *ryūten sazae.*

Book 2

Chapter 2

1. The reigning emperor in 1693 was Higashiyama, who is generally considered 113th in line. Kaempfer's number was arrived at by taking into consideration the alternate emperors of the so-called Northern dynasty of the fourteenth century.

2. Amaterasu; see book 1, chapter 6 note 9, above.

3. Kaempfer refers to the divine rulers. See book 1, chapter 7.

4. For an explanation of these rituals, see Blacker, "Forgotten Practices."

5. The word *shogun* has been added and is used below to translate "weltlicher Kaiser," literally, secular emperor. See "Notes on the Translation" above for an explanation.

6. *Taifu* and *go i* are both used for holders of the fifth rank or higher ranks.

7. Kaempfer: "Maquandairo"; literally, *taifu* without an office.

8. Specific copper plates were never produced. Kaempfer might have wanted to use some of the fifty Japanese watercolors he had brought back from Japan, some of

which he had already copied for this purpose. For these paintings, see B. M. Bodart-Bailey, "The Most Magnificient Monastery and Other Famous Sights: The Japanese Paintings of Engelbert Kaempfer," *Japan Review* 3 (1992):25–44; for Kaempfer's copies, see Bodart-Bailey, "Kaempfer Restor'd," 29–32.

9. While *bugyō* designates a specific title and rank, *bugyō nin* means a commissioned official. Kaempfer generally uses *bugyō* in the sense of *bugyō nin.*

10. Literally, "human emperor," indicating the change from celestial rulers to human rulers.

11. The characters allude to a passage from the official history of the Chinese Sung dynasty, which expresses the sense described by Kaempfer.

Chapter 3

1. Kaempfer's copy is dated 1684. See Gardner, *Descriptive Catalogue,* 578.
2. Gardner, *Descriptive Catalogue,* 582–583.

Chapter 5

1. Gardner, *Descriptive Catalogue,* 580.

Book 3

Chapter 1

1. Kaempfer's assumption that Christianity had at one time as many followers as the other religions listed is incorrect. Schütte estimated that up to 1626 there were between 636,000 and 872,000 Christians. Josephus Franciscus Schütte, *Introductio ad Historiam Societatis Jesu in Japonia, 1549–1650* (Rome, 1968), 426.

2. Kaempfer refers to Aristotle's *Politics.* Aristotle believed that citizens had a variety of duties to perform and therefore required a variety of virtues: " . . . while the precise definition of each one's virtue will apply exclusively to him, there is also a common definition applicable to them all." *Politics,* book III, ch. 3; John Warrington, ed. and trans., *Aristotle: Politics* (London, 1959).

3. Also: *kamiyo nanayo.* For details, see book 1, chapter 6, and Herbert, *Shinto,* 235, 251.

4. *Ishitataki* is more commonly pronounced *sekirei.* The bird has remained a symbol of fertility. See also book 1, chapter 6.

5. These are listed in book 1, chapter 6.

6. Shinto priest, guardian of a shrine.

7. Sacred words of purification of the Nakatomi clan. See Herbert, *Shinto,* 39.

8. The text is from the first chapter of *Nihon shoki,* titled *Shin dai.* See *Nihon shoki,* I, in *Nihon koten bungaku taikei* (Tokyo, 1967), 67:76–77.

9. I have amended the spelling to conform with modern conventions but have not altered the text to conform with that published in *Nihon koten bungaku taikei,* as it

permits insights into the wording used in seventeenth-century Japan. Kaempfer wrote: *Kai Fákuno Fasime Dsjusio Fusó Tatójeba Iujóno sui soni ukunga gotósj. Tentsjino Utsjini itsi butsu wo seosu katats Igeno gotósj Fenquas ste sin to nar kuni tóko datsno mikotto to goos.*

10. A more literal translation of the Japanese text is: "At the creation of the world, land and soil were floating, like fish sporting in water. Between heaven and earth a thing was born shaped like a reed-shoot. It changed and became a god called earthly-eternally-standing-lord." See Herbert, *Shinto,* 244–245. On *kuni toko tatsu no mikoto,* see additional notes to *Nihon shoki, Nihon koten bungaku taikei,* 67:545.

The manuscript available to Dohm continues with further explanations (Dohm, 1:256–257). I presume Kaempfer realized later that these belonged to the chapters on Confucianism and Buddhism and left them out in the manuscript now in the British Library.

Chapter 2

1. Plural of Latin *fanum* = shrine, sanctuary, temple.
2. Not just the chamber, but the whole shrine is called *hongū.* Perhaps a slip of the pen.
3. Literally, "horse pictures." They originally depicted horses and were donated instead of the animal.
4. Kaempfer: "geistliche Pfaffen." This sentence negates the statement above, that the *kannushi* are not "religious priests." Kaempfer apparently wants to convey that while they are called "religious priests," he does not consider them as such. In the manuscript, the "geistliche" (religious) is crossed out and replaced by "weltliche" (secular) in what appears to be Scheuchzer's writing.
5. Kaempfer: "bürgerliche streithändel." This should read "ecclesiastical."
6. Generally known as commissioners of temples and shrines.
7. *On* pronunciation for Amaterasu.
8. Kaempfer: "Koosju" for Jap. "Kōshi."
9. Kaempfer: "Sjutosju" for Jap. "judō shū."
10. The Cimmerii were a people believed to live in continuous darkness in mythological times.
11. "A work of the greatest merit."
12. The implication is that people eating these animals remain unclean for longer periods.

Chapter 3

1. A prayer from the *Engishiki,* the sentence meaning "The gods are on the heavenly plain."

2. In the narrow sense, *reibi* was the equivalent of *sanjitsu* (the three days): the first, fifteenth, and twenty-eighth of each month, which were celebrated as holidays. Kaempfer seems to use the word in the wider sense of holiday.

3. *Sekku* = seasonal festival.

4. Kaempfer: *sinistera fata.*

5. Kaempfer: *sui juris.*

6. Kaempfer most probably refers to what is now known as *hago ita,* battledores, which at that time were usually only about thirty centimeters long. See Ema Tsutomu, et al., ed., *Kinsei fuzoku jiten* (Tokyo, 1967), 318–319.

7. In book 1, chapter 10, Kaempfer explained that pieces of dried abalone were fixed to presents as a sign of good fortune, because these had been the most important food of their ancestors.

8. Dohm's manuscript apparently included a passage on the preparation of *amasake* (sweet rice wine). This is also explained in book 4, chapter 1.

9. *Hina* are small dolls. Originally these were part of a purification ceremony and thrown into the river to float away. They were therefore simple and made of paper, clay, or straw. Ōshima Akeo, et al., ed., *Minzoku tambō jiten* (Tokyo, reprint 1990), 145; Kawaguchi Kenji, et al., *Nenchū gyōji girei jiten* (Tokyo, reprint 1987), 68–69. Thus Kaempfer's number of one thousand could be correct. Dohm (1:270) and presumably also Scheuchzer (2:25) take the "one thousand" to mean the price of the dolls, for which I see no justification.

10. A genus of plants of bitter or aromatic taste, including common wormwood, mugwort, and southernwood.

11. This passage is obscure. It is not clear whether the dolls or the visitors have the trays set in front.

12. *Hōjō* = releasing captive animals; *rō* = cage, basket, bamboo container.

13. *Futsu* is dialect for *yomogi* (artemisia) in Nagasaki and other parts of Kyushu. *Nihon kokugo daijiten,* 9:419.

14. Kaempfer: "beÿfuß"; can also mean "mugwort."

15. While in Western sources the spelling *peiron* is common, it is usually transcribed as *peeron* in Japanese.

16. Dohm (1:271) has an additional sentence on *chimaki,* rice cakes wrapped in leaves.

17. Kaempfer relates this story in greater detail in section 8 of "Theae Japonensis historia," book 3, chapter 13, of *Amoenitates Exoticae,* pages 621–623. There he indicates that the island was close to Taiwan or Formosa and that the king fled to the nearby province of Fukien on the Chinese mainland. (Also Dohm 1:272; 2:453–454.) In China these celebrations on the fifth of the fifth month are known as the dragon boat festival, which is in honor of the poet and minister Ch'ü Yüan (332–395), who fell into disgrace at court and drowned himself. In Nagasaki the boat races are now held throughout the summer.

18. Fukien.

19. It was introduced in 1655. See Inaba Chiyomi, *Nagasaki hitori aruki* (privately published, 1988), 45.

20. Dohm gives an additional story about the statue of a lion whose eyes were supposed to turn yellow. His text specifies that the following passage refers to Mauri ga shima. This is also confirmed by the text of "Theae," mentioned above.

21. Kaempfer forgets to mention that it is paragraph 8 of section 13. Dohm's text (1:273) includes some additional information found in "Theae."

22. *Shichiseki* is the *on* pronounciation for *tanabata.*

23. Dohm's text (1:273) adds the story of Inugai and his wife Tanabata, who are separated by the Milky Way and are able to meet only on this day of the year. If it rains, they cannot meet, and the harvest will be good. Therefore the Japanese sit up all night waiting for a drop of rain.

24. The ninth day of the ninth month.

25. Kaempfer speaks from experience. The Dutch were marshalled to watch these performances all day. The festival is described in greater detail in book 4, chapter 4.

26. Tenman Tenjin is Sugawara Michizane (845–903), the Heian statesman banished from Kyoto to Dazaifu. This paragraph is full of repetition, and the next sections are incomplete, indicating most probably that this was merely a draft. Dohm (1:275–276) has additional information.

27. This is the shrine of Susano o, who killed the eight-forked *(yamata)* serpent. Herbert, *Shinto,* 313–317.

28. Kaempfer: "Osju wo nino Mikotto."

29. Literally, imperial court.

30. The first book of *Nihon shoki.* Kaempfer's *Nihon ōdaiki* is *Dai Nihon ōdaiki.* See book 2, chapter 3, "Translator's Note."

Chapter 4

1. All the country to the north of the old Shirakawa: today's Fukushima, Miyagi, Iwate, and Aomori prefectures.

2. The statesman Sugawara Michizane.

3. Kannon is a Buddhist deity, but Kaempfer's informants obviously conveyed to him that the worship of Kannon did not belong to the mainstream Buddhist tradition.

4. Tenshō daijin is the *on* reading for Amaterasu, but Kaempfer refers to the god throughout as a male deity.

5. An honorific title formerly used for Shinto priests, originally a Chinese court rank.

6. Kaempfer used *shinsha* in the previous chapter; a follower of Shinto.

7. Taboo, impurity.

8. Divine punishment.

9. Kaempfer: "Itznòbe." Perhaps the author of a traveling guide *(dōchūki).* Possibly Kikuya Shichirobei, the publisher of *Dōchū kagami,* which Kaempfer had in his possession. British Library, Sloane Or. 75. f.7 (1); Gardner, *Descriptive Catalogue,* 606–607.

10. Kaempfer: "strassen" = *chō* = 109 meters or 119 yards.
11. The Outer Shrine at Ise.
12. The Inner Shrine at Ise.
13. *Ama no iwato* means "heavenly rock door."
14. Cypress.

Chapter 5

1. The character used is that for *fusu,* the name meaning "the one who lies down in the mountains."
2. See Carmen Blacker, *The Catalpa Bow* (Torquay, 1975), 196–197.
3. Kaempfer refers to the blind *biwa hōshi,* who shaved their heads, but were not priests, and belonged to a society with its own hierarchical structure with headquarters in Kyoto. See note 9 below.
4. The traditional sword of the samurai.
5. This is generally described as a box with a small door and legs, to stand up when put down.
6. A lotus.
7. Buddhist: a symbolic sign made with the fingers.
8. The four heavenly kings.
9. The chapter ends here. Scheuchzer's addition dealing with "the government of the blind" is taken from Kaempfer's notes (Sloane 3062, f. 37). As these notes also contain other important material, they should be published separately.

Chapter 6

1. Kaempfer's transcription for Pali *Thambara Gautama* (glorious Gautama). I thank Professor Saitō Teruko for this information.
2. King Chao (Zhao-wang), who was the fourth successor of King Wu; both were kings of China.
3. The date Kaempfer heard in Siam is the one traditionally accepted for the birth of Buddha. Those given to him in Japan were created to permit Shinto gods to become reincarnations of Buddha.
4. Magadha is modern Bihar province in Bengal.
5. *Sennin* = hermit. Alara Kalama.
6. Dandaka.
7. Kaempfer: Cynosus; Cynosura = the constellation of the Lesser Bear.
8. Scheuchzer (2:61) added a sentence about Emma seeing the crimes of men in his looking-glass; this is not contained in the manuscript.
9. *Sonja* = Buddhist saint. Ananda and Kassapa.
10. *Hokke kyō* means "lotus sutra."
11. *Kyō* = a sutra, Buddhist scripture.
12. The Chinese mythical emperors Yao and Shun.
13. Lao-tzu.

14. The province of Ch'u.

15. The phrase "and the immortality of the soul" is added in Scheuchzer's writing.

16. Confucius.

17. The Province of Lu.

18. One *shaku* = .994 foot, one *sun* = 1.2 inches, making Confucius nearly ten feet tall.

19. For details, see pages 407–408 below.

20. This contradicts the statement made above but is what the manuscript says.

21. Latin: rules of conduct.

22. Kudara.

23. The statue is known as Zenkōji Nyōrai; the temple is in Nagano city, Nagano prefecture (formerly Shinano). Opponents of Buddhism had thrown the statue into a ditch at Osaka, Naniwa (Tsu no kuni), but it was saved by Honda Yoshiteru in 602, and finally the above temple was built in 641. Nakayama Keishō, *Zenkoku ishibutsu ishikami daijiten* (Tokyo, 1990), 613–614.

24. The story is incorrect. The temple was built in the first year of the reign of Empress Kōgyoku (641). Kimmei is believed to have reigned 539–571.

Chapter 7

1. Confucius

2. *The Elementary Learning.* The work was written in the Sung period. Kaempfer states only that Confucius "described" and not wrote the work.

3. Mencius.

4. These are: the Great Learning, the Doctrine of the Mean, the Confucian Analects, and the Works of Mencius.

5. Generally translated as "wisdom."

6. Kaempfer seems to refer to *ruizoku aratame no hō* (law for the examination of related families [of Christians]) of 1687; *Gotōke reijō,* no. 229 in Ishii Ryōsuke, ed., *Kinsei hōsei shiryō sōsho* (Tokyo, 1938), 2:113.

7. Ikeda Mitsumasa (1609–1682).

8. Ikeda Tsunamasa (1638–1714).

9. This contradicts established historical interpretation. See Bodart-Bailey, "Persecution of Confucianism," 307–312.

Book 4

Chapter 1

1. *Takayama* means "tall mountain"; *taka boko,* "tall pike."

2. The text mistakenly states "164." See Nagasaki shiyakusho, ed., *Nagasaki shishi, Tsūkō bōeki hen* (Nagasaki, 1934), 450–457.

3. Nagasaki Kotarō Sadatsuna is believed to have been an official of the Kamakura bakufu who arrived in the area around 1222. Nagasaki Jinzaemon Sumikage (1547?–1622) was the thirteenth generation. Kinzaemon married a daughter of Ōmura Sumitada and was baptized with Sumitada in 1563. Nagasaki was opened to international trade in 1571, and the first city streets were laid out. Jinzaemon lost his domain of some 970 *koku* in 1587 when Hideyoshi placed the area under his direct control. Inaba, *Nagasaki hitori aruki,* 190–191, 196.

4. *Fuka e* means "deep bay," *iri e,* "small bay," "arm of the sea"; *fuka bori,* "deep trench" or "deep canal."

5. *Bun tsuke nushi* = the owner of a plot.

6. Toyotomi Hideyoshi (1536–1598) assumed the title of *taikō* (retired regent) in 1591.

7. The brothel keeper's hold over his customers is compared to the bit by which the horse is controlled.

8. A place where water is stored.

9. Literally: bonze of Bungo.

10. Fire extinguishing tools.

11. Horses were similarly protected. See Bodart-Bailey, "The Laws of Compassion," 169.

12. A gold and copper alloy.

13. The ritual was known as *bosa age* (placing the deity in the temple) and *bosa nose* (returning it to the ship). Maso bosatsu (Ma-tsu p'u-sa, Bodhisattva Maso) was a Chinese sea god. See Nagasaki shiyakusho, ed., *Nagasaki shishi, fuzoku hen* (Nagasaki, 1925), 460–463. Also chapter 9, note 24, below.

Chapter 2

1. During the Edo period a "no kami" following the name of a province was simply a title bestowed by the bakufu; at times it indicated the name of their domain. It is interesting, however, that Kaempfer's informers still connected the word with its wider etymological history.

2. Kawaguchi Munetsune, Genzaemon, Settsu no Kami, Nagasaki *bugyō,* 1680–1694. Hotta Masaatsu, ed., *Kansei chōshū shokafu* (Tokyo, 1964–1967), 9:384.

3. Yamaoka Kagesuke, Jūbei, Tsushima no Kami, Nagasaki *bugyō,* 1687–1694. He was previously employed as *sakite gashira,* head of the shogun's advance unit, whose duty it was to clear the streets of undesirable elements before the shogun's procession. *Tokugawa jikki,* 5:595, B, Jōkyō 4.2.18; *Shokafu* 17:352.

4. From Malay *tahil, taïl* = weight. Used as a weight of silver in the East. See appendix 2.

5. Miyagi Masazumi, Tonomo, Echizen no Kami, Nagasaki *bugyō,* 1687–1696. *Shokafu* 10:320.

6. Also: *naka oku koshō:* the personal servants of the lord permitted to enter his personal rooms: the *naka oku.*

7. Kaempfer: *Judiciis virorum Illustrium.*

8. Kaempfer notes the name of the family as Takaku, but Kure argues that he must be referring to Takashima Shirō Hyōe Shigenori (1681–1715), whose earlier name was Gontarō and who succeeded to the headship of the house on the death of his father, Takashima Shirō Hyōe Shigemura in 1691 and became *machi toshiyori* in 1695. See Engelbert Kaempfer, *Edo sanpu kikō*, trans. Kure Shūzō (Tokyo, 1928–1929), 2:212.

9. Takagi Seiemon Shigekata, 1681–1705. His father died in 1685. He succeeded to the headship of the house in 1686 and was made *machi toshiyori* in 1688. Kure, *Edo sanpu kikō*, 2:212; *Nagasaki sōsho* 3:306.

10. Literally, outer city.

Chapter 3

1. *Hassaku* means literally the first day of the eighth month. On this day the farmers presented some of their first rice crop to their superiors and the day became one of giving presents.

2. Kaempfer: *moderaminis inculpatæ tutelæ.*

3. Kaempfer: *Facientis culpam procul dubio habet, qui quod potest corrigere, negligit emendare.* Kaempfer refers to C. III of *Distinction LXXXVI Gratianus* of *Corpus Juris Canonici,* a medieval collection of canon law, first mentioned in the sixteenth century. The original reads: *Facientis proculdubio culpam habet, qui quod potest corrigere negligit emendare.* E. Friedberg, ed., *Corpus Juris Canonici* (Leipzig, 1879; reprint, Akademische Druck-u. Verlagsanstalt, Graz, 1959), p. 1, 298.

4. The words "the street register by the *nichi gyōshi*" have been added from Dohm (2:36), as there is a line missing in Sloane 3060 (f221 v). One of Dohm's manuscripts obviously contained the missing words, which were not available to Scheuchzer (2:122) and could hardly have been invented.

5. Literally, "Emperor Taikō": Toyotomi Hideyoshi, 1536–1598.

6. *Jū momme* = 10 *momme*, that is, a total of 8,000 *momme* or mace. The *jū momme* unit was convenient for foreigners because it corresponded to one tael.

7. That is, 3,000–4,000 *momme.*

8. Kaempfer: *secundum naturam esse commoda cujuscunque rei eum sequi, quem sequuntur incommoda.* Kaempfer seems to refer to the *Corpus Juris Civilis* consolidated by the Byzantine emperor Justinian I (483–565), also known as the Code of Justinian. Together with the *Corpus Juri Canonici,* mentioned above, it formed the basis of German law. Bernhard Windscheid, *Lehrbuch des Pandektenrechts* (reprint, Scientia Verlag, Aalen, 1963), 6–7.

9. Suetsugu Heizō Shigetomo, *daikan,* 1669–1676. His great-grandfather, Heizō Masanao (d. 1630), had become Nagasaki *daikan* in 1619, after his accusations had caused the previous *daikan* to fall. Shigetomo's grandfather, Heizaemon Shigesada, did not use the name Heizō. Kokushi daijiten henshū iinkai, ed., *Kokushi daijiten,* 8:43; Inaba, *Nagasaki hitori aruki,* 194–195.

10. Kaempfer: "Susunda gasima." However, the offender, Kageyama Marutao, was executed on Hadakajima. Morinaga Taneo, ed., *Hankachō* (Nagasaki, 1958), 1:28.

11. Takagi Sakuemon Muneo (1657–1697). Kure, *Edo sanpu kikō,* 2:255. Kaempfer does not seem to realize that Sakuemon was also merely a "mayor" *(machi toshiyori)*, like the two men assisting him. Nagasaki Shiyakusho, ed., *Nagasaki sōsho* (Nagasaki, 1926), *Jō,* 3:501.

Chapter 4

1. Kyoto.

2. See notes 9 and 10 of book 1, chapter 6, above.

3. Kaempfer must be referring to the custom of shaving the front portion of the head.

4. A camellia tree.

5. Kaempfer seems to refer to *hakama.*

6. Kaempfer refers to Shinto.

7. *Yamabushi,* the priests of Shugendō, use the Buddhist titles of *ajari* and *bettō,* but many worship *kami* (Herbert, *Shinto*, 519).

8. Kaempfer seems to refer to the teaching of Lao-tzu, which he fails to distinguish from that of Confucius, even though he discussed this distinction in book 3, chapter 7, p. 132 above.

9. The first Tokugawa shogun, Ieyasu, 1542–1616.

10. The *jingi kan,* the government office in charge of Shinto worship, was transferred to the Yoshida family in 1590, and the family was influential in religious appointments, ceremonies, and the like (Herbert, *Shinto,* 125–126, 520).

11. Buddhist law.

12. *Jūji* = resident priest; *oshō* = abbot.

13. Kaempfer: "Tsjaksju dira oder Tsjansju dira." This reflects the earlier pronounciation and writing of *chi* + *ya.*

14. This should read Fukusaiji.

15. Alternative pronounciation of Fukushū dera.

16. This should read Sōfukuji.

17. Ingen Ryūki, 1592–1673, became the founder of Manpukuji temple at Uji, Kyoto.

18. *Mukuri* = *mōko* = the Mongols; *kokuri* = *Kōkuri* = Kokuryo = Korea. Ingen came to Japan after the fall of the Ming dynasty, when the Ching armies were subjugating the country.

19. The date is usually given as 1654.

20. Confucianism.

21. A small shrine.

22. Ingen was succeeded by Mokuan Shōtō (1611–1684), not Sokuhi Nyoichi (1616–1671). However, together with Ingen and Mokuan, the latter was known as one of

the Three Writers (*san pitsu*) of the Ōbaku sect. Fujiyamabō Hyakka Jiten Henshubu, ed., *Kokumin hyakka daijiten* (Tokyo, 1936), 10:392.

23. The first thirteen abbots were all Chinese. *Kokushi daijiten,* 2:469.

24. These are generally referred to as "commissioners of temples and shrines."

Chapter 5

1. More commonly, Jorge Alvares, a Portuguese ship's captain who provided Xavier with a written description of Japan in 1547 in Malacca. Kaempfer mixes him up with a young Japanese samurai who fled Japan on Alvares' ship, known as Anjirō, or Paulo Yajirō. Alvares introduced him to Xavier, and he accompanied the fathers to Japan. See Georg Schurhammer, *Franz Xaver; Sein Leben und Seine Zeit; Asien (1541–1549)* (Freiburg, Basel, Wien: Herder, 1971), 2:51, 60–73. Frois refers to him as Paulo de Sancta Fé. Luis Frois, *Die Geschichte Japans,* ed. and trans. G. Schurhammer and E. A. Voretzsch (Leipzig: Asia Major, 1926), 1–4.

2. The Society of Jesus.

3. Saint Francis Xavier, 1506–1552, known as "the Apostle of the Indies."

4. Jacques-Auguste de Thou, 1553–1617, French statesman, bibliophile, and historian, a pioneer in the scientific approach to history. His Latin *Historia* covered the events of 1543–1607. The work has not been available at the time of writing, but Montanus, *Atlas Japannensis,* 33, notes that this passage is contained in book 81 of *Historia.*

5. Kaempfer refers to Matthew 11:12: "Since John the Baptist came, up to the present time, the kingdom of heaven has been subjected to violence and the violent are taking it by storm."

6. Hidyoshi's first edict expelling the Jesuits was promulgated in 1587. The first Christians were executed in 1597, as Kaempfer states on page 182 below.

7. Schütte cites Luis Frois, according to whom there were more than 16,000 baptisms between October 1589 and October 1590 and 30,000 in the period August 1587 to October 1590. *Introductio ad Historiam Societatis Jesu,* 412.

8. Kaempfer: "Kraken." A Norwegian mythical sea monster of enormous size, and the word used by the Portuguese might have been adapted accordingly.

9. 1 *Kings* 9:28: "And they came to Ophir, and fetched from thence gold, four hundred and twenty talents, and brought it to king Solomon." Its locality is uncertain.

10. This incident is not corroborated in Japanese sources, and Captain Moro has not been identified. *Nihon kirisuto kyō rekishi daijiten* (Tokyo, 1988), 1414, entry *Moro mitsusho jiken.*

11. Sakakibara Hida no Kami Motonao (1586–1648), Nagasaki *bugyō* from 1634 to 1640.

12. Baba Saburō Saemon Toshishige (?–1657), Nagasaki *buygō* from 1636 to 1652.

13. Kanei 13 corresponds to 1636 and not 1637, as stated by Kaempfer earlier. Also, such orders had already appeared several years prior to the date mentioned by

Kaempfer. See Nakamura Tadashi, *Kinsei Nagasaki boekishi no kenkyū* (Tokyo, 1988), 154–157.

14. Sakai Sanuki no Kami Tadakatsu, *rōjū* from 1631 to 1638.

15. Matsudaira Izu no Kami Nobutsuna, *rōjū* from 1633 to 1662.

16. Doi Ōi no Kami Toshikatsu, *rōjū* from 1610 to 1638 (when he became *tairō*).

17. Abe Bungo no Kami Tadaaki, *rōjū* from 1633 to 1666.

18. Hotta Kaga no Kami Masamori, *rōjū* from 1633 to 1651.

19. Also *gōtō* = a wild and cruel robber.

Chapter 6

1. Also Couckebacker, Nicolaes, resident director of the Dutch trading settlement from 1633 to 1639.

2. *Quid non mortalia pectora cogis, Auri sacra fames!* Virgil, *The Aeneid*, III:56. The English translation by C. H. Sisson (Manchester: Carcanet Press, 1986), 57, has been chosen. Kaempfer compares the Dutch to the king of Thrace, who at the fall of Troy abandoned his allies to join the victorious enemy armies of Agamemnon and murdered Polydorus, whose education had been entrusted to him, taking posession of the latter's gold. A few lines later, Virgil's text refers to "the place where hospitality was profaned," echoing Kaempfer's sentiments about Japan.

3. The manuscript has lettering next to the sites and buildings in the description below. No doubt Kaempfer had intended to have his copperplate printer produce the relevant illustration. As the only known drawing of Deshima in Kaempfer's hand (p. 190) has no lettering, it has been omitted from the text. The woodblock print of Deshima with lettering found in Dohm (2:73) is believed to have been produced after Kaempfer's death in accordance with this description and the sketch reproduced here. Schmeiβer, "Changing the Image," 149.

4. A large joist, with six sides, traversed with iron pointed spikes over six feet long, crossing each other, used to check cavalry charges and stop breaches.

5. Chapter 10 below.

6. An ancient Greek and Roman measure of length, most commonly one-eighth of a Roman mile. In the English Bible it is rendered by furlong.

7. A club spiked with nails.

8. See page 167 above.

9. The conclusion must be that the foreigners were charged ten times as much as the locals, for three times *jū momme* is thirty mace.

10. Kaempfer left a gap in the text. The word *kozukai* has been supplied in accordance with the letter of employment between Kaempfer and his "student," Imamura Genemon, cited in Katagiri Kazuo, *Oranda tsūji Imamura Genemon* (Tokyo, 1995), 21.

11. A *mon* is a family crest, coat of arms.

12. Kaempfer never wrote the chapter as intended but left only notes. Most of these have been translated in chapter 10 of this book, but the order on procedures in case of fire is extremely sketchy and has been omitted.

13. Kaempfer refers to the men of Cheng Ch'eng-kung (1624–1662), who had received the imperial surname Chu from the refugee court at Nanking and therefore was popularly called Kuo-hsing-yeh, "Lord of the Imperial Surname." The Dutch turned this into "Koxinga." His mother was Japanese. E. O. Reischauer and J. K. Fairbank, *East Asia: The Great Tradition* (Boston, 1958), 355–356.

14. Also Tayouan, Taiwan: the Dutch Fort Zeelandia, completed in 1634 and lost in 1662 when the Dutch were finally completely expelled by Koxinga. At that time the site was given its modern name, An-p'ing.

15. Also Kelang, modern Chilung.

Chapter 7

1. Johannes Camphuis, resident director at Nagasaki, 1671–1672, 1673–1674, and 1675–1676.

2. Kaempfer: "Kammer tolmetschen," lit., chamber interpreters.

3. Kaempfer: "teütsch," which he uses for both Dutch and German.

4. Middle.

5. Seal.

Chapter 8

1. Kaempfer uses the term *prauen,* which he explains in book 5, chapter 11, as flat-bottomed rowboats, flexible enough to bend when passing over rocks.

2. Presumably Kaempfer refers to Johannes Camphuis, who served three times as resident at Nagasaki and as governor general at Batavia from 1684 till his death in 1695, and who shared with Kaempfer some of his personal experience. See Bodart-Bailey, "Writing *The History of Japan,*" 20–30.

3. *Kanban bōeki*, lit., signboard trade; the system of trading as described by Kaempfer below.

4. Fine striped silk or cotton fabric. A.T. Vermeulen, ed., *The Deshima Dagregisters, their original tables of contents*, Vol. 2, 1690–1700, Intercontinenta, No. 8 (Leiden, 1987), 159.

5. Also *peling,* silk fabric from China and India. Vermeulen, *The Deshima Dagregisters,* 157.

6. Persian silk fabric named after Gilan in northern Iran. Sometimes the Dutch East India Company ordered it also in China and Tonkin. Vermeulen, ed., *The Deshima Dagregisters,* 154.

7. Also: armoisin, armesine, ormesine; silk fabric made in various parts of Europe, but the name was applied to similar goods made in China. W. H. Moreland, ed., *Relations of Golconda in the Early 17th Century* (London, 1931), 62n4.

8. Silk from Tunkin. C. C. van der Plas, *Tonkin 1644/45: Journaal van de Reis van Anthonio van Brouckhorst* (Amsterdam, 1955), 110.

9. A silk shawl from the Coromandel Coast. Vermeulen, *The Deshima Dagregisters,* 158.

10. Kaempfer: "Tsitsen"; originally painted calicoes imported from India.

11. Gunny is a coarse material used chiefly for sacking and made from the fibers of jute or from sunn-hemp.

12. Literally, "from Salem"; a blue cotton cloth formerly made at Nellore, Tamil Nadu (former Madras) in India.

13. Kaempfer: "Paracellen"; also percallas; a closely woven cotton fabric similar to fine white cambric. P. van der Velde and T. Vermeulen, ed., *The Deshima Dagregisters their original tables of contents* (Leiden, 1990), 3:216.

14. Also cordovan: Spanish leather made of goat skin tanned and dressed from Cordova, Spain.

15. Ointment made of powdered sandalwood.

16. Camphor from Baros on Sumatra and Borneo was of a higher quality than that from China. See Robert Stevens, *The Complete Guide to the East-India Trade* (London, 1766), 135.

17. Also Achin, Acheen; then sultanate, now province on the northwestern tip of Sumatra. For a description see Stevens, *The Complete Guide,* 115.

18. Also: stick-lac; the dark red resinous incrustation produced on certain trees by the puncture of an insect, *coccus lacca* or *laccifer lacca.*

19. Kaempfer: "Rosmale"; Malay-Javanese *rasamalla,* the resin of the plant Liquidambar altingia of Tenasserim, used for medicinal purposes and as incense.

20. An astringent substance obtained from Acacia Catechu.

21. Also "putchock," most probably from Southern Hindi *pachak*, root used for making medicine and joss-sticks. Apparently a variety of roots went under that name: *Aplotaxis auriculata (Oxford Dictionary); Saussurea Lappa* Clarke, fam. *Compositae* (Lith, *Encyclopaedie van Nederlandsch-Indie,* 3:285–286).

22. Also: Massan de Vaecu. Bezoar, a concretion found in the stomach or intestines of a number of animals was valued as an antidote. See Charles Lockyer, *An Account of the Trade in India* (London, 1711), 49–51.

23. Kaempfer: "Atsjaar," from Hindi *acyar:* pickles.

24. Mercurous chloride.

25. Kaempfer: *Pancado;* in Japanese: *ito wappu shōhō,* regulations instituted in 1604 according to which the foreigners had to sell their silk in bulk at a fixed price instead of in individual private sales. See *Kokushi daijiten,* 2:719.

26. This document is translated in book 4, chapter 10.

27. The name given by ancient writers to the valley of the Phasis (modern Rion) River at the eastern end of the Black Sea; regarded by the Greeks as a land of fabled wealth.

28. This incident happened under François Caron (1600–1673), Dutch resident director at Hirado, 1639–1641, and was also known to the British. See Alexander Hamilton, *New Account of the East Indies* (London, 1727; reprint, London, 1930), 163.

29. Yokoyama Yozaemon, dates unknown.

30. For details about the life and work of Caron, see C. R. Boxer, ed., *A True Description of the Mighty Kingdoms of Japan and Siam by François Caron and Joost Schouten* (London, 1935).

31. The Kyoto *shoshidai:* the shogunal deputy in Kyoto.

32. *Beschrijvinghe van het machtigh Coninckrijk Japan,* 1645.

33. Inaba Mino no Kami Masanori, senior councilor *(rōjū),* 1657–1681.

34. Sakai Uta no Kami Tadakiyo, senior councilor, 1653–1666, then great councilor to 1680.

35. The fourth Tokugawa shogun, Ietsuna, 1641–1680.

36. This chandelier can still be seen at Nikkō.

37. Ushigome Chūzaemon Shigenori (1622–1687), Nagasaki *buygō,* 1671–1681.

38. Ōkubo Kaga no Kami Tadatomo, senior councilor, 1677–1698.

39. Kawaguchi Settsu no Kami Munetsune.

40. In chapter 7 of book 1 Kaempfer mentions that the decreasing output of the mines was said to be the cause of the restrictions. On the shortage of bullion, see B. M. Bodart-Bailey, "A Case of Political and Economic Expropriation: The Monetary Reform of the Fifth Tokguawa Shogun," *Papers on Far Eastern History,* 39 (March 1989):179–180.

41. *Cabessa, bariga,* and *pee,* from Portuguese "head," "stomach," and "foot," meaning "first, second, and third quality."

42. Andreas Cleyer, mentioned above.

43. An island near Singapore.

44. Also "sawaas." Elsewhere (Sloane 3061, f. 133v), Kaempfer noted that *sawaas* meant *sakku do* and was an alloy of gold and copper. The word *sakku do* most probably stems from *zakku to* = the sound of metal, or metal armor. The Japanese-Portuguese dictionary *Vocabvlario da lingoa de Iapam* of 1603 has *Zaccuto* as *Que declara o modo de vestir as armas accommodadoas a seus lugares* (f. 327v), which is difficult to translate but could be taken to mean: that which indicates the [right] way of wearing armor in its [right] place. See also *Shogakukan Nihon kokugo daijiten,* 5:72.

45. Kaempfer: "Rollang."

46. The twenty-fifth section of the eighth book of the Lotus sutra *(Hokke kyō),* also known as *fumonbon,* dealing with salvation through Kannon, the goddess of mercy (Avalokitesvara).

Chapter 9

1. Seres was derived from *sericus* (silk) and was used for the eastern people from whom silk was first obtained.

2. Kaempfer refers to the fall of the Ming in 1644.

3. The amount of trade was limited in 1685, but the number of ships was limited only in 1688/9. The number of ships from different ports varied from year to year. *Nagasaki shi shi, Tsūkō bōeki,* 211–214.

4. Kaempfer: "Hoksju oder Foktsju oder Fuckutsju"; Jap.: Fukushū.
5. Kaempfer: "Cantoo oder Canton."
6. Kaempfer: "Nefa"; Jap.: Neifa.
7. Kaempfer: "Sintsjen"; Jap.: Senshū.
8. Kaempfer: "Kootz oder Kootsja"; Jap.: Kōshū.
9. Kaempfer: "Sjam oder Sijam."
10. Kaempfer: "Cammon"; also known as Cua Nam, Southern Gate, in Vietnamese. (I thank David Marr for this information.) Jap.: Kōnan. The district included the port of Hoi An or Faifo (also Jap.: Kai an), where Japanese merchants had settled before the closure of the country; vessels from Kōnan are regularly listed in Japanese sources, for example, Nagasaki Shiyakusho, ed., *Bakufu jidai no Nagasaki* (Tokyo, 1913), 108.
11. Kaempfer: "Cabotsja oder Cambodia."
12. Kaempfer: "Fudasan," which is the correct Japanese name. The center of the worship of Kannon (Kuan Yin), however, is situated near Ningpo and not Fu-chou.
13. Kaempfer: "Kootsji oder Cosjin Sjina."
14. There is no large island with the name of Tani in the Ryūkyūs. It has been suggested that Kaempfer meant Patani, which was written with characters commonly pronounced "Tani." Kure, *Edo sanpu kikō,* 2:491; Shimada Izao, et al., ed., *Wakan sansai zue,* 18 vols. (Tokyo, 1986), 3:286.
15. Kaempfer's numbers add up to sixty-three only. An early eighteenth-century order lists an additional seven junks from Nanking. (*Bakufu jidai no Nagasaki,* 108). Scheuchzer (2:251–252) changes the sixteen junks from Canton into coming from Nanking, adds five from Canton, and adds others from unknown destinations. Dohm (2:124) follows Scheuchzer with regard to Nanking, but adds seven from Canton.
16. Kaempfer: Sjakkattara = Jakarta. The spelling used in the text is that of the contemporary *Tōtsūji esho nichiroku,* in Tōkyō Daigaku Shiryō Hensanjo, ed., *Dai Nihon kinsei shiryō,* pt. 3 (Tokyo, 1955), 1:158.
17. Kaempfer: "Poking oder Peking."
18. The *daikan* Suetsugu Heizō. See chapter 3, pp. 166–167, above.
19. Deshima; Kaempfer had explained in book 4, chapter 6, that *de* means "in front" and *shima* means "island."
20. Fiber obtained from the young leaves of *Corypha Gebanga* of the palm family, used for ropes, especially for fishing nets. See J. Paulus, *Encyclopaedie van Nederlandsch-Indie* (Leiden: Gravenhage, 1917), 1:532–533.
21. Ginseng. Kaempfer did not distinguish between the sugar root and the true ginseng. See Muntschick, "The Plants that Carry his Name," 89.
22. Mukai Gensei (1656–1727), the third son of the famous doctor Mukai Genshō (1609–1677), who had moved from Nagasaki to Kyoto in 1658 to serve the court (*Yōgakushi jiten,* 695), hence Gensei's claim of being an "imperial" physician.
23. Chinese for bodhisattva. Kaempfer: "Puse."
24. See book 4, chapter 2, note 13. The characters for the Chinese sea god Maso are also read *bosa* in the expressions *bosa age* (placing the deity in the temple) and *bosa*

nose (returning it to the ship). Kaempfer spells the name "Bossa" and refers to the deity as male, although the characters show the deity to be female (*Nagasaki shishi,* 460). The deity is also described as an incarnation of Kannon. Nishikawa Joken, *Nagasaki yawa gusa,* cited in Inaba Chiyomi, *Nagasaki hitori aruki* (Nagasaki, 1988), 274.

25. Kaempfer: "Weijangs" for the Indonesian Wayang.

26. Kaempfer: "Liquea"; elsewhere Kaempfer uses "Liqueo."

27. The fall of the Ming and establishment of the Ch'ing dynasty in 1644.

28. Satsuma subjugated Ryūkyū in 1609.

29. *Hime* = princess, young lady of noble birth. *Himegai* is also known as *igai,* a hard-shelled mussel, *Mytilus coruscus. Takaragai* is the cowrie or porcelain shell.

Chapter 10

1. See Bodart-Bailey, "Preliminary Report on the Manuscripts of Engelbert Kaempfer in the British Library."

2. Title used for Ieyasu; lit., Great Lord of the August place. Note that unlike elsewhere here I have translated the Dutch *Keyserlycke* literally.

3. Sloane 3060, f. 471. Kaempfer's *katakana* transcription of this order states the correct date, namely, Keichō 14 (1609; f. 472).

4. Sloane 3060, 470 v; the text corresponds to the order cited in Takayanagi Shinzō and Ishii Ryōsuke, ed., *Tokugawa kinreikō* (Tokyo, 1959), 6:407.

5. *Loco Sigilli* = the place of the seal.

6. Sloane 3060 f. 476; as the modern pronunciation of the names is given below, Kaempfer's transcription has been given here.

7. That is, the order issued by Hidetada. What follows are additional instructions issued by Hidetada's senior ministers.

8. Title used by the Japanese for the Dutch resident and director of the trading post.

9. Sloane 3060, f. 473, and *Tokugawa kinreikō*, 6:408, are the same except for the name of the addressee in *kana. Tokugawa kinreikō* has "Kenreika Horowaru." According to Kaempfer (f. 474v), "Hanrei Borowara" was a transcription of the name of Henrick (Hendrick) Brouwer (Dutch resident 1612–1614); as the *kana* in Kaempfer's Japanese order seems the more likely one, it has been used here.The signatories acted as Hidetada's senior ministers in positions that would later be called *rōjū*, senior councilors.

10. *Hitobito onchū*, a form of respect used for the addressee of a letter. Kaempfer above translated only the term *hitobito* as "people, people" but noted correctly that it was a form of respect used in letters (476v).

11. Sloane 3060, f. 486, 489; *Tokugawa kinrei kō*, 6:408. The addressee is Matsuura Iki no Kami Takanobu; he was the domain lord of Hizen 1603–1637 and is therefore addressed as Hizen no kami.

12. Sloane 3060, f. 480v–482.

13. *Tokugawa kinrei kō,* 6:409.

14. The portion in quotation marks has been taken from Nagasaki shi yakusho, ed. *Nagasaki shishi, Jishi hen* (1937), 418. All versions in Kaempfer's documents (Sloane 3060, f. 479, 483) have dropped the word *kakushioku* (to hide), and the last sentence does not make sense in view of the foregoing. Kaempfer had noticed that the word *toga* had been dropped in his copy of the order written by a Japanese hand and inserted it in *katakana.*

15. Miyagi Tonomo, Echizen no Kami, Masazumi, Nagasaki *bugyō,* 1687–1696.

16. Yamaoka Jūbei Tsushima no Kami, Kagesuke, Nagasaki *bugyō,* 1687–1694.

17. Kawaguchi Settsu no Kami Genzaemon, Munetsune, Nagasaki *bugyō,* 1680–1693.

18. The portion in quotation marks has been taken from *Nagasaki shishi, Jishi hen,* 418.

19. 1692.

20. Sloane 3060, f. 469. The passage is written in note form, with a number of additions and abbreviations, some of which have been omitted.

21. See Kaempfer's Prologue, pp. 28–29, above.

22. See van der Velde, "The Interpreter Interpreted."

23. The Japanese document is in the British Library, Oriental Collections, Or. 14480/2. It has been published in Katagiri, *Oranda tsūji Imamura Genemon Eisei,* 21–22. Kaempfer's translation: Sloane 3060, f. 477.

24. Yoshikawa Gibuemon was the *otona,* or mayor, of the island of Deshima, and, as Kaempfer explained in his prologue, was responsible for the Japanese servants of the Dutch.

Book 5

Chapter 1

1. Minamoto no Yoritomo (1147–1199), founder of the Kamakura Bakufu.

2. Hendrick van Buitjenhem, resident director at Nagasaki from October 21, 1690 to November 9, 1691. Buijtenhem had held this position twice previously in 1684–1685 and 1687–1688. He was to serve again in Nagasaki in 1692–1693.

3. Cornelis van Outhoorn, resident director from November 9, 1691 to October 29, 1692. Van Outhoorn had previously served as director in 1688–1689 and was to serve again in 1695–1696. His brother, Willem van Outhoorn, was governor general at Batavia from September 1691 to August 1704.

4. The Dutch resident director, who was commonly referred to by the Japanese as "captain" *(kapitan).*

5. Miyagi Tonomo, Echizen no Kami, Masazumi, Nagasaki *bugyō* from 1687 to 1696.

6. Narabayashi Chinzan, 1648–1711, interpreter and doctor, founder of the Narabayashi house. He had become a senior interepreter in 1686. See *Yōgaku shi jiten,* 531.

7. The word *bugyō* is here used in the sense of *bugyō nin,* meaning "official in charge."

8. Two copies of the "small travel book" described here *(Edo dōchūki),* which Kaempfer bought and brought back secretly, are in the British Library (OR 75, f. 3 and 4).

9. See book 4, chapter 8, note 44 above.

10. See p. 273.

Chapter 2

1. Literally, "Eastern sea route."

2. Kaempfer is not consistent in first mentioning 325, then 326 miles; the distances given add up to neither, and Scheuchzer (2:292) therefore changed the figures.

3. Wistaria, camellia, azalea, deutzia, Japanese snowball (*Viburnum Opulus* L. var. *Sargentii* Takeda).

4. The name used for the lower course of the Sagami river, the upper course of which was in the province of Musashi.

5. Kaempfer: "Askagava in. . . .": the province is missing and has been supplied. The following sentence was added in the margin in what appears to be Kaempfer's writing.

6. The Rokugō bridge was washed away in 1688 (*Kokushi daijiten).*

Chapter 3

1. Kaempfer: "Nin no mar," obviously a mistake for *san no maru; soto kamae* means "outer enclosure" and not "outer protection." The translation "outer protection" and *Nin no mar* were added in the margin of the text.

2. In this translation standard modern equivalents are used.

3. The saying by Horace, *Ars Poetica* 139, is: *parturiunt montes, nascetur ridiculus mus* (Mountains will be in labor, and an absurd little mouse will be born).

4. Tenshō daijin is Amaterasu; Hachiman is the god of war.

5. Ainu.

6. *Illicium religiosum* Sieb. et Zucc.: Japanese star anise.

7. Agrimony: *Agrimonia Eupatori* L. var *pilosa* Makino.

Chapter 4

1. "Miseratsie": Kaempfer uses the Japanese adjective *mezurashii* (or *mezurashiki* = rare, extraordinary, and wonderful) and turns it into a German noun.

2. Well known for its beautiful orange, reddish color.

3. Russian for "god."

4. Literally: alternating shelves. Shelves do not run the full width but differ in length and are juxtaposed in an irregular pattern.

5. Kaempfer: "Kursji"; used in Persian for a very similar arrangement, namely, a low, square table with a brazier underneath and covered with a blanket.

6. At the time, there was a clear distinction between a steam and hot-water bath. The former was the norm, and the latter only gained popularity in the second half of the Tokugawa period. See Yanagida Kunio, *Furo no kigen*, in *Yanagida Kunio shū*, 14 (Tokyo, 1962).

7. See book 5, chapter 6, below.

8. *Manjū* were introduced from China into Japan during the early Kamakura period. *Nihon kokugo daijiten*, 18:474; *Kinsei fuzoku jiten*, 221–222.

9. Arrowroot: *Pueraria Thunbergiana* Benth.; also known simply as *kuzu*.

10. Now usually *karō*, but Kaempfer's "Laxa" seems to be a contraction of *karōtsu*, which according to the nineteenth-century work *Morisada mankō* is a Chinese term for *sobakiri* (wheat noodles). *Kinsei fuzoku jiten*, 430.

11. Japanese pepper tree, prickly ash, *Xanthoxyum piperitum* DC.

Chapter 5

1. The original states twenty thousand, but this seems to be a slip of the pen in view of the figures stated elsewhere in this chapter.

2. A lacquered traveling box carried at the end of a pole.

3. *Tate kasa:* a ceremonial umbrella wrapped and tied up, the shape and wrapping being determined by the status of the owner. For further explanations and illustrations, see Ogawa Kyōichi, *Edo bakuhan daimyō ke jiten* (Tokyo, 1992), 3:192–194 and unnumbered front pages.

4. *Daikasa*: like *tatekasa,* this is a wrapped and tied-up umbrella indicating the rank of the owner. Its shape resembles a large, flat hat. By the eighteenth century, this umbrella had no practical use. *Kinsei fuzoku jiten,* 134–135.

5. The five northern provinces of Iwaki, Iwashiro, Rikuzen, Rikuchū, and Mutsu. Today these are contained in the four provinces of Fukushima, Miyagi, Iwate, and Aomori.

6. According to *Morisada mankō* (*Kinsei fuzoku jiten,* 521), the boards were roughly three centimeters wide and twelve to fifteen centimeters long; this work, written between 1837 and 1853, notes that the boards were no longer worn by pilgrims but only by actors on the stage dressed as pilgrims.

7. Shōtoku Taishi (574–622), the son of Emperor Yōmei, who acted as regent for his aunt, Empress Suiko, and is credited with having introduced Buddhism into Japan.

8. Mononobe Moriya (d. 587), a descendent from an ancient clan who opposed the introduction of Buddhism. With his defeat, the clan became extinct.

9. The character used is that for *fusu,* the name meaning "the one who lies in the mountains." See book 3, chapter 5, above.

10. This contradicts Kaempfer's statement in chapter 5 of book 3 that the mountain priests sometimes serve at a shrine.

11. The Lotus sutra, the chief text of the Tendai sect.

12. Also *segaki e:* a rite for feeding the hungry ghosts of departed souls. Formerly it was held throughout the year; nowadays it is mainly held at Obon.

13. See *shikimi* above.

14. Hundred-handed god of Greek mythology.

15. Here the meaning of *sakana* is not "fish" but the variety of snacks served with *sake* (*saka* = sake, *na* = snacks). For a description, see book 5, chapter 6, p. 283.

16. See Boxer, *A True Description,* 48.

Chapter 6

1. See note 15 to chapter 5 above.

2. *Tōjin* also meant "foreigner" or was used as a derogatory term meaning "crazy fellow."

3. The Kyoto deputy.

4. Abe no Seimei (921–1005) was a famous astrologer and *in-yō* (cosmic dual forces yin and yang) scholar of the Heian period. Born into a noble family in Sanuki province, Shikoku, he achieved fame in Kyoto, was promoted to high rank at court, and became the founder of the Tsuchimikado line.

5. The following legend exists in a number of versions and has been retold in many stories and popular plays.

6. "When deciding which days are good or bad for the beginning of a journey, make the day I want to set out a good one."

Chapter 7

1. The word "Tuesday" *(dienstags)* was added in a different hand and has therefore been omitted.

2. Kyushu.

3. Arnoldus Montanus, *Denckwürdige Gesandtschafften der Ost-Indischen Geselschaft in den Vereinigten Niederländern an unterschiedliche Keyser in Japan. . . .* (Amsterdam, 1670). Kaempfer's page number corresponds to the German translation of Montanus' work.

4. Yokoyama Yozaemon.

5. Motoki Tarōemon.

6. Also *bezaibune,* a small Japanese vessel with one sail commonly used at the time.

7. Martaban, name of a town in Pegu; "Martaban jar" is used for a kind of glazed pottery made there.

8. Justus Lipsius (Joest Lips) (1547–1606), Belgian humanist, classical scholar, and historian; see translator's introduction above.

9. Matsudaira (Nabeshima) Hizen no Kami Mitsushige, governed 1657–1695.

10. The ancient Persian kingdom of Media.

11. Kaempfer: "Sanda." Kure (1:231) and Imai (2:216) take this to mean Shiota, which elsewhere Kaempfer refers to as Swota. In my opionion, it is closer to Kaempfer's "Sanga," which stands for Saga. Also Saga seems more appropriate in this listing of major towns and districts.

12. The settlement in question is Tade. Kaempfer's version has been kept because of the explanations that follow.

13. Arima Nakatsukasa no Taifu Yorimoto, governed from 1668 to 1705.

14. See book 1, chapter 3, note 12, above.

15. "In the mountain"; *uchino* means "infield" but is used only as a name.

16. Kaempfer uses the word "prauen," which he describes in book 5, chapter 2.

17. Ogasawara Tadao, governed 1667–1725.

18. *Man koku* = 10,000 *koku,* therefore a total of 150,000 *koku.*

Chapter 8

1. Kaempfer: "cabuja"; *chabune* were small vessels transporting the freight from large ships in the harbors. *Kokugo daijiten,* 7:417.

2. Kyushu means "nine countries" or "nine provinces," but *nishi no kuni* is the *kun,* or alternate, Japanese reading of Saikoku, mentioned below.

3. Kaempfer: "cippus," literally: a pillar on a gravc.

4. The people of Kyushu.

5. "Feke or Fege." The story of the Gempei war recorded by Kaempfer is garbeled. The best-known "hero" of the Heike clan is Taira Kiyomori (1118–1181), who was not an emperor, although it was rumored that his real father was not Taira Tadamori but the Emperor Shirakawa. Kiyomori died of illness while the Taira were still in control of the capital and it was his sons Munemori (1147–1185) and Tomomori (1151–1185) who fought till the end. The young Emperor Antoku (1178–1185), who drowned with his nursemaid at the decisive battle of Dan no ura in 1185, was the son of Kiyomori's daughter.

6. Amidaji was built as a Shingon temple in 1191 by the retired Emperor Goshirakawa to appease the spirit of Emperor Antoku. In 1875 it became the shrine Akama jingū.

7. Mori Mototsugu (1671–1718) succeeded as domain lord and became Hida no Kami in 1690.

8. "Flor"; can also mean crepe.

9. Normally 1½ taels would be one *bu,* but the rate was fluctuating. See appendix 2.

10. "Fiogo oder Sinongi."

11. "Nord t. Ost"; t. = tet, Dutch for "to." Kaempfer does not specify how much north of east, but as he uses the convention north-northeast and so on, it must be less than fifteen degrees. Consequently the translation "slightly" has been chosen. (I thank Dr. L. Sternstein, School of Resource and Environmental Management, ANU, and Professor B. Terwiel, University of Hamburg, for discussing this point with me.)

12. Kaempfer has "Awa."

13. *Sso sjino kso*, literally, "hodgepodge of dung." The proper name is Zōshi no iso, meaning "beach of many stones." *Kuso* is a swearword and was most probably used to express the sailor's dislike of this area.

14. Mori Yoshinari, governed 1682–1694, Lord of Hagi castle; his domain included Nagato and Suo.

15. "Haff von Sivo"; *nada*, however, means "open sea" or "ocean having strong and high waves."

16. Kaempfer refers to Ji (no) Kamuro, "Kamuro on the land," situated on the island of Yashiro, which carried this name to distinguish it from Oki (no) Kamuro, mentioned later, a settlement of the same name on a much smaller island off the coast of Yashiro facing the open sea (*Kadokawa Nihon chimei daijiten* [Tokyo, 1988], 35:228). But as the characters of names were not standardized (i.e., Yashirojima either with the character for "eight" or "house"), the character for "below" could well have been in use.

17. *Oki* means "offing," "open sea"; according to Japanese records, Ji no Kamuro had seventy-one houses in 1737. *Kadokawa Nihon chimei daijiten,* 35:228.

18. Kaempfer must have believed that the island chain on which Kamagari and Mitarai are situated is part of the mainland. See also his comments on Iwagi below.

19. (Asano) Matsudaira Aki no Kami Tsunanaga, governed 1673–1708.

20. "Sjiro motto Fonno" *(shiro moto dono)* means "the lord of the domain's castle." The fifth shogun's daughter, Tsuruhime, was married to the son of the Lord of Kii, Kenchūnagon Tsunanori, not the Lord of Imabari castle. That was Matsudaira (Hisamatsu) Sadanobu, who governed 1676–1702 (Ogawa, *Daimyō ke jiten,* 2:679–680). It appears that throughout this part of the journey Kaempfer's informant was not reliable.

21. The text is ambiguous. For a discussion of the exact location of these fortifications and identification of "Tarumi," see Kure, *Edo sanpu kikō,* 1:262–264.

22. Iwagimura is situated on Iwagishima, that is, the island of Iwagi.

23. Shioya means "valley of salt."

24. Perhaps Momojima; see also Kure, *Edo sanpu kikō,* 1:265.

25. The priest Kūkai (774–835), founder of the Shingon sect.

26. Asano Takumi no Kami Naganori (1667–1701), who had inherited his fief of 53,500 *koku* in 1675, was ordered to commit suicide after injuring Kira Yoshinaka within Edo castle and was revenged by the so-called Forty-seven Rōnin.

27. "Fimesji oder Fimedsi."

28. Since 1681 the lord of Himeji castle was Sakai Uta no Kami Tadataka (1648–1720). *Daimyō ke jiten,* 2:527.

29. "Takasangen oder Taksanni."

30. A hemp summer kimono.

31. That is, twenty thousand *koku.* However, Kaempfer's statement is incorrect. In 1682 Matsudaira Wakasa no Kami Naoakira became lord of Akashi castle; on that occasion his fief was increased to sixty thousand *koku. Daimyō ke jiten,* 2:494–495; also Kure, *Edo sanpu kikō,* 1:276.

32. Kaempfer seems to refer to Awaji.

33. Kaempfer: "Fiogo." I have omitted the sentence: "This locality is also known as Finōgi."

34. "Feiki oder Fage." The work was carried out in 1161 by Taira Kiyomori.

35. The legendary Roman hero Marcus Curtius. The story goes that in 362 B.C. a deep gulf opened in the forum, which the seers declared would not close until Rome's most valuable possession was thrown into it. Realizing that nothing was more precious than a brave citizen, Curtius leaped into the chasm, which immediately closed (*Encyclopaedia Britannica,* 1969).

36. Odagiri Tosa no Kami Naotoshi, Osaka *bugyō* from 1686 to 1692.

37. Nose Izumi no Kami Yorisuke (also: Yorihiro), Osaka *bugyō* from 1688 to the twelfth month of Genroku 3 (1690). When Kaempfer arrived, Nose had finished his duties, but his successor had not yet arrived.

Chapter 9

1. Kaempfer refers to the *gokasho,* the five large cities directly administered by the shogunate, as discussed in book 4, chapter 1.

2. This is incorrect and should read 34.40 degrees North.

3. Kaempfer refers to Lake Biwa, which he later calls "the lake of Ōtsu."

4. Kaempfer refers to the measurement of *ken,* which was 0.994 fathom. However, the exact length of one *ken* showed slight regional variations.

5. "Eine frone" = forced labor, servitude, also, a courthouse. Kaempfer jokingly alludes to the bath in such terms on a number of occasions, presumably because the Europeans were not keen to bathe daily as demanded by the Japanese.

6. The castle of Kumamoto.

7. Kaempfer refers to Katō Higo no Kami Kiyomasa (1562–1611), who in 1588 was given 520,000 *koku* in the province of Higo and became the Lord of Kumamoto castle. Later the province attached to the title *no kami* did not usually indicate possession of land in this province, but here it did.

8. The Kyoto *shoshidai*, generally known in English as "Kyoto deputy."

9. A weapon used by infantry in the sixteenth and seventeenth centuries, consisting of a long-handled spear, the blade having one or more lateral cutting projections.

10. Kaempfer uses the word "Korb" for the simple *kago* as described in chapter 1 of book 5 above.

11. This should obviously read "February." In the following entries of the manuscript, the word "Martii" (March) was crossed out and corrected to "Februarii."

12. "Tsadunilte bäume." The sound is somewhat removed, but Kaempfer seems to refer to *Aleurites cordata,* the tung oil tree.

13. From 1669 the Lord of Yodo castle was Ishikawa Tonomo no Kami Noriyuki (Norifumi). *Daimyō ke jiten*, 2:427–428; see also Kure, *Edo sanpu kikō,* 1:308.

14. "Fusjmi oder Fusjimi."

15. Most probably the famous Fushimi Inari shrine.

16. Matsudaira Inaba no Kami Nobuoki (1630–1691), who had just taken up his duties (Genroku 4, 2.15) and died later that year. *Shokafu*, 5:4.

17. Koide Awaji no Kami Morihide (Aritoshi).

18. Maeda Aki no Kami Naokatsu.

19. Kaempfer's "vintent" comes from *vinto tinto:* Portuguese red wine.

20. This should read "eastern"; Scheuchzer (3:20) changed this accordingly, most probably consulting the map of Kyoto contained in Kaempfer's documents (British Library, Or. 75. f. 16).

21. Kaempfer refers to Nijō castle and the picture contained in the fifty *meisho-e* (pictures of famous sights; British Library Add. Ms. 5252, f. 45), which he had brought back from Japan and had begun to copy as illustrations for his book. However, a copy of the illustration of Nijō castle is not extant, and the original has been used here.

22. Kaempfer refers to the *shūmon aratame no jō,* the Laws for the Examination of Sects. See Bodart-Bailey, "Persecution of Confucianism," 302–306. The figures mentioned cannot refer to the population of Kyoto, which amounted to roughly half a million and is given accurately below. I suggest they refer to the total number of people under the control of the Kyoto *shoshidai.*

23. The chapter ends here. The material Kaempfer refers to is contained in his notes (Sloane 3062, folio 18v and 27) but had not been edited for publication. It is written in a mixture of German, Latin, and Japanese in very small writing and at times is extremely difficult to decipher. Scheuchzer (3:22–25) amplified what he could read, and Dohm (2:236–238) translated Scheuchzer's text.

24. Buddhist temples.

25. Shinto shrines.

26. Residences of the daimyo of the various provinces.

27. Kaempfer first writes out the number in Japanese, then divides the figure using the Japanese unit of ten thousand: *man.*

28. The four sects as well as Monto *shū* (Shin *shū*) mentioned below are among the ten sects, which split off from the main Jōdo sect after the death of the founder, Shinran Shōnin (1173–1262).

29. To the right of the *aratame,* which has been translated above, is a column with notes in a mixture of Japanese, Latin, and German which obviously were not meant for publication. The upper section of these notes consists of explanation of various terms that are already explained in the main text and therefore have been omitted. The second section consists of notes on the Jōdo sect that are not found in the main text and have been added here.

30. Abbreviation for *namu amida butsu.*

31. Another name for the Shin *shū* sect of Buddhism; see note 28.

Chapter 10

1. "Ōtz oder Oitz."

2. "Jesan oder Fiesan"; the meaning is "august mountain."

3. Oda Nobunaga (1534–1582) burned Hieizan in 1571.

4. "Dsedsje oder Sjesji."

5. Honda Oki no Kami Yasuyoshi (1647–1718). The reference to Hakata is difficult to explain.

6. Kaempfer refers to Gozutennō sha, dedicated to the ox-headed god, identified with Susano o, the patron of the nearby village Naka no shō. Today the shrine is known as Shinotsu jinja. Kodama Kōta, ed., *Tōkaidō bunken nobe ezu* (Tokyo, 1977–1985), 22:8.

7. The leaves are hollyhock *(tachiaoi).*

8. "Tsetta, Tsjitto, auch Sjetta."

9. An addition, "especially by the Chinese and Japanese," seems to be in Scheuchzer's hand.

10. Tawara Tōta is the name of the hero who assisted the dragon (Ōtsu Shi Rekishi Hakubutsukan, ed., *Ōtsu no densetsu* [Ōtsu, 1988], 138). He is Fujiwara no Hidesato, who in 940 killed the rebellious Taira no Masakado.

11. Perhaps Kōbō Daishi (Kūkai, 774–835); also, many such irreverant stories are told of Ikkyū Sōjun (1394–1481), but this one could not be traced.

12. "Noodsi oder Nosji."

13. "Kusatz oder Kusatzu."

14. Black bamboo: Phyllostachys nigra.

15. "Tabara oder Tebura."

16. Also Ume no ki; Kaempfer has "Menoki."

17. See book 4, chapter 8, note 21, above.

18. The grindstone can still be inspected today.

19. "Mikade oder Mikame jamma."

20. Katō Sado no Kami Akihide (1652–1712) was appointed junior councilor in the tenth month of Genroku 3 (1690), not long before Kaempfer passed his castle. *Tokugawa jikki,* 6:88.

21. The word *tororo* means grated yam and not simply yam, as Kaempfer seems to assume.

22. Kaempfer: "Finakawa." Hinaga lies at the Tenbaku river, but *kawa* is not part of its name, as Kaempfer states below.

23. Kaempfer's route maps are difficult to read and only the stretch from Kambara to Edo has been reproduced.

24. A clam.

25. "Kuwanna, Kfana oder Qano."

26. Matsudaira Etchū no Kami Sadashige (1644–1717).

27. Genyūin is the posthumous name of the fourth shogun, Ietsuna (1641–1680), who was the elder brother and not the uncle of the reigning fifth shogun, Tsunayoshi. Kaempfer took this story from his notes of Daniel Six's diary (British Library, Sloane 3061, f. 94); it cannot be traced in Japanese sources, unless it is a garbled version of that of Senhime (1597–1666), Hidetada's daughter and widow of Hideyoshi's son

Hideyori. After the fall of Osaka, she married the son of Honda Tadamasa, who was lord of Kuwana castle, but in 1626 was widowed again. She was known as Kuwana hime, and many stories grew up around her. Kondō Moku, ed., *Kuwana shi shi* (Nagoya, 1959), 176–178.

28. Olof Rudbeck (1630–1702), *Atlantica* (Uppsala, 1675–1698). Rudbeck wrote in Kaempfer's autograph book on August 18, 1681, when Kaempfer visited him in Uppsala. Meier-Lemgo, "Stammbuch," 163.

29. Kaempfer refers to his journey from Moscow to the Caspian Sea in 1683. See Meier-Lemgo, *Reisetagebücher,* 34–35.

30. The house of Owari descended from Ieyasu's ninth son, Tokugawa Yoshinao (1600–1650), and was one of the Three Related Houses *(gosanke).*

31. The Atsuta jingū burned down in 1597 and was rebuilt by Toyotomi Hideyori in 1606. It was renovated by the fifth shogun in 1703 (*Kokushi daijiten*). Kaempfer might be referring to repairs. See book 5, chapter 13, note 12 below.

32. Only one sword is kept there. Kaempfer's informant obviously misinterpreted *mitsurugi* (*mi* = august + *tsurugi* = sword) as meaning *mitsu tsurugi* (three swords). Kure, *Edo sanpu kikō,* 1:518.

33. The Kasadera Kannon.

34. "Josjida oder Jöhtsjida."

35. As elsewhere, Kaempfer uses the term *bugyō* in the sense of *bugyō nin,* meaning a person charged with official duties.

Chapter 11

1. A Dutch term for a small rowing boat, which Kaempfer explains below.

2. "Kakinga oder Kingawa."

3. See illustration on p. 278.

4. Tanaka Castle was in the possession of Ōta Settsu no Kami Sukenao. *Daimyō ke jiten,* 1:245; Kure, *Edo sanpu kikō,* 1:502.

5. "Suraga oder Scjringa."

6. Kaempfer is mistaken: one *koban* = four *bu,* consequently 1.25 ducats. See appendix 2.

7. Posthumous name of the second Tokugawa shogun, Hidetada (1579–1632).

8. Posthumous name of the first Tokugawa shogun, Ieyasu (1541–1616).

9. Kaempfer's information is garbled. The Lord of Sumpu had been the third shogun's younger brother Tokugawa Tadanaga (1606–1633), whom the second shogun, Hidetada, planned to install as his successor. After Hidetada's death, Iemitsu exiled Tadanaga to Ueno Takazaki castle, where he committed suicide.

10. "Foreigners, have you got something for sale?"

11. "Jesira oder Jesiri."

12. "Kuno oder Kono."

13. See Kaempfer's *Flora Japonica* in *Amoenitates Exoticae,* reproduced, edited, and translated into German by Wolfgang Muntschick (Wiesbaden, 1983).

14. "Jü oder jü matz."

15. "Fudsi oder Fusi."

16. "Fudsi, Fusji, oder Fusijamma."

17. "Cӯnosus'—Greek: Kunosoura = Dog's tail = constellation at the North Pole known as the Lesser Bear (Ursa Minor), that is, the Pole Star used in the sense of "guide."

18. Also *kanzeni, zeni,* or *mon:* the smallest coin.

19. German coin worth ten pfenning.

20. Minamoto Yoshistune (1159–1189), who was the younger, and not older, half-brother of Yoritomo.

21. Kaempfer brought back a number of these guides which are now in the British Library, Or. 75, f. 3, 4, 7.

22. "Dsoo oder Ssjo," a pagoda.

23. "Ströhmling" = *clupea harengus membras,* a kind of small herring native to the Baltic; the word is used here in a general sense.

24. Governor general at Batavia; see appendix 1.

25. The word means "honorable" (i.e., shogunal) guardpost.

26. Abbreviation for *namu amida butsu:* hail to thee, Amida Buddha.

27. The description of the temple Hakone Gongen and its treasures was added in the margin, but apparently in Kaempfer's hand. It corresponds to the listing in temple records (Edo Bakufu Chiri Hensan Shirabekata, ed., *Shinpen Sagami kuni fudōki kō* [Tokyo, 1975], 18–25) and was most probably contained in one of Kaempfer's *dōchūki* (travel guides). Some of the items are now in the National Museum, Ueno, while most of the remainder are stored in the museum at Yumoto.

28. Gold and copper alloy; see book 4, chapter 8, note 44, above.

29. One *sun* = 3.03 cm; one *bu* = 3.03 mm.

30. "Ein Ama gewebtes Himmels kleid." This is ambiguous and could mean either "a heavely robe woven by a nun," "a heavenly robe woven by a woman diver," "a heavenly robe of flax," or "a heavenly robe woven in heaven." *Shinpen Sagami,* 24, has "a heavenly feather robe."

31. N. sect stands for the Nenbutsu sect of Shingon Buddhism, founded by Kōbō Daishi, or Kūkai.

32. Soga Tokimune (1174–1193), brought up as monk at the temple before avenging his father together with his brother.

33. "Hatta oder Fatta."

34. "Sorinsj."

35. The temple is Shōgenji, famous for the worship of Hōkō Jizō during the Tokugawa period; "double Jizō" because the temple owns two Jizō statues, which is unusual. The temple has been relocated, but the statues still exist.

36. See note 32 above.

37. "Kattama oder Kasamatz."

38. "Odowara Isj (iisch)."

39. An astringent substance obtained mainly from Acacia Catechu used in medicine and in the arts.

40. Inaba Mino no Kami Masayuki was transferred from Odawara castle to Takada castle in Etchigo in the twelfth month of Jōkyō 2 (1685); Ōkubo Kaga no Kami Tadatomo (1632–1712) became senior councilor in 1677 and lord of Odawara castle in 1686.

41. "Banrju oder Bendju"; the name of the area is given to the lower course of the Sagami river.

42. The story cannot be traced. However, *makura* does mean a cushion, and a secondary meaning is "an item to which one is always close"; a secondary meaning of *kura* is a seat. Nobles in disgrace might well have been forced to take the tonsure and enter one of the many monasteries. But Kamakura is not an island, and Kaempfer seems to be describing the island of Enoshima, which is clearly marked on his map, fitting his above description.

43. This was the description Kaempfer gave of Hachijō in book 1, chapter 3. The text is vague, and Kaempfer might well have meant it that way.

44. The Miwa peninsula.

45. Kaempfer refers to Shōjōkō ji, where the abbot died in the ninth month of Genroku 4 (1691) (Kure, *Edo sanpu kikō,* 1:424), which means that he was still alive the first time Kaempfer passed. This explains the ambiguity of the text. See also Kodama, *Tōkaidō bunken nobe ezu,* 2:34.

46. *Gawa* means river. *Kanagawa* is believed to be an abbreviation for *kami nashi gawa,* meaning the river with no upper course *(Nihon kokugo daijiten).*

47. The word is difficult to decipher. It has been read as French *boisage,* meaning "timbering, scaffolding."

48. "Tsisi oder Tsisicku."

49. Hachiman is, like Mars, a god of war.

50. Kaempfer does not seem to realize that *Suzu* is not a place name but refers to the sound the stone makes when tapped. The stone is still in existence, but the shrine is now called Iwai Jinja.

51. Kaempfer refers to a wooden bell tower erected at Hongokuchō 3 chōme in 1626. The tower was famous for "sending Edo to sleep and waking the city up." Haga Tōru, "Kane wa Ueno ka Asakusa ka?" in *Edo no kurashi 122 hanashi,* edited by Nihon Fuzokushi Gakkai (Tokyo, 1995), 147. The inn where the Dutch stayed was known as Nagasaki ya and was situated next to today's exit 4 of JR Shin Nihonbashi station.

Chapter 12

1. Kaempfer was slightly out. The correct reading should be 35°40′.

2. Kaempfer had his map tilted the wrong way: The river runs toward the south, the arm around the castle branches off toward the west, and the five separate streams run in an easterly direction.

3. The two "outer castles" are the fortifications of the *sotobori* and *uchibori;* the "secondary castles" appear to be the *ni no maru* and *san no maru,* because later Kaempfer describes them as lying next to each other; apparently he was not aware of the *nishi no maru.* This is understandable, as ground-plans of the castle were kept secret, and depictions were only schematic.

4. The keep of Edo castle burned down in the Meireki fire (1657) and was not rebuilt. But many maps and travel guides *(dōchūki)* continued to show the castle with its keep in the center of Edo, and Kaempfer might well have consulted these when completing this chapter at home.

5. "*Impluvia.*"

6. See chapter 11, town of Ejiri, p. 338 above.

7. Ieyasu's religious posthumous name: Tōshō Dai Gongen (The Great Avatar of the Brilliant East).

8. Posthumous name of the second shogun, Hidetada.

9. Posthumous name of the third shogun, Iemitsu.

10. Posthumous name of the fourth shogun, Ietsuna.

11. See book 4, chapter 8.

12. See footnote 19, chapter 9, book 5, above.

13. Matsudaira Inaba no Kami Nobuoki was made Kyoto *shoshidai* (Kyoto deputy); see *Tokugawa jikki,* 6:101, 15D, 2M, Genroku 4.

14. Makino Bingo no Kami Narisada was officially not a councilor but the grand chamberlain *(gosoba yōnin);* also Kaempfer indicates that he was treated as a senior councilor. Similarly, the chamberlain *(soba yōnin)* Yanagisawa Yoshiyasu is listed as junior councilor.

15. *Go* is used here as an honorific and does not mean "five," as also in the expression *waka go rōjū* below.

16. Generally: *wakatoshiyori.*

17. The number (1) has been supplied as it had been omitted from the original.

18. "Tempel Herren," literally, lords of temples.

19. Matsuura Iki no Kami Takashi; later that year he was also appointed *jisha bugyō.* See note 39, chapter 14, below.

20. Kaempfer refers to the office of *shūmon aratame yaku,* the office for the examination of sects. The post was created in 1641 and was first referred to as *kirishitan bugyō,* literally, Christian magistrate. It was staffed by a chief inspector *(ōmetsuke)* and a magistrate of building works *(sakuji bugyō),* who performed the functions of the office simultaneously with their other duties. Ikeda Shōichirō, *Edo jidai yōgo kōshō jiten* (Tokyo, 1984), 208.

21. Kaempfer: ". . . dem grossen Reichs Rath Makino Bingo seinem Favoriten . . ." The text does not make it clear who is the favorite of whom, but in line with previous explanations one may assume that Makino Narisada was the shogun's favorite.

22. Makino Narisada (1634–1712) was fifty-seven years old.

23. The idea of a ball at Edo castle sounds odd, but Kaempfer expressly chose

the word "Ball," which in the seventeenth century also meant entertainment with dancing.

24. See *Tokugawa jikki,* 6:102, 30D, 2M, Genroku 4.

25. Kaempfer: "Hollanda Capitain!"

26. The informal audience was first held in 1682 (*Tokugawa Jikki,* 5:438, 28D, 2M Tenna 2). Kaempfer states the correct date elsewhere.

27. The manuscript has been corrected in what appears to be Scheuchzer's hand, and these corrections have been ignored in the translation.

28. The date of birth of Tsunayoshi's *midaidokoro* Nobuko varies by a few years in different documents, but her age was about forty. Takayanagi Kaneyoshi, ed., *Shiryō Tokugawa fujinden* (Tokyo, 1967), 141.

29. "3 geistliche Richter," literally, three religious judges.

30. "2 Commissarii oder Curatores extranearum": the two officials in charge of the *shūmon aratame yaku* mentioned above.

31. "Diese geschminckte Hauβwürmer," literally, these painted house worms.

32. "Fenster=thüren"; obviously a reference to *shōji.*

33. Since 1688 the Lord of Hakata was Kuroda Hizen no Kami Tsunamasa. His son (not grandson) Yoshiyuki (1682–1710) had his first audience with the shogun during Kaempfer's visit to Edo. Kure, *Edo sanpu kikō,* 2:490–491; *Tokugawa Jikki,* 6:101, 15D, 2M, Genroku 4.

Chapter 13

1. "Schedelstete" (Schedelstätte), a word used in Luther's translation of the Bible for the mountain Golgatha (Latin: Mons calvariae). Mark 15:22: "And they bring him unto the place Golgotha, which is, being interpreted, the place of a skull." Also Matt. 27:33; John 19:17.

2. The lord of Kii, or Ki no Kuni, at the time was Tokugawa Mitsusada (1626–1705). His son Tsunanori (1665–1705) had been betrothed in 1685 to Tsunayoshi's daughter Tsuruhime (1677–1704). Judging from the age, Kaempfer's party was passing Tsunanori.

3. Kaempfer refers to Tanaka Castle, which was in the possession of Ōta Settsu no Kami Sukenao. His father, Suketsugu, had been *Osaka jōdai* from 1678 to1684. *Daimyō ke jiten*, 1:245; Kure, *Edo sanpu kikō,* 1:502.

4. "Casjes": Kaempfer refers to *mon.*

5. "Nitssaka oder Misisacka."

6. "Waggabasj oder vielmehr Wackabeijasi oder Wakabaési."

7. "Iosttzida oder Iosida."

8. "Kosoi." The village was Motojuku; Kaempfer's "Kosoi" is most probably based on Hōzōji, referring to the area over which the buildings of the temple were scattered. See Kodama, *Tōkaidō bunken nobe ezu,* 13:19.

9. "Stätg. Fidzka oder Fusikava" appears in the margin.

10. "Primus Regni Senator." Abe Bungo no Kami Masatake (1649–1704), who was senior councilor 1681–1704, was returning from Kyoto, having presented the new Kyoto deputy to the court. *Tokugawa jikki*, 6:101 (18, 19D, 2M, Genroku 4) and 103 (21 D, 3 M, Genroku 4).

11. Sō Tsushima no Kami Yoshizane (1639–1702).

12. See book 5, chapter 10, note 31. Kaempfer might be referring to repairs by the Lord of Owari, who belonged to one the Three Related Houses and therefore is referred to as "king." (I have inserted "local" as Kaempfer's use of the German "König" differs from the modern English "king.")

13. See book 5, chapter 10, note 32, above.

14. The manuscript has the additional phrase "nebst einem Graben" ("as well as a moat"). Presumably this is a mistake.

15. "Faz oder Fas."

16. "Iakuts oder Isj Iakutz."

17. Mori Yoshinari; see book 5, chapter 8, note 14, above.

18. "Wada oder Wanda."

19. "Meino oder Meijenú."

20. Kaempfer refers to Mukadeyama, literally, the centipede mountain; see p. 327.

21. Literally: "Nassumi, also called Natzummi or Nadsame by some people."

22. "Nagasj"; as there is no settlement of that name, it has been taken as a distortion of Magari.

23. Kaempfer gives the name of the long village as Sjettà and that of the large village as Zetta. Both are variants of Seta, a stretched-out settlement that Kaempfer mistook for two separate villages.

24. Honda Oki no Kami Yasuyoshi (1647–1718).

25. A German city traditionally famous for its markets.

26. See illustration on p. 321.

27. "Tsugannin sage Tschuganin."

28. For Kaempfer's sketch of the temple's layout and of the large San mon, see p. 381.

29. Kaempfer describes the Ōhōjō; see Bodart-Bailey, "The Most Magnificent Monastery," 27–28.

30. Kaempfer is not quite correct; see Bodart-Bailey, "The Most Magnificent Monastery," 28–29.

31. "Gnôthi seautòn," from Aristotle's *Rhetoric* (*Rhet.* 2, 21 etc.).

32 . Kaempfer refers to the temple's collection of *e-ma.* The picture Kaempfer describes is still there but portrays the young Buddha. See B. M. Bodart-Bailey, "Kyoto Three Hundred Years Ago," *Nichibunken Newsletter,* 9 (May 1991):8.

33. "Ziwon Iasakki, sage Sjiwon jassakki."

34. Kaempfer refers to the Yasaka Pagoda, which had only five stories; see Bodart-Bailey, "Kyoto Three Hundred Years Ago," 8–9.

35. Kaempfer refers to the famous *butai,* or platform supported by the pillars.

36. The temple has disappeared, but part of the wall remains; see Bodart-Bailey, "Kyoto Three Hundred Years Ago," 10–12.

37. A hollow iron bowl struck with an iron or wooden stick. Here, however, Kaempfer refers to the famous bell cast by Toyotomi Hideyori, the inscription of which Ieyasu took as an excuse to attack Hideyori. The bell can still be seen at Hōkōji, the temple where the Daibutsu once stood.

38. In chapter 15 of book 5, Kaempfer notes correctly that there were only 1,033 statues.

39. Traditional cries to mark the rhythm of a dance and so forth.

40. Kaempfer refers to Osaka.

41. "Tenoizi oder Tenosi."

42. I have supplied "of our leader." The passage is unclear, and there is no reference to this incident in the official Dutch record, the *Deshima dagregisters,* ARA, NFJ 104, pp. 84–85.

43. In the manuscript "Sonnenaufgang" (sunrise) has been corrected to "Sonnenuntergang" (sunset) apparently in Scheuchzer's hand. Sunrise makes more sense, as the following passage specifies that their last meal had been at 5 P.M. the previous day. Arriving "three hours before sunrise," it was naturally difficult to procure a meal, and therefore they were told to go to sleep till the morning.

44. Kuroda Hizen no Kami Tsunamasa (1659–1711).

45. "Marianen," a contraction of *maruyama* (literally, round mountain), the prostitutes' quarter at Nagasaki.

46. "Iwaggi oder Iwangi."

47. "Muggo oder Mukko."

48. Nordkaper = North Atlantic right whale, black right whale: *Delphinus Orca* L.

49. "Sso"; grass writing.

50. *Iris japonica* Thunb. Makino, *Makino's New Illustrated Flora of Japan,* 869.

51. Shepherd's purse: *Capsella Bursa-Pastoris* Medicus. Makino, *Makino's New Illustrated Flora of Japan,* 213.

52. Aazalea: *Rhododendron lateritium.*

53. Nabeshima Tango no Kami Mitsushige (1632–1700).

54. Mathaeus Abouts, who went on the journey to Edo. The previous year he had remained in charge of the Dutch on Deshima during the director's absence. Itasawa Takeo, *Nichiran bunka kōshōshi no kenkyū* (1959), 99.

55. *Peiron:* boat races introduced from China in 1655 and still held today.

56. The fifth month of the lunar calendar—hence the rainy season.

57. "Herbst barken"; presumably barges for the autumn trade. Both Scheuchzer (3:135) and Dohm (2:320) ignore the "herbst."

58. Kaempfer uses the meaning of the Dutch word "Lichtmis" (libertine, rake) for German "Lichtmessen," which simply means "candle mass."

59. "Jacht Wieck auf See"; here Kaempfer translates the Dutch name into German, but the second time he uses the Dutch name, which is used here throughout. Later he also uses the spelling "Wÿk op See."

60. Miyagi Kenmotsu Kazumichi, in office 1681–1686.

61. Kaempfer apparently refers to the sale of the private goods of the Dutch merchants, which was held on a special day after the company's goods had been sold. See book 4, chapter 8.

62. This had been requested by the shogun at the last audience.

63. The festival is still referred to today as *okunchi.* Alternate names are *kunichi* or *kugatsu kokonoka.* As the names denote, the festival is usually held on the ninth of the ninth month (see book 4, chapter 4). Both the festival and the Dutch trading days were unusually late that year.

64. That is, both the outgoing and incoming Dutch directors.

65. The island of Takaboko in the harbor of Nagasaki.

66. The Dutch merchant Pieter van Dÿck, the second in command at the Nagasaki trading station. ARA, NFJ 104, 1691–1692, 12.

67. Yokoyama Yozaemon, also known as Brasman by the Dutch.

68. Kafuku Kizō, known as Sijmbe, Kiso, Kizo by the Dutch.

69. Motoki Ryōi, known as Sadaje by the Dutch.

70. "Secundum acte et probata."

71. Yamaoka Jūbei, Tsushima no Kami, Nagasaki magistrate.

72. *Inter parietes proprios."*

73. "Ima gada"; the lord of Agata (Nobeoka) castle was Arima Suō no Kami Kiyozumi. All his land was confiscated on 22.10 Genroku 4 (1691). *Tokugawa jikki,* 6:123.

Chapter 14

1. "Tensi"; now Sakurababa Tenmangū jinja. Both Tenmangū and Tenshin / Tenjin indicate the veneration of Sugawara Michizane. Before Meiji it was also known as Ifuku ji. The Dutch resident traditionally held his farewell parties there. Nagashima Masaichi, *Nagasaki gaidō,* Shinwabunkō No. 9 (Nagasaki, 1973), 33; Kure, *Edo sanpu kikō,* 2:2.

2. The German verb *bestreuen* requires no object. The word *sand* has been supplied in accordance with Kaempfer's earlier statement.

3. *Kotake* means "small bamboo."

4. "Isjino"; Kuroda Ise no Kami Nagakiyo.

5. "Itsusima"; this island could not be located. Perhaps Ōminaseshima.

6. "Iusima"; the village of Yū on Yashiroshima would have been on their left. Kaempfer appears to refer to Katashima, placed opposite Yūi and belonging to it inasmuch as Yū's inhabitants had a right to collect firewood and cut grass on the island. *Kadokawa Nihon chimei daijiten, Yamaguchi ken,* 35:259. Imai (2:365) suggests Yurushima, but that island lies a fair distance away.

7. See book 5, chapter 8, note 20.

8. Pine trees.

9. Kaempfer refers to Kōzenji, a temple belonging to the Higashi Honganji branch of the Ikkō sect or Jōdo *shinshū.* Kure, *Edo sanpu kikō,* 2:25.

10. Kaempfer: "Sjuke." This locality could not be identified, but it does not appear to be a slip of the pen, as it is also on Kaempfer's map (Sloane 3060, f. 505). Perhaps Kaempfer mistook Japanese *shuku* (post station) for the name of a locality.

11. Yamazaki is situated on the left bank of the Yodo while all other localities mentioned are on the right. Also on Kaempfer's map it is on the left bank (Sloane 3060, f. 505). The monasteries and temple are those on the mountain above Yamazaki, for the manuscript available to Dohm carried the additional information that one of the temples was called Shōnin dera or Mokujiki Shōnin dera, which is a temple known as Kannon dera today. Yet Kaempfer's party is unlikely to have traveled through Yamazaki, because that would have meant two unnecessary river crossings within a short distance.

12. Iwashimizu Hachiman.

13. Kaempfer introduces an element of mockery by attaching the ending *-sava,* frequently found in names of settlements, to the word *kubō* (shogun) to create a new name for Edo (unless it was a slip of the pen and was supposed to be *kubō sama).* Jacatra (Jaccatra) was the name of the Javanese settlement before Batavia was built and was still in use to designate certain areas (i.e., Fort Jacatra). See Susan Abeyasekere, *Jakarta, A History* (Oxford University Press, 1989), 6, 32, 36. At the end of the chapter Kaempfer again refers to the "superior at Jacatra."

14. According to the Japanese calendar it was the eighth day of the second month. The fourth shogun, Ietsuna, died on the eighth day of the fifth month Empō 8 (1680), and the eighth day of each month was being observed as a commemorative day (see below, 23rd April).

15. Ōsawa Ukyō no daibu Mototane (1656–1697).

16. The Ōsawa were *kuge* and together with the Kira and Hatakeyama families provided the envoys despatched to the court with the New Year's greetings. See, for instance, *Tokugawa Jikki,* 6:1, 1.1, Genroku 1.

17. "Des gleichen Mia Okosju." Kaempfer seems to refer to the *kōdō,* which was built after the *Taiseiden* at Shōheizaka, Yushima. *Kokushidaijiten: Shōheizaka.*

18. See *Tokugawa jikki,* 6, p. 133, 13.2, Genroku 5. The fifth shogun, Tsunayoshi, was the first Tokugawa ruler who himself had studied the Confucian classics and actively sponsored this philosophy.

19. Yanagisawa Yoshiyasu (1658–1714) rose from a lowly position to become grand chamberlain and the most powerful minister of the shogun. An abundance of stories circulated as to what kind of entertainment the shogun received when visiting his mansion. See Bodart-Bailey, "Councillor Defended."

20. Kaempfer refers to the so-called Laws of Compassion *(shorui awaremi no rei)* issued by the fifth shogun. See Bodart-Bailey, "The Laws of Compassion."

21. "12 Japanischen Jetto" = *eto* = the sexagenary cycle, the Japanese and Chinese zodiac signs. See book 2, chapter 2, above.

22. The governor general of the Dutch East India Company at Batavia.

23. The phrase ". . . daβ Sie fragten ob man solches aus der Kunst müste haben" is obscure. Scheuchzer (3:168) leaves it out; Dohm (2:348) changes it to ". . . mit einem algemeinen Beifal, den nur die Kunst erwarten kan, . . ." (approx.: with general applause which can only be expected from an artistic performance).

24. While resident at Hirado, until their forced move to Deshima in 1641, the Dutch East India Company had been under the jurisdiction of the Lord of Hirado.

25. Kaempfer made a mistake. Ieyasu was Tsunayoshi's great-grandfather. Moreover, on this day, the eighth day of the month, ceremonies were obvserved for the fourth shogun, Ietsuna, Tsunayoshi's elder brother (*Tokugawa jikki*, 6:134). See above, March 25th.

26. Although the location of Atago points to Zōjōji, Ietsuna's grave is at Kaneiji, Ueno. Temples with imperial princes as abbots, such as Kaneiji, are referred to as *gosho. Nihon kokugo daijiten,* 4:855.

27. "Karkematta": "Respectfully understood."

28. "Miseratis"; *mezurashii* means "precious, rare."

29. Kaempfer refers to a *daisu.*

30. "Gobo basj"; the chamberlains.

31. Kaempfer uses the Japanese *medetai:* "worin ich ihm *medite zuwünschte.*"

32. *Torreya nucifera Sieb. et Zucc.*—Japanese nutmeg.

33. *Paulownia tomentosa* Steudel. Kaempfer's "sun" or "rose" was the imperial chrysanthemum crest.

34. An antidote to poison, containing opium.

35. A song.

36. The square style of the Japanese phonetic syllabary, often used to write foreign words.

37. "Koobojin"; Kaempfer seems to refer to the temple at the bank of the Kanda river, in front of which stood the famous Ocha no mizu well (near the front of today's Juntendō hospital). Old drawings show the well surrounded by a high fence and covered by a roofed structure. After the Meireki fire (1657) the temple was supposedly moved to Komagome, and with the widening of the river in the Manji period (1658–1661), the well is said to have been destroyed. Yet remains of the well could still be seen on the steep river bank at the beginning of the eighteenth century (*Kokushi daijiten*, 2:862–863). Kaempfer's report provides evidence that the well (though dry) and remains of the temple were still in place in 1692.

38. "Medithé" = fortunate.

39. Matsuura Iki no Kami Takashi became commissioner of temples and shrines *(jisha bugyō)* on 25.11, Genroku 4 (1691) (*Tokugawa jikki,* 6:125). He succeeded Ogasawara Sado no Kami (Etchū no Kami) Nagashige, *jisha bugyō* from 3.12, Genroku 3 (1690) to 26.8, Genroku 4 (*Tokugawa jikki,* 6:117).

Chapter 15

1. In book 5, chapter 11, p. 348, Kaempfer explained that there were two small carved figures of horses.

2. The lord of the province of Kii, Tokugawa Mitsusada, a member of the *gosanke* (Three Related Houses), or his son. See book 5, chapter 13, note 2, above.

3. The name of the temple is Chōkōsan Jōtaiji (Shōtaiji). The gate was particularly splendid because this was the family temple of the Inaba family, who rose to influence with Kasuga no Tsubone. Imai Kingo, *Ima mukashi Tōkaidō doku annai* (reprint, Tokyo, 1994), 68.

4. "Tempel Sorinsj oder Forinsi."

5. "Smoke baths" is not the translation of *miya,* which means "shrine." I presume Kaempfer means a place where the souls are cleansed by the smoke of incense.

6. In chapter 11 of book 5 Kaempfer identified this temple as Kiyomi dera.

7. Kaempfer mistakenly has "Sÿriga" for "Suruga."

8. Literally: "the stone of the pine that cries at night." The stone is generally referred to as *Yo naku no ishi* (the crying at night stone). One explanation is that it blocked the steep mountain road and presented such a problem for travelers at night that it brought tears to their eyes. (Kodama, *Nobe ezu*, 9:15). Another is the story that a pregnant woman was killed there, but the child was saved and revenged the mother. The spirit of the mother turned into a stone that cried every night until Kōbō Daishi broke the spell (Imai, *Ima mukashi Tōkaidō doku annai,* 140–141). There is also a shrine called Yo naku matsu (the pine that cries at night) which shows how the stone and the pine tree became interchangeable. The stone has now been moved to the eastern entrance of the Nissaka tunnel of highway no. 1 (Kodama, *Nobe ezu,* 9:15).

9. *Yome ga ta* means "field of the daughter-in-law." Asai Ryōi's *Tōkaidō meishoki,* edited by Asakura Haruhiko, (Tokyo, 1979), 1:228, and Kodama, *Nobe ezu,* 9:21–22, both relate that the daughter-in-law had to plant a field of hemp during one morning. When the mother-in-law arrived to inspect the work, she was struck by a thunderbolt. Hence there is also a *shūtome ga ta* (field of the mother-in-law). A ginkgo tree was planted in remembrance of the daughter, which Asai Ryōi's work published in 1659–1660 claims was still there.

10. Presumably Kaempfer means 1 *chō* = 2.45 acres. However, *Tōkaidō meishoki* (chapter 3) and *Nobe ezu* (9:21) have 1 *tan* = .245 acres, which is more likely.

11. Accupuncture needles.

12. Rice cakes wrapped in oak leaves.

13. Hōzōji; see book 5, chapter 13, above.

14. "Die See Musasj Sjiro" could not be identified. However, Kasadera has a memorial site for Miyamoto Musashi (1584–1645) (Imai, *Ima mukashi Tōkaidō doku annai,* 212), and the sea could be seen from there.

15. *Shōzu ga uba* (also: *datsu eba*) is an old woman believed to be sitting at the river crossing to hell, taking away the clothes of the sinners. Kure, *Edo sanpu kikō,* 2:93,

has a photo of the figure, but the temple was burned down during World War II (Kodama, *Nobe ezu,* 15:23).

16. "Asta oder Atzta."

17. Garden bamboo.

18. While Kaempfer refers to two priests in this sentence (one sitting before, the other after the stone and cross), in the following sentences he describes just one of the priests without indicating the change from plural to singular.

19. "Skimmi" is Japanese star anise, commonly placed before religious statues and on graves.

20. Kyoto.

21. This should read five hundred years ago. See Bodart-Bailey, "The Most Magnificent Monastery," 25–26.

22. Posthumous name of the fourth shogun, Ietsuna (1641–1680).

23. The shoguns were not cremated but enshrined, and therefore the temple would have had at the most some hair or nail-clippings of the rulers.

24. "Jedo busche angethan." The interpretation of the abbot having a "bush" on his robe or holding a "bush" chosen by Scheuchzer (3:191) and Dohm (2:366) respectively is contradicted by the verb *angetan,* which means "dressed in" or "wearing." I take "Busche" to be a variant of the north-German "Buxe" (= trousers) and believe Kaempfer is referring to a *hakama.*

25. See book 5, chapter 13, note 30, above.

26. Kaempfer refers to the Sanmon of Chion-in, but is mistaken in the number of columns. See Bodart-Bailey, "The Most Magnificent Monastery," 29.

27. The temple no longer exists, but a similar chapel, where the Buddhist sutras are stored in a cupboard set on a wheel, which is turned to gain merit, can be found at Seiryō-ji, Saga, in the west of Kyoto. See also Bodart-Bailey, "Kyoto Three Hundred Years ago," 9.

28. See book 5, chapter 13, note 34, above.

29. A statue of *Shōzu ga uba;* see note 15 above. The statue is still there today.

30. The ears of those killed in Hideyoshi's campaigns against Korea (not Ezo) of 1592 and 1597.

31. See illustration on p. 381.

32. Kaempfer seems to have mistaken the figure of Basūsennin (Vasu) for that of the historical Buddha. The statue is one of the *nijūhachi bushū*, the twenty-eight attendants of Kannon. Its height is 156 cm. The temple is known as Sanjūsan gendō.

33. Thousand-armed Kannon.

34. The record was achieved in 1686, when a nineteen-year-old youth shot 13,053 arrows in twenty-four hours, of which 8,133 hit the target. The length of the veranda, which had the target at one end, is 118 meters. For Kaempfer's illustration, see Bodart-Bailey, "Kaempfer Restor'd," 30.

35. Nara was the capital from 710 to 784. Kaempfer refers to the large Buddha of Tōdaiji.

36. "Eiwónimatz oder Eisonomatz."

37. The temple had only a five-storied pagoda. Of Kaempfer's sketch (illustration on p. 430), only the explanations written in ink remain. The drawing of the plan in pencil has faded beyond recognition. The lettering in Kaempfer's text has therefore been omitted.

38. Japanese wisteria.

39. Mitsuya had three temples, of which only one remains, and the "idol" cannot be identified. It has therefore been suggested that this is the name of a temple (Imai, *Ima mukashi Tōkaidō doku annai,* 2:417; Kure, *Edo sanpu kikō,* 2:121; Saitō Makoto, trans., *Edo sanpu nikki* [Tokyo, 1977], 313), but a temple of this name cannot be traced. Old maps, however, show a tea house *(cha ya)* where the entertainment is likely to have taken place, which in turn might have had a statue with a similar-sounding name. Tamaoki Toyojirō, ed., *Osaka kochizu shūsei* (Osaka 1980), map no. 10.

40. Kaempfer's "Katama" is somewhat different in sound, but Hama Mikage (today: Mikage) was the port from which the stones (known as Mikage *ishi*) were shipped. *Kadokawa Nihon chimei jiten,* 28:1401.

41. Kaempfer obviously refers to the whole journey from Satsuma.

42. Literally: "frequently here and there some people are made to shed some hair because of the dogs." Kaempfer uses difficult-to-translate humor, which, however, is important to note because it indicates his perception of the so-called Laws of Compassion that supposedly oppressed the population.

43. "Namanda"; *butsu* has been supplied where Kaempfer uses the short form.

44. II Samuel 24:15. *Ekirei* = *ekibyō,* an epidemic.

45. Literally: "a hundred ten thousand times," i.e., one million times.

46. The eighth day of the fifth month according to the Japanese calendar, the day on which the fourth shogun, Ietsuna, died in 1680.

47. Sanskrit: Skanda, guardian deity, one of the eight generals serving the king of the South of the Four Heavenly Kings *(shi tennō),* usually portrayed with hands raised in prayer with his sword resting on his arms in a horizontal position.

48. Temple of the Zen sect. Kōdaiji is the name of the temple.

49. The second abbot of the temple, the Chinese monk Sengai (Donzui), began handing out *kayu* (rice gruel) in 1681. The kettle was made in 1682 and is still there.

50. *On* reading for "Kiyomizu."

51. No similar word for prayer flag could be traced; perhaps *Kayadhan,* Pali: a cloth tied around the waist.

52. Punishment by which the delinquent's body is smashed with a wheel-like structure. Kaempfer most probably used this figuratively to indicate crucifixion.

53. Philippines: Bantan peninsula.

54. Perhaps the Babuyan Islands north of Luzon.

55. "10. oder tausend Kistens"; this is either a slip of the pen or is supposed to denote a large, unknown number of boxes.

Appendix 2

1. Takizawa Takeo, *Nihon no kahei no rekishi* (Tokyo, 1996), 9. Other sources used for the information contained below include *Nihon rekishi daijiten,* entry "Keichō kingin," and Teruoka Yasutaka, "Saikaku jidai no kahei," in Ihara Saikaku, *Nihon eitaigura* (Tokyo, 1967), 321–328.

2. See above, p. 217.

3. *Nihon rekishi daijiten,* entry "Keichō *tsūhō.*"

4. *Nihon kokugo daijiten,* 10:407. At Kaempfer's time one *momme,* a unit of silver, was roughly one-sixtieth of a gold *ryō.*

5. See above, p. 217 (book 4, chapter 8).

6. *Kinsei fuzoku jiten,* 536–537.

7. See Valentijn, *Oud en Nieuw Oost-Indien,* 4:356.

8. Later the government also attempted to fix internal exchange rates. See Bodart-Bailey, "A Case of Political and Economic Expropriation," 185.

9. For details, see Joe Cribb et al., *The Coin Atlas* (New York, 1990), 47–48.

10. See above, p. 338.

11. See above, pp. 262 and 434.

12. See above, pp. 139 and 140 (book 4).

13. See above, p. 425 (book 5, chapter 13).

Glossary of Japanese Terms

The meanings given are those appropriate to Kaempfer's text.
For additional meanings, a dictionary should be consulted.

aidagin	broker's fee
ama no iwato	"heavenly rock door," behind which Amaterasu (Tenshō daijin) hid in a cave and deprived the world of light
amasake	sweet rice wine
Amida	Amitabha
Anan sonja	Buddha's disciple Ananda
Arara sennin	Buddha's teacher Alara Kalama
aratame	population survey
atotsuke	traveling box, fastened at the back of a horse's saddle
awa mori	alcoholic beverage made of millet
azuki	red beans
ban	guard
bashi	same as *hashi*—bridge
Benzaiten	Sarasvati, the goddess of good fortune
bezaisen	small Japanese vessel with one sail
bikuni	nun of a special order, usually attached to but not living within a temple
Bitchū	modern Okayama prefecture
Bizen	modern Okayama prefecture
bosatsu	bodhisattva, a Buddhist saint
bōzu	Buddhist priest, a bonze
bu	coin worth one-fourth *ryō*
bugyō	magistrate; also used by Kaempfer for *bugyō nin,* a commissioned official
bukkyō	the Buddhist faith
Bungo	province in Kyushu, modern Ōita prefecture
bungo sō	lit.: bonze of Bungo, a Christian
Bunjo	mythical figure; according to one legend, she turned into Benzaiten
buppō	Buddhist law or doctrine
bushi	samurai, a soldier
butsu	Buddha, Buddhism, a Buddhist statue
butsu dō	Buddhism
Buzen	modern Fukuoka prefecture

byōsho	ancestral shrine, mortuary tablet
chabune	small freight vessel
chi	wisdom
chijin godai	five generations of terrestrial gods of Shinto
chigai dana	irregular shelves
chigyō	a (rice) stipend
Chikugo	modern Saga prefecture
Chikuzen	modern Fukuoka prefecture
chin	used as personal pronoun by the emperor when referring to himself in speech
chō	measurement usually of 60 *ken,* 109 meters, 119 yards; a street, town quarter; see appendix 2
chōshi	city messenger
chōshi no mono	city messenger
chū	middle
chūgoshō	also: *naka oku koshō:* valets, personal servants of the lord permitted to enter his personal rooms: the *naka oku*
chūjō	court title of the fourth rank
chūnagon	court title of the third rank
chūtō	one of the five Buddhist precepts: not to steal
Dai Nihon ōdaiki	a chronological account of the first 113 Japanese emperors, beginning with Jimmu Tennō, by Yoshida Mitsuyoshi (1598–1672), first published in 1649
daidokoro mono	kitchen staff
Daijingū	Ise shrine
daijō daijin	court title of the first rank
daikan	intendant, shogunal agent
daimyō	great territorial lord
daimyōjin	name or title for an important god
dainagon	court title of the third rank
Dainichi nyorai	Mahāvairocana, Dainichi Buddha
dairi	emperor; the Imperial court; the Imperial palace
Dandoku	Mount Dandaka
danna	congregation of a temple
Daruma	Bodhidharma
Deshima	man-made island in the harbor of Nagasaki on which the Dutch were located; also Dejima
dō	same as *michi;* the Way
dōchūki	travel guide
dōshin	a lower military official and solider (for a detailed description, see book 4, chapter 2)
Edo	Tokyo

efumi	stepping on Christian images
ema	votive picture, originally of a horse
en nichi	festival day of a temple or shrine
En no gyōja	founder of Shugen dō, the order of the *yamabushi*
Enma ō	king of hell
ensho gura	ammunition store
eta	outcast
eto	the twelve astrological signs that make up the sixty-year cycle
Ezo	Ainu, Hokkaido
fuda no tsuji	location for official announcements
Fudō myō ō	Acala, the God of Fire
fujō	unclean
Fuku shū	Fukien
funa ban	boat guard
funagura	boat sheds
furo	Japanese bath; at Kaempfer's time, a steam bath
futsu mochi	Artemisia dumplings
gawa	same as *kawa*—river
gege	commoner, as opposed to *kuge,* a Kyoto aristocrat
Gekū	see Gekū miya
Gekū miya	Outer Shrine at Ise
genkan ban	guard at the entrance of a residence
genkan chō	register kept at the *genkan ban*
Genroku	era name for the years 1688–1704
gi	justice, righteousness
Gion	ox-headed deity, Gozutennō
go	honorific prefix
go hyaku kai	the five hundred rules or "admonitions" to be observed by Buddhist priests
go i	court title of the fifth rank
goban dokoro	shogunal guard house
goban gashira	head of the shogunal guard
gobansho	see *goban dokoro*
gōdō	a wild and cruel robber
godō	spiritual enlightenment
gogatsu gonichi	the fifth day of the fifth month; also known as Boys' Day
gokai	the five Buddhist precepts
gokasho	the five cities directly under shogunal control
gokuraku	Buddhist paradise
gokuya	prison
gongen	an avatar, an incarnation of Buddha; the deified Tokugawa Ieyasu

gonin gumi	corporation of five households
goō	pills made of paper by the *yamabushi*
gorōjū	see *rōjū*
gosanke	the Three Related Houses of the Tokugawa family
gosekku	the five festivals
goshuin	the ruler's cinnabar seal
gosoba	lit.: at [the lord's] side; the lord's chamberlains and personal attendants
Gozutennō	see Gion
gū	alternative reading for *miya*
gyo	honorific prefix
Gyō	Chinese mythical emperor Yao
gyōja	ascetic
hachi no maki	eighth volume
hachibun	one-eighth of the purchase price of a house to be paid to the council of the street
hachiku	black bamboo *(Phyllostachys nigra)*
Hachiman	god of war
Hakubaji	temple of the white horse
hamaguri	clam
hana gin	lit.: flower money, a tax collected from the foreign trade
hana shikimi	see *shikimi*
hasamibako	lacquered traveling box carried at the end of a pole
hashi	bridge
hassaku	lit.: the first day of the eighth month. On this day the farmers presented some of their first rice crop to their superiors, and the day became one of giving presents.
hassaku gin	money paid on the first day of the eighth month
hatamoto	bannermen, minor vassals of the Tokugawa shogun
hatchō gane	musical instrument of eight bells
Higo	modern Kumamoto prefecture
Hikozan	mountain in the province of Buzen, climbed by *yamabushi* of the Tōzanha
hime gai	hard-shelled mussel. (*Mytilus coruscus*)
hina	doll
hissha	scribe
hito aratame	registration of the population
hito jichi	hostage
Hizen	modern Nagasaki prefecture
hōjōrō	cage for animals for the Buddhist ceremony of *hōjō,* "setting free"
Hokke kyō	Lotus sutra of Buddhism

Hokke shū	Hokke sect of Buddhism
hon tsūji	regular interpreters
hongū	main shrine
honji	main temple
honmaru	main, central building or keep of a castle complex
Honzanha	a sect of *yamabushi*
hora no kai	conch shell
hotoke	Buddha, Buddhist gods
hyakuninban	lit.: hundred-man-guard; guard at Edo castle
Hyakusai	Kudara
i	rank, position
ichi bu	one *bu;* one-fourth of one *ryō*
ihai	mortuary tablet
Ikkō *shū*	Ikkō sect
imi	taboo, impurity
imori	water lizard
in	seal
in	symbolic sign made with the fingers
in	the principle of yin of Chinese philosophy
in yō	the interacting principles of yin and yang in Chinese philosophy, the cosmic dual forces
inari	fox
inusō	"conjuring strokes" of the *yamabushi*
irataka no juzu	long rosary of the *yamabushi*
Isanagi	progenitor of the terrestrial gods
Ise	location of Ise daijingū, the Grand Shrine of Ise
Ise miya	Grand Shrine of Ise dedicated to Shinto's most important deities
ishi tataki	same as *sekirei,* a wagtail
Izumi	modern Osaka prefecture
Izumo no ōyashiro	Izumo Shrine dedicated to the god Susano o
jain	one of the five Buddhist precepts: not to commit adultery
jigoku	Buddhist hell
jijū	court title of the first rank
jikkai	the ten Buddhist precepts
Jikokuten	one of the Four Dewas, or Four Heavenly Kings
jin	humanity
jinja	Shinto shrine
jinsha	humane, virtuous person
jisha	building of a Buddhist temple
jisha	Buddhist temples and Shinto shrines
jisha bugyō	commissioner of temples and shrines

jisha go bugyō	see *jisha bugyō*
jishi gin	land tax
jishinban	guard of a street performed by the citizens
jishonin	owner of plot; landlord
Jizō	Ksitigarbha bodhisattva, guarding deity of children, pregnant women, and travelers
jō	upper
Jōdo *shū*	Jōdo sect of Buddhism
jōgyōji	permanent city officials
Jōkyō	era name for the years 1684–1688
ju dō	Confucianism
jū momme	ten *momme*
judōsha	a Confucian
judōshi	teacher of Confucianism
judōshū	Confucian sect
jūji	resident priest
jūninshū	group of ten soldiers, denoted the *tomi ban* at Nagasaki
junrei	pilgrimage, especially to the thirty-three most important Kannon temples
kachi	foot soldiers
kado	door, gate
kai mono tsukai	purveyors
kaji dōgu	fire extinguishing tools
kama	scythe, sickle
kami	god, soul, spirit; also: title of a feudal lord
kami michi	same as Shinto
kami na tsuki	lit.: month without gods; October, the month when the gods leave their temples to reside with the emperor
kamishimo	ceremonial dress: an over-jacket with stiffened shoulders *(kataginu)* and divided skirt *(hakama)*
kamme	monetary unit; one *kan* equals one hundred *ryō* or taels
kampaku	court title of the first rank
kana	Japanese phonetic writing system
kana za	treasury
kanaban nakama	guild of the officials of the treasury
kanban	abbreviation for *kanban bōeki,* lit.: signboard trade, a system of trading goods. The word is used by Kaempfer for the sales of foreign goods.
kanjin bikuni	begging nun
kanjin bōsu	begging monk
kanmotsu	taxation
Kannon	Avalokitesvara, the Goddess of Mercy

Kannon gyō	twenty-fifth section of the eighth book of the Lotus sutra, also known as *fumonbon*, dealing with salvation through Kannon, the goddess of mercy
kannushi	shinto priest or shrine warden
kanoe uma	according to the sixty-year cycle, the name appropriate for the year 1690
kanoto hitsuji	according to the sixty-year cycle, the name appropriate for the year 1691
kansen	also *kanzeni, zeni,* or *mon:* the smallest coin; see appendix 2
kappa	coat
karajiri	horse with a saddle only
karō	elder regents of a lord's household
karō	wheat noodles
karōtsu	see *karō*
kasen gin	honorarium, brokerage fee
kasho	city plot
Kashō sonja	Buddha's disciple Kassapa
Kasuga dai myōjin	tutelary deity of Kasuga shrine
katabira	hemp summer kimono
katana	sword
kawa	river
kazu	number
keiko tsūji	apprentice interpreter
keisei machi	prostitutes' quarter
ken	now: 1.82 meters, 1.99 yards; in the Edo period there were regional variations
kinchū sama	the emperor
kirishitan bugyō	commissioner in charge of Christians
Kirisutandō	Christianity
kitō	prayer, exorcism
kitsune	fox, often believed to be an evil spirit
kitte no shitagaki	official record of travel permits granted
kō	honorific used for the emperor
ko tsūji	junior interpreter
koban	monetary unit equivalent to one *ryō*
kogashira	official title; lit.: small head
kogatana	knife
kogumi	small corporation
kogumi gashira	head of a small corporation
kogumi oya	see *kogumi gashira*
koku	measurement: 47.654 U.S. gallons, 5.119 U.S. bushels
Kokuzō bosatsu	Akasa-garbha bodhisattva

komegura	rice store
Kōmokuten	one of the Four Dewas, or Four Heavenly Kings
kongō zue	staff of the *yamabushi* and other religious
konpura nakama	see *kai mono tsukai*
kōsen	commission, brokerage
Kōshi	Confucius
koshō	page, valet
kozukai	errand boy, servant
kugatsu kokonoka	see *kugatsu kunichi*
kugatsu kunichi	ninth day of the ninth month, celebrated as *kunichi,* the festival of the god Suwa in Nagasaki
kuge	Kyoto aristocracy
Kumano *no bikuni*	nun attached to the Kumano temple; see *bikuni*
Kumano *no goō*	supernatural pills from Kumano
kumi gashira	head of a corporation
kunichi	see *kugatsu kunichi*
kusu no ki	camphor tree
kutsuwa	horse bit, brothel keeper
kuzu	arrowroot *(Pueraria Thunbergiana)* Benth.
kuzu kazura	see *kuzu*
kyō	Buddhist scripture
kyō	the capital: Kyoto
kyūnin shū	lower samurai receiving an annual stipend
ma	evil spirit
machi	street, ward, measurement; see appendix 2
machi toshiyori	city administrator, mayor
Magada koku	Magadha province: modern Bihar, Bengal
mairu	humble form for "to come," "to go"; used specifically for visiting temples and shrines
man	ten thousand
manjū	buns, usually with a sweet bean-jam filling
maro	personal pronoun used by the emperor for himself in writing
Maruyama	prostitutes' quarter at Nagasaki
Maso Bosa	Chinese god of the sea
massha	subordinate Shinto shrine
matsu	pine
Matsudaira	family name of the Tokugawa, bestowed as special honor also on other families
matsuji	branch temple
matsuri	religious festival
matsuru	to celebrate
Mauri ga shima	legendary island, near Fukien

mawari ban	guard or watch doing the rounds
medetai	lucky
medetō	congratulations
metsuke	inspector
mezurashii	something rare and worthy of admiration
mi	honorific prefix
mi okuri bune	guard boats escorting foreign ships out of the harbor
michi	same as *dō,* a way
mikado	emperor
mikoshi	portable shrine
mikoto	title used for the early Shinto deities
miya	Shinto shrine
miya suzume	"temple sparrows," guardians of secondary shrines
Miyako	Kyoto
mizunoe saru	the year 1692 according to the sixty-year cycle
mō	monetary unit; one-tenth of one *rin;* as weight: one-thousandth of one *momme*
mogō	one of the five Buddhist precepts: not to lie
momme	monetary unit: a mace; 60 *momme* = 1 *koban*
mon	family crest, coat of arms
mon	small brass coin; see appendix 2
monban	guard of the gates
monzeki	title of aristocratic abbots
Morisaki dai gongen	deity of the Morisaki shrine
Mōshi	Mencius
mukuri kokuri	*mukuri* = *mōko* = the Mongols; *kokuri* = Kōkuri = Kokuryo = Korea; disbelievers
Musashi	modern Saitama prefecture and Tokyo city
myōjin	honorific name or title for a god
nai tsūji	private interpreter
naidaijin	court title of the second rank
Naigū	also: Naikū, the Inner Shrine at Ise
nakatomi barai	Shinto ritual of purification
Namanda	see Namu amida butsu
Namu amida butsu	a prayer: hail to thee, Amida Buddha
nanori	personal name of a samurai
negi	Shinto priest
nenban	official serving in annual rotation
nenban toshi yori	elders of the *nenban*
nenbutsu	prayer to Amida; see Namu amida butsu
nenbutsu kō	brotherhood or voluntary prayer association
nengō	era name

nengu	annual tax
nengyōji	officials serving one year only; in Nagasaki, the go-between officials between the magistrates and mayors
nengyōji beya	room of the *nengyōji*
ni no maru	the second castle, keep, or building within a larger castle complex
nichi gyōshi	messenger employed by a street
Nikkō dera	the Tōshōgū at Nikkō, a temple dedicated to the first Tokugawa shogun, Ieyasu
nin nō	Japanese calendrical system counting from A.D. 660, which is believed to have been the beginning of the government of the first emperor, Jimmu
Nihon ōdaiki	see *Dai Nihon ōdaiki*
nishi no kuni	lit.: the western country: Kyushu
Nishidomari	guard station overlooking Nagasaki harbor
norikake	horse carrying a pack on each side with material spread in between to form a flat seat for the rider
norimono	palanquin
ō	honorific prefix (meaning "large")
ō	honorific title for the emperor
ō dai shin ō	hereditary emperors, beginning with Jimmu
ō tomi	the "exalted retinue" of a god in a religious procession
ō tsūji	upper, chief interpreters
ōban	a large coin; seven gold *koban;* see appendix 2
oboe	memorandum
Ōdaiki	see *Dai Nihon ōdaiki*
ōgosho	title used for the first shogun, Ieyasu
ōgumi gashira	heads of great corporations
ōgumi oya	see *ōgumi gashira*
ōharai	Shinto purification, exorcism
oi	according to Kaempfer, the *yamabushi*'s pouch for personal belongings; otherwise described as a box with a small door and legs, to stand up when put down, carried on the back by *yamabushi* and other religious
ōkura	shogunal grain storage
okurina	posthumous name
ōmetsuke	chief inspector
Ōmine	sacred mountain of the Honzanha sect of *yamabushi*
omote	the front
on	honorific prefix
onjū	one of the five Buddhist precepts: to abstain from alcohol
oranda	Dutch

Oshioni no mikoto alternative name for the god Susano o
oshō abbot
Ōshū all the country to the north of the old Shirakawa: today's Fukushima, Miyagi, Iwate, and Aomori prefectures
otabi tokoro the place to which the gods travel
ōteguchi main gate of a castle
otona ward or street headman
ōyashiro *kun* pronunciation of *taisha,* before World War II, the Izumo Shrine, but now a title used also by a number of other important shrines
Papenberg island in the harbor of Nagasaki: Takaboko yama
Peiron Chinese dragon-boat festival introduced at Nagasaki in 1655
rei decorum, propriety
reibi same as *sanjitsu* (the three days): the first, fifteenth, and twenth-eighth of each month, which were celebrated as holidays. Kaempfer seems to use the word in the wider sense of holiday.
rin small monetary unit of varying value
Rinzai *ha* Rinzai school of Zen
Ro Chinese province of Lu
rōjū senior councilor
Rōshi Lao-tzu
rōya prison
ryō see *koban*
ryōbu shintō most dominant stream of Shinto during the Tokugawa period, accepting Buddhist gods as reincarnations of Shinto deities
sadaijin court title of the second rank
Saikoku Western country: Kyushu
saji lower-class city messengers
sakana snacks served when drinking *sake*
sakazuki *sake* cup
sake rice wine
sakuji bugyō magistrate of building works
sama title: lord
san no maru the third castle, keep, or building within a larger castle complex
sangatsu sannichi the third day of the third month, the Girls' Festival
sangū pilgrimage to Ise
sanshō Japanese pepper tree, prickly ash *(Xanthoxyum piperitum* DC)
satori spiritual enlightenment
satsuki azalea *(Rhododendron lateritium)*
satsuki the fifth month of the lunar calendar (the rainy season)

segaki	rite for feeding the hungry ghosts of departed souls, formerly held throughout the year but nowadays mainly held at *obon*
seichō kaki	senior scribes
seijin	sage
Seitenjiku	West India
sekibyō	the pox
sekku	see *reibi*
sesshō	one of the five Buddhist precepts: not to take life
Settsu	modern Hyōgo prefecture
sha	Shinto shrine
Shaka	Shakyamuni; Gautama; the historical Buddha
shaku	measurement: 30.3 centimeters, .994 foot
shakujō	the staff of the god Jizō with four rings on top
shanin	Shinto priest
shichigatsu nanoka	see *shichiseki tanabata*
shichiseki tanabata	festival of Tanabata on the seventh day of the seventh month
shikimi	Japanese star anise (Illicium religiosum *Sieb. et Zucc.*)
shin	alternate reading for *kami*
shin	heart
Shinano	modern Nagano prefecture
shinbatsu	divine punishment
Shindai ki	the first book of *Nihon shoki*
shinja	alternate form of *shinsha*
shinsha	person who follows the religion of Shinto
shinshū	Shinto or people who follow the religion of Shinto
Shintō	the Japanese native religion, Shinto
shintōshū	see *shinshū*
shisho	the Four Books of Confucianism: the Great Learning, the Doctrine of the Mean, the Confucian Analects, and the Works of Mencius
shita yaku	lower-class samurai, performing a variety of official functions
shitennō	the Four Devas, or four guardian deities or heavenly kings
Shō ō	the Chinese King Chao (Zhao-wang)
Shōgaku	the Confucian classic, *The Elementary Learning*
shōgatsu	New Year
shōmyō	lesser territorial lords
shōnagon	court title of the fourth rank
shōnin	title used by the Ikkō sect for its priors
shōshō	court title of the fourth rank
shu	unit of silver; sixteen *shu* = one *koban*
shū	faith, religion, religious sect
shukke	Buddhist monk
shuku	post station

Shun	Chinese mythical sage king
shūshi	religious sect
So	see Sokoku
sobashū	chamberlain
sobayōnin	grand chamberlain
sode no shita	lit.: under the sleeve; a bribe
sojō	petition
Sokoku	ancient Chinese province of Ch'u
Sōtō *ha*	see Sōtō *shu*
soto kamae	outer enclosure of a castle
soto machi	outside city, a division of the city of Nagasaki
Sōtō *shu*	the Sōtō sect of Zen
sowaas	alloy of gold and copper
sugi	Japanese cedar tree
sui furo	Japanese bath
Sumiyoshi daimyōjin	tutelary deity of Sumiyoshi
sun	measurement: one-tenth of one *shaku:* 3.03 centimeters, 1.2 inches
Suruga	modern Shizuoka prefecture
Suwa	tutelary deity of Suwa
Suwa miya	Suwa shrine
suzu kake	belt with tassels worn around the neck by *yamabushi*
tael	six tael = sixty *momme* = one *koban*
taifu	court title of the fifth rank or above
Taikō	title taken by Toyotomi Hidoyoshi
tairō	great councilor
Takabokoyama	island in the harbor of Nagasaki
takama no hara	heavenly fields of Shinto
takama no hara kami todomari	a prayer from the *Engishiki,* the sentence meaning "The gods are on the heavenly plain"
takara gai	cowrie or porcelain shell
takara yaku	official of the treasury
tame	a place where water is stored; infirmary of a prison
Tamonten	one of the Four Dewas, or Four Heavenly Kings
tango no sekku	see *gogatsu gonichi*
tanomu no sekku	see *shichiseki tanabata*
tarate	lotus flower
Tate	see Tateyama
Tateyama	mountain in Nagasaki
tayū	honorific title formerly used by Shinto priests, originally a Chinese court rank
tedai	senior official assisting a *daikan*

tei	title used for the emperor
ten	heaven
Tendai	Tendai sect of Buddhism
Tenjiku	India
Tenjin	deified Sugawara Michizane
tenjin shichi dai	seven generations of gods of Shinto
tenjō bito	Kyoto aristocracy
tenshi	title used for the emperor
Tenshō daijin	Amaterasu, the son god(dess), the highest god of the Shinto pantheon
Tenshō kōdaijin	same as Tenshō daijin
tera	Buddhist temple
tokin	hat or decoration worn on the forehead by *yamabushi*
toko	alcove of a room
toko waki	secondary alcove
Tomachi	one of the two guard stations overlooking Nagasaki harbor
tomi daka	watchtower
tomiban	guard scanning the distance, mostly the sea
tono sama	title: lord, prince
tori fuda	small branded wooden docket permitting passage
torii	ceremonial gate of a Shinto shrine
toshiyori	elder
Tōzanha	sect of *yamabushi*
Tsu no kuni	Naniwa, modern Osaka
tsubaki	camellia
tsubo	the square area of one *ken* or fathom; also a small garden at the back of a house
tsuchinoe tatsu	the year 1688 according to the sixty-year cycle
tsuchinoto mi	the year 1689 according to the sixty-year cycle
tsuetsuki	inspector, overseer
tsuitachi	first day of the month
tsūji	interpreter
tsūshin	official messenger
uchi machi	inner city, part of the city of Nagasaki
udaijin	court title of the second rank
ujigami	tutelary deity of a location
ura	the back
uta	song or verse
wakagorōjū	see *wakatoshiyori*
wakatoshiyori	junior councilor
wakizashi	short sword
yaku ryō	salary

Yakushi	Bhechadjaguru, the Physician of Souls, God of Medicine
yama	mountain
yamabushi	one who "lies" in the mountains, a mountain priest
Yamashiro	present Kyoto prefecture
Yamato	modern Nara prefecture
yarimochi	lance bearer
yashiro	Shinto shrine
yatsume no waranzu	straw sandals
yō	principle of yang of Chinese philosophy
yoriki	military officials (for a detailed description, see book 4, chapter 2)
yūhitsu	scribe
yui itsu	Shinto sect
zazen	religious meditation as practiced by the Zen sect
Zen *shū*	Zen sect
zeni	small brass coin; see appendix 2
Zōjōten	one of the Four Dewas, or Four Heavenly Kings
zushi	small shrine

Bibliography

I. Manuscripts

Algemeen Rijksarchief, The Hague: ARA, NFJ 104.
British Library Add. Ms. 5252, f. 45.
British Library, Oriental Collections, Or. 75, f. 3, 4, 7, 15, 16, Or. 14480/2.
British Library, Sloane 2912, 2921, 2923, 3060, 3061, 3062, 3063.
Niedersächsische Landesbibliothek, Hannover, Leibniz Briefe 1007.
Staatsarchiv Detmold, L 16 O K: Engelbert Kaempfer's will.

II. Published Works

Abe Tokiharu. *Illustrated Fishes of the World in Color (Genshoku gyorui daizukan).* Tokyo, 1987.

Abeyasekere, Susan. *Jakarta, A History.* Oxford University Press, 1989.

Adelung, Johann Christoph. *Grammatisch-kritisches Wörterbuch der Hochdeutschen Mundart.* Vienna, 1808.

Aoki Okikatsu. *Tōmon jissaku.* In *Nihon keizai taiten,* vol. 20. Tokyo, 1966–1971.

Asai Ryōi. *Tōkaidō meishoki,* edited by Asakura Haruhiko, 2 vols. Tokyo, 1979.

Barthold, V.V. *La décourverte de l'Asie.* Paris, 1947.

Blacker, Carmen. *The Catalpa Bow.* Torquay, 1975.

———. "Forgotten Practices of the Past: Kaempfer's Strange Description of the Japanese Emperor." In *The Furthest Goal: Engelbert Kaempfer's Encounter with Tokugawa Japan,* edited by B. M. Bodart-Bailey and Derek Massarella. Folkstone, 1995.

Blussé, J. L. "The Story of an Ecological Disaster: The Dutch East India Company and Batavia (1619–1799)." In *Strange Company: Chinese Settlers, Mestizo Women, and the Dutch in VOC Batavia.* Dordrecht, 1986.

Bodart-Bailey, Beatrice M. "A Case of Political and Economic Expropriation: The Monetary Reform of the Fifth Tokugawa Shogun." *Papers on Far Eastern History* 39 (March 1989).

———. "Councillor Defended: *Matsukage Nikki* and Yanagisawa Yoshiyasu." *Monumenta Nipponica* 34.4 (1979).

———. "Kaempfer Restor'd." *Monumenta Nipponica* 43.1 (1988).

———. *Kenperu to Tokugawa Tsunayoshi.* Translated by N. Naka. Tokyo, 1994.

———. "Kyoto Three Hundred Years Ago." *Nichibunken Newsletter* 9 (May 1991).

———. "The Laws of Compassion." *Monumenta Nipponica* 40.2 (1985).

———. "The Most Magnificent Monastery and Other Famous Sights: The Japanese Paintings of Engelbert Kaempfer." *Japan Review* 3 (1992):28–29.

———. "The Persecution of Confucianism in Tokugawa Japan." *Monumenta Nipponica* 48.3 (1993).

———. "Preliminary Report on the Manuscripts of Engelbert Kaempfer in the British Library." In *British Library Occasional Papers,* edited by Yu-Ying Brown. London, 1990.

———. "The Significance of the Chamberlain Government of the Fifth Tokugawa Shogun." In *A Northern Prospect: Australian Papers on Japan.* Japanese Studies Association of Australia, 1981.

———. "Tokugawa Tsunayoshi (1646–1709), A Weberian Analysis." *Asiatische Studien/Études Asiatiques* 43.1 (1989).

———. "Writing *The History.*" In *The Furthest Goal: Engelbert Kaempfer's Encounter with Tokugawa Japan,* edited by B. M. Bodart-Bailey and Derek Massarella. Folkstone, 1995.

Bodart-Bailey, Beatrice M., and Derek Massarella, ed. *The Furthest Goal: Engelbert Kaempfer's Encounter with Tokugawa Japan.* Folkstone, 1995.

Bowers, John Z., and Robert W. Carrubba. "Drug Abuse and Sexual Binding Spells in Seventeenth Century Asia: Essays from the *Amoenitatum Exoticarum* of Engelbert Kaempfer." *Journal of the History of Medicine and Allied Sciences* 33.3 (1978).

Boxer, C. R., ed. *A True Description of the Mighty Kingdoms of Japan and Siam by François Caron and Joost Schouten.* London, 1935.

Caron, François. *Beschrijvinghe van het machtigh Coninckrijcke Japan.* 1645.

Caron, François, and Jod. Schouten. *Wahrhaftige Beschreibungen zweyer mächtigen Königreiche Jappan und Siam.* Nürnberg, 1663.

Chassigneux, Edmond. "Rica de Oro et Rica de Plata." *T'oung Pao* 30 (1933):70.

Ching, Julia. "China und die Autonomie der Moral: der Fall des Christian Wolff." In *Gegenentwürfe: 24 Lebensläufe für eine andere Theologie,* edited by Hermann Häring and Karl-Josef Kuschel. Munich: Piper, 1988.

Cholmondeley, Lionel Berners. *The History of the Bonin Islands.* London, 1915.

Claudius, Matthias. *Ein Tropfen aus dem Ozean,* edited by Gunter Albrecht. Berlin, 1975.

Cooper, Michael. *They Came to Japan.* Berkeley, 1965.

Cortazzi, Hugh. *Isles of Gold: Antique Maps of Japan.* New York, 1983.

Cribb, Joe, et al. *The Coin Atlas.* New York, 1990.

Dahlgren, E. W. "A Contribution to the History of the Discovery of Japan." *Transactions of the Japan Society of London* 11 (1913).

Dohm, Christian Wilhelm. *Nachricht die Urschrift der Kämpferischen Beschreibung von Japan betreffend.* Lemgo, 1774.

Doitsu Nihon Kenkyū Jo, ed. *Doitsu jin no mita Genroku jidai Kenperu ten.* Tokyo, 1991.

Du Mans, Raphael. *Estat de la Perse.* 1660; Paris, 1890.

Edo Bakufu Chiri Hensan Shirabekata, ed. *Shinpen Sagami kuni fudōki kō.* Tokyo, 1975.

Ema Tsutomu et al., ed. *Kinsei fuzoku jiten.* Tokyo, 1967.

Encyclopaedia Britannica. 1969.

Friedberg, E., ed. *Corpus Juris Canonici,* 2 vols. Leipzig, 1879; reprint, Graz, 1959.

Frois, Luis. *Die Geschichte Japans,* translated and edited by G. Schurhammer and E. A. Voretzsch. Leipzig, 1926.

Fujiyamabō Hyakka Jiten Henshūbu, ed. *Kokumin hyakka daijiten.* Tokyo, 1936.

Gardner, Kenneth B. *Descriptive Catalogue of Japanese Books in the British Library Printed before 1700.* London, 1993.

Gay, Peter, *The Enlightenment: An Interpretation.* London, 1967.

Gebhard, J. F. *Het Leven van Mr. Nicolas Cornelisz Witsen.* Utrecht, 1881.

Gerhardt, C. I. *Die philosophischen Schriften von Gottfried Wilhelm Leibniz.* Hildesheim, 1961 (facsimile Berlin 1890 edition).

Gesner, Conrad. *Historiae animalium.* Tiguri, 1551–1587.

Gibert, Lucien. *Dictionnaire historique et geographique de la Mandchourie.* Hong Kong, 1934.

Gilbert, W. S. Libretto of *The Mikado or the Town of Titipu,* first produced London, 1885.

Goldsmith, Oliver. *The Citizen of the World.* In *Collected Works of Oliver Goldsmith,* edited by Arthur Friedman. Oxford, 1966.

Gottsched, Johann Christoph. *Erste Gründe der gesamten Weltweisheit.* Hildesheim, 1983 (facsimile of the 7th edition of Leipzig, 1762).

Grimm, Jacob and Wilhelm. *Deutsches Wörterbuch,* 42 vols. Leipzig, 1860.

Haga Tōru. "Kane wa Ueno ka Asakusa ka?" In *Edo no kurashi 122 hanashi,* edited by Nihon Fuzokushi Gakkai. Tokyo, 1995.

Hamilton, Alexander. *New Account of the East Indies.* London, 1727; reprint, London, 1930.

Haren, Onno Zwier van. *Proeve, op de leevens-beschryvingen der nederlandsche doorlugtige mannen: behelzende het leeven van Joannes Camphuis.* Tezwolle, 1772.

Hay, John, ed. *De Rebus Japonicis, Indicis & Peruanis Epistolae Recentiores.* Antwerp, 1605.

Herbert, Jean. *Shinto: The Fountain-head of Japan.* London, 1967.

Hotta Masaatsu, ed. *Kansei chōshū shokafu,* 26 vols. Tokyo, 1964–1967.

Hotta Masatoshi. *Yōgen roku.* In *Zoku zoku gunsho ruijū,* vol. 13. Tokyo, 1906–1909.

Hüls, Hans. "Zur Geschichte des Drucks von Kaempfers 'Geschichte und Beschreibung von Japan' und zur sozialökonomischen Struktur von Kaempfers Lesepublikum im 18. Jahrhundert." In *Engelbert Kaempfer zum 330. Geburtstag,* edited by Hans Hüls and Hans Hoppe. Lemgo, 1982.

Hüls, Hans, and Hans Hoppe, ed. *Engelbert Kaempfer zum 330. Geburtstag.* Lemgo, 1982.

Ichthyological Society of Japan, ed. *Dictionary of Japanese Fish Names and Their Foreign Equivalents (Gyorui zukan).* Tokyo, 1981.

Ijsbrants [Isbrant, Ysbrants] Evert, Ides (van Glückstadt). *Driejaarige Reize naar China.* Amsterdam, 1704, 1710.

Ikeda Shōichirō. *Edo jidai yōgo kōshō jiten.* Tokyo, 1984.

Imai Kingo. *Ima mukashi Tōkaidō doku annai.* Reprint, Tokyo, 1994.

Inaba Chiyomi. *Nagasaki hitori aruki.* Privately published, 1988.

Ishii Ryōsuke, ed. *Gotōke reijo.* In *Kinsei hōsei shiryō sōsho,* 2. Tokyo, 1938.

Itasawa Takeo. *Nichiran bunka kōshōshi no kenkyū.* 1959.

Kadokawa Nihon Chimei Daijiten Hensan Iinkai, ed. *Kadokawa Nihon chimei daijiten.* Tokyo, 1988.

Kaempfer, Engelbert. *Amoenitatum exoticarum politico-physico-medicarum fasciculi V,* . . . Lemgo, 1712.

———. *Die Briefe Engelbert Kaempfers,* edited by Karl Meier-Lemgo. Wiesbaden, 1965.

———. *Disputatio Medica Inauguralis Exhibens Decadem Observationum Exoticarum* . . . (Leiden, 1694), translated by H. Hüls and Rohtraut Müller-König. In *Engelbert Kaempfer zum 330. Geburtstag,* edited by Hans Hüls and Hans Hoppe. Lemgo, 1982.

———. *Edo sanpu kikō,* translated by Kure Shūzō, 2 vols. Tokyo, 1928–1929.

———. *Edo sanpu nikki,* translated by Saitō Makoto. Tokyo, 1977.

———. *Flora Japonica,* translated and edited by Wolfgang Muntschick. Wiesbaden, 1983.

———. *Geschichte und Beschreibung von Japan,* edited by Christian Wilhelm Dohm, 2 vols. Lemgo, 1777–1779; facsimile, Stuttgart, 1964.

———. *The History of Japan, Giving An Account of the ancient and present State and Government of that Empire; of Its Temples, Palaces, Castles and other Buildings; of Its Metals, Minerals, Trees, Plants, Animals, Birds and Fishes; of The Chronology and Succession of the Emperors, Ecclesiastical and Secular; of The Original Descent, Religions, Customs, and Manufactures of the Natives, and of their Trade and Commerce with the Dutch and Chinese. Together with a Description of the Kingdom of Siam. Written in High-Dutch by Engelbertus Kaempfer, M.D. Physician to the Dutch Embassy to the Emperor's Court; and translated from his Original Manuscript, never before printed, by J. G. Scheuchzer, F.R.S. and a member of the College of Physicians, London. With the Life of the Author, and an Introduction.* London, 1727.

———. *Exercitatio politica de Majestatis Divisione* (Danzig, 1673), translated into German by R. Müller-König. In *Engelbert Kaempfer zum 330. Geburtstag,* edited by Hans Hüls and Hans Hoppe. Lemgo, 1982.

———. *Nihonshi,* translated by Imai Tadashi. Tokyo, 1973,

———. *Die Reisetagebücher Engelbert Kaempfers,* edited by Karl Meier-Lemgo. Wiesbaden, 1968.

Kant, Immanuel. *Kants Werke.* Reprint, Berlin, 1968.

Kapitza, P. "Japan in der deutschen Literatur des 17. und 18. Jahrhunderts." In *Bonner Zeitschrift für Japanologie.* Bonn, 1981.

———. "Lessings *Tonsine*-Entwurf im Kontext europäischer Japonaiserien des 18. Jahrhunderts." *Doitsu bungaku* 63 (1979).

Katagiri Kazuo. *Oranda tsūji Imamura Genemon Eisei*. Tokyo, 1995.
Kawaguchi Kenji et al. *Nenchū gyōji girei jiten*. Reprint, Tokyo, 1987.
Kodama Kōta, ed. *Tōkaidō bunken nobe ezu*, 24 vols. Tokyo, 1977–1985.
Kodama Kōta et al., ed. *Nihonshi sōran*, 9 vols. Tokyo, 1993.
Kokushi Daijiten Henshū Iinkai, ed. *Kokushi daijiten*. Tokyo, 1980.
Kokushi Kenkyū Kai, ed. *Buya shokudan*. In *Kokushi sōsho*, ser. 2. Tokyo, 1917.
Kondō Moku, ed. *Kuwana shi shi*. Nagoya, 1959.
Kraft, Eva S. *Andreas Cleyer: Tagebuch des Kontors zu Nagasaki auf der Insel Deshima*. Bonn, 1985.
Krieger, Leonard, *The Politics of Discretion: Pufendorf and the Acceptance of Natural Law*. Chicago, 1965.
Kuroita Katsumi, ed. *Tokugawa Jikki*. In *Shintei zōho kokushi taikei*. Reprint, Tokyo, 1976.
Lach, Donald F. *Asia in the Making of Europe*, 2 vols. Chicago, 1965.
Larousse, Pierre. *Grand Dictionnaire Universel Du XIXe siècle*. Paris, 1866–1879.
Leibniz, G. W. *Politische Schriften*, edited by H. H. Holz. Frankfurt, 1966.
Lidin, Olof G. *The Life of Ogyū Sorai, a Tokugawa Confucian Philosopher*. Lund, 1973.
Lith, P. A. van der, et al. *Encyclopaedie van Nederlandsch-Indie*. Gravenhage, no date.
Lockyer, Charles. *An Account of the Trade in India*. London, 1711.
Lotsy, J. P. "Over de in Nederland aanwezige botanische handschriften van Rumphius." In *Rumphius Gedenkboek*. Haarlem, 1902.
Makino Tomitaro. *Makino's New Illustrated Flora of Japan*. Tokyo, 1962.
Massarella, Derek. "Epilogue." In *The Furthest Goal: Engelbert Kaempfer's Encounter with Tokugawa Japan*, edited by B. M. Bodart-Bailey and Derek Massarella. Folkstone, 1995.
———. "The History of *The History*." In *'The Furthest Goal: Engelbert Kaempfer's Encounter with Tokugawa Japan*, edited by B. M. Bodart-Bailey and Derek Massarella. Folkstone, 1995.
Meier-Lemgo, Karl. *Engelbert Kaempfer, der erste deutsche Forschungsreisende, 1651–1716*. Stuttgart, 1937.
———. *Engelbert Kaempfer erforscht das seltsame Asien*. Hamburg, 1960.
———, ed. "Das Stammbuch Engelbert Kaempfers." *Mitteilungen aus der lippischen Geschichte und Landeskunde* 21 (1952).
Montanus, Arnoldus. *Atlas Japannensis, Being Remarkable Addresses by way of Embassy from the East-India Company of the United Provinces to the Emperor of Japan*, translated by J. Ogilby. London, 1670.
———. *Denckwürdige Gesandtschafften der Ost-Indischen Geselschaft in den Vereinigten Niederländern an unterschiedliche Keyser in Japan. . . .* Amsterdam, 1670.
Moreland, W. H., ed. *Relations of Golconda in the Early 17th Century*. London, 1931.
Morinaga Taneo, ed. *Hankachō*, 16 vols. Nagasaki, 1958.
Muntschick, Wolfgang. "The Plants that Carry his Name: Kaempfer's Study of the Japanese Flora." In *The Furthest Goal: Engelbert Kaempfer's Encounter with*

Tokugawa Japan, edited by B. M. Bodart-Bailey and Derek Massarella. Folkstone, 1995.
Murdoch, James. *A History of Japan*. Kobe, 1903.
Nagasaki Shinbunsha, ed. *Nagasaki ken dai hyakkajiten*. Nagasaki, 1984.
Nagasaki Shiyakusho, ed., *Bakufu jidai no Nagasaki*. Tokyo, 1913.
———, ed., *Nagasaki shishi, fuzoku hen*. Nagasaki, 1925.
———, ed. *Nagasaki shishi, Jishi hen*. 1937.
———, ed., *Nagasaki shishi, Tsūkō bōeki*. Nakasaki, 1938.
———, ed., *Nagasaki sōsho*. Nagasaki, 1926.
Nagashima Masaichi. *Nagasaki gaidō*. Shinwabunko No. 9. Nagasaki, 1973.
Nakada Norio. *Ekū hen setsuyōshū taizen kenkyū narabini sakuin*. Tokyo, 1975.
Nakamura Tadashi. *Kinsei Nagasaki bōekishi no kenkyū*. Tokyo, 1988.
Nakamura Tekisai. *Kimmōzui*, edited by Sugimoto Tsutomu. Tokyo, 1975.
Nakayama Keishō. *Zenkoku ishibutsu ishikami daijiten*. Tokyo, 1990.
Niess, W. *Hexenprozesse in der Grafschaft Buedingen*. Buedingen, 1982.
Nihon Daijiten Kankō Kai, ed. *Nihon kokugo daijiten*. Tokyo, 1980.
Nihon kirisuto kyō rekishi daijiten. Tokyo, 1988.
Nose Yukio. *Encyclopaedia of Fishes (Sakana no jiten)*. Tokyo, 1989.
Numata Jirō et al., ed. *Yōgaku shi jiten*. Tokyo, 1984.
Oda Akinobu, ed. *On'eiroku haizetsuroku, Nihon shiryō sensho*, vol. 6. Tokyo, 1970.
Oestreich, Gerhard. *Geist und Gestalt des frühmodernen Staates*. Berlin, 1969.
Ogawa Kyōichi, ed. *Edo bakuhan daimyō ke jiten*, 3 vols. Tokyo, 1992.
Olearius, A. *Vermehrte Newe Beschreibung der Muskowitischen und Persischen Reyse*. . . . Schleswig, 1565; reprint, Tubingen, 1971.
Ōshima Akeo et al., ed. *Minzoku tambō jiten*. Reprint, Tokyo, 1990.
Ōtsu Shi Rekishi Hakubutsukan, ed. *Ōtsu no densetsu*. Otsu, 1988.
Paulus, J. *Encyclopaedie van Nederlandsch-lndie*. Gravenhage, 1917.
Philippi, Donald L., trans. *Kojiki*. Tokyo, 1968.
Plas, C. C. van der. *Tonkin 1644/45: Journaal van de Reis van Anthonio van Brouckhorst*. Amsterdam, 1955.
Ravina, Mark. "State-building and Political Economy in Early-modern Japan." *Journal of Asian Studies* 54.4 (1995):997–1022.
Reischauer, E. O., and J. K. Fairbank. *East Asia: The Great Tradition*. Boston, 1958.
Rodrigues, João. *This Island of Japon: João Rodrigues' Account of 16th-Century Japan*, translated and edited by Michael Cooper. Tokyo, 1973.
Rudbeck, Olof. *Atlantica*. Uppsala, 1675–1698.
Rumphius, Georgius Everhardus. *D'Amboinsche Rariteitkamer, of eene Beschryvinge van aller Hande*. . . . Amsterdam, 1705, 1741.
Sakamoto Tarō and Inoue Mitsusada, ed. *Nihon shoki*. In *Nihon bungaku koten taikei*. Tokyo, 1967.
Sakihara, Mitsugu. *A Brief History of Early Okinawa Based on the Omoro Soshi*. Tokyo, 1987.

Schmeißer, Jörg. "Changing the Image: The Drawings and Prints of Kaempfer's *History of Japan.*" In *The Furthest Goal: Engelbert Kaempfer's Encounter with Tokugawa Japan,* edited by B. M. Bodart-Bailey and Derek Massarella. Folkestone, 1995.

Schurhammer, Georg. *Franz Xaver: Sein Leben und seine Zeit.* Freiburg, 1971.

Schütte, Josephus Franciscus. *Introductio ad Historiam Societatis Jesu in Japonia, 1549–1650.* Rome, 1968.

Schwanold, Heinrich. "Engelbert Kämpfers Testament." *Lippische Mitteilungen* 5 (1907).

Shimada Izao et al., ed. *Wakan sansai zue,* 18 vols. Tokyo, 1986.

Spate, O. H. K. *The Spanish Lake.* Canberra, 1979.

Stevens, Robert. *The Complete Guide to the East-India Trade.* London, 1766.

Sugimoto Tsutomu, ed. *Waran jii.* Reprint, Tokyo, 1974.

Takayanagi Kaneyoshi, ed. *Shiryō Tokugawa fujinden.* Tokyo, 1967.

Takayanagi Shinzō and Ishii Ryōsuke, ed. *Tokugawa kinreikō.* Tokyo, 1959.

Takizawa Takeo. *Nihon no kahei no rekishi.* Tokyo, 1996.

Tamaoki Toyojirō ed. *Osaka kochizu shūsei.* Osaka, 1980.

Teruoka Yasutaka. "Saikaku jidai no kahei." In Iharara Saikaku, *Nihon eitaigura.* Tokyo, 1967.

Terwiel, B. J. "Kaempfer and Thai History: The Documents Behind the Printed Text." *Journal of the Royal Asiatic Society* 1 (1989).

Toby, Ronald P. *State and Diplomacy in Early Modern Japan.* Princeton, 1984.

Tōkyō Daigaku Shiryō Hensanjo, ed. *Tōtsūji esho nichiroku.* In *Dai Nihon kinsei shiryō,* pt. 3. Tokyo, 1955.

Treue, W. *Wirtschaft, Gesellschaft und Technik in Deutschland vom 16. bis zum 18. Jahrhundert.* Handbuch der deutschen Geschichte, 12. Reprint, Munich, 1974.

Urada Tōru. *Dōbutsu bunrui meijiten.* Tokyo, 1972.

Valentyn, François. *Oud en Nieuw Oost-Indien,* 8 vols. Dordrecht, 1724–1726.

Velde, Paul van der. "The Interpreter Interpreted: Kaempfer's Japanese Collaborator Imamura Genemon Eisei." In *The Furthest Goal, Engelbert Kaempfer's Encounter with Tokugawa Japan,* ed. B. M. Bodart-Bailey and Derek Massarella. Folkstone, 1995.

Velde, Paul van der, and T. Vermeulen, ed. *The Deshima Dagregisters, their original tables of contents,* 3. Leiden, 1990.

Vermeulen, A.C.J., ed. *The Deshima Dagregisters, their original tables of contents,* vol. II, 1690–1700. Leiden, 1987.

Virgil. *The Aeneid,* translated by C. H. Sisson. Manchester, 1986.

Voltaire, F. M. A. de. *Essai sur les moeurs et l'esprit des nations.* Paris, 1963.

Wada Sei. "The Native of the Lower Reaches. . . ." *Memoirs of the Research Department of the Toyo Bunko,* no. 10 (1938).

Warrington, John, ed. and trans. *Aristotle: Politics.* London, 1959.

Windscheid, Bernhard. *Lehrbuch des Pandektenrechts.* Reprint, Aalen, 1963.
Witsen, Nicolaas. *Noord en Oost Tartarye.* Amsterdam, 1692, 1705.
Yanagida Kunio. *Furo no kigen.* In *Yanagida Kunio shū,* vol. 14. Tokyo, 1962.
Yasuoka Akio. "Ogasawara Shotō kizoku mondai." In *Kokushi daijiten,* edited by Kokushi Daijiten Henshū Iinkai. Tokyo, 1980.
Zeeden, Ernst Walter. *Europa im Zeitalter des Absolutismus und derAufklärung.* Stuttgart, 1981.

Index

Italicized page numbers refer to illustrations.

About the Translator

Beatrice Bodart-Bailey received her doctorate from the Research School of Pacific and Asian Studies of the Australian National University. She has published books and articles on a wide range of topics on early Tokugawa Japan, including a book on Engelbert Kaempfer and the Fifth Shogun in the well-known Japanese Chūkō Shinsho pocket book series. She is currently professor of Japanese economic history at Kobe University and a founding member of the Faculty of Comparative Culture at Ōtsuma Women's University, Tokyo.